D0398619

THE PROMISE OF PRAGMATISM

John Patrick Diggins

THE PROMISE OF PRAGMATISM

Modernism and the Crisis of Knowledge and Authority

The University of Chicago Press
Chicago and London

John Patrick Diggins is Distinguished Professor of History at the Graduate School and University Center, City University of New York. Of his eight other major books, the most recent is *The Rise and Fall of the American Left* (1991).

The University of Chicago Press, Chicago 60637
The University of Chicago Press, Ltd., London
© 1994 by The University of Chicago
All rights reserved. Published 1994
Printed in the United States of America
03 02 01 00 99 98 97 96 95 94   1 2 3 4 5
ISBN: 0-226-14878-5 (cloth)

Library of Congress Cataloging-in-Publication Data

Diggins, John P.
  The promise of pragmatism : modernism and the crisis of knowledge and authority /
John Patrick Diggins.
    p.   cm.
    Includes index.
    1. United States—Intellectual life—20th century.   2. Pragmatism.   3. Philosophy,
American—20th century.   I. Title.
E169.1.D495   1994
144'.3'0973—dc20   93-11686
                                                                              CIP

To
Arthur Schlesinger, Jr.

Should anyone be able to dissolve the unhistorical atmosphere in which every great event happens, and breathe afterward, he might be capable of rising to the "superhistorical" standpoint of consciousness that Niebuhr has described as the possible result of historical research. "History," he says, "is useful for one purpose, if studied in detail: that men may know . . . the accidental nature of the forms in which they see and insist on others seeing. . . ." Such a standpoint might be called "superhistorical," as one who took it could feel no impulse from history to any further life or work, for he would have recognized the blindness and injustice in the soul of the doer as a condition of every deed; he would be cured henceforth of taking history too seriously, and learnt to answer the question how and why life should be lived. . . . Whoever asks his friends whether they would live the last ten or twenty years over again will easily see which of them is born for the "superhistorical standpoint": they will all answer no. . . . Some will say they have the consolation that the next twenty will be better; they are the men referred to satirically by David Hume:

> "And from the dregs of life hope to receive
> What the first sprightly running could not give."

We will call them the "historical men." Their vision of the past turns them toward the future, encourages them to persevere with life, and kindles the hope that justice will yet come and happiness is behind the mountain they are climbing. They believe that the meaning of existence will become ever clearer in the course of evolution; they only look backward at the process to understand the present and stimulate their longing for the future. They do not know how unhistorical their thoughts and actions are in spite of all their history. . . .

But the question to which we have heard the first answer is capable of another; also a "no," but on different grounds. It is the "no" of the "superhistorical" man who sees no salvation in evolution. . . . How could the next ten years teach what the past ten were not able to teach?

—Friedrich Nietzsche,
Thoughts Out of Season

Contents

Acknowledgments

"The trouble with you and your pals, John Diggins, is you lack respect for authority." So concluded the Juvenile Court Judge in San Francisco in the early 1950s, an opinion reached for the grievous offense of drinking beer and playing pool under the legal age of eighteen.

Many years later I started out to write a book on authority, assuming its foundations rested on knowledge and morality, logic and rational proof, the intrinsic truth of the idea itself. All I found was power, as though education began with Henry Adams and ended with Friedrich Nietzsche. About to drop the subject, I decided to continue to pursue it to see if the philosophers of pragmatism had answers to questions that refused to go away. Thus my first acknowledgment of indebtedness for undertaking this book goes to the judge who put me on probation for displaying insufficient respect toward a subject that has followed me like an intellectual shadow.

Appreciation also goes to David Harlan, James Hoopes, Ross Posnock, and Christina von Koehler for reading parts of the manuscript and offering helpful criticisms, to Salena Fuller Krug and her perceptive copy-editing, and to Doug Mitchell for his advice and encouragement. I am especially grateful to Louis Menand, whose thorough, critical evaluation of the entire manuscript forced me to reconsider some of my assumptions—always a good thing.

The book is dedicated to my colleague and friend, Arthur Schlesinger, Jr., whose urbane writings in American history influenced me to enter the field, and whose scholarship and politics manage to inhabit the best of both worlds—Jamesian pragmatism and Niebuhrian realism.

SOURCES
Henry Adams Papers, Massachusetts Historical Society, Boston
John Dewey Papers, Morris Library, Southern Illinois University,
    Carbondale
Sidney Hook Papers, Center for Dewey Studies, Carbondale, Illinois
William James Papers, Houghton Library, Harvard University,
    Cambridge
Horace Kallen Papers, Center for Dewey Studies

Papers originally appearing as articles have been revised for use in this
book. For use of these materials I thank the following journals: *The American Scholar, Ethics and International Relations, New England Quarterly, Partisan Review, Political Theory, Social Research.*

Introduction

On the evening of December 7, 1941, hundreds of New Yorkers crowded into Cooper Union's "Great Hall" auditorium to hear the famous philosopher John Dewey speak on "Lessons from the War in Philosophy." The lecture pertaining to the First World War had been planned in the summer, part of a series that had already featured the anthropologist Margaret Mead and the theologian Reinhold Niebuhr speaking on the same subject from their respective disciplines. Shocked by the news of Pearl Harbor, the audience sat in silent gloom as Dewey, eighty-two years old and his face pale and tense, approached the podium. Slowly he began his speech, the hands trembling, sweat beads streaming down his forehead and misting the upper part of his glasses, the voice crackling with uncertainty. Moments before he spoke, his thoughts had turned back to the First World War and what he later concluded was his disastrous decision to support America's military intervention. Wondering if events ever repeat themselves, Dewey could only ask himself whether anything had been learned from the last war. And the present war? Could the lofty wisdom of philosophy be made to illuminate the tragic ravages of history?

"I have nothing, had nothing, and have nothing now, to say directly about the war," Dewey told an audience anxious to hear some reassuring words. Intellectuals in particular, he went on, must be careful not to generalize too hastily lest they end up justifying the course of events—what the theologian calls "apologetics" and the psychoanalyst "rationalizations." In his prepared statement Dewey had written that the earlier war had taught philosophy the value of some unified view of human beings so that "ideas and emotions, knowledge and desire" might be more integrated. But of the present war Dewey could only say in his improvised

1

remarks that philosophy can neither discern the direction of events as they develop nor judge their meaning afterward. "Philosophy, intellectual operations, in general, are likely to come after events. This is a sort of *ex post facto* enterprise and very often by the time philosophy is formed, events have changed so much there isn't much for ideas to lay hold of."[1]

Dewey's dilemma would have earned the sympathy of the great American historian Henry Adams. The philosopher advised Americans of the difficulty of gaining knowledge prior to experience; the historian had earlier advised Americans of the even greater difficulty of doing so after experience. Nothing obscures truth so completely as the experience of studying historical experience.

Pragmatism, America's one original contribution to the world of philosophy, had once promised to help people deliberately reflect about what to do when confronting "problematic situations." This instrumental approach to knowledge remained more characteristic of Dewey's pragmatism than that of William James or Charles Sanders Peirce. Dewey's more public-oriented philosophy proposed to bring reflective intelligence to bear on society so as to help define ends and select the means to reach them. But in his speech at Cooper Union, Dewey had come to the same conclusion that Adams had a half-century earlier. Adams had studied history to find the clue to controlling power; Dewey looked to philosophy to develop a methodology for dealing with an environment of disruptive change. Both sensed that the rush of events often left the mind grasping for explanations.

A certain Hegelian pathos stalks Adams and Dewey. In the nineteenth century Adams regarded slavery as an evil, but he could not say which faction of the Republican party had the right response to southern secession: the faction advocating the resort to force or that proposing negotiation. Only the future could judge. Similarly, Dewey knew that European fascism posed a demonic threat, but with the outbreak of the Second World War in 1939 he considered the "method of coercion" and that of "discussion," only to conclude that force and violence could not be justified even in America's confrontation with Adolf Hitler. Perhaps Hegel was right to believe that philosophical knowledge could only be retrospective, and even then, like the Owl of Minerva taking flight at dusk, it arrives too late to be of use.

Pragmatism advises us to try whatever promises to work and proves to be useful as the mind adjusts to the exigencies of events. Does pragmatism

---

1. A transcript of Dewey's speech, including the improvised remarks, is in the Dewey papers, 102 53/14; the description of Dewey's emotions at the time of the event was obtained from his relatives by Charles F. Howlett and conveyed in his *Troubled Philosopher: John Dewey and the Struggle for World Peace* (Port Washington, N.Y.: Kennikat Press, 1977), 3–4.

itself work? To raise that question risks going against the American grain. For much of the twentieth century the school of thought known as pragmatism has enjoyed a charmed life. Older progressive scholars hailed pragmatism for breaking the deductive chains of nineteenth-century conservative ideology and thereby making possible the advent of modern liberal reform thought.[2] More recent scholars have likened pragmatism to the European currents of poststructuralism and deconstruction in order to place the future of philosophy in the realm of linguistic processes rather than in reason and logical proof. Pragmatism never meant to provide "foundations" on which to ground knowledge, we are told, but simply ways of thinking, talking, and writing about specific situations that are not so much known as described. Rhetoric, conversation, narration, and discourse are presently offered by the neopragmatist as a means of coping in the modern world.

The neopragmatist Richard Rorty has been criticized by fellow pragmatists for taking Dewey's scientific-oriented philosophy and reformulating it as a linguistic enterprise. Yet Dewey himself had been sympathetic to literature and its ambitions to understand the world as well as write about it. In 1939 the young literary scholar Lionel Trilling sent Dewey a note of appreciation for an essay on Matthew Arnold that the philosopher had written in 1891. Dewey's essay encouraged Trilling to proceed with his book-length study despite the criticisms Arnold's work had been receiving in the radical depression years. In the essay, which had appeared in the theological *Andover Review*, and in unpublished materials and lecture notes, Dewey seemed haunted by Arnold's meditations on modernity. The most crucial issue Dewey faced as a young philosopher was the dualism between nature and spirit and all its ramifications for matter and mind, science and morality, and other chasms that estranged man from God. "No verse of Matthew Arnold is better known," Dewey wrote in his notes, than that describing "modern man" as

> Wandering between two worlds, one dead
> The other powerless to be born.

Reading Arnold, Dewey knew the meaning of alienation as a kind of cosmic loneliness. Bereft of spirit, the natural world becomes a chilling

2. See, for example, Henry Steele Commager, *The American Mind: The Integration of American Thought and Character since the 1880s* (New Haven: Yale University Press, 1950). Commager represents perhaps the last voice of the progressive spirit of Vernon L. Parrington. For a postprogressive analysis of pragmatism that remains within the spirit of liberalism, see Morton White, *Social Thought in America: The Revolt against Formalism* (Boston: Beacon Press, 1949).

void, and modern man can no longer feel at one with the universe. "Nature, in ceasing to be divine, ceases to be human," wrote Dewey. Arnold had taken refuge in poetry to contemplate what could not be found in modern empirical philosophy: the imagination of moral possibility in a world of mechanical necessity. "Here, indeed, is just our problem," Dewey concluded. "We must bridge this gap of poetry from science. We must heal this unnatural wound. We must, in a cold reflective way of critical system, justify and organize the truth which poetry, with its quick naive contacts, has already felt and reported."[3]

How, then, to "organize the truth," which in the future might only be accessible to the literary imagination? One way, taken up by the modernist writer, was to forget truth as unity and convey experience as it happened without any sense of order or meaning.

Three decades after he had written on Arnold, just after James Joyce's *Ulysses* had appeared in 1922, Dewey observed that intellectuals mistakenly choose only two ways to confront a world in which events have lost their meaning. "We revive 'the classics.' Or we become extreme modernists and string words together in a jumble, feeling that if we can only get as many shocks from the words as we do from things and render the sequence of words as jumpy and blind as the sequence of events, we shall have proved our competency to keep even, up-to-date, with the most recent events."[4] Dewey's description of the modernist literary world, where traditional narrative, action, and drama seem to give way to contingency and simultaneity, would perhaps have pleased Adams, the historian who ended his career portraying the world rushing toward "chaos" and "entropy," the specter of a disintegrating "multiverse."

The literary artist no less than the philosopher is interested in the relationship of mind and reality and language and the world. But as a philosopher Dewey was committed to the logical clarification of ideas, and thus he offered pragmatism as a way out of the worldview presented by the "extreme modernists." Convinced that after Darwinism there could be no return to classical knowledge and its timeless truths, Dewey also convinced himself that the problems of modernism were more apparent than real. To the pragmatist the discrepancies and contingencies of the universe should not provoke meaninglessness and anxiety. On the con-

3. John Dewey, "Wandering between Two Worlds," Dewey mss., 105 53/18. First published under the title "Poetry and Philosophy" in the *Andover Review* in 1891, Dewey's essay on Arnold is reprinted as "Matthew Arnold and Robert Browning," in *Character and Events*, ed. Joseph Ratner (New York: Henry Holt, 1929), 3–17. Lionel Trilling to John Dewey, Jan. 11, 1939, Dewey mss.

4. Dewey, "Events and Meanings," in *Character and Events*, 125–29; the essay first appeared in the *New Republic* in 1922.

trary, life must be seen as a challenge and an adventure, and a universe that is potential and "unfinished" presents abundant opportunities to create meaning through the exercise of intelligent control.

But before Dewey reached his optimistic conclusion about the promises of science and intelligence he had some anxious moments pondering the implications of modernism. In an unpublished paper on Leo Tolstoy, Dewey dwells on the incommensurability of thought and experience, while noting that the Russian novelist insisted that genuine morality revealed itself only in conduct. Tolstoy made "too absolute a separation" between the physical and moral and the individual and social to satisfy Dewey. But he admired the sincerity with which the writer struggled with philosophical issues. Tolstoy's teachings prompted Dewey to make the following observation:

> For at least a hundred years professed philosophy has been increasingly perplexed with two great questions: How are the results and methods of modern science, bound up with a purely mechanical view of the world, compatible with man's moral interests that proclaim the supremacy of purpose and thought? And how is the increasing preoccupation of man with the things of the material world, the multiplication and cheapening of commodities that relate to the senses and appetites, related to man's ideal interests, what somewhat indefinitely we call his "spiritual interests." Even from the side of abstract and technical philosophy there are two seeming contradictions or antimonies: Man's increasing intellectual command over science . . . seems to reveal mankind absolutely caught and helpless within a vast unrelenting mechanism which goes its way without reference to human value or care for human purpose; Man's command over the means of life, his industrial conquest, seems only to have sharpened prior existing social inequities, to have led to devotion to the means of life at the expense of its serious and significant ends—a noble free and happy life in which all men participate on something like equal terms.[5]

An awareness of the dualism between nature and spirit that enhances the means of control while diminishing a conception of moral ends might be regarded as one definition of the modernist sensibility. But Dewey should be regarded as a halfway modernist, a brilliant philosopher who, sensing the implications of modernism, did everything possible to avoid its conclusions. Unlike some twentieth-century existentialist writers, Dewey could not bring himself to believe that life could go on as sheer

5. Dewey, untitled address on Tolstoy, Dewey mss., 102 60/29.

activity without the world satisfying our need for some basis of human value and meaning.

> What a picture of life as an eternal Sisyphus forever engaged in an aimless activity whose sole result is to intensify its aimlessness by accelerating the pace. It is of business conceived as such a life and life as such a business that George Santayana mordantly remarked that those who dedicate themselves to it may have the proud happiness of knowing that when life is extinct upon the globe, the earth may, because of them, cast a slightly different shadow across the moon's crater.[6]

The Dewey who wrote of the contradictions and antimonies of existence is the Dewey admired by Trilling, the philosopher as anguished humanist struggling with the problems of modernity and experiencing the humility of doubt. This early Dewey seldom emerges in scholarly writings on the philosopher.[7] But it bears mentioning that Trilling esteemed Adams for much the same reason he appreciated Dewey. If the philosopher worried about the dualism of spirit and nature, the historian agonized over the tension between politics and ethics. America cannot dismiss Adams, Trilling wrote in 1952, the year of Dewey's death. His somber convictions may yield deeper truths, and if his despair offers little hope, it radiates the power of darkness and makes the American mind more a treasure to behold than a tool to be used. "We come to see, as William James saw," wrote Trilling of the philosopher's attitude toward the historian, "that there is a kind of corruption or corruptingness in the perfect plenitude of his despair. With James we understand that Adams's despair is the chief condition of its own existence, and that the right to hope is earned by our courage in hoping. And when we see this, we turn on Adams, using against him every weapon on which we can lay our hands." Should Adams, then, be dismissed unambiguously?

> But we shall be wrong, we shall do ourselves a great disservice, if ever we try to read Adams permanently out of our intellectual life. I have called him an issue—he is even more than that, he is an indispensable element in our intelligence. To

6. Dewey, untitled fragment, Dewey mss., 102 60/25.

7. Excellent exceptions are Neil Coughlan's slender monograph, *Young John Dewey: An Essay in American Intellectual History* (Chicago: University of Chicago Press, 1973), which shows the importance of Dewey's turning to psychology to overcome dualism; Bruce Kuklick's *Churchmen and Philosophers: From Jonathan Edwards to John Dewey* (New Haven: Yale University Press, 1985), which shows the lingering Calvinist tensions; and Paul L. Conkin's *Puritans and Pragmatists: Eight Eminent American Thinkers* (New York: 1968), which esteems Dewey as "the best of the Puritans" (402).

succeed in getting rid of Adams would be to diminish materi-
ally the seriousness of our thought. In the intellectual life there
ought to be frequent occasions for the exercise of ambivalence,
and nothing can be more salutary for the American intelligence than to remain aware of Adams and to maintain toward
him a strict ambivalence, to weigh our admiration and affection for him against our impatience and suspicion.[8]

American historians have come close to reading Adams out of our intellectual life because his mocking presence seems an insult to the nation's
creed of optimism and progress, an intellect that erodes whatever it
touches. To relate Adams to the study of pragmatism may seem doubly
insulting to the historian who demands a precise context for the study of
ideas. By no means can Adams be categorized as a pragmatist; how, then,
does he fit into the actual historical setting of discourse and debate out of
which developed a specific set of ideas? The contextualist wants to know
the birth certificate of a text and the conscious intent of its author. The
assumption is that the ideas of a given text are the constructions of
the conditions that supposedly brought the text into being, and thus the
"meaning" of ideas and their text may be reduced to a context that it is
the historian's obligation to establish. This work obviously sins against
the contextualist's commandments by violating the canons of authorial
intent and ignoring the historically conditioned character of texts. Adams
and Dewey scarcely intended to scrutinize each other's writings, let alone
engage in a dialogue of argument and counterargument (Adams does so
with James). Yet the history of ideas need not be so unduly restricting as
to relegate their importance solely to their particular setting. Ideas may
be appreciated for their validity as well as their genealogy, and when
evaluating ideas for the problems they illuminate, we can use one author
to interrogate another so that ideas speak to our condition as well as theirs.
Various thinkers in this study will be treated as though they were in a
conversation with one another, with Adams looking over their shoulders
as they compose their thoughts on texts that the author has critically
examined. In juxtaposing Dewey to Adams, one may better appreciate
the affirmations of pragmatism as an effort to overcome the negations of
modernism.

Modernism may be defined in a number of ways, but each definition
returns to the problem of belief and the limits of cognition. The idea of
order and objective truth becomes untenable to the modernist, as do all
traditional modes of acquiring knowledge. Modernism arose in the late

8. Lionel Trilling, "Adams at Ease," in *A Gathering of Fugitives* (New York: Oxford
University Press, 1980), 127–28.

nineteenth century when Darwinism challenged the idea of divine creation and left religious dogma in shambles. Man without God was also left, as Arnold put it, wandering between a world that had been lost and a world that had yet to be found. With God dead, the problem of creating meaning fell to men and women, especially writers like Herman Melville and Emily Dickinson, who gazed into the void to see if the intellect could be at home with the unknown and face the look of death. The modernist can neither believe nor rest content in disbelief.

What, specifically, is modernism? As a way of reacting to the modern world, modernism is the consciousness of what once was presumed to be present and is now seen as missing. It might be considered as a series of felt absences, the gap between what we know is not and what we desire to be: knowledge without truth, power without authority, society without spirit, self without identity, politics without virtue, existence without purpose, history without meaning. Such dualisms and gaps had been known since Plato, but traditionally it had been assumed that the faculties of mind or the forces of faith would enable humankind to resolve them. Today the contemporary "postmodernist" offers a different message: we should go beyond modernism and take a more relaxed look at things, either by comprehending how knowledge, power, and society function, by viewing history without purpose and meaning as simply the longing of human desire for its completion, or by giving up trying to explain the nature of things and being content with studying how beliefs come to be justified. To Dewey, who in some ways anticipated postmodernism (minus the later Parisian verbal fuss), all such absences and their desire for fulfillment could be traced to the dualism of nature and spirit, a false outlook that fails to recognize that mind evolved from matter and thus can neither be separated from it nor reduced to it. Dewey could agree with the postmodernist that philosophy has been trying futilely to prove what is not there; but while the postmodernist seems to delight in exposing the illusions of thinking, Dewey had long been convinced that the classical questions of philosophy have no practical bearing in daily life. In offering pragmatism, Dewey gave America something to be used; in resisting it, Adams held out for something to be worshiped.

Why did Adams refuse to embrace pragmatism as a solution to the problems of modernism? Was it because the historian and heir of illustrious presidents looked backward and had little interest in the future? Hardly. The future obsessed him. Still, a common impression sees Adams as a lost soul who cannot accept modernity and instead pines nostalgically for the vanished world of his ancestors. Yet if there was one thing Adams remained convinced of, it was the inevitability of change and transformation regardless of the political and moral costs. With Adams one feels the universe of power, force, energy, and motion, a universe without purpose, meaning, or hopeful human destiny. With Adams one also feels more inside the mind of a European than an American. In some respects he looms as an American counterpart to Friedrich Nietzsche, the German philosopher who recognized a truth that Adams prized in Pascal's meditations: reason can prove only the limits of reason and the contingent, even arbitrary, character of all thinking. Like Nietzsche, Adams came to sense that knowledge of the past had become as problematic as expectations of the future had become pessimistic. Both thinkers saw how foolish it was to have once assumed that the study of history would shed ever more light on the meaning of existence. "The worst of it is that, as historians, we have wholly lost confidence in our own school," Adams wrote to a friend in 1912, now aware that new currents in intellectual life had left the historian with no certain access to history itself. "I am overwhelmed with astonishment to see how futile and feeble our critical faculty was, and how idiotically we took it."[9] As with Nietzsche, Adams also came to the conclusion that when one knows history cannot be readily understood, the modernist must be prepared to endure irony and accept that "Why?" finds no answer.

That conclusion would also be reached by Reinhold Niebuhr, the theologian who offered some telling criticisms of Deweyan pragmatism in the 1930s. With his sense of the irony of intentions and consequences, the pretensions of virtue and innocence, and the sins of pride and egotism, Niebuhr enriched liberalism and helped to prepare America to face the world of modernity. More than other American thinkers, even more than the domination-struck deconstructionists of our era, Niebuhr enabled us to think about power and its deceptions. In contrast to Dewey and the tradition of the European Enlightenment, Niebuhr rejected the assumption that sufficient knowledge would emerge to constitute a challenge to power. Adams, too, doubted that the intellect would ever master the riddles of power. Both thinkers shared, even if by coincidence, the Nietzschean perspective that the best answer to power is suspicion.

But the early Adams, it should be pointed out, possessed the youthful hopes of the later pragmatists. Although Adams and Dewey had different temperaments and intellectual outlooks, they both assumed that events can be dealt with by bringing science to bear upon historical understanding. Both viewed existence as precarious, and each believed the endless movement of power must be mastered and controlled. "Striving to make stability of meaning prevail over the instability of events is the main task

9. Henry Adams to Frederick Bliss Luquiens, Apr. 8, 1912, in *Letters of Henry Adams*, ed. J. C. Levenson et al. (Cambridge: Harvard University Press, 1988), vol. 6, 529–31.

of intelligent human effort," advised Dewey.[10] Adams agreed, but after writing volumes of history he could find neither meaning nor pattern that would yield purpose or prediction. Later in his career he would discover that modern physics had uncovered indeterminacy in the very structure of matter. Looking forward with apprehension to the twentieth century, Adams projected a world of clashing historical events as random as the micro-universe of subatomic particles. Dewey regarded science as a kind of secular salvation against the assaults of modernism. But Adams was the first historian to relate the implications of modern physics to history, and his fear of the "cosmic violence" that would be released by atomic energy invoked a Calvinist mood of damnation.

The British scholar E. H. Carr has asserted that history can be written "only by those who find and accept a sense of direction in it."[11] The Marxist as well as the pragmatist would like to believe in the rationality of history to assure themselves of a progressive view of the world and the human condition within it. As a historian, Adams resembles Max Weber, the German social scientist who also doubted that the meaning of the world could be derived from analysis alone, discerning instead that consequences defy intentions, and that power continues to escape knowledge in a world in which reason as "rationalization" brings domination instead of freedom. Yet when juxtaposing the historian to the philosopher, a curious reversal of roles occurs. Dewey offered America a philosophy for doing without the conventional concepts of truth. Traditionally it should have been the historian who questions the possibility of truth and the philosopher who feels he must continue to pursue it. Hegel explains why philosophy that aims at the timeless will always be embarrassed by history that shows all thinking as immersed in time: "Philosophy aims at knowing what is imperishable, eternal, and absolute. Its aim is truth. But history relates the sort of thing which has existed at one time but at another has perished."[12]

The "imperishable, eternal, and absolute" are precisely the notions pragmatism set out to purge from philosophy. Pragmatism proposed a philosophy that could dispense not only with classical philosophy but with history as well. For just as truth is unknowable, the past is unrecoverable. Oriented toward the future, unburdened by the classical problems of knowledge and truth, rejecting the perished past as incapable of being represented (made present) in thought, pragmatism nevertheless offered

10. Dewey, *Experience and Nature* (1925; New York: Dover, 1958), 40–77.

11. E. H. Carr, *What Is History?* (New York: Knopf, 1964), 176.

12. Hegel is quoted in Kenneth Schmitz, "Why Philosophy Must Have a History: Hegel's Proposal," in *Doing Philosophy Historically*, ed. Peter Hare (Buffalo: Prometheus Books, 1988), 253.

the promise that modern man could somehow study the world scientifically and live it spiritually.

Neopragmatism, which emerged in the early 1980s due in large part
to the searching, profoundly provocative writings of Richard Rorty, offers
a different promise: that we study the world historically and live it conver-
sationally. With the "linguistic turn" in modern thought, philosophy no
longer has as its task the clarification of truth, morality, and virtue. Instead philosophy is to be conceived as a language activity in which ideas
are examined for their edifying import and intellectual history is studied
to find out how beliefs have come to be justified. The neopragmatist is
haunted by Martin Heidegger's nightmare: "Does this abyss consist only
in the fact that reason resides in language, or is language itself the
abyss?"[13] Either way, truth is lost for good, and the task is to find out
not what is knowable but what is useful. Whether the point of traditional
philosophy was to interpret the world or to change it, the point of "postphilosophy" is to find ways of legitimating what we say instead of proving
what we know.

In 1979, in an address to the American Philosophical Association,
Rorty shocked his colleagues by announcing "the end of philosophy." As
did Adams nearly a century ago, Rorty concluded that the "mind as
mirror" turned out to be an illusion, a desperate Cartesian assumption that
the cognitive faculties could accurately reflect, represent, and replicate the
world as it really is. With knowledge no longer having any basis in ideas
that faithfully correspond to reality, philosophy should forsake pursuing
theories of truth and look to language and literature to develop new moral
vocabularies based on conventions, however contingent and conditional.
Rorty calls for philosophy continuing as "conversation," the arguments
and discourses used by thinkers to defend and justify their thoughts
without reference to anything beyond the language that expresses the
thoughts. William James would most likely have been sympathetic to the
neopragmatist effort to make satisfying beliefs take the place of truths
once regarded as timeless, necessary, and unconditional. Yet it will be
seen that James could lose patience with endless talk that avoids taking
immediate action, while at the same time recognizing that "all human
thinking gets discursified" in verbal transactions.[14] Although Rorty excludes Charles Peirce from his "post-philosophy" project, the founding
father of American pragmatism could easily have taken part in its activities
even while rejecting its convictions—especially the claim that our beliefs

13. Martin Heidegger, *Poetry, Language, Thought,* ed. Albert Hofstadter (New York:
Harper, 1971), 191.

14. William James, "Pragmatism's Conception of Truth," in *The Writings of William James,*
ed. John J. McDermott (New York: Modern Library, 1967), 435.

can rest conditionally on nothing more than the contingency of conventions. Rorty himself excludes Peirce because he continued to believe in the eventual possibility of reaching truth. Yet one can imagine the garrulous Peirce eagerly participating in a Rortyan conversation. John Jay Chapman ran into Peirce one evening at New York's Century Club and conveyed the experience in a midnight letter to his wife:

> I am too tired to write . . . I happened to sit down next to Charles Peirce, and stayed talking to him ever since, or rather he talking. He is a most genial man—got down books and read aloud. He began by saying Lincoln had the Rabelais quality. It appears he worships Rabelais. He read passages in Carlyle in a voice that made the building reverberate. . . . He then talked about—plasms—force, heat, light—Boston, Emerson, Margaret Fuller, God, Mammon, America, Goethe, Homer, Silver, but principally science and philosophy—a wonderful evening. It was ask and have, and, but that he talked himself positively to sleep with exertion, he would be talking yet.[15]

Peirce would certainly have been able to keep the conversation going. To Dewey language was more tool than talk. Dewey liked to use the expression "the problems of men" to suggest that if pragmatism offers itself as a "problem-solving" instrument, it is intended for the practical problems thrown up by history and society and not the theoretical issues of knowledge and truth inherent in philosophy itself, issues that preoccupied Adams as well as Peirce. But once we leave Peirce—who regarded culture as more than a matter of behavior and adaptation, and restricted inquiry to scientific matters of the most theoretical nature—and move on to James and especially Dewey, with his determination to make philosophy redemptive in all aspects of life, pragmatism itself becomes problematic. Could it actually solve the classical questions of philosophy? The dualism of nature and spirit left Dewey with "this unnatural wound." How was it to be healed? Rather than offering solutions to such agonizing theoretical problems, pragmatism simply denies any need to worry about them. "We do not solve them," Dewey said of philosophical questions; "we get over them. Old questions are solved by disappearing."[16]

In what sense are problems of philosophy solved by dropping out of sight? Thirty years after Dewey made the statement above, he offered a convincing explanation of what he had in mind:

15. John Jay Chapman to Minna Timmins Chapman, August 11, 1893, in *John Jay Chapman and His Letters*, ed. M. A. DeWolfe Howe (Boston: Houghton Mifflin, 1937), 94–96.

16. Dewey, "The Influence of Darwinism on Philosophy," in *The Philosophy of John Dewey*, ed. John J. McDermott (Chicago: University of Chicago Press, 1981), 41.

It may be remarked incidentally that the recognition of the relational character of scientific objects completely eliminates an old metaphysical issue. One of the outstanding problems created by the rise of modern science was due to the fact that scientific definitions and descriptions are framed in terms of which qualities play no part. Qualities were wholly superfluous. As long as the idea persisted (an inheritance from Greek metaphysical science) that the business of knowledge is to penetrate into the inner beings of objects, the existence of qualities like colors, sounds, etc. was embarrassing. . . . Given the old idea that the purpose of knowledge . . . is to penetrate into the heart of reality and reveal its "true" nature, the conclusion was a logical one. It was "solved" by the discovery that it needed no solution, since fulfillment of the function and business of science compels disregard for qualities.[17]

That science need not grasp the inherent quality of a thing but instead study its relations and connections with other things was certainly a revolutionary breakthrough in modern thought. But could this discovery be extended to topics beyond the reach of science? On this question Peirce was more cautious than Dewey or James. "I also want to say that after all pragmatism solves no real problems," Peirce wrote to James in 1904. "It only shows that supposed problems are not problems. But when one comes to such questions as immortality, the nature of the connection of mind and matter . . . we are left completely in the dark. The effect of pragmatism here is simply to open our minds to receiving evidence, not to furnish the evidence."[18]

Dewey's faith in experience reinforced his conviction that scientific inquiry could be extended to society and history. The proposal that philosophy give up the search for foundational truths resulted in making philosophy itself historical as well as scientific. In *Experience and Nature* (1925), Dewey insisted that "objects of natural science are not metaphysical rivals of historical events." Instead of searching for timeless essences, the pragmatic philosopher investigates events and developments as part of the changing character of reality. Ancient Greek philosophers strove to know the immutable and eternal; the modern philosopher seeks the pattern of order within change so as to bring knowledge to bear on power and control. "The legitimate implication of the preference for worthy objects of appreciation is the necessity of art, or control of the sequential

17. Dewey, "Time and Individuality," in *John Dewey: The Essential Writings*, ed. David Sidorsky (New York: Harper Torchbooks, 1973), 140.
18. Charles S. Peirce to William James, Mar. 7, 1904, in *Collected Papers of Charles Sanders Peirce*, ed. Arthur W. Burks (Cambridge: Harvard University Press, 1958), vol. 8, 190.

order upon which they depend; a necessity which carries with it the further implication that this order, which is to be discovered by inquiry confirmed by experimental action, is the proper object of knowledge."[19]

Although Dewey understood that historical knowledge could scarcely be "confirmed by experimental action," he nonetheless believed that pragmatism could illuminate history, since historical events, like scientific objects, have a relational character. Aristotle wrongly assumed that individuals and things develop from some fixed essence and move toward some indwelling end, but "potentialities must be thought of in terms of consequences of interactions with other things. Hence potentialities cannot be known till *after* the interactions have occurred." Dewey emphasized the word *after* because he remained convinced, at least a year before Pearl Harbor when he wrote these passages, that history reveals its "temporal seriality" and "sequential order" when events have been actualized. History is like a theater where the audience observes how things turn out. But at the beginning of the play, before the performance has gotten fully under way, one knows nothing and can predict nothing, since social interaction has yet to occur and history has yet to tell its story:

> Individuality conceived as a temporal development involves uncertainty, indeterminacy, or contingency. Individuality is the source of whatever is unpredictable in the world. The indeterminate is not change in the sense of violation of law, for laws state probable correlations of change and these probabilities exist no matter what the sources of change may be. When a change occurs, *after* it has occurred it belongs to the observable world and is connected with other changes. The nomination of Lincoln for the presidency, his election, his Emancipation Proclamation, his assassination, after they took place can be shown to be related to other events; they can also be shown to have certain connections with Lincoln's own past.[20]

Convinced that in experience are connections waiting to be established through inquiry, Dewey assumed it possible to discern more historical relations than could even Lincoln himself, who confessed, years after the Civil War had broken out, to not knowing why it occurred. According to Dewey, if inquiry moves from the individual to the social and the potential to the actual, knowledge becomes possible because it now has access to observable outcomes as history manifests its hitherto hidden relational character. Adams, one needs to emphasize, was closer to Lin-

19. Dewey, *Experience and Nature*, 148–49.
20. Dewey, "Time and Individuality," 145–46.

coln in being perplexed by events and closer to Peirce in appreciating the cognitive limits of science, which should temper philosophical pride with a little intellectual humility.

Henry Adams could neither solve the old questions of philosophy and history nor allow them to disappear. If theoretical knowledge can no longer sit in judgment of practical thought, if thought verifies itself only in action, then we are left with power and its effects. The pragmatists, Peirce excepted, were innocent of power in technological developments and bureaucratic structures; Adams, like Nietzsche, Weber, and Michel Foucault, became almost obsessed by the autonomy of power and the unconscious human submission to its symbols. He also had a Niebuhrian vision of the human condition in which power rationalizes its actions as writers resort to the sounds of language to conceal the sins of thought.

Whither American philosophy? Having declared the end of philosophy, Rorty advocates taking up history to learn how beliefs come to be formed socially, while at the same time dismissing those beliefs philosophically. By looking at history along with philosophy as a branch of literature, the scholar can demonstrate not how ideas are validated by reason and the rules of logic but how they are legitimated and justified in order to win acceptance. Several figures in American intellectual history, Thorstein Veblen and the Progressive historians Carl Becker and Charles Beard, undertook such an exercise almost a century ago, only to conclude that there is no correlation between what Americans profess as their legitimating beliefs and what they do in the actual world of power and interest. Adams himself studied the Middle Ages to convey the rapture of religious faith as well as demonstrate how theology found its legitimation in art and ritual, but he concluded that there could be no going back to historically surpassed forms of belief without surrendering the integrity of the intellect. Pragmatism, whether Dewey's instrumentalism or Rorty's conversationalism, aims at adjusting and coping rather than knowing. Adams seemed to want to provoke life into leaving him maladjusted by setting out to know the unknowable. Estranged from the political and philosophical universe of his ancestors, Adams chose to leave open the intellectual wounds of modernity in order to push thought to the edge of the abyss. As long as he lived, the life of the mind lived in defiance of its limits. Rorty advises philosophers to give up the search for the foundations of knowledge. Adams once likened older philosophers to pearl divers who, having never touched bottom and reached the oyster bed, continue to assume it is there. America's greatest historian was its deepest diver.

Today neopragmatists hail early American pragmatists for demonstrating the futility of many philosophical questions and thereby presaging the European poststructuralists of our era. Specifically the pragmatists are praised for refuting essentialism and foundationalism, which presume that the truth of things exists prior to knowledge, and for being aware that all knowledge is mediated by forms of representation and that the self is itself a social construction. Neopragmatists and poststructuralists have enjoyed considerable influence on the American campus. Yet several important American thinkers understood the meaning of finitude and fallibility without subscribing to pragmatism as the only way out. The philosopher George Santayana, one of Dewey's leading critics, explained why thought is inherently representational:

> Let the reader meditate for a moment upon the following point: to know reality is, in a way, an impossible pretension, because knowledge means significant representation, discourse about an existence not contained in the knowing thought, and different in duration or locus from the ideas which represent it. But if knowledge does not possess its object how can it intend it? And if knowledge possesses its object, how can it be knowledge or have any practical, prophetic, or retrospective value?[21]

In pragmatism knowledge need not possess its object since it transforms or "reconstructs" it in the act of knowing it. Thus Dewey rejected the idea that knowledge must seek an antecedent reality. But pragmatists, poststructuralists, and deconstructionists were not the first to sense the "metaphysics of presence," the illusion that our ideas about the world are immediately present to the knowing mind. This issue, now called the "logocentric fallacy," may be as old as philosophy itself, and certainly as old as American history, which began, intellectually at least, with Calvinists warning us that all pretense to the sufficiency of reason amounts to the sin of pride.

One aim of this work is to bring out the limitations of pragmatism from a historical perspective, and to do so by often going beyond philosophy and its technical arguments to the larger dimension of American culture and politics. But a confession is in order. Because I am more struck by its limitations than by its possibilities, because I see pragmatism as having failed to fulfill many of its promises, by no means do I insist that modern thought must overcome its skeptical impasse and return to the shining certitudes of an earlier age. Dewey would be the first to agree with Adams that the historian's education ill prepared him for the twentieth century because it rested on premodern assumptions.

Where, then, did Dewey and Adams most differ? It is not a case of one thinker becoming aware that truth could no longer be established in philosophy and the other clinging to some vision of certainty in history.

---

21. George Santayana, *Reason in Common Sense* (1905; New York: Collier, 1962), 104.

Where they differed involved nothing less than the promises of inquiry. Dewey ardently believed what Adams came to doubt. According to the philosopher, inquiry begins in an indeterminate, problematic situation, and proceeds by converting that situation into one that is more stable and determinate and that draws the original "discordant" elements into "a unified whole."[22] Adams also set out to look for "unity" without appealing to anything transcendent or supernatural. As a historian, Adams could agree that the drive to know reflects the seeker's desire for the unification of experience, as opposed to searching for some external object that stands outside and imposes itself on finite experience. Hence the meaning of history for both thinkers must be found within history itself. But the coherence, unity, and wholeness promised by pragmatism at the end of inquiry was nowhere to be found. In four words Adams confessed his failure: "Experience ceases to educate."[23]

In dealing with Dewey and Adams it is difficult to know whether one is dealing with different sensibilities or different realities. Consider their outlooks toward their native America. Dewey grew up convinced that America had been encrusted in dogma and doctrinal rigidity, residues of religious traditions and conservative orthodoxies in economic thought. Significantly, Dewey titled his autobiographical essay "From Absolutism to Experimentalism." Now a common assumption holds that Adams saw history not progressing but regressing from "order" to "chaos." This point of view characterizes his later explorations of medieval history and his well-known charting of the dissipation of energy from "unity" to "multiplicity." But in his earlier study of American history he concluded, contrary to Dewey, that the development of the Republic defies all absolutes and fixed theories. After the decline of New England Puritanism in the eighteenth century, the American people ceased looking to doctrines and ideologies and instead responded to the exigencies of change. Even the founding of the new federal government was regarded as an "experiment" in the "new science of politics." How could pragmatism rescue America from the "acids of modernity" (Walter Lippmann) when Americans had been practicing pragmatists long before the philosophy of pragmatism had been born?

In his nine-volume study of the administrations of Thomas Jefferson and James Madison, Adams depicted political leaders behaving pragmatically and allowing their decisions to be determined by "circumstance" rather than by "principle," by the calculation of consequences rather than by a stubborn adherence to ideology. Even Jefferson's Declaration of

22. Dewey, *Logic: The Theory of Inquiry* (1938; New York: Holt, Rhinehart, 1966), 110–19.
23. Henry Adams, *The Education of Henry Adams* (New York: Modern Library, 1934), 294.

Independence presaged Rorty's advice on language supplanting philosophy. As Carl Becker pointed out, the document was less a matter of
logical consistency and rational proof than felicitous rhetorical persuasion.
The Constitution itself scarcely confined America's political culture to a
theoretical straitjacket that restricted growth and change. The *Federalist*
authors scorned the "theoretic" thinker who believed America could be
guided by "reason" rather than by "experience." With the new Constitution, government itself would leave behind political philosophy as it legitimated its actions as a matter of practical necessity.

History is no friend of truth grounded in theoretical foundations. After
the Revolution and its "self-evident" truths, and after the framers drew
upon theory to secure liberty by balancing power without resorting to
such foundational truths, America developed in ways that identified liberty with the power to grow and expand, to move out beyond its origins
in an effort to be more than itself by appropriating whatever it was not,
a driving force of energy that the Greeks called *dynamus* and that Adams
would liken to the industrial dynamo. American history, instead of having
a determinate character based upon its originating principles, became a
series of events and developments that were nothing more than their
effects. As products of that history, would Americans remain unknown
to themselves? Could political thought be anything more than mind limp-
ing after energy?

A century before Rorty announced the "end" of philosophy, Adams
discerned the American political mind coming to its end in ceasing to
have any significant role in American history. No idea could stand in the
way of America's drive to expand the perimeters of its power and make
possible the development of further experience. American history itself
shared with pragmatism the assumption that life progresses toward the
better since its meaning, always contingent, awaits the future and shuns
the past. As Santayana put it, "A sense of potentiality and a sense of
riddance are . . . the two poles of American liberty." Abraham Lincoln
fully grasped the dilemma of governing in a political culture where pragmatic potentiality bid riddance to moral commitments based upon past
ideals. Lincoln lamented that the "mystic chords of memory" struggled
faintly to be heard in a democratic culture that preferred change to commitment and growth to guilt. The meaning of American history is to
supersede itself and leave no traces of time and tradition. American history itself embodied almost everything the pragmatists asked for in philosophy and indeed in what they regarded as the true, "dynamic" self: openness, adaptability, and a readiness to grow beyond what has been.[24]

24. George Santayana, "Emerson the Poet," in *Santayana on America*, ed. Richard C.
Lyon (New York: Harcourt, 1968), 275; on Lincoln, see John P. Diggins, *The Lost Soul of
American Politics: Virtue, Self-Interest, and the Foundations of Liberalism* (New York: Basic,
1984), 296–346.

If America's political culture started on a pragmatic ethos that rendered the Republic responsive to the environment and open to experience, where would it lead? In Adams's account, instead of leading to unity, wholeness, rational purpose, and conscious direction, American history simply drifted with the course of events and the movement of power, often taking unexpected turns, while ideas had little capacity to shape a changing reality in the image of some ideal, and theory quietly fell by the wayside as Americans did what they desired to do and could get away with. With no defining moment to sustain the Republic's "first principles," American history developed with no overarching purpose other than endless action and reaction as the American character seemed to change everything but itself. The difficulty with pragmatism was not that it succumbed to "acquiescence," as its critics charged, but rather, like American history itself, it was all anticipatory, instructing Americans, in Dewey's words, to treat "life experiences" as "potential disclosures of meanings and values that are to be used as a means to a fuller and more significant experience." And if the past itself cannot be an object of experience? "An American philosophy of history must perforce be a philosophy for its future."[25]

The pragmatist focuses on the future, since the past has no ontological status in that it is over, gone, done with, theoretically thinkable but practically irrevocable. Santayana saw this fetish of the "dominance of the foreground" as typically American in its prevalent absorption in present affairs in view of subsequent consequences. Santayana could agree with the pragmatists that truth and reality escape representation, that philosophy operates as a "discourse," that is, a "language" instead of a "mirror"; that intelligence functions naturalistically to satisfy needs and purposes, and that existence is contingent and transitory. Yet Santayana was closer to Adams in seeing human beings as creatures in a world of flux that cannot be known by exploring experience alone. Instead of tempting thought beyond its depth, practical knowledge sustains belief in progress by fixating itself on the future. "Grant this," Santayana observed of the pragmatist privileging the eventual over the actual, "and at once the whole universe is on its feet again; and all that strange pragmatic reduction of yesterday to to-morrow, of Sanskrit to the study of Sanskrit, of matter to some human notion of matter, turns out to have been a needless equivocation, by which the perspectives of life, avowedly relative, have been treated as absolute, and the dominance of the foreground has been turned from a biological accident into a metaphysical principle."[26]

25. Dewey, "What I Believe," *Forum* 83 (1930): 176–82; *German Philosophy and Politics* (New York: Holt, 1915), 132.
26. Santayana, "Dewey's Naturalistic Metaphysics," in *Santayana on America*, 124. Santayana's description of philosophy as "discourse" is in his *Skepticism and Animal Faith* (1923; New York: Dover, 1955), 179.

Although Deweyan pragmatism claimed to have eliminated metaphysics, Santayana saw it as simply projected onto the future where action entailed belief and belief required some certainty of judgment. There remains another implication in the assumption that truth is to be verified to the extent life is conceived as an endless experiment. In this philosophy of expectancy, pragmatism shares with Marxism and capitalism the assumption that the meaning of history and the purpose of life are no longer matters of thought but of action. All three modernist propositions, despite their obvious political differences, presuppose that the meaning and significance of the present await the future, that nature is responsive to human initiative, that the philosopher's responsibility is to be effective and useful rather than to search for preexisting ideas to which the mind must be congruent, and that objects take on meaning and value only when undergoing change. With pragmatism in particular, the use of experience only prepares us for further experience, without experience itself being immediately self-illuminating or self-rewarding. The assumption that truth and value are produced in future action rather than revealed in present reflection holds out the promise of success, and as such pragmatism becomes not so much a philosophy as a story of the upward movement of life, a hopeful vision that appeals to America's romantic imagination:

> Gatsby believed in the green light, the orgiastic future that year by year recedes before us. It eluded us then, but that's no matter—to-morrow we will run faster, stretch out our arms farther. . . . And one fine morning—
> So we beat on, boats against the current, borne back ceaselessly into the past.[27]

Pragmatism advises us to "beat on" and not allow ourselves to be "borne back ceaselessly into the past." Always looking ahead, pragmatism counsels adjustment and adaptation on the assumption that ideals, or at least something of meaning and value, are expected to emerge from experience and hence need not be regarded as external to it. Pragmatism reorients the meaning of history from retrospective reflection to prospective confrontation. Whether or not Dewey would go so far as to say that the present postpones its own fulfillment so as to exist for the sake of the future, he did advise fellow philosophers to look to experience in order to cope with events.

But Adams saw that history itself dissolves the cognitive import of experience to the extent the historian asks for explanations for events and receives none. Surely history is the sum and substance of human experi-

27. F. Scott Fitzgerald, *The Great Gatsby* (1925; New York: Scribner's, 1953), 182.

ence; yet the happenings of history may elude the intellect's quest for meaning and understanding. The historian interrogates history when he asks the reason of things. What do people experience when they experience experience? Is the knowledge supposedly derived from experience found in reality prior to reason's reflections? Is it grasped or constructed? To the pragmatist such questions are poorly formulated, for experience is not known but anticipated, expected to be "had" in the future, and knowledge that is prospective need not refer to its object that it is in itself but only as it will be experienced. Since the past itself cannot be experienced, or even reexperienced, history is not so much known as acted upon, and Dewey encouraged Americans to act and look forward with hope.

As a historian Adams looked backward into the nature of past events, and even at contemporary unfolding developments, and found no rational principle of explanation, no interpretive scheme that would meaningfully connect sequences and discern patterns, no answer to the demand "Why! Why!! Why!!!"[28] Continually disappointed by the experience of trying to derive knowledge from experience, Adams liked to see himself suffering from what he called, somewhat playfully, the "anxiety of truth." Pragmatism promised to relieve such anxiety by showing us not what to think but how to think and how to move confidently ahead instead of dwelling behind in a metaphysical wondersickness. If Adams dove deep and found nothing, Dewey taught Americans how to swim on the surface and how to conceive nature for the purpose of using it. In his early years Adams tried swimming in the treacherous currents of modern thought, assuming mind was a truth-knowing faculty, and he ended up drowning in his own doubts. Dewey would gladly have thrown him a lifejacket, a methodology for staying afloat by coping with the instant conditions of experience. Would Adams have grabbed it? Could the philosopher save the historian?

28. Adams, *Education*, 92.

1

The Disenchantment of the World

The Flowering of Intellect and the Decline of Knowledge

The novelist Gore Vidal once asked Eleanor Roosevelt if she had known Henry Adams. "Oh, yes!" she replied, recalling a scene that took place in 1916, just two years before Adams's death:

> "He was such a kind man, so good with children. They would crawl all over him when he sat in his Victoria. He was very tolerant. But," and she frowned, "we did not agree politically. I remember the first time we went to his house. My Franklin had just come to Washington" (as assistant secretary of the navy) "and I of course was very shy then and could never get the courage to speak up, particularly with someone much older. Well, my Franklin made some remark about President Wilson, about how well he was doing. And Mr. Adams just laughed at him and pointed toward the White House and said, 'Young man, it doesn't make the slightest difference who lives in that house, history goes on with or without the president.' Well, I just couldn't keep quiet. 'Mr. Adams,' I said, 'that is a very terrible thing to say to a young man who wants to go into politics and be of use to other people.' Oh, I made quite a speech."
>
> "And what did Mr. Adams say?"
>
> "I can't remember. I think he just laughed at me. We were always good friends."[1]

Perhaps Adams could laugh because what he knew hurt too much. More than any other American intellectual, Adams carried the burden of

1. Gore Vidal, "The Adams' Fall: II," *New York Review of Books* (April 1, 1976), 23.

the crises of liberalism of the late nineteenth century all the way to his grave. He knew that the three main currents of early American political culture had run dry. New England Puritanism, that seventeenth-century wellspring of spiritual idealism, failed to survive the frontier environment. As a result a Protestant ethic that had emphasized hard work, duty, and moral striving had given way to a sensate culture of wealth, leisure, and opportunity. Classical Republicanism, the second current that had arrived in America by way of Renaissance humanism and English Whig ideology, a political doctrine of "civic virtue" that Adams's great-grandfather had scrutinized, failed to survive the American Revolution. When creating the Constitution the *Federalist* authors, like John Adams, looked to the self-regulating "machinery of government" to compensate for the absence of a virtuous citizenry dedicated to the public good. And the third current, the Enlightenment with its tenuous balance of reason and passion and its faith in "self-evident" truths, had succumbed to new discoveries of the irrational forces within man and the deterministic forces within nature and history. Man, once regarded as a rational creature capable of intellectual and moral progress, was now conceived as little more than a "feeble atom or molecule" at the mercy of unconscious drives and infinite mechanisms. Thus the simple institutions that had once promised to preserve the Republic—free elections, a free press, and free public schools— could no longer be counted upon to assure that reason would prevail in public life. Now, Adams lamented, it hardly mattered who was in the White House. History is governed by power, force, and energy, and political leaders, rather than guiding the rushing movement of history, would simply follow it, even to its doom.[2]

How Henry Adams came to this somber conclusion will be discussed in the following chapter. Why he did is a question that needs to be addressed here. For today many scholars tend to attribute his grim views to social and political factors, with the result, whether intentional or not, of minimizing the seriousness and urgency of his reflections. Assuming that Adams had inherited his family's passion to lead the country, some scholars also assume that he was suffering from the frustrations of political impotence and the "status anxieties" of social dislocation.[3] Thus Adams is depicted as "the powerless patrician,"[4] an American aristocrat manqué who, in writing about power, only revealed his resentment in not possessing it. Yet Adams had made it clear to his family that he never felt cut

2. Adams, *Education*, 3–39.
3. Richard Hofstadter, *The Age of Reform: From Bryan to F.D.R.* (New York, 1955), 71–81.
4. E. Digby Baltzell, *The Protestant Establishment: Aristocracy and Caste in America* (New York, 1966), 90–93.

out to seek political office;[5] and his social life was richly fulfilling and his intellectual status so secure that he could delight in publishing anonymous novels. Even William James believed that Adams's fear that civilization was progressing toward its doom was simply a projection, a personal need to feel that history would culminate in negation only because his own long life was approaching cessation. However valid James's diagnosis, the philosophy of pragmatism that he offered was simply too prosaic and robust to be troubled by the problems that afflicted Adams. So too was the platform of Progressive reform envisioned by President Theodore Roosevelt, whose emphasis on the "manly virtues" had no place for an intellectual effete like Adams, a point of which H. L. Mencken loved to remind Americans.[6] Years later, when the promises of progressivism collapsed in the aftermath of World War I, members of the postwar "Lost Generation" would appreciate Adams's indictment of the easy assumptions that had propelled America into the bloody trenches of the western front. The disenchanted Adams seemed to be the exception, as was Herman Melville in the nineteenth century, to Henry James's observation that Americans lack "the imagination of disaster."

An impression current in historiography sees pragmatism as the victory of "uncertainty" over the sunny certitudes of nineteenth-century American culture.[7] If one regards uncertainty as presupposing deeper confidences, the pragmatists may be read differently. Although Dewey dispensed with past ideas of truth, he found certainty in scientific methodology; although James rejected orthodox religion, he assured Americans they could be certain about beliefs that brought satisfaction; although the eccentric Peirce could scarcely organize his own life, he looked to organized, systematic inquiry as certain to yield truths independent of human vagaries. The pragmatists confidently identified with the future; Adams identified the past as the more haunting burden of uncertainty. "The habit of doubt; of distrusting his own judgment and of totally rejecting the judgment of the world; the tendency to regard every question as open . . . all these are well-known qualities of New England character."[8] Comparing the last Puritan to the first pragmatists, one sees how the philosophers carried Victorian optimism over into the brave new world

5. Henry Adams to Charles Francis Adams, Jr., Feb. 9, 1859, in *The Letters of Henry Adams*, ed. J. C. Levenson et al., 6 vols. (Cambridge, 1982), vol. 1, 18–25.

6. Mencken's preference for T.R. to Henry Adams is in his *Prejudices: A Selection*, ed. James T. Farrell (New York: Vintage, 1955), 68.

7. James T. Kloppenberg, *Uncertain Victory: Social Democracy and Progressivism in European and American Thought, 1870–1920* (New York: Oxford, 1986).

8. Adams, *Education*, 6.

of experimentation, where all human problems were then regarded as ultimately solvable.[9]

A psychohistorian could ignore Adams's own confessions and trace his interrogating doubts to personality disorders. The grief and possible guilt he suffered with his wife's suicide; the outburst of anti-Semitism in 1893, when he blamed the world's banking crisis on Jewish financiers; the "anxiety of influence" he faced in the challenge of living up to the stature of his ancestors; his fascination with the irrational and ironic and the specter of chaos; his determination to wrest philosophical answers from historical questions; his ambivalent attitude toward women as embodying power and virtue; his secret prayers to the Virgin asking forgiveness—does not all this suggest a neurotic personality? More likely, the various episodes of Adams's career have a significance beyond his life, and ramifications in European intellectual history as well. The problems of modernism were peculiar neither to Adams nor to the pragmatists.

To interpret Adams within the broader movement of European culture suggests that other thinkers could arrive at similar conclusions during the fin de siècle, even when writing in different geographical settings. In this instance the "context" of Adams's ideas, the purported conditions and circumstances from which his thoughts supposedly sprang, is less important than the thoughts themselves. European thinkers suffering from neither power frustrations nor status anxieties also felt the limits of knowledge and the eclipse of authority, and hence registered the crisis of liberalism that had been brought on by the corrosions of modernism. In recent years this crisis of liberalism—supposedly constant since World War I—has been linked to "poststructuralism," which is the culmination of modernism in a worldview where language is the only reality and behind words lurks the meaningless void. Today philosophers and literary critics link American intellectual history to European poststructuralism by returning to the writings of James and Dewey. The deeper link may be with Adams, the historian who, sensing the "abyss of ignorance," whimsically concluded that "silence is best." Intellectuals, of course, can seldom remain silent—to paraphrase Auden; despairing of knowing, they go on writing. But Adams's connection with contemporary European intellectual currents may be better appreciated by taking note of European writers who presaged the crisis of knowledge and authority by trying to give literary shape to chaos and disorder.

One writer who would have recognized the significance of *The Education*

9. For a disenchanted reaction to the hopes of science and pragmatism, see Joseph Wood Krutch, *The Modern Temper* (1929; New York: Harvest, 1956).

of Henry Adams was Thomas Mann, whose novel *Buddenbrooks* records the same theme of a long family tradition coming to an end as the twentieth century begins. The failure of the genealogical imperative haunted both writers, and it is no coincidence that each questioned whether the traditional forms of narration, either in the novel or historical prose, could continue to rest on the assumption of linear unity. The sense of unity and continuity was also essential to the concept of family, and the connection between authority and tradition could hardly have been overlooked when Adams discovered he and his new wife would be deprived of the blessing of children. In 1874, two years after Adams married Mariam Hooper, he wrote a review of Fustel de Coulange's *The Ancient City.* "The mystery of generation was to the ancient Romans what the mystery of creation is to our own age. The belief that generation was due entirely to males, that the female was only passive, receptive, and had no other share in it, caused the father to be alone regarded as the possessor of the mysterious spark of existence, and gave to him the peculiar sacredness which characterized the Roman *paterfamilias.*" And if, as in *Buddenbrooks* and the *Education,* the son defies the authority of the fathers and allows the chain of genealogy to be broken? "The domestic hearth was the alter. . . . Neglect of the worship, or failure to make regular offerings, was therefore a crime like parricide. To allow the family to become extinct, so that no one should be left to carry on the worship and supply the offerings, was a compound of parricide and suicide."[10]

The suicide of Adams's wife, who took cyanide in 1885 in despair over her father's recent death, is not mentioned in the *Education.* But the emotion, if not the fact, permeates the last chapters of the book, just as sickness and death permeates Mann's *The Magic Mountain* and *Death in Venice;* and it is notable that both authors, Mann in his Joseph stories and Adams in his explorations of medieval religion, will try to recapture the eternal sources of man's spiritual values. Both authors depicted the work of the dying artist as evidence of alienation and the poet's victimization by a commercial society that suppresses the creative instinct—the theme of Adams's last and most neglected book, *The Life of George Cabot Lodge.*[11] Above all, both believed that the writer's main responsibility was to place his subject genealogically in order to render a patrilineal connection between past and present. Thus the *Education* opens "under the shadow of the Boston State House" where "in the third house below Mount Vernon Place, February 16, 1838, a child was born, and christened later by his uncle . . . as Henry Brooks Adams." Mann similarly advised the

10. Adams, "Coulange's *Ancient City," North American Review* 118 (April 1874): 390–97.
11. Adams, *The Life of George Cabot Lodge* (New York and Boston, 1911).

writer that the genetic approach provides the link of knowledge that could give a sense of meaningful order. "A work of art must have long roots in my life, secret connections must lead from it to early childhood, if I am to consider myself entitled to it, if I am to believe in the legitimacy of what I am doing."[12] But the legitimacy of what Adams as well as Mann is doing becomes problematic when the genealogical tie exhausts itself. Thus the *Education* and *Buddenbrooks* identify descent of their own respective heritages with the passing of history itself. Both works depict power, wealth, respectability, and civic duties, while in the background lurks drift, decay, and dissolution, as though the decreasing energy of the universe gave birth to the increasing sensitivity of the artist. The doctrine of evolutionary progress seems to be reversed, for it is the sense of civilization's decline that coincides with the flowering of intellect. In Mann and Adams we encounter the evolution of the human mind to the point where it had developed the most refined consciousness, only to discover that it was rapidly becoming estranged from a universe it could neither comprehend nor control. For Adams "the last lesson—the sum and term of education" occurs with the dying of his sister. Describing the deathwatch over his sister's fatal and painful illness after she was stricken with lockjaw in Switzerland, Adams is overwhelmed by the serenity of Lake Geneva and the Alps and, by contrast, the terrors of the human mind, which "felt itself stripped naked, vibrating in a void of shapeless energies, with resistless mass, colliding, crushing, wasting, and destroying what these same energies had created and labored from eternity to perfect." The mind could not be at rest with the stillness of nature or the silence of God:

> The idea that any personal deity could find pleasure or profit in torturing a poor woman, by accident, and insane temperaments, could not be held for a moment. For pure blasphemy, it made pure atheism a comfort. God might be as the Church said, a Substance, but He could not be a Person.[13]

In Adams and Mann we are in the presence of two dimensions of modernism—the sense that the continuity of thought has been broken and that the awareness of death brings to consciousness the absurdity of existence.

Adams has been described as an "antimodern modernist," a displaced elitist who fled America's changing, democratic environment to seek order

---

12. Adams, *Education*, 3; Mann is quoted in Patricia Drechsel Tobin, *Time and the Novel* (Princeton, 1978), 58.

13. Adams, *Education*, 289.

and meaning in the Middle Ages.[14] Yet other writers, the philosopher Charles S. Peirce and the novelist James Joyce, for example, regarded themselves as promodern modernists and still looked to the Middle Ages for illuminating perspectives on the modern world.[15] Another writer in another environment, Max Weber, went beyond the Middle Ages to ancient Rome, Egypt, and Israel in an effort to find answers to the riddles of history. Comparing Adams's reflections to those of Weber, we can further appreciate why the sensibility of modernism springs from more than one context and why intellectual history can be the study of ideas held by different thinkers whose curiosities belong to each other even more than to their own specific time and place.

Politics and Ethics

In the skeptical minds of Adams and Weber the personal and the theoretical cannot easily be separated. Both minds were responding to problems that, while possibly felt in the inner recesses of their psyches, originated in philosophical issues involving the crisis of knowledge. In the writings of Adams and Weber the reader also feels the ordeal of liberalism in its confrontation with modernism. The American and the German writer witnessed the rise of industry and technology, wrote about science as methodology, and visited industrial exhibitions in Chicago and St. Louis, and each came away disturbed as well as moved by the new age of energy. Not only did Adams and Weber realize there was no turning back to a previous era, they also felt sharply the split between natural science and the human spirit, a split that rendered unbridgeable the realm of power and the realm of value. For Adams too sensed what Weber called the "disenchantment of the world" and Dewey the "unnatural wound," an awareness that the universe had been reduced to a mechanical specter no longer capable of producing the rich supernatural illusions that had once sustained the mind. Perhaps Adams and Weber felt the threat of science to religion more than other thinkers because during their childhoods their households had reverberated with the ideas of William Ellery Channing, the Boston Transcendentalist and favorite theologian of Weber's mother. Channing taught that to achieve power over one's self was more important than gaining power over the world. Adams and Weber would also come to value religion not as a blind custom but as an ethic involving self-control and sacrifice. Yet both writers would also recognize that Christianity

14. T. J. Jackson Lears, *No Place of Grace: Antimodernism and the Transformation of American Culture, 1880–1920* (New York, 1981).

15. Umberto Eco, *The Middle Ages of James Joyce*, trans. Ellen Esrock (London: Hutchinson, 1989); for Peirce on the Middle Ages, see chapter 4.

failed to inspire its followers to keep their eyes on otherworldly ideals. In 1897, about a decade before Weber published his now-famous *The Protestant Ethic and the Spirit of Capitalism*, Adams saw that the Protestant Reformation must be interpreted as more than a theological dispute. "Doubtless the protestant reformation had an intensely religious side to intensely religious men, yet the connection between protestantism and economy was close, and that between the protestant mind and the economic mind was closer still." But Adams, unlike Weber, believed that the corruptions of materialism antedated the rise of Protestantism and capitalism. In the Middle Ages the Catholic "church itself turned religion into a trade, and made every priest a huckster."[16] Although Adams and Weber recognized that Christianity ultimately failed in its spiritual mission, both would continue to probe the nature of religion as a subjective experience to be understood from the point of view of the believer, an exercise that often reflected their own need to see whether life had a "final meaning." And here these two anguished skeptics met one of the central challenges of modernism: the problem of meaning drives men toward belief in God, and thus the scholar studies religion because of its psychological revelations and social consequences. Neither Adams nor Weber believed that they could sustain the role that religion had once played; they studied it much as a modern anthropologist studies a "cultural system" of symbols and images. Perhaps the alienation of the modern mind is best manifested as one watches it trying to understand what it cannot believe.

What was true of religion was also true of politics. Both Adams and Weber wrote on politics as a vocation, and each understood why it would be difficult to conceive politics as it had been conceived in such historical epochs as classical antiquity, the Renaissance, and the Enlightenment, as morally redemptive. The modern conflict between politics and ethics deeply troubled both writers. In a visit to the United States in 1904, Weber observed firsthand the workings of the boss system and its political machines, and he came away convinced that capitalism had penetrated the body politic. As did Tocqueville in the previous century, Weber saw in America a vision of the future, and especially disturbing were nonideological political parties bureaucratically organized and founded on patronage. Politics had more to do with striving toward power than with accepting authority, not to mention duty and responsibility. He regarded engagement in public life without illusions as a feat of "heroic individualism." But he used the term *Betrieb* to describe politics as a "business," an

16. Adams is quoted in Charles A. Beard's introduction to Brooks Adams, *The Law of Civilization and Decay* (1896; New York: Vintage, 1955), xxviii–xxix.

organized activity that ran mechanically on its own momentum, indifferent to moral considerations; American political parties in particular were
all platform and no principle (*gesinnungslos*). Adams, too, remained convinced that American business had corrupted politics in its shameless
scramble for profit and power. Thus both writers felt estranged from the
classical tradition of politics that was no longer available to them, while
still feeling deeply the moral obligation, inherited from their family lin-
eage, to serve their country. Yet both could only be skeptical of all efforts
to reconstruct society in the light of the republican ideal of civic duty,
the Christian commandment of love, or the socialist principles of justice
and fraternity.

Adams and Weber also remained skeptical of science as a means to
social reconstruction. Where American pragmatists would look to science
as a tool for controlling the forces of nature and history, Adams and
Weber, while seeing in science the methodological imperative of objectivity, also saw it as an augmenting system of power that emanates from
knowledge and will only to stand over and even against its human origins.
The logic of science is predictability, calculation, manipulation, the tendency to rationalize all aspects of life as society becomes more and more
bureaucratized and routinized. In Adams as well as in Weber there is a
sense in which man is the creature and creator of his own means of
alienation. As man reshapes the world through scientific activity he also
allows technique and mechanism to establish dominion over reason and
spirit. For Adams this inexorable tendency toward rationalization would
lead to the "mechanical dissolution" of history, for Weber to the "iron
cage" of bureaucratic society. Both writers shared a modernist awareness
that as man manipulates nature to increase his power he creates forces
over which he has less and less control. And both were haunted by the
thought that modern man may worship power the way primitive man
had worshiped the gods.

Above all, what Adams and Weber shared most fundamentally was a
profound sence that the mechanization of society requires an opposing
principle to represent the creative and spiritual forces of life. Thus both
would appreciate William James's efforts to explore the irrational basis of
human actions—though Adams would question whether James's psychology could provide the foundations for religious belief. But however they
differed over James, both Adams and Weber looked to some emotional
force that could revive feeling and passion and thereby possibly reverse
the scientific tendency toward rationalization. In Weber's view, the mindless momentum of bureaucratic structures and cultural traditions, which
are themselves governed by pragmatic adaptation to reality leading to
routine regulations, could be broken only by the appearance of "charis-

matic authority." Weber sensed that a pragmatic approach to social relations would lead to systematic calculation of consequences based upon practical expediency, and this deadening routinization would erode ideals to the point where only a "charismatic breakthrough" (to use Wolfgang Mommsen's phrase) could bring about the birth of new value-oriented behavior. The charismatic leader, on the basis of some extraordinary or divine gift, would be able to introduce into history emotions that endow life with meaning and value, spiritual emotions that could possibly arrest the technical forces of "disenchantment." In Adams's view, charismatic authority would be found in the symbol of the Virgin Mary, whose miracles and mysteries defied reason and logic yet aroused the devotion of the masses. Both writers attributed feminine qualities to charisma; both also resorted to what Weber called "ideal types," abstract models or pure categories invented by the scholar so that we may have a point of reference for observations on reality. It did not trouble Adams and Weber that such projections had no basis in empirical reality. The ideal type of charismatic authority and the Virgin as symbol and myth simply constituted what their minds pictured them to be. For both authors the real problem was reality itself, the world of power as opposed to the realm of value. Thus to challenge the relentless drive toward complete rationalization, Adams offered "the Dynamo and the Virgin," the juxtaposition of the specter of reason, technique, and control to the symbol of hope, mercy, and freedom.

It should be noted that Adams and Weber were writing during the heyday of science and technology, which was bolstered by the heritage of the eighteenth-century Enlightenment. That both would see a response to the rigorous logic of science in the spontaneous passion of charismatic authority suggests the extent to which the modernist intellect felt estranged from the Enlightenment. Although they continued to believe in the values of liberty and reason, they saw reason itself threatening to eliminate all that was irrational and mysterious, not merely the superstitions of the past, but the surprises of the future that confound scientific determinism and make freedom possible. Yet while Adams and Weber recognized that there could be no return to the unmodified concepts of the Enlightenment, they remained in some respects heirs of that great philosophical tradition. For Adams and Weber were also liberal humanists with a skeptical need to question everything. If they no longer could endorse eighteenth-century doctrines of reason and progress, they still remained committed to the principles of detachment and objectivity. At times Adams could be so objective that he was able to look at himself as though he were another person. One contemporary described Adams as "the only man in the world who could sit on a fence and watch himself go by."[17] The humorous observation suggests another feature of the modern mind that troubled Adams and Weber: the self can know itself only as spectator, in contemplation rather than action. And, curiously, what Adams came to know about himself bears significantly on what Weber sublimated into a theory of knowledge and value.

Watching his father and mother doing their daily chores, the young Max Weber grew up to sense the existence of two distinct spheres: the masculine world, where human relations are mediated through official papers and documents, and the feminine world, where emotions are felt but seldom spoken. From these observations Weber went on to develop a dual perspective wherein the paternal sphere involves the world of power and action and the maternal the world of thought and feeling. Ultimately this insight came to be applied to a methodology for the social sciences that distinguished the empirical mode of logical analysis from the moral demands of value judgment. And Weber could never make up his mind which sphere should prevail, possibly because, as Arthur Mitzman suggested, he could never decide whether to side with his father and the external world of affairs or with his mother and the internal world of affections.[18] Henry Adams did decide only to come to believe that he had committed an unpardonable sin.

Shortly after Adams died, on March 27, 1918, a poem was found in his coat pocket, "Prayer to the Virgin of Chartres." The poem reveals much about Adams's lifelong struggle with authority, whether it be the authority of politics, history, science, art, religion, or, perhaps more emotionally, women. For the poem illustrates Adams's uncanny perception of the relationship of both religion to women and faith to love, those inescapable subjects that begin in rational thoughts and end in sleepless nights. Like Weber, Adams sensed a world divided by the emotions of gender, and in identifying certain aspects of Christianity with the more compassionate qualities of womanhood, he was turning upside down a tradition of thought that began with Machiavelli, continued in Gibbon, and fructified in Nietzsche. That tradition had blamed the decline of classical, masculine virtue on the Christian religion, whose ethical system supposedly rendered political life weak and effeminate, replacing pride with humility, strength with suffering. In several of his writings, as we shall see, Adams challenges the macho critique of Christianity and matriarchy by recounting the numerous instances in history when women wielded power over men. But in the secrecy of his poem to the Virgin,

17. The contemporary, the Kansas editor Ed Howe, is quoted in Ernest Samuels's introduction to *The Education of Henry Adams* (1918; Boston: Riverside, 1973), x.

18. Arthur Mitzman, *The Iron Cage: An Historical Interpretation of Max Weber* (New York: 1969), 39–74.

Adams explains, with almost the same mode of reasoning Freud employed to explain the oedipal tension between son and father, why he betrayed his mother and in doing so possibly denied the feminine side of his own character. Every man's "sin," lamented Adams, originated in rejecting the "majesty of grace and love" of Mary in order to embrace the "Primal Force" that is the world of men. Even Christianity dictated to Jesus that he "be about [his] Father's business." Adams feels he has committed the same transgression in trying "to find the father's clue" and in the process losing "what I now value more, the Mother—you!" Having rejected the mother in order to "claim the father's empire for my own," Adams now believes that in identifying with the father all men merely reveal the power-drive within themselves that culminates in the worship of the Dynamo, the symbol of reason, law, and organized force. For Adams this revelation is especially acute since he had earlier assumed that by following his father's advice and thoughts he would find the "clue" to power. But his "education" concludes with the awareness that power is as elusive as love is mysterious and that, in fact, as we shall see, the two are mutually related as expressions of force and energy, whether it be the love of power or the power of love. Thus his final plea to the Virgin is a plea for knowledge and understanding. "Help me to know! Help me to see! Help me to feel! Help me to hear!" It is also a plea for forgiveness and absolution on the part of a thinker whose thoughts have exhausted themselves in a rational search for rational answers:

Help me to bear! not my own baby load,
But yours; who bore the failure of the light,
The strength, the knowledge and the thought of God,—
The futile folly of the Infinite. [19]

The same tension between the spiritual and the rational characterized Max Weber's perspectives. Both Adams and Weber recognized that the inexorable spread of secular rationalism would extirpate animism and leave the world as a pile of matter to be mastered by the manipulations of science. And a philosophy that turned toward science, as did pragmatism, would have to confront the universe on its own terms. With matter no longer seen as consisting in inherent qualities but as functions and motions in which either men or molecules are regarded as events, and with knowledge no longer answering the question why but how, pragmatism aimed to master events by means of technical control. Such a stance, to be successful, could compel the philosopher to collaborate with power and

19. Adams, "A Poem to the Virgin of Chartres," in A Henry Adams Reader, ed. Elizabeth Stevenson (Garden City, N.Y., 1958), 348–53.

the forces of change. An event-oriented philosophy leaves the philosopher with no prexisting idea to which the intellect must be consonant. Perhaps James disdained the "bitch-goddess" of success" because he sensed that philosophy could become the instrument of power that human intelligence itself manufactured. But how could pragmatism escape the dilemma when its definition of knowledge defers to science as the reliable discipline that experiments in order to produce observable effects, a process wherein the meaning of an object can be known only by gaining power over it?

Somewhat the same implications pertain to the question of value as they do to power. In redefining philosophy as the study of events and occurrences, the pragmatist denies to objects meaning and value other than what happens to them as a result of human control and manipulation. With the intellect seeking knowledge not for the sake of knowing but for the purpose of altering and transforming, what can be known, measured, and valued is change itself. Pragmatism set out to liberate philosophy from religion and theology, but in ending up with the power to produce change as the purpose of knowledge, and with thought itching with eagerness to act, American philosophy differed little from the standards of judgment in politics and economics, where both voter and consumer are to be delivered from discontent by the promise of "Change!" In reducing knowlege to experience and making a fetish of change, could pragmatism prevent America from succumbing to a politics of instrumental domination and an economics of commercial action?

Whatever the answer, Adams and Weber doubted that scientific philosophy could arrest the process of secularization and rationalization that gave industrial society a life of its own, symbolized in the logic of the Dynamo and the laws of bureaucracy. The scientific worldview also sheds little light on the meaning of life and death and the riddle of good and evil. For answers to such issues the philosopher turns to religion to appreciate a system of symbolic representations or to study the wholesome effects of the variety of faiths. But religion is experience and not knowledge, immediate qualities of feelings and emotions, of which Dewey wrote, "since they are bad there is no need to know them."[20] Adams and Weber could accept Dewey's and James's conviction that the emotional phenomenon of religion must be seen as it exists and as it functions without criticizing it from the point of view of knowledge and truth. Yet, as Niebuhr noted in commenting upon James, the pragmatist's affirmative attitude toward religion excludes the darker side of things, especially the Calvinist sense of sin and anxiety about salvation—which Adams could trace to his ancestors and the riddle of free will, and Weber to the origins of capitalism

20. Dewey, *Experience and Nature*, 264.

and the fate of freedom. Moreover, instead of enhancing the will to believe, religion could open up deeper, more complex emotions, such as the terror that feels the beauty of the sublime, emotions that tempt thought beyond its depth and elude the demand of the will. Significantly, Adams and Weber saw the connection between the meaning of religious experience and the mystical springs of eroticism. Weber described how possession gives way to submission and reason to passion as the lover "knows himself to be freed from the cold skeleton hands of rational orders, just as completely as from the banality of everyday routine."[21] Perhaps it was because Weber and Adams could not undergo such a surrender to authority, the sacrifice of intellect either to rigorous claims of religious belief or to the irrational passions of romantic love, that they each experienced life as an ordeal to be faced stoically. When asked why he studied, pondered, and wrote so much, Weber replied that he wanted to see how much he could "endure."[22] Adams asked the Virgin "who bore the failure of the light" to help him shoulder the same burden.

The Cunning of Irony

Adams shared with European thinkers like Mann and Weber the same consciousness of modernism, of the mind's quest for the basis of truth and value in a contemporary world where all knowledge is indeterminate. Yet despite the parallels there remain some differences, not the least of which was the contrast between Mann's desire to cling to the values of the Enlightenment and Adams's conviction that the eighteenth-century world of his ancestors was gone forever. Several crucial differences also separate Adams from Weber.

One curious difference is that Adams saw little value in America's Puritan heritage (except, perhaps, to amuse himself by equating modern scientific determinism with Calvinist predestination in order to suggest that in both science and religion one cannot escape damnation). Weber, in contrast, saw in Calvinism evidence that ideas as well as material forces are viable in history, especially those of a religion that provided no soothing opiate but instead made lifelong sober diligence in one's "calling" both the agony and the ecstasy of Christianity. Two decades after Adams's death Puritanism's rich intellectual legacy became a subject of scholarly

21. Weber, "Religious Rejections of the World and Their Direction," in From Max Weber: Essays in Sociology, ed. H. H. Gerth and C. Wright Mills (New York, 1946), 347; Reinhold Niebuhr, introduction to William James, The Varieties of Religious Experience (New York: Collier, 1961), 5-8.
22. Marianne Weber, Max Weber: A Biography (New Brunswick, N.J.: Transaction, 1988), 196-99, 471-72.

discourse. But Adams never considered the possibility of reconciling certain aspects of Calvinism with modernism or pondered the thought that a sense of sin and Christian irony would help illuminate, if not redeem, the corrupting nature of modern politics. Adams saw himself as estranged from all religious and political traditions, and he could hardly agree with Weber that it was the practice of religion, and not necessarily its truth, that provided the basis of social reality and human solidarity.

If the truths of religion were never meant to be subjected to empirical investigation, what of the authority of tradition and the lessons of the past? Could history itself be a science? Both Adams and Weber believed that historical understanding depends upon causal relations and that science aspires to causal explanation. But whereas Weber rejected the idea that scientific knowledge is identical to the discovery of laws, Adams tried to apply the newly discovered laws of physics to history in a last desperate effort to see if history had a future. It is commonly assumed that Adams went off the deep end when he turned to the second law of thermodynamics to chart the dissipation of energy and the emerging specter of entropy. But after writing nine volumes on American history Adams was unable to comprehend history the way Weber believed it should be comprehended. In his early writings Adams made use of the methodological principle that Weber would later develop: that history required not only empirical investigation but interpretive understanding. Since men in the past have motives upon which they act and reasons and purposes that render their actions meaningful, the task of the historian is "that of interpreting the meaning which men give to their actions and so understand the actions themselves."[23] But Adams could barely find any meaning in American history. The people of the young republic were in a constant state of motion, with little capacity for reflection and no sense of moral striving toward ends higher than the mundane necessities of existence:

The American people went to their daily tasks without much competition or mental effort. . . . Every day a million men went to their work, every evening they came home with some work accomplished; but the result was a matter for census rather than for history. The acres brought into cultivation, the cattle bred, the houses built, proved no doubt that human beings, like ants and bees, could indefinitely multiply their numbers, and could lay up stores of food; but these statistics offered no evidence that the human being, any more than the

23. Weber is quoted in Lelan McLemore, "Max Weber's Defense of Historical Inquiry," *History and Theory* 23 (1984): 277–95.

ant and bee, was conscious of a higher destiny, or was even mechanically developing into a more efficient animal.[24]

For Adams the problem of history remained the problem of consciousness. America was propelled by practical intelligence but moving blindly without theoretical vision. A people unaware of the meaning of their activities communicate almost nothing to the historian who sets out to understand their experience.

The problem of politics, meanwhile, remained the problem of paradox. Should the scholar study political action in light of the intentions of the actor or the results of the action taken? Both Adams and Weber believed that consequences are more important than intentions, and in this sense they shared the pragmatist's conviction that the objective outcome of a course of action deserves more attention than the subjective motives for undertaking it. Yet both went beyond the pragmatists in perceiving an ironic relation between the intentions of political programs and the unexpected consequences of pursuing them. What Weber termed the irony of unintended consequences is a perfect formulation of Adams's description of Jefferson as he left office in 1808, sadly aware of the paradoxical relation of his political programs to the original meaning of his political philosophy:

> Loss of popularity was his bitterest trial. He who longed like a sensitive child for sympathy and love left office as strongly and almost as generally disliked as the least popular President who preceded or followed him. He had undertaken to create a government which should interfere in no way with private action, and he created one which interfered directly in the concerns of every private citizen in the land. He had come into power as the champion of States-rights, and had driven States to the verge of armed resistance. He had begun by claiming credit for stern economy, and ended by exceeding the expenditure of his predecessors. He had invented a policy of peace, and the invention resulted in the necessity of fighting at once the two greatest Powers in the world.[25]

Increasingly seeing history as irrational to the extent he failed to bring it under some law of cause and effect, at times seeing only the cunning of irony, Adams grew less certain about science as a mode of investigating human experience. Yet if Adams and Weber parted company on the

---

24. Adams, *History of the United States of America during the Administrations of Thomas Jefferson* (1889–91; New York: Library of America, 1986), 749.

25. Ibid., 1239.

promises of social science, they did share similar doubts about morality as a rational proposition. Weber's Kantian background sensitized him to dualism, particularly the dualism between fact and value, what "is" and what "ought" to be. Adams also recognized the fundamental dichotomy between the descriptive and the normative when he told Harvard students that it is one thing to accumulate empirical data and another to teach ethical dicta. Was science, then, incompatible with morality?

According to Weber, the presence of dualism, which had kept alive the "pure flame" of conviction and ethical conscience, was "hampered" by two scientific worldviews. First, the physical sciences assumed that unchanging invariant natural laws govern life; hence what is normatively right was identical with the "immutably *existent*"; second, an "unambiguous evolutionary principle" later came to dominate thought in which the normative right waited upon the "inevitably *emergent*."[26] The latter view would be taken up by the pragmatists, who treated human culture in biological terms and believed it impossible to evaluate life from any other point of view than behavior and adaptation. Morality would be not so much defined or demonstrated but, as Weber put it, part of the "inevitably emergent." It would turn not necessarily on what "is" or what "ought" to be put on what the future will bring forth.

One can begin to understand why pragmatism became America's original school of philosophy and the nation's peculiar philosophical outlook. A country born of the repudiation of the old world would find congenial a philosophy that told its people to think ahead because the future is the biological order of human growth. In this respect Darwinism built upon and continued existing American attitudes. America's heritage of Jeffersonianism and Emersonianism subordinated the past to the "sovereignty of the present" in order to liberate thought from the dead weight of tradition. The framers of the Constitution looked to the new "science of politics"; they believed that all previous efforts at establishing republican liberty had failed, just as, a century later, the pragmatists believed that all prior philosophical efforts at establishing truth and morality had failed. Perhaps it is not surprising that the radical Tom Paine would inveigh against antiquity; but even Abraham Lincoln, a rare political leader with a sense of the tragic who recognized that the past weighed heavily in the inherited guilt and sin of slavery, urged Americans to "think anew" and "disenthrall" themselves from the past. Whether trying to abide by theology or adapt to biology, America looked ahead with hope and backward with dread. "William James," John Dewey wrote in 1929, "was well within the bounds of moderation when he said that looking forward instead of

26. Weber, *Methodology of the Social Sciences* (New York: Free Press, 1949), 51–52.

backward, looking to what the world and life might become instead of to what they have been, is an alteration in the 'seat of authority.'"[27]

But Adams and Weber were historians, and, more struck by the physical rather than the biological sciences, were completely modern in recognizing that science had become divorced from philosophy and its traditional quest for foundations and first principles. The idea of a quest implies searching to get at the truth of things by thinking thoughts that are true to the way things are and consistent with other thoughts. The quest came to an end with Darwinism, the theory of evolution that demonstrated the nature of things to be a succession of events in which nothing is fixed and everything is change and transition. No longer could the reality of things be a matter of photographic representation, copied in the mind like a "kodak fixation," as Dewey put it, for modern science cannot reveal what things are but only what effects they have when experimented upon. With pragmatism, then, ideas are tested in experience in view of their observable outcomes, as opposed to being measured against some standard that is atemporal and external to experience. Similarly, the rational meaning of ideas would lay in the future since only the future, and not the past, could be subject to alteration and control. Philosophy once saw itself as finding knowledge; James and Dewey joined modern science in declaring that knowledge is produced rather than discovered. Pragmatism looks to what follows on the assumption that to "verify" is to "make true." The pragmatists also accepted what Weber described as an "unambiguous evolutionary principle" in that they not only regarded knowledge and value emerging from practical human effort but also assumed a kind of Darwinian theory of life that saw truth as that which survives the scrutiny of continuous inquiry as well as the reality of biological struggle.

What could very well survive, of course, is not truth but power, not what is intrinsically valid but what has the capacity to win acceptance and enjoy legitimacy; not, as James would put it, what is in an idea but what happens to it as believers respond to it. Curiously, while Adams related history to modern physics, Dewey related philosophy to Darwinian biology. Dewey could readily accept the relativistic implications of quantum mechanics; the idea that the act of measurement itself changes the thing being measured reinforced Dewey's conviction that knowing makes a difference. But modern physics seems to be more congruent with contemporary poststructuralism, where power remains a riddle when its effects are registered without its causes being necessarily known. In biology animate organisms possess an inherent power to move, whereas in physics objects are moved by something other than themselves. More-

---

27. Dewey, *The Quest for Certainty* (1929; New York: Capricorn, 1960), 285–86.

over, Dewey's biological orientation made philosophy a species of history as part of a single process subject to naturalistic explication. Science encompasses history to the extent that facts are events in the world of nature observable to the philosophical eye. History is homogeneous with nature, but not, it should be emphasized, the natural world of physics that Adams had peered into, not the "multiverse" of leaps, disruptions, and spontaneous occasions, but instead the organic world of unity and continuity, intelligible occurrences and events, and the reassuring sight of growth as the potentiality of spirit in the heart of matter. The "uncertainty principle" came from modern physics and not biology, to which pragmatism was perfectly adaptable.

Science: Experimentation, Rationalization, or Acceleration?

Unimpressed with Darwinism and pragmatism, haunted by the reality of power and the limits of morality, Adams and Weber felt the tension between philosophy and science as keenly as they did that between politics and ethics. As historians Adams and Weber could hardly endorse evolutionary progress, since history may have been moving not upward but downward, from the high ideals that characterized the virtuous principles of republicanism and the spiritual origins of capitalism to the material realities of the present. They were also dualists in seeing no solution to matter and spirit and power and morality and in counseling the limits of knowledge in dealing with anything beyond the forces of nature.

Dewey continued to believe that pragmatism could overcome all such dualisms and that knowledge would be sufficient to a given "problematic situation." Yet in 1949, three years before his death, he came upon Weber's writings and acknowledged that "one of the most distinguished sociologists of the last century" has made us aware that modern science cannot answer to the basic human need for "meaning."[28] Quite an admission for a proponent of pragmatism, a philosophy that once held that any idea having no potential experimental meaning is itself meaningless. As historians, Adams and Weber recognized that any effort to arrive at the meaning of things required not scientific experiment but interpretive understanding, the challenge of penetrating the quality of human experience that eludes an empirical analysis of its ambiguous elements. To strive to be a rational thinker in what may be an irrational universe posed one of the challenges of modernism that these two modernist thinkers faced. While science asks us to observe the practical effects of things when they

28. Dewey, "Philosophy's Future in Our Scientific Age," in *John Dewey: The Later Works, 1925–1953*, ed. Jo Ann Boydston (Carbondale, Ill.: Southern Illinois University Press, 1989), vol. 16, 372.

are experimented upon, and while artists and other creative intellectuals could continue to portray the things of the modern world, the historian still felt obligated to give reasons for things and events after they occurred.

Or while they are still occurring or perhaps expected not to occur. When it came to the relevance of the past, Adams and Weber would agree with the pragmatists that retrospective knowledge must be brought to bear upon the present in order to allow us to glimpse the future. Yet neither thinker saw clear signs of progress over the horizon, nor did they see history following a regular course that promised the realization of human potentialities. In their prophetic vision the past weighed so heavily on other cultures that each doubted whether the achievements of the West may be relevant to the rest of the world. In a remarkable coincidence, Weber and Adams speculated on the future of Czarist Russia in 1906, and each arrived at the same conclusion about the improbability of witnessing the rise of democracy as a result of economic development and technological advance:

> It is utterly ridiculous to attribute elective affinity with democracy or even freedom (in any sense of the word) to today's advanced capitalism—that inevitability of our economic development—as it is now imported into Russia and as it exists in the United States. Rather, the question can be phrased only in this way: How can democracy and freedom be maintained in the long run under the dominance of advanced capitalism? They can be maintained only if a nation is always determined not to be ruled like a herd of sheep. We individualists and partisans of democratic institutions are swimming against the stream of material constellations. Whoever desires to be the weather vane of a developmental tendency may abandon those old-fashioned ideals as quickly as possible. The rise of modern freedom presupposed unique constellations which will never repeat themselves.[29]

> —Weber

> The Czar's empire was a phase of conservative Christian anarchy more interesting to history than all the complex variety of American newspapers, schools, trusts, sects, frauds, and Congressmen. . . . Studied in the dry light of conservative Christian anarchy, Russia became luminous like the salt of radium; but with a negative luminosity as though she were a substance whose energies had been sucked out—an inert residuum—with movement of pure inertia. From the car win-

---

29. Weber is quoted in Guenther Roth and Wolfgang Schluchter, *Max Weber's Vision of History* (Berkeley: University of California Press, 1979), 201–2.

dow one seemed to float past undulations of nomad life—
herders deserted by their leaders and herds—wandering
waves stopped in their wanderings—waiting for their winds
or warriors to return and lead them westward; tribes that had
camped, like Khirgis, for the season, and had lost the means
of motion without acquiring the habit of permanence. They
waited and suffered.

The Russian people could never have changed—could they
ever be changed?[30]

—Adams

Two decades after these cautionary observations were penned, Dewey
answered Adams's question affirmatively after a visit to the Soviet Union.
The philosopher's impressions will be discussed in a subsequent chapter.
Suffice here only to mention that Dewey's positive assessment defied
Weber's warning that "old-fashioned ideals" like democracy would have
to be "abandoned" if one desired to swim with, rather than against, the
stream of twentieth-century collectivist movements. The pragmatic temperament thinks in terms of possibilities rather than actualities, of actions
and events that are coming into being rather than the constellation of
forces that have occurred in the past and cannot be repeated. Dewey
would see in Stalin's Russia "a new world in the making," one that would
outgrow the brutal necessity of the revolution from which it hatched its
bloody birth. Dewey described uncritically the Marxist conviction that
"in the dialectic of history the function of Bolshevism is to annul itself;
that the dictatorship of the proletariat is but an aspect of class war, the
antithesis to the thesis of the dictatorship of bourgeois capitalism existing
in other countries; that it is destined to disappear in a new synthesis."[31]
Nothing was further from Weber's view of Bolshevism than the illusion
that it had emerged to negate and overcome capitalism and that it would
succeed in doing so because of the "dialectic of history."

The problem of Dewey's misplaced hopes is not only his momentary
rapture with Hegelian dialectics. He also believed a peasant population
capable not only of being changed and transformed but even of being
regenerated, because Russia seemed to embody his two basic articles of
faith: experimental science and progressive education. Pragmatism, which
looks to the future to undo the past, remains the last philosophy in modern
times to see progress growing out of the expansion of scientific intelligence
alone.

In Dewey's version pragmatism took on another article of faith—

30. Adams, *Education*, 408–9.
31. Dewey, *John Dewey's Impressions of Soviet Russia and the Revolutionary World*, ed. William
W. Brickman (1929; New York: Teachers College, Columbia University, 1964), 44–112.

democracy. It was the combination of scientific intelligence and democratic idealism that inspired Dewey to support America's entry into the First World War. What Dewey advocated—a just peace settlement that would expand democracy to the monarchial powers of Europe—seemed disastrous to Weber. It would be "a miserable heritage," Weber wrote in 1917, for Germany to learn that "the outside world forced democracy upon us."[32] Although Weber urged programs of parliamentary reform that would make Germany more democratic and less authoritarian, democracy itself he regarded as a solution that carried the seeds of its own problems. Democracy would generate new forms of domination in strong, charismatic leaders, technocratic experts, bureaucratic administrators, and—the theme of Adams's novel *Democracy*—"machine" politics driven by bribery and corruption. Dewey may have been aware of the seamy side of democracy; in fact, he could hardly be bothered by corruption, as will be noted later in the book. Nonetheless, his politics during the First World War seemed to be unpragmatic in that he failed to consider the consequences of forcing democracy on others, especially by using military means to achieve political ends. Since means and ends are organically inseparable, he had always insisted, only democratic methods can fulfill democratic objectives. Yet during the war Dewey's dilemma went to the heart of American liberalism. As a Jeffersonian democrat, he remained convinced that people must participate in their own political reformation; as a Wilsonian internationalist, he convinced himself that the war and Allied victory could be the means of bringing democratic ends to the German people, whose role was presumably to participate in their own defeat.

Contrary to current scholarly impression, Weber was closer to the *Federalist* authors than to Dewey and the Jeffersonian tradition. The task was not simply to make the world safe for democracy; rather it was, in a paraphrase of Madison, to make democracy worthy of governing others by demonstrating it is capable of governing itself. Like Adams, Weber saw that modernity profoundly affected the promises of democracy by weakening the values of independence, morality, and self-control. Neither believed that democracy could restore ethics to politics so that government might be something more elevating than a mechanism of interest and power. If anything, Adams and Weber looked to the responsibilities of leadership as the true vocation of politics.

Dewey's dictum that things are as they are experienced, that knowledge remains within the human organism's experiential participation in the

---

32. Weber is quoted in Wolfgang Mommsen, *Max Weber and German Politics* (Chicago: University of Chicago Press, 1984), 259–69.

world, was one view pragmatism offered to overcome the loss of older
ideas of knowledge based on absolute foundations beyond the world.
Adams and Weber had a deep hunger for experience, an intellectual curiosity that took them back to the ancient world and to the far corners of
the contemporary non-Western world, where they investigated everything from peasant mentalities to Buddhist meditations. Yet they had to
confront the difficulties of attributing coherent meaning to the actions of
those they studied or observed. Looking to history and society to appreciate events as they are experienced by others, they saw tensions, ironies,
antinomies, and a plurality of irreconcilable value spheres. In a passage
Adams could identify with, Weber even suggested that human behavior
defies instrumental explanation:

> The impossibility of purely pragmatic history is determined
> by the fact the action of men is *not* interpretable in such purely
> rational terms, that not only irrational "prejudices," errors in
> thinking and factual errors but also "temperament," "moods,"
> and "affects" *disturb his freedom*—in brief, that his actions too—
> to a very different degree—partake of the empirical "meaning-
> lessness" of "natural change."[33]

Weber makes us aware of what Adams sensed: things can be experienced and still not understood.

Weber shared Adams's, and Dewey's, view of history as the present
age's reflection on its future as well as its past. But Weber's vision of
history remained less pessimistic and deterministic than Adams's specter
of entropy and doom and closer to the pragmatist's vision. Weber had all
along opposed the Marxist notion that history followed invariant laws of
development, and had he been aware of Adams's effort to emplot the end
of history according to the laws of physics, he would have continued to
uphold his own conviction that history was a matter of will, contingency,
and the spontaneous appearance of charismatic leaders—an indeterminist
view similar to that in James's essay "Great Men and Their Environment."

On the subject of authority Weber may also be closer to the pragmatists
than to Adams. One definition of modernism, as indicated in the Introduction, is the presence of power and the absence of genuine, legitimate
authority. Unlike Adams, who had searched futilely the annals of American history to find traces of authority worthy of his respect, Weber saw
various forms of authority surviving in the sheer momentum of existing
institutions, even in the routinization of religion and the bureaucratization

---

33. Weber is quoted in Alan Sica, *Weber, Irrationality, and Social Order* (Berkeley, 1988),
181.

of politics. Similarly, American sociologists would relegate all authority to the rules of society, while some pragmatists believed scientific method could serve in place of all traditional forms of authority. What Weber shared with American sociologists and pragmatists was the need to find sources of stability in a world of flux and change. But while Weber worried that permanency could lead to the petrification of "soulless" forms of instrumental authority, Adams's worries went deeper and presaged the implications of the present nuclear age. For Weber, science meant rationalization, the development of more complex institutions of organization and control; for Adams, science meant acceleration, the advent of increasingly rapid paces of change brought on by the release of new forms of energy. "The world did not double or treble its movement between 1800 and 1900," he wrote in 1909, "but, measured by any standard known to science—by horsepower, calories, volts, mass in any shape—the tensions and vibration and volume and so-called progression of society were fully a thousand times greater in 1900 than in 1800." Adams's anxiety about the scary rush of history grew more acute after the turn of the century, when he described Madame Curie dropping on the world "the metaphysical bomb she called radium." But as early as the American Civil War he saw the handwriting on the wall. "Man has mounted science and is now running away with it," he wrote to his brother in April 1862, while the newly invented *Monitor* and *Merrimack* were maneuvering to blow one another out of the water. "I firmly believe that before many centuries more, science will be the master of man. The engines he will have invented will be beyond his strength to control. Some day science shall have the existence of mankind in its power, and the human race commit suicide by blowing up the world."[34]

Weber believed that science could mitigate the problem of modern authority's eclipse by bringing forth social organizations based upon routine procedures, and the American philosopher Dewey believed that all the disputes that had once been arbitrated by conventional authority would resolve themselves to the extent that man masters the experimental methods of scientific inquiry. Adams believed not only that "science will be the master of man" but that scientific reason would undermine authority and leave humankind worshiping power itself. Adams feared that modernity had separated consciousness from the external world in order to understand nature by experimenting with it rather than by contemplating it. Thus while to the pragmatist science meant liberation, to Adams

34. Adams, "The Rule of Phase Applied to History," in *The Degradation of Democratic Dogma*, ed. Brooks Adams (1919; New York: Capricorn, 1958), 297; Henry Adams to Charles F. Adams, Jr., Apr. 11, 1862, *Letters*, vol. 1, 289–92.

it meant subordination to what man had manipulated into existence—the Dynamo and the expanding constellations of energy. Adams would agree with Weber that in the modern universe of power, humanity meets its "fate."

The "Thirst for the Deed," the Bolshevik Revolution, and "Romantic" Pragmatism

To treat Adams and Weber in tandem illustrates some of the unexamined assumptions in American pragmatism. Although Weber never engaged American thinkers in dialogue, his use of the term "pragmatic" may suggest how philosophy left behind the world of knowledge and moral tension to enter the world of power unprepared for the ironies and dilemmas of politics.

As a critic of *Naturalismus*, the theory, held firmly by Dewey, that value judgments could be drawn from scientific data, Weber insisted that values are a matter of choice and thus can be rendered neither empirically valid nor commensurable with other subjective preferences. He objected to a *rationale Pragmatik* in social theory. The term "adaptation" (*Anpassung*) should remain in biology, for a "pragmatically conditioned" social life only adds to the "shallowness of our routinized daily existence." Weber distinguished the realm of value from the realm of experience and even regarded value conflicts as an "eternal battle of the gods." He contrasted an ethics of intent based upon moral conviction (*Gesinnungsethik*) to an ethics of responsibility based upon the test of consequences (*Verantwortungsethik*). Although Weber believed both ethics require one another, he also observed that in "every-day life" people "do not become aware and do not even wish to become aware of this intermixture of hostile values, be it for pragmatic or for psychological reasons." The very term *pragma* had no ethical import for Weber, and thus *Das Pragma der Gewaltsamkeit* signified the employment of force to control the distribution of power. But while pragmatism subscribed to a naturalistic fallacy in regard to values and implicated itself in the regulative techniques of manipulation that follow from the orderly procedures of science, it also contained an entirely opposite impulse, one that follows from the impatience of will and imagination of desire and results in the paradox of conceiving freedom as both an act of creation and the imposition of control.[35]

---

35. Weber, *Soziologie, Universal-Geschichtliche Analysen, Politik*, ed. Johannes Winckelmann (Stuttgart: Alfred Kroner, 1973), 306; *Wirtschaft und Gesellschaft*, ed. Johannes Winckelmann (Tübingen: J. C. B. Mohr [Paul Siebeck], 1972), 32, 361; on naturalism, see Max Weber to Heinrich Rickert, April 18 and 19, 1908, in *Max Weber Gesamtausgabe*, ed. M. Rainer Lepsius and Wolfgang J. Mommsen (Tübingen: J. C. B. Mohr [Paul Siebeck], 1990), vol. 2, 527–30;

When Weber was pondering the Russian Revolution of 1905, he wondered why Marxism gained ascendancy in an undeveloped country lacking the conditions of social revolution. Weber attributed the coincidence to the *Pragmatik rationalismus* of the Russian intelligentsia, whose "thirst for the 'deed'" compelled its members to leave doctrine behind as they defied historical determinism in order to make history happen. Weber observed that pragmatic politics embodied an *Erfolgsethik*, an ethic aiming at success that allows flexibility of means to reach desired ends. Curiously, Weber uncovered, as early as 1905, a latent pragmatic ingredient in socialism that would later be explicated by Sidney Hook in *Towards an Understanding of Karl Marx* (1933) and elegantly expressed in Edmund Wilson's *To the Finland Station* (1940). But it was first pronounced in the writings of Max Eastman, a former teaching assistant of Dewey's who would, with the Bolshevik Revolution of 1917, see Lenin as the "pragmatic genius" of modern political thought, the "engineer of the revolution" who dramatized how ideas could be put into practice and how truth and justice could be made real through "experimental intelligence."[36]

By no means do such exuberances suggest that pragmatism carried the seeds of what later was called the "totalitarian temptation," a suseptibility characteristic of intellectuals that Dewey (after a brief visit to Russia) and Hook (after a few wayward years) did everything to resist. But from a Weberian point of view, the betrayal of the October Revolution inhered, at least in part, in the pragmatic justification for the seizure of power. Both Weber and Eastman had befriended anarchists and admired their incorruptible integrity and suspicion of any system of organization that violated individual liberty. But Weber perceived what eluded Eastman: a pragmatic desire for the deed frees history from determinism only to create new conditions of domination as action becomes systematized into structures of power that culminate in the bureaucratic state. In this respect pragmatism offered as a solution what a Weberian may see as the problem. Looking upon life as an experiment, the pragmatist imposes conscious control on events as a means of rendering experience rational in the realm of human action. In Weber's analysis, action itself, though

---

Weber, *Methodology*, 18–25; also valuable is the two-part essay by Ernest Moritz Manasse, "Moral Principles and Alternatives in Max Weber and John Dewey," *Journal of Philosophy* 41 (1944): 29–48, 57–68.

36. On Weber and the pragmatic "thirst for the 'deed'" he discerned among Russian Marxists in 1905, see Lawrence A. Scaff and Thomas Clay Arnold, "Class and the Theory of History: Marx on France and Weber on Russia," in *A Weber-Marx Dialogue*, ed. Robert J. Antonio and Ronald M. Glassmann (Lawrence: University of Kansas Press, 1985), 207–10; on Max Eastman, see John P. Diggins, *Up from Communism: Conservative Odysseys in American Intellectual History* (New York: Harper and Row, 1975), 17–73.

essential to sociological understanding by way of a causal explanation of motives, could, instead of creating values, confound intelligence with irony and purpose with paradox. If the early capitalist assumed economic acquisition would be the means of attaining spiritual salvation, the Leninist assumed that party dictatorship would be the means of realizing freedom (an illusion against which Weber warned Georg Lukács), while the pragmatist assumes thinking instrumentally is the means of solving the problem of history by making it rationally synonymous with humankind's emergence out of the state of nature from the embryo to the dynamo. To call upon philosophy to take to the field of action is characteristic of modernism, the will to praxis that carries reason over into the treacherous world of politics and power, the murky world of the unpredictable, uncertain, ironic, and irrational; the world in which, as Adams might have put it, we can experience almost everything and still come away knowing almost nothing.

Experience! Dewey's collapsing the problems of philosophy into the processes of experience comes perilously close to reconciling desire with deed. In Dewey's naturalistic outlook, experience meant the interaction of agency with its environment, of mind operating on sense data in a continuous process of moving toward a world that is knowable to the extent it is amenable to our desire to control it. This essentially biological formulation has ironic political implications. Henceforth ideas no longer have significance other than as instruments; the implementation of ideas necessitates action; and all ideas require power for their realization. In this respect pragmatism signals the "end" of philosophy as did Marx in his earlier eleventh thesis on Feuerbach, where the point is not to interpret the world but to change it. In 1917, historical necessity yielded to a pure act of will; political intervention by means of party organization, with the result that political theory died as it became political fact. Philosophy ceases in that political action is freed from theoretical constraint. Perhaps it would be more accurate to say that theory, no longer capable of claiming truth as an object of knowledge, continues as language as well as action. For the pragmatist and revolutionary must translate into politics ideas that inspire change but do not correspond to reality. Without access to the objectively real, the philosopher settles for the processes of knowing instead of the thing known. Yet the emphasis on process enables the thinker not to know the world but to appropriate it with his own words and concepts. As Nietzsche put it, once one describes life as a process made up of our own perspectives on it, philosophy is "directed not at knowledge but at taking possession of things." Nature has no "ends" and experience may yield no "means" to reach what is created instead of found. "With 'end' and 'means' one takes possession of the process (one invents a process that can be grasped); with 'concepts' however, of the 'things' that constitute the process."[37]

To change the world is to take possession of the language that describes it. That the will to power tempts the pragmatist as much as the revolutionary could suggest that modern thought has profound political implications. Actually it has none, or at least none that can be attributed to a familiar political position. Richard Rorty has been criticized for relating Dewey to Nietzsche and thereby relativizing truth and knowledge. Rorty has responded, sometimes with the controversy surrounding Martin Heidegger in mind, by insisting that pragmatism and poststructuralism have no specific political orientation, that action and description can move in any ideological direction. His position may be reinforced by recalling that in American intellectual history some pragmatists became Leninists, a few flirted with fascism, and many others, including Eastman and Hook, turned into vigorous anti-Stalinists while remaining staunch pragmatists. What pragmatism represented was not so much radicalism as "romanticism," the willingness to plunge into a contingent world of possibility. And the "thirst for the deed," as Weber put it, suggests the need to escape the aridity of abstraction and contemplation, a need felt by conservatives as well as radicals. Even the prince of conservative philosophy, Edmund Burke, railed against metaphysics in favor of a politics based on "circumstances." As Louis Hartz put it, any philosophy that looks for truth in action has a rendezvous with romanticism, and there one is apt to meet the strangest of bedfellows:

> When revolutionary norms move into the realm of reality they become romantic. The implementation of ideals requires a departure from rationalism. By his own route the revolutionary adopts precisely that romantic mood of indeterminacy and complexity that gets defended in reactionary thought. In the world of action the Revolution and the Reaction meet; both the revolutionary and the conservative are justifiably distrustful of thought. Georges Sorel, a syndicalist revolutionary, can therefore be put alongside Burke. Sorel feared that people will only dream of radical achievement; he wanted them to act and reject thought, and he was an irrationalist frightened of systematic thinking as potentially crippling. Sorel therefore blasted abstractions as Burke did.
>
> The problem of action united the revolutionary and the conservative in the realm of romanticism. The conservative wants to defend a pattern of activity, a preexisting standard of behav-

---

37. Nietzsche, quoted in Keith M. May, *Nietzsche and the Spirit of Tragedy* (New York: St. Martin's, 1990), 148.

ior. Thought can function as a component of action, but never at a long distance. The conservative seeks to defend current reality while the revolutionary wants to create a new world. Yet to the extent that both the revolutionary and conservative share an action element, in each case there is a romantic component.[38]

Students of American history have been led to believe that pragmatism stands for a progressive, action-oriented, experimental outlook towards life, while conservatism takes its stand on fixed, orthodox ideas. The impression is reinforced by the Marxist insistence that capital and labor are diametrically opposed ideas, with the former fixated on such doctrines as natural law and the latter liberating itself through practical activity. Adams and Weber would remind us that the conservative-as-capitalist is also a romantic willing to take his chances with contingency. And Adams in particular would see, as did Nietzsche, that both the pragmatic philosopher and the prehensile capitalist, in their desire to command the world and put it to use, are at war with physical nature and the natural condition of "chaos."

History: Evolution or Alienation?

Juxtaposing Adams and Weber to Dewey brings out one of the most questionable assumptions of American pragmatism, Dewey's organic vision of progress. Comparing their respective philosophies of history, we are offered entirely different orientations and expectations, so different that one can only wonder why the pragmatist could be convinced that science would supplant philosophy. Dewey's assumption that history, as the study of human development, could be scientifically intelligible rested on the principles of evolution and the metaphor of nature as a successive continuum from the lower to the higher. That assumption had no basis in the new physics (discussed in the next chapter), where the story of energy was more perplexing than the story of species, where macro-properties of phase transitions are random and irreversible and thus frustrate any search for orderly patterns or signs of progress in the struggle for existence—save for the survival of strength without spirit and the increase of intelligence without conscience.

Does history itself dramatize simply evolution or does it also convey the darker specter of alienation? Is it an account only of the ascent of mind out of matter or also of the eventual rationalization of energy into structure? And if human values are the measure, is the later always the

---

38. Louis Hartz, *The Necessity of Choice: Nineteenth-Century Political Thought* (New Brunswick, N.J.: Transaction, 1990), 84.

better? From the womb of raw nature Dewey saw humankind arising as an "organism" of intelligent adaptation, a progressive elevation away from bondage to instinct to rational control and eventually to community and human solidarity. Ironically, Adams perceived what Joseph Wood Krutch later termed the "paradox of humanism": the earlier and lower forms of life have already realized more perfectly the selfless solidarity to which modern philosophy aspires. Intelligence should also be humbled when compared to instinct. "The quality that developed the eye and the wing of the bee and the condor has no known equivalent in man." It was typical of Adams to show us that what we held as convictions could turn out to be conceits. Could the potentiality of intelligence overcome the human deficiency of instinct?[39]

The assumption that out of history evolves the faculty of rational intelligence with which the problems of history can themselves be solved may also turn out to be more problematic, even for a "problem-solving" philosophy. Adams and Weber saw reason itself as anxious, impelling humankind to seek in vain what is desired but cannot be obtained: freedom from insecurity and insignificance to ward off a precarious and meaningless world. Thus the historians saw men and women turning to religion as an answer to suffering and the fear of death. To Dewey the presence of religion suggested no failure of nerve but simply the imagination's capacity to project, further evidence of the self's yearning to be in harmony with the universe. The major question that worried Dewey about religion was whether it could be reconciled with science. Adams and Weber saw religion as denying the absence of what the imagination desperately desired to be present; anxiety about the salvation of the soul led to either work or worship, and whether productivity or prayer, God's presence was presumed as much from fear as from faith. Seeing the coldness of scientific inquiry as subversive to religion, Adams could share Weber's view of the post–World War I era as "a polar night of icy darkness."[40]

Dewey's answer to the dark chill of alienated existence was to nestle together with others in the "great community" in order to identify with society and uphold cooperation as the sole path to progress. That Dewey looked to democracy to succeed where philosophy had failed makes one wonder how he can be associated with European postmodernism. The philosopher Rorty has rightly shown how Dewey used his brilliant critical faculties to bring philosophy to an end as an epistemological search for

39. Krutch, *The Modern Temper*, 27–55; Adams, *The Degradation of Democratic Dogma* (1919; New York: Capricorn, 1958), 291.
40. Weber, "Politics as a Vocation," in *From Max Weber*, 128.

foundational knowledge. But the comparison with Nietzsche, however playfully provocative, is ultimately misleading. Nietzsche's greatest American exponent was H. L. Mencken, and what Mencken wrote about the pragmatists should perhaps be left unsaid to academics who seem to prefer to "critique" everything but themselves. Had Dewey pondered Melville, there might have been some reason to see Nietzschean raptures and agonies in pragmatism as a tragic philosophy of life. But to go from Melville to Dewey is to go from the sublime to the sober—or to what Mencken said of Dewey's gentle, safe temperament, "the highest bearable sobriety."[41]

In their desire to turn a trend into a tradition, perhaps to make "American studies" hip along with the latest Parisian fashion, many scholars (Giles Gunn, Richard Poirier, Cornel West, et al.) write on the pragma-

---

41. Mencken regarded the pragmatists as pious reformers and, as philosophers, timid Rotarians who enjoyed "the acclamation of all right-thinking and forward-looking men." Although he did begrudge some respect for James and Dewey, along with Thorstein Veblen, he saw American thinkers building a methodological bridge of confidence over the abyss that haunted Nietzsche's outlook, thereby trusting democracy, technology, and belief to succeed where philosophy and religion had failed and truth refused to reveal itself. See H. L. Mencken, "'The Great Thinker' in America," in *The Intellectuals*, ed. George B. de Husar (Glencoe, Ill.: Free Press, 1960), 139–49; Mencken's important book on Nietzsche has recently been reissued with a valuable introduction by Richard Flathman: H. L. Mencken, *Friedrich Nietzsche* (1913; New Brunswick, N.J.: Transaction Books, 1993); Rorty's comparison of Nietzsche and the pragmatists is in "Nineteenth-Century Idealism and Twentieth-Century Textualism," in *Consequences of Pragmatism* (Minneapolis: University of Minnesota Press, 1982), 139–59.

A comparison of Dewey and Nietzsche may help explain what troubles me about pragmatism. In seeking to clarify and at times even systematize the processes of knowing as ways of belief, pragmatism not only makes beliefs serve as truths but comes close to substituting procedure for passion. In its "method" one wishes for a little madness, for Captain Ahab the metaphysical seeker as well as Starbuck the practical navigator. Nietzsche held out for that which is worthy of us as residing beyond us and eluding our will to knowledge and power, something that transports us into feelings of mystery and rapture. Adams as well as Melville could agree with Nietzsche that when skepticism "mates" with longing, mysticism is born. In Deweyan pragmatism there is no ecstasy, no Dionysian music, no charismatic illumination. In turning philosophy over to science and the practical endeavors of everyday life, pragmatism turns thought over to "the men who get their enjoyment and satisfaction out of the cast-off veil rather than out of gazing with rapture at whatever still remains veiled after the unveiling. They care more for the search after truth than for truth itself." So wrote Gorham Mumson of Nietzsche's targets, in *The Dilemma of the Liberated: An Interpretation of Twentieth-Century Humanism* (1930; Port Washington, N.Y.: Kennikat Press, 1967), 290. Nietzsche ridiculed a "new species of philosopher . . . coming up over the horizon," those "philosophers of the future" who see themselves as *experimenters*." He punned on the German expression "experiment" (*versuchen*), which could mean "to attempt," "to be tempted," and "temptation" itself. See Friedrich Nietzsche, *Beyond Good and Evil*, trans. Marianne Cowan (1885; Chicago: Gateway, 1955), 49.

tists and then return to Emerson, and from the Transcendentalist a leap is made to Nietzsche, and from the German philosopher it is only a short step into the purgatory of French poststructuralism. True, Nietzsche admired Emerson, but all this skipping around is questionable, not only because intellectual history takes on the moves of hopscotch (a game into which I often leap), but rather more because Dewey's profound legacy in the eighteenth-century Enlightenment is lost from sight. Adams and Weber could be both postmodern and closer to the older counter-Enlightenment. Like the philosophers of the Constitution who saw fallen humankind driven by "passion" and "interest" and thus incapable of responding to reason, they too discerned irrationality at the basis of even practical striving on the part of human beings unconscious of the meaning of their actions. Dewey, in contrast, carried forward the more optimistic message of the Jeffersonian Enlightenment and the promise of the human species rationally working the materials of earth. In turning to Darwinism, and in ignoring Veblen's warning about the persistence of the "barbaric" archaic traits of predation, Dewey also sustained the eighteenth-century assumption that knowledge and science would be the antithesis of power and its corruptions. The very institutions that Dewey looked to for society's possible reformation—science, politics, education—Adams had also looked to in his younger years as the guiding sources of the Republic. But Dewey's faith in evolutionary progress scarcely prepared him for the ironies inherent in growth and development. Institutional expansion brought with it conditions of domination as a consequence of the technical imperatives of organization, and even knowledge became an instrument of control as the pragmatist's ideal of scientific method left the laboratory to reemerge in business enterprise as scientific management. Dewey assumed, as did Jefferson, that education and democracy would disarm power. Adams and Weber were closer to the *Federalist* writers in their Niebuhrian understanding of power and conflict as the inevitable expression of freedom and the insufficiency of reason.

Adams, Weber, and Niebuhr all retained a Calvinist sensibility toward finitude, doubt, irony, and the inscrutabilities of existence. Such a sensibility puts them in touch with contemporary poststructuralists, those "masters of suspicion" who, like the thundering theologians of olden days, turn consciousness back upon itself to remind us of the abyss of nothingness and the limits of reason. Given these possible parallels, the effort made in recent years to connect American pragmatism with more modern developments in European thought provokes curiosity but suspends credulity. At first one might have assumed that this curious academic enterprise would go the way of all fleshly trends; instead it has become widely accepted and today enjoys the status of a "paradigm." One wonders.

Between the biological optimism of American pragmatism, where meaning simply means adjusting to the rational, evolutionary processes of nature, and the cultural pessimism of European postmodernism, where meaning eludes all transcendental cravings, lies a world of difference. The attempt to assimilate European postmodernism into America's progressive traditions may turn the pragmatist into a politician, which H. L. Mencken once described as a clergyman who promises to free sinners from hell. The following chapters address conventional scholarship in order to examine critically the unrealistic political hopes of American pragmatism, especially Dewey's version, a philosophical stance that can perhaps sustain optimism by asking from thought little more than the expectations of experience. Adams, and those who have followed in the shadow of his skeptical temper, could hardly endorse Dewey's assumption that science, secular education, and professional training would strengthen democracy, reform society, and, in the idea of the "great community," provide a humanistic answer to the alienation and anomie of modern life. The American people, it now seems clear, played out the darker thoughts of Adams, Weber, and Veblen in living not "for" but "off" politics and becoming bureaucrats and consumers slouching toward suburbia, where community simply meant real estate. Pragmatism sprang from native grounds, and the pragmatic interpretation of life sustained America's hope in the will to believe in what satisfied belief. Yet the old promises of pragmatism remain unfulfilled, while the claims of neopragmatism remain unexamined beyond the disciplines of philosophy and literacy theory. Since the neopragmatist advises us to forsake philosophy and turn to history as a language activity, it is appropriate to begin with Henry Adams. "One sought no absolute truth," wrote Adams almost a century ago. "One sought only a spool on which to wind the thread of history without breaking it."[42]

Without that spool, without the connective core of historical narration, does experience alone yield understanding? Much of pragmatism rests on no foundation other than the need and desire to believe that Dewey's "organic whole" can be constructed from history's contingent parts. In turning away from metaphysics toward the study of facts and events, pragmatism assumes historiography can deliver philosophical conclusions. In the absence of truth, pragmatic inquiry still promises to arrive at meaning and understanding, a goal Henry Adams never reached.

42. Adams, *Education*, 472.

2

Who Bore the Failure of the Light:
Henry Adams

The Hand of the Father

The Education of Henry Adams is, among other things, a discourse on power. The problem of power and its responsiveness to reason is inevitably linked to the problem of legitimate authority and its acceptance by those who consent to its exercise. Throughout his intellectual life Henry Adams struggled with both of these problems. One of the characteristics of the modernist mind is its awareness of the phenomenological nature of all knowledge, that is, knowledge as a purely descriptive observation that does not necessarily require a logical explanation of the object being observed. The idea that authority is essentially phenomenological, something directly experienced without the mediation of the reflective mind, occurs in the opening pages of the *Education* in a scene from the author's childhood in the home of his grandfather John Quincy Adams. The six-year-old Henry is refusing to go to school, and his mother, embarrassed by the behavior of her son in her father-in-law's house, is about to give in when suddenly the door of the library opens and the ex-president comes slowly down the stairs. "Putting on his hat, he took the boy's hand without a word and walked with him, paralyzed by awe, up the road to the town." Henry was surprised when the eighty-year-old grandfather, instead of turning back under the hot morning sun, did not release the boy's hand until they had traveled the entire mile to the schoolhouse. Many years later, Adams humorously noted that after receiving this first lesson in political philosophy he knew that Locke and Rousseau must be revised. Whatever the origins of authority relations, they are not initiated by the consent and will of men, especially young men:

The point was that this act, contrary to the inalienable rights of boys, and nullifying the social compact, ought to have made him dislike his grandfather for life. He could not recall that it had this effect even for a moment. With a certain maturity of mind, the child must have recognized that the President, though a tool of tyranny, had done his disreputable work with a certain intelligence. He had shown no temper, no irritation, no personal feeling, and had made no display of force. Above all, he had held his tongue. During their long walk he said nothing; he had uttered no syllable of revolting cant about the duty of obedience and the wickedness of resistance to law; he had shown no concern in the matter; hardly even a consciousness of the boy's existence.[1]

The behavior of the young Adams by no means suggests blind obedience. In Adams's mind submission to unlawful authority could never be justified. A few pages earlier in the *Education* Adams had observed that his intellectual environment had been "colonial, revolutionary, almost Cromwellian, as though he were steeped, from his greatest grandmother's birth, in the odor of political crime. Resistance was the law of New England nature; the boy looked out on the world with the instinct of resistance."[2] The New England principle of resistance could be grasped immediately, especially by youths "who naturally look upon all force as evil" and thus regard as a "duty" both the political opposition to evil and moral hatred of it. John Adams and John Quincy Adams, in struggling against British tyranny in the eighteenth century and southern slavery in the nineteenth, were carrying on the New England habit of resisting oppression not only to realize political liberty but to preserve republican morality. In the light of Henry Adams's family history and his own lifelong puzzlements about the nature of power, it was natural for him, "an American in search of a father,"[3] to desire to seek the unspoken authority of a moral force, even if it could only be felt in the iron grip of his grandfather's hand. As a youth who once felt the silent presence of authority, later as an intellectual who would sense his alienation from the world of power, and ultimately as a skeptical humanist who feared that reason could possibly destroy what it wanted to understand, Adams was not so much interested in discussing the formal properties of authority as he was in exploring the nature of an aesthetic experience when genuine authority manifests itself as the power of moral beauty.

That power reached sublime expression in *Mont-Saint-Michel and*

1. Adams, *Education*, 13.
2. Ibid., 7.
3. Ibid., 229.

Chartres. Written as a companion piece to the *Education*, the Chartres narrative is meant to enliven our vision of authority as an artistic proposition rather than a political principle. Although Adams is now writing about others who lived centuries ago, the genealogical imperative is still present. "The new artist drops unwillingly the hand of his father or his grandfather; he looks back, from every corner of his work, to see whether it goes with the old."[4] The homage to filial piety runs through the body of Adams's work. The firm hand of the father expresses the force of tradition, the "handing down" of knowledge and moral guidance that gives to the artist, and to the young, the historical sense that enables them to be "at home" in the world and thus assent to the roots from which they had sprung. When Adams complains of the "failure" of his education he is lamenting this filial rupture. He realizes he can neither accept nor transmit the moral certitudes so confidently possessed by his illustrious ancestors. Henceforth Adams would bear the burden of modernism: the "futile folly" of trying to use old standards of knowledge to get beyond the new problems of knowledge in order to speak truth to power.

Toward the end of the *Education* Adams tilted one of his chapters "The Abyss of Ignorance," an expression that parallels Mann's description of moral chaos as "sympathy with the abyss." Before Adams reached that modernist conclusion, his lifelong search for the true foundations of authority involved the investigation of three institutions that in the past had provided fundamental answers to ultimate questions: politics, history, and religion. The first institution purported to offer a system of human relations based upon republican ideals, the second a system of knowledge based on the facts of human experience, and the third a system of symbolic meanings based on man's cravings for transcedence. In theory each institution could exercise authority insofar as man's obedience could be inspired by virtue of their respective claims to justice, truth, and salvation. Adams found he could submit to neither politics, nor history, nor religion.

"This taste for politics is a perfect mania in us," Adams wrote to his mother, Abigail Brooks Adams, in 1860.[5] And well it should. Adams's genealogy ran to his father, Charles Francis Adams, Lincoln's foreign ambassador to England; John Quincy Adams, America's sixth president; and John Adams, second president and author of some of the most profound treatises in eighteenth-century political philosophy. In *A Defense of the Constitutions of the Government of the United States of America* (1787–88),

---

4. Henry Adams, *Mont-Saint-Michel and Chartres* (1904; Garden City, N.Y.: Anchor, 1959), 117–18.

5. Henry Adams to Abigail Brooks Adams, Sept. 7, 1860, *Letters*, vol. 1, 201.

John Adams explained why one could be reasonably hopeful for the future of the Republic. Noting that the colonists had rejected both royalty and the "pious mystery" of religion when constructing a government, Adams assumed that authority was now safely lodged in the people themselves.

> The people were universally too enlightened to be imposed on by artifice; and their leaders, or more properly followers, were men of too much honor to attempt it. Thirteen governments thus founded on the natural authority of the people alone, without a pretense of miracle or mystery, and which is destined to spread over the northern part of that whole quarter of the globe, are a great point gained in favor of the rights of mankind. The experiment is made, and has completely succeeded; it can no longer be called in question whether authority in magistrates and obedience in citizens can be grounded on reason, morality, and the Christian religion, without the monkery of priests, or the knavery of politicians.[6]

Young Henry Adams would grow up to call into question many of his great-grandfather's assumptions about the nature of constitutional government and the future of the Republic. "It's my policy to encourage rebellion to every authority but my own," he wrote to his mother.[7] Adams's rebellion eventually led him to return, toward the end of his life, to the very forces that his great-grandfather believed America had successfully escaped: medieval Catholicism, its miracles and mysteries. How are we to account for this curious turn in American political thought?

Clearly it had little to do with the Adams household itself. John Adams believed that his exemplary leadership would establish the Republic on the best foundations conceivable. On the mantelpiece of the dining room of the White House was carved a line from one of Adams's letters to Abigail: "May none but honest and wise men ever rule under this roof." His son John Quincy Adams also believed that in America high political office could be a moral reward rather than the goal of party machination. In turn his son Charles Francis Adams taught Henry that politics required the synthesis of moral theory and public duty. He also believed that a courageous leader could draw on ethical principles that endured the exigencies of experience, and that the first profile in political courage could be found in the life of John Quincy Adams. "In my opinion," Charles Francis Adams told Henry and his brothers, Brooks and Charles Francis Adams, Jr., "no man who has lived in America has so thoroughly constructed a foundation for his political life as your grandfather. His action

6. John Adams, *A Defense of the Constitutions of the Government of the United States of America,* 3 vols. (1787–1788; New York: DeCapo, 1971), vol. 1, preface.

7. Henry Adams to Abigail Brooks Adams, Mar. 25, 1860, *Letters,* vol. 1, 101.

always was deducible from certain maxims deeply graven on his mind."
One maximum was the classical idea of civic virtue, the citizen's commitment to the public good rather than private interests. "The eternal and
immutable laws of justice and morality are paramount to all legislation,"
declared the grandfather, who called upon all republican citizens to dis-
charge their duties to God and their "government of which *virtue* is the
seminal principle."[8]

Henry Adams could share such ideas—at least in theory. Down to
1850, Adams reflected in the *Education*, political leadership was assumed
by those earlier trained in such professions as law, medicine, business,
or letters. "In politics the system required competent expression; it was
the old Ciceronian idea of government by *the best* that produced the long
line of New England statesmen. They chose men to represent them because they wanted to be well represented, and they chose the best they
had."[9] In the midst of the Civil War Adams could still be hopeful about
the future of politics. "I pass my intervals from official work," he wrote
his brother Charles in 1863, "in studying De Tocqueville and John Stuart
Mill, the two high priests of our faith." Adams may have admired
Tocqueville as a fellow gentry intellectual who placed his talents at the
service of republicanism. But the lesson he drew is puzzling. "I have
learned to think De Tocqueville my model, and I study his life and works
as the Gospel of my private religion. The great principle of democracy
is still capable of rewarding a conscientious servant."[10] One wonders if
Adams had sufficiently grasped what Mill had regarded as the most disturbing observation in Tocqueville's *Democracy in America:* in a liberal
society deference succumbs to egalitarianism and the suspicion of elites,
and hence in America the best and the brightest are not elected to political
office.[11] In some respects this dilemma had been presaged in both the
Federalist, where Madison warned that the adjudication of factional quarrels could not be resolved by great leaders since the Republic cannot
count upon their appearance; and in John Adams's *Defense of the Constitutions*, where it was argued that "virtue" would be the effect, and not the
cause, of "a well ordered constitution."[12] Both Madison and Adams
looked to the "machinery of government" to sustain the Republic, to the

8. Gore Vidal, "Adamses: The Best People, I," *New York Review of Books* (Mar. 18, 1976),
20; George Hochfield, *Henry Adams: An Introduction and Interpretation* (New York, 1962), 5,
89.

9. Adams, *Education*, 32.

10. Henry Adams to Charles Francis Adams, Jr., May 1, 1863, *Letters*, vol. 1, 350.

11. John Stuart Mill, "M. de Tocqueville on Democracy in America"; first appeared in
Edinburgh Review, 1840; reprinted in *John Stuart Mill on Politics and Society*, ed. Geraint L.
Williams (Glasgow, 1976), 186–247.

12. *Federalist*, no. 10; John Adams, "The American Prospect," in *The American Enlightenment*, ed. Adrienne Koch (New York, 1965), 267.

soundness of its political architecture and not necessarily to the moral qualities of its people or the virtuous principles of its leaders. The Transcendantalists Emerson and Thoreau saw the implication of this institutional solution and drew the somber conclusion that in America politics required neither inspiration nor dedication. And later Max Weber, who observed that in America politics had become the pursuit of power for its own sake, drew the equally somber conclusion that politics and ethics were incompatible. But young Henry Adams had grown up to believe that in the American Republic the wisest and worthiest would be both recognized and rewarded.

The Failure of Classical Ideals

Belief in the classical ideals of politics strongly impressed itself on Adams's childhood mentality. The gentlemen he observed running the affairs of government were "statesmen, not politicians; they guided public opinion, but were little guided by it." Not only did the young Adams fail to see what Tocqueville so amply documented, public opinion as the "tyranny of the majority" that hindered leadership; he also believed that in the early years of the Republic "politics offered no difficulties, for there the moral law was a sure guide." No one doubted the expansion of reason and social perfection, Adams recalled of his youth, and even in the midst of European revolution and the advent of ominous economic changes the ideals of middle-class government and social progress continued to prevail.

> Even the violent reaction after 1848 . . . never for the moment shook the true faith. No one, except Karl Marx, foresaw radical change. What announced it? The world was producing sixty or seventy million tons of coal, and might be using nearly a million steam-horse power, just beginning to make itself felt. All experience since the creation of man, all divine revelation or human science, conspired to deceive and betray a twelve-year-old boy who took for granted that his ideas, which were alone respectable, would be alone respected.[13]

Even though family pride dictated that he enter public service, Adams begged his brothers to cease urging him to do so.[14] When Charles paid him the compliment of saying that he combined the qualities of William Seward (Lincoln's secretary of state), Horace Greeley (New York *Tribune*

---

13. Adams, *Education*, 25–33.

14. Fear of failure may have had something to do with his reluctance to enter politics. See Henry Adams to Charles Francis Adams, Jr., Nov. 3, 1858, *Letters*, vol. 1, 4–5.

editor and political reformer), and Edward Everett (president of Harvard, governor, and uncle of Henry and his brothers), Adams exploded. "Do you suppose I'm a statesman like Seward or that my amiable play-philosophy would ever set me up to guiding a nation; do you imagine that I have a tithe of Greeley's vigor, originality and enterprise; are you so blinded by the tenderness of your fraternal affection as to imagine that the mantle of Cicero has fallen upon my shoulders, or that I inherit the pride and ample pinion that the Grecian sophist bore?"[15] Adams's plea of incompetence concealed a deeper sentiment of impotence. At the age of twenty-one, a time when many young people feel the future is theirs for the taking, Adams saw himself as a spectator who preferred to watch history run its course. "I am tired of trying to direct what I have no power over," he wrote to Charles in 1859.[16] Even as a young man Adams felt in his heart two convictions that would never cease worrying his mind: history is not a rational process, and the classical argument that politics must be based on reason is an argument that itself is not based on reason. Adams did not come to these conclusions lightly. On the contrary, they derived from four episodes in his education: direct observation of the workings of American politics, the Civil War and what he regarded as the crisis of America's political institutions, his own experience in the theater of European politics, and the corruption of politics by big business interests during and after the Grant administration.

A young man who valued most the qualities that existed least, Adams discerned some miraculous moments in the behavior of American politicians. After Jacksonian democracy had transformed politics from the classical principle of duty to the liberal passion of opportunity, a disinterested commitment to civic virtue and the public good became a rarity in the conduct of political parties and their leaders. But the behavior of Thurlow Weed, assistant to Secretary Seward, was an exception to Adams's growing conviction that politics had fallen into vulgar hands. "The trait that astounded and compounded cynicism was his apparent unselfishness. Never, in any man who wielded power, did Adams see anything like it." But Adams also saw that a man of virtue may not be able to hold his own ideals for long. Weed may have possessed the balance and confidence necessary to Adams's father during the sensitive negotiations with England at the time of the Civil War; Senator Charles Sumner may have enjoyed the egotism essential to the rough game of politics; and John Hay, Adams's close friend, may have had the intelligence to subordinate short-run interests to more enduring international settlements during the

15. Henry Adams to Charles Francis Adams, Jr., Feb. 9, 1859, ibid., 20.
16. Henry Adams to Charles Francis Adams, Jr., Mar. 13, 1859, ibid., 28.

Open Door policy in China. But such talented statesmen failed to anticipate not only the entry of the masses into history that would upset traditional spheres of influence diplomacy; they also failed to foresee that
politics itself was becoming a matter of skilled dexterity and management
rather than moral leadership and virtue. Adams saw that American politics could never be elevated toward the realization of classical ideals because the party system itself presupposed the division and factionalism
that classical republicanism had regarded as destructive to the public
good. In English Whig ideology the idea of "opposition" was anathema
to the extent that it had rendered inevitable the spectacle of competitive
interest politics. But in America almost from the beginning of the Republic political parties were born and took their shape in opposition to one
another, and their leaders struggled to promote legislation favorable to
their own constituencies while obstructing all efforts of the rival party.
Eventually Adams could not deny what Tocqueville had earlier observed
in America: since the ruling passion of a democracy is "envy," politics
itself could be little more than "the systematic organization of hatreds."[17]

Adams was twenty-three when the Civil War broke out, an event that
seemed to demonstrate that routine political hatred would not stop at
even bloody fratricide. He had not yet become so disillusioned with politics that he was incapable of seeing moral purpose in history. He trusted
Seward and Lincoln to see the Republic through its crisis, and he pleaded
with his brother Charles to arrange for him a commission in the army.
The cause of the South was "the last convulsion of the slave power" and
Adams was "glad that the beast was so near her end," he had written to
his brother just before the outbreak of hostilities.[18] Yet Adams recognized
that the Civil War had dramatized the moral embarrassment of America's
political institutions: a Constitution that had been designed to preserve
liberty had also protected slavery. From the South's point of view, the
old classical idea of independence from executive tyranny led to the doctrine of states' rights, and the right of local self-determination made black
slavery an offshoot of white freedom. On this stance the South would
not yield, and the Northern Republicans could never make up their minds
whether to resort to force to destroy slavery or to prevent disunion, even
if the latter meant keeping slavery in the South while controlling its
expansion into the West. In "The Great Secession Winter of 1860–61,"
Adams pondered the implications of a republican party of conciliation
that "could not win and must lose." Since the Republican party was
hopelessly divided, "the task of Mr. Lincoln was one which might well

17. Adams, *Education*, 7, 102–3, 147.
18. Henry Adams to Charles Francis Adams, Jr., Dec. 18, 1860, *Letters*, vol. 1, 208.

have filled with alarm the greatest statesman who had ever lived. He had to deal with men and measures that would have taxed the patience of Washington and required the genius of Napoleon." That the conflict between North and South had no political solution, and was ultimately resolved by "brute force, that final tribunal to which human nature is subjected or subjects herself without appeal," led Adams to ponder the whole meaning of the Republic. Some people say "our theory of government is a failure," he noted in references to the republican theory of checks and balances that had broken down in 1860. Yet Adams was not ready to conclude that the Republic devised by his ancestors had failed to stand the test of secession. Indeed Henry Adams looked upon the coming of the Civil War with the same hope with which John Adams had once looked upon the outbreak of the Revolution: it would be the Republic's supreme test of "integrity."[19]

Yet as the Civil War followed its bloody course Adams was plagued by the same thought that haunted Lincoln: the possibility that man was no longer in control of events. Adams began to refer to himself as "a full-blown fatalist," informing Charles that what "disgusts me is the consciousness that we are unable to govern" the movement of affairs. The notion that the world goes on independently of man's will and effort sensitized Adams's mind to the riddle of fate and freedom (the Civil War had the same effect on Oliver Wendell Holmes, Jr., as we shall see). He now toyed with the idea that he would later develop into a stoical philosophy of history—"that a man of sense can only prove his possession of a soul, by remaining in mind a serene and indifferent spectator of the very events to which all his acts most eagerly contribute. This has been in one form or another the result of every philosophical system since men became conscious of the inexplicable contradiction of existence."[20]

What did much to render existence inexplicable was politics itself. In the chapter "Political Morality" in the *Education* Adams described his experiences in London as an assistant to his father during the Civil War. Charles Francis Adams had been making every effort to prevent England from recognizing the Confederacy. He eventually succeeded in this ordeal of tact and patience in dealing with parliamentarians like Earl Russell, Lord Palmerston, and William Gladstone. But Henry depicted the various maneuvers as though he were emerging from a nightmare in which the meaning of action remained impenetrable to rational analysis. Adams confessed that he could barely distinguish who was supporting the Union

19. Henry Adams, *The Great Secession Winter of 1860–61 and Other Essays*, ed. George F. Hochfield (New York, 1963), 3–21.
20. Henry Adams to Charles Francis Adams, Jr., Oct. 30, 1863, *Letters*, vol. 1, 403.

and who was conspiring against it. While statesmen played their roles as
public actors, political behavior itself seemed to lack a conscious motive.
Was Palmerston a true friend of the Union? Was Gladstone really the
enemy? Adams likened his situation to a scene from a Henry James novel,
where character is described from all perspectives but never fully penetrated. Palmerston appeared to be moving against the Union, yet turned
out to be cautiously neutral: Russell, strong and determined, proved weak
and vacillating; Gladstone, "the sum of contradictions," seemed to represent the finest ideals of British statesmanship, only to reveal a confused
mind and a Napoleonic disdain for truth. Adams found he had to revise
his estimate at every step of the negotiations, and he labored over the
lessons taught by his experience with Whitehall. "Never was demonstration more tangled. Hegel's metaphysical doctrine of the identity of opposites was simpler and easier to understand." Adams tried to bring reason
to bear upon politics, and he attributed intelligence to his English antagonists, but when he found there was no conspiracy afoot he still was at a
loss to explain how he was to act when he could not fathom the actions
of others. Later in life, when he read Russell's memoirs and learned that
its author now admitted he had been at fault in a mistaken policy decision,
Adams observed that even guilt is no substitute for understanding. "The
true issue lay not in the question of his fault, but of his intent. To a
young man, getting an education in politics, there could be no sense of
history unless a constant course of faults implied a constant motive."[21]
To Adams a confession of fault remains irrelevant to behavior that still
needs to be explained. Whether or not events are intended, we need to
understand them causally, and hence political knowledge requires as-
signing motives to actions.

Adams's skepticism about the possibility of political knowledge had
already been aroused in his travels through Italy in 1860. Adams was not
altogether sure that the tumultuous clamor of Italian politics could learn
much from American traditions; nor was he sure that Garibaldi always
kept in focus his two separate goals—a free Italy and a united Italy.
Indeed an audience with the great Italian leader left him disturbed; not
only did Garibaldi remain in the dark as to the historical significance of
is actions, but Adams himself could not fathom the strange fusion of
idealism and opportunism characteristic of Italian political life. "The lesson of Garibaldi, as education, seemed to teach the extreme complexity of
extreme simplicity; but one could have learned this from a glow worm."[22]

21. Adams, *Education*, 145–66.
22. Ibid., 95; Henry Adams to Charles Francis Adams, Jr., June 15, 1860, *Letters*, vol.
1, 173.

Adams sensed that the type of mind Garibaldi represented, an energetic revolutionary who articulated conflicting forces like patriotism and commerce, would be a political symbol of the future, but he did not know what to make of a leader whose actions could not be predicated according to rational political principles.

The fate of Italian civilization also haunted Adams, as it did other New England Brahmins. In Rome he had been reading Edward Gibbon, and the riddle of the decline of glory and the fall of empire plagued him. "Rome," he reflected, "could not be fitted into an orderly, middle-class Bostonian, systematic scheme of evolution. No law of progress applied to it. Not even time sequences, the last refuge of the helpless historian, has value for it." Rome dwarfed students of politics and history, and Adams found himself standing on the steps of the Church of Santa Maria di Ara Coeli repeating "Why! Why! Why!!!"[23]

Would the American Republic follow the Roman and go the way of all flesh? Such a prospect occurred to Adams when he returned to the United States to find his country sunk in scandal. The revelations of fraud and bribery in the Grant administration raised the classical specter of the corruption of public virtue by the force of commerce; the New York Gold Conspiracy illustrated the new power of finance capitalism; and the takeover of Cornelius Vanderbilt's Erie Railroad by the rogues Jay Gould, Jim Fisk, and Daniel Drew seemed the first step toward the creation of "an empire within a republic." Henry and Charles exposed the intricate operations of the latter in *Chapters of Erie* (1869), and in a novel later published anonymously, *Democracy* (1880), Henry dramatized the extent to which senators accepted bribes almost as the normal transaction of politics. Henry Adams was aware that the spectacle of republican corruption by commercial temptation had worried English statesmen in the Walpole era.[24] Although the source of corruption now differed, coming not from ministerial intrigue within government but from corporate entities without, the result would be the same as economic power continued to penetrate the institutions of political authority. Worse still, the public seemed at times more amused than appalled by the machinations of buccaneer capitalists like Gould and Fisk. Although Adams never became familiar with the writings of Thorstein Veblen, he shared Veblen's perception that people are impressed by wealth and power however they are obtained, even, and perhaps especially, through bold, dramatic exploits. "The fascination of amassing wealth without labor," noted Adams, had

23. Adams, *Education*, 92.
24. John Patrick Diggins, *The Lost Soul of American Politics: Virtue, Self-Interest, and the Foundations of Liberalism* (New York, 1984), 252–76.

now come to capture an American mentality that once had been imbued with the Protestant ethic. Those who labor will never achieve glory or fame, but those who possess wealth will rule even in a democracy. With the worship of wealth, money becomes a sovereign power unto itself. While Adams could agree with Marx and the socialists on the fetish power of money as a symbol, he was less sure that lucre itself explained very much. For one thing, money seemed to have no lasting value, and Americans would spend and waste it as much as they desired to possess it. Moreover, the money fetish not only misleads the masses but it as well misleads social critics who believe they can put the solution before the question. "Please," Adams wrote his brother Brooks, "give up that profoundly unscientific jabber of the newspapers about MONEY in capital letters. What I see is POWER in capitals also. You may abolish money and all its machinery, the power will still be there."[25] Money remained for Adams merely the form through which power now expressed itself. And if modern man regarded the force of money as sovereign and even supernatural, such attitudes reflected the decline of political authority and religious faith. More than money, humankind lusts after power, the world of the father. Hence the dilemma: how to discipline through intelligence what is desired by instinct?

The answer to that question, Adams became more and more convinced, could not be found in politics. An understanding of human nature, he observed in the *Education*, was the first task of political philosophy, and the whole purpose of acquiring a political education is "to control power in some form." Years earlier, when investigating the corruption of American politics in the postwar era, Adams followed the classical tradition and undertook "a recurrence to the fundamental principles of the Constitution" in the hope of finding an answer to the problem of power. But in the *Education* he concluded that "the moral law had expired—like the Constitution," convinced that "the system of 1789 had broken down, and with it the eighteenth-century fabric of apriori, or moral, principle." Although the Constitution depended upon neither moral principle nor natural law, it did rest on a set of assumptions about mixed government and checks and balances that promised to control power. Adams now realized that new forms of corporate power had eluded the mechanisms the framers had devised. The Constitution's premises appeared to be "delusive" and "chimerical" because the politcal authority of the state proved impotent to subordinate the economic power of the business inter-

25. Henry Adams to Brooks Adams, April 12, 1906, in *Henry Adams and His Friends: A Collection of Unpublished Letters*, ed. Harold Dean Cater (New York, 1970), 583; hereafter cited as Cater.

ests. And in the absence of sovereign political authority, capitalism worked through bribery, patronage, lobbies, rings, party bosses, and political machines to seek its illicit ends. Thus like Max Weber, Adams concluded that in America the political system had been penetrated from without by business and corrupted from within by bosses. "On that line, too, education could go no further. Tammany Hall stood at the end of the Vista." Adams and Weber shared a conviction that Theodore Roosevelt and other Progressive reformers refused to concede: the union of corporate capitalism and political machines would forever frustrate republican ideals. To the more sensitive Adams it seemed that politics itself, once conceived as a noble profession, had lost all sense of shame. "Politics have ceased to interest me," he wrote Henry Cabot Lodge in 1876. "I am satisfied that the machine can't be smashed this time. As I feared, we have ourselves saved it by a foolish attempt to run it, which we shall never succed in. The caucus and the machine will outlive me. . . . When the day comes on which it will be considered as disgraceful to be seen in a caucus as to be seen in a gambling house or brothel, then my interest will wake up again and legitimate politics will get a new birth."[26]

For Adams that day never came, although he continued to involve himself in efforts at political reform. When we find him in the last years of his life in 1916 telling young Eleanor and Franklin Roosevelt that it makes no difference who is president, and roaring with laughter at their sense of shock, we feel the pain of the moralist who can now only joke about the ideals he once held. "The world has so lost its sense of humor," he wrote a few years earlier, "that it can't laugh—damn it, it can't even cry."[27]

History and the Problem of Consciousness

A year after Adams wrote to Lodge expressing his disgust with politics, he resigned his professorship at Harvard University. In the *Education* Adams had described undergraduate life as directed more to producing a graceful social type of "charm" and "self-possession" than to studying Karl Marx and August Comte, whose absence from the curriculum offered further evidence that Harvard prepared students for life in the eighteenth century, not the twentieth.[28] Education in Germany, where Ad-

26. Adams, *Education*, 36, 180, 280–81; Adams, *Great Secession*, 97–128; Henry Adams to Chanler Francis Adams, Jr., June 4, 1876, *Letters*, vol. 2, 279.

27. Henry Adams to Margaret Chanler, Feb. 10, 1910, in Cater, 679.

28. Adams complained specifically that Marx's *Das Kapital* was not taught at Harvard when he was an undergraduate, forgetting, perhaps playfully, that he graduated in 1858 and Marx's work was not published until 1867. On the whimsical nature of Adams's complaints, see Carl Becker, *Everyman His Own Historian* (New York, 1935), 143–68.

ams had studied civil law, proved even more antiquated as professors mumbled unchallenged convictions and students went through the motions of taking notes. And in his travels, his experiment in "accidential education," Adams would later boast that he could "know only what accident had taught him," knowing full well that one cannot derive general truths from particular occurrences. Still, Adams conceded that Harvard had the effect of leaving him full of questions, and therefore undergraduate education succeeded in weakening "the violent political bias of his childhood" and opening his mind to new ideas. Yet if the development of intellect could free the mind of bias, it still left the mind hungering for knowledge. This awareness that the mind posed the very questions it could not answer had troubled Adams even earlier when he had accepted an appointment as assistant professor in Harvard's history department. "I know nothing about Medieval History," he told President Eliot when he first tried to refuse the position. Irony? False humility? Perhaps. For Adams would offer the first seminar in history at Harvard; he knew enough about medieval history to write a classic on art and religion, worked to make research materials available to undergraduates, felt "pleased as punch about my Ph.D.s," and delighted in describing to his students in colonial American history why they should be proud to be Americans. "There he is, the British aristocrat! The sum of all wickedness and tyranny! We licked him! Ha! Ha! (with savageness). We are a great people!"[29]

Although Adams found teaching a challenging vocation, he also felt that the purpose of education was not only to impart the facts of history but to interpret their meaning as well. At a time when the tides of relativism were about to engulf the various academic disciplines, he remained convinced that education, even though it may weaken bias and liberate the mind, could be of little value unless it led to some certainty of objective truth. Like the philosopher Charles S. Peirce, Adams sensed the dilemma of trying to teach when there are no truths to be taught. Thus Adams pondered the responsibilities of being in a position of intellectual authority and having nothing authoritative to say.

> Not that his ignorance troubled him! He knew enough to be ignorant. His course had led him through oceans of ignorance; he had tumbled from one ocean into another till he had learned to swim; but even to him education was a serious thing. A parent gives life, but as parent, gives no more. A

29. Adams, *Education;* Henry Adams to the Corporation of Harvard College, Dec. 14, 1875, *Letters,* vol. 2, 244; Henry Adams to Sir Robert Cunliffe, July 6, 1874, *Letters,* vol. 2, 199.

murderer takes life, but his deed stops there. A teacher affects eternity; he can never tell where his influence stops. A teacher is expected to teach truth, and perhaps may flatter himself that he does so, if he stops with the alphabet or the multiplication table, as a mother teaches a truth by making her child eat with a spoon;' but morals are quite another truth and philosophy is more complex still. A teacher must either treat history as a catalogue, a record, a romance, or an evolution; and whether he affirms or denies evolution, he falls into the burning faggots of the pit. He makes of his scholars either priests or atheists, plutocrats or socialists, judges or anarchists, almost in spite of himself. In essence incoherent and immoral, history had either to be taught as such—or falsified.[30]

Whether one could find useful a history that displayed little more than incoherence and chaos was a prospect that would trouble Progressive intellectuals like Charles Beard, an admirer of Adams. But Adams's first efforts at historical scholarship began with a more confident assumption about the possibility of discovering a usable past. Shortly after he resigned from Harvard Adams published *The Life of Albert Gallatin* (1879). To Adams, Gallatin's public career offered a textbook study in the highest principles of practical statesmanship by a Swiss-born friend of America. He admired the several capacities in which the Secretary of the Treasury had served the young Republic and thereby helped it establish itself in the eyes of the people as a just source of power.[31]

Jefferson stood for reduction in the national debt, efficiency and economy in government, and elimination of military expenditures. Gallatin, who displayed "essentially a scientific and not a political mind," helped convince Jefferson of the necessity of continuing Hamilton's banking system and import tariff, and he urged the president to negotiate the Louisiana Purchase and to undertake military expenditures and economic embargoes as a means of preparing the country to oppose England, measures that would definitely increase the scope of government power. The weakness of the Jeffersonian system, Adams stressed, lay in its "rigidity to rule," its devotion to a "system of doctrine [that] had all the virtues and the faults of *a priori* reasoning." Although "humane" and "philanthropic" and appealing to "the best instincts of mankind," Jeffersonian ideology made too little allowance for "human passions and vices," relied "too absolutely on interest and reason as opposed to prejudice and habit," and was too willing to renounce openly the use of force as an instrument of statecraft. Adams summed up the dilemma inherent in Jeffersonian ideal-

30. Adams, *Education*, 300–301.
31. Henry Adams, *The Life of Albert Gallatin* (Boston: J.B. Lippincott, 1879).

ism as follows: the Jeffersonians believed that "government must be ruled by principles; to which the Federalists answered that government must be ruled by circumstances."[32]

Gallatin had recognized that peace and frugality were necessary if the Republican principles of government were to be fulfilled. But both Gallatin and Jefferson were caught short by the country's state of military unpreparedness when Britain seized American vessels in 1805, leaving the administration with no alternative but submission or war, both options being fatal to Republican principles. Adams noted that Gallatin, having moved from the Treasury to the foreign service, soon came to understand that the contingencies of events and not commitment to principles governed political affairs and he learned "how to accept defeat and adapt himself to circumstances, how to abandon theory and move with his generation." Such wisdom disillusioned the former Treasury secretary, who began to feel himself a political liability in the Madison administration. Yet Gallatin never surrendered his Jeffersonian faith in the future of democracy, and he held out ultimate hope that someday convictions would count more than circumstances. Adams admired deeply this idealist without illusions, a statesman who was neither a Machiavellian nor a moralist and thus "became neither a cynic nor a transcendentalist philosopher."[33] Alienated by a world of power, Gallatin nevertheless chose to confront that world rather than simply renounce it.

In many respects Gallatin's dilemma became Adams's enigma: the dialectical relationship of principle to power. Principle may be corrupted by power, yet a firm exercise of power is necessary to control history, itself an aspect of the force thwarting the fruition of principles; and all principles, even democratic ideals, require the use of power for their realization. How, then, can political power be joined to some scheme of knowledge so that it might lessen its threatening and coercive character? On this question Gallatin succeeded only in showing Adams how to endure failure, for the more he tried to impose principle on politics the more he clashed with Congress. "The moral of his life," Adams wrote of Gallatin to Henry Cabot Lodge, is "the inevitable isolation and disillusionment of a really strong mind . . . the romance and tragedy of statesmanship."[34] Adams as well as Gallatin knew that to whore after power itself was the sin of vanity. Yet the historian still felt obliged to show how power could be made legitimate and transformed into genuine authority. Despite his first brush with the complexities of knowledge and power, Adams re-

32. Ibid., 272.
33. Ibid., 76–493.
34. Henry Adams to Henry Cabot Lodge, Oct. 6, 1879, *Letters*, vol. 2, 376.

mained convinced that history might be the only place where truth could be found. Acting on such faith, he spent the entire decade of the 1880s working on the nine-volume magisterial classic, *The History of the United States of America during the Administrations of Thomas Jefferson and James Madison* (1885–1891).

The context is crucial. Around the time Adams began his full-scale exploration into early America, Friedrich Nietzsche had attacked the cult of historical study as a false morality of memory that unmans will and imagination, and by the end of the century a host of European writers were denying the status of history as a scientific discipline with claims to intellectual authority. This revolt against positivism had no initial impact on Adams, who started the *History* assuming that the past could be discovered through the recovery of factual data and that the study of history would yield objective knowledge. Confident that history could be approached scientifically, Adams set out to discover the patterns and tendencies that could be considered as the necessary laws of the movement and flow of power, a task that required ascertaining the exact sequence of human activity, the precise causal relations between events that render them comprehensible. Against the disorders of contemporary politics, history offered the last hope of finding enduring principles of explanation; and Adams wanted to assert his own intellectual authority not by making history, as did his ancestors, but by comprehending it. "From cradle to grave this problem of running order through chaos, direction through space, discipline through freedom, unity through multiplicity, has always been, and must always be, the task of education," he later reflected. While doing archival research for the *History*, Adams wrote to a friend that "one man may reasonably devote his life to the effort of impressing a moral on the national mind, which is now almost a void." Faced with that void, Adams did not feel his goal was extravagant or eccentric. "One sought only a spool on which to wind the thread of history without breaking it."[35] Adams could believe in the authority of history because he believed in the rationality of human events illuminated by the mind's capacity for causal understanding. In his premodernist outlook, Adams approached history with the faith of Emerson, who summed up his optimistic credo in his essay on Montaigne:

> We are natural believers. Truth, or the connection between cause and effect, alone interests us. We are persuaded that a thread runs through all things: all worlds are strung on it, as beads; and men, and events, and life, come to us, only because

35. Henry Adams to Hugh Blair Grigsby, Sept. 1, 1879, ibid., 371; Adams, *Education*, 472.

of that thread; they pass and repass, only that we may know the direction and continuity of that line. A book or statement which goes to show that there is no line, but random and chaos, a calamity out of nothing, a prosperity and no account of it, a hero born from a fool, a fool from a hero—dispirits us. Seen or unseen, we believe the tie exists. Talent makes counterfeit ties; genius finds the real ones. We hearken to the man of science, because we anticipate the sequences of natural phenomena which he uncovers. We love whatever affirms, connects, preserves; and dislike what scatters or pulls down.[36]

However confident Adams felt when undertaking the *History*, as the volumes began to appear in the late 1880s he felt the same emotion that Emerson said "dispirits us." So "dreary" did he feel the enterprise had become that he could scarcely "boil up my old interest in history" to finish the project.[37] Emerson insisted that the "genuis" and "man of science" would perceive the "thread that runs through all things," and Adams wanted to find the "spool" on which such a thread could be wound. He did not find it, and unlike Emerson, he knew that simply to define "history" as "autobiography" is to confuse the object with the subject. Many years later literary scholars and some historians would regard the *History* as a masterpiece that ranks with Gibbon's *The Decline and Fall of the Roman Empire*.[38] Adams dismissed it as a "failure" as though he taunted history to disappoint him. Considering what Adams was searching for, we must take seriously his own verdict.

In the *History* and elsewhere Adams set out to achieve two interrelated goals: to recover a past example of political thought and political leadership that could be relevant to the modern age, and to develop a philosophy of history that would provide the "spool" that enabled the historian to connect all things through the thread of interpretation. The first search led Adams to consider three ingredients of American intellectual history as manifested in the years of the Jefferson and Madison administrations (1800–1817): religion, classical politics, and the Enlightenment.

America's Puritan conscience lingered like a dark shadow around the mind of Henry Adams. Although he would, as we shall see, later delight in invoking the Calvinist doctrine of predestination to reinforce his own sense of scientific determinism, he believed New England Puritanism narrow and intolerant even by seventeenth-century standards.[39] He also

36. Ralph Waldo Emerson, *Representative Men* (New York: Hurst, n.d.), 124.

37. Henry Adams to Charles Milnes Gaskell, Dec. 12, 1886, *Letters*, vol. 3, 48–49.

38. See Ivor Winters, *In Defense of Reason* (Denver, 1937), 414–30, for a comparison of Adams and Gibbon.

39. Henry Adams to Henry Cabot Lodge, July 31, 1876, *Letters*, vol. 2, 283–84.

found Unitarianism, the nineteenth-century watered-down version of Puritanism, too shallow to offer spiritual guidance in the modern age. It was not only that Unitarians turned a wrathful God into a benign friend. More significant was Adams's perception that religion was being made to serve man's needs rather than God's purposes, however mysterious. Adams would later chide William James for believing that the problems of faith could be answered by the promises of hope. And as he wrote of the placid mental calm of the early nineteenth-century Unitarian clergy, Adams criticized a theology that would dismiss on grounds of reason whatever challenged reason itself. Unitarianism "founded new churches on what seemed to resemble an argument that the intellectual difficulties in their path must be unessential because they were insuperable."[40] Adams, who enjoyed a kind of Melvillean attraction to the insuperable and inscrutable, wanted to see America with a religion that would challenge its people, not comfort them.

Adams also wanted to see America abide by political ideals, not just mouth them. He knew that classical republican ideals had weak roots in America. After 1800 the New England states were either rushing into the modern world of science and industry or listening to Fisher Ames and the Essex Junto despair over the threat of mass democracy to republican liberty. The Middle Atlantic states remained indifferent to political theory, and their leader, Alexander Hamilton, an ambitious visionary who saw the necessity of economic development, was always tempted by a "Napoleonic" adventurism that in fact spurred him into his fatal duel with Aaron Burr. Only in the southern states did the residues of classical politics resonate. Thomas Jefferson's "Southern Republicanism" derived from the conviction that America had wrung power from the monarchy and that henceforth the young nation could preserve freedom by remaining simple and rural, utilizing commerce as a handmaiden to agriculture while avoiding full industrialization and urbanization. Adams observed that in the South classical republicanism had been transformed into an "idyllic conservatism" based upon the simple truths of field and farm. Southern political thought rested on the "axiom that Virginia was the typical society of future Arcadian America. To escape the tyranny of Caesar by perpetuating the simpler and isolated lives of their fathers was the sum total of their political philosophy." But the backward orientation of southern agrarian thought contrasted favorably to the grubby image of Yankee capitalism, and Adams quotes William Channing to show how easily one could be seduced by the image of the virtuous Virginian gentle-

40. Henry Adams, *History of the United States of America during the Administration of James Madison* (New York: Library of America, 1986), 1308.

men' "They *love money less* than we do; they are more disinterested; their patriotism is not tied to their purse-strings. Could I only take from the Virginians their sensuality and their slaves, I should think them the greatest people in the world. As it is, with a few great virtues, they have innumerable vices."[41]

So much for the image. Once in power, the Jeffersonian Republicans violated their own classical doctrines. President Jefferson went back on his commitment to legislative sovereignty when he used the powers of the executive office to negotiate unilaterally the Louisiana Purchase; went back on his commitment to an agrarian republic when he adopted Hamilton's program for banks, tariffs, and economic development; went back on his commitment to local government when he approved federal expenditures for roads and canals; went back on his commitment to a small republic when he commissioned the Lewis and Clark expedition to explore the possibilities of westward expansion; and, above all, went back on his commitment to states' rights when he and Madison authorized an embargo against England and forced New England states to go along with it. That the Jeffersonians simply out-federalized the Federalists indicated to Adams that in American history no party would be able to stand on principles alone.

Historians of our day have minimized Jefferson's inconsistencies in order to emphasize his concern for the small-scale "ward" system of local government as a means of keeping alive the flame of republican liberty. Yet Jefferson waxed nostalgic for his precious little wards when out of office, and he did so only in private correspondence.[42] His public career, however, suggested to Adams some deeper lessons in America's political history. With no party being capable of abiding by principle, what became of the fate of classical republicanism? Although politics as civic duty had been the inspiring principle of republicanism, Adams saw politics as economic and political opportunity—the unspoken truth of the American way of life. Thus politics itself, the very activity that had once promised to regenerate civic virtue, actually eviscerated it to the extent that government simply became a public means of fostering private ends. In Jefferson and Madison's America, Adams found politicians of both parties who

41. Henry Adams to Henry Cabot Lodge, May 15, 1876, *Letters*, vol. 2, 267; Henry Adams, *History of the United States of America during the Administration of Thomas Jefferson* (New York: Library of America, 1986), 5–179.

42. The neoclassical interpretation, which sees Jefferson upholding the local "ward" system of politics to sustain the ancient ideals of civic participation, was first argued in Hannah Arendt's *On Revolution* (New York, 1968); for a critique see John Patrick Diggins, "Theory and the American Founding," in *Theory in America*, ed. Denis Donoghue et al. (New York, 1988).

"care nothing for fine-spun theories of what government might or might not do, providing government did what they wanted."[43]

In America politics would betray principle and surrender to whatever shifting factions wanted. And those who resisted? In an earlier study of John Raldolph, Adams depicted the Virginian as a republican visionary who could not compromise and accept politics and the party system as inherent in America's historical development. Thus Randolph saw, or thought he saw, the increasing national consolidation in the years after 1800 as a corruption of the "pure" principles of republican liberty, which had always meant resistance to the expanding power of government. In Adams's sympathetic estimate, Randolph suffered from too much theory to the point of paranoia. A stubborn doctrinal vision that saw the movement of history as conspiratorial could lead, as it did with Randolph, to madness. Adams preferred confessions of ignorance to the pretensions of omniscience.[44]

Adams's *History* is scarcely an American jeremiad, an angry sermon against the nation's backsliding from ancestral ideals. But if Adams is not a doctrinaire ideologue bemoaning the betrayal of principle, neither is he a pragmatist who looks to the world of action to find what had been lost to reflection. Adams did not have to wait until the pragmatists came along to advise Americans to reject all ideas that cannot be translated into action. The case of Jefferson illustrated the fate of a philosopher who leaves his study to assume political office. "Here," Adams emphasized, referring to Jefferson's encounter with history as the theater of contingency in which the actor adapts his character to circumstances, "lay the danger, and here came the ultimate shipwreck. It is obvious at the outset that the weak point of what may be called the Jeffersonian system lay in its rigidity of rule. That system was, it must be confessed, a system of doctrinaires, and had the virtues and faults of *a priori* reasoning." The virtue of Jeffersonian theory was its high moral conviction that responded to the dictates of conscience. Yet it was bound to wreck itself on the shoals of reality. "Far in advance, as it was, of any other political effort at this time, and representing, as it doubtless did, all that was most philanthropic and all that most boldly appealed to the best instincts of mankind, it made too little allowance for human passions and vices; it relied too absolutely on the power of interest and reason as opposed to prejudice and habit; it proclaimed too openly to the world that the sword was not one of its arguments, and that peace was essential to its existence."[45]

43. Adams, *History* (*Jefferson*), 440.
44. Henry Adams, *John Randolph* (Boston: Houghton Mifflin, 1882).
45. Adams, *Gallatin*, 76–493.

Adams's observations on Jefferson presage Weber's and Niebuhr's critique of pacifists who would cling to their ethical integrity regardless of consequences. But Jefferson was willing to sacrifice the integrity of his theoretical system in order to be a successful president, which meant expanding the power of government in order to cope with changing circumstances. Yet Adams discerned that politics cannot adapt flexibly to every contingency and still adhere to principle. Jefferson presided over the growth of the young Republic, even supporting Madison and the war against England in 1812, and in the process the "Jeffersonian system" lost its identity. Jefferson succeeded in politics by ceasing to practice philosophy.

In Jefferson's and Madison's America, Adams saw people and their political leaders behaving practically and shunning all ideas that might constitute a judgment on action by virtue of standing above it. Political parties were instruments of action rather than conviction, and a course of action would be determined by circumstances rather than principle. But whereas the pragmatic philosopher assumes that experience will result in knowledge, Adams doubted that Americans had any knowledge of what they were doing or where history was taking them. In Adams's view the pragmatic cult of action negated reflection and precluded the possibility that American history could be guided by conscious human purposes. The lesson seemed to be not that political parties would be opportunistic but that they would simply move with the processes of economic change and, without being aware of any inconsistency, seize the powers they had once renounced. Since the Jeffersonian Republicans were the first to sacrifice principle to experience, Adams could be both amused and appalled by a party that believed in freedom yet followed history rather than determining it. "I am at times almost sorry that I undertook to write their history," he complained to Samuel Tilden in 1883,

> for they appear like mere grasshoppers kicking and gesticulating on the middle of the Mississippi River. There is no possibility of reconciling their theories with their acts, or their extraordinary foreign policy with dignity. They were carried along on a stream which floated with them after a fashion, without much regard to themselves.
>
> This I take to be the result that students of history generally reach in regard to modern times. The element of it is a science. My own conclusion is that history is simply social development along the lines of weakest resistance, and that in most cases the line of weakest resistance is found as unconsciously by society as by water.[46]

46. Henry Adams to Samuel Tilden, Jan. 24, 1883, *Letters*, vol. 2, 491.

In pragmatism the course of events becomes the course of experience; action incarnates thought and in the process leaves older ideas behind in order to adapt to new conditions. In this respect American history evolved pragmatically, and the historian tries to acquire knowledge of what Americans made of themselves by studying their actions as well as their thoughts. But did Americans reflect on their actions as features of their own consciousness?

This question of reflective consciousness has scarcely troubled many modern American historians, particularly those of the cold war generation. In the 1950s, when the term *ideology* rang with the curse of old-world class struggles, Americans were told that the "genius" of their politics lay in their anti-ideological "pragmatic" temper and prudent nondoctrinaire character.[47] Early American history, according to this "consensus" school of thought, came to its senses when its people left behind all "theory" and "dogma" and allowed themselves to be guided by experience, on the assumption that values were "given" in action rather than found or expressed in thought. But in Adams's interpretation of the same events, a pragmatic adjustment to a changing environment, while necessary, defeats conscious purposes and leaves Americans with no scheme of values other than the satisfaction of success. Before 1800, Adams observed, people in certain regions of America tried to live for ideals that resided in conscience:

> The Pilgrims of Plymouth, the Puritans of Boston, the Quakers of Pennsylvania, all avowed a moral purpose, and began by making institutions that consciously reflected a moral idea. No such character belonged to the colonization of 1800. From Lake Erie to Florida, in long, unbroken line, pioneers were at work, cutting into the forest with the energy of so many beavers, and with no more express moral purpose than the beavers they drove away. The civilization they carried with them was rarely illumined by an idea; they sought room for no new truth, and aimed neither at creating, like the Puritans, a government of saints, nor, like the Quakers, one of love and peace; they left such experiments behind them, and wrestled only with the hardest problems of fronter life. No wonder that foreign observers, and even the educated, well-to-do Americans of the sea-coast, could seldom see anything to admire in the ignorance and brutality of frontiersmen, and should declare that virtue and wisdom no longer guided the United States![48]

47. Daniel J. Boorstin, *The Genius of American Politics* (Chicago: University of Chicago Press, 1953).
48. Adams, *History* (*Jefferson*), 121.

Could Americans commit themselves to any theory of politics, not to mention the demands of "civic virtue"? Classical republicanism, based on the conviction that liberty meant independence and resistance to power, seemed to evaporate after 1800, as the Jeffersonians allowed themselves to be carried along by the stream of power and the nation transformed itself from an agricultural to a commercial society. If classical politics failed to survive the momentum of economic change, the Enlightenment failed to survive the meaning of historical events, at least to the extent that Adams could demonstrate that many of the events between 1800 and 1816 defied explanation. Without a meaning-endowed subject determining events, significance resided in action rather than in thought. Yet actions could hardly be traced to theory, and if Americans identified progress with pushing ahead, they lacked any conceptual understanding of the changes they wrought. Small wonder that Adams came to the conclusion that one must falsify history if it is to be taught for moral or political purposes. For the suspicion that grips Adams as he moves toward the conclusion of his magnum opus is that history may be neither reasonable nor rational.

History was unreasonable because it remained indifferent to human intelligence and defied any sequential pattern or logic of development. The Jeffersonians and the Federalists would recognize this implicitly and perhaps unconsciously, when each party subordinated its respective theories to the adjustments of situation. The result of this pragmatic compromise was the surrender of principles to circumstance. "The practical system which resulted from sixteen years' experience seemed to rest on the agreement not to press principles to a conclusion." Like latter-day consensus historians, Adams saw how political ideas were overtaken by events as the changing environment came to absorb the political mind. But rather than celebrate the "genuis" of America's anti-ideological character, Adams lamented it as the sacrifice of reason and purpose to history and process. Not only did American history lack any theoretical self-justification, and not only must the historian confess his inability to arrive at meaning and understanding by establishing sequential relations, but history itself could even be irrational in that there is no logical connection between the course of historical actions and the leaders' motives for performing them. Adams criticized Jefferson as a "theorist" who was "prepared to risk the fate of mankind on the chance of reasoning far from certain in its details." Yet Jefferson was a theorist and pragmatist at the same time without knowing it, a leader who took his bearings from reason only to allow the necessity of experience to dictate his political actions. And all the while Jefferson believed that history would conform to his principles and that the world would respect them. "He was superficial in his knowledge, and a martyr to the disease of omniscience."[49] Such a righteous mentality led Jefferson to bring about events and developments that his principles and policy were meant to avoid. Above all Jefferson desired peace, and he retained a republican fear of standing armies; but in the long run his passion for peace and refusal to be more aggressive toward France in 1805 may have resulted in England's seizure of American vessels and the War of 1812. Jefferson desired to preserve America as an agrarian republic; but the embargo resulted in America becoming a manufacturing nation that would be soon committed to industrialization and the attendant evils of urbanization. To Adams the lesson seems to be clear: we cannot understand the movement of history in terms of the motives of those who claim to control it.

The same lesson applied to the historian. If the problem of human behavior is motivation, the problem of historical understanding is causation. Adams could resolve neither. Even though Adams tried to understand Jefferson's motives, he was not altogether sure a different course of action based upon different motives would have resulted in different consequences. He could of course speculate, but speculation is not science. Political behavior seemed susceptible to ambiguous and ironic turns, and Adams sensed the difference between understanding actions in terms of motives and explaining events in terms of causes. Adams was honest enough to realize that he had set out to explain more than he could comprehend. Indeed certain parts of the *History* read like the chapters on cetology in *Moby Dick*: the more information we have about the varieties of whales and their peculiar habits, the more ignorant we are when encountering the white whale. After devoting much time to unraveling the gist of the vast diplomatic exchange between England and the United States, after chronicling in great detail the day-to-day negotiations and counternegotiations among Madison, Canning, and Napoleon, after studying the actions and reactions to the embargo, the Non-Important Act, the British Orders in Council, and Napoleon's Berlin and Milan decrees, after describing at length the martial spirit of young western warhawks like Henry Clay and John C. Calhoun—after all such accounts Adams does not allow the true cause of the War of 1812 to emerge from his narrative. He started out by making the establishment of sequence his measure of historical understanding, but his masterpiece concludes in volume 9 with a series of ponderous questions that only the future could answer. History seemed to be impervious to any truth, revealing only a succession of events brought about by some vague sense of "force."[50]

---

49. Adams, *History (Jefferson)*, 100.
50. Adams, *History (Madison)*, 1345.

Adams's acute sensibility about the limits of historical knowledge bears all the weight of what would come to be called today modernism and even postmodernism. American history constituted a field of continuous but not necessarily related actions that yielded no unifying principle of explanation. To some postmodernist thinkers, especially those also sensitive to the problems of linear, causal understanding, history as narration might be elevated to the status of art in that its meaning would lie in the forms through which the actions were expressed. History as an aesthetic expression actually antedates modernism. A century ago, just after Adams finished the *History*, Benedetto Croce published *La Storia ridotta sotto il concetto dell'Arte* (1893). The Italian idealist philosopher argued that history is closer to art than to science to the extent that both disciplines seek to comprehend things and happenings in their unique particularity rather than classifying them within categories of universal laws. Adams was as much artist as scientist. Yet even though he delighted in ironic commentary, and was willing to break the thread of narration to offer telling observations on the clash of character and events, he was more interested in understanding history than in simply giving it expressive form. His unfulfilled desire to find meaning in events themselves, as opposed to their representations, led to his radical despair of truth. His despair about the limitations of consciousness had similar implications. Consciousness had once been regarded as the precondition of being free by virtue of understanding what was happening. But Adams saw early-nineteenth-century Americans undertaking actions with little awareness of what they were doing and even less knowledge that they might be creating new structures of power independently of their intentions.

In Adams's generation it was almost an axiom of academic scholarship that the proper study of history was the study of past politics. But Adams saw how history reaffirmed the meaning of present politics, where power, force, and energy had replaced authority, ideas, and principles. He also saw how science had failed to explain both history, where "facts can never be complete, and their relations must always be infinite," and politics, where the ideals of government as a deductive system proved as delusive as the ideals of obedience as a moral proposition.[51] History and politics alike seemed to be determined by the inexorability of power and interests. Knowledge that facts rather than ideals shaped human will and determined events only strengthened Adams's conviction about the "ineluctable malady" of power as the primary reality. Although the author of the *History* felt incompetent to explain events and judge behavior, he could at least prove change, and indeed it was the specter of irreversible histori-

51. Adams, *Education*, 410.

cal change that began to obsess him toward the end of the century. By 1900 the very concept of history took on a different meaning:

> Historians undertake to arrange sequences—called stories or histories—assuming in silence a relation of cause and effect. These assumptions, hidden in the depths of dusty libraries, have been astounding, but commonly unconscious and child-like; so much so, that if any captious critic were to drag them to light, historians would probably reply, with one voice, that they supposed themselves required to know what they were talking about. Adams, for one, had toiled in vain to find out what he meant. He had even published a dozen volumes of American history for no other purpose than to satisfy himself whether, by the severest processes of stating, with the least possible comment such facts as seemed sure, in such order as seemed rigorously consequent, he could fix for a familiar moment a necessary sequence of human movement. The result had satisfied him as little as at Harvard College. Where he saw sequence, other men saw something quite different, and no one saw the same unit of measure. He cared little about his experiments and less about his statesmen, who seemed to him quite as ignorant as himself and, as a rule, no more honest; but he insisted on a relation of sequence, and if he could not reach it by one method, he would try as many methods as science knew. Satisfied that the sequence of men led to nothing and that the sequence of their society could lead no further, while the mere sequence of time was artificial, and the sequence of thought was chaos, he turned at last to the sequence of force, and thus it happened that, after ten years' pursuit, he found himself lying in the Gallery of Machines at the Great Exposition of 1900, his historical neck broken by the sudden irruption of forces totally new.[52]

Science and the Fate of the Universe

The new forces that had suddenly erupted to prostrate the bewildered Adams were the radium rays recently discovered by Marie and Pierre Curie. While studying history Adams had been struck by what he thought was the mechanistic nature of historical processes and the possibility that the past could be understood through laws governing the motion of material bodies. The historian "cannot but become conscious of a silent pulsation that commands his respect, a steady movement that resembles in its mode of operation the mechanical action of Nature herself."[53] In the

52. Ibid., 382.
53. Adams, *Great Secession*, 287.

History Adams had set out to show how the "severity of nature's processes" might be brought under control. Prior to the new physics, Adams had no patience with historians who viewed events as contingent and even capricious. Edmund Burke, referring to the risk English barons took in petititoning King John for the restoration of ancient liberties, had written: "But the history of those times furnishes many instances of the like of want of design in the most momentous affairs, and shows that it is in vain to look for political causes for the actions of men, who were most commonly directed by a brute caprice, and were for the greater part destitute of any kind of fixed principles of obedience or resistance." Adams responded in the margins of Burke's text: "This is the worse kind of principle for a historian. It is merely an excuse for laziness." So determined was Adams to view history as scientifically intelligible that he saw no dualism between mind and nature. "My philosophy teaches me," he wrote from London during the Civil War, "that the laws that govern animated beings will ultimately be found to be at bottom the same with those that rule inanimate matter."[54]

After the discovery of radium, matter no longer appeared inanimate and subject to some law for the explanation of its behavior. Madame Curie's "metaphysical bomb" made science appear as violent and as irrational as history itself. The spontaneous, explosive behavior of radium atoms suggested that randomness inhered in nature itself. In the *Edcuation* Adams termed the rays "wicked," "anarchical," "patricidal," and "chaotic" once he realized that their violation of the laws of mechanisms shattered once and for all his hopes of discovering basic laws governing the movement of history. That man craved order while nature as well as history yielded only chaos and disobedience to human reason signified to Adams that man and nature are alienated one from the other. This conclusion would never be accepted by pragmatic philosophers, who affirmed the organic continuity between man and nature in order to deny dualism. But for Adams the "historical neck" of the continuity had been "broken" forever.

Adams may have overdramatized his visit to the Great Exposition to create the effect of an epiphany, but the profound intellectual reorientation warrants such an effect. For Adams is doing nothing less than reversing Giambattista Vico's dictum and turning the whole idea of progress and liberation on its head: if man cannot understand his own actions even though they are his own creations, and not those of God or nature, he

54. Adams's criticisms of Burke are on p. 442 of Burke's "Abridgement of English History," in *The Works of the Right Honorable Edmund Burke*, rev. ed., vol. 12 (Boston: Little, Brown, 1866), Adams mss. Adams's remark on animate and inanimate is in his letter to Charles Francis Adams, Oct. 2, 1863, *Letters*, vol. 1, 395.

may still understand the movement and direction of history insofar as history is no longer made by the conscious actions of man. Thus while history as a mode of explanation no longer appeared valid, history as the embodiment of some unleashed power emerged as the terrible secret of human destiny. Adams's growing conviction that power had been disjoined from authority led him to reify history itself, which no longer stood for knowledge of what happened but for knowledge of what will come to be. The historian of the American past now became a philosopher of history, and as such he reconceived history not as politics and diplomacy but as a fateful process of force, energy, and power, a process that could be plotted according to the new laws of physics. Convinced that knowledge of the universe must now be found in objective forces independent of men, Adams developed a "dynamic theory of history" to present to the society of American historians.

The theory was spelled out in two speculative essays, "The Rule of Phase Applied to History" and "The Tendency of History," the latter written as an address to the American Historical Association. The conviction that history might become estranged from the faculty of historical understanding had haunted Adams since the Civil War, when he first sensed, as a journalist reporting on military strategies and miscalculations, the impression that events are determined by impersonal forces. Three decades later he became more convinced that the Jefferson and Madison administrations, no less than Lincoln's decisions and General Grant's tactics, demonstrated the inefficacy of statesmanship when confronted with the power of events as brute fact. But while writing the *History* Adams could only vaguely sense that mind and experience had become alienated, that the consciousness emanating from mind could barely grasp the unconscious processes of nature. Not until he addressed himself to the American Historical Association did he feel confident to claim that he now understood the forces of nature sufficiently to predict the future of history; and the latest discoveries in science, which he drew upon to support his arguments, led to a conclusion that seemed to be a conviction nurtured by suspicion—that history had no future.

Adams's "Rule of Phase," "The Tendency," and also "A Letter to American Teachers of History," all attempt to develop a philosophy of history on the basis of scientific explanation of the universe. Drawing upon a variety of sources, including Lord Kelvin's second law of thermodynamics on the dissipation of heat energy and Willard Gibbs's theory of the transformation of the chemical phases of solids, liquids, and gases, and perhaps on his own brother Brooks's cyclical and cataclysmic theories in *The Law of Civilization and Decay*, Adams worked out a fantastic historical scheme and mathematical formula in which the universe was following nature's course and constantly expanding its energy without replenishing it, and human thought was passing through phases of knowledge in which its life force was being dissipated, slowing down like a spent motor as it moved through the religious, mechanical, and electrical stages of development and decay. These tendencies resulted in entropy, the process by which an ordered universe goes over into a state of disorder and the unified laws of the world give way to disunity and multiplicity as all phenomena formerly governed by a structured, law-bound order become increasingly random and directionless. Employing the "law of squares," the mathematical formula in which each phase is shorter than the previous phase, Adams predicted that, given the escalating rush of history, the process of disintegration would culminate in 1917, when the last phase (the "ethereal") reached its termination, and by 1921 life as we know it would pass over into something else as the "reservoirs" of energy exhausted themselves.[55]

Adams's application of the laws of physics to human affairs scarcely received a warm reception by historians of his era and has remained a continual source of controversy among scholars. Did Adams deliberately misuse scientific theories to play a practical joke upon the historical profession, or was he being ironic and registering his objections to the pretensions of science by showing the futility of its logic? Was he displaying his own ambiguity toward a positivism that would undermine humanistic knowledge and insight, or did he really believe he was offering America a vision of the future, a vision that now appears an uncanny warning about the implications of such developments as radioactivity, nuclear fission, and the release of atomic energy?[56]

On the matter of science, the consensus of conventional wisdom in Adams scholarship regards him as more crank than prophet. Many writers agreed that Adams had distorted and simplified the second law of thermodynamics and read into the phenomenon the inexorable dissipation of heat in order to satisfy his own obsession with doom. Yet Adams could well have been attracted to contemporary theories of energy because they revealed the universe to be not inexorable and mechanical but instead paradoxical and ironic. Contemporary controversies over the second law involving physical chemistry and energy physics raised the possibility

55. Henry Adams, *The Degradation of Democratic Dogma* (1919; New York: Capricorn, 1958), 123–305.

56. For differing interpretations of Adams's grim historical speculations, see William Jordy, *Henry Adams: Scientific Historian* (New York, 1952); Lewis Mumford, "An Apology to Henry Adams," *Virginia Quarterly Review* 38 (1962): 196–217; Vern Wagner, *The Suspension of Henry Adams: A Study on Manner and Matter* (Detroit, 1989).

that such developments as entropy happen at random as molecules move from a disorderly to an ordered state and heat from a colder to a warmer body.[57] It may be the case, as Cushing Strout has suggested, that Adams could never be at peace with a universe of disorder that can generate unpredictable patterns of order.[58] But Adams's penchant for chaos was more than personal. Like Weber, Adams was challenging the Victorian idea of orderly progress by describing stable equilibrium as slow death. Adams's own library, it bears noting, contained numerous books in French and German on science, and on the page margins of several are penciled queries in which Adams questions an author's description of the flow of electric current or the behavior of molecules or the gravitational relation of the moon to terrestrial waves. It seems clear that as much as Adams once sought a mechanical explanation for everything, he also came to appreciate, as did contemporary scientists like Henri Poincaré and Ernst Mach, theoretical problems posed by irreversible phenomena. In a printed copy of an address by his friend Clarence King, "Catastrophism and the Evolution of the Environment," Adams underlined the words "uniformitarianism pure and simple received a fatal blow" and the "mysterious energies we call life." The paradoxical idea that a natural catastrophe could be the moment of life's birth, that destruction and creation are related, appealed to an ironist whose restless rationality valued the irrational wherever it could be found.[59]

Max Weber, it will be recalled, had assumed that modern science and technology would issue in new institutionalized forms of authority as life became more routinized and rationalized; and John Dewey, as we shall see, would look to scientific inquiry to stabilize the disruptive character of the environment and thereby enable man to control the forces of nature. Adams's rejections raised the playful but more unsetting thought that nature would resist human mastery because at bottom "she" was meant to be rebellious and disobedient. As did the scientists Max Planck, Louis Dollo, and the young Albert Einstein, Adams recognized that the random conduct of molecules and haphazard mutations could not be easily dismissed as unknown variables that would average out in statistical aggregates. The fact that science, like history, followed no linear process but

---

57. On this point I am much indebted to the article by Keith R. Bunch, "Henry Adams, the Second Law of Thermodynamics, and the Course of History," *Journal of the History of Ideas* 48:3 (July–Sept. 1987): 467–82.

58. Cushing Strout, "The Broken Arch of Henry Adams's Life," *Reviews in American History* 18 (1990): 530–35.

59. Clarence King, "Catastrophism and the Evolution of the Environment," in Henry Adams mss.

instead reversed itself in disruptions and catastrophes meant that man's deepest dream of order was a desperate illusion that could be sustained only to the extent that scientific inquiry ceased.

> If the silent, half-conscious, intuitive faith of society could be fixed, it might possibly be found always tending towards belief in a future equilibrium of some sort, that should end in becoming stable; an idea which belongs to mechanics, and was probably the first idea that nature taught to a stone, or to an apple; to a lemur or an ape; before teaching it to Newton. Unfortunately for society, the physicists again abruptly interfere, like Sancho Panza's doctor, by earnest protests that, if one physical law exists more absolute than another, it is the law that stable equilibrium is—by definition—one that has no history and wants no historians.[60]

For Weber the sociologist, and for Dewey the pragmatist, the task of the intellectual was to explain what makes society possible and scientific progress hopeful. For Adams the historian the task was to explain what makes events and developments discontinuous, random, indeterminate, and irreversible. "The child born in 1900," he observed of the new universe revealed by contemporary physicists and biologists, "found himself in a land where no one had ever penetrated before; where order was an accidental relation obnoxious to nature; artificial compulsion imposed on motion; against which every free energy of the universal revolted; and which, being merely occasional, resolved itself back to anarchy at last." The new physics seemed to hint at an explanation to the riddle that has perplexed the poststructuralists in our time: why the chaos of irrational energies succumbs to order and institutionalization only to be overthrown again; why freedom reduces to domination and then disruption. The discovery of the "new multiverse" had relevance for the historian, for it

> explained much that had been most obscure, especially the persistently fiendish treatment of man by man; the perpetual effort of society to establish law, and the perpetual revolt of society against the law, it had established; the perpetual building up of authority by force, and the perpetual appeal to force to overthrow it; the perpetual symbolism of a higher law, and the perpetual relapse to a lower one; the perpetual victory of the principles of freedom, and their perpetual conversion into principles of power; but the staggering problem was the outlook ahead into a despotism of artificial order which nature abhorred. The physicists had a phrase for it, unintelligi-

60. Adams, *Degradation*, 243–44.

ble to the vulgar;—"All that we win is a battle,—lost in advance,—with the irreversible phenomenon in the background of nature."[61]

Adams was the first scholar in the Western world to relate developments in physics to the study of history in an effort to show that there could be no such thing as a stable equilibrium when phenomena are irreversible and events random. The pragmatic philosophers would also turn to science for knowledge, and Peirce and James in particular would not be troubled to find the universe indeterminate, since spontaneous happenings can spur on purposive activity and lead to habits of control. What struck Adams about the discovery of radium rays was that they had "wrecked" the universe by rejecting, as Karl Pearson had pointed out in *The Grammar of Science*, order, beauty, and benevolence. "Suddenly, in 1900, science raised its head and denied," Adams exclaimed, observing how the new physics now repudiated certainty, universality, order, and harmony. The scientific dream of reducing explanations to simple formulations collapsed with the "new multiverse." What man had wanted from the old notion of the universe the new science could no longer provide.[62]

Adams's speculations on the fate of the universe can only be dismissed as the product of an eccentric mind if similar thoughts of other thinkers are ignored. The speculations of Auguste Comte, H. G. Wells, and others also depicted the human mind as having passed through phases, which dramatized a conceptual similarity between history and irreversibility. Consider, for example, the possible connection between Kelvin's idea of energy dissipation and what Wells called "heat death." Physicists in the twentieth century were relieved to find the solar system more stable than it had been assumed to be in Adams's era. But Adams's obsession about entropy also concerned the way humankind abused natural disorder for the sake of convenience in having a psychological sense of order and physical comfort. "Always and everywhere the mind creates its own universe, and pursues its own phantoms; but the force behind the image is always a reality,—the attractions of occult power." As Adams saw it, industrial society would do everything to make science serve its ends, not those of nature. Having no commitment to authority and discipline, modern man

> was bound to accelerate progress; to concentrate energy; to accumulate power; to multiply and intensify forces; to reduce friction, increase velocity and magnify momentum, partly because this was the mechanical law of the universe as science

61. Adams, *Education*, 458.
62. Ibid., 451–52.

explained it; but partly also in order to get done with the
present which artists and some others complained of; and finally,—and chiefly—because a rigorous philosophy required
it, in order to penetrate the beyond, and satisfy man's destiny
by reaching the largest synthesis in its ultimate contradiction.

The assault on nature by science, Adams observed, stemmed from both
the anarchist dream of freedom and innocence and the bourgeois dream
of order and inertia. Whatever the political motive, the human impulse
to increase the energy at society's disposal violated nature's tendency to
oppose any concentration of energy as alien to its will and to revert to
disorder, chaos, even destruction.[63]

In Adams's era American society had seen the rise of coal, steam, and
electrical power as well as dynamos, turbines, and combustion engines.
All such developments signified man's predatory relationship with an
environment that had once taken its life from biological spontaneity and
diversity. Today some of Adams's observations have an almost biblical
prophecy about generations coming and going and the earth abiding
forever.

Like Friedrich Nietzsche, Adams also believed that Western culture
was on a catastrophic course because its inhabitants insisted that nature
answer to their wishes for power and comfort. Both thinkers questioned
Darwinism because they saw the drive for mastery as alien to nature and
the drive for progress as conceit and self-deception. Both came to question
the eighteenth-century Enlightenment assumption that scientific advance-
ment meant moral as well as material progress. Adams chided the "cheerful optimism which gave to Darwin's conclusion the charm of human
perfectibility." Adams saw no law of progress operating in the nation's
capital, where the spirit of the Constitution was defied and the heritage
of the Founders ignored. "The progress of evolution from President
Washington to President Grant," he quipped in the *Education*, "was alone
evidence to upset Darwin." By unveiling a universe of laws that produce
chaos instead of cosmos, Adams had no trouble upsetting the easy assumptions of the "Gilded Age." The age may have celebrated population
growth and the achievements of science as indicative of the success of
Homo sapiens as an increasingly perfectible organism; but both the drive
to grow and the drive to master could demand so much of nature as to
doom the earth as a human habitat.[64]

Adams shared Nietzsche's conviction that behind the drive to force
nature into yielding its secrets was the human will to power masquerading

63. Adams, *Degradation*, 304; *Education*, 406–7.
64. Adams, *Degradation*, 128; *Education*, 266.

as the pursuit of knowledge. But Adams could scarcely share Nietzsche's critique of Christianity as a "slave morality" that equated meekness with virtue. For in turning to the "new multiverse," Adams was using science the way his earliest ancestors had used religion: to instill the terrors of the unknown. If Adams's reification of science and history suggested the modernist nightmare that nature and reason are alienated, it also suggested the old Calvinist riddle of salvation and submission. "To me, the new economic law brings or ought to bring us back to the same state of mind as resulted from the old religious law, that of profound helplessness and dependence of an infinite force that is to us incomprehensible and ominipotent.[65] The ancestral shadow hovered over Adams's imagination. John Adams had doubted America's claim to a special national "virtue"; Henry also challenged the conceit of American uniqueness. In *Democracy* he chided those proud Americans who believed themselves exempt from the "operation of general laws" of history that doom every republic to corruption; and in *Esther* he obliquely questioned, as we shall see in the following chapter, William James's conviction that mere belief in free will can make freedom happen, breaking the mechanical cycle of cause and effect that governs the "iron-block" universe. The Jeremiah theme of perishability, of the subversion of freedom and virtue by power and luxury, ran in his blood, and no doubt he enjoyed a macabre sense of the humor of developing a capricous theory of history to dramatize the precariousness of human existence. "Thank God I was never cheerful," he remarked to a friend. "I come from the happy stock of the Mathers, who, you remember, passed sweet mornings reflecting on the goodness of God and the damnation of infants."[66]

Adams's moments of humor could scarcely conceal his deeper moods of horror. If the theological fatalism of Puritanism returned in the form of scientific determinism, Adams could face that prospect only with fear and trembling. "My belief," he wrote his brother Brooks in 1902, "is that science will wreck us, and that we are like monkeys monkeying with a loaded shell; we don't in the least know or care where our practical energies come from or will bring us to." Science alienated man from nature by providing man the knowledge to unleash its energies but not the values to control them. "Prosperity never before imagined," he wrote in 1904, "power never wielded by man, speed never reached by anything but a meteor, has made the world nervous, querulous, unreasonable, and afraid." In one of the final chapters of the *Education*, aptly titled "The Height of Knowledge," Adams summed up in three words all he had

---

65. Henry Adams to Brooks Adams, May 4, 1900, *Letters*, vol. 5, 102.
66. Henry Adams to Elizabeth Cameron, Dec. 20, 1914, *Letters*, vol. 6, 671–72.

learned from politics and history: "Power is poison." And in a letter
written to the historian Henry Osborne Taylor in 1905, he spelled out
the shuddering implications of a world experiencing the sudden birth of
massive energy and the darkening twilight of authority:

> The assumption of unity which was the work of human
> thought in the middle ages has yielded very slowly to the
> proofs of complexity. . . . Yet it is quite sure . . . that at the
> accelerated rate of progression shown since 1600, it will not
> need another century or half century to tip thought upside
> down. Law, in that case, would disappear as theory or a priori
> principle, and give place to force. Morality would become
> police. Explosives would reach cosmic violence. Disintegra-
> tion would overcome integration.[67]

The race between enlightenment and energy, between education and
catastrophe, became for Adams a race between authority and power.
How could this process of accelerating distintegration be reversed, the
process by which law would be transformed into force, morality into
police? The question required Adams to return again to history, not to
the American past but to the Middle Ages, the age of faith, worship, and
hope. The key to the alienation of power from authority was to find that
moment in history when these two forces were seen as one and the same.
The challenge of overcoming alienation was to find the basis for reunify-
ing man with nature and God, to find man feeling the presence of power
within himself because he experienced the meaning of authority beyond
himself. The key to authority lay in religion, or so it seemed when Adams
allowed the needs of his imagination to flee the demands of his mind.
Faith required a willing suspension of disbelief, and Adams was willing
to try to reconstruct authority by giving his emotions full rein. If genuine
authority cannot be found in modern world, it may still exist as an idea,
an image or symbol entertained by the imagination. Artistic effect could
convey what scientific analysis would deny—that we believe in what we
appreciate, value, and savor, not what we know, understand, and control.

Four Problems of Modernism: Authority, Faith, Art, Love

Mont-Saint-Michel and Chartres engages the reader as a spiritual odyssey
into the medieval world of poetry, architecture, hagiography, and philosophy, from the *Chanson de Roland* to the stained-glass windows and pointed
arches of Chartres, and from the symbol of the Virgin Mary to the *Summa
Theologiae* of Thomas Aquinas. The cathedral represents for Adams the

---

67. Henry Adams to Brooks Adams, Aug. 10, 1902, in Cater, 529; Adams, *Education*,
499; Henry Adams to Henry Osborne Taylor, Jan. 17, 1905, in Cater, 558–59.

finest flowering of Christianity, the triumph of faith and joy over fear and pain; and the building itself, with its geometrically arranged portals, apses, glasswork, and statuary, celebrates the concrete expressions of unity and harmony, the spiritual goal of all humankind. At the center stands the statue of Mary, a symbol radiating the mystery of grace and love and a shrine expressing the authority of goodness against the power of the oppressor—"an authority which the people wanted, and the fiefs feared." The scene of the mass, evoked by Adams to capture her magnificient presence, enables the reader to be almost at one with the crowd of worshipers who lift their gaze above the altar and see, "high over all the agitation of prayer, the passion of politics, the anguish of suffering, the terrors of sin, only the figure of the Virgin in majesty."[68]

The capacities to believe, trust, respect, worship, and adore, capacities that enable humankind to devote its energies to ends beyond itself, to the veneration of the Virgin and the construction of Chartres—these became for Adams the meaning of genuine authority. A symbol that could draw on spiritual power to elevate and purify all believers could perhaps discipline and refine the larger society itself. The worshiped presence of the Virgin would help ease the burden from which humanity aspired to realize its deepest need—harmony, unity, wholeness.

Although political heir to New England Puritanism, Adams was scarcely proposing a classical Protestant solution to the problem of knowledge and authority. Indeed his keen grasp of Mary's appeal was more psychological than theological, and his perceptions were not without his characteristic irony:

> No one has ventured to explian why the Virgin wielded exclusive power over poor and rich, sinners and saints, alike. Why were all the Protestant churches cold failures without her help? Why could not the Holy Ghost—the spirit of Love and Grace—equally answer their prayers? Why was the son powerless? Why was Chartres Cathedral in the thirteenth century—like Lourdes today—the expression of what is in substance a separate religion? Why did the gentle and gracious Virgin Mother so exasperate the Pilgrim Father? Why was the Woman struck out of the Church and ignored in the State? These questions are not antiquarian or trifling in historical value; they tug at the very heart-strings of all that makes whatever order is in the cosmos. If a Unity exists, in which and toward which all energies centre, it must explain and include Duality, Diversity, Infinity—Sex![69]

68. Adams, *Mont-Saint-Michel and Chartres*, 210.
69. Ibid., 288–89.

The Holy Ghost, Adams reasoned, offered a coldly abstract proposition, while Mary hovered as a real and intimate presence. The Trinity
offered a God of judgment and justice, but the people wanted above all
not strict justice but "protection, pardon, and love." The Church presented a theodicy to explain God's ways to man, but Mary questioned a
God who would create man in order to punish him. The masses identified
with Mary's rebellion against authority. "The people loved Mary because
she trampled on conventions; not merely because she could do it, but
because she liked to do what shocked every well-regulated authority. Her
pity had no limit." Nor did her power: "Mary's wish was absolute law,
on earth as in heaven. For her, other laws were not made. Intensely
human, but always Queen, she upset, at her pleasure, the decisions of
every court and the orders of every authority, human or divine; interfered
directly in the ordeal; altered the processes of nature; abolished space;
annihilated time."[70] Mary emerges as an impulsive anarchist undermining
all that is logical, abstract, impersonal, and objective. A saint, she subverts authority in order better to express it.

In conventional scholarship Adams's return to the Middle Ages represents a search for order and unity. But Adams's treatment of Mary suggests that he was searching the distant past not so much for unity as for
spontaneity. In the figure of Mary he pitted the subjectivity of "charismatic" authority against the objectivity of traditional and "rational-legal"
authority, sensing with Weber that only a continual revitalization of the
former could prevent the latter's routine systematization and eventual
bureaucratization—the modern phenomenon of "rationalization" that
brings death to the inner life of the spirit. Mary is depicted as a passionate
rebel so that her arbitrary acts can upset the dullness of habitual obedience
and ritualistic authority. She is capable of such acts because, unlike God,
she is "human" by virtue of her imperfections and thus able to bestow
subjective favor by demonstrating the true meaning of pity and help,
justice and goodness, love and mercy, and all the life-enhancing qualities
that cannot be translated into law. "If the Trinity was in essence Unity,
the mother alone could represent whatever was not Unity; whatever was
irregular, exceptional, outlawed; and this was the whole human race." As
a charismatic figure Mary would rescue the authority of Christianity by
rehumanizing its meaning:

> Mary concentrated in herself the whole rebellion of man
> against fate; the whole protest against divine law; the whole
> contempt for human law as its outcome; the whole unutterable
> fury of human nature beating itself against the walls of its

70. Ibid., 292.

prison-house, and suddenly seized by a hope that in the Virgin man had found a door of escape. She was above law; she took feminine pleasure in turning hell into an ornament; she delighted in trampling over every social distinction in this world and the next. She knew that the universe was as unintelligible to her, on any theory of morals, as it was to her worshippers, and she felt, like them, no sure conviction that it was any more intelligible to the Creator of it. To her, every suppliant was a universe in itself, to be judged apart, on his own merits, by his love for her—by no means on his orthodoxy, or his conventional standing in the Church, or according to his correctness in defining the nature of the Trinity. The convulsive hold which Mary to this day maintains over human imagination—as you can see it at Lourdes—was due much less to her power of saving soul or body than to her sympathy with a people who suffered under law—divine or human—justly or unjustly, by accident or design, by decree of God or by guile of Devil. She cared not a straw for conventional morality, and she had no notion of letting her friends be punished, to the tenth or any generation, for the sins of their ancestors or the peccadilloes of Eve.[71]

When we read *Mont-Saint-Michel and Chartres* with the problem of authority in mind, we may understand why Adams delighted in calling himself a "conservative Christian anarchist." Authority cannot be based on law, which may only regulate behavior but never inspire it. Neither can it be based on power, which is the means by which authority is overthrown, not necessarily established or sustained. Nor can it be based on an omnipotent God, since a sovereignty that commands its creations denies them their will and his own as well. And although "chaos is the law of nature" and "order the dream of man,"[72] authority cannot be based simply on order without succumbing to a deadening monotony and uniformity. Instead, authority must be founded on ideals that are ontologically self-justifying, ideals that have a compelling inner power of persuasion, spiritual ideals that touch the mind's desire to transcend itself. The symbol of Mary served Adams's purpose of finding a source of authority that could remain immune to the secular corruptions of time and the skeptical forces of science: her arbitrary actions could not be codified nor her irrational nature comprehended.

Adams conceived authority as a characteristic of the relations between leaders and followers. He remained fascinated by the "convulsive hold"

71. Ibid., 307–8.
72. Adams, *Education*, 451.

Mary had on the modern imagination because he remained intrigued by
the attitudes and values that mediate between authority and its subjects.
Only an image that could command such devotion could discipline the
energies of the human race by elevating them to higher ends. The construction of Chartres stood as a symbol of such spiritual power, and
worship of the Virgin helped his burden of existence. Thus through
his sinuous prose of imaginative empathy, Adams's descriptions of the
celebration of the mass and of the Virgin's miracles facilitated a reliving
of the religious experiences that he was trying to convey to modern man,
a sense of the sacred that derives from a figure of human virtues and
supernatural powers. Ultimately Mary becomes the symbol and shrine
of authority because she is also the symbol of freedom, the "hope of
despair" and the "door of escape" through which weak, finite man may
identify with infinite goodness and feel the power of love within himself.
In the Virgin the idea of authority reached its apotheosis and the problem
of alienation found its answer.

In the figure of St. Thomas Aquinas, however, the idea of authority
begins its subtle but certain demise, and man's relation to God becomes
a problem without a solution. The last chapters of the *Chartres* narrative
trace the movement of thought from the scholastic nominalism of Abelard
to the mysticism of St. Francis, a process that culminates in Aquinas's
attempt to reconcile reason and faith, the "logic of God" with the "love
of God." Aquinas also tried to resolve the problem of God's will and
man's freedom, the riddle of evil as the privation of good, and all the
Christian paradoxes confronted by the dry logic of scholasticism. In the
process man's reason destroyed God's mystery. Man, Adams wryly observed, "could be as absurd as he liked; but God could not be absurd.
Saint Thomas did not allow the Deity the right to contradict Himself,
which is one of man's chief pleasures."[73] Hoping to explain God to man,
Aquinas succeeded only in alienating him from God.

Aquinas assumed he was establishing the truth of Christianity, but it
was not the intuitive truth that appeals to the inner eye of the believer.
Rather than providing glimpses of beauty and perfection, scholasticism
involves a strenuous intellectual effort to order the world through reason.
Adams sees Aquinas building his theology as architects had built cathedrals, but the two materials with which both monuments are built, faith
and reason, would eventually tear apart medieval culture. In the last
passages of the *Chartres* text, Adams describes the faulty methodological
reasoning of Thomistic philosophy as similar to the precarious structural
equilibrium of the cathedral. "Perhaps the best proof of it is their apparent

73. Adams, *Mont-Saint-Michel and Chartres*, 385–422.

instability," Adams observes of both philosophy and architecture. "Of all the elaborate symbolism which has been suggested for the Gothic cathedral, the most vital and most perfect may be that slender nervure, the springing motion of the broken arch, the leap downward to the flying buttress—the visible effort to throw off a visible strain—never let us forget that Faith alone supports it, and that, if Faith fails, Heaven is lost."[74]

With the passing of Mary's spiritual hegemony, which reigned by virtue of a charisma of illumination, it fell to St. Thomas to try to resolve the problem of authority, to prove that the Church's exercise of power could be justified by reference to a natural order of man created by Divine Providence. But Aquinas's mechanistic mode of reasoning, wherein God is depicted as a "Prime Motor" propelling an orderly universe, demystified the spiritual dimension of Christian aspiration. The entire edifice of Aquinas's architecture of ideas rested on a tenuous text.[75] Authority too rested on spiritual faith, that ineffable force uniting man with that which reigns above himself. Yet faith and reason could never be reconciled. Adams shared with Weber the view that "the tension between religion and intellectual knowledge comes to the fore whenever rational, empirical knowledge has consistently worked through to the disenchantment of the world and its transformation into a causal mechanism."[76] Both Adams and Weber suspected that the methods of reason would not only substitute an impersonal world for a universe of organic unity but would call into question the very basis of faith. When men try to reason out the grounds for their beliefs, they begin the descending journey from cosmos to chaos, from belief to doubt, and ultimately to the modernist predicament that leaves man with the ability to question everything and the capacity to affirm nothing. Attempting to locate authority beyond knowledge, in something to be believed rather than known, Adams sought to rescue the idea of authority from what Walter Lippmann would later call the "acids of modernity."

Did he succeed? The contemporary intellectual who desires to reconcile religion, politics, and science, the thinker who sees no conflict between ethics, power, and method, needs to ponder the dilemmas Adams faced in trying to make relevant his ideas of spiritual authority. First of all, the only way Adams could save the religious idea of authority from politics and science, from the abuses of power and the negations of reason, was to aestheticize the concept itself. Truth, observed Adams, may only be

74. Ibid., 421–22.
75. The whole project of postmodernism would also be supported not so much by religious faith as by narrative discourse. See chapter 11.
76. Max Weber, "Religious Rejections of the World," 350.

an "empirical relation," but art touches our moral imagination, and the Virgin's authority can be experienced as "beauty," "love," and "truth," which "stares everyone in the eye and begs for sympathy."[77] It should be noted that this deep aesthetic sensibility bears some resemblance to the Puritan Jonathan Edwards's interpretation of authority as assent to the imperatives of "true virtue," which challenges man's artistic comprehension, enabling us to appreciate "disinterested benevolence" in terms of its beauty rather than of its benefits.[78] Indeed, John Winthrop's "city upon the hill" would, like Chartres, succeed only to the extent that the regenerating power of "love" and "grace" could be sustained by imperfect, fallen men and women. Yet Adams's idea of authority seems almost empty of religious content. His veneration of the Virgin calls for Christianity to be purged of its Calvinist elements of anger and punishment so that a new theology of love could replace an older theodicy of suffering and damnation. But Adams got rid of of the substance along with the shadow. In eliminating entirely the primacy of God in his concept of authority, Adams eliminated love as a strenuous moral obligation and translated it into a vague aesthetic intuition. Without the imperatives of Christian piety ("Thou shalt love"), Adams can appeal only to our capacity for wonder and not for obedience. His exquisite portrait of the Virgin offers us a vision to contemplate and behold, a charismatic symbol whose anarchistic energies cannot be translated into Christian ethics nor her mystical imagery into political philosophy.

Sensing the dualism between religion and politics, between the sacred and the profane, Adams made no attempt to translate the spiritual authority of adoration into the modern political authority of obligation in order to reconcile the conflict between Christian cosmology and its sociology. He remained indifferent to authority's relations to the practical needs of society, and he ignored some of the most pressing issues of a truly political character: the laws of sovereignty, the balancing of freedom and order, the duty to obey. Indeed, the Virgin's authority rested not so much on a final truth as on a series of ecstatic moments created and sustained by sentiment, affection, reverence, and even illusion. From her miracles and impulsive acts of defiance, which could inspire but never legally command, man could hardly derive eternal principles on which to ground political authority and stabilize human affairs. At the same time, had Adams attempted to reconcile the spiritual and the political he would have had to sacrifice his ethic of love to develop a system of rules, itself

77. Adams, *Mont-Saint-Michel and Chartres*, 361, 421.
78. Jonathan Edwards, "The Nature of True Virtue," in *Jonathan Edwards: Selections*, ed. Clarence Faust and Thomas H. Johnson (New York, 1962), 349–71.

an admission that genuine authority had become nothing more than the power of law to impose itself as morality became synonymous with police. From a Weberian perspective, it was necessary that Adams's idea of authority remain antipolitical and even irrational, for the very concept of politics had become identical to the manipulation of rules, and rationality had become identical to the following of rules.

Just as authority had to remain beyond the reach of politics and reason, so did it need to transcend knowledge and belief. Adams's epistemological presuppositions transformed the idea of authority into mythology and phenomenology, a quality of aesthetic experience that cannot be disturbed by the inquiring mind. "He had his wish but he lost his hold on the results by trying to understand them," Adams recalled of all syncretic approaches to knowledge. In religion as well as science he could never forget Bacon's warning against trying to know the unknowable as much as one desired to do so. Nor could he address himself to the issue of whether faith inspires a devotion to authority or whether authority instills the necessary faith that makes devotion to it possible. Such a question could be answered only by allowing man to see what it is he believes, and why, and this knowledge would kill the believing spirit—even, as we shall see, the philosopher's "will to believe."

The Virgin "typified an authority which the people wanted" in an age when "man held the highest idea of himself as a unity in a unified universe."[79] That age of faith had long passed, and Adams now saw himself in an age of analysis, with power everywhere and authority nowhere. Encountering the "abyss of ignorance," he felt the depths of alienation. Education, instead of offering man the choice between truth and repose, only sensitizes the mind to its own limitations, leaving a "certain intense cerebral restlessness"; politics, instead of inspiring human association and civil obligation, presents only the spectacle of deception, manipulation, the clash not of men but of "forces"; philosophy, instead of defining the ulterior nature of things, consists merely in giving man "unintelligible answers to unsolvable problems"; science, instead of explaining phenomena on the basis of causal relations, can only describe processes some of which demonstrate the dizzying exhaustion of energy that would culminate in "cosmic violence"; and history, instead of accounting for events by discovering motives in order to evaluate actions according to principles, simply leaves us pondering causeless events that have no rational explanation. So much for the disciplines. As for the family and religion, the two solid foundations that had in the past provided a sense of order, Adams saw as little hope in institutions as he did in ideas. "The family

79. Adams, *Mont-Saint-Michel and Chartres*, 232, 289–91; *Education*, 435.

was extinct like chivalry," enduring more as an "atmosphere" than as an "influence." The modern church could no longer fulfill the capacity for worship, and Adams could only wonder why it was that religion, "the most powerful emotion of man, next to the sexual instinct, should disappear."[80]

Did Adams suffer from the will to disbelieve? One can only wonder why he was so willing to conclude that all authority had disappeared. He never saw much significance in the penetration of social institutions by the new authority of science or even the enduring secular authority of the traditional nation-state. The advent of industrial technology appeared to him as merely a further expansion of the release of coal, steam, and electricity as forms of energy, and the emergence of corporate power and wealth he would never deign to endow with the dignity of authority. But what Adams saw as transitory others saw as permanent. Max Weber perceived in science not the harbinger of darkness and chaos but the expression of organization and efficiency, and the decline of Western religion meant not the loss of men's capacity for reverence but a transformed religiosity leading to the "ethic" of material success and the cultural authority of wealth. Similarly, American sociologists and philosophers would look to the functional properties of society itself as the foundations of order and authority to which all people must adapt. Adams, in contrast, believed that the "new science" would prove "hostile" to the older institutions of church, state, and property.[81] A Weberian perspective suggests why the opposite occurred. While science may purge authority from the human and spiritual realm, it will enable business, politics, technology, and bureaucracy to be legitimated precisely because they become part of the empirical, routine operations of society and thus take on the status of rightful authority. Adams was not blind to the advent of managerialism and other sociological tendencies that reflected the impact of science on society. On the contrary, he equated the symbol of the Virgin with the symbol of the Dynamo, depicting modern man worshiping at the altar of power. But power itself, even, and perhaps especially, organized, integrated industrial power, seemed to Adams the negation of true authority, a false god that could never foster human feelings and help man to achieve the inner harmony and unity necessary to control the insensate mechanisms of modern life.

Thus Adams, to anticipate the content of subsequent chapters, would oppose two ideas offered by American sociologists and philosophers to solve the problem of power in industrial America: the idea of society

---

80. Adams, *Education*, 145–66, 268–313, 379–90.
81. Adams, *Degradation of Democratic Dogma*, 123–31.

itself, the rightful source of authority, and the idea that there is no distinction between power and authority. Adams would never be able to go along with Charles Cooley and George Herbert Mead and regard the norms of society as worthy of obedience. "Society I know it not!" Adams exploded; "society has no unity; one wandered about it like a maggot in cheese."[82] Nor would he be capable of going along with William James and John Dewey and view all relations as power relations, with power defined not as domination but as the ability to have effect. For although Adams would see power everywhere, even in positive symbols like the Virgin, he distinguished power from genuine authority, efficacy from sovereignty. Power, a product of human effort, can also move independently of one's will and understanding; authority is that which should stand above the movement of power and constitute a judgment of it. In history he failed to find a transcendent "principle" that would govern "circumstance"; hence even the Constitution that the framers devised to control power had "expired."

The Virgin as the imaginative construction of Adams's own mind indicates that the modern mind seeks refuge in art, the realm where instinct and feeling can survive the encroachment of science and analysis and preserve value from the relentless assault of fact. That theme emerges in Adams's last book, *The Life of George Cabot Lodge*, where, as in Thomas Mann's *Buddenbrooks*, the poet's "instinct of revolt" offers artistic expression as the answer to social disintegration. Years ago Brooks Adams called *Mont-Saint-Michel and Chartres* "a Gothic pilgrimage," and Kenneth Burke called it "a rebirth ritual."[83] More recently, literary scholars and intellectual historians have probed the depths of Adams's aesthetic sensibility from the point of view of structuralism, semiotics, and deconstruction.[84] Adams, who had turned to the French historian Michelet in his aesthetic reconstruction of the Middle Ages, would probably welcome such interpretive efforts, for he knew that he could never formulate precisely what he was trying to say and, indeed, he chose not to have the *Education* and the Chartres book published because he believed he could not develop for either work the appropriate principle of literary form. He may have

82. Henry Adams to Charles Francis Adams, Jr., Nov. 13, 1963, *Letters*, vol. 1, 406; *Education*, 197.

83. Brooks Adams is quoted in J. C. Levenson, *The Mind and Art of Henry Adams* (Stanford, 1957), 270; Kenneth Burke in Stanley Edgar Hyman, *The Armed Vision* (New York: Vintage Books, 1955), 338.

84. John Carlos Rowe, *Henry Adams and Henry James: The Emergence of a Modern Consciousness* (Ithaca, 1976); Hayden White, "Method and Ideology in Intellectual History: The Case of Henry Adams," in *Modern European Intellectual History: Reappraisals and New Perspectives*, ed. Dominick La Capra (Ithaca, 1982), 280–310.

consoled himself by reminding his friends that Augustine and Rousseau had also "failed" in their personal confessions. But he also realized that his last books were meant to be artistic, not didactic. "The two volumes have not been done in order to teach others, but to educate myself in the possibilities of literary form," he wrote in 1908. To Barrett Wendell he explained the limitations of various styles such as allegory and epic. "Between artists, or people trying to be artists, the sole interest is that of form," and hence his last two works were "hazardous, not as history, but as art." In *Mont-Saint-Michel* he agreed with the nineteenth-century writer Ernest Renan that the images of the Virgin and St. Francis offered human ideals too precious to be resisted merely because they were illogical. Perhaps he would have agreed also with the philosopher R. G. Collingwood that the historian had a right to reenter the mind of the Middle Ages in order to experience the "true ignorance" of those who felt the only thing worth comprehending was the incomprehensible—God.[85]

As artistic creations Adams's last two works offer a plethora of analytic modes for the modern literary critic. The strategy of impersonal narration; the juxtaposition of character and will to history and force; the self reflecting on itself as an exercise in authorial omniscience and, conversely, the scientific effort to eliminate the self ("to dismiss the Ego for a moment!");[86] the problem of meaning and its referents; a narration dramatized by the silence of chronological gaps; a text whose context is generated within the text itself; the decentering of the subject on the part of a third person who can discover neither himself nor the exact object of his angst—all such devices suited Adams's purposes. So too did his sense of humor and comic relief, the well-placed jest that varies the emotional tense of the text; and his brilliant sense of irony, the mind's ability to devise a way to deal with the wounds of the heart.

Other authors, particularly the literary intellectuals of the Lost Generation, would also look to art to create a world in which the mind can function against the assaults of modernity. But Adams, even though he employed his imaginative talents to create the Virgin as an ideal object of veneration, was too much the skeptic to believe that art would be sufficient to validate ideals simply because it could express them. Like William James, Adams had also in his early years toyed with the idea of becoming an artist. With James, however, the emotion ran deeper, and in his later years, when the artist within him became part of his buried

85. Henry Adams to Barrett Wendell, Mar. 12, 1909, in Cater, 644–46; Henry Adams to Edith Morton Eustus, Feb. 28, 1908, in Cater, 614–15; on Adams's valuing "true ignorance," see Denis Donoghue, foreword to R. P. Blackmur, *Henry Adams* (New York, 1980), xiii.

86. Henry Adams to Professor . . . , Jan. 1, 1909, in Cater, 781.

self, he advised the philosopher to approach reality as a painter or sculptor approaches a canvas or stone. To Adams, as we shall see in the following chapter, such advice would allow the mind to create the world rather than to understand it. While the imagination can satisfy the emotions, the whole point of education for Adams was to use the mind to know and represent accurately what existed outside it. "The fact, which all the psychologists insist on, that the mind really reflects itself, is to me the most exasperating thing in the world," he complained to the poet George Cabot Lodge.[87] Although James as a psychologist would have no trouble with that dilemma, and although Dewey would treat it as a false issue in philosophy, Adams regarded the problem of mind and knowledge, the knower and the known, as essentially unresolvable. Thus for the historian the modernist affirmation of art as a source of truth and authority would remain problematic.

So too would another issue that troubled the modern mind at the end of the nineteenth century—the problem of love. This issue has scarcely been explored in American intellectual history. Yet it would be deeply felt by a number of important writers, especially those of the prewar Greenwich Village rebellion and of the postwar Lost Generation. For Adams love would be as precarious as it was painful. Even the level-headed John Dewey allowed love to bring out the poet in him, perhaps because he sensed that philosophy could not respond to the passions of the heart. Religion, art, and love all entail the problem of belief in something that has authority over us by virtue of its power to incite the imagination. All three offer images that the mind reflects on, all suggest that the mind hungers to find fulfillment beyond itself, and all depend upon beauty as the vision of completion and perfection. It was Adams's genius to see that the problem of love was also, as in the case of politics, the problem of power.

A few years after Adams's death T. S. Eliot observed that the author of the *Education* remained immaturely restless because of his incapacity for sensual experience. The observation appears accurate, for Adams remained something of a voyeur when it came to sex. When in the South seas in the 1890s he described, in numerous, lengthy letters to Elizabeth Cameron, the visual delights of native customs. "You can imagine the best female figure you ever saw, about a six foot scale, neck, breast, back, arms, and legs, all absolutely Greek in modelling and action," he wrote of the Siva dance. "Naked to the waist, their rich skins glistened with cocoanut oil. Around their heads and necks they wore garlands or green leaves in strips like seaweeds, as though the girls came out of the sea."

87. Henry Adams to George Cabot Lodge, Apr. 22, 1903, in Cater, 541.

Adams described how his companion John LaFarge "quivered" and "gasped" at the spectacle. "Anyone would naturally suppose such a scene to be an orgy of savage license. I don't pretend to know what it was, but I give you my affadavit that we could see nothing in the songs or dances that suggested impropriety."

But Adams did see, as would other modernist thinkers, a tense relationship among religion, sex, and eroticism. "The highest erotism," wrote Max Weber, "stands psychologically and physiologically in a mutually substitutive relation with certain sublimated forms of heroic piety." Whereas mature religious love rests on the rational need to procreate and on the regulative institution of marriage, eroticism indicates a passionate union with others that is felt as a complete identification. In many non-Western religions eroticism is considered not deviant but divine. "We must not forget," wrote Georges Bataille, "that outside of Christianity the religious and sacred nature of eroticism is shown in the full light of day, sacredness dominating shame." In Japan Adams observed the sexual power of religious symbols. "Phallic worship is as universal here as that of trees, stones, and the sun," he wrote of the Buddhist temples. "I came across shrines of phallic symbols in my walks, as though I were an ancient Greek. One cannot quite ignore the foundations of society."[88]

It was safe for Adams to write such letters to Elizabeth Cameron, the only person to whom he could pour out his romantic emotions unconditionally. Adams had been devastated by the suicide of his wife, who gave him for twelve years "everything I most wanted on earth."[89] But for Elizabeth Cameron he later felt surges of the heart that have no parallel in his earlier letters describing his fiancée just before his wedding. He could express the deepest soul's desire to her because she was happily married. Occasionally he would make light of such feelings to her by citing his age, but he also knew that he could communicate the depth of his emotions and at the same time be assured that the situation rendered consummation impossible. In the Chartres narrative he projected this emotional state into his account of Tristan and Isolde, where romantic passion can be sustained only to the extent it cannot be fulfilled. Did Adams feel, with the medieval courtiers, that love resulting in sexual intimacy could mean the end of desire, or did his diffidence about sex reveal a more modernist awareness of the problem of love and belief?

Adams's attitude toward women reveals a great deal about his attitudes

88. Henry Adams to Elizabeth Cameron, Oct. 2, 1890, *Letters*, vol. 3, 290–91; Henry Adams to John Hay, Aug. 1, 1886, *Letters*, vol. 3, 33–34; Weber, "Religious Rejections of the World," 348; George Bataille, *Eroticism: Death and Sensuality* (San Francisco: City Lights, 1986), 134.

89. Henry Adams to E. L. Godkin, Dec. 16, 1885, *Letters*, vol. 2, 643.

toward both religious and political authority. Admiration for the female sex runs through the *Education* and the novels *Democracy* and *Esther*, and in two anthropological discourses, "The Primitive Rights of Women" and *Tahiti: Memoirs of Arii Taimai*, Adams delighted in recounting the power women commanded over men. The almost universal reverence for women in the Middle Ages in the Chartres narrative reads as though it were a world we have lost. Long before the feminist in our time made her case for "the second sex," Adams showed how the Virgin could inspire artists, court ladies seduce monarchs, and Polynesian princesses head tribal cultures. But Adams was not a writer who could entertain an idea without experiencing a contradictory emotion. Thus while describing women's conquests, he also recognized that women express their power by demanding and receiving man's love and adoration, and this often depends on man's complete surrender of mind and will. "Men were valuable only in proportion to their strength and their appreciation of women," he observed in reference to the heroine of *Democracy*. The paradox of the sexes is that neither man nor woman can expect their opposite to be both virtuous and romantic, that is, to maintain their integrity and independence and at the same time to "fall" in love and hence be out of control.[90] Ultimately what troubled Adams about women was not their strength and power but their irrationality and complexity. "The charm of women is the Hegelian identity of opposites," he wrote Lucy Baxter in 1890. "You can assume nothing regarding them, without assuming the contrary to be equally true." The problem with "civilized women," he complained to Clarence King, is their impulsive fickleness. "She will run away *with* you, if you insist; but she will as easily run away *from* you." But Adams well recognized that it is precisely women's passionate, unpredictable nature that endows them with power as spiritual as it is sensual; hence the Virgin herself is depicted as a sex goddess whose infinite energies offer one expression of force that the scientific mind could never master. In the *Education* Adams wonders why sex, "the highest energy ever known to man," remains unknown to the American mind, where it is seen as sin rather than as fecundity and potency, the miracle of life that even the Dynamo cannot reproduce. "An American Virgin would never dare command; an American Venus would never dare exist." Neither the radiance of spirit nor the pleasure of beauty would be felt as force in an America deadened by the mechanisms of science and industry and devoted to increasing horsepower. Unable to identify with a source of power beyond

90. Henry Adams, "The Primitive Rights of Women," in *The Great Secession*, 333–60; *Tahiti: Memoirs of Arii Taimai* (1901; Ridgewood, N.J.: Gregg Press, 1968), 1–21; *Democracy: A Novel* (1880; New York: Airmont, 1968), 57.

itself, the soul has no object for its inward passions. "No American had ever been truly afraid of either," Adams observed of the Virgin and Venus, realizing that if we are to experience the sublime mysteries of love we must also be prepared for the sudden terrors of fear. America would do neither.[91]

Nor, it must be added, would Adams, who sensed that the same dilemma is true of religion and the surrender of reason to faith. For Adams makes clear that the Virgin's whims are as ungovernable as a lover's moods. Adams praised the medieval age for doing what neither he nor his modern heroines could do. Adams could no more give his life to the Virgin than his heroines in *Democracy* and *Esther* could give their lives to their many charming and powerful suitors. In the first novel, the woman is to accept the political reasons of her lover; in the second, his religious faith; both offers would mean the loss of freedom and control. Even in the medieval age, all that mattered, Adams wrote of man's worship of the Virgin, was "his love for her," at once the most simple offer and the most impossible obligation. In a letter to George Cabot Lodge, Adams admitted that he, like other men, was "afraid" of "his women" as he was "of himself"; and he confided to Clarence King that "sex is altogether a mistake" and that gender division is an "irreparable" blunder of nature.[92] In his last years, when Adams thought he saw the prospect of a world out of control, a universe of "chaos" and "entropy," masculine will and self-control seemed to be the last remnant to cling to for a sensitive intellect who may also have felt feminine impulses within himself. Modern man fears the irrationality and destruction of feminine power as much as classical man, represented by Adams's ancestors, feared the arbitrariness and corruption of political power. And in neither male nor female can love conquer fear.

Adams would remark that the few women in his life meant more to him than the fall of empires, and in the *Education* he confessed that the only valuable knowledge he gained from studying history was his "ignorance" of women, adding as an arresting aside: "The woman who is known only through man is known wrong." Referring to a novelist who never had a wife, Adams told John Hay that the bachelor knew women only from "the mere outside."[93] Yet what Adams knew not as a husband but as a lover was the terrible secret: not only did love require irresistible

91. Henry Adams to Lucy Baxter, Mar. 25, 1890, *Letters*, vol. 3, 231; Henry Adams to Clarence King, Apr. 22, 1891, *Letters*, vol. 3, 466; *Education*, 383–85.

92. Henry Adams to George Cabot Lodge, Apr. 27, 1903, in Cater, 544–45; Henry Adams to Clarence King, Apr. 22, 1891, *Letters*, vol. 3, 467.

93. Adams, *Education*, 353; Henry Adams to John Hay, Sept. 24, 1883, *Letters*, vol. 2, 513.

submission, it also demanded total possession. Feeling he had made a mistake in following Elizabeth Cameron to England, Adams quoted to her lines from Elizabeth Barrett Browning:

Know you what it is when Anguish, with apocalyptic *Never*,
To a Pythian height dilates you, and Despair sublimes to Power?

Adams wanted to run away, telling Mrs. Cameron, "I cannot sublime to power, and as I have learned to follow fate with docility surprising to myself, I shall come back gaily, with a heart as sick as ever a man had who knew that he should lose the only object he loved because he loved too much." Adams was anguished by the pain he must be causing her, yet confessed that he dreaded "the solitude of hotels and the weariness of self-self-self." He then informed her that he would busy himself in study and writing, "if only I still knew a God to pray to, or better yet, a Goddess; for as I grow older I see that all the human interest and power that religion ever had, was in the mother and the child, and I would have nothing to do with a church that did not offer both. There you are again! You see how the thought always turns back to you."[94] Adams finally bid adieu, leaving everything to Kismet and fate.

In Adams the romantic and religious longing are one and the same, no matter how much the Christian church had warned against such an identity. The desire to possess Mrs. Cameron arose from the same emotion as the desire to know God. It is the desire of the seeker to be at one with some majestic power so as to become whole. And it is the riddle of power that one must either emotionally submit to it or rationally resist it. But Adams could not allow himself to be completely overwhelmed by the power of love, nor could he be completely indifferent to it. Far from being a skeptic, Adams hungered for the unattainable and unknowable, whether it be woman or God. Without realizing one or the other, he could neither "sublime" to power nor be obedient to authority.

"Are we . . . to go back to Faith?" Adams asked the medieval scholar Henry Osborn Taylor in 1915. "If so, it is to be early Christian or Stoic?" Adams himself preferred the stoicism of Marcus Aurelius and even that of Eastern Buddhism. Thus his life approaches its end almost on the same emotional basis on which it had begun. One part of his temperament chose reason, nature, and the stoical imperative of knowing oneself; the other, as indicated in his poem "Buddha and Brahma," led him to agree with Eastern philosophers that one cannot act with true knowledge of the meaning of one's actions—that, in short, conduct and reason are

94. Henry Adams to Elizabeth Cameron, Nov. 5, 1891, *Letters*, vol. 3, 556–61.

unrelated.[95] Thus while Adams wanted to return to the classical ideals of
the eighteenth century, he also remained convinced that the principles of
the Enlightenment would not catch up with American energy; and the
regulation of society's energies required a firm grasp of reality, a theory
of history based on causal understanding that eluded him. A political
leader like Theodore Roosevelt or Adams's close friend John Hay might
try to grasp the forces of history and bend them to his will, and the
philosopher Dewey would explain to America why the First World War
demonstrated the logical connection of force and reason. But Adams
doubted that truth could ever reside in power, and he would not presume
to control force by becoming its agent in order to identify his will with
the movement of history. Instead Adams offered America the deeper
wisdom of darkness, as Conrad Aiken put it in his poem *The Kid:*

> Ring within ring he uncovered the pain:
> Found light in darkness, then darkness again:
> World whorled in world the whorly of his thought,
> Shape under series the godhead he sought.[96]

In the following chapters America's pragmatic philosophers will come
forward with answers that might help a skeptic like Adams ease his pain.
The pragmatists would defend the authority of knowledge as the power
to act; Adams conceived authority as a transcendent principle meant to
control power. Pragmatists would use history by making the past serve
the present, and instead of striving for causal understanding, they would
look to the continuing social consequences of events; Adams insisted that
insofar as true scientific history must assume a necessary sequence of
cause and effect, any history that aims to serve the present without establishing that sequence will simply be falsified. Pragmatists would demonstrate that ethics and knowledge are reconcilable; Adams felt that what
he desired was at war with what he knew. Pragmatists would base the
will to believe on human need; Adams had no belief, only the need for it.

Henry Adams would be intellectually incapable of following the rest
of American culture in making the transition from modernism to pragmatism. Why? He knew too much. Adams was one of the first modern
minds to see the problem of force as a moral, and not simply a physical,
fact; and he was the first to state the dilemma of modernism in political
and scientific, and not just literary or cultural, terms: the mindlessness

95. Henry Adams to Henry Osborn Taylor, Feb. 15, 1915, in Cater; "Buddha and
Brahma," in *A Henry Adams Reader*, ed. Elizabeth Stevenson (New York, 1958), 341–47.
96. Aiken's poem is quoted in John Raymond, "Henry Adams and the American Scene,"
History Today 13 (1963): 309.

of power and the powerlessness of mind to resist it. Big business and its putsuit of profit, science and its relentless release of energy, politics and its networks of influence were all forms of power, and against such institutions Adams saw that "no authority exists capable of effective resistance."[97] America's pragmatic philosophers would attempt to establish such an authority by showing how the mind can deal with force and power while dispensing with older concepts of truth, at the same time regarding the world as responsive to human yearnings. About that effort Adams would remain, if not entirely convinced, at least curious. "Let's try pragmatism," he quipped to a friend in 1908. "Send for William James!"[98]

97. Adams, "The New York Gold Conspiracy," in *The Great Secession*, 157–90.
98. Henry Adams to Anna Cabot Mills Lodge, Feb. 13, 1908, in Cater, 612–13.

3

The Pragmatic Affirmation:
William James and the Will to Believe

James and Adams's "Serial Law Fallacy"

William James had wrestled with many of the same personal and philosophical problems that had troubled Adams, a close friend whom he had known for more than forty years. The philosopher no less than the historian wanted to find a way to cope with a world unhinged from the traditional sources of authority, a world not of a "block universe" but with its "lid off."[1] The path Adams had chosen, however, seemed to James to lead nowhere.

James had read *Mont-Saint-Michel and Chartres* and sent Adams "a paean of praise," complimenting his "frolic quality" of prose and wondering where he "stole all that St. Thomas." James shared much of the historian's religious hunger and also remained interested in attitudes toward the supernatural. Yet James found Adams's vision of history bewildering. Adams had seemed to identify the coming end of history with the approaching end of his own life, a kind of deathbed determinism that could only make James wonder how one could explicate the very forces he could not control. Thus James, who in 1910 had just seen a heart specialist in Paris and knew that the end was near, summoned up almost in his dying breath all his resources to refute Adams. "To tell you the truth," he wrote a few weeks before his death, referring to Adams's "Letter to American Teachers of History," "it doesn't impress me at all, save by its wit and erudition." James chided Adams for refusing to meet "his Maker" by performing a final positive intellectual act instead of writing a "tragic

---

1. William James, "Monistic Idealism," in *The Writings of William James*, ed. John J. McDermott (New York, 1968), 497–511.

subject." Even more disturbing to James was Adams's equation of history with physical laws, his confusing the quantity and distribution of energy and its flow and direction, and his inability to recognize that while man may be caught in the historical state of entropy, man's mind may still act upon the world. All the evidence was not in to comprehend the full implications of the second law of thermodynamics, James insisted. Unless mind, nature, and history are regarded as synonymous, there is no reason not to hope that human agency would break the mechanical cycle of cause and effect and become a principal cause itself. Above all, the dissipation of energy as heat in the physical world cannot be translated into the exhaustion of intellectual energy in the human world. On the contrary, the modern mind can do more with less expenditure of energy and effort:

> The *amount* of cosmic energy it costs to buy a certain distribu-
> tion of fact which humanly we regard as precious, seems to
> be an altogether secondary matter as regards the question of
> history and progress. Certain arrangements of matter *on the
> same energy level* are, from the point of view of man's apprecia-
> tion, superior, while others are inferior. Physically, a dino-
> saur's brain may show as much intensity of energy-exchange
> as a man's but it can do infinitely fewer things, because as a
> force of detent it can only unlock the dinosaur's muscles, while
> the man's brain, by unlocking the feebler muscles, indirectly
> can by their means issue proclamations, write books, describe
> Chartres Cathedral, etc. and guide the energies of the shrink-
> ing sun into channels which would never have been entered
> otherwise—in short, *make* history. Therefore the man's brain
> and muscles are, from the point of view of the historian, the
> more important place of energy-exchange, small as this may
> be when measured in absolute physical units.
> The "second law" is wholly irrelevant to "history"—save
> that it sets a terminus for history in the course of things before
> that terminus, and all the second law says is that, whatever
> the history, it must invest itself between that initial maximum
> and that terminal minimum of difference in energy level.[2]

Adams's deterministic view of history not only violated James's belief in voluntarism, it also offended his deepest metaphysical outlook. In "The Notion of Reality as Changing," an essay written a year before his death, James made oblique reference to Adams's conviction that he could plot the future from the past by identifying, or "triangulating," the constant succession of forces that enabled him to see forward as well as backward:

2. William James to Henry Adams, June 17, 1910, *The Letters of William James*, ed. Henry James (Boston: Atlantic Monthly Press, 1920), 344–47.

A friend of mine has an idea, which illustrates on such a magnified scale the impossibility of tracing the same line through
reality, that I will mention it here. He thinks that nothing
more is needed to make history "scientific" than to get the
content of any two epochs (say the end of the thirteenth and
the end of the nineteenth century) accurately defined, then
accurately to define the direction of the change that led from
one epoch into the other, and finally to prolong the line of that
direction into the future. So prolonging the line, he thinks, we
ought to be able to define the actual state of things at any
future date we please. We all feel the essential unreality of
such a concept of "history" as this; but if such a synechistic
pluralism as Peirce, Bergson, and I believe in, be what really
existed, every phenomenon of development, even the sim-
plest, would prove equally rebellious to our science should the
latter pretend to give us literally accurate instead of approximate, or statistically generalized, pictures of development of
reality.[3]

The "synechistic pluralism" that James and his fellow philosophers
had worked out, the idea that reality consisted in endless unactualized
possibilities, could hardly be compatible with the universe that Adams
had conceived. What James objected to was the presumption that through
the universe runs a principle or force endowed with the ontological status
of a logical axiom. Such a presumption resulted in the "serial law" fallacy
wherein "the cause of a cause is the cause of its effects." James denied
that a straight line of "sameness" or "causality" could be traced, for no
one kind of causal activity continued indefinitely in history. One could
not emplot a line of progress or decline and trace it to the same cause,
whether it were the force of faith that led to medieval unity, or the
mentality of reason, science, and energy that led to the discord of modernism. Such a scheme implies a rational continuity of causation that rules
out the novelty and contingency of historical reality. For all his
learnedness, James could never bring himself to believe in ultimate answers to the problems of philosophy; but if he was certain about anything
it was the futility of Adams's search for causal laws and final outcomes.
James could readily sympathize with Adams's heroic attempt to offer
America "the consciousness that he and his people had a past, if they
dared but avow it, and might have a future, if they could but divine it."[4]
Yet James remained certain that one could not arrive at truth merely by
thinking historically. Lacking the status of observable reality, the past by
itself could never be the fount of truth and authority.

3. James, "Notes on the Notion of Reality as Changing," in *Writings*, 301–4.
4. Adams, *Education*, 420.

The problems of seeking truth in history could hardly bother William James. With other modernist thinkers, James believed that knowledge of the past would always be mediated by the practical concerns of the present; and with pragmatists like Dewey, he could never be convinced that anyone should be bound to something that did not spring from his own nature and experience. This stance had separated Adams from James as early as 1880, when the latter wrote an essay in the *Atlantic*, "Great Men, Great Thoughts, and Their Environment." In an attempt to refute Herbert Spencer's Darwinism for emphasizing the impersonal forces governing history, James insisted that any attempt to deny individual initiative conjures up "an ancient Oriental fatalism," a "metaphysic creed . . . disguising itself in 'scientific' plumes." Adams, though no Darwinist, complained to James that he had little patience with "hero worship like Carlyle's." Instead Adams believed, as did, incidentally, thinkers as disparate as Marx and Tolstoy, that the actions of military heroes neutralized each other, and he also wondered whether even great intellectuals can be sure that their thoughts are determined by intellect and will alone.[5]

Adams and James pose conflicting temperaments. On the one hand, we have Adams, with his grim vision of the law-bound totality of a universe gone over to randomness and disorder and of a history whose fate defies human intervention; on the other, James, with his buoyant vision of an open-ended universe in which man is free to order it according to his will and imagination. The historian quarreled with God, the philosopher praised the tenacious soul. Adams found there was no enduring truth; James believed truth could be made to happen. These contrasts, however, belie all that Adams and James shared in common. Both grew up in the post–Civil War milieu, where the Transcendentalism of the 1840s lingered on as the last promise of inner peace and harmony before science and Darwinism would unveil a harsher view of nature. Their families were acquainted and they had been colleagues at Harvard in the 1870s. As with other writers who came of age during the height of the "genteel tradition" in American culture, Adams and James went through early personal and spiritual ordeals. Both had difficulty choosing a fulfilling vocation, and each felt inner doubts about the religious creed and moral precepts on which he was raised. Both thinkers thus faced the crisis of authority that afflicted the high culture of the late nineteenth century, the deepening awareness that the assumptions and values of tradition were succumbing to the forces of modernity. And perhaps more than all other contemporary thinkers, both saw the problematic relationship of

5. Henry Adams to William James, July 27, 1882, *Adams Letters*, vol. 2, 465–66.

authority and freedom to knowledge and belief—what can we know for sure, and on what epistemological grounds can we base our actions as well as our convictions? This question in turn was bound up with the rise of natural science as a mode of investigation, a new empirical methodology that sent the historian searching for a science of the past and the philosopher for a science of the mind. Each writer, feeling himself in the grip of forces he sought to describe, looked to either history or philosophy for an accounting of the world. Both became almost obsessed with the problem of time, memory, consciousness, and the recovery of past experience; and each believed that in the control of power, whether historical or psychological, whether in the course of events or in the operations of the mind, lies the fate of civilization.

There was, in short, a hint of metaphysical desperation in both thinkers' pursuit of knowledge, as if old-fashioned religious salvation could now be gained through new scientific means. However their outlooks might differ, the great pressing concerns of their personal lives became the issues of their historical and philosophical speculations. Some of the most revealing aspects of their biographical reflections are confessions of helplessness. In the *Education* Adams describes finding himself face to face "with the harsh brutality of chance, the terror of the blow" felt when watching his sister die. In the "sick soul" section of *The Varieties of Religious Experience* James has a hallucination of a catatonic epileptic and fears that he himself may someday be reduced to such a state.[6] Both writers knew that human existence always involves the possibility of self-destruction.

Adams's wife took her own life, and James contemplated doing so in 1866. "No one is educated who has never dallied with the thought of suicide," James reflected. Adams, watching his sister Louisa die in pain, concluded that God could not be a "person"; James was certain He could "surely be no gentleman." The sensitive mind usually requires a sense of justification to make life bearable, and for James no less than for Adams this meant a search for some basis of authority that could not only relieve the ordeals of personal experience but also illuminate the conditions of daily existence. With traditional religion no longer capable of providing the sanctions of conduct, both writers had to find ways of dealing with a world they did not fully understand. Both figures, in short, confronted the first challenge of modernity, which would be the intellectual ordeal of the twentieth century, the pluralization of perspectives dramatizing the twilight of the mind as it coped with uncertainty, bleakness, and darkness. Adams wanted to know how to endure "the failure of the light," and

6. Adams, *Education*, 285–89; William James, *The Varieties of Religious Experience* (1902; New York: Collier, 1961), 138–39.

James felt the same responsibility for wresting meaning from the void of meaninglessness. So did the philosopher's brother, Henry James, who esteemed Adams for "his rich and ingenious mind, his great resources of contemplation, resignation, speculation." The novelist spoke for his brother and his friend when he described the modernist predicament. "We work in the dark—we do what we can—we give what we have. Our doubt is our passion, and our passion is our task."[7]

This chapter explores how the American mind met the crisis of modernity, in this instance a crisis that saw the American mind divided against itself. James would describe this predicament as a conflict between the "tender-minded" thinker who, like one half of himself, insisted that human will and desire could make a difference, and the "tough-minded" thinker who, like Adams in his darkest moments, insisted that we live in a world in which human action may be incapable of influencing the inexorable course of history. James was certain that modern man could live with uncertainty; Adams remained uncertain of James's own certainties.[8]

The "Murdered Self" and the Riddle of Consciousness

If modernism challenged the concept of history as a linear narrative of progress, it also challenged the conventional concept of the self as a single, conscious center reaching out to constitute its objects. Since James felt acutely the problem of the self, especially his own self, and since he believed strongly that a given philosophy could well reflect the philosopher's own temperament, perception, and aspiration, perhaps some discussion of the relationship of personality to philosophy is in order. John Dewey also insisted that one aim of philosophy is to express man's interests and satisfy his needs. "Every living thought," wrote Dewey, "represents a gesture made toward the world, an attitude taken to some practical situation in which we are implicated." The journalist Walter Lippmann, who had studied with James at Harvard, was so struck by Dewey's observation that he embellished it with his own corollary. "We may add that the gesture can represent a compensation for a bitter reality, an aspiration unfulfilled, a habit sanctified. In this sense philosophies are truly revealing. They are the very soul of the philosopher projected, and to the discerning critic they may tell more about him than he knows about

7. William James to Benjamin P. Blood, *James Letters*, vol. 2, 39; James on God not being a "gentleman" is quoted in Bertrand Russell, *A History of Western Philosophy* (New York, 1945), 811; Henry James is quoted in Alfred Kazin, "In Honor of William and Henry James: Special Section," *New Republic* 29 (Feb. 15, 1943): 218; and his description of Adams is in Louis Auchincloss, *Henry Adams* (Minneapolis, 1971), 32.
8. James, "The Present Dilemma in Philosophy," in *Writings*, 362–76.

himself. In this sense a man's philosophy is his autobiography; you may read into it the story of his conflict with life."[9]

In some ways James's explorations of intellect and emotion may be interpreted as "a compensation for a bitter reality" and his adoption of the philosophy of pragmatism as "the story of his conflict with life." James's own father, Henry James, Sr., was a bundle of contradictions. Son of an Irish immigrant who had become a millionaire during the Jacksonian era, Henry, Sr., spent many years in a successful effort to break his father's will and inherit early a fortune to which he felt entitled. Thereafter he scorned money-grubbing, led a life of leisure, toured Europe in high style, and preached the values of hard work. Pressured by his father to get down to serious business, William toyed with one vocation after another in a futile effort to satisfy the patriarch's confusing moods. The father once spoke of art as a noble endeavor, but when William decided to become a painter, his father now hinted that art was feminine and science the truly "manly" vocation. When William finished medical school, his father worried that the pursuit of science would cultivate a skepticism threatening to religious belief. The father once regarded philosophy as the highest form of knowledge, but as William became interested in the discipline, the father judged it too technical to lead to spiritual truths. "I originally studied medicine in order to be a physiologist, but drifted into psychology and philosophy from a sort of fatality," James later reflected in 1902. On one occasion James referred to his "murdered self," leaving the impression that he had abandoned his original true vocation of art, what Lippmann would have called "an aspiration unfulfilled."[10]

One wonders if James's struggle over the choice of a vocation stemmed directly from neurotic paternal tensions or whether it was characteristic of a late-nineteenth-century generational dilemma. Henry Adams, it will be recalled, had been pressured to enter politics and government service; he too spent many years pondering his proper function in society as well as the problem of free will and the meaninglessness of existence; and he also tells us that he "drifted into the mental indolence" of studying history only to discover late in life that art remains, after all other disciplines have failed, the one activity that can redeem man. Modernism may be just as important as Freudianism in explaining James's struggles for self-definition. If knowledge is alienated from reality, how does one decide to

9. Lippmann, quoted in Ronald Steel, *Walter Lippmann and the American Century* (Boston, 1980), 85.

10. James's quote and the psychological account of his early life are drawn from Howard M. Feinstein, *Becoming William James* (Ithaca, N.Y., 1984), 298.

live in the real world, where there remains no fixed foundation on which to think?[11]

Whether James's tortured path to a healthy, productive life can be explained through psychoanalytical categories remains a controversy among Jamesian scholars.[12] Perhaps it is more edifying to consider that a young thinker who once suffered from insomnia, eye trouble, and painful backaches as well as suicidal thoughts went on to offer America a philosophy of exuberance and uplift. He impressed his students as a welcome oddity, a dynamic, vibrant professor who dressed casually, displayed little respect for respectability, and defied academic convention by inviting questions in the classroom. He was "always throwing off sparks," said one student of his lectures. "To see him," said another, "was never to forget what it means to be alive." Gertrude Stein, one of the most daring of modernist thinkers, could never forget her classes with "Professor William James" as she went on to become a Parisian collector of Braque, Matisse, and Picasso, artists who also valued the contingent and spontaneous. Effervescent despite continuing bouts with ill-health, James approached philosophy as an outdoorsman and wanted Americans to approach life as though each morning were a new beginning. His sister Alice once remarked that William captured his own spirit when he told her his New Hampshire summer house had fourteen doors, each opening outward.[13]

Given James's early emotional stresses, it is not surprising that he devoted himself to the study of psychology after having spent a few years teaching physiology. His masterpiece, *Principles of Psychology* (1890), remains a seminal work, a pioneering effort in what later would be called psychotherapy (although it fell into disfavor for almost a century when its author turned his back on psychology to take up philosophy, religion, and even spiritualism, the occult, and mind cure). As a psychologist James would dispute Adams's casual remark that "the history of the mind concerned the historian alone."[14] But the two disciplines of history and psychology had much in common. For James also approached the study of

11. Adams, *Education*, 36.

12. A solid scholarly work critical of the psychological approach is Gerald E. Myers, *William James: His Life and Thought* (New Haven, 1966); R. W. B. Lewis is also skeptical of Freudian speculations in *The Jameses: A Family Narrative* (New York, 1991).

13. On student remarks about James as teacher, see Paul Boller, Jr., "William James as Educator: Individualism and Democracy," *Teachers' College Record* 80 (Feb. 1979): 587–601; Alice James's remark is in Lloyd Morris, *Postscript to Yesterday* (New York: Random House, 1947), 332.

14. Adams, *Education*, 401.

the mind as an empirical scientist, and he too assumed it was conditioned by the past. Human experience, whether national or individual, required an understanding of causal relations. But how could one distinguish cause from effect? James believed that mental states arose from physical antecedents, which in turn were influenced by the mind's activity, and therefore the ontological dualism between mental and physical processes could no longer be maintained. Initially Adams and James undertook the same search for sequences based on descriptive analysis alone, apart from conventional religious or metaphysical categories. But whereas Adams initially searched for causal determinism, only later to welcome a modern "multiverse" of randomness, James, after overcoming the fatalist fears of his youth, could never believe that every event had a necessitating cause.

Nor could James rest with the dimensions of psychology alone. All the subjects he desired to explore—mind, self, emotion, perception, time, memory, attention, thought, reality, morality, religion, knowledge, belief—required philosophical inquiry and speculation. Above all, James became preoccupied with self-knowledge, introspection, and personal consciousness. Exploring the interior operations of the mind also concerned other modernist thinkers who sought to understand history and their place in it. Adams, who had doubted whether the masses of Americans were aware of the meaning of their historical and political actions, was no less interested in the problem of consciousness. Although he told his brother that introspection was a "heartrending" ordeal, and although he chided James for refusing to see that probing the self only leads to a regressive thinking about thinking, Adams could not resist the temptation. "Do you understand," he once quizzed his brother, "how, without a double personality, *I* can feel that *I* am a failure? One would think that the *I* which could feel that must be a different *ego* from the *I* which is felt."[15] Does introspection require a double personality? Auguste Comte ridiculed as absurd the notion that a person could separate himself into two, with one half reasoning and the second half observing the first half doing the reasoning. But we might recall the reporter who said that Henry Adams was the only man he knew who could sit on a fence and watch himself go by. The third-person voice of the *Education* offered the author's reflections on what thoughts had passed through his own mind. But Adams doubted that retrospection any more than introspection could lead man out of the "abyss of ignorance." James had no such self-doubts about the promises of self-knowledge.

15. Henry Adams to Charles Francis Adams, Jr., Feb. 14, 1862, *Adams Letters*, vol. 1, 281–82.

In his provocative essay "Does Consciousness Exist?" (1904), James attempted to demonstrate exactly what could be proven by probing the phenomenon of self-reflection. His celebrated discovery was that consciousness does not exist, at least not as a static entity that may not be known but must be postulated as essential to human awareness on the part of the knowing subject. Since experience involves not isolated moments but indeterminate continuities, consciousness can only be a relation that exists when the known object is encountered by the knowing mind. Similarly, since mental states are transitive, the mind is not a timeless, all-knowing presence, and since awareness itself has no entity it cannot be introspectively established. Thus James substituted for a single state the notion of a "stream" of thought and consciousness, an exciting idea that would be adopted by modernist writers like James Joyce and John Dos Passos to treat experience as indeterminate and to use the flow of words to dramatize simultaneity. Whether or not objects could be known without the interposition of the mind's own ideas and concepts, James insisted that "pure experience" does not play tricks that separate the knower from the known. The philosopher's claim that a reflective consciousness of the self must be distinguished from the object of knowledge falsely "maintains that I cannot know without knowing that I know." On the contrary, the interpretation of experience is simply a function of context.

> Experience, I believe, has no such inner duplicity; and the separation of it into consciousness and content comes, not by way of subtraction, but by way of addition—the addition, to a given concrete piece of it, of other sets of experience, in connection with which severally its use or function may be of two different kinds. The paint will also serve here as an illustration. In a pot in a paint-shop, along with other paints, it serves in its entirety as so much saleable matter. Spread on a canvas, with other paints around it, it represents, on the contrary, a feature in a picture and performs a spiritual function. Just so, I maintain, does a given undivided portion of experience, taken in one context of associates, play the part of the knower, of a state of mind, of "consciousness"; while in a different context the same undivided bit of experience plays the part of the thing known, of an objective "content." In a word, in one group it figures as thought, in another as a thing. And since it can figure in both groups simultaneously we have every right to speak of it as subjective and objective both at once.[16]

16. James, "Does Consciousness Exist?" in *Writings*, 169–83.

One wonders whether James would have agreed with the abstract expressionists of the 1950s, the "action painters" who proclaimed that the picture painted and the act of painting cannot be distinguished, that art is both thing and thought, what it is and what the artist does. Believing that we interpret experience in answer to our practical needs, James insisted that we need not distinguish consciousness (thought) and its object (thing). Toward the latter part of the twentieth century, in the period of postmodernism, the identity of subject and object itself came to be questioned. The argument would now be advanced, as we shall see in the concluding chapter, that there is no conscious subject, but only structures and objects, things without intentional thoughts; a Jackson Pollack canvas with no perceiving Pollack dripping paint; a novel by Joyce, who disappears from the text, perhaps drowned in his own "stream" of indeterminate prose. But James had no wish to bury the living mind in the dead structures of what later would be called "deconstruction." To James the mind remained irreducible to external structures because it "is at every stage a theatre of simultaneous possibilities."[17]

In *The Varieties of Religious Experience* James cites the works of Freud, Otto Breuer, and other pioneering psychologists to discuss what he called the "subliminal consciousness." It is perhaps no coincidence that James became absorbed by the mysteries of the mind and religion right after suffering from cardiac problems. "The fact that we *can* die, that we can be ill at all is what perplexes us," he wrote in *Varieties*.[18] James felt that knowledge of the workings of the mind might hold the key to explaining his own neurosis and loss of mental energy. But he was also concerned about the collective unconsciousness of society as a whole, and, as would the Swiss psychologist Carl Jung, James grew mystical about the possibility of unconscious psychic forces connecting a person's neurological and mental systems to the larger universe. "There is a continuum of cosmic consciousness, against which our individuality builds but accidental fences, and into which our several minds plunge as into a mother-sea or reservoir."[19] In "The Energies of Men" (1906), James spoke of the "twilight region," which, like the athlete's "second wind," offered a storehouse of unsuspected powers to anyone who would activate them. James's concern about human vitality and dissipation paralleled in many ways the contemporary discussion of the second law of thermodynamics. Building on the law, the German physiologist Hermann von Helmholtz formulated

17. William James, *The Principles of Psychology* (New York: Henry Holt, 1890), vol. 1, 288–89.

18. James, *Varieties of Religious Experience*, 123.

19. James, "Final Impressions of a Psychical Researcher," *Writings*, 798–99.

a theory of displaced energy in which human nervous forces were likened to electricity and both were regarded as running down, with no new means of replenishment. In this respect the writings of James as well as those of Adams reflected growing American concern about the phenomenon of energy and how it related to life and death, science and religion, and, in Theodore Roosevelt's era, politics and the triumph of will over inertia. Yet James's sense of the subconscious as the source of psychic energy differs profoundly from Adams's sense of man's blindness to his own predicament.

The phenomenon of explosive energy Adams had seen everywhere, not only in radium rays and the Dynamo but in the Virgin as a rebellious goddess. Adams felt the subconscious was a seething "chaos," a storehouse not of vital energies but of alien emotions as mysterious as the captivating presence of women. His interest in medieval saints, Egyptian queens, and Tahitian princesses suggested to him the power of sex as well as religion. "Early women became a passion," he wrote of his research in the *Education*. "Without understanding movement of sex," he observed of women always moving in the unbroken, constant line of maternity and reproduction, "history seemed to him mere pedantry." While early women leaders indicated the possibilities of freedom and independence, Adams believed the dilemma of modern woman would remain as long as she continued to look toward men whose "instinct of power was blind":

> The typical American man had his hand on a lever and his eye on a curve in his road; his living depended on keeping up an average speed of forty miles an hour, tending always to overcome sixty, eighty, or a hundred, and he could not admit emotions or anxieties or subconscious distractions, more than he could admit whisky or drugs, without breaking his neck. He could not run the machine and a woman too; he must leave her, even though his wife, to find her own way, and all the world saw her trying to find her way by imitating him.
>
> The result was often tragic, but that was no new thing in feminine history. Tragedy had been woman's lot since Eve. Her problem had always been one of physical strength and it was as physical perfection of force that her Venus has governed nature. The woman's force had counted as inertia of rotation, and her axis of rotation had been the cradle and the family. The idea that she was weak revolted all history; it was a palaeontological falsehood that even an Eocene female monkey would have laughed at; but it was surely true that, if her force were to be diverted from its axis, it must find a new field, and the family must pay for it. So far as she succeeded,

she must become sexless like the bees, and must leave the old
energy of inertia to carry on the race.[20]

In "The Energies of Men" James does discuss women, but only to suggest
that tapping the unconsciousness affords them more power to carry out
their conventional duties. When discussing men, James spoke of the need
of "unlocking" latent energies that either individual flabbiness or social
convention had blocked. Such energies would enable men to break bad
habits like drinking and gambling and to practice yoga, and "energy-
releasing ideas" like patriotism and honor could enlarge the reach of power
and achievement. But in the case of women James wanted to illustrate
the "humbler examples" of energy in the service of society.

> John Stuart Mill somewhere says that women excel men in
> the power of keeping up sustained moral excitement. Every
> case of illness nursed by wife or mother is proof of this; and
> where can one find greater examples of sustained endurance
> than in those thousands of poor homes, where the woman
> successfully holds the family together and keeps it going by
> taking all the thought and doing all the work—nursing, teach-
> ing, cooking, washing, sewing, scrubbing, saving, helping
> neighbors, "choring" outside—where does the catalogue end?

James then discusses a prize given by the Académie Française for each
year's best example of "virtue":

> The academy's committees, with great good sense, have
> shown a partiality to virtues simple and chronic, rather than
> to her spasmodic and dramatic flights; and the exemplary
> housewives reported on have been wonderful and admirable
> enough. In a report for this year we find numerous cases, of
> which this is a type; Jeanne Chaix, eldest of six children;
> mother insane, father chronically ill. Jeanne, with no money
> but her wages at a pasteboard-box factory, directs the house-
> hold, brings up the children, and successfully maintains the
> family of eight, which thus subsists, morally as well as materi-
> ally, by the sole force of her valiant will.[21]

Adams would have preferred to see the prize go to the woman who
took off in "spasmodic and dramatic flights," women like the heroines in
Democracy and *Esther*, who defied man's unconscious instinct for power
and domination. James wanted to release energies in order to better control them. He could scarcely regard sex as one of the primal energies

---

20. Adams, *Education*, 442–46.
21. James, "The Energies of Men," *Writings*, 671–83.

struggling to express itself. While Adams perceived sex and religion as intimately linked as two expressions of power involving submission to and salvation by another, James denied any connection between "religious consciousness" and "sexual consciousness" because each domain partook of different "contents." One half of James's mind probed the unconscious as a Victorian moralist who wanted not so much to uncover repressed emotions as to unleash healthy energies.[22] But in his writings on religion, as opposed to sex, James was more daring than Adams in turning religion into psychology in order to identify it with freedom rather than authority. In *The Varieties of Religious Experience* the eccentrics and abnormal harbor higher spiritual insights, as though the divine found its proper outlet in the deviant. In *Varieties* the reader feels the full emotional force of religion as much as in Adams's *Mont-Saint-Michel*. Indeed James shows why religion will continue as an indispensable human feeling and not die out, as Adams assumed it would in depicting Aquinas's failure to reconcile it with reason. James sought to reconcile it with experience.

"Did you ever read the *Confessions of St. Augustine*, or of Cardinal de Retz, or of Rousseau, or of Benvenuto Cellini, or even of our dear Gibbon?" Adams asked James in 1908. Henry Cabot Lodge, in his editor's preface to the *Education*, wrote that Adams used to say, "half in jest," that he once thought of completing Augustine's *Confessions* but soon realized he was moving in the opposite direction, from "unity to multiplicity." In Adams's own Author's Preface he quotes Rousseau: "I have shown myself as I was . . . I have unveiled my interior." Most educators and scholars of the nineteenth century, Adams continued, were reluctant to expose themselves for what they were. No models exist for such self-scrutiny. Even Rousseau's *Confessions* offered an example of the egoist only to warn against the Ego. All that remained after the Ego had been effaced was the "manikin," the dummy on which "the toilet of education is to be draped in order to show the fit or misfit of the clothes. The object of study is the garment, not the figure." Although Adams stated that the "tailor adapts the manikin as well as the clothes to his patron's wants," thereby implicitly endorsing the pragmatic dictum that philosophy should serve practical human needs, he was not at all certain that the human creature knows who he is or what he wants or ought to want. James had asked "Does Consciousness Exist?" By using the image of the bare, passive manikin instead of the conscious, active subject, Adams treated education more as a matter of adaptation than of introspection. Is, then, self-consciousness a fiction, an invention that is draped rather than discovered? Characteristically, Adams waxed ironic and suggested that the

22. James, *Varieties of Religious Experience*, 28–29.

garment-draped manikin may be real, since it "has the same value as any other geometrical figure of three or more dimensions, which is used for the study of relation. For that purpose it cannot be spared; it is the only measure of motion, of proportion, of the human condition; it must have the air of reality; must be taken for real, must be treated as though it had life;—Who knows? Possibly it had."[23]

Who knows indeed. Relations can be established and motions measured by the empirical mind. Beyond that? James sought to resolve the riddle of consciousness by redefining it as a continuous "stream" in which religious emotions could surface to be psychologically analyzed by the scientific temperament. Adams remained a restless dualist convinced that the known world of the empirical mind would be real, but not real enough for the metaphysical mind that sought to penetrate beyond it. For whatever reason, Adams always felt that what James denied inhered in experience—its "inner duplicity." In one of his last publications, "Buddha and Brahma" (1915), he implied why education must deal with the "garment" and not the "figure," with the real world of space and motion and not the inner consciousness that desires to transcend it.

> . . . we, who cannot fly the world, must seek
> To live two separate lives; one, in the world
> Which we must ever seem to treat as real;
> The other in ourselves, behind a veil
> Not to be raised without disturbing both.[24]

Beyond Rationalism and Empiricism

Although James looked to the cultural supremacy of his own class as the guardian of morality, he shared Adams's skepticism about politics and business as spheres of public ethics. James even viewed institutions as being not so much the embodiment of authoritative ideals as their systematic perversion. "We 'intellectuals' in America," he wrote at the time of the Dreyfus affair, "must all work to keep our precious birthright of individualism free of these institutions [church, army, aristocracy, royalty]. *Every* great institution is perforce a means of corruption—whatever good it may do. Only in free personal relations is full ideality to be found."[25] In his early years as a medical student James became horrified

23. Henry Adams to William James, Feb. 17, 1908, *Adams Letters*, vol. 4, 119–20; Adams, *Education*, xv-xvi.

24. Henry Adams, "Buddha and Brahma," in *A Henry Adams Reader*, ed. Elizabeth Stevenson (Garden City, N.Y., 1958), 341–47.

25. William James to William Salter, Sept. 11, 1899, *James Letters*, vol. 2, 100–101.

by the thought that man may be merely a mechanism fated to act in a universe of ironclad laws. Later his passion for freedom expressed itself in a revolt against institutions, a deep antipathy to those forces of organization and bureaucratization that the German philosopher Max Weber saw as inevitable. "I am against bigness and greatness in all their forms," James wrote in 1899. He preferred "the invisible molecular moral forces" that are capable of "rending the hardest monuments of man's pride, if you give them time. The bigger the unit you deal with, the hollower, the more brutal, the more mendacious is the life displayed. So I am against all big organizations as such."[26] That James could utter such quasi-anarchist thoughts suggests that at least some members of his class no longer felt that large institutions could be relied upon to guide the country. Adams, it will be recalled, described himself as a "conservative Christian anarchist," and he too saw institutions corrupting ideals. Although Adams could not foresee any institution surviving the twentieth century, his disdain for politics as "the systematic organization of hatreds" conveyed the same Jamesian animus. Both the historian and the philosopher feared that if the individual mind failed, its place would be taken by the mega-structures of organization. Both felt the chill of modernity.

James especially wanted man to be independent of institutions because he wanted him free of any external pressures of power or authority. For James authority could never be part of the conventional opinions of officialdom, the received wisdom passed down through established systems and structures. Nor could authority be founded in the final truths of philosophy, the eternal principles of thought that are meant to command our obedience. In "The Moral Philosopher and the Moral Life" (1891) he even denied that authority had anything to do with truth, a concept that presupposes a standard external to the individual to which he must conform. For man's "passional nature" was such that he could only conform to that which he desired, and thus there could be no notion of truth, morality, or goodness independent of our personal support. James remained convinced that the problem of authority was merely the opposite side of the problem of freedom, and that both problems were bound up with the crisis of cognition and belief that characterized late-nineteenth-century scientific thought. "As the authority of past traditions tends more and more to crumble," James wrote in *A Pluralistic Universe* (1909), "men naturally turn a wistful ear to the authority of reason or the evidence of present fact. They will assuredly not be disappointed if they open their minds to what the thicker and more radical empiricism has to say. I fully believe that such an empiricism is a more natural ally than

26. William James to Mrs. Henry Whitman, June 7, 1899, *James Letters*, vol. 2, 90.

dialectics ever were, or can be, of the religious life."[27] James offered modern man a fresh outlook, enabling him not only to escape the paralyzing skepticism of Adams but to live without the long hand of authority, which Adams had always felt on his shoulder.

Traditionally, in the course of Western intellectual history and political philosophy, the authority of truth frequently rested on two fundamental postulates: the existence of a universe governed by certain regulative principles that guided human as well as natural phenomena, and the possession of a mind that managed to rise above its own epistemological limitations, as well as those distortions stemming from the "interests and passions," in order to apprehend the ultimate nature of reality. The crisis of this sense of objective truth did not originate in the fin de siècle. Many eighteenth-century thinkers, the *Federalist* authors, for example, accepted a universe of natural laws but remained less certain that the human mind was capable of perceiving them. Thus Madison followed Hume in claiming that all governments rest on shifting "opinion," not eternal truth.[28] The pragmatists, too, would regard that which is accepted as more important than that which is known, since knowledge itself could at best be only tentative and never yield absolute truth; and the pragmatists shared the framers' conviction that "experience" is a more reliable guide than "reason." But the framers were premodernists in upholding certain absolutes such as inalienable natural rights, and they could never be convinced that public opinion generated from democratic participation and discussion would lead to a truer and juster society. Where James was more interested in what people would act upon than what they would believe in, the framers insisted that actions needed to be controlled precisely because beliefs could not be instilled. The framers were both rationalists and empiricists, thinkers who assumed that human reason need not rely upon divine revelation, yet advocates of a new "science of politics" who believed that the laws of the physical world and the lessons of historical experience could be applied to human affairs. In this respect James was heroically attempting to transcend the limitations of both rationalism and empiricism so that America could enjoy the best of both philosophical traditions.

James was fond of contrasting the rationalist and the empiricist: the "tender-minded" philosopher who stuck to principles, ideals, and a single, monistic vision that reassured convictions about religion and free will; and the "tough-minded" philosopher who went by facts, sensation, and

27. James, "The Moral Philosopher and the Moral Life" and "An Overview," *Writings*, 610–94, 804.
28. *Federalist*, no. 49.

a pluralistic vision that ended in being fatalistic, irreligious, and pessimistic.[29] These categories, as James well knew, could scarcely explain Henry Adams or even himself. Each writer absorbed the teachings of modern science only to arrive at profoundly different conclusions on almost every subject under the sun, including the proper place of women. Adams may be regarded as a quintessential modernist thinker in that he felt the exhaustion of both rationalism and empiricism even while recognizing the value of each. The *Education*, an exercise in heightened retrospection, attempted to use these waning philosophical categories. Simultaneously Adams was both a rationalist, who based his explanations on the operations of his own mind and thought-processes, on reason itself; and an empiricist, whose accounts of life drew upon the nature of things and events, on experience itself. For Adams the combination of these intellectual operations, of mind reflecting on events, led only to a series of negations and frustrations. The solution to Adams's dilemma, from a Jamesian perspective, was to relax the questioning intellect in order to appreciate the relations, associations, and connections that made some semblance of coherence possible. The answer to the frustrations of mind was the flow of experience.

James, of course, was by no means addressing Adams when he developed a daring new theory of reality and the mind's place in it. But he was attempting to break through the philosophical impasse of modernism—a rationalism that had vainly tried to find universals in its clear premises, and an empiricism that had confined itself to finding its necessary proofs in isolated data. In James's estimate the philosophical corollaries of idealism and materialism had also lost their hold on the modern mind; if the former was too cerebral to take into account the physical, the latter was too coarse to take into account the mental. How, then, to take into account the physical *and* the mental, matter and mind, object and subject, reality and thought? James's answer was to demonstrate that such dualisms collapse when we experience the world as continuous, constantly changing and shifting as we interact with its flux and flow.

James's new theory of "radical empiricism" sought to limit rationalism and discursive thought as intrusive to experience. James contended that "everything real must be experienceable somewhere, and every kind of being experienced must somewhere be real." To turn Hegel on his head, James might have said that the real was not the rational but the experiential, not thought in the abstract but encounters that have effect and make a difference in ways that tie things together. "The relations between things, conjunctive as well as disjunctive, are just as much matters of

29. James, "The Present Dilemma in Philosophy," in *Writings*, 362–76.

direct particular experience . . . [as] the things themselves." The radical
nature of James's idea of empiricism was to offer the new notion of "pure
experience" to subvert the older notion that experience could be made to
stand still as the philosopher analyzes its component parts to distinguish,
for example, thoughts and feelings derived from experience from the external objects that had formed them. In some ways James was asking
philosophers to cease being philosophers and to approach life as it is
lived through by the nonphilosopher. To a modernist thinker like Adams,
whose troubles may have been made more acute by his clinging to the
categories of older philosophies, James's message would have been clear:
the antiquated, theoretical constructions of mind try to analyze the contents of experience at the expense of arresting its flow or "stream." In
contrast to James's writings on religion and psychology, with radical empiricism philosophical discourse would be regulated by observable criteria. James wanted modern man to approach experience not with chastened
confusions but with innocent acceptance. "The baby," he wrote in what
became a memorable statement, "assailed by eyes, ears, nose, skin and
entrails at once, feels it as one great blooming, buzzing confusion." The
barrage of this sensory input is overcome by the child's innate faculties
of association and discrimination, out of which impressions of normal
habitual recurrences are formed.[30]

In addition to suggesting that philosophical dualisms have already been
conquered in the crib, James sought to distinguish his version of empiricism from the contemporary British empiricism in vogue at the time. The
latter was more of an epistemological tribunal that had established criteria
of evidence for accepting or rejecting as unreliable certain knowledge-
claims regarding the elements of experience as separate entities. By dispensing with conventional canons of validity, by regarding relationships
and continuities as just as real as the items related, James gave philosophical legitimacy to all kinds of experience, personal and spiritual as well as
physical and factual. And, in making room for the subjective as well as
the objective, James paved the way for making American philosophy
receptive, later in the twentieth century, to such modernist modes of
thought as existentialism and phenomenology. The philosopher John
Wild has shown how both James's and Martin Heidegger's idea of "self-
becoming" originates in anxiety about sickness, failure, and death; and
how Maurice Merleau-Ponty, like James before him, tried to prove that
conceptual thinking must give way to direct sensible encounters so that
knowledge, or the act of knowing, could be as much felt as found. As

30. William James, "A World of Pure Experience," in *Writings*, 194–214; *Principles of Psychology*, vol. 1, 488; *The Meaning of Truth* (New York, 1909), xii-xiii.

did James, European existentialists and phenomenologists also substituted choice and action for thought and reflection.[31]

Convinced that both the ontological status of the universe and the knowing faculties of the mind had become problematic, James convinced himself that truth and authority could no longer be found, but instead must be produced. In "Humanism and Truth" (1904) James transferred the ultimate locus of legitimacy to man himself, to his self-generating powers and emotions. "Must not something end by supporting itself? Humanism is willing to let finite experience be self-supporting."[32] With James American philosophy leaves behind the burdens of Henry Adams.

The Right to Choose One's Own Beliefs

The kind of universe Adams had conceived—where all events are some-how causally related, where the movement of history proceeds by a vague dynamic of expansion and contraction of energy, or even where, paradoxically, certain phenomena in the physical world mischievously disobey the laws of mechanics—seemed to James the conceit of omniscience. Not only was the finite mind incapable of perceiving an "iron-block" universe, but such a conception left no room for change and indeterminacy, the "loose play" of events, not the "actualities" but the "possibilities" that could be appreciated by recognizing the rich diversities of experience. In James's pluralistic universe, history remained essentially open-ended ("unfinished"), and it thus provided the moral battleground where the forces of human effort, evil as well as good, would struggle for supremacy. Clearly authority did not lie in unity.[33]

James's penchant for seeing openness in history convinced him that no institution, doctrine, idea, or faculty was sovereign, even the human mind. James was too steeped in psychology to ignore the extent to which the mind's operations are tied to the neural-biological processes of the body. The mind was not a pure organ of cognition but an instrument motivated by interests and preferences. Consciousness, too, was not an entity or substance or a condition suggesting a final state of knowing, but rather a process or "stream," James's liquid metaphor implying a Whitmanesque continuous becoming, where each flowing moment of consciousness supersedes that which preceded it. Both mind and consciousness interact with the external world and thus are not causally deter-

31. John Wild, *The Radical Empiricism of William James* (Garden City, N.Y., 1970).

32. William James, "Humanism and Truth," in *Pragmatism and Other Essays* (New York, 1963), 180.

33. James, "The One and the Many" and "The Dilemma of Determinism," in *Writings*, 258–70, 587–609.

mined. What affects the environment and activates the mind is our "volitional nature," the intensity of our desires and the power of our will. Mind is selective and consciousness teleological, and the objects that mind perceives and consciousness dwells upon are considered in light of our practical and subjective concerns. This was one meaning of "radical empiricism," that nothing could be known outside of experience, and what was known was influenced by what was felt from within. Occasionally James approached the phenomenon of mind almost as would an artist. "The mind works on the data it receives very much as a sculptor works on a block of stone." The notion of approaching life as an artist shaping his materials offered one answer to the crisis of modernity. "In our cognitive as well as our active life we are creative," advised James.[34] The proposal that true knowledge is tantamount to creative vision abolished the epistemological gap between thought and reality by replacing conceptual knowledge with perceptual experience. But did James's formulation help resolve the problem of modernism?

European thinkers like Nietzsche had also considered the stance of artist as a way out of the nihilism of modernity. While Nietzsche could share James's belief in willpower and the autonomy of the self (both admired by Emerson), Nietzsche also felt that the will to envision and shape the world as an artist may be only another example of power parading as aesthetic imagination, a case, that is to say, of the will forcing its own wishes on reality and then regarding what had been imposed as a discovery. Henry Adams, who regarded the will as simply the ego writ large, also doubted that artistic vision could suffice to replace the loss of older categories of conceptual knowledge. Even as an amateur watercolorist in Tahiti, Adams felt the limits of perception. "I can see that my way of seeing is just the way I do not want to see," he wrote the artist John LaFarge.[35] Adams was referring to the discrepancy between will and knowledge, what he would like to paint and what he could paint, the reaches of imagination and the limits of technique. But in *The Life of George Cabot Lodge* (1911) he considered other issues that would have rendered problematic a view of the mind's activities as similar to those of a sculptor working on stone. Substitute society for stone and the artist encounters resistance and recalcitrance to being reshaped—together with indifference to his very existence.

Although James himself had once aspired to be an artist, his primary concern in his later years was to resolve issues in technical philosophy.

34. James, *Principles of Psychology*, vol. 1, 360–73; *Pragmatism: A New Name for Some Old Ways of Thinking* (New York, 1907), 256.
35. Quoted in Ernest Samuels, *Henry Adams: The Major Phase* (Cambridge, 1964), vol. 2, 26.

His reference to the activity of the artist was perfectly legitimate in this respect. For James's quarrel was with the prevailing philosophies of materialism and idealism. He had little patience with the materialist's claim that the universe consisted of matter and motion, out of which the mind evolved as a conditioned product, and the idealist's conceit that human thought could deal with unobservable objects independent of itself. James sought to liberate the mind from materialism and idealism. His own reconception of the mind involved some artistic effort at verbal description, but it also derived from his psychological observation of behavior. In James's daringly brilliant new account the mind was no longer seen as a machine responding to stimuli nor as a mirror reflecting a preexisting order. Similarly, the mind knew its objects not as a separate fixed entity but as a process of its own function of wanting to know. With James philosophy offered not so much the condition of knowing as it did the options for living. Methodical doubt yielded to the deeper demands of desire.

In his famous essay "The Will to Believe" (1896) James carried this phenomenological approach to knowledge to its most extreme formulation, offering a radical stance on religion that had ironic implications for the political problem of authority and the philosophical problem of truth. Before we can know anything, James pointed out, we must first want to know something, and thus behind man's rational faculties lies a deeper "passional nature" that influences thought. In situations that are "live," "forced," and "momentous," often perplexing moral situations in which we need to act and choose before we have the necessary information, we must draw upon our free will and choose a "live option," a choice whose truthfulness is inherent not in the hypothesis itself but in our willingness to act upon it. What matters is purpose, effort, will, deliberate exercises of resolve that enable us to make decisions and act and thus not to be deprived of that experience which may confirm our beliefs. In arguing that man can create truth by acting upon certain propositions (such as belief in God), James came close to making action the final expression of knowledge and arbiter of belief, and human will the ultimate agent of authority. Man is what he wills, and he may choose what he becomes and how he perceives reality by freely choosing belief. Thus in the literal sense of the term man can "authorize"; he can originate and bring into existence, if not the reality of God Himself, belief in God as a phenomenon; and insofar as the universe remains unfinished, man can remake it through imagination, will, and effort.[36]

James's willful, subjective emphasis upon action, and acting upon, as

---

36. James, "The Will to Believe," *Writings*, 717–35.

tantamount to knowledge upset Peirce, who insisted that the psychological effects of belief have no bearing upon its philosophical validity. James would modify his position, as we shall see. Other philosophers wondered whether James was arguing a species of discredited metaphysics, which F. H. Bradley had wryly defined as thinking up bad reasons for good beliefs. James himself was replying to the English philosopher W. K. Clifford, who had denied any warrant for believing in anything except that which is scientifically verifiable. Clifford's rule resulted in what philosophers call "evidentialism": our beliefs ought to be determined by evidence, and the strength of our beliefs ought to be proportionate to the strength of the evidence. But James's point was that in critical situations one cannot, as Peirce would advise, patiently accumulate evidence as a member of a community of inquiry. In "The Sentiment of Rationality," James cites Clifford and Thomas Huxley as examples of philosophers who look to the "long run" for the kind of proof scientific procedure provides. Their determination to be right, James observed, leads them to fear error more than they desire a truth that may result from desire itself. "The part of wisdom in what one desires is one of the indispensable preliminary conditions of the realization of its object." James used an example of being stuck high on an Alpine mountain and having to decide to make a perilous leap without prior evidence of the ability to do so, or hesitating and from fatigue falling into the abyss. Believe and act or doubt and perish! "There are then cases where faith creates its own verification."[37]

James's attempt to justify the right to believe has traditionally been interpreted as a declaration of philosophical freedom against the advocates of scientific determinism. But if James was rescuing philosophy from science, he was also liberating modern religion from its Protestant heritage in Calvinist determinism. James sought to take religion away from the theologians and deliver it to the people as though it were a long-lost passion. In "The Will to Believe" James begins by telling his audience that "I have brought with me tonight something like a religious sermon on justification by faith to read to you."[38] That James saw himself delivering a hopeful sermon rather than a rigorous philosophical treatise may have had something to do with his emotional relationship with his father. For James's long interest in the psychology of religious experience was also bound up not only with his therapeutic concerns but also with the "voice" of his "father's cry"—"that religion is real."[39] James could not accept his

37. James, "The Sentiment of Rationality," *Writings*, 337.
38. James, "Will to Believe," 717.
39. Ralph Barton Perry, *The Thought and Character of William James: Briefer Version* (New York, 1964), 41; for a psychological study of James and his relation to his father, see Feinstein, *Becoming William James*.

father's monistic idealism and doctrine of revealed truth, but he desired
to sustain the "gospel of moralism" that had been instilled into him as a
youth, the ethical precepts of character and integrity that he tried to
accommodate in his pluralistic philosophy. Thus, like Henry Adams,
James turned to religion, not organized religion but the "lawfulness of
voluntary faith," as the saving remnant of authority, and he too perceived
the indispensable link between authority and opinion, between the idea
of faith and the mind of the faithful. Yet while James would have no part
of Adams's philosophy of history and his anxiety about knowledge, Adams would have no part of James's psychology of religion and his theory
of truth.

"Towards Action and Towards Power"

Modernists were not the first intellectuals to believe they could advance
knowledge by doubting truth. But they were among the first to feel the
void in discovering there may be no deeper truths to unconceal, as Plato
had promised in his allegory on the cave. James realized that older concepts of truth had to be rejected in order to make the modern mind
relevant to the twentieth century. But modernists like Adams, Weber,
Nietzsche, and Heidegger might have seen in James's will to believe the
will to power. In their view James's easy identity of thought and thing
could result in an unacknowledged, aggressive subjective determinism out
of which the impulse to dominate the earth through scientific means
would flow. The dark shadow of power haunted the modernist, who
wondered whether an alien world could be subjected to human mastery.
Sharing, if not by knowledge then by temperament, Nietzsche's view
that nature could be contingent and resistant in response to man's drive
to dominate, Adams also saw that the drive sprang not from human
strength and will but from fear and weakness. "Man's function as a force
of nature was to assimilate other forces as he assimilated food. He called
it love of power. He felt his own feebleness, and he sought for an ass or
a camel, a bow or a sling, to widen his range of power, as he sought a
fetish in a planet in the world beyond." The human power-drive may be
energized by fetishistic illusions, but it is real nonetheless. Without a clear
concept of truth to provide standards for judging the use of knowledge,
knowledge becomes power as it classifies and organizes the world in order
to control it even in the name of freedom. Adams also shared Nietzsche's
conviction that truth is duplicitous to the extent that man assumes he can
disclose it objectively. "The historian must not try to know what is truth,
if he values his honesty; for, if he cares for his truths," warned Adams,
"he is certain to falsify his facts."[40] History remained for Adams a vast,

40. Adams, *Education*, 475.

cosmic movement without meaning in which truth might be interpreted but never known, an interpretation that could falsify facts with the pretense that the world is being presented as it really is. The possibility that an intellectual might unknowingly produce truth while assuming he is discovering it awakened the modern mind to its own deceptions.

Did James succumb to such self-deceptions? Yes and no. While James had no trouble with being told that his philosophy amounts to making truth rather than knowing it as an act of discovery, he also admonished the "closet-philosopher" who would impose his idea of truth on society as if he knew whereof he spoke. In his reflections on moral life, if not on philosophy itself, James was fully aware of the temptation to make ungrounded pronouncements. Although often regarded as a philosopher of will, power, and self-fulfillment, in moral and public philosophy James could also be a philosopher of self-restraint. There almost seem to be two Jameses: the psychologist who instructs individuals on how to conceive truth and belief for their own needs and purposes, and the moralist who cautions thinkers to shun the role of public philosopher or else they will end up wielding power in the name of knowledge. In his first book, *Principles of Psychology*, James describes consciousness as purely a personal possession such that among individual minds "there is no giving or bartering between them." Thoughts exist in isolation. "Absolute insulation, irreducible pluralism, is the law." In later writings James becomes more of a communitarian and describes people as living off each other's ideas, even "trading" their respective truths. Whether or not he was inconsistent in describing the mind functioning differently in different settings, he valued the distinction, which Dewey regarded as spurious, between subjective life and social existence. Moreover, by separating private truth from social authority, James brilliantly avoided a Nietzschean critique of the will to believe as the will to power in which knowledge functions as a tool of domination.[41]

In developing a new approach to the idea of truth, James acknowledged his indebtedness to Charles S. Peirce. His declaration that "there can be no difference which doesn't make a difference" was derived from the Peircean principle that ideas turn on their practical consequences.[42] But where Peirce, as we shall see, sought truth in the larger public domain, in which a consensus might be arrived at by scientific inquirers, James tended to believe that the deepest and most meaningful experiences involved the particular and personal. Later, in response to his critics, James would attempt to give pragmatism a less privatized dimension. But when

41. James, *Principles of Psychology*, vol. 1, 226.
42. James, "Philosophical Conceptions," *Writings*, 349.

he thought of truth he first thought of the possessive "we" and "our," implying that it belongs to "us."

The pragmatist thinker, James explained, "turns his back resolutely and once for all upon a lot of inveterate habits dear to the professional philosopher. He turns away from abstraction and insufficiency, from verbal solutions, from bad *a priori* reasons, from fixed principles, closed systems, and pretended absolutes and origins. He turns towards concreteness and adequacy, towards facts, towards action and towards power." A pragmatist need not make his ideas copy reality or cohere with a larger structure of thought. For truth is not a possession in the form of an abstract mental idea. Instead it is the outcome of an action that is meant to confirm or disconfirm a proposition. "What, in short, is the truth's cash-value in experimental terms?" asked James in worldly language Americans could appreciate. "The moment pragmatism asks this question, it sees the answer: *True ideas are those that we can assimilate, validate, corroborate and verify. False ideas are those we can not.*" In this respect truth does not reside in an idea as a "stagnant property" reflecting a fixed reality. In a world that is forever changing truth itself becomes the result of change, a consequence of experience and a product of human action. "Truth happens to an idea," James insisted. "It *becomes* true, is *made* true by events. Its verity *is* in fact an event, a process, the process namely of its verifying itself, its verification. Its validity is the process of its validation." To the extent that true ideas enable us to adapt to situations, and to the extent that they result in greater fulfillment and "satisfaction," the pragmatist regards the true not only as the useful but also as the good. "The true," advised James, "*is only the expedient in the way of our thinking, just as the right is the expedient in the way of our behaving.*"[43]

James's brave attempt to work out a new approach to the idea of truth generated considerable controversy in the early part of the twentieth century and is still debated today among students and professors of philosophy. Arthur O. Lovejoy once praised James for bringing to philosophy "the artist's freshness and purity of vision," a precious quality that enabled his fellow philosophers to see through the "deadening" limits of older categories and classifications. Nevertheless, Lovejoy offered a telling critique in "The Thirteen Pragmatisms" (1908) and elsewhere. Lovejoy pointed out that James had unknowingly put forward two different theories of truth with no single criterion of meaning to unite them. One version of James's idea of truth—which presaged the later school of logical positivism—presented a verificationist theory of meaning wherein ideas

43. James, "Pragmatism and Radical Empiricism" and "Pragmatism's Conception of Truth," ibid., 311–17, 429–43.

are validated by their predictive import. But James also reasoned in ways that made the meaning of a proposition turn on the future consequences that resulted from believing in it independently of the truth or falsity of the proposition itself. In the latter case anything one believed in would be meaningful if belief in its truthfulness had positive consequences. The British philosopher G. E. Moore also critized James's claim that truth can be made to happen by believing in its possibility. If an Indian's rain-dancing convinces the tribe that it will rain tomorrow, and indeed it does, can one say that their belief in benevolent spirits caused the rain to fall? Another British philosopher, Bertrand Russell, saw James's concept of truth as an example of modern America's worship of action, power, and success. And Marxists seized upon James's reference to "cash-value" to dismiss pragmatism as the decadent philosophy of a desperate capitalist system.[44]

Some of these criticisms fall to the ground like off-the-wall impressions. How would a corporate capitalist determined to control markets react to a philosophy that offered no rational guarantees and defined the moment of truth as a "leap" into the unknown? The view that James's pragmatism amounted to a power philosophy has some validity to the extent that almost all efforts to resolve issues in modernism had to come face to face with power, either as actualization or as domination. But it was James, not John D. Rockefeller, who denounced the "bitch-goddess of success." Of all the critiques of James's idea of truth, Lovejoy's surgical dissection continues to be scrutinized by contemporary thinkers. Although James was fond of Peirce's saying that "there can be no difference which doesn't make a difference," does it follow that there can be no important difference between accepting as true ideas whose consequences have been verified and accepting as true ideas whose consequences would be better for one's personal and emotional life? Are beliefs true because they can be proven or are they true because they improve one's well-being? In responding to his critics, James acknowledged there was a difference between believing in God and the actual existence of God; yet believing itself, he insisted, may bring forth personal, spiritual experiences that could do more for the world than all the dry, lifeless exegeses of "dogmatic" theologians. Here James seemed to have coined a volunteerist,

---

44. Arthur O. Lovejoy, *The Thirteen Pragmatisms and Other Essays* (Baltimore, 1963), 1–30, 79–112; G. E. Moore, *Philosophical Studies* (London, 1922), 141; Bertrand Russell, *Philosophical Essays* (London: Allen and Unwin, 1966); for a Marxist critique, see V. J. McGill, "Pragmatism Reconsidered," *Science and Society* 3 (1939): 299–322; T. A. Jackson, *The Logic of Marxism and Its Critics* (London, 1936); for more recent evaluations, see Ellen Kappy Suckiel, *The Pragmatic Philosophy of William James* (Notre Dame, Indiana, 1982), 91–121; and Armand A. Mauder, "William James's Notion of Truth," *Monist* 57 (April 1973): 151–67.

along with the verificationist, theory of truth. When it came to human needs rather than knowledge itself, James made the consequences of believing an idea the criteria of its truthfulness. We choose beliefs that promise the greatest rewards and not necessarily the greatest rigor. "'What would be better for us to believe': This sounds very like a definition of truth. It comes very near to saying 'what we ought to believe': and in that definition none of you would find any oddity. Ought we ever not to believe what it is *better for us* to believe? And can we keep the notion of what is better for us, and what is true for us, permanently apart? Pragmatism says no, and I fully agree with her."[45]

The idea of truth as a betterment that results in "satisfaction" led some critics to regard pragmatism as too individualistic and hedonistic, what J. A. Hobson then called the "go as you please philosophy." or what perhaps in the 1960s would be hailed as "doing your own thing." James attempted to answer his critics by pointing out that his philosophical stance had certain "logical" demands and "theoretic" requirements. These criteria deserve examination before one can clear James of the charge of excessive individualism in order to make him into a "public" philosopher.[46]

In "Pragmatism and Humanism" (1907), James discusses freedom and its various constraints stemming from sensations forced upon us, encounters with primary experience, inner relations that mediate between thoughts and things, social benefits due to others, and prior truths that linger in the mind of the community as well as the individual. Indeed, at times James seems to want to cling to the coherence theory of truth by emphasizing the importance of what can be assimilated, and even to a rough version of the corresponding true by interpreting the unobservable from the observable so that a prediction that finds its verification in new facts "brings old and new harmoniously together." In his later years James moved toward a realist position in insisting that thought cannot go unchecked and uncontrolled by that to which it refers. At times James made the idea of reality itself essential. With no reference to their objects, James advised, ideas lose their "cognitive lustre." In *The Meaning of Truth* (1909) a newer James emerges, an older philosopher who, responding to pragmatism's critics, now leans more toward realism than constructivism, more toward knowledge as agreement and conforming rather than creation and transforming, more toward an object of belief with reference to the real than the activity of will that works upon the real and reshapes it. Perhaps

45. James, "What Pragmatism Means," *Writings*, 376–90.
46. Hobson is quoted in Lovejoy, 83; James, "What Pragmatism Means," 385; "Pragmatism's Conception of Truth," 442; for a view opposite to the one argued here, see George Cotkin, *William James, Public Philosopher* (Baltimore, 1990).

James wanted to please Dewey and demonstrate that knowledge could have a public matter rather than a private cognition, and experience could be shared rather than solitary. In *Pragmatism* (1907) James seems even to be warning those who took literally his earlier "The Will to Believe" (1896):

> Woe to him whose beliefs
> play fast and loose with
> the order which realities
> follow in his experience;
> they will lead him nowhere
> or else make false connexions.[47]

One could well conclude from such a passage that James wants us to defer to the true and real that exists independent of human thought. Clearly if we fail to take into account what is there beyond ourselves we shall make false judgments. Yet if we accept the world as it has been represented to us we forsake the opportunity to become part of its ongoing nature by becoming its interpreters. Thus James's answer to Adams's sense of the meaninglessness of chaos and entropy is to endow the world with meaning and purpose:

> In our cognitive as well as in our active life we are creative.
> We *add* both to the subject and to the predicate part of reality.
> The world stands really malleable, waiting to receive its final
> touches at our hand. Like the kingdom of heaven, it suffers
> violence willingly. Man *engenders* truth upon it.[48]

For all James's belated deference to realism, to knowledge constituted by the object, he could never bring himself to believe that the things that mattered most could emanate from any source other than our subjective selves. On moral and religious issues in particular he was less inclined toward realism and objectivity and instead grounded knowledge and judgment in desire and preference. There is no moral order in which objective truth resides, and facts in themselves can make no demands upon our passional nature, which has more to do with the impulses of desire than with the imperatives of duty.

One senses that James did not so much contradict himself as leave his ideas open to varying interpretations by readers who have their own needs

---

47. James, "Pragmatism and Humanism" and "Pragmatism's Conception of Truth," *Writings*, 449–61, 429–43; *The Meaning of Truth* (1909; Cambridge: Harvard University Press, 1975), 78–122; *Pragmatism: A New Name for Some Old Ways of Thinking* (1907; New York: Longman's, Green, 1947), 205.

48. James, "Pragmatism and Humanism," *Writings*, 456.

to be met. His essay "The Moral Philosopher and the Moral Life" can be read to support just about any political value. "Whether a God exist, or whether no God exist, in yon blue heaven above us bent, we form at any rate an ethical republic here below." James's notion of republicanism has little to do with civic virtue in the classical sense of subordinating private interest to the public good. Instead James advocated rearranging things so as to maximize the realization of desire and minimize the extent of human dissatisfaction. "The course of history is nothing but the story of men's struggles from generation to generation to find the more and more inclusive order. *Invent some manner* of realizing your own ideals which will also satisfy the alien demands." Typically, James then explains why custom and community must be respected and, the obverse, why they must be defied. "The presumption in cases of conflict must always be in favor of the conventionally recognized good. The philosopher must be a conservative, and in the construction of his casuistic scale must put the things most in accordance with the customs of the community on top." The next paragraph then makes clear why freedom and justice can conflict with community and conventional morality. "And yet if he be a true philosopher he must see that there is nothing final in any actually given equilibrium of human ideals, but that, as our present laws and customs have fought and conquered other past ones, so they will in turn be overthrown by any newly discovered order which will hush up the complaints that they still give rise to, without producing others louder still." An essay that uses the term *moral* twice in its title concludes by explaining why no philosophy of morality and ethics can apply to the changing nature of modern social life. "In point of fact," James exhorts, "the highest ethical life—however few may be called upon to bear its burdens—consists at all times in the breaking of rules which have grown too narrow for the actual case. There is but one unconditional commandment, which is that we should seek incessantly, with fear and trembling, so to vote and to act as to bring about the very largest total universe of good which we can see."[49]

James's pragmatism, in contrast to Peirce's and Dewey's, is too pluralistic, if not anarchistic, to give purpose and direction to thought by advocating organized inquiry and cooperative intelligence as a means of addressing social problems. Thus while James could urge a creative role for the philosopher facing a malleable physical world, he advised the philosopher to stand aside and become a mere spectator when it came to facing the struggles in the social world. James wanted to see the excluded included, and he sympathized deeply with the marginals and misfits. But

49. James, "The Moral Philosopher and the Moral Life," *Writings*, 610–28.

he refused to advocate programmatic causes or preach ethical idealism because only a God, "a divine thinker with all-enveloping demands," is sufficiently omniscient to adjudicate conflicting values and define the common good. The world-bound philosopher has no foundations on which to build a moral system, and any effort to do so will do more in the long run to oppress than to liberate the human condition:

> Pent in under every system of moral rules are unnumerable persons whom it weighs upon, and goods which it represses. . . . See the abuses which the institution of property covers, so that even today it is shamelessly asserted among us that one of the prime functions of the national government is to help the adroiter citizens grow rich. See the unnamed and unnamable sorrows which the tyranny, on the whole so beneficent, of the marriage institution brings to so many, both of the married and the unwed. See the wholesale loss of opportunity under our *regime* of so-called equality and industrialism, with the drummer and the counter-jumper in the saddle, for so many faculties and graces which could flourish in the feudal world. See our kindliness for the humble and the outcast, how it wars with that stern weeding-out which until now has been the condition of every perfection in the breed. See everywhere the struggle and the squeeze; and everlastingly the problem of how to make them less. The anarchists, nihilists, and free-lovers; the free-silverites, socialists, and single-tax men; the free traders and civil-service reformers; the prohibitionists and anti-vivisectionists; the radical darwinians with their idea of the suppression of the weak,—these and all the conservative sentiments of society arrayed against them, are simply demanding through actual experiment by what sort of conduct the maximum amount of good can be gained and kept in this world. . . . What closet-solutions can possibly anticipate the result of trials made on such a scale? Or what can any superficial theorist's judgment be worth, in a world where every one of hundreds of ideals has its special champion already provided in the shape of some genius expressly born to feel it, and to fight to death in its behalf? The pure philosopher can only follow the windings of the spectacle, confident that the line of least resistance will always be towards the richer and the more inclusive arrangement, and that by one tack after another some approach to the kingdom of heaven is incessantly made.[50]

James's pragmatism originally promised belief, will, action, and power. But the above passage indicates he urges caution when facing social con-

50. Ibid., 624–35.

flicts in which there can be no clear solution. In contrast to Dewey, James would not attempt to derive social ethics from scientific naturalism in order to render pragmatism a public philosophy. One cannot, as Dewey would later claim one could, use reflective intelligence to move from the "desired" to the "desirable" since human desires cannot be ordered and often can only be realized at the cost of frustrating other desires. Thus philosophers who take up causes become partisans and lose all sense of objectivity in claiming they know the public good. In this instance James is closer to Nietzsche and Adams (the "conservative Christian anarchist") in seeing that knowledge claims in the name of moral order are little more than the will to power. "All one's slumbering revolutionary instincts waken at the thought of any moralist wielding such powers of life and death," exclaimed James.)"Better chaos forever than an order based on any closet-philosopher's rule."[51]

Truth as Pleasure, Knowledge as the Disposition to Believe

In the first decade of the twentieth century pragmatism came under considerable criticism. It seemed to be a philosophy of power and success at the expense of truth and morality, a philosophy that had eliminated epistemology and thus left the modern mind with no access to the real, a philosophy taught and practiced by those who seemed to prefer the chaos of endless change to the coherence of purposeful order. In "Pragmatism's Conception of Truth" (1907), James attempted to answer the critics. John Dewey and F. C. S. Schiller, the Oxford-trained philosopher who would later teach in the United States, have "suffered a hailstorm of contempt and ridicule," James complained. Pragmatists like Dewey and Schiller are not destroying all objective standards in rethinking the concept of truth, he patiently explained. "Schiller says the true is that which 'works.' Thereupon he is treated as one who limits verification to the lowest material utilities. Dewey says truth is what gives 'satisfaction.' He is treated as one who believes in calling everything true which, if it were true, would be pleasant."[52]

Dewey would also have to address the issues of whether truth and the process of its verification are one and the same and whether true ideas are those that satisfy interests and fulfill needs. Dewey's confrontation with his critics will be taken up in a subsequent chapter where the ethical problems of pragmatic philosophy will be explored. What bears mentioning here is that, despite James's coming to the defense of fellow philosophers, American pragmatism constituted no united front when it came

51. Ibid., 623.
52. James, "Pragmatism's Conception of Truth," *Writings*, 442.

to James's rather eccentric variations. Not only the older Peirce but even the younger Dewey grew disturbed as they watched James redefine the mission of American philosophy. In public Dewey often defended America's most popular philosopher. "Mr. James says expressly that what is important is that the consequences should be specific, not that they should be active. When he said that general notions must 'cash in,' he meant that they must be translatable into verifiable specific things. But the words 'cash in' were enough for some of his critics, who pride themselves upon a logical rigor unattainable by mere pragmatists."[53] Privately Dewey had serious misgivings about James's "The Will to Believe" and other bold declarations of self-sovereignty. Dewey was more interested in establishing a valid criterion for knowing on the basis of doing rather than in developing a stance for believing on the basis of feeling. To Dewey James's position seemed to rely on an emotional inwardness that had little reference to either public awareness or the uses of cool, reflective intelligence.

In unpublished manuscripts Dewey wrote that "passion is not as wholly exclusive of reflection as Mr. James' statements taken literally imply." The use of reason need not result in "chilling objects." Dewey also had second thoughts about his own earlier account of the mind's operations when he later discerned in it "too much the stream of consciousness."[54] What troubled Dewey was James's subjective individualism, which seemed almost oblivious to any social context. "The individual qua individual is the organ or instrument of truth but not its author," he wrote to James in 1891. Dewey, to be sure, had great affection and admiration for the magnanimous James, but even years before "The Will to Believe" appeared he did not hesitate to offer advice to the senior pragmatist. In a long letter to James, Dewey retold a story that had been related to him by a journalist whose attempt to investigate a subject had been blocked by his publisher. The journalist soon found that it was "not any one newspaper but rather the social structure that prevented freedom of inquiry." The journalist went on to identify "the question of inquiry with, in philosophical terms, the question of the relation of intelligence to the objective world." The lesson? Dewey told James that the journalist's difficulties disabused him as a philosopher of "idealism" and made him consider that such realities as "class interests" can affect inquiry. It is not enough, concluded Dewey, that philosophical knowledge satisfy subjective needs; it must also "secure the conditions of its objective expres-

53. Dewey is quoted in R. W. Sleeper, *The Necessity of Pragmatism: John Dewey's Conception of Philosophy* (New Haven, 1986), 93.

54. John Dewey, ms. 102, 61/3, n.d.; John Dewey to Brok Brod [?], Mar. 12, 1914, Horace Kallen mss.

sion."[55] Herein lies one of several differences separating Dewey from James: the former sought to render philosophy relevant to society so as to change its conditions; the latter believed philosophy could help to regenerate the individual by changing his emotions. But whether concerned about the public or the private, about social reform based upon intelligence or self-transformation based upon willpower, neither philosopher believed that change required knowledge of the past.

What is the place of history in the pragmatist's account of knowledge? Dewey would address this question fully as a matter of theory and, as we shall see, a precondition of practice. James also had to face the fact that a pragmatic theory of truth ruled out any accurate knowledge of the past, since events in the past could be neither changed nor verified. Was history therefore unknowable? James tackled this question in an imaginary dialogue between the antipragmatist and his foe:

> Anti-Prag.:—But I thought you said a while ago that there is a truth of past events, even tho no one shall ever know it.
>
> Prag.: Yes, but you must remember that I also stipulated for permission to define the word in my own fashion. The truth of an event, past, present, or future, is for me only another name for the fact that if the event ever *does* get known, the nature of the knowledge is already to some degree predetermined. The truth which precedes actual knowledge of a fact means only what any possible knower of the fact will eventually find himself necessitated to believe about it. He must believe something that will bring him into satisfactory relations with it, that will prove a decent mental substitute for it. What this something may be is of course partly fixed already by the nature of the fact and by the sphere of its associations.
> This seems to me all that you can clearly mean when you say that truth pre-exists to knowledge. It is knowledge anticipated, knowledge in the form of possibility merely.[56]

In his later years Henry Adams came to see that knowledge of the past is conditioned by the knowing. James went further. Because there is no cognizable preexisting reality to which knowledge can conform, truth resides in the knower's disposition to believe. Whatever the philosophical validity of this position, the irony is delicious. Consider the juxtapositions. Adams is a determinist who ultimately confesses his inability to

55. John Dewey to William James, Nov. 22, 1891, Dewey mss.; John Dewey to William James, June 3, 1891, James mss.
56. James, "A Dialogue," *Writings*, 446.

see anything but change, randomness, and the chaos of indeterminacy. James is a volunteerist who insists that historical truth can be found only to the extent that it is "to some degree" predetermined. Truth cannot exist, even in the past, prior to its instantiation, that is, its becoming present to the historian who is inclined to believe it. James remained convinced that people will find themselves "necessitated to believe" whatever truth will bring them into "satisfactory relations with it." The conviction derived from the pragmatist's assumption that the rationalist concept of truth, which amounted to, in James's vivid words, "the notion of a reality calling on us to 'agree' with it, and that for no other reasons, but simply because its claim is 'unconditional' or 'transcendent,'" is completely incapable of demonstration. If knowing makes a difference to the thing known, the knower can hardly expect to know the thing in itself, and therefore must settle for "a decent mental substitute for it" and regard knowing as a future possibility rather than an immediate actuality. The correspondence theory of truth must be replaced by the verificationist theory, in which the nature of truth is provided by its own criterion. If truth remains separate from its means of verification, if it asks us to agree with it without providing the means of doing so, how can the inquirer ever know it?[57]

James acknowledged that what we come to know "may be partly fixed by the nature of the fact and by the sphere of its associations." But there is no way to know if the real may be "partly fixed"—a curious phrase—since the nature of the real cannot be discovered to reside outside the procedures by which it is tested and its practical effects observed. Unlike Peirce, James did not believe the real can exist unaffected by our thoughts about it. But how we think about things is precisely the problem in a philosophy that identifies truth not only with verification but with satisfaction.

If people are free to choose their beliefs as a "live option," and if truth cannot exist outside its subject, can it impose itself upon our attention and run against our disposition to believe in what we want to believe? It may be the case that we tend to apprehend what we have already vaguely desired; and Hegel, the philosopher who insisted that paradoxes clarify rather than obscure things, defined freedom as the recognition of necessity. Although James denigrated Hegel's "block universe" in order to give man freedom of will and choice, he also seemed to imply that freedom is obedience to our impulses toward gratification. Hence the exercise of the faculty of will is preceded by a "truth" that the subject comes to know as it "preexisted" in his own disposition to act upon it, because what is true must answer to the need to be satisfied. Satisfied with what?

---

57. James, "Pragmatism's Conception of Truth," *Writings*, 433–42.

James's reasoning derives from the pragmatist's biological assumption that humankind is disposed to believe in whatever promotes survival, self-preservation, success, and other rationally desirable needs. But such reasoning denies the skeptic, not to mention the masochist, the freedom to see truth as discomforting and unsatisfactory. For all James's troubles about the existence of human affliction, he continued to identify truth with pleasure rather than pain. Many modernist thinkers, particularly European, could scarcely see as true that which conforms to human desires. Émile Durkheim, whom James occasionally quoted, pointed out, in his lectures on pragmatism at the Sorbonne in 1913, that truth, instead of being desirable, attractive, and inherently good, can be disconcerting, disabling, and possibly despairing.[58] Do people really want the mirror of truth held up to themselves? Or, as T. S. Eliot put it, do they avert their gaze because they cannot stand too much reality?

Juxtaposing Eliot to James could lead readers to assume that the author advocates abandoning pragmatism and returning to some form of absolutism. On the contrary, I agree with Reinhold Niebuhr that James helped America enter the world of modernity by liberating religion and philosophy from doctrinal abstractions and relating them both to life as it is actually experienced. Yet while the more existentialist Niebuhr believed the modern thinker should address the problem of power and justice, James still clung to the issue of knowledge and truth. On the ruin of rational illusions, James heroically strove not to discard the idea of truth but to give it a new meaning.

The problem with James's reconceptualizing orthodox ideas of truth is the lack of a reference, a means of connecting subject to object, the processes of thinking to the thing thought. The reference theory of knowledge holds that the meaning of a word is what it refers to. Without reference, and without knowledge based in either correspondence or coherence, in the recalcitrant character of reality or the internal demands of consistency, truth cannot be traced or found in the phenomenon of knowledge and thus becomes a subject without an object, thought without a necessary thing, rhetoric without the reality of the real. James's defenders have been quick to point out how the philosopher, in his later works written in response to his critics, emphasized that thought must cohere with society's sentiments and be in agreement with the real. This is how James put it in *The Meaning of Truth*:

> The Pragmatist calls satisfactions indispensable for truth building, but I have everywhere called them insufficient unless reality be also incidentally led to. . . . For him, as for his

58. Émile Durkheim, *Pragmatism and Sociology*, ed. John J. Allcock, trans. J. C. Whitehouse (New York, 1983), 74–75.

critic, there can be no truth if there is nothing to be true about. Ideas are so much flat psychological surface unless some mirrored matter gives them cognitive lustre. This is why I have so carefully posited "reality" *ab initio*, and why, throughout my whole discussion I remain an epistemological realist.[59]

Here a distinction needs to be made between what James says and what he can prove. The most James can say, as a concession to his critics, is that the real ought to be conceived to be logically independent of the knowing subject. But he could hardly concede that it could be causally independent, since he had already defined truth as that which "happens" to an idea. Earlier he had proclaimed that "mind engenders truth upon reality" and that "the belief creates its own verification—wish was father to the thought." James might later call himself an "epistemological realist"; the challenge was to demonstrate how philosophy gives us knowledge of the real when pragmatism had advised us to forget about any antecedent reality, since it cannot be known apart from the activity that experiences it. Truth, the actual object of knowledge, cannot occur on its own; it remains dependent upon the knowing and acting self for its existence. John Jay Chapman was one of several critics who recognized that Jamesian pragmatism had no determining conditions beyond the self. "I have a notion," he wrote James, "that I could tell you what is the matter with pragmatism—if you would only stand still. A thing is not truth till it is so strongly believed in that the believer is convinced that its existence does not depend upon him. This cuts off the pragmatist from what truth is."[60] James would not allow philosophy to stand still in a world under the absolute dominion of change. Rather than be cut off from the real, he would race after it.

Pragmatism and Its Paradoxes

Although Henry Adams appears to have been unfamiliar with James's "The Will to Believe," he did engage in a thorough critique of the seminal inquiry that preceded it, the philosopher's two-volume *The Principles of Psychology* (1890). Adams confined his thoughts to marginal comments made on his copy of the 1902 edition of *Principles* (his great-great-grandfather John Adams engaged in the same marginalia exercise when he did critiques of the works of the eighteenth-century *philosophes*). In one respect it is curious that Adams remained skeptical of the promises of

59. James, *The Meaning of Truth*, 106.
60. Chapman is quoted in Edmund Wilson's discerning essay on him in *The Triple Thinkers* (New York: Oxford, 1963), 155.

the "new psychology" that was rapidly establishing itself as an exciting discipline at the turn of the century. For no less than James was Adams a man of deep feeling, sensitive to moods and emotions and perplexed by consciousness and memory. Yet although a meditative thinker, he professed in the *Education* to be averse to any form of self-contemplation. "Of all the studies, the one he would rather have avoided was that of his own mind. He knew no tragedy so heartrending as introspection."[61] The confession is a bit apocryphal, for the status of mind in the universe was one of Adams's preoccupations, and he realized that the acceptance of authority turned on the character of the assenting mind. As with many intellectuals confronted by the negations of modernism, Adams also liked to watch his own mind think.

Adams rejected James's approach to the traditional mind-body problem, wherein consciousness was seen as a sort of container through which simple, unmediated ideas passed. In an attempt to overcome the dualism of mind and object and combine the physical as well as the mental side of human existence, James argued that consciousness is a series of continuous states in which impressions combine to form images and apprehend relations, and thus the activity of consciousness is selective and purposeful rather than receptive and passive. Responding to *Principles of Psychology*, Adams felt that James had no real definition for consciousness, and he would not allow him to resort to such metaphors as "stream," "flow," or "theater" to conceal his ignorance. Adams agreed with "limiting the meaning of consciousness to the personal self of the individual," and he also underscored in pencil his emphasis that "*the cortex is the sole organ of consciousness in man.*" But he doubted that consciousness was a "cause" or "selecting agency." He also questioned whether consciousness was really a cognitive process that could subdue the emotions or whether it could even lead to "understanding."

Adams, who often wondered whether something other than himself moved his own mind, remained skeptical of the efficacy of mind to comprehend its own nature; and any exercise in thinking about what took place when thinking occurred led him to a kind of Freudian awareness that the mind might be divided against itself. In the *Education* he had observed that "the only absolute truth was the subconscious chaos below, which everyone could feel when he sought it."[62] In his response to James's work, he was certain that the mind was more a "dissolving unit" than an integrating agency, an observation that led him to wonder whether the rational faculties were even capable of accommodating the life-enhancing

61. Adams, *Education*, 432.
62. Ibid., 433.

"instincts." But above all, Adams could not bring himself to believe that the will could tame the emotions that preyed upon the mind. "The emotions," wrote Adams in the margin of James's book (perhaps thinking about the suicide of his wife), "ought to be involuntary nervous reactions incident to self-preservation. The mystery is in their astounding sensitiveness to the stimulant. How can a whisper kill? How can an external immaterial suggestion act on a physical organ? How can a thought outside the body, penetrate and kill the body? Why is will powerless to control it?"[63]

Adams's suggestion of a healthy will crippled by a sick mind presented James's philosophy with a paradox: man may be regarded as a self-actualizing creature only if he understands the causes of his actions, but he may understand them only by tracing the motives of his actions to inscrutable forces (or "feelings") beyond the control of the will. And if the mind is determined in its actions by antecedent causes unknown to consciousness, then it cannot be determined by reasons that are more willed than true. Scientism and voluntarism appeared to be at an impasse:

> James: All is fate . . . a resultant of what pre-exists. . . . This is really no argument for simple determinism. There runs throughout it the sense of a force which might make things otherwise from one moment to another, if it were only strong enough to breast the tide.
>
> Adams: If what? A man says: "I must die." Suppose he says: "I mean to live forever!" Will it breast the tide?
>
> James: Psychology will be psychology, and social science as much as ever (as much and no more) in this world, whether free-will be true in it or not. Science, however, must be constantly reminded that her purposes are not the only purposes, and that the order of uniform causation which she has use for, and is therefore right in postulating, may be enveloped in a wider order, on which she has no claims at all.
>
> Adams: Or why not in disorder? The whole dispute is whether order exists as an ultimate law of nature.
>
> James: [The heroic mind] can face [sinister and unwelcome experiences] if necessary, without for that losing its hold upon the rest of life.
>
> Adams: And supposing it decides not to face them? Is it a different will or is it less of an effort?

63. Adams's marginal observations are quoted in Max I. Baym, "William James and Henry Adams," *New England Quarterly* 10 (1937): 717–42.

> James: He [the hero] can *stand* this universe. He can meet it
> and keep up his faith in it in presence of those same
> features which lay his weaker brethren low.
> Adams: Twaddle![64]

One might conclude from the Adams-James dialogue that the historian offers us knowledge without hope and the philosopher courage without wisdom.[65] This is far from the crux of the matter. Indeed if James had his moments of doubt and despair, Adams desired no less to believe in the possibility of transcendence:

> It was surely no fault of his that the universe seemed to him real; perhaps—as Mr. Emerson justly said—it was so; in spite of the long-continued effort of a life-time, he perpetually fell back into the heresy that if anything universal was un-real, it was himself and not the appearance; it was the poet and not the banker; it was his own thought, not the thing that moved it. He did not lack the wish to be transcendental.[66]

Adams's lament reminds one of an observation made a half-century later by the literary scholar Lionel Trilling: "Only the self that is certain of its existence, of its identity, can do without the armour of systematic certainties."[67] Adams was perhaps no more uncertain about his self than James had been about the state of his "sick soul" just before he had his earlier anxiety attacks. The complexities of personality make it difficult to conclude that Adams found hope for authority in the vision of medieval unity while James saw the possibility of freedom only in a universe of modern diversity. Actually both thinkers were staking their claim to truth and authority by exposing the limits of knowledge, especially positivist and empirical knowledge. Even as scientific thinkers each came to believe in the efficacy of religion and spiritual vision as sources of hope, and each regarded the human subject as the source of the believer's convictions about the object of his beliefs, even "the reality of the unseen." Thus the message of the symbol of the Virgin and that of the essay "The Will to Believe" are strikingly identical: an idea or image is valued by the results it produces in the subjects who believe, adore, love, and act upon their convictions. Belief in the Virgin and belief in the will to believe become credible by virtue of the power to get things done. Although Adams's

64. Ibid., 740–42.
65. The observation that James offered America courage instead of wisdom is from Santayana's marvelous essay "William James," reprinted in *Santayana on America*, ed. Richard Colton Lyon (New York, 1968), 73–88.
66. Adams, *Education*, 63.
67. Lionel Trilling, *The Opposing Self: Nine Essays in Criticism* (New York, 1959), 37.

idea of religion implied more a state of possession than an action, the Jamesian penchant for the practical consequences of a creed could be found in the most mystical of faiths, even in miracles. "Of all Mary's miracles," wrote Adams, "the best attested, next to the preservation of the Church, was the building of it." "Who gains promotions, boons, appointments," wrote James, "but the man . . . [whose] faith acts on the powers above him as a claim, and creates its own verification."[68] James likened his theory of knowledge to "a credit system."[69] In this sense at least Adams was a pragmatist *malgré lui*, even though he had no sympathy for James's entire approach to knowledge and truth. Indeed, from Adams's point of view, James's attempt to bring philosophy and psychology to bear upon the reconciliation of science and religion may have done more to highlight than to resolve the problem of authority and truth itself.

The entire issue between Adams and James turned on the relationship of belief to faith and on the status of mind and will to both. In "The Sentiment of Rationality" (1879) James tried to reconcile the first two concepts: "Faith means belief in something concerning which doubt is still theoretically possible; and as the test of belief is the willingness to act, one may say that faith is the readiness to act in a cause the prosperous issue of which is not certified in advance. It is in fact the same moral quality which we call courage in practical affairs."[70]

The moral quality of courage may have different ways of expressing itself. In *Esther: A Novel*, published under the pseudonym of Frances Snow Compton in 1884, Adams addressed the whole matter of faith as an effort of the mind to be an expression of the will. The novel appears to take the conventional form of a love-plot. Esther Dudley, a young woman of twenty-five, her mother long deceased, finds herself the caretaker of an ailing father and his house. Lonely, uncertain, Esther inwardly craves for some larger transcendent significance while her outward solitary existence gives the impression that she is the ideal prospect for marriage. As in the novel *Democracy*, however, Adams creates a heroine who defies the American "type" of women as longing for the comforts of domesticity. The heroine in the first novel demands virtue in politics; the heroine in the second demands truth in religion. Her suitor, the Reverend Stephen Hazard, must persuade her of the reasonableness of his church to win her hand. At first he begins to dominate her by appealing to the "natural instincts" of her sex to marry and bear children and of women's "need to submit." If it were only a matter of romantic love Hazard would

---

68. Adams, *Mont-Saint-Michel and Chartres*, 110; James, "Will to Believe," *Writings*, 730–31.

69. James, "Pragmatism's Conception of Truth," *Writings*, 433.

70. James, "Sentiment of Rationality," *Writings*, 333.

have triumphed, as Esther came to identify completely with him and felt "she could believe whatever he believed and do whatever he did." But as she listens to his sermons she realizes she belongs to another world than that of the churchgoers and cannot honestly believe a word of his creed. Vainly Hazard tries to convince her that religion, like love, "is the great magnet of life," an irresistible force that cannot be denied. But when Esther later maintains that some people are made for faith and others not, Hazard replies, unaware of the inconsistency, that the skeptic can always overcome doubt—"It is a simple matter of will."

Another character, the palaeontologist George Strong, senses the crux of the problem. "The trouble with you is that you start wrong," he lectures Esther. "You need what is called faith, and are trying to get it by reason. It can't be done. Faith is a state of mind, like love or jealousy. You can never reason yourself into it." How long must one wait until faith comes along? asks Esther, and why is it that even when she wants to submit she cannot on her own resolve and cannot be made to by others? Strong replies coldly that what she really needs is the Roman Catholic Church. "They know how to deal with the pride of will."[71]

For James the will to believe could naturally lead to religion; for Adams the faculty of will could just as easily doubt belief as embrace it. The philosopher identified will with freedom of choice involving live options; the historian-novelist identified will with freedom of resistance against dead doctrines—particularly those man wants to impose upon woman.

While James remained convinced that will and imagination can alter reality and make things come true, Adams could never be persuaded that the content of faith could be voluntarily invoked. In *Mont-Saint-Michel and Chartres* the Virgin's compassionate qualities elicit on the part of her subjects an adoration and love that is felt rather than understood. Unlike James's sense of "belief," Adams's notion of "faith" could not be produced by the exercise of will alone. On the contrary, it is the power of faith that makes possible the activity of will. One cannot reason or will oneself from a state of belief to a state of faith, for while faith remains innocent of doubt, belief is continually exposed to it. And herein lies the modernist predicament. Man's critical capacity to question and inquire, the heritage of the Enlightenment, undermines his capacity to believe and act. With the worm of consciousness at the core of the mind, the mind paralyzes the will because it cannot rest content that it has arrived at truth, particularly when it pauses, James-like, at a tentative belief that has no content other than the utility of belief itself. Faith alone leaves man with no knowledge of his desire for more knowledge, the restless energy that

71. Henry Adams, *Esther: A Novel* (1884; New York: Peter Smith, 1965), 318.

brings forth both the progress of reason and the disillusion of mind. Beliefs are held, but faiths are lived. "You are so fortunate," Adams wrote his brother Charles, "to be able to forget self-contemplation in action."[72]

Faith prepares man for authority by precluding his capacity to dispute it, and faith requires not so much courage and will as an absorbing sense of the sacred, divine, transcendent, those qualities that endow ideas and images with spiritual significance and thereby remove them from the sphere of pragmatic utility. Even the Catholic Church, Adams reminds us, realized the primacy of faith to reason when it was forced to "bow" to the Virgin. Refuting the pragmatist solution to the problem of authority, Adams questioned James's conviction that supernatural beliefs could be affirmed on the basis of natural needs, that religious truth could be reconciled with psychological understanding, and that the will could restore what the mind had destroyed. Only faith could save the world from destruction by its own energies.

The problem of faith as an elusive, super-rational state of mind suggests that modernism may not necessarily be an exclusively modern predicament. Both Adams and James recognized that religion defied the two prevailing modes of philosophical thought: rationalism and its assumption of the mind as a container of immediate, accessible ideas; and empiricism and its assumption that knowledge derived primarily from sensation and perception. Sensing the gray dawn of modernism, Hegel believed that the subjective and objective could be transcended through a long-developing dialectic of self-consciousness that enabled man to appreciate the slow but destined realization of Spirit. Neither Adams nor James could be reassured that modern religion would survive through Hegelian philosophy, which—especially for an American philosopher like Josiah Royce— provided the consoling thought that God is radically immanent and dynamic in history as the unfolding "Absolute." As a "conservative Christian anarchist" Adams could hardly accept a Hegelian dialectic that used negation to move toward a "larger synthesis" to reach the "universal which thinks itself, contradiction and all," thereby denying the chaos and paradoxes of nature. James found Hegelian logic insufferable. "Its necessity, with no possibilities; its relations, with no subjects, make me feel as if I had entered into a contract with no reserved rights, or rather as if I had to live in a large seaside boarding-house with no private bedroom in which I might take refuge from the society of the place." James also shared Adams's doubts that Hegelianism could explain away evil and pain as resolving themselves in evolving dialectical necessities, as though good-

72. Henry Adams to Charles F. Adams, Jr., Feb. 14, 1862, *Adams Letters*, vol. 1, 282.

ness and pleasure would be guaranteed by "Hegel's metaphysical doctrine of the identity of opposites."[73]

Adams recognized, and no doubt James too, that religion as a philosophical proposition had reached an impasse long before Hegel tried to synthesize the sacred and the secular. *Mont-Saint-Michel and Chartres* reads as though the aesthetic beauty of the cathedrals must compensate for the cognitive uncertainties of God. The text contains many references to René Descartes, Blaise Pascal, and the seventeenth- and eighteenth-century controversies over metaphysics and natural theology. The twentieth-century modernist worry that neither metaphysical speculation could discover God's attributes nor empirical investigation prove His existence had troubled philosophy even before the Enlightenment. Adams describes Descartes teaching the "habit of doubt," a habit that Adams himself may have regarded as a curse in the disguise of a blessing. Beginning with doubt, Descartes assumed that reason could explain almost everything as a matter of clear and distinct definitions. Thus for Descartes God's existence guaranteed the presence of order and eternal truths as a logical inference drawn with the certainty of a geometrical theorem. But Cartesian metaphysics becomes the butt of a joke in *Esther* when Hazard tries to convince his flock that the church is no longer afraid of science:

> Analyze, dissect, use your microscope or your spectrum till the last atom of matter is reached; reflect and refine till the last element of thought is made clear; the church now knows with the certainty of science what she once knew only with the certainty of faith, that you will find enthroned behind all thought and matter only one central idea,—that idea which the church has never ceased to embody,—I Am: Science like religion kneels before this mystery; it can carry itself back only to this simple consciousness of existence. I Am is the starting point and goal of metaphysics and logic, but the church alone has pointed out from the beginning that this starting-point is not human but divine.[74]

Translated into the American idiom, Adams suggests, in a moment of wicked humor, that Descartes' logic ends where it began, with thinking man thinking of himself and his possessions:

> Most of the flock were busied with a kind of speculation so foreign to that of metaphysics that they would have been puz-

---

73. Adams, *Education*, 856, 1092, 1192; James, *Essays in Radical Empiricism* (1912; New York: Longman's, Green, 1947), 276–78.

74. Adams, *Mont-Saint-Michel and Chartres*, 639–40, 864–67; Adams, *Esther*, 190.

zled to explain what was meant by Descartes' famous COGITO
ERGO SUM, on which the preacher laid so much stress. They
would have preferred to put the fact of their existence on
almost any other experience in life, as that "I have five million," or "I am the best-dressed woman in the church, therefore I am somebody."[75]

Descartes' assumption that God's existence could be proven by man's
reflective assertion of his own presence only made Adams wonder how a
finite mind could claim to know an infinite mystery. Adams was more
drawn to Pascal, "one of the greatest men between Descartes and Newton," and the "finest religious mind" of the early Enlightenment. Pascal's
seventeenth-century *Pensées*, which were not discovered until 1842, possibly suggested to Adams that the agonies of the modernist mind were but
a continuation of Pascal's conviction that human reason could always deny
what it wanted most to affirm: "Descartes had proclaimed his famous
conceptual proof of God: 'I am conscious of myself, and must exist; I am
conscious of God, and He must exist.' Pascal wearily replied that it was
not God he doubted, but logic. He was tortured by the impossibility of
rejecting man's reason by reason."[76]

The pioneering Adams scholar Max I. Baym once observed that
Adams's "Prayer to the Virgin of Chartres is a metrical stylization of
Pascal's prose-lyric."[77] One does indeed find in the two thinkers the same
condition of man stymied by his desire to embrace the infinite, the same
sense that the heart feels what the mind can never know, the same understanding that science could only produce power but not reveal truth while
falsifying reality with reassuring systems, the same restless succumbing
to action at the expense of meditation, the same sinking feeling that reason
is impotent and irrelevant in the search for God and that man's ignorance
of God relates to his own ignorance of himself, and the same paradox
inherent in man's need to strive futilely after final syntheses when he
really finds pleasure in unresolved paradoxes. Yet here one runs up against
a puzzle. If Adams accepted Pascal's view of human nature as a hopeless
contradiction, why could he not accept Pascal's famous "wager" about
God's existence?

In Adams's thought Pascal stood as a reminder to Saint Thomas that
God was incapable of proof and that He cannot, as Descartes argued, be
thought to exist simply by asserting His existence within us through a

75. Adams, *Esther*, 190.
76. Adams, *Mont-Saint-Michel and Chartres*, 640.
77. Max I. Baym, *The French Education of Henry Adams* (New York, 1951), 202. Baym's
relatively early student is an important and somewhat overlooked work to which I am in
debt.

cognitive effort. Adams had little patience with Descartes' argument that one could begin by doubting everything and end by becoming intuitively aware of everything—especially one's own existence and that of God. But that one might accept God's existence by following "Pascal's famous avowal of it in the simile of the wager" was a proposition that could arouse Adams's curiosity but not his credulity. Pascal's reflections on the human condition Adams described as a "Prometheus lyric," an ordeal of doubt and disquiet in the endless struggle with divinity. Yet to follow Pascal was to enter the church and leave behind every trace of reason, science, and the interrogative mode of skepticism. "The mind that recoils from itself can only commit a sort of ecstatic suicide; it must absorb itself in God; and in the bankruptcy of twelfth-century science the western Christian seemed actually on the point of attainment; he, like Pascal, touched God behind the veil of scepticism." In choosing God one chooses a mystical oblivion that absorbs the observer and transcends the individual self. "In essence, religion was love; in no case was it logic. Reason can reach nothing except through the senses; God, by essence, cannot be reached through the senses; if he is to be known at all, he must be known by contact of spirit with spirit, essence with essence; directly; by emotion; by ecstasy; by absorption of our existence in his; by substitution of his spirit for ours." Adams remained the seeker who was not about to commit "ecstatic suicide."[78]

At several points in "The Will to Believe" James discusses the "celebrated passage" of Pascal's wager. Pascal, James noted, advised man to weigh the advantages and disadvantages of believing in an unknowable God. If such an act of belief could possibly bring man "eternal beatitude," clearly he had everything to gain and nothing to lose. At first James feels that "the language of the gaming-table" is offensive to the mind that requires reasons other than risking and betting for accepting specific religious ceremonies. "It is evident that unless there be some pre-existing tendency to believe in masses and holy water, the option offered to the will by Pascal is not a living option. Certainly no Turk ever took to masses and holy water on its account; and even to us Protestants these means of salvation seem such foregone impossibilities that Pascal's logic, invoked for them specifically, leaves us unmoved." Yet James makes the point that Pascal's wager is not a live option people will act upon, only then to better affirm that indeed it is one when measured against the timidity of the scientific mind. After citing all the contemporary skeptical empiricists who regarded it scandalous to believe in unproved sentiments, James demonstrates that their determination to be disinterested and objective is unnatural and that therefore science, instead of being liberating, is actually repressive. Thus James concludes by describing Pascal's wager as a "regular clincher" to his own argument and by advising readers to follow Pascal when confronted with moral and spiritual questions and consult not science but the heart.[79]

Adams sided with Pascal to demonstrate the limits of reason; James sided with Pascal to dramatize the possibilities of faith. Like Adams, the pragmatists had little use for Descartes and his feigned "paper doubts" (Peirce) about the foundations of knowledge. But James saw more clearly than Adams the uses to which even the pessimistic Pascal could be put. For Pascal anticipated the pragmatist claim that genuine knowledge must address itself not to the past but to the future. In this assumption the pragmatist and Marxist also meet. The point of philosophy is not to interpret the world, for reality cannot be known through thought alone. The aim of philosophy is to change the world. James would have philosophy help individuals to change themselves, and his will to believe was no less than a wager that a God who could not be known intellectually might be experienced emotionally, in practical life rather than in speculative thought. In this respect pragmatism, like Marxism and existentialism, partakes of the modernist predicament that God, nature, and history are no longer the domain of pure theoretical argument. What can be known is now a question of practice.

James tried to sustain the moral teachings of his father by updating traditional religious man with a new understanding of psychological man, a valiant effort to reassert the continuity of generational authority to overcome cultural modernity. In *The Varieties of Religious Experience* James grappled further with this issue by showing that science was concerned with objective knowledge and religion with subjective experience. The British philosopher R. G. Collingwood, "profoundly shocked" by James's book, wrote that "the mind, regarded in this way, ceases to be mind at all." Collingwood believed that the "natural ally" (to use James's expression) of religion was philosophy, not psychology, for while the latter can only account for the emotions that are experienced, the former must determine whether they are true. "To study a man's consciousness without studying the thing of which he is conscious is not knowledge of anything, but barren and trifling abstraction."[80] Perhaps a more gentle verdict was registered by the American philosopher George Santayana. James once told Santayana that he found philosophy a "curse" and rather than probing further into its riddles he was trying to "find a way out." When he em-

---

79. James, "The Will to Believe," *Writings*, 717–35.

80. R. G. Collingwood, *An Autobiography* (London, 1939), 93; *Religion and Philosophy* (London, 1916), 42.

braced psychology, James himself, Santayana observed, "did not really believe; he merely believed in the right of believing that you might be right if you believed."[81]

Believe in what? One of the paradoxes of the pragmatist's response to the crisis of religious authority is that it could very well undermine religion itself. If belief in God's existence answers to a deep human need, cannot an atheist use the same reasoning to arrive at the opposite conclusion? Those who fear God's judgment and His eternal punishment would surely be gratified to discover that it is emotionally satisfying to contemplate His nonexistence. James gave Americans the freedom to believe in whatever they chose to believe existed; but Adams had doubts about God's existence because he, like the Virgin, questioned the nature of a biblical God who created evil and then demanded of man that he overcome it. James liberated religion from the older philosophical criteria of knowledge and truth. Previously it had been accepted that we do not believe without a reason; James showed us that we do not believe without an emotion. But pragmatism can only make God believable instead of the object of belief. Since God cannot be found, we must find grounds for justifying our belief in him. Why?

Although James is usually regarded as a voluntarist who values indeterminism, on matters of religion he seemed more determined than Adams to prove the impossible. For all his cheerful pronouncements of an open-ended, unfinished "pluralistic universe," James sought in religion nothing less than cosmic certainty. He acknowledged that his belief in God grew from his desire to believe "in eternal moral order," the "deepest need in our breast." Belief in God "guarantees an ideal order that shall be permanently preserved."[82] In the end James's religious philosophy can only be regarded as a deep personal conviction that the universe still had divine dimensions that answered to man's need for order. Adams also felt that need, but he knew it was a personal quest that would forever lack metaphysical fulfillment. "Nothing was easier than to take one's mind in one's hand, and ask one's psychological friends what they made of it," Adams wrote in discussing the rise of the "new psychology" in the *Education*. James would have had no trouble making sense of Adams's mind, since they both experienced many of the same emotions as well as thoughts. But for Adams, James's purported philosophical solution to the riddle of God only returned the problem to where it started. "Philosophers agreed that the universe could be known only as motion of mind, and therefore as unity. One could know it only as one's self; it was psychology."[83]

81. Santayana, "William James," 79.
82. James, "Some Metaphysical Problems," *Writings*, 398.
83. Adams, *Education*, 432.

James could readily agree that all knowledge is mediated by the self. But in the philosopher's attempt to make thought respond to need in order that beliefs may produce effects, there is no way of knowing whether the object of knowledge is more willed than true. I need the satisfaction of certainty, unity, and order; therefore, God exists!

James's pragmatic response to the crisis of religious authority also had serious implications in the realms of politics and history. For James had successfully demonstrated that as long as science could not determine choice, man was free to choose; and, good democrat that he was, James was not about to tell Americans what to choose. Here James's advice was more psychological than philosophical, resting on the conviction that man's "passional nature" gave him the right to believe in whatever satisfied his needs and purposes. Yet providing a reason why we believe is a far cry from demonstrating that what we believe is true. Many beliefs, no matter how appealing, can be false because they do not correspond to reality. James, as we have seen, was not troubled by this dilemma because truth as correspondence could no longer be demonstrated, and thus he hoped to show how truth can be made to "happen" by transforming the actual state of things. Deciding to believe is deciding to act on the assumption that the world can be made to conform to our beliefs. The dilemmas inherent in that assumption became manifest during World War I, when every American intellectual had to decide whether to advocate intervention. Those who did decide to call for America's entry were assuming that the world would match their beliefs and hopes. Consider the purposes for which the *New Republic*'s liberals felt the need to enter the war: to control the forces of history (John Dewey), to influence the peace settlement (Walter Lippmann), to revitalize nationalism from its bourgeois slumbers (Herbert Croly), to block Germany's imperial ambitions (Thorstein Veblen), and to ally with the new Soviet state and support its formula of "peace without annexations and indemnities" (Charles Beard).[84] When World War II broke out, some of these same thinkers felt the need to warn America to stay out "no matter what happens," as Dewey exhorted. This issue will be taken up in a subsequent chapter. The point here is that such thinkers allowed their will to respond to their need to believe in a course of action whose rightfulness could only be verified in the realm of action. In this predictive theory of knowledge, the problem of truth is not so much resolved as projected.

In the disillusionment following World War I, James and the philosophy of pragmatism would be attacked by several writers, most notably

84. John Patrick Diggins, "The New Republic and Its Times," *New Republic* 191 (Dec. 10, 1984): 27.

Julien Benda in *La Trahison des clercs* (1927). Benda charged that reactionary nationalists and even fascists had taken to James to exalt the particular at the expense of the universal and direct action at the expense of disciplined meditation. The charge is historically questionable. Fascism regarded truth as a return to the glories of the past, welcomed the release of the irrational in politics, and espoused militarism and imperialism— everything James opposed. The subject of pragmatism and politics will be returned to later in the book in a discussion of totalitarianism and the Second World War. Here one must ask whether pragmatism helped resolve the crisis of authority.

Characteristically, James remained convinced that modern man could live without older ideas of truth and authority if he had the will to believe in himself. Such a resolution liberated the human condition by making the subject aware that he or she could be the author of his or her own actions. Small wonder that the philosophy of pragmatism could be hailed by James as "an alteration in the seat of authority that reminds one almost of the Protestant Reformation."[85] But Protestantism in America had also become identified with individualism, capitalism, and material success; and it was for this reason, among others, that Charles S. Peirce and John Dewey saw the necessity of going beyond James's version of pragmatism to develop a philosophy that would bind Americans to a moral community and provide criteria for decisions that were socially important and politically useful. James's stance had made belief more a matter of subjective conviction than philosophical explanation. Even though he could occasionally wax collectivistic and insist that people can profit by trading on each other's ideas; even though he could talk about the need for ideas to agree with realities and for philosophers to see how "all human thinking is discursified" because "all truth" is a language affair and "thus gets verbally built out, stored up, and made available for everyone";[86] even though, in short, he wanted to see philosophy take a linguistic as well as a public turn, James remained more concerned about the individual and his and her personal freedom and passional volitional nature in a universe where truths clashed rather than converged. His contemporaries also saw him as a pluralist who wanted to keep philosophy open to the eccentricities of feeling and spirit. The individual, Dewey reminded James, can be the "instrument" of truth but not its "author." Moving from James to Peirce and Dewey, American philosophical thought moved into the public sphere; and with Peirce the movement of knowledge no longer lies in belief but in doubt.

85. James, "Some Metaphysical Problems," *Writings*, 404.
86. James, "Pragmatism's Conception of Truth," *Writings*, 435.

4

Doubt and Deliverance: Charles Sanders Peirce and the Authority of Science

"Proud Man/His Glassy Essence"

A scholar once criticized Charles Sanders Peirce's philosophy because he did not seem to be "absolutely sure" of his own conclusions. Peirce took the complaint as praise rather than criticism. After a half-century of philosophical reflection and writing, Peirce felt he was on the right track precisely because he had arrived at no final conclusions. The modernist dilemmas that had troubled Henry Adams and would trouble many twentieth-century thinkers—the inability to move from knowledge to truth and from power to authority—scarcely troubled Peirce. To assume that philosophy could recover truth from the negations of modernism was itself an error. Metaphysicians like Hegel, Peirce liked to remark, possessed the answer before they formulated the question; thus they used philosophy merely to elaborate their own purposes. Genuine philosophy, he wrote, was "meant for people who want to find out; and people who want philosophy ladled out to them can go elsewhere. There are philosophical soup shops at every corner, thank God!"[1]

A contemporary of Adams and James, Peirce came from the same New England Brahmin background and imbibed the same intellectual currents of the latter half of the nineteenth century. A member of the Cambridge "Metaphysical Club," he enjoyed a peripheral association with Harvard University, which he attended as an undergraduate and graduate student. He also experienced some of the same pangs of metaphysical self-doubt that afflicted Adams and James, the wounds of the mind that cripple the spirit. In 1876, on a trip to Europe, Peirce suffered a paralyzing mental

1. *Collected Papers of Charles Sanders Peirce*, ed. Charles Hartshorne and Paul Weiss (Cambridge, 1962), vol. 2, xi, 90.

breakdown that lasted almost the entire year. Years later, around the time Adams was discovering the Virgin Mary, Peirce would also be justifying man's relation to God on aesthetic grounds, claiming that while the reality of God may be an unprovable hypothesis, belief in His existence was too appealing to the imagination to be dismissed as a delusion. Peirce was similarly brought up under the tutelage of a famous father who, like the elder James and Adams, was of "the purest Puritan stock," and he even wrote an unsigned essay on the elder Henry James's Swedenborgian religion, which perhaps provided Peirce a clue to how the younger James could reconcile his spiritual inclinations with his scientific methodology. Benjamin Peirce, the eminent Harvard mathematician, supervised his son's early education, calling upon young Charles to repeat the arguments of the great philosophers of the ages, only to "rip them up and show them to be empty." Spending many evenings with Charles demonstrating the bad thinking habits of traditional philosophers, the father impressed upon his precocious son one lesson he would never forget: the ways of authority and the life of the mind are incompatible.[2]

If one of the conditions of modernism is the capacity to live with unanswered questions, Peirce seemed to be born to face that challenge. In his youth the enigmas of science and mathematics fascinated him. He studied chemistry at the age of eight; at twelve he had set up his own amateur laboratory. The following year he devoured a philosophical treatise on logic. But even while studying the principles of reasoning in science and philosophy, the young Peirce remained more drawn to what seemed, at first glance, to defy reason. He had a keen interest in puzzles, chess moves, card tricks, and code languages, some of which he made up himself. Later in his life he once offered to teach children "cyclic arithmetic" by means of card games. But when asked how he could consistently pick out the seven of hearts from a shuffled deck, he had to write an explanation in a philosophy journal that went on for fifty-eight pages.[3]

Peirce remains one of the most baffling figures in the history of American philosophy. He entered Harvard at the age of fifteen and was a lackluster and undisciplined student, graduating seventy-ninth in a senior class of ninety-one members. He had a stubborn independence of mind

2. Ibid., vol. 1, 4–5; for details of Peirce's life I am indebted to Paul Conkin, *Puritans and Pragmatists: Eight Eminent American Thinkers* (New York, 1968), 193–205; C. Wright Mills, *Sociology and Pragmatism: The Higher Learning in America* (New York, 1964), 123–214; Paul Weiss, "Biography of Charles S. Peirce," in *Perspectives on Peirce,* ed. Richard J. Bernstein (New Haven, 1965), 1–12; Joseph Brent's *Charles Sanders Peirce: A Life* (Bloomington: Indiana University Press, 1993) appeared too late to be used.

3. Martin Gardner, "Mathematical Games of Charles Sanders Peirce: Philosopher and Gamesman," *Scientific American* 239 (1978): 18, 23–26.

and did not suffer fools gladly. He had been brought up in a Unitarian household and went through the motions of belonging to the episcopal church; yet like Adams's heroine in *Esther*, once he heard the sermon he knew he could neither believe nor will to believe conventional religious platitudes. No belief system seemed adequate to Peirce unless he added his own thoughts to it. After college he showed a capacity for hard work and sustained concentration with the U.S. Coast and Geodesic Survey. While doing research reports on such subjects as meteorology, gravity, and pendulum accuracy, he also wrote pioneering essays on logic and returned to Harvard to take a degree in chemistry and win the *summa cum laude*, the first time the prize was awarded. Despite his impressive accomplishments he never landed a permanent academic post. James's enthusiastic recommendations to a position at Harvard failed to convince President Charles Eliot. Aware that Peirce's "purely philosophical activity was known to comparatively few," James also recommended Peirce to a professorship at Johns Hopkins University. "I don't think it extravagant praise to say that of late years there has been no intellect at Cambridge of such general powers and originality," James wrote to President Daniel Coit Gilman. Peirce did hold a part-time instructorship at Hopkins in the early eighties, but his appointment was not renewed. Whether his dismissal was due to his highly technical and obscure lectures or to the improprieties of his personal life remains unclear. During the period he had divorced his first wife and married a French woman, Juliette Froissy.[4]

Peirce led an unstable, semi-bohemian personal life unsettling to the starch-collar respectability of the American academic world. Sometimes difficult and snobbish at social occasions he could also be charming and witty. A well-bred member of polite society, he defied conventions with his undisguised love for fine wines, beautiful women, and risqué affairs. When considering Peirce's personality together with his philosophy, the curious thing about his life-style was not that it was indulgent but that it was inconsistent. Although he praised science as a demanding discipline requiring humility, sacrifice, and self-control, he himself often lacked such qualities. Casual about commitments, he kept irregular hours and was forgetful about personal appearances. In his last years, after squandering a small inheritance and, when he could, living lavishly beyond his means, Peirce found himself penniless and in debt. James secured for him a small fund raised through old friends and students. During the same period Peirce was suffering from cancer and had to take morphine to ease the pain. All the while he kept writing papers—on science, epistemology,

---

4. James's recommendation of Peirce is quoted in John E. Smith's preface to *The Relevance of Charles Peirce*, ed. Eugene Freeman (La Salle, Illinois, 1983), 9.

religion, pragmatism—and although some appeared in the *Nation* and academic journals, no publisher was interested in bringing out a book. He died in 1914, an isolated, obscure figure without readers or followers. Yet heroically he kept thinking and reflecting to the end, sustained by the conviction that his version of pragmatism could answer to the problem of modernity and the crisis of authority.

Today Charles Sanders Peirce stands as a monument to the American mind at its soaring heights. The appearances of worldly failure concealed a genius, perhaps the greatest American philosopher since the eighteenth-century Puritan theologian Jonathan Edwards. Peirce is now recognized in Europe as well as America as the precursor of developments in geology, palaeontology, linguistics, semiotics, logical positivism, structuralism, the sociology of symbolic interaction, Freud's triadic theory of the mind, "binding algebra," binary calculus, phenomenology, the indeterminism of quantum mechanics, and the electric circuit theory later used in computers. Even the German Marxists Karl-Otto Apel and Jürgen Habermas have attempted to see a "logical socialism" in Peirce's theory of inquiry; the Italian semiotician Umberto Eco sees Peirce and Sherlock Holmes as fellow detectives who get to the truth by refined hunches and systematic guesswork as well as inference and deduction; others have found in Peirce's ideas anticipations of the philosopher Karl Popper's theory that scientific truth is tentatively valid until falsified. To thinkers everywhere it seems that Peirce is a philosopher for all problems. In Habermas's estimate, a subject to be discussed in the concluding chapter, Peirce holds the key to cracking open the problem of modernity.[5]

Pragmatism purports to reconcile theory and practice by making the latter the test of genuine ideas. Yet in the case of Peirce, theory and practice, his philosophical stance and his actual life, often stood in conflict. Although he regarded individualism as America's greatest curse, he himself lived and died an individual cloistered in his study in a remote house in Milford, Pennsylvania. Although he believed that the highest expression of science lay in the cooperative spirit and mutual interrogation carried on by a "community of inquirers," he did his greatest work as a solitary thinker impatient with the limitations of others. Perhaps these contradictions, or "compensations," as R. Jackson Wilson put it, are more apparent than real when one considers Peirce's deepest aspirations. No less than Henry Adams did Peirce hunger for unity, and hence he was as uncomfortable with James's pluralism and action-oriented volunteerism as was Adams. One source of unity Peirce found in religion was Christianity's central concept of love. Yet he also believed strongly that science

5. Max H. Frisch, "The Range of Peirce's Relevance," in *Relevance*, 11–37.

would forge unity out of diversity. Where Adams saw science as bringing forth power and energy and accelerating life beyond control and comprehension, and where Weber saw science bringing forth spiritual disenchantment, Peirce remained convinced that science was redemptive rather than destructive. Science could not help but result in unity, since communal and collaborative inquiry would require individuals to subjugate their pride and differences for the cause of truth. So devoted to scientific method was Peirce that he once likened it not only to the promise of religious faith but to the power of romantic love:

> The genius of a man's logical method should be loved and reverenced as his bride, whom he has chosen from all the world. He need not condemn the others; on the contrary, he may honor them deeply, and in doing so he only honors her more. But she is the one that he has chosen, and he knows that he was right in making that choice. And, having made it, he will work and fight for her, and will not complain that there are blows to take, hoping that there may be as many and as hard to give, and will strive to be the worthy knight and champion of her from the blaze of whose splendors he draws his inspiration and his courage.[6]

Adams, who also felt the pull of chivalrous romantic love, could have readily understood Peirce's attraction to a discipline as though it were a person. Indeed both thinkers knew that the modern age meant the triumph of masculinity and individuality and the loss of authority and unity. Peirce also admired medieval Catholicism, which had once offered the world a consensus based on reverence as well as reason. A philosophy based on authority had at one time achieved great things, not the least of which was scholastic theology and its aesthetic expression in towering cathedrals. Peirce could have reminded Adams that the modern dynamo and the Gothic cathedral derived from the same impetus, a commitment, whether by scientists or religious thinkers, to advance knowledge by means of subduing personal penchants and pursuing truth as a mutual endeavor. Although Peirce had no truck with the Catholic conviction that truth resides in papal authority, he did value the way art, science, and religion all came together in the Middle Ages:

> If anyone wants to know what a scholastic commentary is like, and what the tone of thought in it is, he has only to contemplate a Gothic cathedral. . . . Nothing is more striking in

6. Charles S. Peirce, "The Fixation of Belief," in *Philosophical Writings of Peirce*, ed. Justus Buchler (New York, 1955), 121–22; R. Jackson Wilson, *The Quest for Community* (New York: Wiley, 1968), 32–59.

either of the great intellectual products of that age than the complete absence of self-conceit on the part of the artist or philosopher. That anything of value can be added to his sacred and catholic work by its having the smack of individuality about it, is what he has never conceived. His work is not designed to embody his ideas, but the universal truth; . . . Finally, there is nothing in which the scholastic philosophy and the Gothic architecture resemble one another more than in the gradually increasing sense of immensity which impresses the mind of the student as he learns to appreciate the real dimensions and cost of each.[7]

One Peirce scholar, Murray Murphey, suggests that Peirce's great hope in the promises of science derived from his daily observations of his colleagues working cooperatively and selflessly in laboratories and in field research; another, James Hoopes, sees Peirce arriving at the notion of community from his prior study of logic and its relational unity.[8] The scientists' respect for each other's opinions, the striving to reach consensus in formulating theories, seemed to Peirce evidence that the scientific community had an almost religious devotion to the pursuit of universal truth, while logic and semiotics provided the guiding principles. Some German philosophers of our time claim Peirce believed science could not only resolve the problems of modernism but also redeem America by offering an alternative to individualism and capitalism. To suggest here that in America big business would also adopt such pragmatic methods, and thereby make cooperation, getting along, and "togetherness" the goal of managerial science, is to run ahead of our story regarding Peirce's legacy. A more immediate issue is the nineteenth-century ideological legacy against which Peirce himself had to struggle.

To the modernist mind plagued by uncertainty, Peirce asked for one virtue—patience. As a philosopher willing to take on almost any problem, Peirce remained convinced that collective inquiry will yield truth sometime in the future, not "the" truth but increasing approximations of it as error is progressively expunged. Peirce's notion of inquiry encouraged man to doubt, and by doing so to move to sounder footings of knowledge. This meant that philosophy was a continuous exercise of the fallible mind in a community setting. Unlike Adams, who believed that authority and unity could be achieved only at the intolerable cost of submission, Peirce somehow assumed that inquiry and mutual criticism could bring forth

7. Peirce, *Collected Papers*, vol. 8, 11.
8. Murray G. Murphey, *The Development of Peirce's Philosophy* (Cambridge, 1961); James Hoopes, ed., *Peirce on Signs: Writings on Semiotics by Charles Sanders Peirce* (Chapel Hill: University of North Carolina Press, 1991).

unity and that a scientific community engaged in such activity could constitute itself as an authoritative body. In this respect Peirce's quarrel was with the legacy of Emersonian America, with those who regarded themselves as self-reliant individuals, especially those who assumed their minds are so sovereign as to require neither language conventions nor social communities to see truth through the "transparent eyeball." The problem with the American, wrote Peirce with Emerson's heir James in mind, is that he sees himself as an individual and identifies his being with his will. Such identification is an illusion that can only result in frustration:

> The individual man, since his separate existence is mani-
> fested only by ignorance and error, so far as he is anything
> apart from his fellows, and from what he and they are to be,
> is only a negation. This man is,
>
>   . . . proud man,
>   Most ignorant of what he's most assured,
>   His glassy essence.⁹

"Thought Is More Without Us Than Within": Peirce versus James

When Peirce found out what James was doing with, or to, the philosophy of pragmatism, he immediately chose to identify his version of America's single original contribution to Western thought as "pragmaticism"—a term so "ugly," he quipped, as to be safe "even from kidnappers."¹⁰ Peirce, the real founding father of American pragmatism, remained certain that knowledge could not rest on a belief that had no basis other than the resolution and conviction of the individual believer. By identifying the right to act with the will to believe, James's philosophical answer to the problem of modernity had jeopardized the authority of truth itself.

In some respects Peirce's reservations about the philosophy of James resembled Adams's reservations about the politics of Theodore Roosevelt. "He was pure act," Adams wrote of TR, a man of iron will driven by "restless agitation" that sought "unlimited force," a Faustian statesman with "power wielded by abnormal energy" and unaware that the exercise of power required "self-control."¹¹ Adams had seen the identification of will with energy not only in Roosevelt's politics but also in Nietzsche's and Schopenhauer's philosophy. At the fin de siècle philosophers throughout the Western world wondered whether a theory of knowledge

9. Peirce, "Some Consequences of Four Incapacities," in *Philosophical Writings*, 250.
10. Peirce, *Collected Papers*, vol. 5, 276–77.
11. Adams, *Education*, 417.

based upon the power of will would result in the will to power. Significantly, when Peirce used the term "power" it had more to do with discipline than with action, "the creative power of reasonableness, which subdues all other powers, and rules over them with its sceptre, knowledge, and its globe, love."[12] James wanted to make man aware of his resources of power in order to augment them; Peirce wanted to make Americans aware of the need to legitimate power in order to accept authority.

James's "radical empiricism" was one example of a modernist formulation that enhanced the realm of power and freedom at the expense of authority and duty. James's theory, which gave priority to the raw stuff of "pure experience," seemed to Peirce to locate all knowledge in and within experience itself, even the life-history of a single individual. More concerned with the general than the particular, Peirce sought to establish the logical principles of knowledge in which experience is organized and understood. Mathematics represented one mode of thought in which the mind's categories impose the symbolic order of notations on the set of rational numbers. Peirce himself often vacillated between idealism and realism, between the belief that objects are internal to the mind and that they exist independent of consciousness. But Peirce was more systematic than James, whom he liked to tease by remarking that he could clarify certain problems in philosophy for him if only James would give up the impression that he couldn't understand mathematics. James remained convinced that the shortest way to get around the cognitive problem of truth was to make it happen through belief, will, and action. More committed to the objectivity of genuine knowledge, Peirce took the long route and spent his life working on a conceptual analysis of the logic of discovery.

The differences between James and Peirce highlight the rich diversity of American pragmatism. Both were modernists in recognizing that there could be no return to older schools of philosophy. But while Peirce loved to savor ideas, James seemed to fear their seductive temptations if they placed demands upon the individual and constrained the free activity of the mind. In "The Sentiment of Rationality" James emphasized the sufficiency of momentary experience as valid knowledge requiring no necessary explanation; hence successful reasoning had its own inner criteria free of the "ontological wonder sickness" that infected thinkers like Schopenhauer and other seekers pursuing the phantom of foundations.[13] Peirce believed that foundations could be established and the object of knowledge progressively approximated through logic, science, and semi-

12. Peirce, *Collected Papers*, vol. 5, 365.
13. James, "Sentiment of Rationality," *Writings*, 317–44.

otics. But he remained certain that the validity of thinking has no bearing on what the particular thinker thinks is valid. James sought to will belief and inspire action, Peirce to organize it and clarify meaning. For James, truth was a matter of conviction; for Peirce, it remained independent of what the believer believed about it.

James's temperament ran in the opposite direction. He remained suspicious of "systems" based upon logical coherence and other formal properties that presuppose fundamental categories of thought through which truth becomes introspectively discoverable. In his essay "Hegel and His Method," James criticized what he regarded as mental constructions like the dialectic and the idea of negation, which implied an inner necessity unfolding in all things, in mind as well as matter. "Once catch well the knack of this scheme of thought and you are lucky if you ever get away from it. It is all you can see."[14] Though no Hegelian, Peirce did believe that conceptual thinking was essential and that ideas could be part of an evolving, interrelated system. In Peirce's view, James was too anthropomorphic, too willing to make man the measure of all things. This egocentrism seemed to Peirce another example of the nominalistic fallacy of denying the existence of anything beyond the immediate activities of a particular mind. "One must not take a nominalistic view of Thought as if it were something a man had in his consciousness," Peirce wrote to James in 1902. "Thought is more without us than within. It is we that are in it, rather than it in any of us."[15]

The nominalist-realist controversy that had originated in medieval philosophy fascinated Peirce as it had Adams. The nominalist conceit that the knowing subject creates the world with his own categories and verbal descriptions seemed to Peirce to be at the heart of James's difficuties. To Peirce, James seemed to want to make philosophy less the long, arduous search for truth than the springboard for immediate beliefs and actions. Thus he used pragmatism to instruct Americans to turn toward facts, action, and power. The Jamesian "doctrine," complained Peirce, "appears to assume that the end of man is action." Peirce held that action, and the belief that motivated it, would always remain individual and singular, and such categories could not lend themselves to interpreting and evaluating conduct according to general standards and values. Action may be the result of thought, but it is not necessarily its purpose or meaning. Actually, James's equation of philosophy with praxis had some basis in Peirce's original formulation of pragmatism, in which the philosopher was taught to regard first and foremost the "practical bearings" of theoretical ideas.

14. James, "Hegel and His Method," in *Writings*, 516.
15. Peirce, *Collected Papers*, vol. 8, 189.

But later Peirce felt the need to distinguish his pragmatism from that of James in order to save philosophy from the worship of power and action at the cost of scientific authority and community. It may be the case that "we believe the propositions we act upon," wrote Peirce in reference to James. "But pure science has nothing at all to do with action." Science is a matter of observation and verification, a methodological procedure in which the investigator holds to no established beliefs and arrives at conclusions only to see them challenged and changed. "There is thus no proposition at all in science which answers to the conception of belief."[16]

The problem of mind and consciousness seemed less pressing to Peirce, in part because he believed that pragmatism should be more involved with the external world of fact and experience than with the inner world of mind and its emotions. Peirce, to be sure, loved to speculate on phenomenology and would wonder, for example, how a man could be surprised to know that he was surprised. But pondering experience as it immediately presents itself was not enough for Peirce, who wanted the philosopher to rise above his own subjectivity, to appreciate how thinking itself puts one in touch with the mediating thoughts that reach after meaning. Like Adams, he felt that introspection, while irresistible, was an infinite labyrinth of emotions playing hide-and-seek with thought.

Peirce similarly doubted that James had resolved such philosophical riddles as free will and consciousness. Responding to James's "Dilemma of Determinism," Peirce pointed out that freedom cannot be identified with the faculty of will because the act of choosing antedates the will to act.[17] James's denial that consciousness exists as an "entity" Peirce regarded as a false issue. He cited a number of philosophers writing about the phenomenon with a variety of descriptions none of which had the connotations of a fixed state. "This word," Peirce wrote James in reference to his use of *entity*, can only be "a sign the writer is setting up some man of straw whom he imagines to entertain opinions too absurd for definite statement."[18]

Peirce was not altogether sure that James's notion of consciousness as a continuous "stream" could explain very much. The term implied smoothness, but Peirce thought of the turbulence in oceans. How could a smooth, flowing experience explain the disruptions and shocks that shake the mind? Here Peirce raised the same question that Adams had in respect to James's theory of consciousness. Does not the sudden presence of the unexpected in the mind indicate that something other than

16. Peirce, *Collected Papers*, vol. 5, 2; vol. 1, 347.
17. Peirce to James, Mar. 18, 1897, in *Collected Papers*, vol. 8, 209.
18. Peirce to James, Sept. 28, 1904, in *Collected Papers*, vol. 8, 198.

the mind is impinging upon it? The reality of the intruding world remained more real for Peirce, a reminder that objective facts and events cannot be reduced to experience. Even though reality as something that does not necessarily depend upon thought and its representations cannot be known for sure, the existence of an environment makes itself felt through its dyamic interaction with the subject. James could agree that knowledge cannot play fast and loose with its object. But James was ambiguous on this issue, and critics chided him for making knowledge so mind-dependent that truth is produced in action rather than found in reality, a deed rather than a discovery.[19] In his early years James convinced himself that mind could impose, or "engender," truth upon reality. But Peirce was impressed with the degree to which reality can resist man's efforts. Thus he defined "existence" as "that mode of being that lies in opposition" to suggest that a table, for example, is hard, heavy, inert, wide, and opaque. Willfully to refuse to acknowledge the table's existence risks bumping into it. Facts fight for their own existence, Peirce argued, and the manner in which hard facts surprise the mind led him to believe in a "double consciousness" consisting of the ego and his expected ideas and the non-ego, "which is the strange intruder in his abrupt entrance."[20]

Peirce wanted to elevate the idea of consciousness from the individual's encounter with "pure experience" to a grander vision, one in which the thinker is part of an ongoing process of interpretation and communication that rises above the private and subjective. Similarly, Peirce wanted to see philosophy serve truth, not therapy. "No man can be logical who reckons with his personal well-being as a matter of overwhelming moment," he advised James. If James's answer to modernism was to probe the emotions as a psychologist, Peirce's answer was to reaffirm reason as a logician. The former believed that modern man needed to learn how to live without traditional authority, the latter that he needed to find it anew. James sought to get around the correspondence theory of truth by making ideas turn not on the validity of representation but on the intensity of conviction as well as experiential consequences. Peirce wanted the authority of truth to be independent of individual will and desire, and thus ideas must be proven not simply by action but "by some external permanency, by something upon which our thinking has no effect."[21]

A comparison of James and Peirce suggests the ways in which a philoso-

19. See, for example, Paul Carus, *Truth on Trial* (Chicago: Open Court, 1911).
20. Peirce to James, Sept. 28, 1904, in *Collected Papers*, vol. 8, 199–204; Peirce on the "strange intruder" is quoted in W. B. Gallie, *Peirce and Pragmatism* (Edinburgh, 1952), 196.
21. Peirce to James, Mar. 13, 1897, in *Collected Papers*, vol. 8, 187; "The Fixation of Belief," 18.

phy held in common can harbor two uncommon outlooks. Peirce was less concerned with self-realization of desire than with self-control of discipline, less concerned with the responsiveness of the knowing subject than with the actual behavior of the observed object, less concerned with religion as a psychological experience than as a cosmic vision of human evolution, less concerned with belief as that which is acted upon than as that which contributes to stability, agreement, and the development of "concrete reasonableness," and less concerned with truth as a state of satisfaction that each person pursues than as the gradual, systematic convergence of inquirers upon a consensus that all are obliged to accept.

It could be said that Peirce protested too much James's version of pragmatism in order to distance himself from what appeared to be its highly individualistic and almost anarchistic implications. Some philosophers have noted that there was nothing in Peirce's original formulation of pragmatism that made James's emphasis upon will and action illegitimate.[22] But as the historian Hoopes has pointed out, James either never read or did not understand Peirce's essays of 1867–71, where he argued that external reality can be known by the internal mind, and that truth, transcending the conditions of its production by action, can influence thought. Yet in a deeper personal, and larger historical, sense, the differences between the two thinkers may illuminate a tension at the core of the so-called "American mind."

In the years immediately prior to the outbreak of the First World War, Van Wyck Brooks and George Santayana wrote essays in an attempt to analyze this intellectual conflict. In their view the dilemma of the American mind lay in the conflict between theory and practice, between the loftiness of abstraction and the starkness of the concrete, between thought and utility, contemplation and action, between the metaphysical thinker who feels the need to push thought as far as it can go to get at the bottom of things, and the instrumental thinker who, perhaps sensing that there is no bottom, settles for a workable, expedient adjustment to change. The theoretical spirit found expression in Jonathan Edwards, Emerson, and Melville, the practical in Ben Franklin, William Dean Howells, and Thomas Edison. In American pragmatism, however, this distinction between theory and practice breaks down, even though a residue of tensions remains between Peirce and James. The latter could not wait to rush outdoors to put his ideas into practice; the former felt more fulfillment in analyzing the presuppositions of thought and in insisting that "pure

22. See, for example, William J. Gaven, "Peirce and the Will to Believe," in *Relevance*, 145–53; and Vincent G. Potter, "Charles Sanders Peirce, 1839–1914," in *American Philosophy*, ed. Marcus G. Singer (New York, 1985), 21–41.

theoretical knowledge or science, has nothing to say concerning practical matters."[23] But even Peirce had to agree that detached philoshical rationalism was a conceit that denied man's emotional nature and that science was nothing until its theories were tested in practice. The real difference separating Peirce and James was not necessarily the distinction between theoretical speculation and practical application, nor rationalism versus empiricism nor realism versus nominalism. Rather, it was the old dilemma of freedom versus authority. James valued most that which emanated from the self in its encounter with experience shaped by the will; Peirce valued that which the self encountered as having the capacity to be recognized as something permanent and external to the will. In this respect the Jamesian thirst for freedom runs from Jefferson to Thoreau to Mark Twain, while Peirce's search for authority runs from, among other figures, John Adams to Henry Adams.

Several American writers, especially Herman Melville and Henry Adams, are generally regarded in political terms as "conservative" because they write on the subject of authority. A closer look at their works would suggest that they write about it precisely because they want to expose its existing expressions as inauthentic rationalizations based on the false emotions of insecurity or the false arguments of necessity. When Peirce wrote on the "methods of authority" in his first seminal essay, "The Fixation of Belief" (1878), he was also trying to find the basis of true authority for the modern age. Yet when the essay first appeared in *Revue Philosophique*, the French editor and translator did a little rewording to make Peirce sound as though he were the voice of the Paris Commune demanding the destruction of all authority![24] Actually Peirce was deeply concerned about the fate of authority in the face of modernity, so concerned that in some respects he was closer to Adams than to his fellow philosopher James.

Between Realism and Nominalism: Adams and Peirce

The first problem that should be considered in a comparison of Adams and Peirce is the problem of historical knowledge. Adams would become an anguished precursor of modernism; long before relativism became rampant in the twentieth-century mind, leading scholars like Charles Beard into an impasse, Adams was the first historian to confess that historical

23. Peirce, *Collected Papers*, vol. 1, 347; Van Wyck Brooks, *America Comes of Age* (New York, 1913); George Santayana, "The Genteel Tradition in American Philosophy" (1913), in *The Winds of Doctrine and Platonism and the Spiritual Life* (New York: Harper, 1957), 186–215.

24. Gerard Deledalle, "Les articles pragmatistes de Peirce," *Revue Philosophique* 170 (1980): 17–29.

truth had eluded him. Peirce once remarked that "the essence of truth is its resistance to being ignored."[25] But Peirce was referring to the present, not the past, the way in which a brute fact or unexpected thought may intrude upon the mind. Adams loved to admit that he knew the depths of his ignorance but still could not touch truth. The teaching of history at Harvard was thus a torture, since he saw no way to relate its facts to any existing theory and could give it dramatic effect only at the cost of falsifying it. After Gibbon the spectacle of historical method was a scandal. History, like politics, lost both pride and shame. "It was a hundred years behind the experimental sciences."[26]

In his history of the administrations of Jefferson and Madison, Adams had sought to make the sequence of cause and effect his focus of analysis. But the final volume, it will be recalled, concludes with Adams being unable to established the precise causes of the War of 1812, even though he judged the outcome of the war salutary. Later Adams found consolation in the new sciences of radium and thermodynamics, which seemed to replace strict causality with indeterminism and randomness. By the time Adams wrote *Mont-Saint-Michel and Chartres* he knew his exploration into the Middle Ages was more art than science, a narrative in which his philosophical and poetic imagination had free rein.

Peirce did not feel the crisis of historical knowledge acutely reflected in the writings of Adams, Nietzsche, and other modernists, particularly those who sensed that any intepretation of the past may be little more than the scholar's own imposition of the will to mastery in the name of objectivity. On the few occasions when he wrote on history, Peirce questioned the "balancing of likelihoods" in historical testimony, since there was no scientific way of using probability to get at veracity. The historian can formulate a hypothesis to see which relevant facts might be explained by it. And in addition to demonstrating "growth," the lessons of the history of science also demonstrated how progress flourishes when inquiry is uninhibited and how a historical sensibility can therefore free us from the "tyranny of our preconceived notions."[27] But in what sense can historical research be approached in the spirit of scientific inquiry? The philosopher Arthur O. Lovejoy was the first to raise this question. Since pragmatism rests upon a future-based verificationist theory of truth, how can it offer meaningful judgments about that past?[28] Peirce recognized the dilemma. "History would not have the character of a true sci-

---

25. Peirce, *Collected Papers*, vol. 2, 139.

26. Adams, *Education*, 301.

27. Peirce, *Collected Papers*, vol. 7, 89–147.

28. Arthur O. Lovejoy, *The Thirteen Pragmatisms and Other Essays* (Baltimore, 1963): see also Lovejoy's "Present Standpoints and Past History," in *The Philosophy of History in Our Time*, ed. Hans Meyerhoff (Garden City, N.Y., 1959), 173–87.

ence," he wrote, "if it were not permissible to hope that further evidences may be forthcoming in the future by which the hypotheses of the critics may be tested. A theory which should be capable of being absolutely demonstrated in its entirety by future events, would be no scientific theory but a mere piece of fortune telling. On the other hand, a theory, which goes beyond that which may be verified to any degree of approximation by future discoveries is, in so far, metaphysical gabble."[29]

Peirce would not say precisely what kinds of historical knowledge must await evidence forthcoming in the future, other than old documents that may later turn up. But he did conclude by suggesting that all beliefs—religious, personal, etc.—have a basic element of expectation and that "knowledge which should have no possible bearing upon any future experience—bring no expectation whatever—would be information concerning a dream."[30] Peirce refused to cease having expectations about the possibility of historical knowledge being brought to bear upon the present and eventuate in the future. Adams looked backward with despair, Peirce forward with hope. Peirce would have agreed with Adams that the forces of history continue into the present and will have some kind of determining influence upon the future, even though both authors saw the interplay of fate and chance and order and chaos. As a pragmatist Peirce also believed that the past can be studied through the present events that are its effects. Adams, however, was concerned not only with consequences but with causes, not only the persisting influences but also the original impetuses that could make history understandable in light of sequential patterns or some other principle of explanation. To Peirce, in contrast, the past had already actualized itself, and hence there was no point in worrying about it. "If you complain to the Past that it is wrong and unreasonable, it laughs. It does not care a snap of the finger about Reason." Apparently Peirce was not going to lose sleep over the classical adage *Nihil est sine ratione* ("Nothing is without reason"). Peirce was content to conclude that the past may act upon us, but only in ways that make life mechanical rather than creative and habitual rather than resourceful. Thus the true liberating power of mind "must refer to the future."[31] If Adams had only taken the pragmatic turn in modern thought, his troubles would have been over. One may well dwell upon the past historically, but one cannot change it scientifically. What happened, happened. Those who cannot forget the past, to reverse Santayana's dictum, are condemned to rethink what cannot be redone.

29. Peirce, *Collected Papers*, vol. 5, 380.

30. Ibid., 383.

31. Ibid., vol. 2, 44, cited in the valuable article by Joseph L. Esposito, "Peirce and the Philosophy of History," *Transactions of the Charles Sanders Peirce Society* 19 (1983): 157; Peirce, *Collected Papers*, vol. 5, 312.

Peirce's point, of course, was that philosophers should be concerned about the future instead of the past, because even though history provides a "storehouse" of knowledge, the pragmatist can only influence and control future conduct and events. This stance, however, did not prevent Peirce himself from becoming an intellectual historian with a deep interest in the thought of past thinkers whose minds could be analyzed and appreciated apart from the whole question of change and control. Here Peirce and Adams agreed: the crisis of modernity was not so new that past philosophical traditions should be dismissed as having no relevance to it.

Had Peirce known of Adams's *Mont-Saint-Michel and Chartres*, he would perhaps not have chided its author, as James had, for allowing himself to become absorbed in the philosophy of the Middle Ages. Adams regarded the nominalist-realist controversy as a great "scholastic tournament" that pitted Abelard against William of Champeaux. He recognized that the philosophical fate of the Catholic Church hung on the thread of a fierce theological debate, one whose issues had troubled thinkers in the late-nineteenth-century age of science as much as it had troubled earlier thinkers in the age of faith: whether order or chaos was the rule of the universe, whether unity or diversity was the ultimate reality, and whether truth had a real existence outside of human experience. Aware of recent discoveries in modern physics, Adams observed that "science only repeats what the Church said to Abelard, that where we know so little, we had better hold our tongues."[32]

Adams delighted in re-creating the debates between realists and the nominalists: the former assuring themselves of ultimate universals and ideal types, the latter just as convinced that only particulars are represented in language and experienced in perception. Noting that the distinction between the ideal as a form made by God and the ideal as a name imagined by man was as old as Plato and Aristotle, Adams observed that "the whole of philosophy has always been involved in the dispute" between realists and nominalists. Adams also wanted to show that both doctrines would prove dangerous to the Church once their logical implications were pushed to extremes. In dramatically restaging the debate between William and Abelard, Adams sought to demonstrate how the realist position could only result in pantheism and the nominalist one in materialism. In the first instance, the assumption that universals cannot be divided would make every aspect of existence, the bad as well as the good, part of one continuous "divine essence" in which everything is identical and man cannot be held responsible for his actions. In the second instance, the assumption that there is no reality except in the mind that conceives

32. Adams, *Mont-Saint-Michel and Chartres*, 326.

it makes truth tantamount to the limits of factual experience and the activity of knowing.[33]

Adams indicated the ways in which the realist-nominalist dispute extended into the early Enlightenment. As noted earlier, he had sided with Pascal against Decartes, agreeing with the former that at best one might approach God as a "leap" of faith, whereas reason and logic were helpless to prove God's existence simply by asserting man's presence. One part of Adams was a nominalist who believed that the finite cannot comprehend the infinite. On the other hand, Adams was not quite prepared to deny that universals exist and that all reality inheres only in the mind. Such a proposition would leave philosophy where Spinoza left it—with God implicit in all things and no explanation of how human nature became alienated from its universal essence and individual mind and matter from spirit. The following passage consists of notes Adams made on the margins of a text of Barthelemy Haureau's *De la philosophie scolastique* (1850):

> What is an abstract concept?
> Concepts exist, qua mind, or not. What exists qua mind, is real qua mind.
> An abstract concept is either real qua mind, or does not exist.
> If it is real, qua mind, how can it be, as Haureau says, the opposite of reality?
> A triangle is an abstract concept?
> A triangle exists, qua mind, or not?
> If it exists, qua mind, it is real qua mind, not the opposite of reality.
> If it does not exist and is not real, qua mind, how can it remain with the universal form. Or does he mean that, after abstracting the individual from the universal mind, nothing remains but the abstract concept by the universal mind of its own universality?
> Is not this the doctrine of Spinoza?
> What then, can produce individuation either in mind or matter except a third force? and so on ad infinitum?[34]

It was characteristic of Adams to leave things unsettled, as though modern man carried in his breast not the scarlet letter of sin but the question mark of doubt. Adams's ambitious study of early American history, one recalls, also ended with a series of interrogations about the Republic's destiny. Significantly, Peirce had some of the same tendencies

33. Ibid., 328–30, 391–92.
34. Adams, quoted in Baym, *The French Education*, 188–89.

of the probing mind whose aspirations to knowledge knew no limits. He was just as impatient with easy explanations and, like other modernists, delighted in turning them into harder questions. But Peirce went further and refused to leave modern thought in an interrogative impasse. Peirce showed how one can accept all the impediments to knowing and still have access to reality. James saw no genuine antithesis between reality and experience, and Adams came to see experience itself as problematic and thus later quested for something beyond it. Peirce believed truth and reality external to thought and experience; yet they could still be known even if they were representational and not immediate to the mind. Had Adams been aware of Peirce's rare stance, he might have appreciated why both philosophy and history could continue to search for the truth of things in the objective nature of events. Nevertheless, the affinities between Peirce and Adams may explain why both saw limitations in James's version of pragmatism.

For one thing, Peirce had the same quizzical response as did Adams to James's seminal essay, "Does Consciousness Exist?" After quoting James's insistence that the sole organ of consciousness lies in the cortex, Peirce demands more: "The reasoning seems pretty loose for settling all the important questions implied in the statement. What is consciousness anyway?"[35] Although Peirce shared Adams's skepticism toward introspective knowledge, he did not believe that a modernism that begins with the mode of doubt need end in the mood of despair. Adams concluded that the magnificent cathedral of Chartres had been built on faith and that Aquinas's attempt to bring reason to bear on religion threatened the entire edifice of architecture as well as that of philosophy. Peirce felt even more deeply that the power of reason had been demonstrated in the Middle Ages and that the modern philosopher could build his own "architectonic" system of ideas. Moreover, where Adams had assumed that the realist-nominalist controversy had ended in a draw, Peirce declared the realists the winners and proceeded to construct modern pragmatism upon a "critical realism" whose metaphysical postulates rested on the fallibility of meaning rather than the foundations of truth, on what could be infinitely revised rather than ultimately resolved.

If Adams identified with Blaise Pascal and the mind's sobering inadequacies, Peirce identified with Duns Scotus and its infinite possibilities. Peirce praised Duns Scotus as "one of the greatest metaphysicians of all time." The medieval debates between Duns Scotus and the nominalist William of Ockham impressed Peirce as the most dramatic peak of philosophy, the point at which epistemological issues were clarified in intellec-

---

35. Peirce, *Collected Papers*, vol. 8, 64.

tual combat. Identifying himself as a Scotist realist, Peirce felt strongly that the earlier critique of nominalism had important implications for the modern age.[36]

First of all, the critique would save the modern world from relativism by demonstrating that how things come to be known, whether through the modes of signification or any other procedure, need not be synonymous with the things themselves. When Peirce reminded James that thought was "more without us than within," he was distinguishing thought from thing and suggesting, as did the medieval realists, that a thing might be known independently of any immediate thought about it if the philosopher keeps in mind that all knowledge is potential and seeks to move beyond itself. Even if reality remains "without us," that is, non-dependent upon our thoughts, the activity of knowing is driven by the mind's restless desire to know the object of knowing, and nothing can be ultimately unknowable as long as scientific inquiry continues indefinitely. Moreover, Peirce's conviction that reality could always resist false interpretations reinforced his conviction that the real is something other than the will to believe (James) or to deny (Adams). The real retains its general character regardless of what particular people think about it. Such convictions led Peirce to the conclusion that modern philosophy could be in harmony with modern science, since both were based on the medieval insight that "general principles are really operative in nature."[37] It is here, on the question of how modern science is to be interpreted, that Peirce and Adams diverge completely, revealing in the American mind two opposing responses to the challenge of modernity.

The *Education* contains a chapter called "The Grammar of Science," the title taken from the widely discussed book by the British scholar Karl Pearson. It is in this chapter that Adams discusses the implications of Madam Curie's "metaphysical bomb" and other developments that introduced an element of indeterminacy into science. That the emission of radium rays seems to behave erratically, and that a physical law could paradoxically reverse itself so that the dissipation of energy moves from disorder back to equilibrium, suggested to Adams that the traditional mechanical laws of science had to be reconsidered if not altogether rejected. Pearson's *The Grammar of Science* (1882) had already urged caution and humility against the empiricist's claim to metaphysical conceptions of truth independent of sense perception. Science is not explanatory but merely descriptive, and the assumption of causality and prediction is possible only because of the sense impressions of regularity and repetition.

36. Ibid., vol. 4, 22.
37. Ibid., vol. 5, 67.

"Pearson shut out of science everything which the nineteenth-century had brought into it," Adams observed noting that causality, order, harmony, and beauty were now regarded as impressions without foundations. Adams's well-known dictum, "Chaos was the law of nature; order was the dream of man," summed up his response to Pearson's thesis that scientific knowledge is a grammar. Thus the mind creates its own reality based on its will to believe in those comforting convictions that enable man to overcome his estrangement from nature. But the nominalist faces a rendezvous with reality. For the latest discoveries in science are themselves alienating to those "uniformitarians" who assumed they would find in the universe a "larger synthesis." With not a little glee, Adams concluded: "At last their universe had been wrecked by rays, and Karl Pearson undertook to cut the wreck loose with an axe, leaving science adrift on a sensual raft in the midst of a super-sensual chaos."[38]

In Peirce's response to *The Grammar of Science* there is no wreckage to salvage. If Pearson set science adrift it was because he mistakenly assumed that thought has no way of getting beyond itself; that which is in the mind's mediating impressions is all there is. But beyond the sense impressions through which knowledge is built there are deeper attributes of the mind that can apprehend instantly. Peirce criticized the author of *The Grammar of Science* for confounding psychology with logic. The mind may swim in a sea of chaotic impressions but, Peirce insisted, "our logically initial data are percepts." Peirce argued that percepts enable man to know before he is aware of knowing, so that, for example, he sees red itself and not, as the positivists claim, only patches of color. Adams had agreed with positivists like Henri Poincaré that hypotheses are necessary in science to organize sense data and as such are procedural conventions or even the product of the imagination and thus have no basis in reality independent of verification. Peirce, in contrast, held that reality may exist apart from individual thinkers, but the collective process of scientific inquiry eliminates differing individual views and thereby renders reality more accessible to the methodological progression of knowledge. Reality is itself mental, since thought itself is a sign system, and interpretations of reality must survive repeated tests and gain the acceptance of the scientific community. When pressed about the promises of science, Peirce insisted that objects experienced as present in thought have the same features as they exist independent of mind. Peirce's conviction that everything real is eventually knowable enabled him to believe that science had a far sounder foundation than Adams's "supersensual chaos" and that science discovers a reality beyond human conventions and the mind's creations. Thus Peirce's re-

38. Adams, *Education*, 449–61.

sponse to the crisis of modernity was not to bemoan the loss of truth and reality but to celebrate their expected presence, not to despair of the chaos of nature but to delight in its refusal to deny its right to recognition:

> Prof. Pearson, not having fully assimilated the truth that every object is purely mental or psychical, thinks that when he has shown that the content of natural law is intellectual, he is entitled to conclude that it is of human origin. But every scientific research goes upon the assumption, the hope, that in reference to its particular question, there is some true answer. That which that truth represents is a reality. This reality being cognizable and comprehensible, is of the nature of thought. Wherein, then, does its reality consist? In the fact that, though it has no being out of thought, yet it is as it is, whether you or I or any group of men think it to be so or not. The question of whether Hamlet was insane is the question whether Shakespeare conceived him to be insane. Consequently, Hamlet is a figment and not a reality. But as to the inkstand being on my table, though I should succeed in persuading myself and all who have seen it that it is a mere optical illusion, yet there will be a limit to this, and by the photographic camera, the balance, new witnesses, etc., it will, at last, I guess, force its recognition upon the world. If so, it has the characteristic which we call reality.[39]

The real, whether or not independent of what Adams and Pearson thought about it, will make itself known sooner or later. Its existence does not depend upon a modernist mind determined to deny any possibility of direct, unmediated knowledge. Peirce likened "the real" to an intruder; it can come unsought, forcing itself upon our attention. When Adams gave up trying to seek truth and reality in history he found some consolation in earlier philosophers who once failed to find God through reason and logic. "In essence, religion was love; in no case was it logic," wrote Adams, who shared Pascal's painful secret: "The only way to reach God was to deny the value of reason, and to deny reason was skepticism."[40] Reason can reach nothing outside the senses, the spiritual realm where God dwells until He chooses to reveal Himself. For Adams the crisis of modernity had begun in the Middle Ages, when God was assumed to inhabit a sphere impenetrable to reason and human experience. Peirce, in contrast, did not believe the challenge of modernity insurmountable. With heroic audacity he would reconcile reason and religion, logic and

---

39. Peirce, *Collected Papers*, vol. 8, 118; see also Matthew J. Fairbanks, "Peirce and the Positivists on Knowledge," *Transactions* 6 (1970): 111–22.

40. Adams, *Mont-Saint-Michel and Chartres*, 358–61.

love, science and morality, as well as freedom and determinism and chaos and order. With Peirce, modernism enters a new universe where doubt is not so much the end of faith as the beginning of belief, where inquiry aims not to discover truth but to eliminate error, and where science seeks not to exalt power as the release of energy but to establish authority on the basis of methodology.

Synechism, Tychism, and the Dialectic of Doubt and Belief

The foundations for knowing reality became an article of faith to Peirce, who believed he had established them in the constitutive power of thought, and who regarded the continual successes of scientific investigation as the groundspring of all hope. Peirce's faith in the mind's capacity to penetrate the mysteries of the universe contrasted to Adams's puzzlement at what defied explanation: glacial movements, Cro-Magnon cavern paintings, Aquinas's account of free will and Augustine's of grace, and, above all, Darwinism, which to the historian did not add up to a coherent theory. Adams saw too much uniformity and not enough selection and too many forms of life, like the *terebratula* fish, which survived without evolving and thus remained the same from the beginning to the end of geological time. When traveling in the South Seas, Adams often made his own investigations of volcanoes and coral formations in an effort to prove Darwin wrong. He once observed that Darwinism was "pure inference" and was reminded of the Deist who found a watch and inferred a maker. Darwinism could prove to Adams only haphazard change, not conscious direction. Taking progress for granted, Darwinism paid too much attention to the origins of the species; taking nothing for granted, Adams pondered not their origins but their possible extinction.[41]

Peirce saw in Darwinism not blind conflict and struggle but a deeper metaphysical significance pointing to orderly progress arising out of fortuitous variations. He did have some reservations about Darwin's theory of natural selection as the only cause of evolution. (Peirce was familiar with the writings of Adams's close friend, Clarence King, a catastrophist who, in opposition to Darwin, emphasized cataclysmic changes in the environment.) And Peirce rejected the application of Darwin's principles outside of biology to social philosophy and ethics. But Peirce recognized the statistical dimensions of Darwinism, which accounted for the tendency toward variation in the species. And he believed that spontaneous variations indicated only that science need not depend upon the fact of absolute regularity in the universe. Evolution offers both uniformity and indeter-

41. Adams, *Education*, 224–36.

minacy, continuity and contingency, the persistence of laws and the variety of chance. Scientific theories, Peirce held, are organic adaptations and can therefore be revised in response to the irregularities and contingencies of nature.[42]

Peirce's conviction that the methods of science can pursue the ironies and paradoxes of nature reinforced his conviction that evolution was progress. With Peirce there would be no alienation of the thinking mind from a mindless universe, none of the angst that Adams had felt when looking at the icy indifference of the Alps while listening to his sister's death agony. "Philosophy tries to understand," wrote Peirce. "In so doing, it is committed to the assumption that things are intelligible, that the processes of nature and the processes of reason are one."[43] Nor for Peirce would there be any Weberian "disenchantment of the world," no worry that science progresses through mechanistic explanations that strip the world of both human and spiritual meaning. In a way, Peirce's father saved him from modernism, for the son retained from the country's foremost mathematician the conviction that scientific inquiry would ultimately disclose the world's divine scheme. Thus he would never be as troubled as James was wrestling with free will and determinism or as Adams was staring into the abyss. Observing that "change begets order," Peirce saw in Darwinism and the flux of history not the chaos of events but their probability, a perspective that would be reinforced later by his mathematical conviction that statistical analysis eventually encompasses the increasing number of occurrences and thereby reveals their general regularity—a conviction further reinforced in his belief that continuity logically depended upon the infinitesimals that characterize numbers in a continuum with no predecessors or successors. Seeing mind at one with nature, Peirce insisted that the human intellect had a "magnetic turning toward truth." Convinced that mind possessed an inward tendency to rejoin the source from which it had sprung, Peirce saw no great gap between thought and reality. "The mind of man has been formed under the action of the laws of nature," Peirce wrote against Hume's skepticism, "and therefore it is not so very surprising to find that its constitution is such that, when we can get rid of caprices, idiosyncrasies, and other perturbations, its thoughts naturally show a tendency to agree with the laws of nature."[44]

42. Peirce, *Collected Papers*, vol. 6, 197–203; Peter Skagestad, "C. S. Peirce on Biological Evolution and Scientific Progress," in *Relevance*, 348–72.

43. Peirce, *Collected Papers*, vol. 6, 386.

44. Peirce, "Hume's Argument against Miracles and the Idea of Natural Law," quoted in Joseph Dauben, "Peirce and the History of Science," paper delivered at the Peirce Sesquicentennial International Congress, Harvard University, September 1989.

Peirce remained equally untroubled by the omnipresence of force, which Adams had seen as an operating principle in nature that propelled history to move blindly as it followed the path of least resistance. To Peirce force was the phenomenon that accounted for change and motion, which embodies experience and without which there could never be alterations of velocity and direction. How could there be a riddle about the movement of force when one comprehends it by simply studying its effects?

Peirce failed to complete his grand philosophical system; yet, unlike Adams, he could scarcely regard his catholic education as a "failure." Peirce never lost faith in the unlimited potentials of mind. Where Adams saw entropy in the universe, and James a playful indeterminism, Peirce would come to believe that man's mind and the natural world are integral parts of a universe of representation, and that science and religion, unlike history and politics, are concerned less about the past and present than about the future.[45]

Traditionally the American thinker, particularly the Jeffersonian and Emersonian, repudiated the past in the name of the individual's pursuit of "happiness" or the "over-soul." While Peirce had no place for the individual in his outlook, his philosophy did contain some Transcendentalist overtones. He could readily agree with Emerson's definition of the enlightened thinker as one who affirms all that relates and connects and thereby upholds the constitution of the world. He could also agree that the scientist no less than the poet is involved in the contemplation of nature. And Peirce's assumption that the universe was not Adams's discordant "multiverse" but a harmonious whole whose manifest diversity yielded up a deeper unity might suggest ways in which Emersonian optimism survived Darwinian pessimism. But the difference between the poet and the philosopher lay more in the message than in the medium. If Emerson taught Americans to trust the self, Peirce taught them to trust the larger processes of nature.

Consider some features of Peirce's cosmology. His principle of *synechism*, the principle that laws entail the idea of continuity because phenomena are discovered to be continually obedient to them, enabled Peirce to appreciate the reassuring regularities of behavior that in turn form habits of mind. The persistence of general principles operating in nature suggested not only the continuity of true laws but the unactualized possibilities of the future. Peirce also subscribed to the principle of tychism, the theory that pure chance operates in the universe to the extent that

45. Peirce's theories of knowledge and probability are lucidly examined in H. S. Thayer, *Meaning and Action: A Critical History of Pragmatism* (Indianapolis, 1968), 101–20.

there are events and mutations undetermined by prior causes. The phenomena of growth and evolution, Peirce held, cannot be explained by deterministic mechanics to account for sudden variations. What, then, of Adams's worry about the random, explosive behavior of radium rays? Perhaps Peirce would have seen them as spontaneous eruptions that will eventually develop their own laws as constancy gradually replaces contingency. Where Adams saw the universe as tending toward acceleration and disintegration, Peirce interpreted Darwinism to imply that spontaneous origins can evolve into stable patterns. "Now the only possible way of accounting for the laws of nature and for uniformity in general," Peirce wrote, "is to suppose them the results of evolution. This supposes them not to be absolute, not to be obeyed precisely. It makes an element of indeterminacy, spontaneity, or absolute chance in nature."[46]

Adams had embraced modern physics because it seemed to confirm the lesson he had learned from studying history: man dreams of order only to be defied by nature, which forever yields chaos. Peirce's outlook is so different that it is unfortunate the two remained ignorant of one another and hence American history missed a potentially great intellectual confrontation.[47] Peirce saw no disparity between man's dreams and nature's ways. His scheme had an original, primal chaos evolving, through tendencies of adaptation and repetition, into habits of order, and he saw nothing paradoxical or "parricidal" in the irregularities of nature. His *tychism* rendered him closer to James in recognizing that indeterminism meant chance, possibility, and freedom. Yet tychism could also explain order as well as freedom, for chance involves the laws of probability, and thus contingency can explain general features of experience such as regularity. "A chaos . . . being without connection in reality would probably be without existence."[48] One wonders whether Peirce had wanted to have it both ways so that the freedom inherent in the spontaneity of chance could live with the determinism inherent in the regularity of order. One wonders, too, how the historian can apply Peirce's cosmology to the study of the past. Can one generalize from a chance occurrence? Conversely, if

46. Peirce is quoted in Karl-Otto Apel, *Charles S. Peirce: From Pragmatism to Pragmaticism* (Amherst: University of Massachusetts Press, 1981), 150; see also Peter T. Turley, "Peirce on Chance," *Transactions* 5 (1969): 243–54.

47. In a letter to Lady Welby (Mar. 14, 1909), Peirce mentions that many figures he and his father knew among the New England intellectuals, "but not the Adamses"; letter reprinted in *Values in a Universe of Chance: Selected Writings of Charles S. Peirce (1839–1914)*, ed. Philip P. Wiener (Garden City, N.Y., 1958), 416. Although Adams had a lively exchange with James and was well known and admired by Oliver Wendell Holmes, Jr., a member of Cambridge's "Metaphysical Club," the index to the six volumes of Adams letters recently published by Harvard University Press contains no entry on Peirce.

48. Peirce, *Collected Papers*, vol. 6, 419.

history repeats itself sufficiently to produce patterns allowing for generalization, wherein lies freedom?

In some respects, at least at first glance, Peirce and Adams shared a few perspectives in common. Both regarded motion as the crucial object of scientific investigation, and each believed that in the modern age Euclid's preference for the simple explanation over the complex may have to be rejected. Both also recognized that the laws of the conservation of energy and the laws of evolution were in conflict—the former ended in balance if nothing was added or lost, the latter proceeded with growth and change wherein everything adapts or dies, and thus transformation overtakes equilibrium. But where Adams was obsessed with energy, Peirce delighted in symmetry. In his debate with the philosopher Paul Carus, Peirce discussed the mathematical implications of the laws of energy and matter without mentioning dissipation or entropy. One suspects that Peirce had less fear about the state of matter because he had more faith in the status of mind. And whether or not mind and matter interact, Peirce believed that they both partake of thought.

People need to recognize, advised Peirce, that thought operates in the world and is not simply the result of material determinants and the dynamics of motions. When Peirce pointed out to James that "thought is more without us than within," he was suggesting that particular minds rise to the generality of thought when they form habits so that we belong to a larger universe that is not of our making. "Order is simply thought embodied in arrangement," Peirce observed, and habits are mental in that they organize and connect thoughts.[49] Adams, in contrast, doubted that thought could be identical to what was assumed to be without, although in at least one instance he reflected that introspection had led him to sense the same "chaos" in the mind that science was supposedly discovering in nature. But Adams had a different view of the origins of mind. "Thought did not evolve nature but nature evolved thought," he wrote in the *Education*, implying that because mental activity followed biological development, thought may lose the race against energy.[50] Adams remained something of a dualist who sensed the estrangement of mind from nature. As a pragmatist, Peirce would not only anticipate Dewey in his naturalistic critique of dualism; he also seems to have long anticipated the structuralists of the mid-twentieth century in regarding the world as intelligible because man is the product of the same laws of nature he investigates as a scientist. Peirce even created semiology in foreseeing that thinking and acting are verbally conditioned by words and language conventions.

49. Ibid., 336.
50. Adams, *Education*, 485.

"Thus may language is the sum total of myself; for man is the thought," Peirce announced.[51] Life is intelligible to the extent that man constitutes a structure, whether linguistic or otherwise, between the world and himself. To revise and collapse Adams's dualism, a Peircean might say that since thought produces structure, structure contains thought, and man's mind, having evolved from the laws of nature, can think in accordance with nature.

For the pragmatist, of course, man is not only his thoughts expressed in signs and language but also his actions expressed in practical endeavors, and since the pragmatist regards knowledge as a production, it could be said that action evolves thought and truth is its product. Yet for all Peirce's emphasis upon language and the structures of signs and symbolic systems, it is doubtful that Adams's troubles would have been eased by the pragmatic turn in modern thought. As a historian Adams grew depressed precisely because he could see so few politicians, statesmen, and generals who knew what they were doing and why, who could, that is, explain their policies on the basis of their causes so that their actions would be consistent with their intentions. Jefferson assured Americans of a small, simple, virtuous republic in his political rhetoric; in his political action he purchased the Louisiana Territory and made America a continental empire. If "order is simply thought embodied in arrangement," how does one find it in American history when there is no logical sequence of thought and action?

How to find God is another question besetting the modern mind. Peirce's views on the status of religion also contrasted with Adams's worry that the "religious instinct" was dying. Where the historian had tried to appreciate religion as a lost treasure of symbols and rituals, the philosopher insisted that belief in God was "a fundamental belief of the soul" that could never be extinguished.[52] Peirce even undertook the challenging task of reconciling Darwinism, with its emphasis on competition and struggle, with a Christianity based upon compassion and justice. In "Evolutionary Love," Peirce rejected the "Gospel of Greed" of the Social Darwinists, who combined utilitarianism with Manchester economic theory to make the pursuit of self-interest tantamount to the general good. Peirce shared Adams's and James's conviction that religion is not simply a "belief" but a sentiment and instinct that is lived and felt rather than thought and discussed. And Peirce could have agreed with Adams when the latter focused on the Virgin rather than God to suggest that Christianity had

51. Peirce, "Some Consequences of Four Incapacities," 249.

52. On Peirce's religious convictions, see Robert J. Roth, *American Religious Thought* (New York, 1967), 63–84; and John E. Smith, *Purpose and Thought: The Meaning of Pragmatism* (Chicago, 1978), 166–82.

more to do with the forgiveness of sin than with its eternal punishment, and thus is essentially a "religion of love." But when Peirce turns from Christianity to God's existence as a philosophical problem, he does not, as did Adams, dwell upon Aquinas, Augustine, Descartes, and Pascal to show why the problem eludes every effort at rational proof.

Instead Peirce wrote, among other papers, "A Neglected Argument for the Reality of God" to open the modern mind to the possibility that religion has more to do with emotion than reason. In addition to synechism and tychism, Peirce added *agapism* to show the world moving by the power of love as well as continuity and chance. With a sense of aesthetics that Adams would have appreciated, Peirce advised approaching religion with "musement" so that one might spontaneously be drawn into the universe of spirituality. The "normal man" who follows this practice and keeps in mind the interplay of life, chance, and love "will come to be stirred to the depths of his nature by the beauty of the idea and by its august practicality, even to the point of earnestly loving and adoring his strictly hypothetical God, and that of desiring above all things to shape the whole conduct of life and all the springs of action into conformity with that hypothesis."[53]

In view of Peirce's reservations about James's "The Will to Believe," he seems here to contradict his strictures against allowing the subject to be influenced by what he feels to be satisfying and fulfilling, an inconsistency that perhaps stems from Peirce's scholstic-realist assumption that the human mind must in some sense be in touch with truth in order to recognize it when it discovers it. In this respect Peirce could provide reasons for opening the emotions to make love a logical proposition even if founded on a psychological disposition. Adams had sensed with Pascal that reason must be separated from religion or else faith will be exposed to doubt. Peirce not only used logic and reason to validate instinct and emotion, he also tended to view God anthropomorphically, in part to emphasize God's benign nature and also to suggest that although His mind may be unlike ours, "we can catch a fragment of His Thought, as it were."[54] All such approaches to religion avoided the theodicy problem that troubled Adams, Kierkegaard, and other modernist thinkers: why would a God of goodness create evil and bring suffering into the world? Perhaps, Peirce speculated, when writing on the nature as well as the reality of the Divine Creator, "God probably has no consciousness."[55] To Peirce, tracking God down philosophically was no more and no less

---

53. Peirce, *Collected Papers*, vol. 6, 319.
54. Ibid., 346.
55. Ibid., 334.

challenging than verifying knowledge empirically: in religion as well as science, truth is attained in the future.

With other modernists of the late nineteenth century Peirce felt deeply the tensions between religion and science even as he tried to bridge the gulf between the sacred and the secular. Although he knew that his arguments for God's existence offered only a "poor sketch" rather than a convincing proof, he recognized, as he told Lady Welby, that the search for truth did not imply finding it or defining it but holding out for it.[56] He would settle for a clearer view of reality and a more objective basis of knowledge. Similarly, the search for truth had little to do with the pursuit of happiness. A man who delighted in sensual pleasure, Peirce ironically devoted his life to searching for a philosophical system that would free the mind from the crass hedonism and survivalism of recent utilitarian and Darwinian thought. Perhaps only a thinker who could be a rigorous logician as well as a bon vivant epicurean could have felt that "no desire can possibly desire its own satisfaction."[57] It was Peirce's heroic mission to restore the dignity and authority of philosophy, and to do so he felt it necessary to question the meaning of authority itself.

The interrogation of belief and truth and their traditional relation to authority concerned Peirce long before he responded to James's version of pragmatism after the turn of the century. Some of Peirce's best meditations occurred before pragmatism became a subject of controversy not only in the United States but in western Europe. His early writings are usually treated as part of the origins of pragmatism; they also deserve our attention in order to appreciate how Peirce was trying to prevent modern American philosophy from stumbling into the quicksands of relativism.

The Objectivity Question

In his now-famous essay "The Fixation of Belief" (1877), Peirce considered the "method of authority" as one of several approaches to valid knowledge. Unlike the method of tenacity, in which men simply "cling spasmodically" to the views they hold, authority generally functions as an institutional expression of thought. And unlike traditional methods of philosophical discourse, in which thinkers sensitive to different belief systems question among themselves propositions that they may or may not find agreeable to reason, authority is capable of establishing consensus, commanding assent, and preserving the "universal and catholic charcter" of a particular reigning ideology. In addition to sustaining the existing order, authority also creates the living faiths with which men can

---

56. Peirce to Lady Welby, Dec. 14, 1908, in *Values*, 397.
57. Peirce, "The Criterion of Validity in Reasoning," in *Philosophical Writings*, 121.

move mountains (and build cathedrals). If we are to judge a belief system by its results, Peirce would have conceded that the system of authority had reigned successfully for the greater part of human history:

> In judging this method of fixing belief, which may be called the method of authority, we must, in the first place, allow its immeasurable mental and moral superiority to the method of tenacity. Its success is proportionally greater; and in fact it has over and over again worked the most majestic results. The mere structures of stone which it has caused to be put together—in Siam, for example, in Egypt, and in Europe— have many of them a sublimity hardly more than rivaled by the greatest works of nature. And, except the geological epochs, there are no periods of time so vast as those which are measured by some of these organized faiths. If we scrutinize the matter closely, we shall find that there has not been one of their creeds which has remained always the same; yet the change is so slow as to be imperceptible during one person's life, so that individual belief remains sensibly fixed. For the mass of mankind, there is perhaps no better method than this. If it is their highest impulse to be intellectual slaves, then slaves they ought to remain.[58]

The mystical faith of the Middle Ages that Adams had lyricized in *Mont-Saint-Michel and Chartres* would perhaps have seemed to Peirce an attitude fit only for the cowardly intellectual and the unthinking masses. True, Peirce recognized religion as one of the needs of the soul and indeed shared some of Adams's deepest spiritual yearnings—the philosopher's doctrine of agapism suggests the same force of God's love that the historian found in the Virgin. Yet Peirce believed that while man may live by instinct and need, he prevails as a moral being only by committing himself to the promotion of reason and knowledge. With this intellectual imperative, Peirce set out to show why the "method of authority" could not be relied upon as a method of belief in modern civilization.

The scheme of authority, Peirce argued, has generally represented the "will of the state" or that of a "priesthood," and hence it has been used to uphold "correct theological or political doctrines," often by imposing an atmosphere of total thought control that silences all dissent. Under systems of authority disputes are usually settled by a "general massacre" of the opposition on the part of a ruling class whose power is sustained by keeping the masses ignorant or by coercing them into submission. In Peirce's description one finds both the long, dark shadow of the sixteenth-

58. Peirce, "The Fixation of Belief," 14.

century Inquisition and a curious foreshadowing of twentieth-century totalitarianism. "Cruelties always accompany this system; and when it is consistently carried out, they become atrocities of the most horrible kind in the eyes of any rational man." Peirce may have exaggerated such "cruelties" to dramatize the possible incompatibility of authority and reason. But he chastised authority not only because it was undesirable but also because it would prove unworkable. First of all, no institution can endeavor to regulate opinions on every subject; only the most vital matters can be supervised by state or church, and for the rest men's minds must be left "to the actions of natural causes." Moreover, the method of authority, like that of tenacity, is incompatible with man's social nature, his need to interact with others, which results in his experiencing opinions different from his own. In every society, furthermore, there will always be some people who become aware of thinkers in other societies and in other ages who have held different beliefs, and thus they will conclude that their own ideas may be merely a matter of historical accident. Hence knowledge of intellectual history sensitizes the mind, and the mind's awareness of diversity undermines authority.[59]

One aspect of Peirce's many-sided genius may be seen in his anticipation of the problems of relativism and historicism before they became unresolved theoretical issues associated with pragmatism and other expressions of modernism. The notion that reason is itself historical, that all human ideas and ideals are subject to continuous change, could be regarded as either a higher state of understanding the modern condition or the eclipse of truth as a principle of permanence. Peirce could accept neither historicism nor relativism. Consciousness of the contingency of our convictions, an awareness that our ideas turn on who we are and where we happen to be, means only that there can be no reason for our beliefs, since anything accidental has no bearing on what is true or false. In contrast to James, Peirce was an "evidentialist," convinced that while knowledge may originate in belief it must move on toward proof and not go beyond evidence to what James would later call his right to believe in God—"overbelief." Peirce's essay appeared two decades before James's "The Will to Believe." But one can compare the two statements even out of context to highlight how the two philosophers differed on the status of belief: Peirce sought to fix belief, not will it.

Peirce's critique of authority in "The Fixation of Belief" bears some resemblance to Jefferson's philosophy of liberty. The human mind, wrote Jefferson a century earlier, is too idiosyncratic to conform to any philosophy that aspires to uniformity.[60] Yet Peirce sought to offer America more

59. Ibid., 5–22.
60. See Daniel J. Boorstin, *The Lost World of Thomas Jefferson* (Boston, 1960), 61–98.

than the liberal pluralism of Jefferson or the radical empiricism of James. The views of Jefferson and James risked rendering truth relative and making all philosophical convictions simply a matter of individual preference. Although Peirce vigorously opposed the idea of authority as it manifested itself so brutally throughout history, he wanted to restore to philosophy the moral force of objective authority. Taking on this audacious task, he started by analyzing the very premises of epistemology: what do we do when we think, and how do we know that what we think is true?

Peirce's theory of knowledge presupposes a dialectical relationship between belief and doubt. He could agree with Adams and James that it was not truth itself but beliefs that "guide our desires and shape our actions." Yet his awareness that beliefs, unlike absolute truth or transcendent faith, would always be subjected to the skeptical mind did not trouble Peirce. For the "irritation of doubt" that motivates man to question his present beliefs and to move on to a truer belief provides the very means by which conflicting opinions are settled. The experience of questioning one's prior convictions may involve uneasiness and hesitancy, but it leads to the resolution of doubt, and that new state of mind is the sole object of inquiry.[61] Peirce's descriptions of the processes of human thought attempted to elucidate the logic of intellectual and scientific progress, and they may also have reflected a Darwinian conviction that the mind is a faculty of change and adaptation. But the problem that had plagued Adams could still haunt the pragmatist. Adams and other modernist thinkers realized that all beliefs are logically as well as emotionally dubitable, but they also recognized that the inevitability of doubtfulness can be psychologically disorienting and unnerve the will to act. The great Italian leader Garibaldi, Adams observed in the *Education*, succeeded because he neither doubted what he was doing nor understood what he had done. The Middle Ages believed in itself because its theologians made belief the precondition of faith, understanding, and acceptance. From the point of view of the modern mind the truths of the past may have been little more than fictions, yet they worked only to the extent they went unquestioned.

Adam envied his eighteenth-century ancestors and the pilgrims at Chartres precisely because they were free of doubt. Nietzsche, Weber, Kierkegaard, and other modernist thinkers also felt themselves driven to doubt what they most wanted to believe. The intense consciousness stirred by a sense of the confusions and disorders of unbelief was their idea of the permanent human condition. The pursuit of knowledge demands that every faith and proposition be investigated and exposed, but the dissolution of accepted beliefs leaves modern man's wish to be at one

61. Peirce, "Fixation of Belief," 5–22.

with himself and the world essentially unfulfilled. Peirce assumed that the state of belief can become so routine, habitual, and orderly that the mind suffers a quiet death unless irritated into questioning and inquiry by a new sense of discomfort and disorder. Adams, to mention only one modernist, felt that similar doubt and disorder keenly throughout his intellectual life. He also engaged himself in inquiries into different belief systems. Yet he regarded his efforts to do so as a systematic "failure" since his questioning mind could not be stilled by a new belief that answered a psychological need more than an intellectual demand. Thus Adams recognized that the dogmas of the Church must be accepted without argument, although he himself refused to bend and continued to argue. Any disputation would lead to skepticism, and skepticism assaults authority in its relentless questioning of truth.

It is here that Peirce's contributions to the dilemma of modernity can be fully appreciated. Where the modernist intellectuals saw doubt as debilitating, Peirce saw it as liberating; and where they assumed that the authority of truth had been doubted out of existence, he would offer a new method of thinking wherein authority and truth could be reestablished. The possibility that old ideas could be displaced by the mind's probing curiosity had worried Adams; that same possibility encouraged Peirce to see in the falsifiability of ideas hopeful evidence of science's progressive character. No less than Adams did Peirce feel from his earliest years that there was no way to establish truth on infallible foundations. All knowledge is conditional and based on learned inferences rather than immediate intuitions, and scientists in particular question everything, intuitions and percepts as well as sense data, because their method is not foundational but corrigible. Peirce's challenge was to demonstrate that modernism can preserve truth and authority by grounding all knowledge in a self-validating system of inquiry. In rising to that challenge, Peirce sought to demonstrate why civilizations progress and not decline, as Adams would have it, to the extent that belief is exposed to the perplexities of doubt.

Truth as Consensus

Peirce's pragmatic approach to knowledge offered an escape from the dilemmas of modern skepticism. The aim of knowledge, Peirce insisted, was not to discover innate truths by means of the intuitive intellect, a Cartesian exercise that mistakenly assumes that the mind is a self-contained theoretical faculty, one that ignores the role of language and communication, forms of expression that mediate between subject and object and thereby help establish the meaning of things. Nor can the meaning of objects be grasped in their simple, unmediated essence. On the contrary, it is the external nature of phenomena that interests us, the actions and functions of things in their behavior. We clarify the meaning of ideas by observing their "practical bearings," and our beliefs are made valid by anticipating "their conceivable practical consequences" in the everyday world of experience. Mind is the dynamic interplay of belief, doubt, and inquiry; but philosophy has less to do with the interior operations of mind than with the external world of action in which ideas are tested and verified.[62]

The conviction that ideas and propositions can be judged by the results they produce when put into practice, and therefore the effects of an object constitute our conceptions of it, would be the cornerstone of pragmatic philosophy. Peirce, however, remained unsatisfied with his own formulation that the state of satisfaction eases the irritation of doubt. The assumption that a belief is measured in terms of its practical value—a controversial assumption we shall return to when examining Dewey's thought—seemed to Peirce a crude equation of the true with the useful that risked reducing knowledge to the egoistic needs of the individual. Although Peirce's explorations into metaphysics, semiotics, and axiology may not have succeeded in elevating pragmatism above its instrumental character, he was determined to demonstrate that valid beliefs could lead to a kind of binding authority. To do so he set out to show that any reliable approach to knowledge must meet two requirements: the methodology must be empirical and rule-bound and the verification must be public and agreement-bound. Thus Peirce rejected James's early position, in *Principles of Psychology*, that private consciousness can be regarded as the ultimate criterion of experience because individual minds remain separate and there can be "no giving or bartering between them." In contrast to James's conviction that the mind inheres in a state of "absolute insulation" (a view he would later revise, claiming we "trade off" each other's ideas), Peirce sought continuity and communication.[63] But how to avoid allowing individuals to be the judges of their own opinions without compelling every individual to accept the same opinions? How to get the mass of people to agree to what Peirce called the "one True opinion"? To avoid the chaos of intellectual anarchy on the one hand and the tyranny of political authority on the other, Peirce proposed an ingenious way out of an apparent impasse in liberal thought:

> To satisfy our doubts, therefore it is necessary that a method
> should be found by which our beliefs may be determined by

---

62. Peirce, "How to Make Our Ideas Clear," in *Philosophical Writings*, 23–41.

63. William James, *The Principles of Psychology* (1890; New York: Harper, 1950), vol. 1, 226; on the difference between James and Peirce, see Vincent M. Colapietro, *Peirce's Approach to the Self: A Semiotic Perspective* (Albany: SUNY Press, 1989), 76–80.

nothing human, but by some external permanency—by something upon which our thinking has no effect. . . . It must be something which affects or might affect, every man. And, though these affections are necessarily as various as are individual conditions, yet the method must be such that the ultimate conclusion of every man shall be the same. Such is the method of science.

In scientific methodology intellectual assertions would be put to a "community of inquirers" whose collective judgment would control and validate the conditions of belief. "All the followers of science are animated by a cheerful hope that the processes of investigation, if only pushed far enough, will give one certain solution to each question to which they apply it." The nature of empirical inquiry, in which truth-claims remain tentative until accepted and verified publicly, binds successive generations of scientists and professionally commits them to arriving at a consensus that will derive from a "community of the competent." Peirce assumed that the truth that will emerge from scientific investigation will have the character of a "predestinate opinion," for scientists will be carried "by a force outside of themselves to one and the same conclusion," and that "force" is "nothing human" in the sense of arbitrary and accidental; instead it comes from the canons of empirical thought that provide the "external permanency" of rules of evidence to which all investigators are answerable. "The opinion which is fated to be ultimately agreed to by all who investigate, is what we mean by truth, and the object represented in this opinion is the real."[64]

In the larger context of American intellectual history, Peirce's "The Fixation of Belief" turned against two deep traditions: the Jeffersonian conviction that the individual is sovereign and the Emersonian conviction that the self is sacred. Peirce offered pragmatism and scientific inquiry as a means of submerging the individual into the community and allowing the thinker to have access to a reality beyond the self. Science could be objective to the extent that knowledge could be tested with reference to objects outside the self and the self would gladly submit to the judgments of others regarding the external world. To Emerson's Delphic dictum, "Know thyself!" Peirce might have added: To know the world, think with others.

Sociologists and intellectual historians have seen in Peirce's formulation the seeds of the rise of "professionalization" in American life, the beginning of a conviction that would later usher in the managerial society and the administrative state. The conviction implies that only degree-holding

64. Peirce, "The Fixation of Belief," 18; "How to Make Our Ideas Clear," 26–31.

experts and specialists are qualified to make judgments that will take into consideration the public good and general welfare. The pragmatist's commitment to "disinterested" inquiry, and Peirce's condemnation of capitalism as "the gospel of greed,"[65] can also be seen as the first brave effort on the part of an emerging organization of philosophers to address the social problems of industrial America. Yet the view that Peirce's proposals for a scientific community of investigators helped resolve the "crisis of authority" of the late nineteenth century and started America on the road to professionalization is misleading and not a little anachronistic.[66]

For one thing, Peirce had little influence on the thinkers of his time, and most of his proposals in science and philosophy remained unheard-of in the public domain. Moreover, although Peirce trusted the judgment of a community rather than the individual, he distrusted formal organizations as extensions of society's stultifying conventions. Peirce well remembered how Galileo, Kepler, and Bruno worked outside the boundaries of what in their time passed for professional science. While aware of the necessity of scientific associations, journals, research teams, universities, and other resources, Peirce desired to see science open, fluid, and experimental, the fruit of piecemeal discoveries by individuals working on their own apart from the surveillance of directors and bureaucrats. Peirce's sense of the spirit of scientific inquiry would have been uneasy with the professionalization of science. Like Veblen and Adams, Pierce believed that the pretensions of society threatened the procedures of inquiry to the extent that the individual researcher defers to class proprieties.[67] Once the scientific scholar takes on the image of a "gentleman" and the "recognized exponent of good manners" is regarded as the "most learned man," then "the inquiring spirit cannot say that the gentlemen are a lot of ignorant fools. To the moral weight cast against progress in science is added the weight of superior learning. Wherever there is a large class of superior academic professors who are provided with good incomes and looked up to as gentlemen, scientific inquiry must languish. Wherever the bureaucrats are the more learned class, the case will be worse."[68]

To save science from the sins of bureaucracy Peirce insisted that the community of inquirers must remain independent of society and its demands. In his long review of Pearson's *The Grammar of Science*, Peirce

65. Peirce, "Evolutionary Love," in *Philosophical Writings*, 361–74.

66. Thomas L. Haskell, *The Emergence of Professional Social Science: The American Social Science Association and the Nineteenth-Century Crisis of Authority* (Urbana: University of Illinois Press, 1977).

67. Thorstein Veblen, *The Higher Learning in America: A Memorandum on the Conduct of Universities by Businessmen* (New York, 1918).

68. Peirce, "The Scientific Attitude toward Fallibilism," in *Philosophical Writings*, 45.

reprimanded the British author for suggesting that scientists devote themselves to the "welfare of human society" and to "strengthening social stability." Pearson was a socialist and humanist convinced that science could serve the cause of justice and that good citizenship depended upon the public adopting scientific habits of mind. Pearson's position, which closely resembles one that Dewey would develop, Peirce questioned on two grounds: that the value of scientific method does not depend on its immediate promotion of the survival of the species but instead, Peirce held, on its long-term pursuit of truth through the elimination of error; that science can only claim to be an ethical ideal to the extent its disciples practice detached, disinterested inquiry.[69]

What convinced Peirce that scientists could do so? Later in the twentieth century thinkers influenced by postmodernism would dismiss Peirce's stance as the illusion of objectivity and the last, desperate hope of Victorian morality. Peirce himself believed that the rigorous methods of science were themselves intrinsically moral, and if the scientist sinned against reality he could be punished by the entry of facts into the court of judgment. In pursuit of truth the scientist thus follows a logic of discovery responsive to the universal course of evolution and to the consensus of the community of inquirers. Peirce placed great emphasis on the mutual spirit of scientists who shared and respected each other's thoughts and hypotheses in a common effort to advance knowledge. Peirce assumed that science's cooperative ethos could offer an answer to the ruthless competitive individualism of the capitalist system. He had no foreknowledge that American business firms would adopt similar principles of in-house teamwork and input to advance not so much knowledge as profits. Business schools teaching the "scientific" techniques of management would often emphasize the pooling of talent and collective inquiry to solve common problems involving sales or public relations. With the rise of the corporate economy the American capitalist became what William Whyte called the "organization man," the executive whose idea of success was not so much getting ahead as getting along.[70] Ironically, while much of American business would become more integrated, it was science that had to become more competitive with the rise of the cold war as directors of research laboratories vied with each other for government contracts and grants.

Thorstein Veblen offered a different theory to explain why science could be an ethical vocation to the extent it remained independent of society. While Peirce emphasized more the peculiar mode of inquiry, Veblen emphasized the matter scientists worked upon. Veblen assumed

---

69. Peirce, *Collected Writings*, vol. 8, 103–20.
70. William H. Whyte, *The Organization Man* (New York: Simon and Schuster, 1956).

that because scientists deal with the inert materials of earth or the motions of active matter they have a greater tendency to be impartial and objective. Since the basic elements of nature have no subjective character—no feelings, perceptions, or purposes—scientists allow their minds to be tutored to imitate the objective world and to think matter-of-factly. Veblen and Peirce were close in assuming that the laws of nature and the structural regularities of the universe can be known to the extent that the scientist develops habits of mind constrained by the subject being investigated. But where Peirce emphasized the rigor of logical principles and experimental procedures to claim that one could not be morally ethical without being rationally logical, Veblen believed that the scientist develops proper mental habits not so much in teamwork with fellow scientists as in adopting himself to a universe that is at once disenchanted and lacking in any trace of "animism," that is, stripped of all human and spiritual significance.[71]

Veblen's vision of the true scientific mind would have been too much not only for the pragmatist Peirce, who wanted to see a place for God in the world, but also for the modern humanist, who wanted to see a place for man. Veblen's answer to modernity was to allow the machine to take over. His dream was to have engineers and technicians produce a world of intricate mechanisms, precise springs, and efficient gears moving with clocklike predictability in a medium of matter and energy uncontaminated by the biases of society, the superstitions of religion, the pressure of politics, the wasteful inanities of a consumer culture, and a business ethos more devoted to profit than to production. To a future generation haunted by war and the bomb, such a technological vision would seem as alienating as it is threatening, and it may be recalled that Adams had presaged it in his juxtaposition of the Virgin to the Dynamo, the compassionate image of love to the cold symbol of power.

Even more striking is Adams's anticipation of the problems that would be encountered by a scientific community. Adams shared Peirce's concern that scholars as scientists must remain fiercely independent of a society to protect their professional integrity. When he addressed the American Historical Association on this issue Adams seemed to imply that his colleagues enjoyed too much belief and not enough doubt. As president of the AHA, Adams had sent the organization "A Letter to American Teachers of History," actually a one-hundred-page discourse on the implications of new discoveries in science for the writing of history. Modern atomic physics reinforced Adams's conviction that contingency, randomness, and indeterminism characterized historical events as well as evolutionary mutations and particle discontinuities. When a scientist informed Adams that he was wrong in some details of his analysis, Adams

71. Veblen, *The Place of Science in Modern Civilization and Other Essays* (New York, 1919).

replied that it was not physicists but historians he was trying to upset. Before submitting the document Adams waxed almost Peircean in his delight at being the disturber of belief. "I've the notion of printing a letter to Professors," he wrote to a friend. "Pure malice! but history will die if not irritated. The only service I can do to my profession is to serve as a flea."[72] But the AHA paid no attention to Adams's explications of the new physics and mathematics. He wanted to be a thorn in the side of complacency, but his barb was scarcely felt. Nor did the AHA feel the full weight of his warning about the conflict between science and society.

In a letter to Herbert Baxter Adams, the incoming secretary of the AHA, Adams urged that he use the resources of the organization to help make history a scientific discipline. The effort may fail, Adams conceded, but inquiry along empirical lines must proceed if history is to have any rational explanatory value. "Historians will not, and even if they would they cannot, abandon the attempt. Science itself would admit its own failure, if it admitted that man, the most important of all its subjects, could not be brought within its range." Yet if and when history succeeds in converting itself into a scientific discipline it will immediately confront four antagonists: the church, the state, property, and labor. Religion cannot admit of any scientific history that excludes Providence; government will respond to scientific research only if its findings strengthen the state; capitalists will judge science only in light of their vested rights, and workers will do likewise for the rights of labor. If socialism is proved to be more scientific than capitalism, would the universities tolerate science's teachings? If science can introduce labor-saving technology, would not trade unions resist its findings? Could American government withstand a scientific history that would replace eighteenth-century Newtonianism with nineteenth-century Darwinianism and thereby show that the equilibrium of checks and balances had given way to politics as conflict, struggle, and the domination of power and interests? "In whatever direction we look," warned Adams, "we can see no possibility of converting History into a Science without bringing it into hostility towards one or more of the most powerful organizations of the era." Yet Adams insisted that historians must accept all the implications of what they teach regardless of the political consequences. "A Science cannot be played with. . . . The mere fact that it overthrows social organizations, cannot affect our attitude. The rest of society can reject or ignore, but we must follow the new light, no matter where it leads."[73]

72. Henry Adams to Margaret Chanler, Sept. 9, 1909, *Adams Letters*, vol. 6, 272.
73. Henry Adams to Herbert Baxter Adams, Dec. 12, 1894, ibid., vol. 4, 228–34; this letter contains the seeds of the argument Adams later spelled out in "A Letter to American Teachers of History," reprinted in Adams, *The Degradation of Democratic Dogma*, ed. Brooks Adams (New York, 1919), 133–259.

Adams's conclusion is pure Peirce and Veblen: the integrity of science depends upon its autonomy and devotion to "idle curiosity" rather than practical utility. Such a stance meant that science would have to be freed of the political context in which it operated, and perhaps be resistant as well to society's economic pressures. What, then, would be the relation of science to democracy? Given its monopoly of specialized knowledge beyond the reach of laymen, would not science have elitist implications, and would not the community of researchers constitute what Georges Sorel feared would be "an aristocracy of professionals"?[74] The reconciliation of science and democracy would be left for Dewey, while James remained skeptical about the possibility of a superior community of scientists predicting human behavior. The historian remains skeptical for different reasons. One thinks, for example, of the fate of scientific research in the modern world of politics. Consider "the inquiry," a group organized by President Woodrow Wilson after America entered the First World War. Leading scholars like Lippmann and Veblen were called upon to provide research reports bearing upon a just and lasting peace settlement. As Adams might have expected, the reports, some of which tried to protect the sovereignty of small colonial countries, were ignored at the Versailles Conference. From Versailles in 1919 to Potsdam in 1945, the world witnessed the triumph of politics over science. Peirce's great hope was that scientists would, indeed must, respect facts, and that reality was recalcitrant and could resist a triumphant will to power. But as Adams observed, "practical politics consists in ignoring facts."[75] A politics that has power and success as its criteria seldom pauses to ponder the awkward truths of science. Perhaps the only thing the scientist and politician can agree upon is Hegel's modernist dictum that truth resides in power, whether the release of energy or the control of history.

The problem with Peirce's theory of a scientific community is not only his organizational assumptions about independence and autonomy. Another problem lies in the tension between the values he accorded to doubt and the virtues he attributed to community. Peirce remained convinced that his community of inquirers must extirpate the un-Christian pecunciary motives that prevailed in the business world; and in his essay "Evolutionary Love" he declared that "self-love is not love," believing instead that growth comes from merging the self with the interests of others. Peirce's antipathy toward Social Darwinian individualism flowed logically from his religious devotion to community, but it may have had little to do with science. Surely Galileo did not grow by deferring the

---

74. See *From Georges Sorel: Essays in Socialism and Philosophy*, ed. John L. Stanley (New Brunswick, N.J., 1987), 1–60, 257–89.

75. Adams, *Education*, 373.

findings of his research to the *consensus catholicus*. Peirce never entertained the possibility that truth might be an individual possession, and here he broke completely with the Transcendentalists and seemed oblivious to the problem that troubled Thoreau and Tocqueville. In pre–Civil War America they saw the solitary mind feeling the discomforts of doubt as it experienced conflict with the larger community that would tolerate no "irritation" of dissent. A community governed by "public opinion" wants to see its conventions perpetuated and not interrogated. Philosophers may regard opinion as always open to doubt, but it is in the nature of community that its opinions and attitudes are regarded as almost uncontested truths. The great fear of the Puritans, that humankind would conform to the pressures of society and lose sight of God, scarcely posed a problem to Peirce and the pragmatists. Nor did the concerns of the Founders. While the individual may be responsive to appeals to conscience and virtue, wrote the *Federalist* authors, the masses ("factions") are less capable of reason and responsibility and hence need to be controlled.

Peirce breaks with the Puritans, the Founders, and the Transcendentalists by offering a new locus for truth and its ratification. While the individual thinking for himself may be wrong, the community of scientists engaged in a mutual dialogue would reach an agreement that more closely approximates truth by leaving error behind. Somewhat like Oliver Wendell Holmes, Jr., Peirce offered a survival theory of truth: individual investigators suggest hypotheses and truth-claims, but in the continuous process of inquiry other scholars will revise earlier conclusions so that truth becomes the belief ultimately sustained by the community. Curiously, while Peirce wants to see truth as consensus end with the community, he is reluctant to see doubt as conflict beginning with the individual. Yet if it is the case that only the uncertainties of doubt keep the mind alive and inquiry ceases when disputes are settled, the imaginative writer or inventive genius may find himself in radical opposition to tradition, authority, and the consensus of community. Peirce's richly dialectical mind could value doubt only to see it lose its sting as the results of the inquiry it prompts meet with public acceptance. Peirce seemed to imply that communities cannot live without the provocations of doubt and uncertainty, but instead must see them resolved by settling on new beliefs that appease the irritation by issuing in more stable habits and rules of action. Can, then, the pragmatic community live with modernity? Can modern man live with doubt? The energies and passions of the modernist intellectuals, it will be recalled, are charged by doubt and the capacity to live in darkness.

Modernism is the recognition that value conflicts may have no resolution and truth no foundations. Peirce rejected that view and instead tried to develop ways of thinking to overcome all dualisms that left modern man estranged from God and nature. Yet in Peirce one still senses an unresolved tension between his scientific commitments and his religious convictions. The challenge to modernism was to assimilate the achievements of science without losing the spiritual meaning of life. Adams had concluded that the Dynamo had already replaced the Virgin and modern industrial society would worship at the altar of power. Peirce believed that philosophy could elevate science to the level of a religious commitment so that the modern intellect, no less than that of the scholastics of the Middle Ages, would "put into rational light the faith of which they were already possessed."[76] Combining scientific vocation with spiritual aspiration, Peirce believed that philosophers would learn to love truth and scientists would aim at acquiring knowledge purely for the sake of knowing. Yet religious faith may have less to do with learning and knowing than with submitting and accepting. Curiously, when Peirce explained why one should admire the philosopher who chose the method of scientific investigation, he suggested that the "genius of [his] logical method should be loved and reverenced" as he "loves his wife."[77] In likening science to love, Peirce may have been suggesting that one object of inquiry is beauty, a suggestion that would befit his own amorous charcter. More obviously, he wanted to elevate science to the religious ideals of sacrifice and self-denial. But in Peirce's own Christian terms the love with which one loves one's own wife is based on unquestioned fidelity and not on the "irritation of doubt" and the "problematic situation" without which science could never advance. Perhaps Peirce was trying to make a place in science for feeling and emotion and thereby preclude the cold investigator who would deny all sentiment in his quest for knowledge, the "sin" of intellectual pride that worried Nathaniel Hawthorne. Whatever the case, the relationship of science to love remains tenuous: one implies that the forces of nature must be investigated to be controlled, the other that they must be surrendered to as the head yields to the heart.

The modernist doubted that science could fulfill the void left by the collapse of religion, which had made love the mystery of mysteries and truth and reality a matter of faith and the suspending of disbelief, the "promise" of an afterlife. Peirce and the pragmatists circumvented the modernist crisis of truth by shifting emphasis from truth's existence and accessibility to clarifying the meaning of ideas. An idea is true not as a matter of agreement with reality, coherence with a larger system, or its

76. Peirce, *Collected Papers*, vol. 7, 56; see also Yuri K. Melvil, "The Conflict of Science and Religion in Charles Peirce's Philosophy," *Transactions* 2 (1966): 33–50.
77. Peirce, "The Fixation of Belief," 21.

intrinsic defining properties. Since science "works" because it is forever in a state of change and revision, the meaning of an idea also lies in its practical effects, and knowledge becomes an instrument of action in a world of change. The question of reality, however, continued to concern Peirce, perhaps in part because, as John E. Smith has noted, Peirce shared Josiah Royce's unease with the philosophical realists who insisted that the real is independent of being known.[78] Like Royce, Peirce tended toward idealism in recognizing that much of human knowledge deals with the apparent world of signs, symbols, and linguistic representations, whatever it is that remains independent of those signs and ideas. One suspects that Peirce's religious faith in science led him to believe that the investigator is motivated by the assumption that the real can be discovered, or else he would not be dissatisfied with what passes for the real. Of the method of science, Peirce wrote:

> Its fundamental hypothesis . . . is this: There are Real things, whose characters are entirely independent of our opinions about them; those Reals affect our senses according to regular laws, and, though our sensations are as different as are our relations to objects, yet, by taking advantage of the laws of perception, we can ascertain by reasoning how things really and truly are; and any man, if he have sufficient experience and he reasons enough about it, will be led to the one True conclusion. The new conception here involved is that of Reality. It may be asked how I know that there are any Reals. If this hypothesis is the sole support of my method of inquiry, my method of inquiry must not be used to support my hypothesis. The reply is this: 1. If investigation cannot be regarded as proving that there are Real things, it at least does not lead to a contrary conclusion; but the method and the conception on which it is based remain ever in harmony. No doubts of the method, therefore, necessarily arise from its practice, as is the case with all others. 2. The feeling which gives rise to any method of fixing belief is a dissatisfaction at two repugnant propositions. But here already is a vague concession that there is some *one* thing which a proposition should represent. Nobody, therefore, can really doubt that there are Reals, for if he did, doubt would not be the source of dissatisfaction. The hypothesis, therefore, is one which every mind admits. So that the social impulse does not cause men to doubt it. 3. Everybody uses the scientific method about a great many things, and only ceases to use it when he does not know how to apply it. 4. Experience of the method has not

78. John E. Smith, "Community and Reality," in *Perspectives on Peirce*, 101–2.

led us to doubt it, but, on the contrary, scientific investigation
has had the most wonderful triumphs in the way of settling
opinion. These afford the explanation of my not doubting the
method or the hypothesis which it supposes; and not having
any doubt, nor believing that anyone else whom I could influence has, it would be the merest babble for me to say more
about it.[79]

The modernist feels the real world as something unattainable and unde-
monstrable. In view of its elusive and impenetrable character, Peirce upholds the stability and continuity of method. The real may be independent of the thoughts of particular thinkers, yet continuous inquiry can
lead to an agreement by a community of knowers ready to revise their
beliefs in response to new evidence. The real, then, is knowable to the
extent that a community of investigators continue their efforts and inquiry
converges on its object. The real may not be known by being immediately
represented, but it can be indefinitely pursued until it coincides with a
"settled opinion" that results from inquiry.

Did Peirce's formulation resolve the crisis of reality and truth? Perhaps
any answer depends upon what question is being raised. The method of
scientific, or laboratory, inquiry and the method of "settling opinion"
may be two different activities. For the former asks nature to yield its
secrets, whereas the latter asks inquirers to interpret their meaning. Opinions, in short, are settled by consensus. Now consensus is a relation
arrived at among a group of investigators, and the relation itself does not
necessarily tell us that the consensus is true but only that it has satisfied
the criterion of agreement about what is believed to be true. In taking
agreement as the defining characteristic of the true, Peirce is not giving
us an account of the object of consensus independent of the consensus
itself. As a matter of deep conviction he did hold that "truth is the conformity of a representamen to its object, its object, ITS object, mind you."[80]
For he believed that representational signs must not only refer to their
objects but be compelled by them. Yet since in Peirce's universe there is
no dualism between thought and thing, knowledge and reality, consensus
would be hammered out through discourse, whether it be the mediation
of logic or that of signs. Would a committee of inquiry be moved more by
persuasion or by proof to reach a consensus that recognizes no distinction
between the two?

Whatever the shortcomings of Peirce's consensual theory of truth, he
came closer than any modern American thinker to resolving the crisis of

79. Peirce, "The Fixation of Belief," 18–19.
80. Peirce, "The Basis of Pragmatism," in *Peirce on Signs*, 254.

intellectual authority without resorting to older philosophical doctrines, simple religious dogmas, or the traditionally coercive "method of authority" itself. By committing a community of intellectuals to accept the same mode of inquiry, he demonstrated how the credulity of individual belief could be submitted to the credibility of professional verification, thereby binding thinkers to the public certification of their beliefs as reliable knowledge. Convinced that truth and reality remained accessible only to a broad and dedicated community of inquirers, Peirce succeeded in making the problem of intellectual authority a matter of hope rather than despair.

At the same time, however, Peirce felt that he must restrict the range of human concerns on which philosophy—or at least pragmatic philosophy—could speak authoritatively. For Peirce was primarily concerned with questionable beliefs rather than indubitable truths, and he explored not so much the basic foundations on which knowledge depends as the logical and probable consequences of beliefs. The scientific method he formulated did not propose to produce statements about reality but to offer a mode of inquiry, based on the continuous testing and revisability of hypotheses, by which science and philosophy obtain ever truer statements that may increasingly approximate reality. Similarly with ethics. Peirce realized that authority hinged on ethical foundations, that vital sense of the "ought" that inspires conduct, and he wanted passionately to construct a philosophical cosmology that would enable modern man to again believe in something common and general. It was his great hope to demonstrate the relationship of thought (logic), conduct (ethics), and feeling (aesthetics) in order to merge intelligence, goodness, and beauty into a "normative science."[81]

Nevertheless, though science may provide knowledge of the true, the good, and the beautiful, whether reason itself could oblige man to strive to realize such ideals is another matter, and Peirce was too honest to try to gloss over this dilemma. He even recognized, with James and Adams, that "reasoning out an explanation of morality" may undermine the very substance of morality.[82] To Peirce, who believed that empirical procedure constituted a kind of self-training in ethical behavior, it did not seem that man could be at the same time both logical and selfish. Yet it did not necessarily follow that man's moral sensibilities increased in proportion to his scientific capacities. The gap between science and ethics remained unresolved, and the authority of pragmatism became procedural, the au-

81. See Richard S. Robin, "Peirce's Doctrine of the Normative Sciences," in *Studies in the Philosophy of Charles Sanders Peirce*, ed. Edward C. Moore and Richard S. Robin (Amherst, 1964), 271–88.

82. Peirce, *Collected Papers*, vol. 1, 359.

thority of methodology. Ultimately pragmatism committed philosophy to the mere forms of knowledge alone, of knowing how to inquire, not what to believe.

Fully aware of this impasse, Peirce even conceded that the vocation of philosophy must remain distant from the human content of society lest modern science become confused with traditional religious concerns. He insisted that science cannot be a guide to conduct because it deals with the probable, tentative, provisional, whereas human behavior yearns for certainty and regularity. People are willing to act on beliefs that presuppose the constancy of reality; scientific knowledge, in contrast, reacts to the vagaries of experience. Similarly, morality is essentially conservative, always wanting to uphold the old and familiar, whereas science is inquisitive and speculative, even if this means that the community it serves must suffer its "shocks."[83] Thus science cannot speak with effective authority and belief systems cannot contribute to intellectual progress. At the heart of the entire Peircean cosmological edifice one encounters the dilemma that haunted Henry Adams. Science itself is incapable of formulating the body of opinions from which a nation draws its sustenance; and beliefs are powerless to provide a mode of existence that will enhance a rational comprehension of reality. This modernist dilemma, so keenly sensed by Adams and Peirce, and perhaps less so by James, lies in the inescapable recognition of the alienation of intellect from life. Peirce understood well that eighteenth-century Scottish thinkers rested beliefs on "habits" and "instincts," whereas the modern science he propounded required the assumption of "fallibilism," the conviction that all knowledge is tentative and impeachable.[84] Such a conviction led Peirce to share the same attitude held by Adams about the impossibility of being a teacher when there are no truths to be taught:

> The first thing that the Will to Learn supposes is a dissatisfaction with one's present state of opinion. There lies the secret of why it is that our American universities are so miserably insigificant. What have they done for the advance of civilization? What is the great idea or where is the single great man who can truly be said to be the product of an American university? The English universities, rotting with sloth as they always have, have nevertheless in the past given birth to Locke and to Newton, and in our time to Cayley, Sylvester, and Clifford. The German universities have been the light of the whole world. The medieval University of Bologna gave Eu-

83. Peirce, "Scientific Attitude and Fallibilism," 44.
84. Peirce, "Critical Common-Sensism," in *Philosophical Writings*, 293–94.

rope its system of law. The University of Paris and that de-
spised scholasticism took Abelard and made him into Descartes. The reason was that they were institutions of learning
while ours are institutions of teaching. In order that a man's
whole heart may be in teaching he must be thoroughly imbued
with the vital importance and absolute truth of what he has
to teach; while in order that he may have any measure of
success in learning he must be permeated with a sense of the
unsatisfactoriness of his present condition of knowledge. The
two attitudes are almost irreconcilable.[85]

Peirce's distinction between teaching and learning contained serious
implications for the relationship of society to science. While society requires beliefs for its very survival, science itself cannot survive except on
the basis of doubt and negation. How then may science serve society
except by undermining its beliefs? It remained for John Dewey to attempt
a reconciliation of society's needs to the demands of science and to demonstrate as well that there is no conflict between teaching and learning, nor
between science and democracy.

85. Peirce, *Collected Papers*, vol. 5, 405.

5

"The Flickering Candles of Consciousness": John Dewey and the Challenge of Uncertainty

"Imagination in Action": Dewey in Love

The British philosopher and anthropologist Ernest Gellner once offered to explain why pragmatism became the dominant creed in America. It was not only that pragmatism stood for cheerful optimism, Gellner suggested; it also flourished in an environment that knew nothing of "crisis and radical discontinuity." Pragmatism's biological vision was perfectly compatible with its emphasis on stability, continuity, and the criteria of "consensus" based upon the unquestioned premise of "cognitive growth." Gellner's observation, while perhaps partly true, is curious in light of the late-nineteenth-century world as seen by Henry Adams and John Dewey. Both writers knew of the Civil War, clearly the greatest crisis the Republic ever faced, and wherever they looked they saw an environment of conflict and disruption together with the instabilities and uncertainties produced by accelerated change. The reception of pragmatism may have had less to do with America's supposedly vaunted stability than with its deeper distrust of authority and its modernist bias against the old in favor of the new.[1]

1. Ernest Gellner, "Pragmatism and the Importance of Being Earnest," in *Pragmatism: Its Sources and Prospects*, ed. Robert J. Mulvaney and Philip M. Zeltner (Columbia, South Carolina, 1981), 43–65. The point made by Gellner and others about the reception of pragmatism in America needs to be qualified by a reminder that pragmatism in the beginning was not that well received. It met some resistance among public figures who felt truth slipping away, and even among some professional philosophers it seemed a little cavalier about abandoning the foundations of knowledge. In the first decade of the twentieth century leading pragmatists saw themselves on the defensive. Writing to James in 1909, Dewey observed that the publication of the former's *Pragmatism* "amply discharged" the author from any obligation to make himself clear to the public. Of philosophical critics Dewey

While James and Peirce struggled intermittently with the issue of authority, the former rejecting it as a refuge for those seeking false spiritual shelter, the latter dismissing all its prescientific expressions as philosophical anachronisms, Dewey offered the most comprehensive case against authority in modern American intellectual history. Dewey derived from James and Peirce flashes of insight into epistemology, ontology, and metaphysics, and from these brilliant fragments he constructed a whole philosophical universe, a systematic, unified theory of man and society in which there would be no essential need for historical knowledge and belief. In the writings of Dewey authority found its most profound and consistent antagonist and modernism its most vigorous and thoughtful champion. While artists and poets tried to find aesthetic responses to "the shock of the new," Dewey taught Americans not only how to endure such shocks but how to thrive on them.

Dewey was fond of quoting Emerson's adage that all "truth lies on the highway."[2] The philosopher agreed with the poet that the paths by which truth is pursued will suffice for the modern mind. The pragmatist is an intellectual traveler more interested in the voyage than in the destination. For a country that is more concerned about ways and means than about ends and ultimate goals, pragmatism emerged as a philosophy of affirmation about the infinite potentialities of intelligence. Adams, it will be recalled, shared with European thinkers such as Nietzsche the chilling thought that the mind had stretched its limits to the point that it could only doubt, deny, and disturb. America had no need of such traveling companions.

In accepting Dewey's philosophy American culture would leave behind the negations and cosmic skepticism of Adams. Not that Dewey himself was insensitive to the dilemmas of modernism. The popular philosopher, with silver-gray hair, drooping mustache, and quizzical spectacles, courageously faced the problems that had troubled Adams. Dewey admired the historian for his insights into the debilitating nature of American politics. In *Art as Experience*, he complimented Adams's sense of aesthetic beauty and the human need for it, and he too saw that medieval cathedrals, in contrast to "ugly" modern skyscrapers, grew organically with the architect's plans so that the idea and its objective embodiment developed simultaneously. Dewey similarly started out assuming that history could be approached scientifically and that modern science and its methods

---

grew weary "trying to make them understand who do not wish to understand." John Dewey to William James, Mar. 1, 1909, James mss.

2. John Dewey, "Emerson—The Philosopher of Democracy," *The Middle Works*, 1899–1924; vol. 3, *Essays on the New Empiricism* (Carbondale, Ill., 1983), 189.

would supplant classical philosophy and its categories. The philosopher had the same hunger for unification as the historian, and he also sensed that the problem with America was the American mind mired in Lockean individualism. He also believed that any new philosophical stance must begin where Darwinian science had left off, and he too saw the universe as essentially unstable and in need of control. Both saw education as a means of either expanding the mind or testing its limits.

Dewey also resembled Adams in matters other than cerebral. Like Adams, Dewey was a man of feeling, and he also knew the meaning of unrequited romantic love. One does not find Dewey prating of the domestic virtues of women, as did James. Dewey could readily have accepted Adams's warning that to know women only through men was to know them wrongly. Dewey had fallen in love with a graduate student while married to his first wife, Alice Chapman, who died in 1927. The platonic affair moved Dewey to pour out his soul privately in ninety-eight poems that have only recently seen the light of day.[3] The poems make explicit what remained implicit in Adams's correspondence with Elizabeth Cameron: "Of untamed desire / Of thoughts which travel th'untracked wild" and cause the philosopher to awake from his sleep and realize the distance that separates them:

> Generations of stifled worlds reaching out
> Through you,
> Aching for utt'rance, dying on lips
> That have died of hunger,
> Hunger not to have, but to be.

Why explore a philosopher's emotional response to love in a book that deals with the rational dimensions of pragmatism and modernism? In part because the subject suggests that the will to believe may not in all instances lead to freedom, as James assumed, but to its opposite, to the surrender of autonomy, as Freud noted when he observed that "credulity of love" is the most fundamental submission to authority. A peek at Dewey's emotional life may also suggest that modern morality does not necessarily depend upon premodern certainty.

Adams's sense of modernity convinced him that love is a creation of the imagination and that the ability to live for it surpassed the prudence of rational intelligence. Adams's heroines in *Democracy* and *Esther* also saw love as an invitation to marriage, an institution in which filial responsibility threatened emotional fulfillment. After the death of his wife he chose

---

3. Dewey, *The Poems of John Dewey*, ed. Jo Ann Boydston (Carbondale: Southern Illinois University Press, 1977).

to remain single and carried out his love for Elizabeth Cameron at the safe distance of correspondence. Curiously, Dewey chose the same strategy with Anzia Yezierska, a vibrant, attractive Polish-American who attended his seminars during the World War I years. Yezierska made use of Dewey's poems in the novels she later wrote, and the philosopher helped instill self-confidence in her ambitions to be a writer. Reservations about family responsibilities and age differences—he was going on sixty when she was in her early thirties—sobered Dewey out of any thought of consummating the relationship:

> Riches, possessions, hold me? Nay,
> Not rightly have you guessed
> The things that block the way,
> Nor into what ties I've slowly grown
> By which I am possest.
>
> Who makes, has. Such the old old law.
> Owned then am I by what I felt and saw
> But most by them with whom I've loved, and fought,
> Till within me has been wrought
> My power to reach, to see and understand.
> Such is the tie, such the iron band.[4]

The discovery of Dewey's secret love for Anzia Yezierska is by no means a scandal. On the contrary, it indicates the philosopher's capacity for the deepest feelings and the joys of friendship. But in view of Dewey's lifelong commitment to pragmatism, his aching relationship with her represents one instance when philosophy had no answer to the needs of the heart. Adams well recognized this dilemma when thinking about Elizabeth Cameron. Yet the historian could console himself with the Pascalian thought that whatever moved the emotions remained beyond the reach of the intellect. Dewey was reluctant to admit of such dualisms. Again and again he insisted that the ideal is "warranted" to the extent the means are available to reach it. Morever, Dewey refused to acknowledge that private experience could be isolated as an existing reality. "The privacy of enjoyments and sufferings in their occurrence seem to describe a *social* fact," he advised, suggesting that the nature of mental knowledge does not confine itself to introspection alone but instead is conditioned by the public context of moral sentiments and epistemological impediments.[5] Dewey doubted that any form of immediate self-knowledge would elimi-

---

4. Ibid., 3–14.
5. Dewey, "How Is Mind to Be Known?" *Journal of Philosophy* 39 (1942): 29–35.

nate the need for reflection and inquiry, exercises that made the individual aware of the social conditions of his situation and the consequences of acting upon them. The ironies are rich.

As a philosopher Dewey denied that knowledge could mean something intrinsically private that could never be acted upon. As a love-struck poet, he felt all the more deeply precisely what could not be fulfilled in the practical world. Pragmatism promised to take creatures of "desire" and show them how to reach the "desirable." Dewey's love poems evoke the pains and tensions of a mind longing for the impossible. Can pragmatism realize in philosophy what cannot be realized in life?

Dewey became a hero to the Greenwich Village rebels of the World War I years, and it is significant that figures like Floyd Dell, Max Eastman, and Walter Lippmann would go on to write about love and marriage as subjects that fall somewhere between theory and therapy. Adams, one recalls, saw in the perplexities of love the same problem of belief, not the unity of subject and object but the submission of mind and will to something other than the self. "I cannot sublime to Power," he told Elizabeth Cameron. In chapters on love and marriage in *The Modern Temper* and *A Preface to Morals*, authors Joseph Wood Krutch and Lippmann reflected the modernist negations of the "lost generation" of the twenties. To Aldous Huxley and Ernest Hemingway, wrote Krutch, "love is at times only a sort of obscene joke." Lippmann agreed that romantic love must disappoint because it is a momentary pleasure whose immediate fulfillment and simultaneous erosion leave the need for it greater than ever. Emotional illusions like love and sex, Krutch and Lippmann advised, cannot survive their actualization. The liberation of the modern mind from all inhibition is inevitable yet self-defeating, since it destroys the tension, uncertainty, and mystery from which human values are created. Moreover, love is seen in the modern world not as a projection of the romantic imagination but as a crude biological urge, and scientific analysis trivializes the emotion to the point that heartthrobs are reduced to glandular motions. Like Adams, Lippmann and Krutch saw that what holds for romantic love also applies to religious faith:

> We may realize now that the effort to develop the possibilities of love as an adornment of life by understanding it more completely wrecks itself upon the fact that to understand any of the illusions upon which the values of life depend inevitably destroys them; but we realize the fact too late, and even if we should convince ourselves that we have paid too high a price for our rationality, that we should willingly reassume all the taboos of the Victorian if we could feel again his buoyant sense that the meaning of life had been revealed to him through

love, we could no more recapture his illusions by means of an intellectual conviction than we could return to the passionate faith of the Middle Ages merely because, having read Ruskin, we should like to build a cathedral.[6]

In *Art as Experience* Dewey addressed Lippmann and the modernist critique of values like love and religion. He denied the harmful effects of science upon the imagination, and he did so with full awareness of the implications of Weber's "disenchantment of the world." No doubt, Dewey observed, "physical science strips its objects of the qualities that give the objects and scenes of ordinary experience all their poignancy and preciousness, leaving the world . . . without the traits that have always constituted its immediate value. But the world of immediate experience in which art operates, remains just what it was." The advent of modern science does not mean the death of poetry, for humankind has long known the feeling of being "disinherited" from a universe that is alien to its aspirations. Nor does understanding kill love. When two people are said "to fall in love at first sight," Dewey observed, "it is not so instantaneous but the union of two life-histories, the dramatic acting out of habits in an emotionally-charged context." Dewey stressed the role of tension and disharmony in art as essential to creative effort, and he regarded matters of the highest value, both romantic and religious love, as ideals born of the imagination that partake of aesthetic experience and may seek surrogate objects. "The emotion of love may seek and find material that is other than the directly loved one, but that is congenial and cognate through the emotion that draws things into affinity. This other material may be anything as long as it feeds the emotion. Consult the poets, and we find that love finds its expression in rushing torrents, still pools, in the suspense that awaits a storm, a bird poised in flight, a remote star or fickle moon." This phenomenon, Dewey continued, is not a matter of language and metaphor but real emotional identification:

> In all such cases, some object emotionally akin to the direct object of emotion takes the place of the latter. It acts in place of a direct caress, of hesitating approach, of trying to carry by the storm. There is truth in Hulme's statement that "beauty is the marking of time, the stationary vibration, the feigned ecstasy, of an arrested impulse unable to reach its natural end." If there is anything wrong with this statement, it is the veiled intimation that the impulsion *ought* to have reached "its natural end." If the emotion of love between the sexes had not

6. Joseph Wood Krutch, *The Modern Temper* (1929; New York: Harcourt, 1956), 68, 74–75.

been celebrated by means of diversion into material emotionally cognate but practically irrelevant to its direct object and
end, there is every reason to suppose it would still remain on
the animal plane. The impulse arrested in its direct movement
toward its physiologically normal end is not, in the case of
poetry, arrested in an absolute sense. It is turned into indirect
channels where it finds other material than that which is "naturally" appropriate to it, and as it fuses with this material it
takes on new color and has new consequences. This is what
happens when any natural impulse is idealized or spiritualized.
That which elevates the embrace of lovers above the animal
plane is just the fact that when it occurs it has taken into
itself, as its own meaning, the consequences of these indirect
excursions that are imagination in action.[7]

Adams would have had no trouble agreeing with Dewey that the emotion of love can vary its object, and thus he saw the human mind attracted
to the modern Dynamo for much the same reason it has been attracted
to the medieval Virgin. Dewey himself assumed he could find in modern
science some of the cosmic coherence that had once been the sole province
of religion. But Adams could also agree with Krutch that love is "the
wry joke played by the senses and the imagination upon the intellect."[8]
Lippmann even quoted Santayana to give Dewey's analysis a different
twist. "Love," observed Santayana, "is indeed much less exacting than
it thinks itself. Nine-tenths of its cause are in the lover, for one-tenth that
may be in the object. Were the latter not accidentally at hand, an almost
identical passion would probably have been felt for someone else; for,
although with acquaintance the quality of an attachment naturally adapts
itself to the person loved, and makes that person its standard and ideal,
the first assault and mysterious glow of the passion is much the same for
every object." Dewey interpreted the emotion of love as an "arrested
impulse" that could move on to a different object. But Lippmann interpreted Santayana as saying that the riddle of love was not its frustration
but its fulfillment:

This is the reason why the popular conception of romantic
love as the meeting of two affinities produces so much unhap-
piness. The mysterious glow of passion is accepted as a sign
that the great coincidence has occurred; there is a wedding
and soon, as the glow of passion cools, it is discovered that no
instinctive and preordained affinity is present. At this point
the wisdom of popular romantic marriage is exhausted. For it

7. Dewey, *Art as Experience* (1934; New York: Perigee, 1980), 76–77, 338.
8. Krutch, *Modern Temper*, 72.

proceeds on the assumption that love is a mysterious visitation. There is nothing left, then, but to grin and bear a miserably dull and nagging fate, or to break off and try again.[9]

The skepticism of Lippmann's modernist reflections would subvert Dewey's "imagination in action." To the philosopher the sensory world of art demonstrated the inexhaustible connections of the emotions first induced by aesthetic experience. The object or person inducing the emotion may drop out of the picture, but the emotion itself will find a passionate outlet in "other material" and take on "new color" and "consequences." But would not love be dull and redundant if the "mysterious glow" of anticipation were known to lie in the self and not the new object? Does the magnetic force of love lie in the excitement we bring to it more than in the experience we take from it? Dewey could hardly acknowledge the deceits and enigmas of love without acknowledging that experience may be repetitive and without knowledge and value. Thus for Dewey love is not the "great coincidence" of an encounter of man and woman, as Lippmann put it, but instead the continuous activity of the imagination ever in search for "new materials" of aesthetic experience. Elevating romantic love to the level of art, Dewey declared that some aesthetic theories (Hegel's, for one) have demonstrated "a union of necessity and freedom, a harmony of the many and the one, a reconciliation of the sensuous and the ideal."[10] Dewey's war against dualism was personal as well as philosophical. His uncanny ability to reconcile "the sensuous and the ideal" suggests how far he had come from his early religious upbringing.

"An Inward Laceration": The Tension between Religion and Science

Dewey was born in Burlington, Vermont, in 1859, the year Darwin's *On the Origin of Species* was published. In his youth the conflict between religion and science troubled him almost as acutely as it did Adams, James, and Peirce. All four thinkers would get over it as adults, either by resolving the dualism or simply by forgetting the problem. But in his younger years Dewey sensed the yawning gap between spirit and matter. He had been raised by a devout mother, a Congregationalist of serious piety who was forever asking John and his brothers, even in the presence of others, if they were "right with Jesus." The energetic Lucina Dewey, who taught her sons their daily prayers and took them to Sunday services, created a strenuous, demanding religious environment. Dewey never questioned

9. Walter Lippmann, *A Preface to Morals* (1929; New Brunswick, N.J.: Transaction, 1982), 310.

10. Dewey, *Experience and Nature* (1925; Dover, 1958), 359.

the teachings of Burlington's White Street Congregational Church, which retained few traces of Calvinism and its doctrines of election and damnation. He did wonder about the "routine performances" of prayer and sermon even while becoming a Sunday-school teacher himself. Not until he was a junior at the University of Vermont did he experience what might be called a spiritual crisis or turning point. While attending a course in physiology, Dewey encountered a text by Darwin's learned disciple, Thomas Henry Huxley, who was then struggling to liberate the theory of evolution from the "impregnable rock" of Holy Scripture. Awakened by the scientific account of the operation of man's brain and body, Dewey also became interested in Auguste Comte and Herbert Spencer, and he soon found himself in a world altogether different from the Sunday-school rituals of his adolescent years.

The rapture of scientific knowledge proved incapable of turning Dewey into a village agnostic convinced that material reality is all there is and all one needs to know. He still retained his older religious moralism regarding character and will, even though he could hardly dispute Huxley's account of material forces shaping behavior. The tension between science and religion, between new knowledge about reality and an older faith about moral possibility, remained deeply imbedded in the psyche of the mild, shy, self-conscious youth. Many years later he remembered that during this period, when struggling with the conflicting authorities of religion and science while teaching high school in Oil City, Pennsylvania, he had his one experience with the awful unknown. While he sat reading one evening the gnawing doubt again arose "whether he really meant business when he prayed." It was not, he recollected, "a very dramatic mystic experience. There was no vision, not even a definable emotion— just a supremely blissful feeling that his worries were over." Dewey somehow managed to conclude that all his anxieties about spirit and matter were an illusion. What is here is here; the supernatural and transcendent are part of the immediate given, and the finite and natural world can be known and trusted. Freed of the pains of spiritual disquietude, Dewey explained: "I've never had any doubts since then, nor any beliefs."[11]

Dewey may have found a certain tranquillity in his single "mystic

11. Dewey, "From Absolutism to Experimentalism," in *Contemporary American Philosophy*, ed. George P. Adams and William P. Montague (New York, 1930), vol. 2, 13–27; for Dewey's earlier life I have benefited from two valuable studies: Max Eastman, "John Dewey: My Teacher and Friend," in *Great Companions: Critical Memoirs of Some Famous Friends* (New York, 1959), 249–93; Neil Coughlan, *Young John Dewey: An Essay in American Intellectual History* (Chicago, 1975); for the religious background of Dewey's philosophy, see the important work by Bruce Kuklick, *Churchmen to Philosophers: From Jonathan Edwards to John Dewey* (New Haven, 1985). The most informative work is the recent biography by Robert Westbrook, *John Dewey and American Democracy* (Ithaca, N.Y.: Cornell University Press, 1991).

experience." But memory of old-fashioned religious authority continued to weigh upon him. In a brief autobiographical sketch written when he was sixty, Dewey referred to an "inward laceration" inflicted upon him by the conflict between scientific truth and revealed dogma that seemed to divide the universe in two. He had once been overwhelmed, he recalled, by the "sense of divisions and separations that were, I supposed, borne upon me as a consequence of a heritage of New England culture, divisions by way of isolation of self from the world, of soul from body, of nature from God." The chasm between empirical science and moral philosophy became a daily obsession to Dewey; he once remarked that he devoted his entire intellectual life to its solution.[12]

Two contemporary sources enabled Dewey to achieve his desired synthesis. From Darwinism Dewey learned that man was not—as Adams had felt in his bones—distinct from nature but actually an organic extension of the evolutionary process. But the philosophical meaning of that process remained unexplained by Darwin, and for the answer to that riddle Dewey turned to Hegel. Although he never became an orthodox Hegelian, Dewey initially embraced Hegelian philosophy as a "liberation." The very elements of Hegel that Adams found amusing nonsense, the notion that reality is inherently contradictory and that conflicts are fruitful collisions yielding higher synthesis, Dewey seized upon as an answer to dualism. The idea that reality must be seen as a continuity between matter and spirit, emotion and reason, mind and society, and that all reality, the bad together with the good, is part of a process of inner and external struggle toward the realization of its own free and ultimate being, left a permanent impression on Dewey. Hegel's metaphysics of the unifying wholeness and totality of things seemed to resolve once and for all the traditional dualisms that Dewey regarded as the bane of conventional philosophy. By restoring what Dewey called the sense "of unity, of things flowing together," Hegelianism helped modern man overcome the shock of alienation that occurs when one first senses the loss of authority. Henceforth Dewey would identify authority in philosophy with those schools of thought that emphasized the fragmentation of phenomenon, the discontinuity of the self from the world, of mind from body, individual from society, and nature from God. Those who called for authority seemed to Dewey the very thinkers who wanted to confine humankind to its alienated state, to leave us without the intellectual means of overcoming our estrangement from a universe in which we experience what Dewey called "a sense of separatedness," "dividedness," and "loneliness," as though we are forever cut off from something larger than our-

12. Dewey, "From Absolutism to Experimentalism," 13–27; Eastman, 255–62.

selves, that deeper essence that gives our shallow existence meaning and value. Pragmatism would enable man to feel at home in the world.[13]

One way to bring man home from his alienated condition is to show him that the intellectual problems of modernism are more apparent than real. Consider Dewey's approach to two problems that stymied Henry Adams: power and interests. Adams saw American history being determined almost at every turn by the inexorability of power and interests, political and economic forces that overran any assertion of moral authority or ethical principle. Ultimately the Dynamo symbolized power reified and incarnate as Americans worshiped at the altar of science and energy. For Dewey, however, power is simply potency and efficacy, not an alien entity but the human ability to translate thought into action and desire into deed; and interest, rather than suggesting a violation of ideals, is simply what concerns us and commands our attention. The etymology of the term *interesse*, Dewey pointed out, suggests "to be between," the emotional distance that separates the self from its objects. During the period that Adams was writing the *History* and coming to conclude that power and interests had escaped the controls devised by the *Federalist* authors, young Dewey was teaching students that the old eighteenth-century conflicts between "virtue and interests" and "altruism and ego-ism" were philosophically groundless. Since all human action is social in nature and hence involves interaction, man must take account of others and thus regard "what he does as his interests, not for his interests."[14] To Dewey power and interests could hardly invoke the specter of commerce and corruption that haunted Adams, nor could science and technology be anything but benevolent.

Dewey's political philosophy—a subject reserved for a later chapter—required that he take such a position. In rejecting the impression that self-interest must necessarily be immoral, Dewey rejected both the classical idea of "duty" and the Christian principle of "sacrifice." His rejection of traditional political and religious ideas of authority was part of a general critique of the very concept of authority as the enemy of modernity. The idea of authority itself, even though it may have sunk only shallow roots in America's soil, could easily lead to the atrophy of mind and society. In history authority played a negative role by sustaining the superstitions and errors of the past; in education and learning it depended upon coer-

13. Eastman, 263.

14. Dewey, *The Early Works, 1882–1898*, vol. 5, *1895–1898*, ed. Jo Ann Boydston (Carbondale and Edwardsville, Ill., 1972), 122; Dewey, "The Psychology of the Virtues" and "The Psychology of Self-Realization and Its Application to the Egoism-Altruism Controversy," in *Lectures on Psychological and Political Ethics*, ed. Donald F. Koch (1898; reprint, New York, 1976), 181–218.

cion and indoctrination rather than free inquiry; and in contemporary society and politics it functioned to obstruct social change. Dewey had little patience with the classical dualisms of authority and freedom and self and society. If authority resisted change, freedom proved incapable of directing it. The American philosopher dismissed as "absurd" the German notion that freedom and authority could be grasped as a dialectical unity; but in the study of history a synthesis of the two concepts made sense. In the struggles of the past, whether "groups" or "classes," authority stood for collective, institutionalized power and social and political stability, while freedom represented individual aspirations for movement and change. Even when the forces of freedom triumphed, however, the problem of authority remained. For authority had traditionally been conceived as external to the individual, a system of controls and restrictions that humankind had to overcome. The result of this great historical conquest over authority was liberalism, which Dewey saw as exemplified in modern laissez-faire economics and pluralistic politics, both of which identify the individual as the agent of freedom.[15]

Thus what the Founders of the Republic saw as a victory, the triumph of individual natural rights over the power of the state, Dewey saw as a contemporary dilemma, the helplessness of his fellow citizen to act as an individual against the organized power of big business. Dewey also recognized that some philosophers he deeply admired, particularly Emerson and James, gave preeminence to the individual as the fount of freedom as well as authority. In the late twenties and thirties Dewey would subject the liberal legacy to a severe critique at the same time that Walter Lippmann and Reinhold Niebuhr were coming to grips with the problems of liberalism and modernism. All three thinkers, as we shall see, wondered what could be done with an American character that was reluctant to accept the authority of either government, religion, or science.

Neither would Americans accept the full responsibilities of freedom. Although Dewey would continue to have quarrels with Lippmann and Niebuhr, he did share one of their disturbing thoughts that would become characteristic of the modern mind: the mass of men cannot bear the burden of freedom. From his vast reading in intellectual history Dewey realized that almost the entire course of Western culture had conditioned people to be resistant to liberalism. Instead of seeking change, the public feared it, preferring certainty and stability to freedom and experiment. People may speak liberty even while craving authority; and ironically the

15. Dewey, "Authority and Social Change" (1936), reprinted as "Science and the Future of Society" in *Intelligence in the Modern World: John Dewey's Philosophy*, ed. Joseph Ratner (New York, 1939), 343–63; Dewey, *Liberalism and Social Action* (New York, 1935); *The Public and Its Problems* (1927; Denver: Swallow Books, 1954), 96–97.

proponents of authority were not the destroyers of philosophy but its original founding fathers—the Greeks of classical antiquity, the thinkers who taught that nothing is knowable and valuable unless it is unchangeable.

The False Quest for Certainty

Dewey's critique of Greek philosophy, implicit in almost all his texts but spelled out explicitly in *The Quest for Certainty* (1929), derived from his conviction that classical thought rested not only on dubious epistemological grounds; it also rested on ontological fantasies that rendered man confused and alienated. The Platonic notion of eternal "essences" made finite creatures fear the very changing nature of reality that is the rule of life. What gave human alienation its pathos—what made an intellectual like Adams suffer from angst in the face of power and change—was a false belief in absolutes. Even after Darwin showed us that the world must be understood naturalistically, that is, as an ever-changing biological process, some people still believe they have knowledge of something seemingly certain, even if it can only be vaguely sensed, whether it be God, the Virgin, or "pure being." The hunger for certitude is the curse of Greek philosophy. The Greeks, moreover, denigrated practical activity because it involved man with the perils of coping with change; instead they offered a "higher" type of truth to be grasped by the inner operations of the mind alone. Dewey regarded this ancient legacy as a mistaken search for security, a philosophical daydream that asked man to aspire to a transcendent wisdom that, because it could never be reached in the mundane world, left him anxious, guilty, and incapable of practical action. The quest for a "universal Being" can only lead to paralyzing self-doubt, since thought as well as action can never attain more than a tentative, probable truth. "All the fear, disesteem and lack of confidence which gather about the thought of ourselves, cluster also about the thought of the actions in which we are partners. Man's distrust of himself has caused him to desire to get beyond and above himself; in pure knowledge he has thought he could attain this self-transcendence."[16]

Dewey discerned three serious flaws in classical Greek philosophy: it distorted the true operations of the mind; it misconstrued the actual object of knowledge; and it divided and fragmented reality's essential unity. The mind for Dewey could not be a pure faculty of contemplation with the knower as a passive "spectator"; on the contrary, the mind arises in response to immediate practical needs and it functions to modify the contin-

16. Dewey, *The Quest for Certainty* (1929; New York: Capricorn Books, 1960), 6–7.

gencies of existence. And what the mind comes to know in this process are not timeless, antecedent truths; on the contrary, the mind changes what it knows in the act of knowing it. Thus, given the dynamic interaction of mind and environment, reality cannot be perceived apart from experience, and the universe cannot be separated into the real and ideal, a separation that leads to all the false dualisms that Dewey repudiated: man and nature, mind and matter, subject and object, theory and practice, science and morality, fact and value, means and ends. Dewey responded to modernism by showing how the problems that burdened traditional philosophy need not burden the modern mind.

As the high priest of modern American liberalism, Dewey has seldom been regarded as a philosopher of authority. Yet he remained absorbed by the issue, and *The Quest for Certainty* devotes several chapters to the subject, one revealingly titled "The Intellectual Seat of Authority." Dewey could find no satisfactory resolution to the issue in the entire course of Western intellectual history. Even the modern philosophers who influenced his early development left him skeptical. In *German Philosophy and Politics* (1915), a controversial work that some intellectuals took to be an attack on Prussian culture for its alleged responsibility for World War I, Dewey undertook a critical examination of Hegel and Kant with the problems of authority, sovereignty, liberty, and obedience in mind.[17] Dewey could find no democratic vision in Hegel, who located authority in the state as the disciplining agent of human "desire" and the ultimate embodiment of "world spirit." With greater severity he criticized Kant's conception of authority, where reason imposed an ethic of duty on the individual, a dangerous injunction, Dewey observed, that could lead the individual to mistake the dictates of his own reason for obedience to the commands of some external or arbitrary rule, thereby identifying the self with politically constituted authority.[18]

Dewey's critical reaction to Hegelian and Kantian rationalism derived from his antipathy to rationalism in general. Rationalism, which had its origins in Greek thought, was the bane of a philosophy that had come to exercise a tyrannical hold over the Western mind for twenty-five hundred years. By rationalism Dewey meant the invoking of "eternal principles" that purport to explain actions but actually justify them in ways that "mask" the real nature of events. Thus again and again Dewey returned in his writings to the original misbegotten conceptions of Greek philosophy that had equated authority with eternal and universal truth, a notion

17. See Dewey's exchange with Ernest Hocking over the book on German philosophy in *New Republic* 48 (Oct. 2, 1915): 234–36.

18. Dewey, *German Philosophy and Politics* (New York, 1915).

that had influenced Christian doctrine and thus permeated much of modern thought, religious as well as secular. The classical emphasis on universal concepts shifts our attention from the specific context in which the mind functions to the inner logic of the concepts themselves. Greek philosophers also conceived reality to be the world of the eternal, something antecedently existent, whereas the world in which we live and act is the world of experience, a world of change and flux that can never really be known because it is shaped by the shifting "shadows" of impressions and opinion. Here Dewey calmly confronts one of the problems of modernism by asserting that reality cannot be known because the mind has no means of representing it.

How could Dewey be so sure that the unknown could not be known? Peirce, it will be recalled, believed that reality could be known because representations are subject to scrutiny and progressive revision as their objects struggle to have their existence recognized. Dewey denied any distinction between reality and experience and hence did not feel obligated to deal with the problem of representation. For Dewey the criterion of knowing would be observation. In his version of pragmatism, knowledge becomes a form of action that changes things to produce measurable effects. To be and to know is to do and to act.

But classical thinkers, imbued with the rapture of pure "Being," disparaged the world of endless doing and becoming and recognized in philosophy what Henry Adams had discovered in history: experience could never yield truth. As the leading exponent of American pragmatism, Dewey could do no other than to repudiate the classical idea that to know is to grasp the immutable and to invoke authority is to voice the universal.[19]

What seemed to the American philosopher most disturbing was the Greek depreciation of practical activity. That disdainful attitude relegated doers to the low status of working with their hands in order to live and elevated thinkers to the esteemed status of passive contemplation. The same attitude resulted in a separation of practice from theory that legitimated master-slave relationships and made obedience the duty of the laborer and authority the privilege of the thinker. The denigration of practice that accompanied slavery and the harsh social conditions of the predemocratic and prescientific world stemmed from two philosophical premises:

> First, namely, that the object of knowledge is some form of ultimate Being which is antecedent to reflective inquiry and independent of it; secondly, that this antecedent Being has among its defining characteristics those properties which alone

19. Dewey, *Quest for Certainty*, 3–73.

have authority over the formation of our judgments of value—
that is, of the ends and purposes which should control conduct
in all fields—intellectual, social, moral, religious, esthetic.
Given these premises—and only if they are accepted—it follows that philosophy has for its sole office the cognition of this
Being and its essential properties.[20]

Dewey was willing to reject these premises and thus to throw out the
baby along with the bathwater, the Greek conception of authority along
with the classical epistemology on which it rested. With Dewey the "sole
office" of philosophy was not the apprehension of universal ideas through
meditation. The quest for truth and the ultimate nature of things gives
way to the goals not of philosophy but of psychology. The modern philosopher is not to dwell on the problem of objective reality but to immerse
himself in the flux of human experience. But "experience," as we shall
see, becomes a vague, incantatory expression of Dewey's, and here we
begin to encounter some of the problems in the pragmatist confrontation
with modernism. Even if one grants that, after Darwinism, truth can no
longer be regarded as an inherent quality of thought, one can only wonder, with Adams, what one is to learn from experience. Can experience
itself illuminate the nature of moral and political authority, explaining
not only how authority functions and why people obey but the more
difficult question—why they should obey?

It may be well to consider here the Greek conception of authority in
light of Dewey's strictures, especially that conception as explicated by a
modernist thinker with Hellenic proclivities—Hannah Arendt. In classical philosophy knowing and doing represented two discrete activities, and
the political implications of this epistemological dualism could only be
undemocratic: authority resided in knowing and obedience in doing. But
one purpose of this distinction between theory and practice was to locate
authority in a source that would be safe from belief and opinion, from
the shifting moods of sentiment and impression in which men are free
only to conform to the views of each other. As Arendt has observed, the
Greeks structured the principle of authority on truths that can compel
the mind, permanent truths that can judge everyday behavior because
they stand above the realm of human affairs. The aspect of Plato's philosophy that had the greatest influence in the Western tradition was the conviction that the source of the legitimate exercise of power "must be beyond
the sphere of power and, like the law of nature or the commands of God,
must not be man-made." Moreover, the Roman concept of authority,
from which the original term *auctoritas* derives, was rooted in the past,

20. Ibid., 69.

and thus those who acted in the name of legitimate authority conceived themselves as properly returning to historical origins and "augmenting" the republic's founding.[21] Thus whether authority resided in immutable ideas, as with the Greeks, or in the eternal past, as with the Romans, the final source of authority remained either beyond the range of human deeds or in a remote ancestral memory that could be reinvoked but never repudiated.

Dewey had his work cut out for him. Where classical writers looked to transcendent ideas or the historical past for true knowledge, Dewey looked to probable hypotheses and present problems as the place where useful knowledge asserts itself. And where ancient philosophers looked to thought as the ordering agency that would give society ideas at which to aim, Dewey believed that practical activity itself could serve as an ideal by which men could order their lives. Dewey's pragmatic naturalism, locating the origins and validity of ideas in human experience, arrived at a conclusion that turned upside down the assumptions of classical thought: authority, like truth, is neither given by nor revealed to the theoretical intellect, but instead is produced by human activity. Dewey believed that Thomas Hobbes was one of the first political philosophers to recognize that authority does not lie in law alone, whether written or unwritten, but in the power to elicit obedience, and he praised Hobbes's effort to establish the study of politics on a scientific basis, one that would explain political obligation in terms of interest and expediency rather than classical principles or theological commandments.[22]

Dewey wrote his essay on Hobbes in 1918, a year after he had urged liberals to endorse America's intervention in World War I and accept the necessity of force and power in diplomacy. We shall return to that episode in the following chapter. Here it is important to mention that Dewey's Hobbesian reasoning raises a host of troubling questions. If authority derives from everyday experience, how can the contingencies of experience yield order and stability? If authority does not lie in a source external to and independent of man's actions, how can it govern his actions? Henry Adams, it will be recalled, saw "principle" surrendering to "circumstance" at almost every stage of American history. But where Adams concluded that political authority had "expired" in America, Dewey insisted that an understanding of historical circumstances will show us how authority functions in specific situations. Ultimately Dewey was less interested in distinguishing authority from power, than in reconciling authority and

21. Hannah Arendt, "What Is Authority?" in *Between Past and Future: Eight Exercises in Political Thought* (New York, 1968), 91–141.
22. Dewey, "The Motivation of Hobbes's Political Philosophy," *Studies in the History of Ideas* 1 (1918): 88–115.

freedom. In this bold enterprise, one of the noblest efforts in modern democratic philosophy, Dewey confronted a number of traditional philosophical issues whose resolutions had to be demonstrated before authority could be democratized: man's alienated relationship to nature; inquiry and the concept of truth; ethics and moral judgment; and the problem of historical knowledge.

Alienation and the Origins of Mind

The concern of the philosopher, wrote Dewey in his seminal work, *Experience and Nature* (1925), "is not with morals but with metaphysics, with, that is to say, the nature of the existential world in which we live."[23] No less than Henry Adams was Dewey caught up in the problems of the real world, and he too grasped the precarious and unstable state of things that could make man tremble with insecurity. Yet although he insisted with Peirce that pragmatic philosophy aims at clarifying meaning, Dewey remained convinced that the meaning of existence is itself a meaningless issue. Free of that discord between mind and spirit that haunted Adams, Dewey accepted life on its own terms, substituting the concept of "experience" for the problem of existence. Dewey had no quarrel with God or nature. Drawing upon Darwin for a theory of nature, and on Hegel for an ontology that could absorb all dualisms, he developed a philosophical system that purported both to explain man's state of alienation and to offer a solution to it.

At the heart of Dewey's philosophy is his definition of man and nature. Dewey conceived man neither as an estranged spirit divided against itself nor as Adams's "atom or molecule" in a mechanistic universe. Instead man was an "organism" operating within a natural and social environment. A unified creature, man must be understood in biological terms, as a product of nature's evolutionary processes, and his problems must be seen as coterminous with those of nature. Man comes into being, so to speak, when his mind begins to grope toward awareness and consciousness as a result of continuous interaction with a changing environment. From this process arises intelligence, the faculty that mediates between man and nature. The purpose of mind is to comprehend, adapt to, and eventually control an environment of change and flux. Curiously, Dewey saw man's natural condition as almost as dangerous and threatening as did Adams. In the chapter titled "Existence" in *Nature and Experience*, Dewey describes man's relationship to nature as "uncertain," "uncontrolled," "perilous," "inconstant," "contingent," "irregular," and "uncannily unstable."[24] Yet

23. Dewey, *Experience and Nature* (1925; New York: Dover, 1958), 45.
24. Ibid., 40–77.

rather than deplore the precarious character of existence, Dewey celebrates its benefits. Out of the interaction of the organism with a troublesome environment arises man's intellectual growth, his capacity to think, analyze, imagine, plan, and control the processes of nature. Unlike some other writers confronting modernism, especially the humanists and proto-existentialists of the Lost Generation, Dewey did not experience nature as an alien presence, much as Adams had seen, upon his sister's death, the Alps as coldly indifferent to human feeling. Denying any distinction between man and nature, Dewey rendered the environment responsive to human ends by virtue of mastering it.

So formulated, Dewey's pragmatism attempts to resolve the dualism between spirit and nature. Adams had conceived man as a disinherited creature vainly struggling to comprehend an alien world. To Dewey man's sense of confusion and estrangement simply reflected the price of consciousness. He rejoiced in affirming the incompleteness of experience and the vagaries of nature. Life confronts us as a struggle between what is precarious and what is stable in existence, and mind is called into being to minimize the contingent and develop the constant elements. Thus the greater the uncertainties of the environment, the greater the challenge to man's reflective intelligence. "The *immediately* precarious, the point of greatest immediate need, defines the apex of consciousness, its intense or focal mode." Dewey repudiated all philosophical systems that would provide final truths in the false hope of liberating man from his existential condition within nature. Such spiritual liberation would mean death to the life of the mind. It would be conceivably "better," Dewey conceded, if man could accept experience as "given" and feel himself at one with a "closed" and "finished" universe, the great dream of older schools of thought. "But," he added, "in that case the flickering candles of consciousness would go out."[25]

Dewey's conception of man and nature could seemingly resolve almost every issue in philosophy except the two problems that preoccupied Adams: alienation and authority. Unwilling to go to the root of the first problem, Dewey naturalizes what may very well be a spiritual condition. Specifically, he does not explain why man experiences nature as discord and contingency. Darwinism, of course, made Dewey aware that nature continually challenges man's capacity for survival, and historically man has responded to this challenge with magic, rituals, gods, and scientific intelligence. Yet this emphasis on control can be narrowly unilateral, positing man as always responsive rather than deliberative, a creature of need rather than desire. The sense of alienation that gripped other mod

25. Ibid., 312, 349.

ernist thinkers arises from an awareness that nature has been conquered and transformed, yet man remains estranged from it. Man may assault nature not only because its disruptions threaten his existence but also because he encounters a reality alien from his being. If man's being fully coincided with that of nature, he would be without necessity and desire; his aspirations and satisfactions would be one and the same, and he would not feel the need to "neutralize [its] hostile occurrences."[26] Other modernist writers would see the tragic "human condition" as springing from the disquieting awareness that man is part of nature, yet aspires to be more than nature. After such awareness, nature and spirit part company, and man is left with the task of changing the natural world and not necessarily the duty of comprehending it. Pragmatic man identifies knowledge with control rather than understanding, with mastery rather than meaning. That he continues to act upon nature to control its processes may enlarge man's intellectual faculties, as Dewey insisted; whether such practical activity can provide anything more than mere expedient knowledge with which to exploit the natural world remains unclear.

Dewey was, of course, perfectly aware of this human predicament. He happily accepted a definition of existence that depicted active man laboring to organize and control an unfinished and ever-evolving environment. Indeed man's continual need to "readjust" to nature sparked the life of the mind that dramatized the height of human ingenuity. Yet Dewey's biological approach to human development prevented him from seeing also how the insecurities of existence result in the drive toward power as much as in the use of intelligence, a point to be explored later in discussing Reinhold Niebuhr. It is here, in Dewey's account of mind's relation to nature, that one begins to encounter difficulties that have serious implications for the problems of authority and modernity.

The difficulty stems from the pragmatist's refutation of Cartesian rationalism, especially the notion that thought is a fixed possession and mind a pure faculty to which self-evident truths are revealed. Dewey's own explanation of the origin and nature of mind derived from Darwinism. Steeped in the language of "process," "struggle," and "adaptation," Dewey believed that mind and intelligence evolved in response to an unstable environment. Does it follow, then, that the meaning of mind and intelligence can be identified with the response as such? Dewey, as his critics have noted, remained ambiguous toward this question.[27] How

26. Dewey, "The Need for a Recovery of Philosophy," in *John Dewey: The Essential Writings*, ed. David Sidorsky (New York, 1977), 72.

27. Although no severe critic of Dewey, John E. Smith touches on this problem in *The Spirit of American Philosophy* (New York, 1963), 126; a more thorough discussion is in T. A. Goudge, "Pragmatism's Contribution to an Evolutionary Theory of Mind," *Monist* 57 (1973):

can mind respond to a precarious situation unless it first possesses the capacity to perceive the situation as precarious? There is also the riddle of Homo sapiens' creative faculties, such as art and music. Such faculties may have conferred no significant utility to primitive societies struggling to survive. Religious cultures based on human sacrifice—even early Christians going before the lions—defy the evolutionary view of mind as an organ of self-preservation. War and aggression may have a Darwinian explanation, but Jefferson wondered why it is that man is the only living creature that systematically kills its own species on a grand scale. Dewey accepted George H. Mead's theory that self-consciousness derives not from introspection but by communicating with others in spoken language. Yet surely among the most intense levels of self-awareness are the frustrations of love and the fears of death. The result of such private angst may express itself in poetry and prayer, but in what sense can pain and sorrow be regarded as originating in adaptive behavior?

The contemporary ecological crisis would also suggest that man is dangerously maladaptive and often acts against his best interests. The pragmatic view of mind as responding to its biophysical environment can hardly explain why the American mind decided to impose an industrial system on a natural landscape. If capitalism derived from Protestantism, it responded to a religious "ethic" that called upon man to forsake the pursuit of material interests in order to lead a Christian life of frugality and hard work. Dewey's own struggles as a youth with the conflict between spirit and matter grew out of a specific Vermont environment, but it was an environment infused with high moral ideals, and one he chose to flee from rather than adapt to, a "problematic situation" that arose from religion and would be resolved by science. If Dewey's mind was with Charles Darwin, his heart was with Huck Finn.

Although Dewey believed that adaptation is more fruitful and liberating than introspection, there is no reason the reverse cannot be true. A mind that is molded by its environmental context may be fit only to respond specifically to that context and be ill prepared to anticipate and imagine a future environment with a different set of problems requiring a distinctly different response. Thus Henry Adams concluded that the Framers gave America a constitution that successfully dealt with controlling political power in an eighteenth-century environment but left Ameri-

---

133–50; and Gellner, "Pragmatism and the Importance of Being Earnest," 43–65; see also the valuable anthology *Dewey and His Critics: Essays from the Journal of Philosophy*, ed. Sidney Morgenbesser (New York, 1977). The first to point out that pragmatism confuses the meaning of truth with its verification was, I believe, Arthur O. Lovejoy in "Pragmatism and Theology" (1908), reprinted in his *The Thirteen Pragmatisms and Other Essays* (Baltimore, 1963), 44–78.

can government unable to respond in the nineteenth century to the rise
of corporate economic power. Adams's worries would perhaps not trouble
Dewey, who could agree with Oliver Wendell Holmes, Jr., and other
pragmatic theorists that the Constitution needs to adapt to new conditions
instead of deferring to old traditions. But such evolutionary advice would
complicate pragmatism's claim to identify with science and the power of
prediction. Since the mind as a biological phenomenon cannot, in theory,
deal with situations it has yet to encounter, how can it anticipate and
extrapolate?

Dewey remained convinced that mind is an organ created by its function because he refused to regard mind as something distinct from nature.
Others would attribute to "instinct" the qualities Dewey attributed to
intelligence, for many of the endowments of the animal and human
world—the eye, the bird's wing, the sense of smell, and the like—evolved
as elementary prehensions apart from the activity of mind. Dewey seems
to identify mind as originating in the evolutionary processes from which
it developed. Thus his conviction that what the mind knows is conditioned by what it experiences has profound implications for the problems
of truth and authority. To the extent that the thought processes of mind
derive from experience, thought itself cannot escape the contingencies of
experience in order to provide regulative principles of knowledge, not to
mention immutable ideas and universal truths. Dewey maintained, of
course, that philosophy aimed to illuminate the processes of change and
not to discover eternal truths disclosed to the mind. This pragmatic resolution raises the question whether a philosophy that conceives reality as
change and knowledge as control can provide answers to questions that
are not so much biological as moral and political.

The Authority of Scientific Inquiry and the Problem of "Truth"

Although regarded by liberals as the philosopher of freedom, Dewey was
no less a philosopher of authority, and he aspired as much as any conservative moralist to make authority a viable concept in the modern world.
The mind itself could still be the fount of authority, for it is philosophy,
the highest activity of mind, that provides the reflective enterprise that
enables man to take his bearings in a chaotic world. Henry Adams, confronted by the perplexities of that same world, believed that philosophical
discourse could only sensitize the mind to its own limitations, driving
man to hunger all the more for knowledge and truth. Dewey's philosophy
offers a way out of Adams's dilemma, and it does so neither by denying
the reality that Adams had faced nor by forsaking the quest for a basis of
authority that would mitigate man's existential condition. Just as Adams

felt that the aim of education is "to control power in some form," so did Dewey feel that the aim of knowledge is "to control the contingent."[28] If Adams responded to a world of "chaos" and "entropy" by trusting instinct and feeling, Dewey responded by trusting intelligence and reason even while feeling the same need. "The need for authority is a constant need of man," wrote Dewey. "For it is a need for principles that are both stable enough and flexible enough to give direction to the processes of living in its vicissitudes and uncertainties."[29]

To Dewey the problem of authority logically involved the problem of knowledge—how do we come to know what we know, and how do we determine whether our beliefs are true? We do so by thinking, and for Dewey thinking should always be regarded as a contextual necessity rather than as a theoretical curiosity. Thought is prompted by the specific conditions of a given environment, whose discordance and instability confront men with "problematic situations" that activate the mind and initiate the processes of "inquiry." This functional description of thought Dewey termed "instrumentalism," and it differs subtly but significantly from both Peirce's and James's version of pragmatism. Where the latter maintained that inquiry arises from a state of psychological tension and culminates in a new state of belief, Dewey insisted that inquiry aims to alter not only mental states but actual conditions, and it does so by rendering an "indeterminate situation" determinate in order to achieve not only emotional comfort but intelligent control. Unlike James, Dewey became interested in knowledge that could contribute to the public good and not only individual success; unlike Peirce, he saw the thinker moved to inquiry not only by an "irritation of doubt" but also by an encounter with a "problematic situation" whose resolution required cooperative effort. But Dewey did agree with Peirce in the possibility of a permanently valid criterion of knowledge. In Dewey's pragmatism ideas are "plans of operation" that enable man to transform a given situation, and the highest expression of this mode of inquiry may be found in modern scientific methodology.

Dewey followed Peirce in looking to the method of scientific inquiry in the physical world as the model for arriving at true knowledge in all areas of life. The experimental method of the natural sciences, proceeding as it does from the formulation of hypotheses to the testing of theories, offers the best means of resolving conflicts about beliefs and of revising our ideas in response to experience. The self-correcting discipline of scien-

28. Dewey, *Experience and Nature*, 87–89.
29. Dewey, "Philosophy of Education," in *Problems of Men* (New York: Philosophic Library, 1946).

tific method implies that while truth is verified in practice, truth itself remains tentative, since beliefs can never be "so settled as not to be exposed to further inquiry." In *Logic: The Theory of Inquiry* (1938), Dewey makes clear that genuine knowledge involves not what is worth believing from the individual's standpoint but what society judges useful, a judgment that must continually be reexamined.[30]

Dewey was careful not to identify knowledge with experience. He had always been suspicious of epistemology, and he once described that branch of philosophy that deals with the nature of knowing as "that species of confirmed intellectual lockjaw."[31] Dewey believed that the philosopher, whether he or she be an empiricist who looks to experience and change or a rationalist who looks beyond experience and inward to the mind's operations, is vainly looking in the wrong place. Experience itself cannot be a "knowledge affair," nor can the act of thought as meditation. For experience cannot be known until the mind reflects on it, and what the mind comes to know are the effects produced by consciously acting upon problematic situations. Dewey drew a distinction between "knowing" and "having" because he was aware of the epistemological impasse that confronted philosophy in the late nineteenth century: the impossibility of mind claiming direct access to an exact "copy" of reality or of possessing a timeless logic of consistency and self-evidence in a world of endless change and transformation. Dewey insisted that knowledge does not take place until a process of inquiry begins, and the aim of inquiry is to interact with and experiment upon an environment in order to bring about knowable consequences. Dewey would perhaps have found absurd the reporter's description of Henry Adams sitting on a fence watching himself go by. For Dewey rejected the "spectator" theory of knowledge, in which knowing is knowledge of some object passively viewed by the knower. To Dewey, watching and viewing, or anything suggesting the presence of something to see, was unreliable and unusable. Dewey would have Adams the spectator join Adams the stroller. Together they would continue until they bumped up against some problem; then they would take the necessary action to resolve it, after which they would have gained knowledge as the awareness and recognition of the specific consequences that result from inquiry.

If Dewey can be accused of avoiding the issues of epistemology, he can also be admired for demonstrating their insolubility. In one of his early essays, "Knowledge as Idealization" (1887), he showed the impossibility

---

30. Dewey, *Logic: The Theory of Inquiry* (New York: 1938), 8.
31. Dewey, "The Practical Character of Reality," in *The Philosophy of John Dewey*, ed. John J. McDermott (Chicago, 1981), 207–22.

of knowing the immediate existence of objects. The epistemologist wants to know such objects "out there" in the real world. But Dewey explained why all objects as existing entities are empty and devoid of meaning until perceived. Ideas as well as physical objects have existence as impressions, but they too scarcely constitute knowledge. "An idiot," wrote Dewey, "has as many ideas, *qua* existences, as Shakespeare; the delirious patient has, in all probability, more in a given time than his physician."[32] Such ideas exist as physical facts without psychical meaning, as sensations without significance. It is only intelligence in the form of attention, reflection, and inquiry that gives experience meaning and significance. In his early years Dewey related philosophy to psychology to make thought the study of conscious experience in response to practical needs. Thus the mind for Dewey was not a looking glass reflecting the world nor a logical faculty for defining truth; instead it was a problem-solving tool for adjusting to an unstable environment.

And truth itself? Dewey's substituting "warranted assertability" for old-fashioned notions of truth was his prosaic way of saying that propositions are warranted only if their predictions deriving from hypotheses are observed and verified. Dewey's repudiation of the whole notion of truth as an enduring idea capable of being directly present to the mind amounted to announcing the "end" of philosophy long before Heidegger or Wittgenstein, as Richard Rorty has argued. Even before Dewey, Henry Adams wondered what would become of philosophy once it lost its innocence about there being ulterior foundations to knowledge. What would truth be in agreement with if not the real? What would knowledge refer to if not its object? To Dewey knowledge would refer to effects and outcomes, and hence the true would be a property of the future, a confirmed prediction. The classical notion of truth as the agreement of thought with things and with other thoughts seemed to Dewey not only untenable but a scandalous illusion. In "The Experimental Theory of Knowledge" (1906) and "The Development of American Pragmatism" (1922) he explained why truth as coherence and correspondence can no longer be supported.

Truth as pure coherence, when there is simply consistency of one belief with another, proves nothing about a particular truth-claim. One might have mental concepts or even fictions based upon a coherent set of propositions. Statements that are compatible or logically consistent must also be empirically verified. As to correspondence, the claim that the mind can copy the object it represents leaves knowledge in a state of mystery:

32. Dewey, "Knowledge as Idealization," *The Early Works*, vol. 1, *1882–1888* (Carbondale: Southern Illinois University Press, 1975), 176–93.

Epistemology starts from the assumption that certain conditions lie back of knowledge. The mystery would be great
enough if knowledge were constituted by non-natural conditions back of knowledge, but the mystery is increased by the
fact that the conditions are defined so as to be incompatible
with knowledge. Hence the primary problem of epistemology
is: How is knowledge *überhaupt*, knowledge at large possible?
Because of the incompatibility between the concrete occurrence and function of knowledge and the conditions back of it
to which it must conform, a second problem arises: How is
knowledge in general, knowledge *überhaupt*, valid? Hence the
complete divorce in contemporary thought between epistemology as a theory of knowledge and logic as an account of
the specific ways in which particular beliefs that are better
than other alternative beliefs regarding the same matters are
formed; and also the complete divorce between a naturalistic,
a biological and social psychology, setting forth how the function of knowledge is evolved out of other natural activities,
and epistemology as an account of how knowledge is possible
anyhow.[33]

The divorce between epistemology and logic came about because
Locke, Descartes, and other philosophers who assumed truth as correspondence between thought and its object never successfully demonstrated how it could be established. Thus philosophy found itself either
paralyzed with Hume's total skepticism or pondering Kant's extra-
empirical *Ding-an-sich*. But the whole project of philosophy needs to be
rethought, especially the idea of experience. Traditional philosophy,
Dewey pointed out, regarded experience as the exclusive possession of
the private subject and hence sought to ground knowledge in something
extraneous to experience that represented the external world. Why,
Dewey asked, continue to try to prove the existence of the external world
when we find ourselves already in it, as evidenced not only by our interactions with its processes but also by our need to adjust thought and behavior to the "course of nature"? Dispensing with epistemology, Dewey
sought to develop a logic of inquiry to illustrate how the "knowing medium" takes shape, not the relationship between mind and object but the
method for dealing with things to be known based upon our intentions
and purposes. A theory then corresponds to facts not as they exist but
when the theory is applied and carried out and "leads to facts which are
its consequences." Experimental knowledge is always prospective, since
it deals with consequent phenomena. True scientific knowledge addresses
itself to the processes of change that rule nature.

33. Dewey, "The Experimental Theory of Knowledge," in *Philosophy of Dewey*, 186.

Henry Adams saw the significance of the historical triumph of scientific thought much as Dewey did. But Adams remained disturbed at the thought that the advent of science and the turn toward nature meant that humankind had given itself over to the promises of force, energy, and power. Nature can be commanded only by being obeyed, if even by accident. "Evidently a new variety of mind had appeared. Certain men merely held out their hands,—like Newton, watched an apple; like Franklin, flew a kite; like Watt, played with a tea-kettle—and great forces of nature stuck to them as though she were playing ball." Discoveries in science seemed like "the sports of nature," and once thought is seen as evolving from nature, philosophy with its search for unity and foundations is dead, or, more accurately, left to follow something alien to itself—the dynamics of power:

> Except as reflected in himself, man has no reason for assuming unity in the universe, or an ultimate substance, or a prime-motor. The *a priori* insistence on this unity ended by fatiguing the more active—or reactive—minds; and Lord Bacon tried to stop it. He urged society to lay aside the idea of evolving the universe from a thought, and to try evolving thought from the universe. The mind should observe and register forces,—take them apart and put them together,—without assuming unity at all. "Nature, to be commanded, must be obeyed." "The imagination must be given not wings but weights." As Galileo reversed the action of earth and sun, Bacon reversed the relation of thought to force. The mind was thenceforth to follow the movement of matter, and unity must be left to shift for itself.[34]

Such an interpretation of the meaning of science and scientific knowledge, in which mastery of nature requires mind to subjugate itself to the power that resides in matter, could only strike Dewey as alien and confusing. Dewey agreed that Galileo and Bacon had reoriented philosophy from reason to investigation and from the permanent to the changing. But Dewey's logic of inquiry aimed to show why science can serve our purposes: "Inquiry is the controlled or directed transformation of an indeterminate situation into one that is so determinate in its constituent distinctions and relations as to convert the elements of the original situation into a unified whole."[35]

Dewey's faith that humankind can achieve the status of a "unified whole" by making indeterminate situations determinate is reminiscent of

34. Adams, *Education*, 484.
35. Dewey, "The Pattern of Inquiry," in *Philosophy of Dewey*, 226.

a Hegelian's faith in history's unfolding of spiritual wholeness in opposition to the contingency and indeterminacy of worldly things. In inquiry one changes ("converts") the reality that one is trying to know, and thus the subject can no longer feel alienated from its object, nor can spirit be estranged from nature. From Adams's viewpoint, Dewey is trying to find in nature what Aquinas found only in God and not in science: unity, order, sequence, pattern, meaning—everything that renders life determinate and not subject to an alien will. A "unified whole" emerges from nature as human intelligence works upon and refashions its materials. Dewey believed that science makes genuine knowledge possible, and that the purpose of philosophy is to interpret the results of science. Adams saw science as uncovering aspects of nature that were indeterminate, anarchical, even "parricidal," like the discovery of radium, which confirmed the impermanence of matter. To paraphrase Adams: chaos is the law of nature; "a unified whole" the dream of man. With science it is nature, not mind, that reveals a universe that defies the senses, a "supersensuous" universe of an increasing multiplicity of forces demanding to be recognized by an intelligence more controlled than controlling. In abandoning philosophy for science, the pragmatic inquirer follows the attractions of power in order better to control the world.

If science meant to Adams the frightening acceleration of energy and the mindless movement of matter, to Dewey it meant the promising liberation of knowledge and the dispelling of such dualisms that claimed mind and nature are distinct and that being is prior to knowing. For the work of science indicated that one could know the objects created as a result of experimentation. Collapsing the classical distinction between knowledge and action, Dewey believed that we encounter the world in our involvements with it rather than our representations of it. Since there is no way to conceptualize objects independently of our engagements with them, it might be said that Dewey believed that philosophy should be more concerned with coping than with knowing, with results in public action rather than with thoughts in private contemplation, with verifiable outcomes instead of conceptual propositions.

Dewey's verification theory of truth and his notion of a "continuum of inquiry" created a host of problems involving the very meaning of truth, problems inherent also in James's and Peirce's theories, which philosophers are still debating today.[36] All three American pragmatists rejected

36. See, for example, Bertrand Russell, *An Inquiry into Meaning and Truth* (New York, 1940); George Dicker, "Knowing and Coming to Know in John Dewey's Theory of Knowledge," *Monist* 57 (1973): 191–219; Joseph Margolis, "The Relevance of Dewey's Epistemology," in *New Studies in the Philosophy of John Dewey*, ed. Steven N. Cahn (Hanover, N.H.: University Press of New England, 1977), 117–48.

the older correspondence theory of truth, in which beliefs are supposed to derive from knowledge of actual facts that can be accurately represented; and they could not accept completely the coherence theory of truth, in which judgments are true if they partake of logically necessary relations and concern an ultimate reality intelligible to the mind that progressively apprehends it. To the pragmatist truth is never actual but potential, never total but partial and tentative. Whether a potentially true idea be regarded as whatever moves one from a state of doubt (Peirce) or as a volitional belief precipitating action (James) or as "a plan of operation" that equips us to control the environment (Dewey), truth is not a property inherent in an idea but something that happens to an idea in the process of experiencing it. Ideas become true to the extent they either "work efficiently and satisfactorily" (James), enable us to measure their practical consequences and "sensible effects" through scientific inquiry (Peirce), or provide us with "warranted assertibility" with which we can act upon hypotheses and solve problems (Dewey).[37] To be sure, there are distinctions in these definitions; yet they all share one premise: truth is not discovered but produced; it does not exist but comes into being, so to speak, in the act of knowing. Any other formulation of truth—for example, the view that a law or principle exists independently of the knowing mind—must be rejected because it cannot be empirically verified. This raises the question, put to pragmatists by several philosophers, friends and foes alike, whether an idea that is proven to be true was true all along. Are not pragmatists confusing what truth is with how we find it out, thereby mistaking the process for the substance?

The pragmatists replied that one cannot distinguish between the process of inquiry and the object of inquiry, for what is being investigated is determined to a large extent by the hypotheses and questions formulated by the investigator, and the investigator's own concerns are shaped by culture and society. All thinking is conditioned by its context, truth is made rather than found, and reality has no cognizable antecedent existence but instead becomes that which inquiry compels scientific researchers to agree it is for the purpose of solving a specific problem. The pragmatist response to the modernist crisis of knowledge was to make truth not so much a matter of philosophical proof as one of rational acceptance. All that truth can possibly mean is the practical results of inquiry, and society informed by science is the best judge of what works.[38]

To argue that the validity of an idea lies in its practical consequences

---

37. H. S. Thayer, *Meaning and Action: A Critical History of Pragmatism* (Indianapolis, 1968), 120–29, 148–52, 192–99.

38. *Dewey and His Critics,* 167–308.

and workability was hardly original, and the pragmatists were the first to admit that they were merely offering new ways of thinking about old ideas. But the insistence that the meaning of an idea lies in its verification may have done more to obscure the problem of truth and authority than to resolve it. The theory that true knowledge must wait upon experience offered a form of knowledge, and doubtless an accurate one, but not the kind of knowledge for which one had traditionally turned to authority in the past. Traditionally authority implied, among other things, the capacity to give credence to a judgment, make pronouncements on moral and political issues, and declare the lawfulness, rightfulness, or truthfulness of propositions and assertions. Yet pragmatic authority must suspend judgment until the process of verification takes place. Here in Dewey's philosophy emerges another paradox in pragmatism as troublesome as the ones found in James. While Dewey's theory of knowledge offers "plans of action" relating to the future, knowledge is really acquired in the past, after the event, when experience renders its judgment.

What authoritative knowledge traditionally supplied, or purported to supply, was not only the lessons of experience but also some assurance of the reliability of our ideas before they are put into practice. If pragmatic knowledge must always be from hindsight, of what value is it in guiding our thoughts prior to acting? It would be the ultimate irony to conclude that pragmatic knowledge is neither useful nor practical, but one cannot avoid Arthur O. Lovejoy's conclusion, spelled out in "The Thirteen Pragmatisms" (1908), that Dewey's theories about the ex post facto criterion of truth are "as irrelevant and redundant a thing as a coroner's inquest on a corpse is—to the corpse."[39]

Perhaps the most severe criticism of pragmatism concerns its presumed equation of the true and the useful. G. E. Moore pointed out that ideas can be false and useful and true and futile; hence utility itself cannot be the only property of all true ideas. Nor can the true itself be defined by reference to another attribute conducive to utility. To many critics any definition of truth involving what "works," "pays," and brings "satisfaction" was simply too crass to deserve the aura of authority. Santayana, an admirer of James as a "man of the Left" who faced a meaningless world with both bravery and compassion, nonetheless concluded that James's translation of truth into willfulness offered Americans "courage" when they really needed "wisdom," and he chided Dewey for denying the poetic nature of consciousness by "dissolving the individual into his social functions." Perry Miller, the foremost American intellectual historian, likened James's "The Will to Believe" to a pill or a good stiff drink—

39. Lovejoy, *The Thirteen Pragmatisms and other Essays*, 12.

it doesn't really resolve philosophical issues, but it may help us pass a restful night. Bertrand Russell, who rejected as "distasteful" Dewey's use of knowledge "merely as a means to other satisfactions" instead of as a form for articulating "the ends of life," also dismissed James's exploitation of belief in God as an exercise in therapy and benevolence rather than inquiry and philosophy. Lewis Mumford stated the case against pragmatism even more sardonically. "He used philosophy," wrote Mumford of James, "to seek peace rather than understanding, forgetful of the fact that if peace is all one needs, ale can do more than Milton can, 'to justify God's ways to man.'"[40]

Unfair, perhaps, but in pragmatism one finds neither a deep sensibility to alienation nor much anxiety about the eclipse of authority and truth. "The mistake of pragmatism," observed Ernest Gellner, "is to feel too much at home in the world. It knows neither nausea nor vertigo."[41] Certainly the young James knew both. Before we substitute an anguished humanism for an allegedly complacent pragmatism, it is important to keep in mind what the pragmatic turn in modern thought entailed. Directed primarily to the human phenomenon of activity and experience, pragmatism does not ponder the objects of knowledge but only problems of knowing, and all problems include the possibility of their solution—even the problems of authority and modernity.

Dewey shared with Peirce the conviction that the answer to the eclipse of older notions of truth and authority lies in modern scientific methodology. The empirical system of investigation provides the means for resolving conflicts that arise when people hold differing beliefs. A community of inquirers dedicated to verifying ideas through scientific methods would also eliminate the radical subjectivism in James's personal "satisfactory" notion of truth and ensure that practical inquiry yields objective results. In the absence of older philosophical and religious authority, of absolute systems and sacred dogma, science emerges as the only reliable source of authority capable of illuminating experience and directing behavior.

The writings of Peirce and Dewey gave powerful expression to a movement in American social thought that had been developing since the late

40. G. E. Moore, "William James's 'Pragmatism,'" in *Pragmatic Philosophy*, ed. Amelie Rorty (Garden City, N.Y.: Anchor, 1966), 328–38; George Santayana, "William James," 73–88; Santayana, "Dewey's Naturalistic Metaphysics," in *Dewey and His Critics*, 343–58; Perry Miller, introduction to *American Thought: Civil War to World War I*, ed. Perry Miller (New York, 1954), xxxii–xxxiv; Bertrand Russell, *An Inquiry into Meaning and Truth*; Lewis Mumford, "The Pragmatic Acquiescence," in *Pragmatism in American Culture*, ed. Gail Kennedy (Boston, 1950), 40.

41. Ernest Gellner, "The Last Pragmatist, or the Behaviorist Platonist," in *Spectacles and Predicaments: Essays in Social Theory* (New York, 1979), 241.

nineteenth century: the attempt on the part of academic scholars to elevate their various disciplines to the status of an "empirical science" that could enjoy cultural legitimacy. Yet far from resolving what one historian has called "the nineteenth-century crisis of authority," pragmatism may have only compounded it.[42] Although early scholars in the fields of politics, sociology, and economics could now regard themselves as professional "social scientists," the theoretical issues of knowledge remained as intractable as ever. Since Dewey drew on Peirce, it is necessary here to return to the latter's theoretical assumptions. Peirce convinced Dewey that truth and reality are accessible only to a scientific community of inquirers that would carry on investigation indefinitely, formulating hypotheses, testing theories, and revising ideas as a means not necessarily of reaching truth but of clarifying meaning and fixing belief. Dewey extended the community of investigators to include the democratic public itself. No doubt this represented a profoundly radical turn in philosophical thought. As Santayana wryly noted, American pragmatists convinced themselves that they could "humanize truth" by leaving it up to the opinions of the people.[43] Peirce, it will be recalled, believed that the final source of truth lies in the "consensus of the competent"—a belief that rests on the unspoken assumption that there exists a consensus about competency and that the scientific community would be open to ideas originating beyond that community. Dewey could advance the concept of truth no further than Peirce's notion of collective investigation. "The best definition of *truth* from the logical standpoint which is known to me is that of Peirce: The opinion which is fated to be ultimately agreed to by all who investigate is what we mean by truth."[44] Examining the contributions of both Dewey and Peirce, Russell argued that if we accept "ultimately" in a "chronological" sense, "it would make 'truth' depend upon the opinions of the last man left alive as the earth becomes too cold to support life."[45] Dewey and Peirce would no doubt reject Russell's assumption that the meaning of truth implies some final opinion, a notion that would bring knowledge to perfection at the cost of bringing inquiry to cessation. Since nature has no finality, the possibility of a last pragmatist on earth would be, in Dewey's expression, "unwarranted."

With the search for ultimate truth regarded by pragmatists as the pursuit of a phantom, cooperative scientific inquiry became the only recourse for the attainment of reliable knowledge. There seems little doubt that

42. Thomas L. Haskell, *The Emergence of Professional Social Science: The American Social Science Association and the Nineteenth-Century Crisis of Authority* (Urbana, 1977).

43. Santayana, *Winds of Doctrine*, 124.

44. Dewey, *Logic*, 345.

45. Russell, "Dewey's New Logic," in *Dewey and His Critics*, 145.

science offers the last dependable source of authority in resolving conflicts of belief about the physical world—although the work of Thomas Kuhn demonstrates just how difficult it is for a historical framework of empirical discourse (a "paradigm") to question its own assumptions so as to continue the true process of scientific experimentation as new data and theories clash with conventional presuppositions of "normal" science.[46] The real difficulty lies with problems that do not have their origins in scientific inquiry, social and political issues that seem impervious to empirical scrutiny. Indeed the relationship of science to society bears a double burden that modern democracy must shoulder: science may be contaminated by society's beliefs, and society may be contaminated by science's doubts. A scientific community could take on social issues and turn to the public for guidance, as Dewey advised, only to discover that the consensus of expert opinion must yield to prejudices of a democratic majority. Scientific method may succumb to the unscientific pressures of a democratic society, rendering inquiry "adaptive" where it should be adventurous, timid where it should be bold. It was for this reason that Peirce and Veblen insisted that science progresses only to the extent it remains "irrelevant" to contemporary social problems and devotes itself to the canons of "idle curiosity."[47]

As Veblen sensed, the nature of authority in science may prove to be a dubious model for establishing a basis for authority in society and politics. Dewey recognized no distinction between science and democracy, convinced that both represented collective endeavors that could be responsive to empirical procedures. But the distinction had been deeply felt by American political leaders and social philosophers. That beliefs and opinions sustain the political order, and not the critical temperament that questions it, was perceived by Tocqueville as one of the fundamental problems of modern democracy, especially when public opinion asserted itself as an expression of majoritarian tyranny. Lincoln had to face the problem of public opinion and truth in the crisis of slavery (and Oliver Wendell Holmes, Jr., had to take account of it in legal philosophy). Even though Lincoln adamantly opposed slavery on moral grounds, and wisely rejected all "scientific" arguments in defense of racism, he recognized that racial prejudice as "a universal feeling, whether well or ill-founded, cannot be safely disregarded."[48]

46. Thomas Kuhn, *The Structure of Scientific Revolutions* (Chicago: University of Chicago Press, 1970).

47. Thorstein Veblen, *The Place of Science in Modern Civilizations and Other Essays* (1918; New York: Capricorn, 1969, reprinted as *Veblen on Marx, Race, Science, and Economics*), 1–31.

48. Abraham Lincoln, "Speech at Peoria," Oct. 16, 1854, in *The Collected Works of Abraham Lincoln*, ed. Roy Basler (New Brunswick: Rutgers University Press, 1953), vol. 2, 256.

The dilemmas Lincoln faced point up the practical problems of pragmatic philosophy when applied to political reality. A politician must recognize that sentiments and feelings may stand in the way of science and progress. While science may be open to rational discussion and empirical investigation, public sentiments cannot be challenged without jeopardizing the social order. Although political as well as scientific authority serves to resolve differences of opinion, politics itself aims to neutralize conflict, whereas empirical data may maximize it. A science that fails to challenge beliefs could never advance, but a democratic society without unquestioned beliefs might possibly never endure. Thus Dewey's attempt to collectivize the scientific method fails to consider the difficulties of democratizing the Peircean dialectic of belief and doubt; society requires beliefs, only the curious individual doubts; and in actual life beliefs are believed before they are understood. The Virgin and the Dynamo could achieve hegemonic status in medieval and modern society not because they represented scientific objects but rather because they symbolized emotions resistant to rational analysis. No doubt science could expose such beliefs as fictions, but then science would be contributing to the crisis of modernism rather than resolving it.

Dewey's attempt to democratize science and render it responsive to the needs of society went far beyond Peirce's more cautionary stance. Peirce believed that the self-correcting principles of science must come from the scientific community itself. Dewey saw society as sovereign and science as its supreme instrument. Peirce, in contrast, wanted the community of inquirers to monitor its own activities so that the autonomy of science could be protected from the encroachments of society. To Dewey the social conditions of inquiry are part of the problem that needs to be addressed.

Empirical Method and Moral Knowledge

Dewey seldom doubted the adequacy of scientific inquiry to meet every problem society confronted. This was a bold claim, and it is not without its theoretical difficulties. Can a philosophy that offers only procedure instead of answers fulfill its promises to resolve the problems of modernism? The philosopher H. S. Thayer has observed that "Dewey is able to suggest *how* problems are to be encountered and resolved but not *what* the solutions are or should be."[49] This apt formulation derives from Dewey's conviction that because theory and practice and means and ends are united in experience, there is no dualism between the "how" and the "what," since proper empirical procedure will force the latter to emerge from the

49. Thayer, 182.

former. The formulation does not get us very far, although one hastens to admit that the idea of a solution remains no less elusive than the idea of truth itself, as Plato first pointed out in the *Meno*. To search for a solution to a problem implies that you know what you are looking for, else there would be no problem; or, if you do not know what you are looking for you cannot expect to find anything bearing upon the problem. In the concept of a solution we encounter the same paradox inherent in the concept of truth: unless we have some knowledge of what truth is prior to experience, we are unable to recognize it when we presumably find it. Similarly, at least a vague indication of a solution must precede inquiry in order to recognize that a problem exists and to reason backward from its expected solution to its origin and nature. For a problem to become a problem requires some vision of a solution, a sense of "what" we want to do about it, of how things "ought" to be. Dewey's antidualistic stance, however, does not admit of a conflict between the "is" and the "ought," between the descriptive and empirical and the normative and moral. Dewey would agree that there can be no knowledge without problems; the real question is whether there can be problems without knowledge that something is wrong.

Contrary to the claim that Dewey showed us "how" problems are to be confronted but not "what" should be done, Dewey remained unclear on both counts. Using the language of Darwinism, Dewey insisted that "problematic situations" arise where man as a human "organism" encounters "contingent" and "unstable" elements in the environment. Aside from the disruptions of the natural environment that bring disasters on humans, it is difficult to see how this description explains precisely the way in which problems arise in the social world. Poverty and injustice have been with us since man left the caves; slavery existed for two thousand years in Egypt and for two centuries in America—hardly "contingent" phenomena. Dewey refused to acknowledge any separation of social and natural science, assuming that the same methods of investigation could be applied to both realms. Yet the character of social problems may differ profoundly from that of natural problems. Dewey insisted that "a state of imbalance in organic-environmental interactions" explains the genesis of all problems, and hence "to see that a situation requires inquiry is the initial step of inquiry."[50] How, then, does one see a social problem requiring inquiry that will eventuate in a solution? Would not such a perception call for more than biological discomfort and require, indeed demand, some intuitive recognition that the actual situation has fallen short of an ideal? Human slavery, for example, was accepted for centuries as a natural

50. Dewey is quoted in Thayer, 191.

reflection of the order of things; it did not become a problem until its continued presence clashed with political and religious ideals. Yet we still do not know why one generation suddenly finds immoral what another generation regarded as inevitable. The discrepancy between actuality and possibility lies at the heart of social thought. Even to become aware of this discrepancy, not to mention resolve it, requires some understanding that the conditions of the actual world can be transformed by human will. For only a person who can conceptualize a different society from the existing one can experience a "problematic situation," and such a sensibility requires in turn a theory of ethics and the authority of moral philosophy—the most controversial feature of Dewey's pragmatism.

The fear of a gap between matter and spirit had haunted Dewey in his younger years, as we have seen. It may have been this specter that compelled him to devote so much of his intellectual energies to dispelling dualism as a species of false consciousness. Whatever the subject he wrote on during his long and remarkably active life—epistemology, metaphysics, axiology, logic, aesthetics—he faced the awesome challenge of reconciling science and morality. Dewey never lost sight of ethical questions, which became central to the entire corpus of his philosophical writings. Indeed, it would not be going too far to say that the approach pragmatists take toward the interrelated problems of authority, truth, and modernity stands or falls on the adequacy of Dewey's ethical theory. Ethics, the analysis of moral conduct, provides the wellspring of value and the *summum bonum* of ideal ends of human behavior. With the eclipse of truth in scientific philosophy, the fate of authority in the modern world rested more than ever on the future of moral philosophy.

In facing this dilemma Dewey knew what he was up against—a whole tradition in classical thought that had rendered nature irreconcilably distinct and separate from morality, the realm of science, fact, and objectivity from the realm of ethics, values, and subjectivity. He rose magnificently to the challenge of dualism, drawing upon almost every branch of knowledge in order better to absorb, assimilate, and synthesize the supposedly false antinomies of mind. In his early writings Dewey expressed indebtedness to G. W. Leibniz. The seventeenth-century German philosopher possessed a rare perspective for his age: an active concept of intelligence that saw all thinking as a dynamic process that unified subject with object and thought with thing, as well as contingency and continuity, identity and difference, individuality and universality, and the real and the ideal.[51] But ultimately it was Darwinism that left the most lasting impression on Dewey.

---

51. Dewey, "Leibniz's New Essays concerning the Human Understanding: A Critical Exposition," *Early Works*, vol. 1, 427–28.

To the extent that nature encompasses all reality, that mind evolved from nature, and that knowledge derives solely from man's experience with the environment, it follows that human values too had their basis in the natural world. Values have no antecedent status; nor are they imagined or envisioned in an act of theoretical speculation; instead they are experienced in concrete situations. Thus all subjects, moral issues as well as scientific hypotheses, can be submitted to controlled experimentation, since all valid knowledge derives from the same methods of inquiry. Is it correct to continue to believe that science can only describe and not judge, that it can provide only the "means" to an end, whereas the decision concerning what "end" should be pursued remains a moral issue? Far from it. The framing of practical goals—"ends in view" as opposed to ultimate, transcendent ends—is devised in actual problematic situations, since we cannot envisage a goal without at the same time adopting a program of action to reach it. Thus means and ends are organically related in an unbroken continuum.[52]

Dewey never wavered from his naturalistic approach to ethics (although some scholars believe he never was, strictly speaking, "an ethical naturalist").[53] In an early essay, "Logical Conditions for a Scientific Treatment of Morality" (1903), Dewey denied any distinction between empirical inquiry and ethical judgments. Such a dualism misleads philosophers into assuming that moral standards are found in universal conceptions independent of the course of experience, and that, in addition, these standards apply to actions still to be performed by human beings as free agents whose behavior, as individuals, cannot be generalized or objectified. Dewey argued that the individual scientist is also involved in moral judgments that require him to be honest with his data lest his experiment fail. In a manner somewhat similar to Peirce's, Dewey held that the scientist is moved by logic, if not ethics, to the extent he is engaged in judging himself. Dewey believed such acts of judgment could be extended to the social sciences. Thus there was no reason an ethics of science could not be developed, "a kind of hygiene of moral action" that would assess judgments of worth in human relations with the same kind of responsibility and objectivity science applies to physical relations. Standards of right derive from society, and science can help evaluate right by whatever relations promote the good.[54]

52. Dewey, *Quest for Certainty*, 74–139; see also James Gouinlock, *John Dewey's Philosophy of Value* (New York, 1972).

53. Robert L. Holmes, "John Dewey's Moral Philosophy in Contemporary Perspective," *Review of Metaphysics* 22 (1966): 42–70.

54. Dewey, "Logical Conditions of a Scientific Treatment of Morality," in *Middle Works, 1899–1924*, vol. 2 ed. Jo Ann Boydston (Carbondale: Southern Illinois University Press, 1983), 3–39.

Dewey, however, went much further than Peirce, not only in trusting society with standards but also in blurring distinctions in various modes of knowledge. Peirce held that logic could teach people how they ought to think, ethics how they should act, and aesthetics how they can appreciate. Peirce also separated the psychological from the logical so that how people think and act will be distinguished from how they ought to do so. In *Logic: The Theory of Inquiry*, Dewey denied the distinction between the psychological and the logical and argued that the way people think is good or bad depending on whether their thinking leads them to their intended goal. If people follow methods of inquiry that fail to fulfill the ends in mind, the experience of failure and frustration will compel them to adopt better means of thinking. Dewey saw no troubling dualism between means and ends because he regarded ends as given. The historian Louis Hartz has suggested that the reason pragmatism became so peculiarly an American proposition is that America's Lockean political culture, resting on the consensus of liberty, property, and opportunity, never called into question its ends. "It is only when you take your ethics for granted that all problems emerge as problems of technique." Whether pragmatism reinforced liberalism's "conformitarian ethos" (Hartz's expression) is not really the issue. The larger question is whether Dewey's collapsing of means and ends could contribute to a public philosophy capable of addressing social policy issues. Max Weber, for one, had serious doubts about such a possibility. "The distinctive characteristic of a problem of social *policy* is indeed the fact that it cannot be resolved merely on the basis of purely technical considerations which assume already settled ends." To arrive at judgments regarding ends and ultimate values is less a subject of scientific analysis and more "a matter of *faith*."[55]

Dewey's writings on ethics remain perhaps the weakest branch in the philosophy of pragmatism. Yet one can only admire his daring effort to tackle moral philosophy, since he was trying to resolve problems in intellectual history that perplexed other modern thinkers. As long as science and ethics remained separate, the universe would continue without the guidance of morality and intelligence. Unless ethics could be developed into a science, humankind would be unable to gain control of a history subjected to chance, irony, and fate. Thus against the Kantian tradition Dewey argued that ethics did not have to be categorical when it could be conditional, empirical, and testable. Dewey also desired to go beyond conventional ethical theories, such as those of Jeremy Bentham and Thomas Hill Green, and establish morality not on rules involving duty and responsibility but instead on the more flexible and adaptive

55. Louis Hartz, *The Liberal Tradition in America* (New York: Harcourt, 1955), 10; Weber, *Methodology of the Social Sciences*, 55–56.

procedures of scientific inquiry. Morality should be treated, Dewey observed in correcting Bentham, not in the closed systems of logic but in the open landscape of life.[56]

Dewey's ethical theory became the subject of considerable criticism. For the sake of brevity, and at the risk of oversimplification, the criticisms can be reduced to categories of problems involving (1) procedures of investigation, (2) knowledge of the good, (3) moral obligation, (4) criteria of judgment.

The first criticism, raised by the political philosopher George Sabine, charged pragmatists in general and Dewey in particular with failing to keep distinct the factual, causal, and evaluative modes of analysis. A political theory, insisted Sabine in what appears to be the same reasoning used earlier by Max Weber, includes three discrete elements: statements concerning facts, causal analysis explaining behavior, and ethical discussion that both evaluates empirical data and persuades us to choose ends and moral objectives. While the factual and causal are scientific in nature, the evaluative remains distinctly moral and must be approached by a different mode of inquiry.[57] The notion that the descriptive and normative must be kept separate in investigation was, of course, a mere restatement of the dualism that Dewey's naturalism set out to demolish. Yet he still had to demonstrate that the empirically knowable realm of "facts" could be treated in the same manner as the nonscientific subjective realm of "values." His attempt to do so led to the second criticism, that pragmatic philosophy lacks an adequate theory of the good.

In what is perhaps his most controversial assertion, Dewey had argued that we can arrive at moral judgments of the good through scientific means. In making such judgments we are not so much concerned about what has happened, the traditional preoccupation of philosophers determined to assign praise or blame; rather we should be concerned with what will happen. Instead of indulging in useless questions regarding motives of conduct, we should be more interested in consequences, and thus we must strive to remedy situations that make difficult the realization of the good. What the good exactly is, Dewey did not specify, other than to indicate that it inhered in society's laws, which, representing the "demands" of society as a whole, would help broaden the particular "rights" and "claims" of individuals and thereby enlarge our conception of the public good.[58] What we ultimately choose as the good is not a subjective judgment; on the contrary, by using our critical intelligence

56. Dewey, "Ethics," *Middle Works*, vol. 3, 40–58.

57. George Sabine, "Social Studies and Objectivity," *University of California Publications in Philosophy*, ed. G. T. Adams et al., vol. 16, no. 6 (1954), 125–42.

58. A. H. Somjee, *The Political Theory of John Dewey* (New York: Teachers' College, Columbia University, 1968), 35.

we can become aware of what we want to realize and discern the means to realize it. Then, after experiencing the desired result, we can use the same scientific method of cause-effect analysis to inform us whether the proper means have been employed, and we can also reflect on what we have wrought to determine whether the particular quality of experience should be repeated. This is the crux of the matter—Ralph Barton Perry called it "Professor Dewey's paradox"—that we do not define the good but simply "fulfill" it; we cannot, that is to say, know why we choose one good over another, since knowledge, even knowledge of objective consequences, may not necessarily determine our affective preferences.[59] Thus we have no way of judging the value of an object desired, since the intelligence brought to bear on means does not in itself provide a criterion of value to assess the ends that are to be realized. And since the ends are realized in the future, the problem of valuating the good is postponed. As C. I. Lewis noted, Dewey failed to separate the essence or criterion of good and its existential locus in reality, making it impossible for us to bring to experience some knowledge of the nature of the good.[60] If we can only experience the good, not contemplate it, how can we be persuaded to do good before we do it?

The third criticism raised against Dewey's ethical theory relates to the question of obligation. Can empirical knowledge itself make moral demands upon our behavior? Dewey assumed with Peirce that to be objective is to be moral, and he never doubted that ethical judgments could be subjected to scientific considerations alone. In *The Quest for Certainty* he tried to demonstrate how ethical knowledge could be derived from empirical data, the normative "ought" from the empirical "is." All human beings have desires, reasoned Dewey; they strive toward some ends that they regard as good, satisfying, and valuable. Yet man may be misled and seek fulfillment of some crass pleasure or fanciful wish. Thus we must distinguish between the desired as a naked impulse and the desirable as something man believes he wants and, after critical reflections, he knows he should and ought to want. To move between "the enjoyed and the enjoyable, the desired and the desirable, the satisfying and the satisfactory" is to specify what conditions are met and what consequences are fulfilled. Thus for Dewey ethical statements are experimentally justified in that the consequences of an action must fulfill the prediction and continue to bring satisfaction. It should be noted that Dewey's ethical theory involved an almost hedonistic focus on satisfaction and pleasure

59. Ralph Barton Perry, "Dewey and Urban on Value Judgments," in *Dewey and His Critics*, 586–98.

60. C. I. Lewis, review of *The Quest for Certainty*, in *Dewey and His Critics*, 253–64.

and their perpetuation. When he distinguished something that "has been eaten" with that which "is edible" he emphasized that the latter expression cannot be judged apart from its connections with other things and its foreseeable consequences. Morality for Dewey remained a fulfillment of the human organism, and hence judgments about values are judgments about the conditions and consequences that "should regulate the formation of our desires, affections, and enjoyments."[61]

One wonders about an ethical theory that contains no heirarchy of values and has as its goal "our" needs and desires. In moral situations bound up with the welfare of others; in situations presenting alternative ways of behaving, each involving not physical obstacles to overcome but human obligations to meet; in existential situations requiring the agony of choice, how does Dewey enable us to decide upon the right course of action? (Hamlet combined pragmatism with existentialism—"To be or not to be / That is the question"—and the results were disastrous.) Morton White has effectively illuminated the difficulties in Dewey's attempt to render ethics an empirical science, and even though Sidney Hook, Dewey's ardent disciple, has questioned the terminology in White's critique, neither Hook nor any other pragmatist has successfully demonstrated how the exercise of scientific intelligence can by itself command obligation.[62]

This issue troubled Dewey throughout his long career both in teaching and in scholarship. In his unpublished manuscripts there is a draft of his lecture notes on "Desire/The Desirable" written as early as 1911, when he was teaching at Columbia University. Apparently his students had difficulty with the terms and the link between them. In 1950 Dewey returned to the issue, again drafting some personal notes in response to Morton White's critique of the desire/desirable distinction. Thus two years before his death America's greatest contemporary philosopher would still be trying to resolve one of the most vexing issues in ethical theory, the relationship of science to morality as both a cognitive and an objective endeavor. Today philosophers either have given up trying to resolve issues in moral theory or have proposed solutions that suffer from an excess of hubris about the intellectual's capacity to instruct the public on the values it should hold dearest—usually the intellectual's own values, not to say "desires."[63]

61. Dewey, *The Quest for Certainty*, 74–139.

62. Morton White, *Social Thought in America: The Revolt against Formalism* (Boston, 1957), 203–19; Sidney Hook, "The Desirable and the Emotive in Dewey's Ethics," in *John Dewey: Philosopher of Science and Freedom*, ed. Sidney Hook (New York, 1950), 194–216.

63. Dewey, "Desire/The Desirable," lecture notes, Oct. 26–Nov. 21, 1917, 102.62/11, Dewey mss.; 102 59/5, "ca. 1950," ibid.

The fourth criticism of Dewey's theory of ethics turns on the locus of judgment and value. Dewey rejected the idea that moral judgments depend upon insight into transcendent truths, and he denied the so-called emotive school of ethics, in which ethical statements have no cognitive meaning because they cannot explain feelings but only "express" and "arouse" them. With ethics purged from both realms, intuition and emotion, it remained for Dewey to locate moral judgment in experience itself. Convinced that the scientific method could turn all moral issues into questions of experiential fact, he remained equally convinced that no standards of judgment could be external to the situation judged. Any other source of ethical truth—for example, the idea that reason can be brought to bear on moral situations by elucidating rules—seemed preposterous. "The notion that valuations do not exist in empirical fact and that therefore value-conceptions have to be imported from a source outside experience is one of the most curious beliefs the mind of man has ever entertained."[64]

To locate the source of value in experience alone is a proposition riddled with difficulties, and no one has done more to illuminate the ironic consequences of these difficulties than the literary critic Kenneth Burke. "How do we test the success of a value?" asked Burke in his review of Dewey's *The Quest for Certainty*. If we were to accept the criterion of the value's practical usefulness, we would have to admit that all values by which people have organized their lives have functioned successfully, and this includes the repugnant as well as the attractive. "Taboo against murder works, since societies flourish where this taboo is prevalent; a systematic killing of aging parents also works." Surely we ought not accept all values that have arisen to serve human ends. How then do we discriminate and create new values by the experimental methods proposed by Dewey? The "experimental method," wrote Burke,

> would derive its values, not by authority, not by any theory of antecedent absolute good, but by the test. It seems, however, that when carried to its logical conclusion, this method of evaluating values presents difficulties of its own. When judging the effectiveness of a value, for instance, we have to utilize some other value to appraise it. Though we may know the processes whereby people are made fat, lean or middling, we still have to decide whether we ought to make them fat, lean or middling; for there is no judgment inherent in a process. Suppose that we decide to make them lean in order that they may run faster. Then we have founded our value of lean-

64. Dewey, *Theory of Valuation* (Chicago, 1939), 6–7, 58.

ness upon the value of speed in running, which must in turn be founded upon another value, and so on. Where then is our "key value"? By the experimental method there could obviously be no key value, in the sense of its antecedent existence, its acceptance on authority. Even a key value must be dependent upon experiment for its justification, and its worth could be tested only by the adoption of some other value by which to test it.

Dewey tried to handle this dilemma by elevating "intelligence" to the status of an absolute or "key value," an entity that not only functioned to bring about good but is good in and of itself. So defined, the reflective intelligence of pragmatism, functioning as an end as well as a means, enabled modern philosophy to regain its moral heritage and join man in his unending quest for the good life. Yet to elevate intelligence to the status of authority is a circular exercise that relativizes the very concept of authority by endowing it with the power of self-legitimation. Attempting to resolve the problem of authority, Dewey succeeded only in compounding it, as Burke so astutely discerned.

If the arbiter of success is Intelligence, evaluating out of itself, creating the values by which it measures its own success, is this not an intrusion upon the relativistic thinking of pragmatism? Would it not be much like "pure" Intelligence, an absolute? We have done away with the unmoved mover; but do we have in its stead the self-judging judger, the self-measuring measurer, a good so good that it perceives its own goodness?[65]

Attempting to develop a philosophical system in which there would be no need for authority in the traditional sense of the term, Dewey only revealed the difficulty of trying to establish the authority of a belief or value without reaching something absolute, complete, and inescapable, something beyond which it is impossible to go.[66] Yet one cannot help but be impressed by Dewey's heroic effort to resolve the crisis in ethical theory without drawing upon any previous tradition of moral philosophy. He rejected, as we have seen, both the Christian idea of the good as "sacrifice" and the classical idea of "virtue" as the subordination of private interests to the needs of the general public. He also wanted to go beyond Kant's idea of ethics as fundamentally a logic of duty. And he would have had little patience with a later existentialist proposition that man

65. Kenneth Burke, *The Philosophy of Literary Form: Studies in Symbolic Action* (1911; Berkeley: University of California Press, 1973), 382–88.
66. Michael Oakeshott, *Modes of Experience* (London, 1933), 115.

must rise above "being-in-itself" and act in ways that benefit others. As Dewey asked earlier in his career, why should seeking happiness for ourselves be immoral while making it possible for others be ethical?[67] Similarly, Dewey's own ethical stance was not characterological or educative in the sense that man is born with certain tendencies that must be disciplined in order that moral potentialities be fulfilled. As we shall later see, Dewey's educational philosophy aims to dispense with discipline as well as authority. Thus, although Dewey wanted to rescue modern philosophy from its Greek heritage, we are still back with classical thinkers when we consider the question posed by Plato: does man desire the good because it is pleasurable, or is the good pleasurable because it is desirable? Without a "key value," can pragmatism provide standards for preferring some desires to others?

We are now in a position to sum up the many difficulties in Dewey's philosophy as they bear upon the problems of authority and modernism. Inasmuch as pragmatism aims at meeting human needs, it seems fair to ask what precisely pragmatism offers us. It does not give us objects of knowledge, since it confines itself to providing ways of knowing. It does not give us knowledge of truth, since truth has no antecedent existence but instead comes into being in the process of becoming known—and can in fact be transformed by that process. It does not give us accuracy of representation, modes of knowledge capable of grasping an independent reality against which we can check our thought, since knowledge of reality cannot be brought to bear upon the very operation of our own thoughts. It does not, even though it may claim to do so, give us a means of recognizing imperative moral obligations, since value judgments are arrived at only after we experience the good. It does not give us authoritative principles that can regulate human affairs, since human existence is characterized by the inexorable contingencies of experience. It does not give us truths that can compel the mind, since the mind itself is incapable of apprehending truths disclosed to the mind. It does not give us the basis of making present decisions, since all verifiable propositions can only refer to the future. It does not, in short, give us a criterion of judgment, since there is no authority to render it. Ultimately what pragmatism offers us, as Santayana noted, is the benign message that it is better to pursue truth than to possess it, and better to regard as knowledge only those ideas that enable us to change things according to our desires, rather than to regard knowledge as a criterion of judgment that stands over and against our drives and desires.[68]

67. Dewey, "The Psychology of Self-Realization and Its Application to the Egoism-Altruism Controversy," 209.

68. Santayana, "The Philosophy of Bertrand Russell," in *Winds of Doctrine*, 137.

The philosopher Richard Rorty has made the point that "pragmatism is the philosophical counterpart of literary modernism, the kind of literature which prides itself on its autonomy and novelty rather than its truthfulness to experience or its discovery of pre-existing significance."[69] Pragmatism may pride itself on autonomy and novelty, but an examination of Dewey's response to the first and second world wars suggests that what American philosophy needed was a little more humility.

69. Richard Rorty, *The Consequences of Pragmatism* (Minneapolis, 1982), 153.

6

Focusing on the Foreground: Dewey and the Problem of Historical Knowledge

World War I and the Dewey-Bourne Debate

John Dewey was as suspicious of historical authority as he was of adult authority, and for much the same reason. His commitment to evolutionary naturalism and Jeffersonian liberalism precluded his acknowledging that the validity of an idea or institution could be ascertained by finding it temporally prior. The dominion of age and antiquity represented the tyranny of the past, and if the past were deferred to, it could negate the sovereignty of the present and inhibit the will to act. Dewey's future-oriented, activist temperament had far more appeal to the liberal imagination than did Henry Adams's somber reflections. Where Dewey believed he could look to the "cumulative continuity of movement" in historical experience for guidance in the contemporary world, Adams sensed only the discontinuities and disruptions. Where Dewey maintained that immediate problems should determine how the past is to be grasped, Adams realized that presentism would simply mean that the historian could never look historical truth in the face. "Past history," wrote Adams, "is only a value or relation to the future, and the value is wholly one of convenience, which can be tested only by experiment."[1]

Dewey would certainly have linked the reference to "experiment," but he would have had little patience with Adams's futile effort to ascertain the exact sequence of events in order to arrive at causal understanding. Adams's conclusion, uttered upon his resignation from Harvard, that history without truth could only mean manipulation and even self-

1. Adams, *Education*, 488.

250

deception, cut too deeply. For Dewey's progressive disciples were less concerned to prove that history is knowable than to demonstrate in what practical ways it can be usable. To Dewey, history signified neither the drama of human destiny nor the vehicle of moral judgment, nor even the paradigm for establishing general laws of social relations. The first kind of history led to literary conceit, the second to otiose didacticism, the third to a positivistic universalism that denied the particularity and emergent novelty of events. Only pragmatic instrumentalism could show the historian how to use his craft as an instrument of control. Although Dewey himself admired Adams, the philosopher's pragmatic instrumentalism had no place for the historian's anguished humanism. "No future Henry Adams," wrote the avid pragmatist Sidney Ratner, "if he knows Dewey's philosophy, will be likely to write what Adams wrote in 1896: 'As History stands, it is a sort of Chinese play, without end and without lesson.'"[2]

Thus spake the conventional wisdom on the subject. But is it the case that Dewey's philosophy did indeed succeed in resolving the problems that confounded Adams? Since all inquiry begins with the "irritation of doubt," let us begin with the most irritating question of all: Does pragmatism work?

In the past American scholars seemed to be confident that pragmatism resolved the problems of life. Intellectual historians concentrated on its background and development, while philosophers evaluated its theoretical implications in view of the technical issues in philosophy itself. Few historians or philosophers—even such astute critics as Arthur O. Lovejoy, Bertrand Russell, and George Santayana—studied pragmatic ideas in light of their consequences in human behavior. It seems strangely ironic that an intellectual historian or a philosopher would accept the theoretical claims of pragmatism without examining its actual operations in the daily world of experience. Such behavior presupposes the very formalism that pragmatism sought to overcome—the fallacy of accepting at face value what a thinker says rather than what he does, and of treating the propositions of philosophy as tantamount to their validity. The irony lies in the awkward fact that pragmatism may be refuted not so much by logic as by its own criterion of verification: the experience of history may demonstrate that it fails to work in helping us understand history itself.

The outbreak of World War I confronted John Dewey's pragmatism with one of its greatest challenges. He had always held up rational intelli-

---

2. Sidney Ratner, "Dewey's Contribution to Historical Theory," in *John Dewey: Philosopher of Science and Freedom*, ed. Sidney Hook (New York, 1950), 134–52.

gence and the scientific method as the means by which disputes could be settled. To the bitter surprise of many intellectuals, however, Dewey came out in support of America's entry into the war, and he did so with a well-developed rationale that justified his new position. The war, Dewey held in the *New Republic* in 1917, opened up the possibility of employing collective knowledge on an international scale, bringing to foreign as well as domestic affairs the service of the scientific expert in the cause of peace and justice. The war was not only an instrument of integration and socialization; it also compelled the intellectual to reconsider the "intelligent use of force" in international affairs. The war had dramatized the impotence and "moral innocency" of the pacificists, who believed that war could be opposed simply by the exercise of conscience.

> The tendency to oppose war by bringing it under the commandment against murder, the belief that by not doing something, by keeping out of a declaration of war, our responsibilities could be met, a somewhat mushy belief in the existence of disembodied moral forces which require only an atmosphere of feelings to operate so as to bring about what is right, the denial of the efficacy of force, no matter how controlled, to modify disposition; in short the inveterate habit of separating ends from means and then identifying morals with ends thus emasculated, such things as these are the source of much of the perplexity of conscience which idealistic youth has suffered. The evangelical Protestant tradition has fostered the tendency to locate morals in personal feelings instead of in the control of situations, and our legal tradition has bred the habit of attaching feelings to fixed rules and injunctions instead of to social conditions and consequences of action as these are revealed to the scrutiny of intelligence.[3]

Convinced that America's entry into the war could not be resisted, Dewey argued that history could be brought under control only if the intellectual focused on the rush of events and thereby came to understand the inevitability of America's involvement.

> If at a critical juncture the moving force of events is always too much for conscience, the remedy is not to deplore the wickedness of those who manipulate events. Such a conscience is largely self-conceit. The remedy is to connect conscience with the forces that are moving in another direction. Then

3. John Dewey, "Conscience and Compulsion"; this and other war essays appearing in the *New Republic* in 1916–1917 are reprinted in John Dewey, *Character and Events*, ed. Joseph Ratner (New York, 1929), vol. 2, 676–80.

will conscience itself have compulsive power instead of being
forever the martyred and the coerced.[4]

Ultimately Dewey justified America's entry by trying to show the com-
patibility of pragmatism and war, an effort that led him to distinguish
force from violence.

> Common sense still clings to a via media between the Tol-
> stoian, to whom all force is violence and all violence evil, and
> that glorification of force which is so easy when war arouses
> turbulent emotion, and so persistent (in disguised forms)
> whenever competition rules industry. I should be glad to make
> the voice of common sense more articulate. As an initial aid,
> I would call to mind the fact that force figures in different
> roles. Sometimes it is energy; sometimes it is coercion or con-
> straint; sometimes it is violence. Energy is power used with
> a eulogistic meaning; it is power doing work, harnessed to
> accomplishment of ends. But it is force nonetheless, brute
> force if you please, and rationalized only by its results. Exactly
> the same force running wild is called violence. The objection
> to violence is not that it involves force, but that it is a waste
> of force; that it uses force idly or destructively. And what is
> called law may always, I suggest, be looked at as describing a
> method for employing force economically, efficiently, so as to
> get results with the least waste.[5]

Dewey assured himself, and some of the *New Republic* liberals, that
"force is the only thing in the world which effects anything," and thus
those who would substitute law or morality or some other source of
authority in order to resolve conflicts were being unrealistic and, worse,
ineffectual. "Squeamishness about force is the mark not of idealistic but
of moonstruck morals."[6] Dewey may have been correct to argue that the
authority of the state could require the exercise of physical strength if
necessary, just as other writers (Walter Lippmann, for example) would
argue that the United States must enter the war to protect its national
interests and to assure itself of participating effectively in the peace negotiations. But Dewey's view of the war as a potential instrument of social
reconstruction seemed to fly in the face of his view of the war as historically inevitable. As Randolph Bourne replied to Dewey, "If the war is
too strong for you to prevent, how is it going to be weak enough for you

4. Ibid., 580.
5. John Dewey, "Force, Violence and Law," ibid., 636–41.
6. Ibid., 638.

to control and mold to your liberal purposes?"[7] In "Twilight of the Idols," which appeared in *The Seven Arts* in 1917, Bourne became the first writer, as far as I know, to discern in pragmatic philosophy a tendency to equate authority with power and to look to force as a solution to problems.

Before the war Bourne championed Dewey's proposals for educational reform and his ideal of a democracy of citizen participation. But with America's entry into the war, democracy lost its innocence. In his essay "The State," unfinished at the time of his death in 1919, Bourne made a crucial distinction between the normal mechanisms of government during peace and the dangerous mystification of the state during war.

Bourne believed that the central deficiency of pragmatism could be traced to its lack of a "poetic vision," a sense of the true and right as opposed to the efficient and expedient. Lacking such a sensibility, pragmatism could easily confuse the illegitimate power of the state with the constituted authority of government. "War is the health of the state," declared Bourne in what would become an epigrammatic lament for a subsequent war-weary generation. In war, power gravitates away from legitimate institutions and ascends to an emotional abstraction that can enforce its will. In this situation, Bourne argued, the individual reaches his "apotheosis" not in democratic participation but in a total surrender of his being to the state, and the state becomes indistinguishable from the regular machinery of government and takes on the majesty of rightful authority:

> In time of war it is natural that Government as the seat of authority should be confused with the State or the mystic source of authority. You cannot very well injure a mystical idea which is the State, but you can very well interfere with the processes of Government. So that the two become identified in the public mind, and any contempt for or opposition to the workings of the machinery of government is considered equivalent to contempt for the sacred State. The State, it is felt, is being injured in its faithful surrogate, and public emotion rallies passionately to defend it. It even makes any criticism of the form of government a crime.[8]

Most scholars who have reexamined the Dewey-Bourne debates, especially during the height of the Vietnam War, have generally judged Bourne the winner because of his grasp of the weakness of Dewey's rea-

7. Randolph Bourne, "Twilight of Idols," in *War and the Intellectuals: Collected Essays, 1915–1919*, ed. Carl Resek (New York: Harper, 1969), 53–64.

8. Randolph Bourne, "The State," in *War and Intellectuals*, 88.

soning and of the outcome of the war itself.[9] This conclusion seems questionable on several counts. First of all, Dewey's desire to exercise some measure of control over that which was apparently inevitable cannot be dismissed as illogical. The paradox of fate and will has never bothered most great leaders in modern history. Lincoln could act decisively while meditating on Providence, and Jefferson could justify taking deliberate actions that the "course of events" made "necessary." Bourne's offering "poetic vision" as a higher form of knowledge also seems dubious when one considers the political judgments and sense of history displayed by many twentieth-century poets. And Bourne's own sense of the direction of history surely cannot be sustained. When he declared that "war is the health of the state" in 1919, several monarchial regimes and imperial dynasties were crumbling in eastern and southern Europe.

After his untimely death in 1919, Bourne became the prophet and symbolic martyr to the "lost generation" of the twenties. With the failure of Wilsonian democracy and the anti-Bolshevik "red scare," Bourne seemed to have accurately anticipated the reactionary course of events. But in what sense did Bourne expose the weaknesses of pragmatism? It should be noted that Bourne was himself a pragmatist and indeed had earlier explicated Dewey's philosophy for readers of the *New Republic*. Here he agreed with Dewey that "our life is a constant reaction to a world which is constantly stimulating us," and that "our minds are simply the tools with which we forge out our life." Yet after America's intervention, Bourne thought he detected a deficiency in pragmatism. Now Dewey's followers, too willing to act and experiment, "were immensely ready for the executive ordering of events, pitifully unprepared for the intellectual interpretation or the idealistic focusing of ends." Earlier Bourne had agreed with Dewey that thought must yield to action as the true test of knowledge. "We are in situations where we must do something, and it is for the purpose of guiding this doing from the point of view of what has happened or what is likely to happen, that we think. We are not bundles of thoughts and feelings so much as bundles of attitudes or tendencies. We act usually before we 'perceive'; the perception is only important as it enables us to act again." In his wartime debates with Dewey, however,

9. Christopher Lasch, *The New Radicalism in America: The Intellectual as a Social Type* (New York, 1967), 181–224; White, *Social Thought*, 161–79; Alan Cywar, "John Dewey: Toward a Domestic Reconstruction, 1915–1920," *Journal of the History of Ideas* 30 (1969): 385–300; Daniel Levine, "Randolph Bourne, John Dewey, and the Legacy of Liberalism," *Antioch Review* 29 (1969): 234–44; Sidney Hook, "John Dewey and the Crisis of American Liberalism," ibid., 218–32. Levine and Hook defend Dewey against the attacks made during the height of the Vietnam War. See also *The Radical Will: Randolph Bourne: Selected Writings, 1911–1918*, ed. Olaf Hansen, introduction by Christopher Lasch (New York, 1977).

Bourne reversed the priority and insisted that ideals and ends must be analyzed and worked out before action is taken. Of Dewey he observed: "There was always that unhappy ambiguity in his doctrine as to just how values were created." [10]

Dewey assumed that values evolved naturally out of the processes of action, and he therefore hoped that democratic participation and military mobilization could march hand in hand to bring the message of Wilsonianism to Europe and also begin the reconstruction of American society. Bourne came to doubt that values are implicit in action itself, and he asked of pragmatism that it focus more on purposes than on processes and more on vision than on technique.

Dewey's encounter with Bourne had a regrettable effect on the philosopher's future outlook, particularly in the late thirties as world war once again loomed on the horizon. Bourne had insisted that democratic values are incompatible with the necessities of war and that the ends of liberalism could not be achieved through the means of militarism. How, then, would Dewey advise America to face Adolf Hitler?

In 1917, the country's leading philosopher had no difficulty advising Americans how to face the Kaiser. He rejected the warning of Bourne and Max Eastman about the dangers of patriotism in times of war. Instead his defense of the government's military efforts against Germany, and of conscription, legitimated the power of the state and turned it into rightful authority worthy of intellectual and moral support. Yet Dewey's reasoning points up the difficulties in the pragmatic attempt to tie political authority to the philosophical authority of scientific methodology, to the rule of efficiency and the criterion of consequences, "something which concerns results rather than aspirations." [11] For Dewey's advice that the intellectual must "connect conscience with the forces that are moving in another direction"; his observation, made in response to the patriotic hysteria and suppression of civil liberties in 1917, that "the appeal is no longer to reason; it is to the event"; and, not least, his rather desperate effort to distinguish "force" from "violence"—all illuminate with equal poignancy the problems inherent in the pragmatic approach to history. [12] As a pragmatist more concerned with the outcome than with the origins of the war, with future consequences rather than historical causes, Dewey could refer vaguely to "forces" without specifying their political or economic nature and without analyzing the causal factors behind them. How,

10. Bourne, "Twilight of Idols," 53–64; "John Dewey's Philosophy," in the *New Republic* (1915), reprinted in *The Radical Will*, 331–35.

11. Dewey, "Force, Violence and Law," 639.

12. Dewey, "Conscience and Compulsion," 580; "In Explanation of Our Lapse," *New Republic* (1917), in *Character and Events*, 571–75.

then, could he possibly conclude that the war could not be resisted? How could he grasp what was happening when he had no basis for knowing what had happened?

As a historian Henry Adams presaged the problems Dewey would face in coming to terms with historical events. Adams had been brought up to believe that the study of American history was vital to the Republic's memory and identity. But by the end of the nineteenth century the corrosions of modernism had convinced Adams that true, objective historical knowledge was problematic, that historical events, like atomic particles and biological mutations, may be random and indeterminate, and that the most the historian could make out of studying the past was the relentless movement of power alienated from human consciousness and purpose. When the First World War broke out, in August 1914, Adams was resting at Saint-Remy-Les Chauvreuse, recovering from a stroke and studying French medieval music. He immediately left for London and then returned to the United States. The war kept him lying awake at night pondering the end of civilization. While his brother, Charles F. Adams, Jr., was writing to him about the war and comparing the infantry assaults on trenches to the battles of the American Civil War, Henry was thinking about Augustine of Hippo writing *The City of God* before the barbarians descended. Adams also felt that Jefferson's and Madison's embargo policies during the Napoleonic wars had an eerie echo in President Wilson's neutrality policies in response to Germany's unrestricted submarine deployment. When America entered the war, in April 1917, Adams cautiously approved, with the reminder that "behind all the killing comes the great question of what our civilization is to do next." To Elizabeth Cameron, Adams wrote of "our beloved William James," his old friend who once believed there could be a "moral equivalent" to war; and in his last extant letter, to William Roscoe Thayer, on March 15, 1918, Adams stated: "Universities are our American equivalent for a church; they will give you peace. My error in life was in deserting their blessed peace."[13]

John Dewey would never have regarded universities as America's equivalent of a church where the scholar can contemplate in peace and quiet. Pragmatism aimed at applying knowledge rather than pondering it. The purpose of education was to bring scientific intelligence to bear upon public issues, and the very existence of conflict in the world made it imperative that the philosopher involve himself in the necessity of choice and active struggle. The war seemed to offer such an opportunity,

13. Charles Francis Adams, Jr., to Henry Adams, Sept. 17 and Oct. 15, 1914, Adams mss.; Henry Adams to Elizabeth Cameron, Sept. 5, 1917; Henry Adams to William Roscoe Thayer, Mar. 15, 1918, *Letters*, vol. 6, 765–68, 790–92.

and to the extent that Dewey shared Adams's conviction that a central aim of education is to learn how power can be controlled, the philosopher had good reason to advocate America's entry into the war as a means of expanding democracy. But Adams, uncertain of what the past had wrought, went to his grave wondering what the future would bring. Knowledge of history had increased his sense of both ignorance and humility as events seemed to follow no clear, predictable pattern. History expressed itself as the movement of power and interests, but power could only be matched by countervailing power or controlled and legitimated by the authority of objective knowledge. And only through the study of history could one intelligently act on the current of events. Adams's skepticism about the possibility of such action made Dewey's dilemmas all the more challenging. Adams could readily agree with Peirce that history only "laughs" at man's efforts to understand it in rational terms. But for Dewey history would be, particularly during the war crisis, no laughing matter.

In many respects there was no way that Dewey could avoid philosophy's inevitable rendezvous with history. Long before the literary critics of the post–World War II period, Dewey perceived that history is essentially a philosophical question. The implications of studying that which no longer exists trouble the epistemologist if not the archivist. The historian thinks and writes about what happened, but historical events must be reconstructed from textual artifacts. Is the unobservable unknowable? Does history move independently of man, or is its meaning and direction constituted in part by the mind of the historian? Dewey assumed that such questions could only be answered, if at all, in the future—that is, in action rather than thought. Historical events, or, more precisely, the relations among events, could possibly be known if seen as part of a problem to be solved; but the past as knowledge of original occurrences remained beyond recovery. Dewey tried to explain that the past was also at one time "a living present," just as today's present is becoming a vanished past. Denying any dualism between past and present, between events that have occurred and events that are happening, Dewey declared: "There is no history except in terms of movement toward some outcome." Adams could scarcely claim to see the outcome of historical movements. But Dewey believed that one had only to look at the contemporary world to sense "the urgency of social problems which is now developing out of the forces of industrial production."[14] Thus Dewey overcame the crisis of historical knowledge by redefining events not as past occurrences whose character could not be known but as present developments whose problematic nature could be addressed.

14. Dewey, *Logic: The Theory of Inquiry* (New York, 1938), 230–44.

No philosopher, historian, or literary critic of our day has yet to resolve how past events "in themselves" can be knowable. If Dewey's attempt to come to terms with historical events went awry during the First World War, he nonetheless deserves admiration for tackling theoretical issues that stymied other historians, not only Adams but progressive scholars like Charles Beard and Carl Becker. Dewey, a philosopher who saw the mind becoming active when confronting problematic situations and intelligence responding as an instrument of adaptation and control, believed that pragmatism must bring thought into line with the "actual movement of events."[15] And the perils of politics and history appeared beneficial to Dewey, since intelligence would remain dormant unless challenged by the forces of change. For Dewey philosophy could keep alive only by acting upon history. So too could the study of history be kept alive. If Adams concluded, along with later existentialist writers, that history had no meaning, the pragmatist could show Americans how history could depend upon the meaning we give it. History was no impenetrable "contrived corridor" to Dewey as it was to T. S. Eliot, an endless passageway in which nothing is revealed to the proud inquirer. In adressing the issue of history, the pragmatist was determined to overcome one of the basic issues of modernism: history as the "nightmare from which I am trying to awaken."

The Appeal to the Future

The dilemma that Dewey courageously faced confronted the most sensitive minds of the entire World War I generation, in Europe as well as America: the "horror" of unexplained events.[16] To overcome this sense of intellectual helplessness, Dewey advised the troubled liberal to "connect conscience" with the "forces" that were violating it. But Dewey himself made no effort to ascertain some causal relation in order to connect the war with the "forces" that brought it about, so as to know what it is one is fighting for—and against. He had good epistemological reasons for avoiding such an exercise, as we shall see. Yet this strategy meant that Dewey could only think about history from the outside, describing vaguely its nature, movement, and direction; he could not address himself to problems within history itself—the connections, causes, and explanations of events. In Dewey's mode of thinking, the study of history becomes not so much a precise method of inquiry as a vague philosophy of process, not so much a means of knowing what was as a way of believing in what will be. Dewey wanted to get intellectuals to respond to the

15. Dewey, *Individualism Old and New* (New York, 1930), 70; *Liberalism and Social Action* (New York, 1935), 61.
16. Paul Fussell, *The Great War and Modern Memory* (New York, 1975).

processes of history, the "moving forces of events." In doing so, Dewey was assuming that one can control history by becoming its agent, an assumption that comes close to rendering individual judgment indistinguishable from the forces that are shaping it by counseling subjective obedience to objective events. Political consciousness, the ability to reflect on power, follows the forces of history. And since the significance of those forces is itself bound up with the future, the wisdom of Dewey's advice must wait upon events.

The idea that knowledge can be expected and anticipated rather than immediately known is one proposal the pragmatist makes to get around the problems of modernism. For whereas classical philosophers had justified the use of force by appealing to the past, as Hannah Arendt reminded us,[17] Dewey singularly appealed to the future, to the "event which is still to be."[18] He came close, ironically, to identifying with power and advocating what almost amounted to submission to historical destiny— even though, as a pragmatic philosopher, he had no way of perceiving the movement or meaning of history, since the future cannot be known until it is experienced. In Dewey the problem of history, the task of interpreting events, is not so much examined as projected; and the problem of authority, the obligation to legitimate the exercise of power, is not so much explained as postponed.

A fundamental paradox appears to lie at the heart of Dewey's attitude toward history. Although he looked to human experience as the test of truth, historical experience could never be the source of authority. Indeed Dewey's philosophy denied the historian the ability to make reliable judgments about the past. With pragmatism, the professor of history would seem to be almost obsolete, an antiquarian who, as Tolstoy put it, is like a deaf man answering questions nobody has asked him.

Dewey had good philosophical reasons for making the historian aware of the crisis of knowledge in his discipline. No longer could the scholar sustain the claims of both moralism and historicism—the claim that, on the one hand, the study of history could yield ethical truths, and on the other, that it could recapture the past as it actually had been. The idea that the purpose of history is to discover the great moral lessons of the past that we should know in order to obey could hardly be endorsed by Dewey, who saw historical reality as an indeterminate series of unique events from which no clear lessons could be drawn. He also rejected the historicist goal on the ground that historical investigation cannot discover actual reality, since the object of inquiry could possibly be transformed in the act of reconstituting it. Insofar as what happened in the past cannot

17. Hannah Arendt, *On Violence* (New York, 1970), 51–54.
18. Dewey, "The Post-War Mind," in *Character and Events*, 596–601.

be known independent of our present thinking about it, the distinction between history and the historian all but disappeared in Dewey's philosophy.

The collapse of that distinction did not prevent Dewey from valuing the study of history. For one thing, history could demonstrate that philosophical issues arise from a specific historical context that renders dubious the claims of timeless truths. It could also show that the goal of knowledge is not truth but "meaning," the relationship between consciousness and its environment, and that the interaction of mind and nature had its highest expression in scientific methodology. The cultural authority of science in modern civilization could be applied to history, an argument Dewey spelled out in *Logic: The Theory of Inquiry.* "History," wrote Dewey in typical prose, "is an instance of judgment as a resolution through inquiry of a problematic situation." The pragmatic historian, concerning himself not with the actual, perished past but with the effects of the past as it relates to problems in the present, can use his craft as an instrument of social control. Even though history itself may never become a science, because of the contingent nature of social reality and the vanished nature of the past, a scientific temperament could, Dewey wrote in *Experience and Nature,* help the historian begin to control events by demonstrating which qualities of human existence are "pervasive, common, stable."[19]

Dewey's theory of historical inquiry once enjoyed widespread influence. It not only rendered philosophical justification to the "new history" of James Harvey Robinson and Charles A. Beard; it also seemed to offer a rationale for regarding history in the secondary schools as a "problem-solving tool" to be used by teachers of "current affairs." Professional philosophers could hardly protest. "The study of history, conceived in the light of Deweyan philosophy, is instrumental to the future," wrote Columbia University professor Joseph Blau. "We do not merely, in the manner of elementary school children, learn history; nor do we, in the manner of the conservative, learn *from* history. Instead, we employ history as a means of changing human life."[20] How can we employ what we cannot learn? History cannot be accurately interpreted because of epistemological impediments; yet it provides the means of changing what needs to be changed. If the crisis of objective knowledge prevents us from ascertaining the exact origins of a problem, can we still claim to offer a solution to it? Dewey may have given us hope, but did he really enable us to deal with history?

Let us consider three of the most pressing issues of historical study

19. Dewey, *Logic,* 230–44; *Experience and Nature,* 108–10, 147–49, 273–75.
20. Joseph Blau, "John Dewey's Theory of History," *Journal of Philosophy* 52 (1960): 89–100.

itself: causation, judgment, and representation. Pragmatic history cannot
deal with causation because the traditional genetic method used by historians, where it was assumed that a close analysis of a historical development
contributes to our understanding of its nature, not only tells us little
about the order of connection between events but as a method cannot be
subjected to empirical confirmation. Nor can pragmatism engage itself
with moral judgments that involve the vagaries of human intentionality
and may also require standards of judgment external to the situation
judged. And the pragmatist cannot deal with representations of the past
that have no means of scientific verification in the present. Insofar as
genuine historical inquiry arises not from idle curiosity but from our
needs and desires, our knowledge of history will be conditioned by the
questions we bring to it; hence all we can know about the past is not its
objective reality but what has been modified in the act of knowing it in
response to present needs.[21]

21. On history's lack of experimental confirmation, see Sidney Hook, "A Pragmatic
Critique of the Historico-Genetic Method," in *Essays in Honor of John Dewey* (New York,
1929), 156–74. Dewey's ethical theory would not allow the historian to invoke "the qualities
of sin and righteousness, of vicious and virtuous motives" (*Logic*, 494–95). Dewey felt moral
judgments irrelevant for two reasons: first, indulging in questions of praise or blame will
do little to help control history, which requires analyzing the consequences rather than the
motives of human actions; second, we can only experience the processes of history, bad as
well as good; we cannot facilely judge or contemplate them (*Quest for Certainty*, 195–222).
See also John Dewey and J. H. Tufts, *Ethics* (New York, 1908), 318–19; and A. H. Somjee,
Political Theory of John Dewey, 32–38.
   Is there a fundamental conflict between the criteria of pragmatic philosophy and the
requirements of historical knowledge? At first glance, pragmatism and history seem entirely
compatible. Consider, first of all, that the Greek term *historia* originally signified "inquiry,"
one of Dewey's favorite terms. The pragmatist as well as the historian depends upon methods of investigating and authenticating, and to find out what there is to know turns on
modes of inquiry based on evidence as well as on reason. Moreover, pragmatism represented
in philosophy a shift from studying indwelling qualities to studying external processes, not
what exists to be found but what moves and flows in motion and interaction. In this respect
pragmatism seems close to the goals of history, which also aims to know not transcendental
essences but the meaning of natural events. Lastly, pragmatism confines itself to the phenomena of actual experience and shuns all claims that are merely intuitive or have their
origin in something other than the experimental material. The historian, or at least the
old-fashioned historian, also shuns all documents and narrative accounts that make no distinction between fact and fiction. Thus exploration of experience, whether present or past,
appears to be the common aim of philosophy and history.
   Experience, however, takes on an unusual connotation in pragmatism. Dewey took pains
to distinguish the "established doctrine" of classical empiricism from the more recent philosophy of pragmatism. "So far as anything beyond a bare present is recognized by the established doctrine, the past exclusively counts. Registration of what has taken place, reference
to precedent, is believed to be the essence of experience. Empiricism is conceived of as tied
up to what has been, or is 'given.' But experience in its vital form is experimental, an effort to

The three pragmatic reservations about historical knowledge bear emphasizing: (1) history as it actually was is affected by the difference made

---

change the given; it is characterized by a projection, by reaching forward into the unknown; connection with a future is its salient point." With pragmatism experience would be not the foundation of ideas but the means of testing them in experimental procedures. How is historical knowledge possible by "reaching forward into the unknown"? Dewey's answer was to regard the past as a "projected present" in which we come to know it as a result of the practical questions we ask of it, and the questions make a difference to what comes to be known. "No doctrine about knowledge can hinder the belief . . . that what we know as past may be something which has *irretrievably* undergone just the difference which knowledge makes."

To a pragmatist the end of epistemology should also spell the end of history as traditionally conceived. Just as Dewey insisted that there is no way of getting from our inner sensations to the external world as long as the dualism of subject and object, of the knower and the known, continues, so too is there no way of getting from present descriptions and interpretations of the past to the past itself, particularly a vanished past that leaves no remaining effects.

The difficulty of deriving retrospective knowledge from pragmatism may be seen in the following passage. Here Dewey attempts to answer critics who accused pragmatists of seeing truth as the outcome of inquiry rather than as its object, and thereby identifying truth with verification:

> If knowing be a change in a reality, then the more knowing reveals this change, the more transparent, the more adequate it is. And if all existences are in transition, then the knowledge which treats them as if they were something of which knowledge is a kodak fixation is just the kind of knowledge which refracts and perverts them. And by the same token a knowing which actively participates in a change in the way to effect it in the needed fashion would be the type of knowing which is valid. If reality be itself in transition— and this doctrine originated not with the objectionable pragmatist but with the physicist and naturalist and historian—then the doctrine that knowledge *is* reality making a particular and specified sort of change in itself seems to have the best chance at maintaining a theory of knowing which is in wholesome touch with the genuine and valid.

Apply Dewey's advice to historical inquiry and one senses the futility of learning anything about the perished past. How can history itself be in transition? Dewey did not deny the existence of history as an antecedent reality. But he did convince pragmatists that the only things in the world that could be known were those undergoing change and transition, phenomena that could be further manipulated and experimented upon so that the effects of human intervention might be scrutinized. Hypotheses are formed so that the inquirer can introduce change and control its processes. To be pragmatic, history would have to become a science of prediction confirmed by empirical observation. Judgments may be made about the past as propositions, but true, verifiable knowledge depends upon measuring and evaluating the consequences of change itself. History is not so much known as made, a matter of practice and not an exercise in theoretical exploration. No wonder Dewey had little patience with critics of pragmatism who insisted that history can be studied for its own sake and known on its own terms.

The quotes above are from John Dewey, *Creative Intelligence: Essays in the Pragmatic Attitude* (1917; New York: Rhinehart, 1945), 7; *Philosophy and Civilization* (New York: Milton, Balch, 1931), 39–40.

in the historian's effort to know it; (2) because the past is beyond empirical science, nothing can be done about it; (3) thus one must look to the future for knowledge and control. Does history have no significance simply because it is beyond the reach of scientific intervention? When attacking the old individualism of laissez-faire, Dewey protested: "Traditional ideas are more than irrelevant. They are an encumbrance." Adams might agree with Dewey that certain past ideas could not survive the historical context from which they arose, and hence, like the founding principles of the Constitution, they had "expired." Both the philosopher and the historian recognized that change leaves truth behind. But since pragmatism identified itself with the forces of change, if only better to control them, it would be difficult for pragmatism to distinguish itself from power, even in the hope of disciplining it by scientific intelligence. The pragmatist rejects the past as irrevocable and looks to the future as the realm of the possible. Nietzsche as well as Adams would be the first to point out that whatever is possible and can be made to happen excites the will to power. Yet it should also be noted that if power is the promise of the future, authority is the province of the past. For only the past, as Karl Jaspers observed, can speak to us, and because it does it "raises a claim to be responded to." The future, in contrast, cannot speak and lies there waiting to be acted upon as the self-projection of the present. The "terrible forgetfulness" of the present age, Jaspers warned, lies in ignoring the past and denying its authority precisely because it remains unresponsive to our purposes. Even if not immediately transparent to knowledge, the past can be made to live again if one listens to it, debates with it, and possibly learns that progress does not guarantee the superiority of the present. The will to power must be matched by the will not to succumb to oblivion so that the historian can be the guardian of the conscience of experience. "Our true approach to history should be to wrestle with it."[22]

Jaspers, a close friend of Weber's whose thought resembles in some respects that of Niebuhr, believed a sense of the past would mitigate the sins of pride. One has a duty to be faithful to the past as opposed to our natural inclination to forgetfulness. This idea, expressive of modern existential thought, had its predecessor in Lincoln's idea of a sacred covenant with the "spirit of '76." Nowhere is it found in American pragmatism.

In light of the pragmatist's reservations about history as irrevocable, one can understand why Dewey could not, in his own words, "see any

22. John Dewey, "Toward a New Individualism," in McDermott, *Philosophy of Dewey*, 617; John Hennig, "Jaspers' Attitude toward History," in *The Philosophy of Karl Jaspers*, ed. Paul Arthur Schilpp (La Salle, Ill.: Open Court, 1957), 565–79.

grounds for claiming that it should play any large role in the curriculum of elementary education." In *Moral Principles in Education*, Dewey called for the authority of the historian to be supplanted by that of the sociologist. "History is vital or dead to the child according as it is, or is not, presented from the sociological standpoint. When treated simply as a record of what has passed and gone, it must be mechanical, because the past, as past, is remote. Simply as the past there is no motive for attending to it." Unwilling to permit students "to become deeply immersed in what is forever gone by," Dewey advised teachers that "the past is the past, and the dead may be safely left to bury the dead." Dewey drew further upon scripture to authenticate his hostility to traditional history. "Remember," he warned the Michigan University Students' Christian Association in 1892, "Lot's wife, who looked back, and who, looking back, was fixed into a motionless pillar."[23]

Dewey's conviction that "the object of knowledge is always prospective" could only mean that even the historian should submit himself to what Santayana described as "the dominance of the foreground." Such advice as Dewey offered could be accepted only by one who had no quarrel with history—that is, with such retrospective problems as causality and judgment. The very notion of cause implies that things could have been otherwise, and thus we are forced to consider that all judgments, causal as well as moral, depend upon evaluating what did happen in light of what could have happened. Dewey seldom addressed himself to such vexing problems, and at times he seemed to accept the givenness of events, which is a short step from concluding that the best way to comprehend history is to identify with it. In 1917 he took that step.

Dewey's behavior seems inevitable in light of his desire to see the study of history emulate scientific methodology. Convinced that we can understand what history is, and was, only through what it will come to be, Dewey would have the historian convert retrospective statements into prospective hypotheses and judgments that may be subsequently verified. Yet one can only wonder whether such an exercise is possible within the nature of historical study. It is not merely that the scientist may certify knowledge by means of experimentation, while the historian must establish truth by asking questions about the past. The real difficulty is that for history to be a science of prediction the historian would have to offer valid reasons for demonstrating the probability that a sequence of events

23. Dewey, *Moral Principles in Education* (New York, 1909), 36; "History for the Educator," *Progressive Journal of Education* 1 (1909): 1–4; Dewey's reference to Lot's wife intended to make the point that democracy is, like religion, a living faith and not a tradition bound to the past; see "Christianity and Democracy," *The Early Works, 1893–1894* (Carbondale: Southern Illinois University Press, 1971), vol. 4, 3–10.

will happen before it happens. Dewey came close to doing this in 1917, and he would in fact do it in 1939; and in both these encounters with history the methodology of pragmatism tested itself against the real world of events.

Dewey's deep conviction that the past simply as past is wholly unusable, that it is devoid of any knowable antecedent reality, raises two difficult questions for anyone confronting the course of historical events. If only the future can verify our ideas about the past, upon what ideas and beliefs do we act here and now? And, conversely, if the past cannot authorize the present, why are we obligated to return to it? A study of Dewey's encounter with Leon Trotsky and his response to World War II will help us understand why he felt the need to remember the past and why he was condemned to misinterpret it.

The Trotsky Inquiry and the Debate over Means and Ends

In 1937, Dewey was asked by some old friends, among them the anarchist Carlo Tresca and the feminist libertarian Suzanne Lafollette, to go to Mexico as head of a commission of inquiry and examine the charges against Leon Trotsky stemming from the Moscow trials. Trotsky had been accused of directing terrorist attacks on the life of Stalin and other officials, organizing acts of industrial sabotage to undermine the military preparedness of the Soviet Union, and entering into secret agreements with Germany and Japan. When the Dewey commission investigated the charges against Trotsky and published the document *Not Guilty* (1938), 150 American Progressives signed a statement denouncing the verdict and supported the trials as necessary to strengthening Russia in the coming confrontation with Germany. Earlier Dewey had written Bruce Bliven, editor of the *New Republic*, protesting the magazine's pro-Soviet apology for the trial of Sergei Kirov, which instigated the bloody purges, and of denying Trotsky's right of an open hearing in its pages. Not only communists but many liberal fellow-travelers pressured Dewey to disassociate himself from Trotsky, whom they saw as a threat to the Popular Front. That Dewey resisted such pressures is a testament to his rectitude and lasting commitment to truth in politics even though it had eluded modern philosophy. The following letter from Malcolm Cowley to Dewey suggests the kind of advice America's leading philosopher was receiving from one of America's leading literary critics: "Trotsky's policies have had a terribly bad effect. I think that he is now so eccentric that he lets his followers die for him. I wouldn't ever say it in print, but my personal conviction is that he is touched with paranoia, with delusions of persecution and grandeur."[24]

24. John Dewey to Bruce Bliven, May 26, 1937; Malcolm Cowley to John Dewey, June 4, 1937, Hook papers.

When Trotsky was first informed about the commission of inquiry, he had doubts that the aging Dewey—he was seventy-eight in 1937—would be up to the task. "Would he not fall asleep during the hearings?" Isaac Deutscher paraphrased Trotsky as wondering.[25] At the conclusion of the hearings, after seven long days of intense questioning of witnesses and examination of enormous documentary evidence, Trotsky made a passionate and eloquent presentation of his case; he concluded by exclaiming to a hushed audience that the counter-trial

> has not only not destroyed my faith in the clear, bright future of mankind, but, on the contrary, has given it an indestructible temper. This faith in reason, in truth, in human solidarity, which at the age of eighteen I took with me into the workers' quarters of the provincial Russian town of Nikolaev—this faith I have preserved fully and completely. It has become more mature, but not less ardent.
>
> In the very fact of your Commission's formation—in the fact that, at its head, is a man of unshakable moral authority, a man who by virtue of his age should have the right to remain outside the skirmishes in the political arena—in this fact I see a new and truly magnificent reinforcement of the revolutionary optimism which constitutes the fundamental elements of my life.

The audience sat motionless as Trotsky ended his dramatic peroration, then broke into applause when he expressed his "profound respect" for Dewey, "the educator, philosopher and personification of genuine American idealism." "Anything I can say," remarked the white-haired Dewey when he pronounced the hearings closed, "will be an anticlimax."[26]

The deep admiration between Trotsky and Dewey made their ideological differences all the more acute. In early 1938 Trotsky wrote "Their Morals and Ours" in the *New International*, and Dewey responded in the same party journal with a most telling theoretical statement, "Means and Ends." Dewey had been disturbed by the problem of democracy and revolutionary socialism before Trotsky attacked the "banalities" of liberal morality. In Mexico he had questioned Trotsky's version of democracy in action.

25. Isaac Deutscher, *The Prophet Outcast: Trotsky: 1929–1940* (New York, 1965), 371–74.
26. *The Case of Leon Trotsky: Report of Hearings on the Charges Made against Him in the Moscow Trials* (New York, 1968), 584–85. It should be noted that Dewey behaved more as a historian than as a pragmatist during the trial; he was willing to infer knowledge about past events that, in theory, should be unknowable because unobservable. See Allan B. Spitzer, "John Dewey, the 'Trial' of Leon Trotsky, and the Search for Historical Truth," *History and Theory* 29 (1990): 16–37.

Dewey: Was there any organized, recognized method by which, aside from criticism and discussion, the worker could control the committees, the different branches of the Party?

Trotsky: Of the Party or of the Soviet?

Dewey: Of the Party.

Trotsky: It was the right only of Party members to change the Party and to control the Party. In the soviets, it was the right also of non-Party members—the Constitution assured to the workers and peasants the right to remove at any time their representatives to the soviet and to elect new ones.

Dewey: I was not referring to the soviets. I was referring to the governing bodies of the Party.

Trotsky: The bodies of the Party were elected only by the Party members and submitted only to the Party Congress.

Dewey: Under these circumstances, how can you say that it was democratic?

Trotsky: I didn't say it was democratic in the absolute sense. I consider democracy not as a mathematical abstraction, but as a living experience of the people. It was a great step to democracy from the old regime, but this democracy in its formal expression was limited to the necessities of the revolutionary dictatorship.[27]

Dewey did not press Trotsky on the issue of democracy during the hearings. The following year he did reply to Trotsky's stirring and controversial article that did much to divide the American Left in the thirties. Trotsky had attacked anarchists and democrats for shirking the harsh realities of class struggle and allegedly succumbing to "absolute" principles of ethics, vague "moral effluvia" preached to revolutionaries and not to their persecutors. Ridiculing the "theory of eternal morals," Trotsky noted that even utilitarian philosophers insisted that the ends justified the means; while the Jesuits, "more consistent and courageous," taught that a means is condoned or condemned depending on the specific end it serves. Since Marxist morality is governed by the imperative of revolution, "all means are possible which genuinely lead to mankind's emancipation." But the dialectic of means and ends is such that only certain means can lead to that end, only those means that instill "solidarity and unity" in revolutionary workers and imbue them with the "courage" and "consciousness" necessary to carry out their "historic tasks." Addressing himself to American Marxists, Trotsky drew upon episodes in American history to claim that posterity would judge his views in the same light:

Lincoln's significance lies in his not hesitating before the most severe means, once they were found to be necessary, in achiev-

27. *Case of Trotsky*, 356.

ing a great historic aim posed by the development of a young nation. The question lies not even in which of the warring camps caused or itself suffered the greatest number of victims. History has different yardsticks for the cruelty of the North- erners and the cruelty of the Southerners in the Civil War. A slave-owner who through cunning and violence shackles a slave in chains, and a slave who through cunning or violence breaks the chains—let not the contemptible eunuchs tell us that they are equals before a court of morality![28]

Dewey's reply indicated how close pragmatism and Marxism stood in their common opposition to traditional moral authority and common advocacy of a praxis-oriented history. Dewey agreed with Trotsky that "the only alternative position to the idea that the end justifies the means is some form of absolutistic ethics based on the alleged deliverance of conscience, or a moral sense, or some brand of eternal truth." Rejecting an ethics based on rule-bound principles, and believing instead that moral criteria are determined by historical circumstances and social relations, Dewey fully agreed with Trotsky that actions are to be judged in view of goals and that ends and means are interdependent and dialectically related. Dewey also agreed with Trotsky's Marxist goal of "increasing the power of man over nature and abolishing the power of man over man." Nonetheless, Dewey sharply departed from Trotsky's belief that a "law of historical development determines the particular way in which the struggle is to be carried on." Dewey claimed Trotsky had "deduced" from "a fixed law of social development" in Marxism—"a conception inherited presumably from its Hegelian origins"—the conclusion that vio- lent, revolutionary class struggle is the only means of realizing the goals of human freedom. The principle of the unity of means and ends, Dewey argued, requires a scrupulous examination of means to ascertain their "actual objective consequences" in bringing about desired results. Since both Dewey and Trotsky had ruled out moral judgment in historical inquiry, and since both subscribed to a morality of consequences, the philosopher challenged the revolutionary to be more pragmatic.

> An individual may hold, and quite sincerely as far as personal opinion is concerned, that certain means will "really" lead to a professed and desired end. But the real question is not one of personal beliefs but of the consequences that will actually be produced by them. So when Mr. Trotsky says that "dialectical materialism knows no dualism between means and ends," the natural interpretation is that he will recommend the use of

28. Leon Trotsky, "Their Morals and Ours," *New International* 4 (1938): 163–73.

means that can be shown by their own nature to lead to the liberation of mankind as an objective consequence.[29]

Perhaps the only conclusion to draw from the Dewey-Trotsky debate is that no conclusions can be drawn. Obviously Dewey had come a long way from his World War I stance, when he chastised liberals for confusing the rational use of force with violence and refusing to enter the war in order to control history as an instrument of power. But Dewey could not refute Trotsky from any position of theoretical or philosophical authority. To demonstrate the efficacy or futility of class struggle by historical example would be to concede that the past is not gone forever but directly relevant to the present; to demonstrate the same propositions by praxis would be to withhold judgment until the experiment is verified. The late 1930s, however, was not a time when writers were willing to continue suspending judgment, and since the future seemed so bleak, even Dewey and Trotsky looked to the past for hope—a strange perspective for either a pragmatist or a Marxist. Thus in 1939 we find Dewey and Trotsky returning to 1917 as the year in which history revealed its secrets about the nature of power and the prospects of freedom. Both towering figures, the heroes of Western liberalism and Marxism, still held that the rightness of a political action depends on its intended consequences, and both could therefore feel confident in invoking the judgment of history.

Yet while Trotsky possessed a theory of history, Dewey had only a theory of inquiry. In respect to the meaning and direction of events, the revolutionary would be able to assume what the philosopher would be required to explain. In turning to Leninism, therefore, Trotsky could believe that the glorious October Revolution would reenact itself because the nature of history is constituted in terms of recurring patterns and "stages" of development. But in turning to the lessons of Wilsonianism, what conclusions could Dewey draw if history had no determinate character and contained no universal truths about human experience? Seen in this light, the debate with Trotsky appears as a theoretical rehearsal for Dewey's ultimate rendezvous with history. For the approach of World War II compelled Dewey to confront the very question he had put to Trotsky, a philosophical question in search of a historical answer. If Trotsky could not demonstrate that the means of class struggle would lead to the liberation of mankind, could Dewey demonstrate that the methods of democracy would assure the survival of democracy?

World War II and the Double Irony of Philosophy and History

Against the threat of fascism the question Dewey had to face became almost a life-or-death proposition in 1939. With the future of democracy

29. Dewey, "Means and Ends," ibid., 232–33.

in doubt, Dewey addressed himself once again to the question of means and ends in *Freedom and Culture*. Published shortly before the war broke out in September, the book provides another opportunity to observe pragmatic reasoning responding to the demands of the historical moment.

Dewey reaffirmed his defense of the Western tradition of liberalism against a European rationalism that supposedly embodied individuality and freedom in abstract principles of law and order. Contemporary European totalitarianism thus provided further evidence that the excesses of classical philosophy can lead to an absolutism that substitutes the "method of coercion" for the "method of discussion." Along with Peirce and James, Dewey had always believed that the democratic spirit animating empirical method would provide a new basis for authority, a systematic means by which disputes could be settled without resorting to arbitrary, dogmatic authority on the one hand or force and violence on the other. Now more than ever, Dewey reasserted that "democratic ends demand democratic methods for their realization." In 1917 Dewey believed that democracy would be expanded by aligning itself with the forces of history; in 1939 he argued that to resist force with force was to become the captive of the very thing America was fighting—the ideologies of a corrupt and corrupting continent.

> The conflict as it concerns the democracy to which our history commits us is *within* our own institutions and attitudes. It can be won only by extending the application of democratic methods, methods of consultation, persuasion, negotiation, communication, co-operative intelligence, in the task of making our own policies, industry, education, our culture generally, a servant and an evolving manifestation of democratic ideas. Resort to military force is a first sure sign that we are giving up the struggle for the democratic way of life, and that the Old World has conquered morally as well as geographically—succeeding in imposing upon us its ideals and methods.[30]

By the outbreak of World War II, Dewey's philosophical position had reached a theoretical impasse in the realm of politics and world affairs. His dilemma sprang from two basic premises that proved incompatible with each other. Dewey's commitment to freedom led him to assert that democratic ends necessitated democratic means; his commitment to science led him to assert that truth must be judged by the pragmatic norm of results. Although the first assertion might be proved by logic, the second had to be proved by experience, the historically demonstrated consequences of actions and events. Yet experience could easily deny

---

30. Dewey, *Freedom and Culture* (New York: Capricorn, 1963), 175.

what logic affirmed. When perusing *Freedom and Culture*, one will find it difficult to know whether one should approve or condemn the Founding Fathers for resorting to the "methods of coercion" to fight the American Revolution, or whether one should praise or denounce the diplomats of the thirties for employing the "methods of discussion" to oppose Hitler. The first method led to success, the second to failure. Both suggest a cruel paradox: if Dewey made democratic means primary, he may have had to sacrifice democratic ends; if he did the obverse he would have had to violate his whole commitment to the efficacy of intelligence as opposed to force. Dewey's dilemma is all the more compounded by the pragmatist's conviction that whatever means are used, they must be evaluated in terms of the consequences they produce. Why not, then, experiment with different means instead of allowing the ends to dictate the political method to be employed in every situation?

These dilemmas only point up the fact that Dewey's belief in the unity of means and ends is neither logically persuasive nor historically demonstrable. A strict adherence to democratic methods may not result in the expansion of democratic rights, as the American abolitionists discovered; conversely, militant, nondemocratic actions may produce victories for democracies, as the European antifascists discovered. No more than Trotsky could Dewey prove a causal link between chosen means and a desired end. Indeed one suspects that Dewey's unswerving belief in democratic methods derived not from the dubious and inconclusive lessons of historical experience but from the necessary principles of logic, specifically the principle that a democracy cannot contradict itself; it cannot at the same time have and not have the properties of democracy. Whether it was on this basis or simply on an act of faith, Dewey insisted that the answer to totalitarian power was democratic culture, and he supported his argument with numerous references to American history. Since the first and last chapters of *Freedom and Culture* pay homage to the ideas of Thomas Jefferson, a student of history cannot help observing what Dewey apparently passed over: that the Declaration of Independence justifies the means in relation to the end only because the end is not identical with the means. Hence the right of the people to nullify the compact and to resort to power to safeguard liberty, to realize freedom by means of force.[31]

The more the grim realities of history caught up with Dewey, the less pragmatic he became. When his final rendezvous with history occurred with Hitler's invasion of Poland, Dewey did not hesitate to advise America to stay out of the war at any cost. His position drew bitter

31. Ibid., 3–23, 155–76.

denunciations from the "humanist" liberals—Archibald MacLeish, Waldo Frank, Lewis Mumford—who attacked "empirical" politics for its "laboratory insulation" that allegedly permitted the intellectual to flee "the responsibilities of moral choice" and expose all America to "Our Guilt in Fascism."[32] The attacks in the *New Republic* and the *Nation* did much to reinforce the older suspicion that pragmatism could not provide the ethical basis for adopting the "right" course of action because Dewey's philosophy could not derive moral judgments from naturalistic premises, the "ought" from the "is." "On all questions which involve conflict between opposing groups, and consequently a choice, and consequently a definite belief that one mode of behavior is better than some other mode, Dewey is unable to commit himself," wrote Henry Bamford Parkes in *The Pragmatic Test* (1941). "Instead of making choices, he confines himself to the pious aspiration that in the future we shall have a science of human nature comparable to the physical sciences—a development which will apparently preclude us from the necessity of holding beliefs and making decisions." In *The Philosophy of John Dewey*, an anthology of critical essays in the Library of Living Philosophers series, published in 1939, George Raymond Geiger of Antioch College explained why Dewey's philosophy could not answer the needs of the historical moment, since the public needs to know what to think about the war, not how to think about it, a criterion of judgment instead of a procedure of inquiry.[33]

Such arguments would perhaps be more persuasive had nonpragmatist thinkers—Catholics, conservative isolationists, Marxists, natural-law theorists, Christian pacifists, social scientists unburdened with values, bards blessed with poetic vision—displayed a keener grasp of the threat of fascism and the need for intervention. The difficulty with Dewey's position on the war is not that a "pragmatic acquiescence" led to appeasement or that the "method of discussion" proved the illusions of liberal innocence. The real difficulty is that Dewey's position turned pragmatism itself on its head. After spending almost his entire intellectual career advising Americans on how to use history to solve problems, insisting that we study the past in light of the present, Dewey was now approaching the present in light of the past, allowing the experiences of World War I to shape his outlook toward World War II.

Could the lessons of 1917 be invoked to explain the realities of 1939?

32. Waldo Frank, "Our Guilt in Fascism," *New Republic* 102 (1940): 603–8; Lewis Mumford, "The Corruption of Liberalism," ibid., 568–73; Archibald MacLeish, "The Irresponsibles," *Nation* 50 (1940): 618–23.

33. Henry Bamford Parkes, *The Pragmatic Test: Essays in the History of Ideas* (New York, 1941), 95–119; George Raymond Geiger, "Dewey's Social and Political Philosophy," in *The Philosophy of John Dewey*, 337–68.

Dewey now felt that historical experience could indeed offer politically relevant knowledge, and perhaps with the ghost of Randolph Bourne haunting his memory, he was not about to repeat the mistakes of the past. In 1917 he was certain that democracy could align itself with the forces of war; in 1939 he confessed in *Common Sense*, "I hesitate to predict anything whatsoever about the outcome of the present war."[34] World War I encouraged him to advise Americans to keep their focus straight ahead, "with the future, with what is coming next." World War II compelled him to advise Americans to look backward and remember the "dire reaction" that occurred in America as a result of entering the war and the unexpected rise of fascist movements in Europe. Neither the problems of the present nor the probabilities of the future seemed to impinge on Dewey's thoughts when he offered Americans six words of wisdom that transformed pragmatism from a mode of inquiry into an absolute principle and imperative, from the vagaries of knowing history to knowledge of its essential truth: "No matter what happens, stay out."[35] It was now the searing past that came to dominate Dewey's mind and conscience, rendering the great American philosopher less an interpreter of history than its victim.

Obviously Dewey had convinced himself that he had arrived at later truths from earlier errors—realizing, perhaps, that we cannot learn without a little pain, and that history is, after all, philosophy teaching by examples, especially bad examples. The lessons of World War I, the Versailles settlement and demands for its revision, and the "Red Scare" of 1919 indicated that American democracy would collapse under the strain of another international war. This conviction, shared by liberals like Charles Beard and Trotskyists like Dwight Macdonald, reoriented Dewey's entire perspective on events and rendered pragmatism an unworkable tool of historical analysis. For history now emerged in Dewey's mind as something to be feared rather than mastered, a specter from the past endowed with a curious repetitive power that seemingly could be grasped by reason rather than by experiment. In fact, at times Dewey's reasoning appeared to be based on the logic of causal necessity: given war, reaction will follow. And this premise derived from reasoning that can only be regarded as analogical. Since Dewey never bothered to study the causes of both world wars, it is not surprising that he would see parallels between the two and infer similar consequences from presumably similar events. Yet America's encounter with so unprecedented a phenomenon as Nazism raises a question as old as the study of history

34. Dewey, "The Basis for Hope," *Common Sense* 8 (December 1939): 9.
35. Dewey, "No Matter What Happens—Stay Out," *Common Sense* 7 (March 1938): 11.

itself: can a novel event be dealt with by experience? When Dewey drew upon the experiences of the past to deal with the problems of the present, it was as though he had now discovered essential truths that must be heeded regardless of the consequences. This curiously unpragmatic position, which appears now to affirm the absolute character of things and events, suggests the limits of historical knowledge based upon the presumed lessons of experience, especially an experience drawn from a comparison of two discrete and incomparable situations. Mark Twain knew a good deal about the fallacies of reasoning from a partial resemblance to an identical correspondence in order not to repeat history: "We should be careful to get out of an experience only the wisdom that is in it—and stop there; lest we be like the cat that sits down on a hot stove lid. She will never sit down on a hot stove lid again—and that is well; but she will also never sit down on a cold one." [36]

Dewey's stance in the late 1930s only made manifest some of the theoretical problems implicit all along in pragmatic philosophy. A philosopher who hesitated to "predict anything whatsoever" about the war may only have been reiterating the Jamesian dictum on the reality of the uncertain; but one who advised Americans to stay out of the war "no matter what happens" was clearly certain that intervention must be resisted for the very reason that its dire results could be predicted. In Dewey's thoughts one finds no whisper of skepticism about the mind's ability to understand what is happening. Nor is there any suggestion of the "fallibilism" and "temporalism" that intellectual historians regard as the genius of pragmatism. [37] This experimental temperament is surely the ideal of the empirical scholar and pragmatic citizen. But often those who believe themselves to be prepared to revise their positions in accordance with new evidence cannot help interpreting the evidence and events in accordance with their positions. It could be said that Dewey confused memory with understanding, the ordeal of personal experience with an interpretation of historical events.

Yet how does one separate the course of experience from the course of events so as to distinguish the continuous nature of memory and knowledge from what could very well be the discontinuities of historical reality? Can pragmatism provide guides for right action in an ambiguous world? On the one hand we are advised to look to human experience for guidance; on the other we must look to future events because knowledge based on past experience cannot be verified. The only valid knowledge is that

36. Mark Twain, quoted in Arthur Schlesinger, Jr., "On the Inscrutability of History," *Encounter* 27 (Nov. 1966): 15.
37. Philip P. Wiener, *Evolution and the Founders of Pragmatism* (New York, 1965), 190–204.

which derives from experience; yet historical experience cannot guide our actions because present conditions and future events are contingent rather than necessary. Moreover, since acting on ideas changes the conditions on which the ideas were originally formed, and since the consequences of action cannot be predicted, how can we know whether an idea that led to action can explain what resulted from the action taken? Even hindsight cannot confirm foresight, because knowledge of an approaching danger could lead to action to avert the danger and thereby preclude the possibility of knowing through actual experience whether such a danger had really existed; the historian Marc Bloch called this "the paradox of prevision." The same paradox characterizes Dewey's conviction that all historical inquiry should begin in a "problematic situation."

One can only try to illuminate the dilemmas and paradoxes in Dewey's thoughts and behavior in relation to history. It would be far more difficult to refute or revise his ideas, for in order to do so the universe would have to be constituted by the very moral truths and historical certainties that went out with the gaslights of the last century. By what authority can we claim that such older verities are still live options? Dewey realized that the quest for certainty was an illusion of past ages, and he tried to resolve the crisis in historical knowledge by showing how the problems of causality, judgment, and representation can be overcome to the extent that the historian emulates the scientist. We may admire Dewey for offering such advice, but his own conduct in response to historical events suggests the limits of our admiration. Dewey's answer to the problem of understanding history involved two practical efforts: first, in 1917, to identify knowledge with the "forces" of history in order to control power; second, in 1939, to identify knowledge with the lessons of history in order to renounce power. Now the perplexed historian may well wonder whether a philosophy that tells us what we cannot know can tell us what we must do. The intellectual historian, for example—and especially those literary critics who believe we need go no further than the text to evaluate the adequacy of an idea or doctrine—may find it instructive to consider that Dewey's *Logic* appeared in 1938, the year following Trotsky's counter-trial and a year before Dewey took his stand on World War II. In the text he drew upon his vast learning to demonstrate that genuine empirical knowledge cannot deal with occurrences that took place before the present, and that future events are so different from past events, because of the contingent nature of reality, that historical experience is useless in understanding history. When the Trotsky report was published in 1938 it laid before the public six hundred pages of investigation of past events. And when Dewey came out against entering the war the following year, his position implied exactly the opposite of the thesis propounded in *Logic:* now historical knowledge could be knowable and history predictable. So much for theory and practice.[38]

John Dewey had reached his eightieth birthday when World War II broke out; perhaps he was too far along in years to serve as a beacon for younger writers and philosophers. Yet a number of intellectuals had looked to Dewey in the thirties, and thus when he lapsed into silence during the early war years some turned elsewhere for guidance. The philosophy of pragmatism, having bravely risen as a methodology that would replace all traditional forms of authority, had itself lost authority in the eyes of a younger generation.

Ultimately the eclipse of pragmatism involves a double irony. Dewey had offered pragmatism as an answer to the crisis of historical knowledge; yet history itself would demonstrate the limitations of pragmatism as philosophical knowledge. As early as 1908, Arthur O. Lovejoy had observed rather bemusedly a truth that sooner or later was bound to be found out: that pragmatism cannot provide useful knowledge at all. Unable to certify as truthful that which we need to know before we act, pragmatic philosophy cannot provide knowledge precisely when it is most valuable. Verified ex post facto wisdom can tell us little about how to face the future if the past is behind us. The double irony is that the philosopher cannot provide genuine knowledge prior to experience, and the historian cannot do so after experience. In his numerous writings, Dewey valiantly tried to find a way out of this philosophical impasse—of knowledge knowing its limits as intelligence continually proves unequal to experience. But an examination of his career seems only to bear out Hegel's dictum that what we learn from history is that nobody learns anything from history; and an examination of the pragmatic criterion of knowledge in view of the liberal response to European totalitarian "experiments" seems only to bear out Hobbes's observation that truth is hell seen too late.

Dewey may have written philosophical treatises urging historians as well as citizens to keep their eyes on the foreground, but his own mind remained in the grip of the past. Between the logic of inquiry and the

38. In *Logic* Dewey had maintained that history as knowledge of "original occurrences" could not be known because of the lack of any means of empirical verification. During the Trotsky trial, however, Dewey became an old-fashioned Rankean fact-gatherer as he proceeded to take notes, compare dates and allegations, authenticate documents, and cross-examine the accused. Although the concept of truth may have dropped out of modern philosophy, during the trial Dewey felt it imperative to "ascertain the truth" as vital to the cause of justice. Thus in the Trotsky trial Dewey was in no position to deal with prospective statements about future events, which for a pragmatist are the only statements capable of verification. Now it was the character of past events that had to be established in a fact-finding inquiry. (*Logic*, 330–47; "Appendix III: Correspondence," *Case of Trotsky*, 594–603.)

experience of history Dewey symbolized a mind divided against itself, the existential man who, as Kierkegaard might put it, desires to live forward and is condemned to think backward. Had Dewey really been able to "look to future events," as he advised in *Logic*, he would not have allowed himself to assert so dogmatically, "No matter what happens, stay out!" An esteemed philosopher who had courageously declared his independence from history and authority, an intellectual leader whose very conduct, as Trotsky recognized, enabled us to believe once again in old-fashioned virtues and ideals, Dewey became a prisoner of the past, haunted by a memory that now came close to constituting the very seat of authority. One thinks, sadly, of Lot's wife.

One also thinks of Henry Adams. By no means can Adams be regarded as having a grasp of history superior to Dewey's. Rather one thinks of him because he found himself faced with the same dilemma in writing about the Civil War as Dewey faced almost a century later in thinking about the Second World War. Adams recognized that there was no way to judge which wing of the Republican party understood better the course of action that must be taken. Some Republicans wanted to respond to the South's secession with armed force; others felt that to do so would risk responsibility for bringing on a war that America, North and South, neither intended nor desired. A true understanding of the historical circumstances of 1860–61 compelled the historian to acknowledge that the power of prevention or prediction eluded American politics:

> It will be a question that History only can decide, which of the two wings of the Republican party were right; whether that one which saw hope only in an experience of force, or that which saw in the outbreak of a war for which they could be made in any degree responsible, only the cast of a loaded die, by which they could not win and must lose. This was the sum total of the differences of opinion among the Republicans. . . . The difference was wholly one of future policy; not of recorded principle.[39]

It will be recalled that on the evening of Pearl Harbor, Dewey told an audience at New York's Cooper Union that philosophy had no wisdom to offer America upon its entry into the war. Did he now sense with Adams that "only History can decide"? The alienation of mind from history cast into doubt pragmatism's great faith in scientific intelligence. Dewey, of course, was not one to lose faith so easily, as we shall see. But for a dramatic moment he perhaps could sense what Adams had felt in being unable to explain what was happening in the world. The help-

39. Henry Adams, *Great Secession*, 19–20.

lessness of mind in the face of the dizzying succession of events is for the modernist and the classical thinker alike the essence of tragedy. The tumult of history continues without God, and science fails to disclose its meaning.

> Whirl is King, having driven out Zeus.
> —Aristophanes

Yet ultimately the two world wars could hardly daunt Dewey's outlook. To the pragmatist, thinking is not meant to contemplate the significance of events but to use the past in order to reconstruct better experiences in the future. The difference between Adams and Dewey is best expressed in Karl Lowith's distinction between the classical thinker worried about the loss of truth and the modern thinker confident that knowledge progresses in action rather than in retrospection. "The classical historian asks: How did it come about? The modern historian: How shall we go ahead?"[40]

40. Karl Lowith, *The Meaning of History* (Chicago: University of Chicago Press, 1949), 17.

7

Pragmatism and the Problem of Power

The Challenge of Fascism

In 1942, several months after Pearl Harbor, *German Philosophy and Politics* reappeared in American bookstores, a treatise Dewey had written in 1915 in response to the outbreak of the First World War. To Dewey the war-prone tendencies of Germany, whether under the Kaiser or Hitler, derived from German philosophy and its craving for mystical transcendence. In theory the Kantian legacy gave Germans a moral philosophy based on categorical imperatives. In practice, and contrary to Kant's intentions, it instilled in Germans the conceit of believing that such idealistic sentiments were being carried out in the brute world of politics and diplomacy. Hegel, too, must be held responsible for leaving Germans with the impression that the "absolute" dwells in their collective soul and sanctions their actions. German military leaders may act pragmatically in given situations, Dewey acknowledged to the philosopher William E. Hocking when the book first appeared. "What is at issue is the difference between an activity which is aware of its own character, which knows what it is about, which faces the consequences of its activities and accepts responsibility for them, and an activity which disguises its nature to the collective consciousness by an appeal to eternal principles and the eulogistic predicates of pure idealism." With the appearance of the book's second edition, Dewey's devoted disciple Sidney Hook wrote his mentor to remind him that Hegel's owl of Minerva arrives too late to bring the message of philosophy to the real world of politics and history. Hegel's "reason worked self-consciously and only after its work was done did reflection come in and recognize what was done . . . reflection, thought, intelligence is the wisdom that flies by night."[1]

Fascism, along with Stalinism, presents a dilemma to the biological naturalist (including the Marxist as well as the pragmatist) who assumes the evolutionary stage of historical development. How to interpret an ideological phenomenon that defies progress by renouncing reason and reverting to barbarism? Unforeseen in both Liberal and Socialist thought, fascism represented not so much the despotism of the past as the demonic future. Dewey attributed fascism to the same Kantian idealism that he saw resulting in Prussian militarism in the First World War. Both Kantianism and Hegelianism imbued Hitler's weltanschauung with "emotional fusion," a binding solidarity that answered to the spiritual hunger of the German mentality. Dewey recognized that fascism contained several essential ingredients of his own philosophy of democracy, namely, community, personality, and collective activity. But he saw in the German longing for the "absolute spirit" a maladaptive, rigid Kantianism that upheld duty and authority, and a misinterpreted Hegelianism in the hands of Hitler, who denied any separation of the ideal and the real and instead identified both with the destiny of the Third Reich. The curse of Germany was the curse of absolutism.

In Dewey's hands pragmatism became a philosophical resource that would save America from the temptations of absolutism and rigid dogma. Or so it seemed. For Dewey's pragmatism itself contained metaphysical assumptions and absolutes, especially in its imperative of action and certainty about the eventual intelligibility of events, all of which, as Santayana put it, involved "that strange pragmatic reduction of yesterday to to-morrow." Such a reorientation advised America to look ahead and trust future experience because, in Hegel's formulation, "pragmatical" history "takes the occurrence out of the category of the Past and makes it virtually Present."[2] And if present as well as past experience eludes the mind's quest for meaning?

It is significant that when Dewey reviewed The Education of Henry Adams in 1921, he did not use the occasion to examine and question its author's view of the human condition and the mind's alienation from history and power. Instead the philosopher focused on Adams's service in London during the Civil War to give Americans "some instruction" about dealing with England in particular and international relations in general. Dewey

1. John Dewey, German Philosophy and Politics (1915; New York: rev. ed., 1942); John Dewey, letter to New Republic 48 (Oct. 2, 1915): 234–36; Sidney Hook to John Dewey, June 30, 1942, Hook papers.

2. G. W. F. Hegel, The Philosophy of History, Trans. J. Sibree (New York: Dover, 1956), 6.

believed that certain passages in the *Education* were appropriate to the current Washington conference on securing international peace, especially passages on John Hay's taking the diplomatic initiative away from Europe in China at the time of the Boxer Rebellion in the 1890s. Although chastened by the unfulfilled promises of Wilsonianism, Dewey still believed that the "American system" was morally superior to Old World politics.[3]

During the twenties Dewey joined the "Outlawry of War" movement. Dedicated to educating the public on the need for international cooperation, the organization seemed to Dewey preferable to the cynical realpolitik of European nation-states. In 1928, at the time the Kellogg-Briand treaty was being negotiated, a pact that would bind signatory nations to renounce war as an instrument of national diplomacy except in self-defense, Dewey was proffering advice to lawyers and peace foundation officials who worked to sway public opinion behind the treaty. In turn the officials asked Dewey to write an article on the Monroe Doctrine and its present-day implications. Then distraught by the illness of his wife, Dewey had no time to research the proclamation of 1823, but in the Kellogg-Briand Treaty the United States reserved freedom of action in the Western hemisphere, as stipulated in the Monroe Doctrine.[4]

In the thirties Dewey continued as a staunch pacifist to champion the cause of peace. His increasing condemnation of violence—in contrast to his justification of "rational" and "efficient" force in 1916—was one reason he remained unmoved by the communist doctrine that began to influence the intellectual community. Earlier Dewey's former student Hook had written from Berlin trying to convert his mentor. Marxism is entirely "presuppositionless," Hook insisted. A "critique" is not a fixed doctrine. It was Engels, Hook complained, who systematized Marxism by hypostatizing it as a body of infallible truths about nature. "But Marxism is no more a system than is Pragmatism!" exclaimed Hook.[5] Dewey remained skeptical of the Marxist doctrine of class struggle and revolutionary violence. The destruction of capitalism by means of force seemed both undemocratic and unscientific to Dewey, who continued to believe in society's reformation through experimental procedures. The challenge of fascism could best be met not by class warfare in Europe but rather by further developing democracy in America. Dewey's benign melioristic approach taxed the patience of Marxists as well as that of the Christian realist Reinhold Niebuhr. Ironically, Niebuhr argued that the use of force

3. Dewey's review of Adams's *Education* appeared in *New Republic* 19 (Dec. 21, 1921): 102–3.

4. Salmon Levinson to John Dewey, Feb. 8, 1928; Dewey to Levinson, March 2, 1928; March 6, 1928; Dewey papers.

5. Sidney Hook to John Dewey, Jan. 29, 1929, Dewey papers.

in politics derived not from the truths of science but from those of religion.

Niebuhr's place in American intellectual history is more profound than generally presented by historians who associate him with cold war liberalism. Niebuhr's thought antedates the cold war and has more to do with America's confrontation with fascism than with communism. It also involves America's confrontation with its own native liberal tradition. Dewey had assumed that, with science supplanting religion, power could be subdued by reconciling potentially violent issues through means of rational discussion. Niebuhr saw power as expressive of human nature and evil as constitutive of human freedom. The contrast between Niebuhr's Christian realism and Dewey's pragmatic instrumentalism represents a curious moment in the history of political thought. Dewey's belief in "social intelligence" carried forward a tradition originating in the eighteenth-century Enlightenment, which insisted that political theory be founded upon a theory of social change. Many of the *philosophes* argued that no modern political philosophy could be based simply upon assumptions about an unchanging or essential human nature, especially assumptions that rendered intellectual and moral growth problematic. In the 1930s Niebuhr's role was to do precisely that by introducing, or reintroducing, the idea of original sin; in so doing he also combined two sensibilities that, in our contemporary theory, are alleged to be incompatible: essentialism and modernism. Dewey had no difficulty combining modernism with his belief in evolutionary growth and endless change and transformation. But Niebuhr's resort to essentialism may have been more daring. The philosopher gave liberalism an intellect; the theologian gave it a conscience.

The Obscure Object of Power: Reinhold Niebuhr and Original Sin

Like Dewey and several other American intellectuals born in the nineteenth century, Niebuhr had been brought up in an environment of devout Protestant piety.[6] Reinhold's father, Gustav, was a minister in the German Evangelical Synod and a man of liberal sympathies. Reinhold grew up in a German-speaking household with two brothers and a sister in Lincoln, Illinois. He attended Elmhurst College outside of Chicago, then Eden Theological Seminary, and finally the Yale Divinity School, where he felt inferior among the better-prepared students who spoke perfect English. After some reservations about war (in "The Paradox of Patriotism" [*Atlantic*, 1915] Niebuhr noted how nations call upon young

6. For Niebuhr's life I have drawn upon Richard Fox's excellent study, *Reinhold Niebuhr: A Biography* (New York, 1985).

men to risk their lives, the only thing that has "eternal significance," for political ends that have no "eternal value") Niebuhr supported Woodrow Wilson and America's intervention. In the early twenties his disenchantment with Wilsonian liberalism led Niebuhr to flirt with Christian pacifist ideas. But during his tenure as a pastor in Detroit his struggles with the Klan and with industrialist Henry Ford turned Niebuhr into a bitter social critic who came to see entrenched power as unresponsive to prayer or rational persuasion. On the subject of power it could be said that Niebuhr spent much of the rest of his life teaching American liberals that they did not really know what they thought they knew—the basis of the human will to power.

Power has been analyzed in a variety of ways by political scientists. Distinctions abound. Power *to* implies efficacy at bringing about consequences; power *over* implies imposition and control.[7] One can lead to liberation, the other to oppression. However power is defined—as force, might, coercion, the legitimate use of violence, unequal relations of dependency—Niebuhr would agree with Simone Weil that there is never power but "only a race for power"; and he would agree with Hannah Arendt and the American framers that power is not an individual but a collective phenomenon of groups and factions that move in concert and continue to move until resistance is encountered. If power is aggression marching toward its object, and if, as Weil pointed out, power can only be exterminated by abolishing its object, what is its object?[8]

On this question much of modern thought takes its point of departure from the seventeenth-century English philosopher Thomas Hobbes. According to Hobbes, the insecurities of the state of nature compel people to submit to authority. The insecurities themselves derive from the fact that members of the human species are striving for the same goals: gain, security, reputation. The result is competition, invasion, and war of each against all. Niebuhr criticized Hobbes for eliminating religious categories from his political analysis and for demanding, at the same time, unconditional loyalty to the state that is itself implicitly religious.[9] Yet, Dewey hailed Hobbes precisely for eliminating religion and, like Machiavelli, for

---

7. See Goran Therborn, "What Does the Ruling Class Do When It Rules?" in *Classes, Power, and Conflict*, ed. Anthony Giddens and David Held (Berkeley: University of California Press, 1982), 224–48; Steven Lukes, "Power and Authority," in *A History of Sociological Analyses*, ed. Tom Bottomore and Robert Nisbet (New York: Basic Books, 1978), 633–76.

8. Simone Weil, *Oppression and Liberty*, trans. Arthur Wills and John Petrie (Amherst: University of Massachusetts Press, 1973), 56–83; Hannah Arendt, *On Revolution* (New York: Oxford University Press, 1963).

9. Niebuhr, *The Nature and Destiny of Man* (1943; New York: Scribner's, 1964), 100–101, 106.

putting political thought on a scientific basis. Dewey agreed with Hobbes
that the early Christian church had appealed to some indwelling Holy
Spirit as the source of divine law. As a result political obedience had
nothing to do with publicly instituted forms of authority and legality.
Politics, Dewey assumed, required neither heaven nor hell, neither cosmic support nor diabolical fear.[10]

In the 1930s, when Niebuhr had rejected his earlier Christian pacifism
and turned to Marxism for a better perspective on power, he grew impatient with progressive thinkers who refused to see the necessity of class
conflict and perhaps even violence in the struggle for social justice. Niebuhr's *Moral Man in Immoral Society* (1932) appeared during the depths of
the depression, when its author was attempting to synthesize the Marxist
commitment to struggle with a Christian sense of sin. Neither scientific
intelligence nor appeals to piety and goodness could abolish social conflict
in an evil world. Liberals like Dewey, Niebuhr protested, refused to
recognize the subordination of reason to interest in the struggle for power.
It almost seemed as though Niebuhr had now taken Dewey's position in
the latter's earlier debates with Randolph Bourne and the pacifists. Indeed
Niebuhr was trying to awaken the American mind from that same slum-
ber in which Dewey supposedly found the German mind—the false consciousness and self-righteousness of a political stance unaware of its own
character. The use of force and even the resort to violence, Niebuhr
advised, could be justified as desperate means to realize democratic ends
on the part of moral persons willing to take responsibility for their actions
and to suffer the agony of choice and the dread of guilt. From Niebuhr's
perspective what made force and conflict inevitable was not only human
aggression but the moral weakness of the human condition afflicted with
original sin. Thus Niebuhr felt obligated to make a case against Dewey's
simple political innocence as dangerously deceptive. He did so in a 1936
article, "The Blindness of Liberalism," that spelled out the propositions
that a Deweyite subscribes to:

> a. That injustice is caused by ignorance and will yield to edu-
> cation and greater intelligence.
> b. That civilization is becoming gradually more moral and
> that it is a sin to challenge either the inevitability or the effi-
> cacy of gradualness.
> c. That the character of individuals rather than social systems
> and arrangements is the guarantee of justice in society.
> d. That appeals to love, justice, good-will and brotherhood

10. Dewey, "The Motivation of Hobbes's Political Philosophy," *Studies in the History of
Ideas* 1 (1887): 88–115; "Notes on 'The Prince'" (undated), Dewey mss.

are bound to be efficacious in the end. If they have not been so to date we must have more appeals to love, justice, goodwill and brotherhood.

e. That goodness makes for happiness and that increasing knowledge of this fact will overcome human selfishness and greed.

f. That wars are stupid and can therefore only be caused by people who are more stupid than those who recognize the stupidity of war.[11]

The historians Richard Fox and Robert Westbrook, authors of respective biographies of Niebuhr and Dewey, argue that Niebuhr's portrait is unfair and inaccurate. To support their case, they cite passages from Dewey's writings where he is quite realistic about the inescapable presence of force and conflict in social relations.[12] Perhaps this confusion stems from the fact that there are two John Deweys. During the period of the First World War, when Dewey was writing on Hobbes, he was also debating Bourne over America's entry into the war. Dewey's defense of intervention, it will be recalled, distinguished irrational violence from a rational, prudent use of force. Many years earlier Dewey, as a Darwinist, informed students that ethical ideals do not descend from metaphysical heights but are born out of necessity in the real world of conflict, strife, and struggle. Thus it could be said that Dewey realized that all ideas, even the idea of democracy, require some use of power for their realization. The Dewey of the 1930s, however, was a philosopher chastened by the outcome of the Versailles settlement. As indicated in the previous chapter, Dewey remained unswerving in his rejection of force and violence as means of bringing power to bear on hostile predicaments and responding to aggression. Invoking the "method of discussion," Dewey would fight fascism with conversation.

The positions taken by Niebuhr and Dewey in some ways represent the two distinct intellectual traditions in American foreign policy. In his early pacifist period Niebuhr stood for idealism, later moving to a realistic outlook toward history as power and conflict. Dewey moved in the opposite direction, from advocating military might in 1917 to renouncing any exercise of force in 1939. Dewey sided with Jefferson, reason, progress, cooperation, and hope in the human capacity for self-government; Nie-

11. Niebuhr's essay is quoted in Arthur Schlesinger, Jr., "Reinhold Niebuhr's Role in American Political Thought and Life," in *Reinhold Niebuhr: His Religious, Social, and Political Thought*, ed. Charles W. Kegley and Robert W. Bretell (New York: Macmillan, 1961), 125–50. I am indebted to this insightful analysis.

12. Fox, *Niebuhr*, 136–37; Robert B. Westbrook, *John Dewey and American Democracy* (Ithaca, N.Y., 1991), 523–32.

buhr sided with the *Federalist* authors and the necessity of power to counterpoise the irrational passions and interests whose causes cannot be eliminated because they are "sown" into humankind's fallen condition. Historians Fox and Westbrook are right to suggest that Dewey and Niebuhr shared many similar ideas and values and that neither was a naive optimist nor a hopeless pessimist. But it is going too far to insist that Niebuhr had nothing to teach Dewey. "Niebuhr ought to have known," writes Fox, that Dewey would have agreed that reason is hardly disinterested in a social world of conflict and struggle.[13] The observation fails to go to the heart of the issue separating Dewey and Niebuhr. It was not simply that they both saw intelligence as problematic and history as the challenge of events that need to be controlled. The deeper issue is the genesis of power in the story of human evolution.

As a Darwinian naturalist, Dewey treats the human species as an "organism," and he confines his analysis to a biological vocabulary that need not probe the depths of motivation but instead focuses on struggle, adaptation, and survival. Dewey also assumes that the precarious status of existence is as progressive as it is provocative, for the instabilities of the environment give rise to intelligence as an instrument of control.[14] With Niebuhr, however, the very uncertainties and instabilities of life result not in the rational use of intelligence but in an irrational need to find safety in power. "The lust for power is prompted by a darkly conscious realization of its [the ego's] insecurity." Avarice has much the same origin as power. "Greed as a form of the will-to-power has been a particularly flagrant sin in the modern era because modern technology has tempted contemporary man to overestimate the possibility and the value of eliminating his insecurity in nature. Greed has thus become the besetting sin of bourgeois culture." Where Dewey believed the instabilities of existence challenged the mind and brought out its best qualities of rational intelligence and scientific control, Niebuhr saw in the dread of insecurity the origins of power and aggression. Niebuhr's perspective enables us to see why objects of power cannot be eliminated. Arising out of fear, the will to power must forever assert itself to reach a state that is impossible to attain. "Man is tempted by this basic insecurity of human existence to make himself doubly insecure and by the insignificance of his place in the total scheme of life to prove his significance. The will-to-power is in short both a direct form and an indirect instrument of the pride which Christianity regards as sin in its quintessential form." Rooted in sin, the human power-drive cannot be eliminated because pride prevents the ego

13. Fox, *Niebuhr*, 136.
14. Dewey, *Experience and Nature*, 40–77.

from seeing that its purpose in trying to dominate others is futile. "The peril of a competing human will is overcome by subordinating that will to the ego and by using the power of many subordinated wills to ward off the enmity which such subordination creates. The will-to-power is thus inevitably involved in the vicious circle of accentuating the insecurity which it intends to eliminate."[15] Interpreting the genesis of power as the Christian sin of pride that springs from fear, Niebuhr shows why power can seldom know the truth about itself. But knowledge of this Niebuhrian insight can be derived from sources other than Christian. "It is not power that corrupts but fear," wrote Aung San Suu Kyi, the imprisoned Burmese dissident leader and winner of the Nobel Prize. "Fear of losing power corrupts those who wield it and fear of the scourge of power corrupts those who are subject to it."[16]

It may be true, as the historian Fox has observed, that Niebuhr never studied closely Dewey's thoughts but "was constructing an ideal-type opponent who was easy to take down."[17] Still, Niebuhr's critique remains valid. For Dewey not only refused to give much attention to power and its origins, he also had no idea where to look for it other than as some kind of aberration. When Dewey thought at all about power—not as the ability to act and have effect but as control and domination—he usually interpreted it as an example of dislocation and maladjustment, the failure of education and intelligence to catch up with economic development and the rise of big business. He saw American individualism as a cultural lag that could be redressed once political culture redefined itself along more cooperative and collectivist directions. Dewey came close to suggesting that the evils of power would disappear to the extent that the individual merges with the social and members of a democratic society lead lives of mutuality as "an organic whole":

> To learn to be human is to develop through the give-and-take of communication an effective sense of being an individually distinctive member of a community; one who understands and appreciates its beliefs, desires and methods, and who contributes to a further conversion of organic powers into human resources and values. But this translation is never finished. The old Adam, the unregenerate element in human nature, persists. It shows itself wherever the method obtains of attaining results by use of force instead of by the method of communication and enlightenment. It manifests itself more

15. Reinhold Niebuhr, *The Nature and Destiny of Man: Human Nature*, vol. 1, 188–91.

16. Aung San Suu Kyi, "The Glass Splinters," *Times Literary Supplement* (July 12, 1991), 6.

17. Fox, *Niebuhr*, 136–37.

subtly, pervasively and effectually when knowledge and the instrumentalities of skill which are the produce of communal life are employed in the service of wants and impulses which have not themselves been modified by reference to a shared interest.[18]

Dewey assumed that human sinfulness and the temptations to power, the "old Adam," can be properly dealt with so far as individual actions are subordinated to a community of "shared interest." Such an assumption presupposes that a collectivized body politic is more enlightened and moral than its defective human parts, and that interest loses its egoistic character when it is directed toward public rather than private ends. Niebuhr offered an entirely different perspective to suggest why power-driven actions of individuals become even more corrupting when behavior is taken to be a collective phenomenon. Like the *Federalist* authors, Niebuhr insisted that the limitations of human beings as individuals are magnified in political society:

> Individual men may be moral in the sense that they are able to consider interests other than their own in determining problems of conduct, and are capable, on occasion, of preferring the advantages to their own. They are endowed by nature with a measure of sympathy and consideration for their kind. . . . Their rational faculty prompts them to a sense of justice which educational discipline may refine and purge of egoistic elements.
>
> But all these achievements are more difficult, if not impossible, for human societies and social groups. In every human group there is less reason to guide and check impulse, less capacity for self-transcendence, less ability to comprehend the needs of others, and therefore more unrestrained egoism than the individuals who compose the group in their personal relationships.[19]

Niebuhr's analysis of human conduct is not only different but diametrically opposed to that of Dewey, George Herbert Mead, and other pragmatists who rest their hopes on social interaction and the presumed moral superiority of community to individuality. In Niebuhr's view, which impressed Martin Luther King, Jr., the individual human capacity for love and care diminishes in larger organizations where group egotism remains blind to its power-motivated rationalizations.

18. Dewey, *The Public and Its Problems* (1927; Denver: Swallow, 1954), 154–55.
19. Reinhold Niebuhr, *Moral Man and Immoral Society* (1932; New York: Scribner's, 1960), xi–xii.

Dewey's ideas about the meaning of freedom can also be subjected to Niebuhrian scrutiny. Like most liberals, Dewey regarded freedom as the antithesis of authority. Freedom had more to do with progress, and hence it could be identified with scientific inquiry and involvement in social action. In *Freedom and Culture*, Dewey took pains to disassociate freedom from individuality, and he cautioned that it may not have had its origins in the doctrine of natural rights. Dewey also asked a series of questions that made freedom as problematic as power. "What is freedom and why is it prized? Is it wanted as an end or as a means of getting to other things? Does its possession entail responsibilities, and are these responsibilities so onerous that the mass of men will readily surrender liberty for the sake of greater ease?" Dewey doubted that the desire for freedom could be traced to a single motive and suggested instead that the amount of freedom existing at a given period of history depends upon culture and social arrangements. According to Dewey, human behavior has undergone so many changes throughout history that one cannot specify a constant motive for all epochs:

> It is significant that human nature was taken to be so strongly moved by an inherent love of freedom at the time when there was a struggle for representative government; that the motive of self-interest appeared when conditions in England enlarged the role of money, because of new methods of industrial production; that the growth of organized philanthropic activities brought sympathy into the psychological picture, and that events today are readily converted into love of power as the mainspring of human action.[20]

In contrast to Dewey, Niebuhr hardly shied away from attributing human motives to a constant principle, and thus love of freedom and love of power spring from a similar source. For freedom is sin, the assertion of the self, the right to do wrong, especially when the self remains proudly unconscious of its motives. Power is not necessarily the negation of freedom but possibly its expression. Where there is history, there is freedom; where there is freedom, there is sin; where there is sin, there is power.[21]

Not only is power ironically implicated in freedom, it is also implicated in justice. Against the pacifists Niebuhr tried to demonstrate how the exercise of power could be an instrument of justice. To engage in a theoretical critique of power scarcely absolves one from occasions when power, violence, and the shedding of blood may be necessary to prevent evil and promote good. Niebuhr's attitude toward the pacifists who re-

20. Dewey, *Freedom and Culture*, 3–23.
21. Niebuhr, *Nature and Destiny*, vol. 1, 110–12; vol. 2, 257–69.

fused the call to arms against Hitler reminds one of Max Weber's famous essay "Politics as a Vocation." Niebuhr may not have agreed with Weber that politics and ethics are incompatible. But the distinction Weber drew between an "ethic of ultimate ends" and an "ethic of responsibility" is Niebuhrian. In the first instance, moral judgments are made on the basis of the purity of the person's intentions; in the second, the consequences of actions are paramount in arriving at moral decisions. Niebuhr insisted that the pacifist is an absolutist rather than a pragmatist, one who is less interested in the practical results of his or her politics than in preserving the ego's innocence from the guilt that inevitably accompanies the use of power. In this respect Dewey himself could hardly be described as a pragmatist when he announced, after Hitler invaded Poland in 1939, "No matter what happens, stay out!"[22]

Nor can Niebuhr himself be described as simply an antipragmatist. For Niebuhr was quite comfortable with William James's version of pragmatism. He praised *The Varieties of Religious Experience* for taking theology away from theologians and placing it within the experience of human emotions. As a Christian existentialist, Niebuhr appreciated James's sense of uncertainty and contingency, his conviction that life contained secrets impenetrable to science, his revolt against determinism in support of moral choice and responsibility, his strictures against rationalism and abstraction, and his message that the deeper meanings of existence lay beyond politics and public life. With Dewey, however, public life was precisely what America lacked; his political philosophy aimed to address that deficiency as the first step in overcoming it.[23]

Dewey and the Classical Tradition

In the 1920s, the period in which Dewey devoted his philosophical mind to political theorizing, he was responding to two books by Walter Lippmann, *Public Opinion* and *The Phantom Public*. Lippmann had concluded that an informed, civic-minded public had no real existence in America. Later Lippmann would, as will be pointed out in the next chapter, return to the "Great Tradition" of classical thought to seek foundations for modern political philosophy. Why would Dewey become so disturbed by Lippmann's recurrence to classical traditions, and how did he propose to reconstruct America's political culture simply by looking ahead?

It may be helpful to recall that Henry Adams believed there was no

22. Max Weber, "Politics as a Vocation," in *From Max Weber: Essays in Sociology*, ed. H. H. Gerth and C. Wright Mills (New York, 1946), 77–128.
23. Reinhold Niebuhr, introduction to William James, *The Varieties of Religious Experience* (New York: Collier, 1961), 5–8.

going back or forward. He saw that the framers had taken "issue with antiquity" by establishing a republic that fragmented the idea of unified sovereign authority and by devising a new system of government based on modern conceptions of interest and property rather than classical ideals of virtue and reason. Adams's personal library, containing the works of leading political philosophers of the eighteenth and nineteenth centuries, together with his own notations on the page margins, suggests that he continued to search for a solution to the problem of liberal pluralism left by the framers. But Adams found no consolation in the writings of even great conservative thinkers. Edmund Burke and John C. Calhoun had little understanding of human motivation, especially the "passions" that make politics irrational and unpredictable.[24] Only Tocqueville seemed to understand that American history had produced a new species, people who fled political authority and succumbed to social conformity, self-reliant individualists powerless in the face of mass society, wishing to be free and wanting to be led. Tocqueville also knew that the Americans' incessant pursuit of wealth in the name of higher ideals was something new in modern history, a mentality of enlightened self-interest (*L'intérêt bien entendu*) that turned the old notion of classical republicanism upside down by making private greed a surrogate for public duty. But Tocqueville was hoping that the new form of "virtuous materialism" could preserve liberty by channeling the old irrational politics into the sober, disciplined life of labor and entrepreneurship.

Tocqueville did not live to see the industrial transformation of America after the Civil War. As Adams gazed upon the Gilded Age of the late nineteenth century, America became corrupted by the very forces Tocqueville hoped would sustain freedom in the modern world: capitalism, democracy, and frontier individualism. Such forces meant the concentration of economic power and the absence of centralized political authority to oppose it; the commercialization of society and the worship of wealth; and the rise of interest politics, political machines, and the boss system. Noting that both politicians and economists preoccupied themselves with railroad rates, commodity prices, tariffs, taxes, and other issues that touched the pocketbook, Adams believed that America had reached "the very bottom notch of political bathos." In a letter to Moorfield Storey, he pointed to material abundance as the death of the austere ideals of classical republicanism. "It is in reality the vast and rapid accumulation of wealth, thus produced, and most unevenly distributed. This, it goes without saying, is wholly inconsistent with the idea or working

24. Adams's criticisms of Burke and Calhoun are from the marginal notations he wrote in their books in his personal library, now in the Massachusetts Historical Society, Boston.

of Republican government." On his eighteenth birthday, on February 16, 1918, a month before he died, Adams wrote to a friend that he preferred the age of Marcus Aurelius to that of Woodrow Wilson.[25]

To the very end Adams painfully recognized that modernity killed morality once economics triumphed over politics. Sensitive to dualism, he took wicked delight in observing that a society could have an economic system or a moral system but not both. Dewey, however, believed America could have both—a system of politics and economics based upon the inescapable reality of interests, and a system of ethics and morality based upon the possibility of community-engendered ideals.

It has been noted how Dewey, though an admirer of Plato, rejected Greek philosophy as mired in the illusion that ultimate knowledge must be based upon eternal and unchanging principles, an illusion that Darwinism dispelled once and for all. Adams, too, recognized that there could be no return to a preevolutionary state of knowledge. But Dewey had other reasons for turning his back upon the past. If the historian found the tradition of civic humanism dead in America, the philosopher would have found the tradition useless even if alive and well. For Dewey had a different explanation of the corruption and stagnation of republics. Where classical republicans had believed that the coming of wealth and luxury could undermine the citizens' moral fiber, Dewey believed that human development had been stunted throughout history because of material scarcity. Thus the rise of industry and technology, instead of threatening the polity, would free men to live beyond the level of economic necessity and pursue more noble goals and ideals. More is not less but more, the means by which human potentialities may be actualized.

Although Adams and Dewey held different interpretations about the decline and fall of republics, they did agree that the study of history would be of little help in preserving them. Adams, it will be recalled, concluded that if history be taught for didactic purposes it must be "falsified." Dewey agreed. What troubled the philosopher was not only that "our schools send out men meeting the exigencies of contemporary life clothed in the chain-armor of antiquity." Dewey had all along made it clear that a study of the past could seldom serve the needs of the present, since historical experience has no repetitive pattern. But Dewey also perceived a problem that Adams well understood and that champions of classical republicanism would find hard to accept. Can good history produce good citizens? Is it not the case that teaching patriotism requires "avoidance of the spirit of criticism in dealing with history, politics and

25. Henry Adams to Moorefield Storey, August 13, 1910; to "My Dear Carlo," Feb. 16, 1918, Adams mss.

economics. . . . The more indiscriminatingly the history and institutions of one's own nation are idealized, the greater is the likelihood, so it is assumed, that the school product will be a loyal patriot, a well-equipped good citizen." Nietzsche noted how historical knowledge destroyed religious myth by exposing its parables. The modernist mind knows that political authority is subject to the same fate when exposed to critical history.[26]

Dewey had intellectual as well as personal reasons for opposing a recurrence to classical politics. In much of ancient thought man was conceived as having an essential nature that each being strives to attain. In this teleological view the natural and the spiritual are in combat as desire and virtue struggle against one another to possess the soul. Dewey's understanding of mind, grounded in Darwin's evolutionary principles, viewed the intellect as an external phenomenon responding to the exigencies of the immediate environment. In the classical view, mind sought to realize its immutable spiritual essence in accordance with its fixed Being; in the pragmatic view, it struggles to adapt to endlessly changing conditions. Dewey replaced classical introspection with social action.

Yet Dewey had a deep respect for classical political knowledge. In his lectures at the University of Chicago, he continually reminded students of the efforts the ancients made to organize life in ways that would overcome "the divisions and irreconcilable strifes of classes and parties" that afflicted the polis. "We often forget the extent to which our political *ideas* have descended to us from the Athenian Greeks." If skeptical of classical philosophy for denying the validity of experience in favor of permanence, Dewey admired those "Greek writings which reawakened the dormant civic sense." In a letter to Santayana, Dewey explained his identification with his beloved Greeks. "My pragmatism, such as it is, derives from Plato more than from any one else; I mean of course from that strain in Plato according to which 'the science of the whole' is the science of politics."[27]

But the whole of Greek philosophy was precisely what Dewey refused to swallow. While he esteemed ancient social and political philosophy for promoting the civic sense, he criticized its epistemology for promoting the speculative sense. Plato's conviction that life must imitate preexisting celestial forms found no home in pragmatism, which rejected antecedent ideals of perfection for the more immediate world of growth and adaptation. Dewey wanted the philosopher to be both in the world and of it,

---

26. Dewey, "Education as Politics," in *Character and Events*, ed. Joseph Ratner (New York, 1929), vol. 2, 776–81.

27. Dewey's lecture notes on Greek political thought are in his ms. 102 60/23 (undated); John Dewey to George Santayana, Mar. 9, 1910, Kallen papers.

where universals and absolutes had little bearing on problematic situations. Thus he examined, both in published works and in his private notebooks, the writings of Machiavelli and Hobbes. As a modernist thinker Dewey was more at home in the historical world of power, interest, conflict, and struggle, in contrast to the ancient moral world of beauty, harmony, love, and wisdom.

In his unpublished "Notes on 'The Prince,'" Dewey recorded no objection to Machiavelli's advocacy of force and fraud. He wrote out Machiavelli's dictum, "Never behave well unless compelled," not to admonish realpolitik but to analyze it. Machiavelli hated despotism, Dewey noted, and unlike Plato he devoted his life to finding ways it could be overthrown and liberty restored. Dewey similarly admired Hobbes for rescuing politics from theology and, as noted earlier, turning it into a scientific discipline. Hobbes opened up the modern mind to the reality of unending change and conflict. Grounded in the actual world of power struggles, Hobbesianism offered Dewey not so much a formula for absolutism as "a science of human nature operating through the art of social control in behalf of the common good." Hobbes and Machiavelli reinforced Dewey's Darwinian conviction that movement and motion are the only reality, that in the absence of truth adaptation to circumstances is the only strategy, and that civil society is born of human needs, fears, and desires. In Dewey's outlook philosophy and political thought sprang not from Plato's heavenly spheres but from the real world of strife and want. "The development of society has never been through abstract and ethical considerations," he stated to his class in political philosophy in 1892. "Whatever ethical ideals and motives have to do with social development it must be found *in* and *through* the development forced by the necessities of the case and *not* as a separate thing."[28]

Perhaps nowhere is the difference between modern and classical thought better seen than in Dewey's naturalistic ethical theory. In college lectures on ethics and politics, Dewey addressed a series of eighteenth-century problems—"The Psychology of the Virtues," "The Psychology of Self-Realization and Its Application to the Egoism-Altruism Controversy," and "The Significance of the Problem of Knowledge." Machiavelli made Dewey aware that force may be necessary to realize ideals, and he also recognized, with writers like Hobbes, Locke, and Hume, that knowledge is accessible only through direct sense experience, and not through disinterested ideals like "benevolence" and "virtue." Denying any

28. Dewey, "Notes on 'The Prince,'" in Dewey mss. (undated); "The Motivation of Hobbes's Political Philosophy," *Studies in the History of Ideas* 1 (May 1887): 88–115; "Political Philosophy" (1892), 102 62/1, Dewey mss.

conflict between self and society, Dewey also rejected Kant's idea of ethics as the logic of duty. Since all human action involves social interaction, Dewey reasoned, what man does is not so much "for his interests" but simply "as his interests." Dismissing as unreal the distinction between the moral and the empirical, Dewey's naturalistic ethics saw no dualism between "virtue" and "interests" in the classical sense. On the contrary, interests meant little more than the identity of the self with its object, whatever anyone happened to be concerned with as a means of developing "self-realization."[29]

There appears to be a curiosity, if not a contradiction, in Dewey's view of man as thinker and man as actor. In the world of politics that involves collective action, Dewey doubted that man could or should rise to virtue by suppressing his interests. He rejected as unnatural the republican principle of civic responsibility, the Christian principle of personal sacrifice, and the Kantian principle of moral obligation as an unconditional imperative. Indeed Dewey inverted Kant's logical categories. Why should seeking happiness for ourselves be immoral, he asked, while making it possible for others is ethical? Yet the curiosity is that although Dewey denied that man could transcend self-interest in his political and social roles, he did think it possible in pure intellectual activity. Only when the mind loses itself in the playfulness of its own thoughts can it move beyond itself. Whereas Machiavelli and his realistic disciples saw the political mind as constrained by its own subjectivity, Dewey cited Aristotle and Plato to show why "wonder" can free the mind from such a state:

> Wonder is the simple recognition that objects have significance for us beyond the mere fact of their existence. It is accordingly the spring to that activity which shall discover their significance. A wide development of the feeling of wonder constitutes *disinterestedness*, the primary requisite for all investigation. Wonder, as the outgoing activity of mind, necessarily requires a surrender of all purely subjective and selfish interests, and the devotion of one's self to the object wholly for the sake of the latter. It is the love of knowledge; and knowledge is necessarily objective and universal. It is vitiated by the presence of any merely personal interest. When the activity occurs not for the sake of the object, but for the sake of satisfying the personal emotion of wonder, we have, not disinterestedness, but *curiosity*.[30]

29. Dewey, *Lectures on Psychology and Political Ethics: 1898*, ed. Donald F. Koch (New York, 1976), 181–218; John Dewey, *The Early Works, 1895–1898* (Carbondale, Ill., 1972), vol. 5, 4–24.

30. Dewey, *Early Works, 1887*, vol. 2, 263.

Here Dewey seems close to Niebuhr and the framers of the Constitution, who also believed that man as individual could possibly be trusted to behave responsibly and be capable of objective thinking and disinterested conduct. But Dewey as well as Niebuhr and the framers recognized that politics deals not with individuals but with groups and factions acting in concert. Nevertheless, Dewey saw little relevance in Christian and classical traditions to America's political condition. For both those traditions made little allowance for Dewey's passionate belief in self-realization. The pure scientist, poet, or philosopher, Dewey observed, might be capable of feelings directed not toward objects but toward a state of mind induced by knowledge of the objects, which "originate[s] a love for knowing" for its own sake. Such a state, while wonderful, seemed also "abnormal curiosity" that defeats the self from following its healthy growth. "The only way to develop self is to make it become objective; the only way to accomplish this is to surrender the interests of the personal self. Self-culture reverses this process, and attempts to employ self-objectification or knowledge as a mere means to the satisfaction of these personal interests. The result is that the individual never truly gets outside of himself." Could people even as citizens rise above self-interests? Dewey convinced himself that people need not worry about that question as long as they see themselves as part of a "social organism." With his great faith in redemption by socialization, Dewey remained singularly untroubled by the disease that had haunted Adams and earlier exponents of classical republicanism—the disease of political corruption:

> A man when he goes to vote does not put off from him, like a suit of clothes, his character, his wealth, his social influence, his devotion to political interests, and become a naked unit. He carries with him in his voting all the influence that he should have, and if he deserves twice as much as another man, it is safe to say that he decides twice as many votes as that other man. Even if his character is corrupt, and his devotion to politics is from motives of self, it yet remains true that he votes, not as a mere unit, but as representative of the social organism. It is only because society allows him, nay, grants him power on such grounds, that he can use it. His very corruption is the expression of society through him.[31]

This amazing passage is from "The Ethics of Democracy" (1888), which Dewey wrote in response to Sir Henry Maine's influential *Popular Government*. Maine contended that democracy was the rule of numerical aggre-

31. Ibid., 264; Dewey, "The Ethics of Democracy," *Early Works, 1882–1888*, vol. 1, 233–34.

gates that could never produce a general will except by manipulation, and that in mass society sovereignty becomes indistinguishable from power and politics becomes a matter of expediency and corruption. Dewey replied by redefining democracy not as a multitude of competitive atoms but as a "social organism" based upon mutual "interdependence." Here Dewey anticipates some neopragmatists of our time who believe that problems can be resolved, or shown not to have been problems to begin with, by means of "redescription." But why should seeing society as an organism and people behaving interdependently rid the ills of human conduct that exist independently of how they are described? Thinkers from the *Federalist* authors to Niebuhr to Martin Luther King saw collective behavior as presenting a group egoism that resists appeals to intelligence and morality. All society corrupts; social organisms corrupt interdependently.

Religious thinkers like Niebuhr carried on the conviction of Adam's ancestors that humankind is theologically incapable of transcending self-interests because of the curse of original sin. Dewey believed the human species is biologically incapable of doing so, yet the blessings of self-objectification make it unnecessary. Hence the Christian and classical notions of self-denial never made much sense to the naturalist philosopher who learned from Darwin that life signified struggle and self-preservation. For man to become a "unified whole," self-actualization cannot be thwarted. Where, then, should America turn for the reconstruction of political thought and the regeneration of modern society? Invariably pragmatism turns in one direction—to the future.

This future orientation is merely one of several reasons why it strains credulity to see Deweyan pragmatism as a revival of classical republicanism. Dewey values growth as a biological principle; republicanists feared it as a threat to the polis. The Greeks demeaned work and productive activity; Dewey advocated vocational education. The classical philosopher aimed to discipline desire, Dewey to fulfill it. Classical thinkers taught obedience, Dewey experience. Above all, Dewey departed completely from Machiavelli in refusing to bestow glory upon the Founders. As Thelma Levine put it: "There is, strangely, in the writings of Dewey no reference to *illo tempore*, the Great Days of the Revolution, the Constitutional Convention, the Great Men of those heroic and kairotic times; Dewey offers no celebration of the Founding of the Republic."[32]

Dewey's endorsement of progress and industry is perhaps the most

---

32. Thelma Z. Levine, "Pragmatism and the Constitution in the Culture of Modernism," *Transactions of the Charles Sanders Peirce Society* 20 (1984): 1–19.

fundamental reason why he felt no regret in departing from the classical ideals of virtue and duty and the Christian ideals of obedience and benevolence. What Dewey believed essential to America's revitalization was not so much a Machiavellian *ricorso* as a modern advance toward empirical science. Dewey's conviction that scientific authority could replace political and religious authority meant that governance itself could be reconceived as an empirical proposition. Unlike Adams and Weber, Dewey did not see science as the expression of power in industrial society. Instead of seeing science as bringing "disenchantment," Dewey was closer to Marx in welcoming it as liberating, the harbinger of mind's growing awareness of its social and collective nature. Other contemporary philosophers, the French sociologist Émile Durkheim, for one, believed that industrial society was dissolving all organic ties and reducing human relations to an atomistic "dust of individuals." Dewey's challenge was to show how science could restore what others claimed it had destroyed.

The Great Community: Politics as Control

Dewey's writings on political philosophy in the twenties and thirties were in some respects responses to positions taken by Lippmann. The "pundit" seemed to the philosopher too elitist and classical-oriented, too skeptical of modern democracy and citizen rationality. But in his early career as a young professor Dewey had also reflected on the political theories of Kant, T. H. Green, and John Austin as well as those of Hobbes and Hegel.

Dewey remained skeptical of Kant's conception of the rational self as an independent and solitary entity. Instead of seeing cognitive faculties as capable of formal, a priori judgments independent of experience, Dewey was an organicist who regarded human thought processes as active products of social interaction. He questioned Austin's view of law as a series of commands, since such a definition left sovereignty simply as a matter of power with no ethical considerations. People can be crushed by "brute force," he told his students. But "mere force can't command obedience; it has a contradiction in its make up. Men would kick back." Dewey was more comfortable with Rousseau's locus of authority in the "general will" in which people prescribe for themselves the rules by which they live. The notion of sovereignty as flowing by means of consent from subjects to rulers had its origins in the social contract. But the contract theory of government came to be distorted, according to Dewey, by later writers like Tocqueville, who refused to see that the world "suffers more from leaders and authorities than from the masses"; by Herbert Spencer, who postulated individuals as prior to society in place of Rousseau's sense of sovereignty as the supremacy of the general over the particular; and by Lippmann, who denied Rousseau's omnicompetent citizen.[33]

In his major political texts—*The Public and Its Problems* (1927), *Individualism, Old and New* (1928), and *Liberalism and Social Action* (1935)—Dewey returned again and again to the two problems that beset modern American political theory: a liberal legacy that conceives the individual as self-sufficient and asserting his natural rights against the encroachments of government, and a modernist temperament that judges individuals ill prepared for the demands of responsible politics and rational decision-making. To use Dewey's chapter titles, in view of "The Eclipse of the Public," how did he propose to "Search for the Great Community"?

Dewey conceded Lippmann's point that the individual on his own may lack the intelligence to make reasonable political judgments. But to the extent that the individual joins with others in common effort his intellectual and moral faculties are expanded. Dewey used the institution of marriage as an example of how "union" with others brings new levels of awareness and responsibilities. A curious example. Contemporary playwrights like Eugene O'Neill saw the family as a sick institution of mendacious dialogues, repressed thoughts, ironic confrontations, hidden meanings, and neurotic personalities. The more modernist Lippmann, whose own marriage was on the rocks in the late twenties, had no Victorian innocence about the institution.[34] But Dewey's main point was to emphasize that knowledge is a function of "association" and "communication" in a participatory democracy. The act of knowing is not so much an acquisition as a transformation to the extent people decide what is to be done and take common action to do it. "To be a recipient of a communication is to have an enlarged and changed experience. One shares in what another has thought and felt and . . . has his own attitude modified." In Dewey's analysis democracy is synonymous with community, the sovereignty of the general made possible through social interaction and civic participation.[35]

During the depression era Dewey critically analyzed liberalism from a socialist position, and he did so as a historian of ideas, but one who

33. Dewey's discussion of sovereignty and why men would "kick back" is from his lecture notes on Rousseau and Austin (undated), 102 62/1, Dewey mss. For Dewey's political thought I am much indebted to A. H. Somjee, *The Political Theory of John Dewey* (New York, 1968).

34. See Lippmann's discussion of marriage in *A Preface to Morals* (New York, 1929), 307–13.

35. Dewey, *The Public and Its Problems* (New York, 1929), 143–84; *Democracy and Education* (1916; New York: Free Press, 1966), 87.

made the problems of the present the portals to the past. The result was something of a double vision, with liberalism first being described as the legacy that needs to be overcome, and then being dismissed as a false impression the reality of which never existed. In American history, argued Dewey, unchecked individualism led to concentrated units of economic power, monopolies legitimated by the laws of economic development, while the exercise of freedom had become synonymous with the absence of any organized control. Such a liberal reading of history misinterpreted the past by conceiving freedom as arising out of individual, competitive striving, when its true historic source lay in collective struggle and effort. Dewey's reinterpretation of American history may have given comfort to Marxist scholars, but it contained some ironic twists, even for Marxists who took seriously the necessary stages of history. For Dewey could not bring himself to concede that America had a liberal epoch and an individualist mentality. Even before the depression he felt it necessary to challenge Woodrow Wilson's view of American history. "The statement that 'yesterday and ever since history began, men were related to one another as individuals' is not true," Dewey declared in reference to Wilson's *The New Freedom*. Drawing upon the theories of Charles Cooley, Dewey insisted that men had related to one another in close association in which they stood "face to face" in communities of social intimacy and personal responsibility. Dewey believed he could find in the American past what the *Federalist* authors, Tocqueville, and even Marx concluded was an impossibility—a social order not of factional strife but of common interests! And where Henry Adams had traced the disintegration of unifying principles to the eclipse of classical values at the birth of the Republic, Dewey claimed that "American democratic polity was developed out of genuine community life."[36]

Dewey would have been on stronger grounds had he traced communal society to seventeenth-century New England Puritanism. But the eighteenth-century Enlightenment and its doctrines of natural rights undermined "the city upon a hill." Did not Jefferson warn that dependency "begets servility"? Yet for Dewey what once existed had somehow been lost and must now be regained. In *Individualism Old and New* he called for restructuring America's social environment so as to approximate some of the qualities of the Greek polis. Only in a "great community" can individualism be freed from private concerns to achieve true moral growth. Individuality, as opposed to individualism, can flower when men and women take part in a public life of mutual concerns, shared intelligence, and social control guided by scientific inquiry.

36. Dewey, *The Public*, 96–97.

In the thirties Dewey was saddened to see his "search for the great community" recede from view. Illinois Senator Paul Douglas, influenced by *The Public and Its Problems*, started the League for Independent Political Action in an attempt to continue the search. Dewey joined the organization and tried unsuccessfully to solicit funds from the industrialist Cyrus Eaton to launch a third party.[37] Curiously, although liberal intellectuals like A. A. Berle and Rexford G. Tugwell believed they were applying Dewey's experimental methods to FDR's administration, Dewey himself rejected the New Deal as too experimental, a politics of "messing around" and "doing a little of this and that in the hope that things will improve." Specifically, Dewey wanted to see capitalism abolished, since "any compromise with a decaying system is impossible." In *Liberalism and Social Action* Dewey became disillusioned with his faith in communication and "public discourse." What America now needed was not more talk but coherence, direction, and a systematic organization of the means of production. Dewey looked to a "new" liberalism to redeem America through a philosophy of empirical adaptation and social control, and he indicted the "old" liberalism for having conditioned the American people to regard government as their opponent rather than their servant.[38]

Thus by the end of the thirties Dewey had become estranged from both the New Deal liberals and the pro-interventionist liberals, those who supported the welfare state and those who supported the war against Hitler. Dewey judged the New Deal incoherent and liberalism as bankrupt as Wall Street. He himself advocated government intervention domestically but not diplomatically. Was Dewey's own political philosophy coherent?

Robert Westbrook acknowledges that Dewey was "ambiguous" in defining "the public" and the meaning of "interest," and he failed to make clear what citizenship entailed.[39] But the difficulties of Dewey's political philosophy are more serious than a mere lack of clarity and precision. For one thing, he never resolved how democracy arising from local self-government could be necessary to his goal of self-realization, especially when there is no essential self to realize but only a social self to interact with, no government of the self but only government by the whole people, no freedom as the absence of restraint but only collective obedience to participatory democracy, where decisions are left to a majority whose constituencies are themselves governed by nothing more than the contingencies of opinion and the whim of fashion. If people as citizens have a

37. John Dewey to Cyrus Eaton, Dec. 5, 1932, Dewey mss.
38. Dewey, "The Future of Liberalism," *Journal of Philosophy* 32 (April 1935): 225–30; Edward J. Bordeau, "John Dewey's Ideas about the Great Depression," *Journal of the History of Ideas* 23 (Jan.–Mar. 1971): 67–84.
39. Westbrook, *Dewey*, 314–17.

natural desire to participate in democratic politics, what are they seeking? Dewey had no trouble conceding that people are moved by "interest," but interest reflects unfulfilled desires and needs, and desire desires what is lacking. Dewey refused to specify motives, whether materialist or idealist, whether gain for oneself or social justice for others. Nor did he rest politics on older notions of liberty and natural rights. Could politics simply be a process without a purpose?

To Dewey active participation was more important than the constitutional guarantees of representation, and presumably people are moved to participate when they encounter a "problematic situation" that is to be resolved. Politics depends upon the disturbance of stability and adapting to change. Politics can go on only so far as people experience doubt and frustration, for if their desires were ever fulfilled, politics would have destroyed itself by realizing its promise of restoring "organic wholeness" and leaving behind the requisite stimulus of an irritant. It would appear to follow that the *Homo politicus* is fated to create problems as much as to solve them. Does such an ironic twist to Dewey's notion of "creative intelligence" render progress problematic? Does it render doubtful Dewey's claim that pragmatic philosophy could overcome the burdens of the "old" liberalism, the ingrained tradition of Lockean individualism where human beings labored on the materials of life in "a joyless quest for joy"?[40]

Neither Dewey nor his biographers have discerned any great tensions and contradictions in his four commitments: to nature, to politics, to science, and to community. Toward nature, science stands poised as aggressor; the resources of the earth are there not to be beheld but to be transformed by technology. The Dynamo dominates nature and ushers in the kingdom of power. A Weberian might also point out that Dewey's commitment to industrial progress and technology is at odds with his desire to preserve the communal values of primary relationships. Science concentrates knowledge in the hands of technicians who run the machinery of society on the basis of expertise, while politics generates committees, caucuses, lobbies, political action groups, bureaucratic agencies, and other institutions that thwart initiative and spontaneity to the point where citizens lose sight of politics' original purposes. Did Dewey, in short, ever understand that participatory democracy results in more organizations, pressure groups, monitoring and surveillance, endless meetings of deliberation and adjudication, and the multiplication of offices of supervision and regulation? Dewey assumed that everything had to grow in order to affirm itself. But as democratization stifles itself in its own procedures,

40. The description of liberalism as "joyless" is Leon Strauss's in *Natural Right and History* (Chicago: University of Chicago Press, 1953), 251.

power moves away from people toward impersonal institutions that function to perpetuate themselves. Democracy offers no guarantee that power will not become alienated from its legitimate source. Why does power seem always to steal quietly away from people?

It would be interesting to imagine Dewey grappling with this Weberian scenario wherein politics loses its meaning to the structures of officialdom. Could Dewey face the thought that human beings might possibly create the conditions of their own alienation and remain too alienated to realize it? It may be that not only is Dewey's language ambiguous but reality itself is too ambiguous and paradoxical to be contained within his language. Dewey looked upon politics as he looked upon knowledge and saw both as vehicles of power and control. But the control was to be imposed upon the economic forces that came to dominate capitalist society in America. Here arise two ironies.

During the depression Dewey criticized the New Deal for lacking purpose, direction, and systematic social control. The public philosophy and the good society could only be, he was convinced, a society of applied intelligence, a "great community" scientifically planned, designed, organized, and managed along with citizen participation. The irony here is that Dewey's epistemology could give little support to his politics. As Weber might have put it, how could the philosopher speak of a rationally planned economy without working out a rational plan that accurately represented market relationships, price determination, and resource allocation? Having concluded that the world could not be known and represented as it actually is, how could Dewey be so certain that he could control it as he wanted it to be? Presumably to know is to change the object known in order to produce desirable effects. This pragmatic dictum seems to assume that the good society can be brought into existence not necessarily by knowledge of the good but instead by sheer will, effort, and technique directed at the reorganization of society. Although Dewey has been hailed for ridding philosophy of epistemology in order to bring it into the modern world, in this instance he appears to be returning to the eighteenth-century French Enlightenment in his conviction of a rational world responsive to scientific manipulation. Curiously, it was the eighteenth-century Scottish philosophers of market economics who differed from the French in their skepticism of the possibility that the emergent capitalist society could have rational foundations. Adam Ferguson, David Hume, and Adam Smith all saw history and economic development as the product of human action, but not necessarily of human design or purpose. Freedom consisted in allowing people to pursue their material desires, however irrational, unpredictable, and pregnant with the irony of unintended consequences. Dewey's idea of rational social control could scarcely take account of the uncertainty, obscurity, and paradoxes inherent in reality itself. Convinced that a planned society was within human conception and design, he claimed cognitive abilities in politics that his epistemology denied in philosophy.

A second irony arises when we turn to Dewey as teacher and pedagogue. For here Dewey's philosophy allows laissez-faire in educational and moral life that it denies in political life. Seeing the economy as haphazard, he saw schooling as spontaneous. Thus in the schoolroom Dewey advocated hands off, a decidedly noninterventionist philosophy that would impose no system or structure upon the process of learning. Dewey trusted the presumed self-directed activities of education with the same faith with which the capitalist trusts the presumed self-regulations of the market. Whether the "invisible hand" be cooperation or competition, the problem of power disappears from discourse as a "discipline" that need not be learned.

The Child and the Curriculum: Education as Freedom

In no area of American life did John Dewey enjoy more influence than in education. For almost the entire first half of the twentieth century his ideas prevailed in many public and private schools, virtually transforming older, formal systems of instruction and reshaping the outlook of students and teachers alike. Then came the reaction. President Dwight Eisenhower, who served briefly as president of Columbia University, where Dewey had taught for more than a quarter of a century, voiced a common sentiment in *Life* magazine in 1959. "Educators, parents, and students must be continually stirred up by the defects in our educational system. They must be induced to abandon that educational path that, rather blindly, they have been following as a result of John Dewey's teachings."[41]

Max Eastman, once a teaching assistant with Dewey at Columbia, described the beloved philosopher as "the man who saved our children from dying of boredom, as we almost did in school."[42] Critics like Eisenhower, however, charged Dewey with being responsible for the "permissiveness" in the classroom that resulted in excessive experimentation. Did Dewey save American children from boredom only to turn them over to bedlam?

The question needs to be raised, for Dewey's defenders are correct to point out that his influence has been exaggerated and his ideas distorted and abused. The defenders are quick to emphasize that Dewey changed his mind about progressive education after he became aware of what was happening in the classroom in the name of his principles. Yet the issue

41. "Private Letters of the President," *Life* 46 (Mar. 16, 1959): 104–6.
42. Max Eastman, *Great Companions: Critical Memoirs of Some Famous Friends* (New York, 1959), 250.

is more complex. For not only did the practice of progressive education evolve from Dewey's theories, he never reevaluated his theories in light of their failure in practice, nor did he demonstrate how a theory that made "self-expression" the basis of education could overcome a culture that made "self-interest" the basis of the economy.

Academic scholars seldom give much attention to the problems of teaching, especially at the elementary levels of instruction that seem so far removed from the research interest of the luminaries of "higher learning." Dewey, however, was a dedicated educator as well as a scholar, and he devoted a large part of his intellectual career to developing a theory of teaching and learning that would enrich the life of the mind and the fabric of society. He also believed strongly in education as the agency of cultural transmission that would relate knowledge to current issues. The educational environment was crucial to Dewey; it was here that social values could be passed on to the young.

Dewey's *School and Society* was published in 1899, about the same time that Adams began writing the *Education*. Both documents reflect the tensions of cultural modernism, and both, interestingly enough, see the crisis of modernism as the crisis of authority and look to science for an answer to that crisis. It is commonly known that Dewey became a critic and reformer of an educational system rooted in antiquated ideas and teaching techniques. It is also a common impression that Adams was a frustrated elitist who sought to resist the changes taking place in American society in order to uphold older values upon which the survival of his gentry class depended. In fact, Adams shared many of Dewey's complaints about American education. When teaching history at Harvard, he protested the "genteel" and "ornamental" character of the curriculum and wanted to see instruction become more directed toward society and science than to the cultural pursuits of the leisure class. To a friend he wrote of his efforts to make students "understand that all knowledge has not been exhausted by Newton and such. This effort to get rid of rubbish and to utilise good material is one of my labors, I am preaching a crusade against Culture with a big C. I hope to excite the hatred of the entire community, every soul of whom adores that big C. I mean to irritate every one about me to a frenzy by ridiculing all the idols of the University and declaring a University education a swindle."[43]

Adams taught at Harvard during the period when President Charles Eliot was trying to revise the curriculum. Although sympathetic to Eliot's efforts, Adams the "conservative Christian anarchist" felt the inertia of the system would prevail, together with its "elegant scholars" and gentlemen "of refined classical taste." Much like Dewey, Adams wanted to see

43. Henry Adams to Charles Milnes Gaskell, Oct. 4, 1875, *Letters*, vol. 2, 271–72.

"more university men trained to take a hand in the rather rough game of American nineteenth-century life. To do that effectively, they must be brought up in communication with that life." Adams especially knew what the educational reformer was up against:

> Our men in the same devoted temper talk "Culture" till the word makes me foam at the mouth. They cram themselves with second-hand facts and theories till they burst, and then they lecture at Harvard College and think they are the aristocracy of intellect and are doing true heroic work by exploding themselves all over a younger generation and forcing up a new set of simple-minded, honest, harmless, intellectual prigs as like to themselves as two dried peas in a bladder. It is an atmosphere of "culture," with a really excellent instinct for all the very latest European fashion in "Culture." Matthew Arnold should be their ideal. Ruskin and Herbert Spencer, Morris wallpapers, Corot paintings. . . . Such a swarm of prigs as we are turning out, all formed by prigs and all suffering under a surfeit of useless information, is new to human experience. Are we never to produce one man who will do something himself, is the question I am helplessly asking.[44]

Dewey was too kind a man to explode in such a manner. Yet he could not have agreed more about the useless conceits of high culture. Both thinkers knew that the challenges of modernism required a reorientation of education and learning. Both agreed that knowledge was more than an exercise in accumulation and recitation. Yet starting with the same complaints, Adams and Dewey reached different conclusions.

Adams protested that his education, mired in eighteenth-century certitudes, left him unprepared for twentieth-century uncertainties. Dewey similarly protested against an educational system that perpetuated obsolete thoughts under the name of authority. Both felt the wrong ideas were being taught in school. But Dewey, without quite specifying what are the right ideas, managed the uncanny feat of welcoming the loss of authority while still upholding the value of responsibility. Adams judged his life a "failure" because he did not know how to make himself worthy of his ancestors; Dewey set out to rescue students from the false consciousness of guilt.

Modernism as the problem of disbelief unsettled education around the turn of the century as it did other institutions. Who determines which values are to be continued or rejected, and what role does a teacher assume

---

44. Henry Adams to R. Cunliffe, Aug. 31, 1875, *Letters*, vol. 2, 235; for Adams's thoughts on education I am indebted to Piotr Skurowski, "Henry Adams and the Academic Reform at Harvard," *American Studies* 6 (Warsaw University Press, 1987): 85–103.

in the moral education of a nation? The teaching of morality expresses the highest reach of authority, the wisdom that can guide us in our confrontations with ethical decisions. Yet Dewey's war against dualism compelled him to reject the notion that the responsibilities of moral conduct require an absolute foundation of authority. Darwinism had sensitized Dewey to the reality of relativism, the impossibility of finding immutable moral principles governing behavior. Granted that moral ideas and ideas about morality change with different circumstances, can students be taught to do right before they know what the right is?

Although Dewey firmly believed in the necessity of character development, and although he wrote of the "ethical responsibility of the school," he remained convinced throughout his life that "virtue" could not be taught. It will be recalled that Adams insisted that while arithmetic and table manners could be taught to children, philosophy was more difficult and morals even more complex. Dewey similarly felt that moral knowledge hardly qualified as a skill like basic grammar, which students might learn as a body of rules. Plato recognized, he pointed out, the "sophistic" implications in any claim that purported to translate wisdom into goodness. Religion may offer itself as the voice of moral authority; yet religious doctrines, like philosophical speculations, represent little more than opinions buttressed by persuasion. The variety of philosophical systems should caution us against grounding moral authority in any source save science, and the history of religion should caution us against looking to a dogmatic spiritual creed to foster democratic values in the school. In *Moral Principles in Education* (1909), Dewey emphasized that ethical authority resides neither in the cultivation of "good intentions" on the part of students nor in "knowledge of what the right is." Instead the teacher must develop in the students "the power of trained judgment" that can channel their "spontaneous instincts and impulses," thereby enabling them to discriminate among "relevant values" and "relevant ends." Although Dewey did not specify what these values and ends consisted of, he was sure that the pursuit of such goals involved little sustained intellectual discipline and no emotional repression. Once students become aware of the value of concentrating on a "positive end" all repression becomes self-imposed, an expression of human power and not its distortion. "In keeping powers at work upon their relevant ends, there is sufficient opportunity for genuine inhibition. To say that inhibition is higher than power, is like saying that death is more than life, negation more than affirmation, sacrifice more than service."[45]

To what extent should education be directed? This question, often raised by critics of pragmatism, Dewey answered again and again, and

45. Dewey, *Moral Principles in Education* (Boston, 1909), 3–54.

he did so with his naturalistic penchant for the language of biology. One word sums up his entire rationale for learning: "growth." Dewey's educational writings are thick with the metaphors of "development," "formation," "integration," "unification," "assimilation," "adjustment," "continuity," and "progression," all of which convey the forward movement of mind through the resolution of problems. Growth implies potentiality, the ability to develop from immaturity to adulthood, a passage in which the students' "pliable elasticity" enables them to interact with their environment and to modify behavior and acquire new habits through the continuous reconstruction of experience. Insofar as individuals are different in interests and capacities, the educational environment should provide opportunities for personalized growth. Above all, there is no end to the learning process, for each new stage of growth creates the conditions for more developed responses to experience, and thus education, like life itself, can never be regarded as finished. "Since growth is the characteristic of life, education is all one with growing; it has no end beyond itself."[46]

Nor should education be organized and structured according to preestablished principles. Dewey was against any form of systematic instruction that could become empty routine and any fixed method of presenting knowledge that smacked of indoctrination. What must be avoided at all costs are a priori procedures that may frustrate the student's potential for self-directed activity. The "common principles" of "progressive" as opposed to "traditional" teaching Dewey summed up as follows: "To imposition from above is opposed expression and cultivation of individuality; to external discipline is opposed free activity; to learning, from texts and teachers, learning through experience; to acquisition of isolated skills and techniques by drill, is opposed acquisition of them as means of attaining goals which make direct, vital appeal; to preparation for a more or less remote future is opposed making the most of the opportunities of present life; to static claims and materials is opposed acquaintance with a changing world." Learning by "doing" rather than by drill, and knowing from active experience rather than from passive information, not only liberated intelligent inquiry from ritualized deadness but offered the student the best means of emulating the scientific method. Dewey likened learning itself to "play" and "work" that, in contrast to the "toil" and "drudgery" of labor, is not motivated by economic necessity but instead represents a mode of physical activity involving implements through which students find manual and artistic expression.[47]

How does the teacher influence the learning process? Dewey usually

46. Dewey is quoted in Thayer, 180.
47. Dewey, "Traditional vs. Progressive Education," in *Intelligence*, 656–57; "Learning and Doing," ibid., 607–14.

approaches this question negatively rather than affirmatively, pointing out the ways in which instructors prevent genuine learning from taking place. The greatest danger to learning arises from teachers who presume to speak as "authorities," a stance that enhances the ego through the worst forms of self-deception. "As a matter of course," Dewey reminded educators, those who behave in this manner "know that as bare individuals they are not 'authorities' and will not be accepted as such. So they clothe themselves with some tradition as a mantle, and henceforth it is not just 'I' who speaks, but some Lord speaks through me. The teacher then offers himself as the organ of the whole voice of a whole school, of a finished classic tradition, and arrogates to himself the prestige that comes from what he is spokesman for. Suppression of the emotional and intellectual integrity of pupils is the result; their freedom is repressed and the growth of their own personalities stunted." Dewey was hardly advocating anarchy in the classroom. "When external authority is rejected," he wrote in *Experience and Education* (1938), "it does not follow that all authority should be rejected, but rather that there is need to search for a more effective source of authority." Earlier Dewey had proposed that American teachers could learn one source of authority from their own political culture, an argument spelled out in *Democracy and Education* (1916). Education, like democracy, must resist authoritative principles that promise the false security of ready-made truths. Schools in a democracy should give students the opportunity to grow by allowing them the freedom to question; the students should also be able to acquire the knowledge and techniques that enable them to control their physical and social environment. In this situation the relation of teacher to pupil is that of an interpreter to an inquirer, one who guides and directs students' emotional and intellectual energies. Through such procedures, students will learn how to organize their experiences into meaningful steps of investigation that lead to the formation of reflective habits. The teacher "steers the boat, but the energy that propels it must come from those who are learning." Conceiving modern education as the cultural expression of democracy, Dewey offered America the pedagogy of participation.[48]

In regard to subject matter, Dewey also made student "interests" and "needs" the criterion of selecting learning materials. The result was the pupil-oriented curriculum against which Dewey himself would later protest. Initially, however, Dewey believed that abstract, remote subjects had no immediate meaning in a student's life and led to the further isola-

---

48. Dewey, "Individuality and Freedom," ibid., 623; *Experience and Education* (New York: MacMillan, 1938), 1–13, 17–19; "The Training of Thinking," in *Intelligence*, 615; *Democracy and Education* (New York, 1916), 6–9, 81–99, 164–79.

tion of school from society. That isolation resulted from administrative boards' reliance upon traditional "literacy, dialectical, and authoritative methods of forming beliefs." Thus the textbooks and other instructional materials should be drawn directly from the present environment and not from a body of predigested literature that must be learned by rote. Active student involvement based on pragmatic inquiry into immediate problems would guarantee that any subject taught would be "relevant."[49]

Dewey believed that his programs for reform in education would lead to the reformation of society itself. As embryos of society, schools reflect the tensions and problems inherent in the existing social order. In the past a society dominated by class divisions established its educational programs in accordance with the tenets of philosophical dualism. Then learning was seen as an exercise in knowing rather than doing, the acquisition of knowledge for the sake of cultural appreciation rather than social application. Modern progressive schools, where instruction becomes the instrument of cooperative intelligence directed toward the solution of problems, could be the shining center of new methods of learning that would radiate outward and enlighten society as a whole. Democratic participation in civic life would thus be enlarged. As the teacher and scientific expert provided the information and methodology with which to develop intelligent citizens, the cultural lag of prescientific habits could be overcome and students and citizens could plan, direct, and control social change. In Dewey's brave vision, student and society, citizen and public, education and democracy, all grow together.

This brief outline of Dewey's educational philosophy describes a program and vision he clung to throughout his entire intellectual career. With the founding of the Progressive Education Movement in 1919, Dewey's influence in academic circles developed rapidly in the teens, and by the post–World War II period the philosophy of pragmatism had transformed the American school. All along, however, Dewey's ideas encountered resistance. In the fifties especially Dewey was attacked by the conservative Right for allegedly encouraging bedlam in the classroom, and the following decade the radical Left came down hard on him for presumably counseling acquiescence to the status quo. Some of these criticisms echoed those heard in the twenties when intellectuals of the "lost generation" discerned in pragmatism the practical ethos of bourgeois civilization, a false ideology supposedly offering both the pleasures of self-expression and the profits of material acquisition while ignoring the higher pursuits of the mind. Whatever the validity of these indictments, it does seem curious—and not a little humorous—that Dewey the schoolmaster could

49. Dewey, *Democracy and Education*, 180–93.

be charged by conservatives with nurturing anarchy and by radicals with promoting conformity.

The notion that Dewey must be responsible for the excesses of progressive education first developed in the late twenties and turned rancorous by the fifties. Before the full reaction to pragmatic educational theory set in, the new experimental approach stirred widespread excitement. One exuberant manifesto was Harold Rugg and Ann Shumaker's *The Child-Centered School* (1928), with its emphasis on pupil interests and initiative, open-ended inquiry, unstructured curriculum, personality development via social interaction, "life adjustment," and, above all, freedom, creativity, and self-expression.[50] Dewey himself, interestingly enough, grew disenchanted with the chaotic ferment as he began to see all forms of discipline disappear from the classroom. Even before the publication of *The Child-Centered School* he questioned the cult of freedom and creativity. The notion that the students should only be provided materials to which they may respond if they wish, and that the teacher "not suggest to them what they shall do" for fear of violating their "individuality," Dewey found outrageous. "Such a method is really stupid," he exploded. "For it attempts the impossible, which is always stupid; and it misconceives the conditions of independent thinking." To allow the student to follow his own "desires" is to assume that learning springs mysteriously "from uncontrolled haphazard sources." In truth there is "no spontaneous germination in mental life. If he does not get the suggestion from the teacher, he gets it from somebody or something in the home or the street or from what some more vigorous fellow pupil is doing." Refusing to interfere with the student's "personal freedom" not only denies the teacher's "greater background and experience" but the teacher's own rights as well. "The implication that the teacher is the one and only person who has no 'individuality' or 'freedom' would be funny if it were not often so sad in its outworkings." Dewey believed that the answer to the dilemma of the students' interest and the teachers' expertise lay in cooperative effort. "If the teacher is really a teacher, and not just a master or 'authority,' he should know enough about his pupils, their needs, experiences, degrees of skill and knowledge, etc. to be able (not to dictate aims and plans) to share in a discussion regarding what is to be done and be as free to make suggestions as any one else."[51]

That Dewey put quotation marks around the word *authority* in many of his educational writings only indicates how much he loathed the con-

50. See Lawrence Cremin, "John Dewey and the Progressive Education Movement," in *Dewey on Education: Appraisals*, ed. Reginald D. Archambault (New York, 1966), 9–25.

51. Dewey, "Individuality and Freedom," 619–27.

cept. It also suggests that no matter how critically he reacted to the excesses of freedom in the classroom, he remained unwilling to endow the teacher with the status of authority. Thus Dewey left the teacher in a deeply ambiguous position—an instructor who could participate but never pronounce, offer suggestions and share in decision-making but never determine, think what might be best for students but never utter it.

After Dewey had reduced the role of the teacher in order to eliminate any possible compulsion in the classroom, it comes as a surprise to find him being attacked for conceiving education as an instrument of "social control." This indictment came from the New Left of the 1960s generation, which challenged the entire structure of America's educational system, claiming that schooling functions to reproduce the inequalities of society and to sustain the elitist "hegemony" of corporate capitalism.[52] The eminent intellectual historian Christopher Lasch was more discriminate in *The New Radicalism in America* (1967), but he too could not resist the temptation to strike out at the patron saint of modern American liberalism. Dewey, according to Lasch, confused advocacy of social change with "education for citizenship" and hence counseled "conformity" to existing norms. "The very act, of defining the purpose of school in these terms forced Dewey back into the concept of education he wished particularly to avoid, the idea of education as a form of indoctrination in the values of the grown-up world."[53] Although Lasch's interpretation fails to consider how a philosopher who replaced doctrinal thought with methodological analysis could be in a position to indoctrinate, it does lead us to a more fundamental difficulty in Dewey's educational philosophy—the relationship of the school to the society of which it is a part, and the relationship of both to the problems of authority and modernity.

Dewey's philosophy of education attempted to encompass the demands of scientific detachment and social involvement. If schools are to be the agents of social change they will not only have to distance themselves from society but critically question the existing social order, a stance that could lead to a loss of contact with the real world. Conversely, if schools are to integrate themselves into the community and address issues faced by students and local citizens, educators may have to accept the community's values instead of seeking to change them. Insofar as the teacher is obligated to serve the needs of students, is his ultimate responsibility owed to students and their social environment or to his profession and discipline? As a critique of society, pragmatism must stand apart from

52. Samuel Bowles and Herbert Gintis, *Schooling in Capitalist America: Educational Reforms and the Contradictions of Economic Life* (New York: Basic, 1976).

53. Christopher Lasch, *The New Radicalism in America: The Intellectual as Social Type* (New York: Vintage, 1965).

existing institutions; as a program of social change, however, it would have to make education an instrument of politics. In equating education with democracy, Dewey wanted freedom to be expressed through group decisions and shared values. Yet his conviction that shared values are legitimate because they derive from common endeavors leaves unaddressed the question of who is to initiate the criticism of values that may be wrong even though widely shared. The problem is compounded when one recalls that Dewey also equated scientific method with democratic participation. The famous Scopes trial suggests only one of many examples of the will of the people at the local community level—the very fount of political values for Dewey—denying all that he stood for in the realm of intellectual values: the momentous influence of Darwinism upon modern thought.[54]

Despite Dewey's valiant attempt to humanize education, the modernist problems of authority and truth eluded theoretical explanations and practical solutions. Although pragmatism prides itself on being a "problem-solving" methodology, neither Dewey's philosophical thoughts nor the daily classroom experience of progressive schools solved the intractable problems of American education. The difficulty was not that Dewey and progressive educators simply wanted to eliminate authority from the classroom. Even Henry Adams shared the modernist conviction that scientific progress requires the rejection of authority along with all supposedly preexisting truths. The deeper dilemma lay in Dewey's refusal to define any specific "ends" to which education should aspire. Without a philosophy of ends, he could not state on what basis values are accepted or chosen, whether they be those of the student or those of the teacher. Even the value of democracy was taken for granted, just as all value was attributed to experience itself. Dewey advised teachers that "moral principles are real in the same sense in which other forces are real; they are inherent in community life, and in the working structure of the individual. If we can secure faith in this fact, we shall have secured the condition which alone is necessary to get from our educational system all the effectiveness there is in it."[55] To the extent that Dewey saw moral principles inherent in reality, experience itself could not be evaluated by standards external to it. Nor could growth:

> Growth, or growing as developing, not only physically but intellectually and morally, is one exemplification of the principle of continuity. The objection made is that growth might take many different directions: a man, for example, who starts

54. See Frederick Lilge, "The Vain Quest for Unity," in *Dewey on Education*, 52–71.
55. Dewey, *Moral Principles of Education*, 58.

out on a career of burglary may grow in that direction, and by practice may grow into a highly expert burglar. Hence it is argued that "growth" is not enough; we must also specify the direction in which growth takes place, the end toward which it tends. Before, however, we decide that the objection is conclusive we must analyze the case a little further.

That a man may grow in efficiency as a burglar, as a gangster, or as a corrupt politician, cannot be doubted. But from the standpoint of growth as education and education as growth the question is whether growth in this direction promotes or retards growth in general. Does this form of growth create conditions for further growth, or does it set up conditions that shut off the person who has grown in this particular direction from the occasions, stimuli, and opportunities for continuing growth in new directions? What is the effect of growth in a special direction upon the attitude which alone opens up avenues for development in other lines? I shall leave you to answer these questions, saying simply that when and *only* when development in a particular line conduces to continuing growth does it answer to the criterion of education as growing.[56]

In Dewey there is no suggestion that one might aspire to be educated not simply to grow but to realize ends, to achieve goals and purposes beyond the activity of learning itself. The desire to achieve meaning, purpose, and value does not arise from the biological givens of growth. A life that turns on nothing more than growth could be aimless and empty, lacking the tension and direction that comes only from the conscious choice of ends. Here again the problem derives from Dewey's wish to extirpate every vestige of dualism. Convinced that there was no conflict between means and ends, Dewey could argue that how one acquires knowledge would determine what one does with knowledge on the assumption that scientific inquiry issues in moral conduct. Yet why a budding empiricist should not grow into an accomplished embezzler is never explained except as some thwarting of growth itself.

Dewey's efforts to prevent teachers from asserting authority are understandable in view of his desire to liberate the child's natural impulses from intimidation and coercion. He did not want to see teachers proselytize, and he rightly criticized the insidious ways of intellectual seduction that pass for education. Yet one may question, as did Richard Hofstadter in *Anti-Intellectualism in American Life*, Dewey's conviction that all education based on authority invariably produces a conformist mentality.[57]

56. Dewey, "Philosophy of Experience," in *Intelligence*, 664–65.
57. Richard Hofstadter, *Anti-Intellectualism in American Life* (New York, 1963), 382–85.

Voltaire was taught by Jesuits, Hofstadter noted, and one thinks of other examples in intellectual history when the rebellious mind is a direct product of authoritarian schooling (the sardonic student Thorstein Veblen bewildered his pious teachers when he wrote an essay in defense of cannibalism as the economics of recycling). All true education, observed Henry Adams, begins in the act of resistance. All true teaching, it may be added, involves distinguishing between what students are interested in and what may be in their interest to know and learn.

Can such a distinction be made? Dewey addressed this question in one of his least known and yet most important essays, "Interest in Relation to the Training of the Will." How can the teacher gain the attention of students? Dewey doubted discipline would work, since students will seldom be motivated out of fear of punishment. The notion that education is an exercise in effort is also misleading, since strenuous effort (pace James) simply reveals the difficulties of being interested in the uninteresting. However, once students' interests are aroused teachers can be assured that the particular interest has attached itself to an object that now is channeling their "spontaneous impulsive activity." The arousal of interest may induce wants and desires, but to reach the object of desire requires the mediation of thought and reflection, and before long students will find pleasure in developing means as well as fulfilling ends. Hence it is not necessary to make pleasure an end of conduct or to eliminate desire from the moral will. Desire simply moves the will, but does not determine it from a source beyond itself. Students may legitimately follow their interest because it cannot be alien to themselves. "The real object of desire is not pleasure, but self-expression."[58]

Dewey's theory of learning is entirely consistent with his theory of knowledge. The pursuit of learning has no goal to be realized, just as knowledge has no objects to be known. So formulated, Dewey's theory circumvents the problem of desire, value, and motivation. By making self-expression the object of desire, he need not deal with a theoretical issue that had preoccupied philosophers from Plato to Kant: value arises when its object stands outside the self, and is attained only by struggling to overcome obstacles, distance, and difficulties. In equating desire and its satisfactions with self-expression, Dewey assumes, as does the economist, that value is not so much known or appreciated as an object of thought but made and produced in the world of action.

Dewey convinced himself that self-expression cannot, in theory, ex-

58. Dewey's article first appeared in *Second Supplement to the Herbert Year Book for 1895.* John J. McDermott did American intellectual history a great service by retrieving the essay from obscurity and including it in his *The Philosophy of John Dewey* (Chicago, 1981), 421–42.

press itself egotistically. But cannot students be motivated to achieve as a way of expressing their desire to outshine others? Some might desire to express themselves differently and, following the example of Thoreau and Huck Finn, drop out of school. Dewey's point is that as students' interest becomes involved, self-interest is overcome in self-objectification and self-expression. Yet since Dewey's philosophy denies any dualism between subject and object, or any motivation of desire to attain something beyond the self, how is it possible to know when a student is not thinking about himself? Does thinking require an object, or can knowing produce its own object? Whatever the answer, it is difficult to see how Dewey's reasoning helps free students, or teachers, from self-absorption in their own interests.

Dewey has been criticized for offering an educational philosophy that is almost anti-intellectual in its emphasis on practical subjects that confuse vocational training for genuine learning. His preference for science over the humanities has led one critic to claim that the "dimension of speculative curiosity, of wonder and awe, is missing" from Dewey's educational theories.[59] This absence is puzzling. For in Dewey's early writings on learning psychology, that dimension is included with almost poetic passion. Here the philosopher did believe, as indicated earlier in the chapter, in the value of "wonder" and "curiosity" as pure intellectual activity. Dewey even believed that the "love of knowledge" for its own sake promotes "disinterestedness," thereby making the learning process "objective and universal."[60]

Thus although Dewey prized such qualities as wonder and curiosity when explicating the phenomenon of thinking, he tended to ignore them when writing on education. Here Dewey seemed more interested in cooking and carpentry than in chemistry and geometry. It was not theoretical wonder but workshop technique that he emphasized. "The questions, the chemical and the physical problems, arising in the kitchen and the shop, are taken to the laboratories to be worked out."[61] Dewey's emphasis on the practical side of education followed from the pragmatist principle that all ideas should be submitted to a threefold procedure: cooperative inquiry, experimental testing, and judgment arrived at through public consensus. In this respect the humanities would be accorded a subordinate role; for in the past humanistic learning had drawn its truths not from nature but from scripture, literary texts, philosophical treatises, and other

59. R. S. Peters, "John Dewey's Philosophy of Education," in *John Dewey Reconsidered*, ed. R. S. Peters (London, 1977), 120.

60. Dewey, "Intellectual Feelings," *Early Works*, vol. 2, *1887*, 262–63.

61. Dewey, "School and Society," in *Dewey on Education: Selections*, ed. Martin S. Dworkin (New York, 1955), 83–84.

nonempirical sources. Like Veblen, Dewey also viewed literature as a leisure-class activity cultivated by those who wanted to display their superior status by scorning the practical subjects of science and engineering. Hence pragmatism would overturn all remnants of classical culture that had given a higher status to theory and thinking than to practice and doing. But Dewey had three other reasons for upholding technical study over purely cultural pursuits. First of all, his democratic sympathies forced him to recognize that the mass of people are more interested in practical gain than in higher learning. "The simple facts of the case are that in the great majority of human beings the distinctly intellectual interests is not dominant."[62] Moreover, Dewey saw cultural knowledge as private in nature, an accumulation of inner ideas and values that could not readily be shared. "What is called inner is simply that which does not connect others, which is not capable of full and free communication. What is termed spiritual culture has usually been futile, with something rotten about it, just because it has been conceived as a thing which a man might have internally—and therefore exclusively."[63] Finally, culture was useless to the extent to which it concerned the past. Transforming society is more important than appreciating beauty; thus for the pragmatist "culture becomes an ornament and solace; a refuge and asylum."[64]

In Dewey's "problem-solving" curriculum there would be little place for the qualities of truth that emanate from art and literature—aesthetic insight, moral vision, irony, tragedy, catharsis, negative capability, sensate discourse, beauty and sublimity, fear and pity. Dewey recognized the importance of such qualities, but he was more interested in whatever could be utilized and controlled rather than simply appreciated and contemplated. In *Art as Experience* (1934) Dewey acknowledged that aesthetic objects have value to the extent that they produce an aesthetic response and that experience could never be completely understood by reason but only deepened by imagination and aesthetic perception.[65] Thus in its confrontation with modernism, Dewey's pragmatism left the educator with a curious bias: literature may claim the right to describe experience but not necessarily the capacity to render knowledge. "Where shall we find authority, the instruction of which our natures demand?" Dewey had asked early in his career, in a lecture on Matthew Arnold and Robert Browning delivered at Smith College in 1890. "Shall we cease to find it in philosophy, or in science, and shall we find it in poetry?" Dewey feared

62. Ibid., 48.
63. Dewey, quoted in Antony Flew, "Democracy and Education," in *Dewey Reconsidered*, 89.
64. Dewey, quoted in Hofstadter, 388.
65. Dewey, *Art as Experience*, 32–34.

exactly what Adams had felt: disenchanted with science and conventional philosophy, the intellectual would turn more and more toward poetry and art for consolation. But Dewey wondered why whatever may be true for the imagination and the emotions could not also be true for the intelligence. "How can poetry preserve its genuineness and its sustaining force, if it is cut loose from all verifiable accounts of the universe?"[66]

Other thinkers confronting modernism would seek truth and value in modes of knowledge that seemed "higher" precisely because insight and understanding need not be verified but simply felt with personal intensity. In his seminal statement, "On the Teaching of Modern Literature" (1961), Lionel Trilling specified which writers he would assign to students to force them to raise questions "at the behest of wonder and fear." Trilling believed the problems of modernism "really ought to be encountered in solitude, even in secrecy." With Adams, Trilling wanted students to "look into the Abyss" and to appreciate the values of aesthetic ambiguity and moral uncertainty. Trilling cites the protagonist of Thomas Mann's story "Disorder and Early Sorrow":

> . . . that sad Professor Cornelius with his intense and ambiva-
> lent sense of history. For Professor Cornelius, who is a histo-
> rian, the past is dead, is death itself, but for that very reason
> it is the source of order, value, piety, and even love. If we
> think about education in the dark light of despair I have de-
> scribed, we wonder if perhaps there is not to be found in the
> past that quiet place at which a young man might stand for a
> few years, at least a little beyond the competing attitudes and
> generalizations of the present, at least a little beyond the con-
> temporary problems which he is told he can master only by
> means of attitudes and generalizations, that quiet place in
> which he can be silent, in which he can know something.[67]

As a modernist philosopher Dewey was almost alone in orienting education toward science and the challenge of technical mastery. Although Dewey and Trilling admired one another, the philosopher could scarcely look upon the past alone as a source of "order, value, piety, and even love." Nor could the past be contemplated in silent tranquillity. Trilling shared Adams's hope that history and tradition, however dead and gone, might offer some solace to the modern mind. But to appreciate the past as a source of truth and value seemed to the pragmatist the false pursuit of knowledge as something permanent and preexistent. For Dewey the

---

66. Dewey, "Poetry and Philosophy," in *Early Works*, vol. 3, *1889–1892*, 110–24.
67. Lionel Trilling, *Beyond Culture* (New York, 1961), 3–27.

purpose of knowledge and education is not simply to feel the play and pangs of consciousness but to realize "a new truth" by making it happen.

But to make things happen involves planning, design, direction, and control. Dewey had no hesitancy calling for intervention and regulation to bring the forces of capitalism under control. In education, however, Dewey tended to assume the "spontaneous impulsive activity" of children and hence to regard the learning process as in no need of structure and direction. Even though on at least one occasion Dewey grew impatient with progressive educators who refused to exercise classroom control, he nevertheless believed even more that education must be free of all external interference and restraint. The character of human conduct depends upon "whether growth . . . promotes or retards growth in general" and hence whether it "conduces to continuing growth." Curiously, Dewey attributes to intelligence what economists attribute to the market: interference with either cripples growth, and laissez-faire stimulates it. Similarly, the capitalist believes that schoolchildren need the imposition of authority and discipline, and the pragmatist believes that the economy needs the imposition of regulation and control. Both assume that power will take care of itself once the conditions of freedom are allowed to prevail in either the school or the economy, where the object of desire is "self-expression." Both see no evil emerging from the forces of nature, whether nature manifests its truths in cooperation or in competition. One assumes that a society of mutuality could hardly be subjected to sources of domination, sources so invisible that "free" public education is made compulsory; the other assumes that a society of emulation could hardly be tempted to exploitation, since tyranny comes from the state and not from "free" enterprise. Whether they have in mind the child or the consumer, each sees the self as formed by the community, and thus they look to socially induced behavior as uncoerced and healthy. Without knowledge of evil, how are the deceits of power to be detected?

The specter of power haunts the modernist thinker who wants to believe that some other principle operates in the universe. The term *power* is being used here not in Dewey's instrumental sense of the capability of achieving consequences. Power signifies not only *to* but *over* in the Adams-Weber-Niebuhr sense of collective domination rather than self-determination, not the power of belief and action but the human condition of being preyed upon by forces to which citizens have given no clear consent. When the exercise of power is voluntarily accepted by those who experience its effects, it could be said that power has been legitimated and turned into rightful authority. The two thinkers to be discussed in the next chapter, Walter Lippman and Oliver Wendell Holmes, Jr., addressed such subjects as power and authority within, or close to, the paradigm of pragmatism. Lippmann came to the conclusion that he had to break out of the paradigm to find a more genuine foundation for political authority in a public philosophy based upon natural law. Holmes, in contrast, spent much of his life trying to teach America that there was no escape from the world of power and no possibility of finding truth in politics or morality in law.

8

"The Acids of Modernity": Walter Lippman and Oliver Wendell Holmes

The Odyssey of a Political Moralist

When Walter Lippmann's *Essays in the Public Philosophy* appeared in 1955, it arrived on the American intellectual scene at a time when authors of various philosophical and ideological persuasion were making claims on the political soul of Western civilization. Two years earlier, at the University of Chicago, Leo Strauss wrote *Natural Right and History* to insist that the classical values of his beloved ancient world offered the best hope of saving the modern world from pragmatism, scientism, and relativism. At the same time, and at exactly the same institution, the historian Daniel J. Boorstin wrote *The Genius of American Politics* to make the opposite case. America, Boorstin held, needs neither abstract philosophy nor absolute values or any kind of "theory" that would give priority to thought over action. What Americans do in their daily life requires no mediation of concepts, principles, doctrines, and, above all, "ideology," the curse of the Old World. Lippmann's move to natural law was closer to Strauss's idea of natural right than to Boorstin's claim that American "experience" triumphs over all "dogma." With the classical scholar Lippmann saw the contemporary world suffering from too much experimentation and mindless process and not enough direction and conscious purpose. Reflecting, as did Strauss's work, the threat of mass politics, Lippmann's book represented the conservative culmination of years of searching for radical and liberal solutions to the dilemmas of modernity, an odyssey that began with the promise of pragmatism.

The Public Philosophy appeared the same year that saw the first issues of *National Review*, the magazine William F. Buckley, Jr., launched to save America from the heresies of contemporary liberalism. Yet that same year

Louis Hartz published *The Liberal Tradition in America* to argue, more in sorrow than in celebration, that the absence of feudalism as a historical social structure and the presence of Lockeanism as a system of values based on property and opportunity defined the American Republic as a new liberal experiment unburdened by the dead weight of European history and unexplainable by Old World categories. Lippmann's effort to reorient America's political culture partakes, however coincidentally, of both Hartzian anguish and Straussian piety; more specifically, an awareness that history, especially American history, is the problem and that philosophy, especially modern philosophy, contains no solution. All three thinkers recognized that classical republicanism, having its origins in Aristotle's polis, fructifying in Machiavelli's idea of active citizenship, and culminating in James Harrington's exhortations to civic virtue, never made it to American shores. And if it had? Today, some contemporary political philosophers and intellectual historians look to Rousseau as the last great thinker who reconciled the classical idea of virtue with the modern idea of democracy. But Lippmann believed that Rousseau's idea of natural right led not to moral discipline and civic duty but to the defiant, autonomous independence of the individual. Lippmann recognized the libertarian implications of Rousseau while a student at Harvard. Lippmann had taken courses from Irving Babbitt, the controversial professor of French who had declared war on romanticism, modernity, and science in favor for the "inner check" of classical humanism. When Babbitt tried to trace the illusions of socialism to Rousseau's belief in innocent human nature, Lippmann wrote his professor a letter suggesting that the real legacy of Rousseau was not radical socialism but the vigorous individualism expressed in the Manchester school of economics.[1]

Lippmann touched on an insight that remains relevant today. Radicalism undermines authority to create the conditions of freedom, but unrestricted freedom finds its expression in capitalism, the willful, arbitrary workings of the marketplace that refuses to recognize the need for a public philosophy. In his early socialist years, Lippmann chided the creatures of capitalism for making the rich powerful, the middle class pitiful, and the working class miserable. A half century later in *The Public Philosophy*, the word *capitalism* is not mentioned, while the right to property is subjected to a system of moral duties and civic obligations. Even though Lippmann had recently fallen under the influence of Ludwig von Mises

---

1. Lippmann's letter to Babbitt is mentioned in J. David Hoevler, Jr., *The New Humanism: A Critique of Modern America, 1900–1940* (Charlottesville: University Press of Virginia, 1977), 8.

and F. A. von Hayek, he could hardly allow his notion of the public philosophy to be determined by the supposedly self-regulating laws of supply and demand. Were not the Austrian economists simply Rousseauists on the Right? "We must think less about authority and more about liberty," wrote Rousseau in the eighteenth century.[2] Lippmann's whole effort, from his first book on politics to his last meditations on government, was to reverse that dictum.

Lippmann's notion of the public philosophy rested on authority as a commanding idea that transcends the private sphere of life, the arena of interest and power that came to characterize liberal society to the detriment of any vital concept of the state. As with Dewey, Lippmann's quarrel was with pluralism, a legacy that left America plagued by competing interest groups and no sovereign political authority to render the public good. When Tocqueville visited the United States in the 1830s, he confessed his inability to find the center of political authority and remained troubled at the thought that the vicissitudes of public opinion would function as the source of social control. Lippmann similarly discerned the eclipse of authority and the emergence of modern politics as the avenue of personal opportunity rather than civic duty. Like Tocqueville's heir, Raymond Aron, Lippmann recognized that in modern society popular, consensual authority hovered outside the political world and by its very "tyranny" of opinion and fickleness of attitude rendered government subordinate to the masses. In *Drift and Mastery*, Lippmann defined liberalism as "a great gap between the overthrow of authority and the creation of a substitute."[3] Santayana suggested that modern American liberalism represented a curious, if not dangerous, departure from older classical liberalism in that it was less interested in establishing the foundations of freedom by means of resisting power than in augmenting the structures of power for purposes of social control.[4] But Lippmann was not simply interested in power as a technique of issuing orders and eliciting obedience. Somewhat like the old New England Calvinists of the seventeenth century, Lippmann felt that no government could be genuinely legitimate unless its members have consciously and willfully given their consent to it. Lippmann understood that while authority demanded submission, morality required freedom in that its values could only be a matter of choice. Significantly, his first effort at political philosophy rested on the will to believe and choose.

2. Jean-Jacques Rousseau, *The Political Writings of Rousseau*, vol. 2, ed. C. E. Vaughn (Cambridge: Cambridge University Press, 1915), 220.

3. Walter Lippmann, *Drift and Mastery* (New York: Kennerly, 1914), 113–19.

4. George Santayana, "The Irony of Liberalism," *New Republic* 135 (September 24, 1956): 12–15; this essay first appeared in *Dial* in October 1921.

Lippmann was the quintessential political moralist in an age when politics had ceased to be a moral proposition. As with Max Weber, who sensed the same dilemma, the values that Lippmann espoused were often in tension: disinterestedness and commitment, reason and imagination, spontaneity and efficiency, rules and purposes, discipline and desire, and, above all, authority and freedom. Somehow, the legitimacy of the government and the basis of political rights would have to include all these seemingly contradictory values. With these values uppermost, Lippmann's search for the authentic foundations of government took him across the terrain of twentieth-century thought in a kind of backward movement. Bravely starting out with science and pragmatic humanism, which made the source of values man-centered, Lippmann ended up in a theological universe of natural law, where metaphysical values were to be discovered and obeyed. His heroic odyssey attempted to move the modern human condition beyond existence to the realm of essence. Turning away from pragmatism, and indeed almost all varieties of modern, existential thought, Lippmann convinced himself that the preservation of freedom depended on rediscovering a concept of truth through the uses of old-fashioned reason. For all his earlier sensitivity to "the acids of modernity," Lippmann offered America a public philosophy that held out the premodern possibility of direct knowledge of the truth of things. Much like a long-forgotten Cartesian, Lippmann seemed to assume that the act of thinking could clarify and define the essential ideas that mattered, and that therefore the mind could know its object. Even Henry Adams, who also returned to Aquinas, Descartes, and medieval philosophy to get a better perspective on the dilemmas of modernity, knew better than to try to resuscitate antiquated philosophic systems based as much on faith as on reason. Lippmann's odyssey is curious for many reasons, not the least of which is the question of whether the American Republic really required the foundation of medieval philosophy for its legitimacy.

Science and the Legitimacy of Government

Lippmann felt deeply the burdens of modernism, perhaps because he had entered the premodern world that Van Wyck Brooks aptly labeled "the age of confidence." He was born in New York City in 1889, an era that basked in the warm glow of Victorian optimism. After attending a select boys' school in New York, he went to Harvard in 1906 at a time when the walls of academe were cracking and the fissures seeping with iconoclasm. Lippmann joined the rebellious and impish John Reed and the solemn and sensitive T. S. Eliot in taking to writing essays and poems. The diverse temperaments of his two contemporaries had their counterparts in the diverse minds of his two mentors: the philosophers James and Santayana. So impressed was James by the precocious Lippmann that he crossed Harvard yard to compliment him for his essay against Anglophile elitism. James's philosophy had a liberating impact on Lippmann and indeed on many of the prewar generation of rebels. The Jamesian vision of an "unfinished" universe to be acted upon and molded according to human desire was irresistible. But another, more contemplative, side of Lippmann was drawn to Santayana and his idea of "essences," principles and ideals that may not exist in reality but rather come into existence as objects of the mind's prolonged and discriminating reflection. As much as Lippmann wanted to see the world changed, he also had a need to believe in principles that transcended the vicissitudes of change. "I love James more than any other great man I ever saw," he wrote to Bernard Berenson a decade after graduating from Harvard, "but increasingly I find Santayana inescapable."[5]

But the Santayana side remained dormant in Lippmann's early career. Thus no contemporary who had read Lippmann's early books could have predicted where his thinking would take him by midcentury. His first two books, *A Preface to Politics* and *Drift and Mastery*, resonate with hope, despite the awareness of the complexity of problems facing America and the world. From the philosophy of pragmatism, especially James's version, Lippmann gained faith in human ingenuity and the creative potential of the intellect confronting life not as a given datum but as something to be shaped by will, purpose, and effort. Just as James had advised that in an open-ended universe there will never be a time when all the facts are known, and thus one must act prior to the certitudes of knowledge, Lippmann exhorted the political thinker to move ahead armed only with methods of inquiry rather than blueprints and final answers. "We cannot wait in politics for any completed theoretical discussion of its methods: it is a monstrous demand." True social knowledge requires experimentation to produce new conditions, and thus all learning awaits results and outcomes. "We have to act on what we believe, on half-knowledge, illusion and error. Experience itself will reveal our mistakes; research and criticism may convert them into wisdom. But we must act, and act as if we know the nature of man and proposed to satisfy his needs.[6]

Pragmatism enabled Lippmann to believe that politics could derive its legitimacy from science. Curiously, the framers of the Constitution assumed the same thing, yet Lippmann rejected their political architecture

---

5. Quoted in Ronald Steel, *Walter Lippmann and the American Century* (Boston, 1980), 21.

6. Walter Lippmann, *A Preface to Politics* (1914; Ann Arbor: University of Michigan Press, 1962), 83–84.

and balancing mechanisms based on Newtonian formulas. In Lippmann's estimate, the Constitution was all procedure and no spirit; it touched people negatively as prohibitions rather than positively as fulfillment. True enough, perhaps. But a Weberian might point out that Lippmann's own synthesis of politics and science can lead to the same impasse.

Lippmann refused to believe that politics as a method of inquiry need involve itself with values: "Politics is not concerned with prescribing the ultimate qualities of life. When it does so by sumptuary legislation, nothing but mischief is involved. Its business is to provide opportunities, and not to announce ultimate values."[7] In the Progressive era, Lippmann complained, political discussion dealt with such mundane matters as the tariff, trusts, currency, and civil service. Lippmann referred to such issues as "a fixation upon instruments" on the part of reformers who were reluctant to see "the enlargement of political issues."[8] Lippmann was closer to Weber than to the pragmatists in seeing that politics could result in routine functions, administrative rules, and bureaucratic structures. Yet how could Lippmann call for a broader view of politics without introducing the whole question of values that he felt should be excluded from civic discourse? One possible answer is that, like James and particularly Dewey, Lippmann assumed that science itself could provide a mode of thinking and analysis without depending on the abstract moral categories of conventional reason, which failed to take account of humankind's emotions and subconscious drives. So confident was Lippmann in the possibility of enlightened leadership guided by the higher professionalism of scientific thought that he believed business conduct could be changed so that the entrepreneur would be, as Thorstein Veblen expected of the engineer, more interested in production than profit, dedicated to making goods rather than money. "That subtle fact—the changing of business motives, the demonstration that industry can be conducted as medicine is—may civilize the whole class conflict."[9]

While Lippmann advocated elevating politics to a science that could function independently of values and older moral principles, he complained that the framers of the Constitution had rendered American government too scientific to the point that the "machinery of government" had become routine and indifferent to ethical and aesthetic considerations. When drafting the Constitution, the framers had also excluded political ideals, that is, ethical imperatives that would obligate conduct. As Arthur O. Lovejoy noted, the framers were mainly concerned with predicting

7. Ibid., 152–53.
8. Ibid., 1–33.
9. Ibid., 48.

what people would do rather than instructing them on what they "ought" to do.[10] And what they were expected to do was pursue their own interests acting collectively as "factions." The framers also denied that enlightened leaders would be needed in the new republic for two reasons: Future generations cannot count on the appearance of great leaders, and the Constitution would be so wisely constructed that it will be, as James Russell Lowell later put it, "a machine that would go of itself."

Lippmann protested such a notion as the "machinery of politics," as did other social scientists like Weber and Woodrow Wilson. All three thinkers recognized that politics conceived as a mechanistic phenomenon would remain indifferent to moral considerations and involve itself with structural arrangements and instrumental rationality. Yet what the framers bequeathed to America was offered as "the new science of politics," a break from both Christian and classical traditions. Lippmann described the framers as Newtonian philosophers lacking in feeling, vision, and imagination, so mechanistic and behavioristic as to exclude from politics Jamesian volunteerism and Henri Bergson's *élan vital*. In politics, Lippmann declared, "the goal of an action is in the final analysis aesthetic and not moral—a quality of feeling instead of a conformity to rule."[11] Thus to be legitimate, government had to be, even more than scientific, aesthetic, and artistic, emotionally satisfying and fulfilling, the experience of perceptual pleasure.

Lippmann never took the trouble to explain how a "quality of feeling" could be objectified so that rational intelligence could rechannel human instincts toward worthy political ends. Thus in his second book, *Drift and Mastery* (1914), he now realized that emotion and action could hardly be the basis on which to develop a political philosophy. Such natural tendencies merely led to aimless drift. What was needed was mastery, control, discipline. Dewey, as indicated earlier, would argue along similar lines in the twenties. But while Dewey believed social control was necessary to liberate America from the hegemonic impediments of individualism, Lippmann believed that America had already liberated itself from all vestiges of authority. Dewey identified authority with conservatism and assumed that democracy had to be liberal and progressive almost by definition. Obviously he had not learned from Tocqueville the same lesson that Lippmann tried to convey to his teacher Irving Babbitt: when authority disappears, freedom and democracy find their natural expression in capitalism and individualism. Thus Lippmann saw the dilemma

10. Arthur O. Lovejoy, *Reflections on Human Nature* (Baltimore: Johns Hopkins University Press, 1961), 1–66.

11. Lippmann, *Preface to Politics*, 152.

of modernism in the historic fact that liberty and freedom had been won from the forces of oppression and now man must learn to govern himself. "The sanctity of property, the patriarchal family, hereditary caste, the dogma of sin, obedience to authority—the rock of ages, in brief, has been blasted for us." The struggle against an inherited conservatism has succeeded; the burden of modern man is to learn how to use an inherited liberalism that otherwise will lead to "the chaos of the new freedom."[12]

In contrast to Dewey, Lippmann could scarcely see much hope in having democracy return to its purported roots in "community." Wilson's "new freedom" called for returning power to small towns and away from corporate structures, to the habitats of petit entrepreneurs, "the man on the make." Labor as well as business seemed indifferent to the public good. In Lippmann's analysis, business wants freedom and labor wants power. A Niebuhrian could perhaps suggest that freedom is the power to impose one's will and power is the freedom to do so. But in his early years Lippmann had no patience with religion. Dogmatic religions, like despotic governments, may have provided stability in the past, but they also inhibited the fulfillment of humankind's spiritual potential and capacity for self-government. The Catholic Church in particular—the very institution Lippmann would later turn to for the doctrine of natural law— "tried to make weakness permanent" by indoctrinating the pseudo virtues of "poverty, chastity, and obedience."[13]

The only viable option remaining for Lippmann was pragmatism and the "discipline of science." Science had no Weberian connotations for Lippmann, who believed that empirical thinking could serve humanity's deepest desires. Something of a Freudian as well as a pragmatist, Lippmann assumed that the irrational could be channeled without repressing human freedom. Yet in the absence of traditional authority, how could science be the basis for the legitimacy of government?

In his pragmatic phase, Lippmann, like James, confused will and action with purpose and goals, and he looked to experience to settle all matters. But experience to Lippmann did not represent past experience. As with James and Dewey, Lippmann turned to science rather than to history, to future consequences rather than to past traditions. Estranged from the Newtonian, mechanistic world of the eighteenth-century framers, Lippmann sought to find a new basis of politics in the ideas of an array of twentieth-century thinkers ranging from Freud to Graham Wallas. But whomever he drew on, Lippmann's pragmatic persuasion meant that the

12. Walter Lippmann, *Drift and Mastery*, ed. William E. Leuchtenburg (Englewood Cliffs, N.J., 1961), 17, 100–116.
13. Ibid., 146–51, 170.

legitimacy of government would be based not on its historical origins but on its subsequent performances. What Hannah Arendt said of Marxism also applies to pragmatism: Each establishes its rationale and claims to legitimacy by appealing to the future rather than the past. In pragmatic philosophy, the method of verification refers to what is to come, what does not yet exist but can be brought into being. In this respect, the legitimacy of government lies in its fruits and actions and not the sources of its foundations. As our contemporary poststructuralists might put it, legitimacy is a production rather than a discovery, something made rather than found. The legitimate authority of a government derives not from what it is as a concept but from what it does in its procedures and practices. A strict pragmatist thus looks to future experience as the test of a government's legitimacy and justification for obedience. Whereas conservative thinkers like Burke and Hegel insist that the origins of a regime's authority must remain veiled in secrecy, the pragmatic political philosopher demands that government perform in full view of the public. Ultimately, government has no more status than a hypothesis, a tentative idea or experiment awaiting proof. The pragmatist thinks under the spell of the future, or what Santayana called "the dominance of the foreground."

In Lippmann, however, one senses a hesitancy about pragmatism and its sanguine preoccupation with the foreground. In the closing pages of *A Preface to Politics*, Lippmann expresses sentiments that would have perplexed James and Dewey: "Why this age should have come to be what it is, why at this particular time the whole drift of thought should be from authority to autonomy would be an interesting speculation. It is one of the ultimate questions of politics."[14]

Autonomy was the basic value most prized by James, who regarded nothing worthy of legitimate belief unless it sprang from the freely determining self. Dewey would have hailed the story of humankind moving out from under the constraints of authority as evidence of the history of progress. Nor did James and Dewey feel there were "ultimate questions" in politics or philosophy that must be confronted once and for all. The best way to overcome such questions is to forget them or, as Dewey put it, allow them to disappear from mind.[15]

The mind and character of Walter Lippmann was such that he would never be able to put aside the ultimate questions of politics. Unlike the pragmatists, he had difficulty believing that action and practice would confirm or disconfirm the truthfulness of an idea and establish the legiti-

14. Lippman, *Preface to Politics*, 237.
15. John Dewey, *The Influence of Darwinism on Philosophy and Other Essays* (New York: Peter Smith, 1951), 19.

macy of a regime. Part of Lippmann always felt that theory and speculative thought should precede practice and possibly determine it. Some of his studies were offered as "prefaces" precisely to elevate politics and moral thought above the demands of concrete situations in order to search for foundations or first principles. Thus after questioning the legitimacy of Madisonian pluralism, his next important effort in political thought was to question the adequacy of Jeffersonian democracy.

From Pragmatism and "The Phantom Public" to Natural Law

Lippmann's *Public Opinion*, written shortly after the end of the First World War, reflects the disenchantment of the era, a sort of analytic counterpart to Hemingway's *A Farewell to Arms*, where democratic ideals are also questioned as adolescent verbiage. Members of the "lost generation" derided the language of politics; Lippmann "deconstructed" it by showing how its rhetoric and metaphors evoke images that have little basis in reality. The book is prefaced with a passage from Plato's *Republic*, Book 7, deep in the caves, where shadows are taken for substance.

The pragmatist's desire to reshape the world collapsed with the Versailles settlement, and Lippmann wondered whether democracy, dependent as it is on the will of the governed, can rely on an electorate sufficiently informed to understand what is happening in the world. His reconsideration of his earlier hopes for democracy's revitalization resulted in *Public Opinion*, perhaps his most reflective and somber book, and also another work that came close to despair, *The Phantom Public*. Both books challenge the validity of liberal democracy by suggesting that to invest authority in the people may be foolish when people's thoughts are determined by the distortions of the mode of information. A reader of *Public Opinion* could easily come away convinced that democracy can no longer claim the privilege of human reason. But does democracy require reason for its legitimation?

When Madison drew on Hume in the *Federalist* to declare that "all governments rest on opinion," he anticipated a problem that would later be discerned by Tocqueville and even more acutely felt by Lippmann. Tocqueville had seen that public opinion could be a form of majoritarian conformity that would stifle dissent and endanger individual liberty. But with Lippmann, mass opinion becomes even more threatening to the presuppositions of democracy and republicanism alike, for in Lippmann's analysis, sovereignty no longer necessarily resides in the legislature, as it had been assumed in both Lockean and classical politics, but now belongs to the press and the media in general, institutions that shape the very opinions on which citizens base their decisions and from which popular consent is "manufactured." Readers experience the "news" of the day as "episodes, incidents, eruptions," and to the extent that the public mind is subjected to the techniques of communication—stereotyping, image formation, and prejudice—the "omnicompetent citizen" so precious to Jefferson is a lost species.[16]

In a way, *Public Opinion* is a misnomer, for there was nothing public about the disparate, fleeting opinions bouncing around inside the heads of people who received impressions without analyzing them. In the book, Lippmann praised Machiavelli for grasping that all judgments are subjective because of the interest-bound conditions of perception that go unacknowledged in public discourse. "The world, as he found it," Lippmann wrote of Machiavelli, "was composed of people whose vision could rarely be corrected," people who "see all public relations in a private way" and hence are forever "involved in perpetual strife." Machiavelli's solution to the crisis of a republic was to advise political leaders to engage in a *ricorso*. But Lippmann does not follow Machiavelli's explanation of why republics must go through rituals of renewal by a return to the revivifying principles of the original founding. Instead, Lippmann proceeds to discuss Tocqueville and then Jefferson, particularly the agrarian environment that shaped the latter's thought. Here, the problem of epistemology and politics begins. Jefferson's world presupposed a small, self-contained community where all people not only knew one another but felt competent to manage public affairs because they believed the external world corresponded to the "pictures" they had of it in their heads. Jeffersonianism was based on a community of consensus that would be unable to deal with the very problems that both Machiavelli and the *Federalist* had to confront: the obliteration of the public good when all people see only privately and when a large republic must deal with communities that identify liberty with locality.

In searching for whatever might give American government a sense of legitimacy, a rationale that would make its authority acceptable, Lippmann seemed to recognize that a public philosophy based on the spirit of commonwealth and public good had been obscured at the Philadelphia convention in 1787. He also understood what some of our contemporary historians seem reluctant to acknowledge: that civic virtue and the public interest will be defeated by the very institution that classical republicans expected to nurture such ideals, namely, politics. As the Federalist age gave way to Jacksonian democracy, the pressure of mass politics resulted in patronage and logrolling. Lippmann explained why Madison's hope that representatives would "refine and enlarge" the views of their districts proved unfounded, and not only because, as Madison was also aware,

16. Lippmann, *Public Opinion* (1922; New York: Macmillan, 1960), 1–47.

congressmen would respond to the demands of their immediate constituencies. The problem was that representatives preferred the security of a false picture of reality to the risks of trying to grasp what needed to be done for the good of the whole. The representative "needs to know the local pictures, but unless he possesses instruments for calibrating them, one picture is as good as the next."[17] What undermines the public good is propinquity, the tendency to mistake the provincial for the general.

For Lippmann, the problem of representation was ultimately not so much political as epistemological. In *Public Opinion*, he suggested that the political misinformation plaguing the American people might be corrected by a bureau of experts capable of screening and organizing the news to make it more intellectually responsible. By the time he wrote *The Phantom Public* three years later, Lippmann doubted that the "medium of fictions" that kept people from understanding the external world could be penetrated. No one, neither administrative experts enlightened by scientific intelligence nor the masses moved by interests, neither the few nor the many, can claim a privileged grasp of the objective truth about the public good. America, it seemed, left political man where Machiavelli had found him, a private creature whose "visions could never be corrected." The *res publica* commanding citizens and directing the course of events is a "phantom."

What Lippmann assumed to be a discovery had been seen as a reality two centuries earlier. In their reply to the opponents of the Constitution, the *Federalist* authors rejected the notion that some vague, harmonious, general public consciousness would emerge from contending factions; in his reply to the French critics of the Constitution, John Adams depicted the shibboleth of "the people" almost like Lippmann describing "the public"—a linguistic construction with no corrresponding object in the real world. There is no such thing as "the people" as a collective entity, Adams insisted, since citizens as "a whole body" never gather, reason, or act together.[18] The difference is that Lippmann wanted people to do so, whereas the framers saw unanimity as threatening. Lippmann seemed to feel that only a coherent, unified concept of the public could render government philosophically legitimate; the framers defended and justified—and thereby legitimated—the new republic by identifying liberty not with unanimity but with diversity.

Lippmann's quest for a public philosophy turned on the idea of authority as a unifying principle, the very idea that disappeared from American history almost at the moment of the republic's conception. Henry Adams

17. Ibid., 263–92.
18. John P. Diggins, "John Adams and the French Critics of the Constitution," in *To Form a More Perfect Union: The Critical Ideas of the Constitution*, ed. Herman Belz, Ronald Hoffman, and Peter J. Albert (Charlottesville, Va., 1992), 107–33.

and Charles Beard discerned this loss in the late nineteenth century, as did Hannah Arendt closer to our times. The U.S. Constitution, in dispersing power the better to control it among the various branches of government, had so fragmented authority as a supreme sovereign idea that it was virtually "abolished" as a principle in the American political state.[19] The original abolition of authority did not trouble Lippmann, who still held to the pragmatist conviction that the fount of value necessary to establishing political legitimacy need not be rediscovered by tracing the origins of the American system of government:

> The democratic fallacy has been its preoccupation with the origin of government rather than with the processes and results. The democrat has always assumed that if political power could be derived in the right way, it would be beneficent. His whole attention has been on the source of power, since he is hypnotized by the belief that the great thing is to express the will of the people, first because expression is the highest interest of man, and second because the will is instinctively good. But no amount of regulation at the source of a river will completely control its behavior, and while democrats have been absorbed in trying to find a good mechanism for originating social power, that is to say, a good mechanism of voting and representation, they neglect almost every interest of man. For no matter how power originates, the crucial interest is in how power is exercised. What determines the quality of civilization is the use made of power. And that cannot be controlled at the source.[20]

Lippmann came close to assuming that power was something to be exploited rather than explained, as though its legitimacy depended on its efficacy. But whether power is to be used or controlled, its exercise requires justifying principles that cannot be established by looking to results alone. As his mentor Santayana could have reminded Lippmann, the use and control of power may make a government effective, but the legitimacy of a government depends on the origins of its authority.[21]

By the end of the twenties, when Lippmann's *A Preface to Morals* appeared, he had, whether intentionally or not, changed his mind about the source of value and the legitimacy of government. The book appeared the same year (1929) as Dewey's *The Quest for Certainty*, a treatise that sought to liberate America from the residues of classical habits of thought

19. Hannah Arendt, *On Revolution* (New York: Viking, 1963).
20. Lippmann, *Public Opinion*, 196.
21. Santayana, *Dialogues in Limbo* (1948; Ann Arbor: University of Michigan Press, 1957), 100.

grounded in the universal and eternal. After Darwinism, Dewey insisted, there can be no return to Greek philosophy and its assumption that only the unchangeable is knowable. Lippmann asked Americans to look to ancient thinkers like Plato and Socrates, for the "basic elements of modern morality" can be derived from Hellenic as well as rational and religious sources. The orientation of knowledge is now not simply prospective, as it is for the pragmatist, but decidedly retrospective. *A Preface to Morals* marks a break with James's pragmatism and a turn to Santayana's Platonism and the imaginative richness of life of the mind apart from practical, utilitarian considerations. Lippmann could no longer subscribe to Dewey's conviction that participatory democracy together with scientific inquiry will resolve the problem of authority. The legitimacy of government called for more than an empirical methodology content to control change by adjusting to it. Legitimate rule must be based on self-understanding derived from knowledge of the order of nature. Lippmann's book, although engaged in a confrontation with modernism, gave fresh expression to such old and unfamiliar ideas as "goodness," "virtue," "loyalty," "discipline," "spirit," and "piety."[22] Lippmann even turned to great religious leaders of the past to learn how to achieve "the reeducation of desire," an inner transformation that would enable modern man to begin to approximate the "pure knowledge" attained only in a state of "disinterestedness." Lippmann had moved beyond the liberal world, where the legitimacy of government rested in part on the necessity of humankind's submitting to government to preserve life and property. Lippmann was more the conservative moralist examining the values that would enable modern man to govern the self by bringing human desires into harmony with the natural order of things.

In some respects, Lippmann's treatise on moral philosophy was a preface to his later *The Public Philosophy*. A quarter-century separates the two books, the decades of the thirties and forties when Lippmann wrote about the depression, the New Deal, totalitarianism and the outbreak of the Second World War, and the advent of the Cold War.[23] The urgency of these subjects perhaps explains why *The Public Philosophy* is more intellectually desperate than *A Preface to Morals*. In the latter text Lippmann wrote:

> When men can no longer be theists, they must, if they are
> civilized, become humanists. They must live by the premise

22. See John P. Diggins, introduction to Walter Lippmann, *A Preface to Morals* (1929; New Brunswick, N.J.: Transaction Books, 1982), ix-liii.
23. On Lippmann's response to these events, see Steel, *Walter Lippmann and the American Century*, 285–556.

that whatever is righteous is inherently desirable because experience will demonstrate its desirability. They must live, therefore, in the belief that the duty of man is not to make his will
conform to the will of God but to the surest knowledge of the
conditions of human happiness.[24]

In *The Public Philosophy*, Lippmann is no longer sure that the answer to
the crisis of religious faith is secular humanism and that experience can
validate the righteousness of beliefs and desires. The grounds of legitimacy must have a transcendent source.

The historical context of *The Public Philosophy* antedates its publication
in the placid Eisenhower years. Lippmann started the book in the late
thirties and then shelved it after the outbreak of war. Appalled by the
failure of Western democracies to take a vigorous stand against the forces
of aggression, Lippmann saw almost everywhere the collapse of political
leadership. In the United States, the executive branch had been enfeebled
by pressure groups and responsive to public opinion rather than the true
national interests. Ultimately, the crisis was less institutional than conceptual; it involved the loss of belief and conviction due to the disappearance
of the "traditions of civility," vital traditions that once gave coherence
and direction to society because its members believed they were being
ruled by transcendent, universally valid principles.

The traditions of civility had little to do with the "night watchman"
theory of government of classical liberalism, the minimal state limited to
the right of property, the enforcement of contracts, and the protection of
citizens against crime. Lippmann's idea of political rights was more positive and ennobling than the idea of "negative" liberty as resistance to the
molestations of the state. In the thirties, when Lippmann wrote *The Good
Society* in response to the rise of totalitarianism, he invoked, almost inter-
changeably, the idea of common law and higher law in the defense of the
rights of men and women. Nazism and Stalinism convinced Lippmann
that only people of religious faith possessed the fervent beliefs to oppose
totalitarianism. In a column on the Bill of Rights in 1939, Lippmann
spoke of "inalienable rights" as deriving from the structure of the universe
and the "nature of things" and from "the Creator," eternal sources that
no finite regime can abrogate nor can popular majorities violate without
jeopardizing freedom.[25]

While Lippmann had no difficulty securing the idea of rights and liber-

24. Lippmann, *A Preface to Morals*, xvii.
25. Lippmann's 1939 essay "The Bill of Rights" is reprinted in *The Essential Lippmann*,
ed. Clinton Rossiter and James Lare (New York: Vintage, 1965), 130–33.

ties in familiar philosophical sources, even if he credited such sources with the character of truth that he had earlier denied, he did have trouble trying to find the philosophical traditions that would impress on the modern mind the idea of duty and responsibility. The burden of *The Public Philosophy* was to convey insights into the meaning of authority in a modern political culture that loves to dispute it.

In this endeavor, the philosophy of pragmatism on which Lippmann had based his earlier studies proved almost useless. James's conviction that the individual self can engender knowledge and reality by willing truth into existence had no bearing on obligations to obedience, and Dewey's conviction that freedom is identified not with government but with the collective efforts of the masses of people did more to deify democracy than to direct it. In *The Public Philosophy*, Lippmann quotes a long passage from Peirce to the effect that "truth" will be arrived at "in the long run" as long as inquiry continues unobstructed.[26] But earlier in *A Preface to Morals*, Lippmann criticized Peirce for defining truth as that which is "fated to be ultimately agreed to" by a community of investigators.[27] What passes for truth is simply that which satisfies curiosity and settles opinion. If truth is whatever wins acceptance, how can true political authority be legitimated except by the caprice of public opinion?

In order to find firmer ground for legitimate authority, Lippmann distinguished the realm of existence from the realm of essence, where objects only touch the senses from where they are actually "present to the mind." To the poststructuralists of our day, Lippmann's belief in the realm of essence would be dismissed as another example of the "logocentric fallacy," the belief that the knower can have direct, unmediated access to the object known. But belief in the possibility of that "esoteric wisdom," as Lippmann put it, was necessary to his ambition to move on to an even higher belief in natural law. Lippmann offered that idea to replace the modern, pragmatic view of a pluralistic universe of endless change and "buzzing confusion." Natural law had less to do with the "practical ideals" of the existential world than with "the realm of being" that cannot be proven to the sense organs.

The philosopher Morton White took Lippmann to task for assuming that natural law was a self-evident concept accessible to the rational mind. Noting that Dewey, Veblen, and Holmes had repudiated the idea of natural law, White delighted in demonstrating that it had no epistemological status in modern philosophy—although, curiously, White seemed lit-

26. Lipmann, *Essays in the Public Philosophy* (1955; New York: Mentor, n.d.), 102–3.
27. Lippmann, *Preface to Morals*, 129.

tle troubled by this deficiency when in subsequent books he documented the importance of the natural law tradition to the ideas that went into the making of the American Revolution and its resultant Constitution.[28]

Lippmann never specified what he meant by the idea of natural law. A set of self-evidently just rules? A dictate of right reason? Knowledge of the lawful will of God? Nor did it seem to trouble him that natural law could not be rendered rationally demonstrable. Perhaps Lippmann might have replied that many liberal doctrines suffer the same deficiency. John Locke and Thomas Aquinas are in the same boat when it comes to offering political beliefs without philosophical foundations. "The first principle of a civilized state is that power is legitimate only when it is under contract," wrote Lippmann in *The Public Philosophy*.[29] Yet, as Lippmann noted, the contractual theory of the basis of government had been repudiated because there is no historical evidence of the existence of an original social contract. Fictions are not necessarily false, nor are myths misleading when politically useful. But Lippmann felt drawn to natural law theory in contrast to the social contract, because he experienced it as true rather than useful; or perhaps another way of putting it is that his aesthetic sensibility enabled him to appreciate how other thinkers in the past assented to it:

> The crucial point, however, is not where the naturalists and supernaturalists disagreed. It is that they did agree that there was a valid law which, whether it was the commandment of God or the reason of things, was transcendent. They did agree that it was not something decided upon by certain men and then proclaimed by them. It was not someone's fancy, someone's prejudice, someone's wish or rationalization, a psychological experience and no more. It is there objectively, not subjectively. It can be discovered. It has to be obeyed.[30]

Ultimately, Lippmann's idea of legitimacy rested on what Catholic thinkers call the doctrine of objective knowledge, the capacity of an idea like natural law to impose itself on our knowledge and conviction because it resides in the realm of essence discoverable beyond the realm of human existence. To a Nietzchean, of course, the whole idea is an illusion on the part of desperate thinkers who cannot accept their beliefs as interpreta-

---

28. Morton White, *Social Thought in America; The Revolt against Formalism* (1957; Oxford University Press, 1976), 264–80; see also White, *The Philosophy of the American Revolution* (New York: Oxford University Press, 1978) and *The Philosophy of the Federalist* (New York: Oxford University Press, 1988).

29. Lippmann, *Public Philosophy*, 128.

30. Ibid., 133.

tions but insist on treating them as discoveries. Fortunately, the *Federalist* authors were closer to Nietzsche, and to Hume, in realizing that natural law, along with "common law," "statute law," "maritime law," "ecclesiastical law," and "the law of corporations," would be a matter of contentious interpretation because of the imperfection inherent in the "organ of conception."[31] Lippmann always believed that skepticism was the enemy of legitimate political authority; the framers saw it as the friend of liberty.

The Battle for America's Political Mind: Lippmann versus Dewey

One thinker who insisted that the framers were wrong to distrust democracy in the name of liberty was John Dewey, the leading exponent of the philosophy of pragmatism and America's most influential educator. Dewey had long assumed that America's political culture had its origins not in the pessimistic suspicions of the *Federalist* authors but in Jefferson's more optimistic faith in human intelligence and moral progress. During much of the first half of the twentieth century, Dewey and Lippmann vied with one another to be the voice of modern American liberalism. As we saw, Dewey wrote *The Public and Its Problems* in response to Lippmann's *Public Opinion* and *The Phantom Public*, works the philosopher regarded as among the most severe indictments of democracy "ever penned." Although troubled by Lippmann's critique, Dewey came close to admitting that he had no clear answer to an American polity that rules but cannot govern because of the "eclipse of the public."[32] Dewey shared Lippmann's desire to make mass opinion more rational, see the state as the legitimate organ of the public interest so that the dualism of the individual and the social could be overcome, and have intellectuals and scholars participate in America's political reformulation to answer the cynicism of H. L. Mencken and his Nietzschean lampoons against democracy. For years, Dewey remained respectful of Lippmann's political commentaries even while noticing his elitist and cosmopolitan tendencies, which went against the philosopher's hope that the modern state could somehow inculcate citizen participation by invoking older community values once found in face-to-face relations. But Dewey sensed Lippmann's conservative turn long before *The Public Philosophy* appeared. In 1941, writing to novelist James T. Farrell, Dewey observed that as a popular journalist, Lippmann was telling his readers how pleased he was to discover that the founders had gotten America off to a good start because

31. *Federalist*, no. 37.

32. John Dewey, "Public Opinion," *New Republic* 30 (3 May 1922): 286–88; also, Dewey's *The Public and Its Problems*, 110–42.

they had been educated in the classics. "I can't but feel that L's devotion now to classical learning and the Great Tradition is another case of Jewish inferiority compensatory reaction," Dewey complained. Lippmann's search for enlightened political leaders possessed of a firm sense of authority seemed to Dewey the height of folly. "About Lippmann—it would be hard to find a more egregious example of concocted ignorance."[33]

Dewey's reference to Lippmann's alleged Jewish "inferiority" complex was as dubious as it was desperate, a grouchy way to dismiss unwelcome intellectual positions by reducing them to ethnic dispositions. But Lippmann's later effort to associate the framers with Catholic natural law theory had its own desperation. Ironically, in his earliest writings Lippmann had argued just the opposite, depicting the framers as technicians who bequeathed to America a "machinery of government" that had no place for aesthetic vision or moral obligation. The *Federalist* authors were certainly closer to this empirical portrait. Adopting the new "science of politics," the framers drafted a Constitution that left nothing to the imagination and everything to institutional procedures.

Dewey and his disciple Sidney Hook felt deeply the conservative development of Lippmann's political philosophy because at one time the journalist had been, or appeared to be, a staunch defender of pragmatism and secular humanism.[34] But it could be said that Lippmann foresaw the postmodernist implications of pragmatism a half-century before Richard Rorty and Jürgen Habermas returned to American philosophy to develop new ways of thinking about politics and society that required no metaphysical foundations. The idea that philosophy could survive without claiming to know the true and the real and that politics could be regarded as an endless experiment rather than a recourse to first principles or an upholding of past traditions Lippmann recognized as the message of pragmatism during the First World War era. Lippmann saw in the rejection of foundationalism what might be called the beginning of inventionalism, the urge to make up in activity what cannot be discovered in theory. Without foundations, there is no need to believe that knowledge must be gounded in, or have a cause or origins in, something immediately given, self-evident, unconditional, indubitable, a self-explanatory, self-justifying presence unaffected by our thoughts about it, a bottom on which thought is said to rest. In a curious afternote to a review of Dewey's *German Philosophy and Politics*, Lippmann departs from the book itself to observe

33. John Dewey to James T. Farrell, 18 February 1941, Dewey mss.

34. See Hook's introduction to a later edition of Lippmann's *A Preface to Morals* (New York: Time-Life Books, 1964), ix–xxii, where the philosopher praises the journalist for showing that while ethics may be embedded in religious practices and beliefs, such ideals are logically independent of them.

the momentous historical significance of the philosophy of pragmatism. "When he says that the true American philosophy must be one of radical experiment," Lippmann wrote of Dewey, he

> is urging on us something never done before by any other people. He is urging us consciously to manufacture our philosophy. There would be no more complete break with the tradition of thought. The whole value of philosophies up to the present has been that they found support for our action in something outside ourselves. We philosophized in order to draw sanction from God, or nature or evolution. The theory was that our philosophies determined us; we conformed to them. Now comes Professor Dewey to argue that we ought to make our philosophies for our own needs and purposes.[35]

Although Lippmann hailed pragmatism as politically liberating during his early years, he also saw it as philosophically debilitating. A philosophy that aspired to serve one's own purposes could confuse need for truth and identify the intentions of action with the definition of the situation to be acted on. The contemplative Lippmann was more at ease with a philosophy that would suspend purpose and action in the process of inquiry in order to reduce subjectivism. But subjective self-interpretation and narration is precisely where neopragmatism has ended up today in the writings of Rorty. Since the act of knowing an object alters it in the process of interpreting it, since there can be no accurate correspondence between the knower and the known, since indeed philosophy as representation has "ended," philosophy must, Rorty contends, take the "linguistic turn" and continue as language and conversation, an exercise not in what we know but in how we speak, write, and engage in other discursive practices. Significantly, Lippmann had noted that with pragmatism, philosophy became more an expression of a series of "autobiographies," self-revealing perspectives "from which you can learn more about the men who made them than about the world they strive to interpret." Thus Lippmann asked and answered his own question in a manner that presages Rorty's reformulation of pragmatism as a philosophy of self-creation by means of language and redescription:

> What justification is there for this ultimate impudence which would allow a people to make its own philosophy? The justification is in the fact that people have always made their own philosophies. They have made them unconsciously, and be-

35. Lippmann, "The Footnote," *New Republic* 2 (17 July 1915): 284.

cause they did not know how or why they had made them, the systems if they worked well seemed very noble.[36]

Lippmann remained uncomfortable with such a justification, for by applying pragmatism to politics, the search for the legitimate foundations of government becomes a matter of the will to believe in ideas that have no sanction in transcendent sources, not only in natural law but in historical origins or objective truths. Pragmatism offered uncertainty and plurality as an answer to the exhausted past ideas of authority. Lippmann saw that a philosophy that consciously made its own world would turn legitimacy into expediency and authority into contingency. It may be useful but hardly noble, not to mention truthful.

Until the end of his life Lippmann held to the conviction that government must have foundations in knowledge rather than in belief and on authority rather than on power. His last, unfinished manuscript was titled "The Ungovernability of Man." When we turn to Oliver Wendell Holmes, we encounter a thinker singularly untroubled by Lippmann's worries about contingency and expediency. Instead of searching for foundations, Holmes would give the American character a "fighting faith."

Holmes' Quarrel with the Pragmatists

When men have realized that time has upset many fighting faiths, they may come to believe even more than they believe the very foundations of their own conduct that the ultimate good desired is better reached by the free trade in ideas—that the best test of truth is the power of truth to get itself accepted in the competition of the market, and that truth is the only ground upon which their wishes can safely be carried out. That at any rate is the theory of our Constitution. It is an experiment, as all life is an experiment.

John Dewey began his essay on Oliver Wendell Holmes, Jr., published in the *New Republic* in 1928, quoting the above statement from the legal philosopher's writings. Dewey informed his readers that this "brief passage" contained three essential principles of the modern "liberal faith": the direction of life by the conclusions of intelligence, the determination of that direction though freedom of thought and expression, and the acceptance of life as a continuous experiment with no fixed ends to be realized. Holmes possessed the requisite humility, Dewey commented, to recognize that judicial decisions must take into account consequences and that the judge's own values must defer to the beliefs of others in "free

36. Ibid.

competition in the open market of ideas." Dewey particularly praised Holmes for rejecting the deductive method of formal logic and for declaring what appeared to be the essence of pragmatism: "The Constitution is an experiment, as all life is an experiment."[37]

Dewey may have embraced Holmes as a fellow pragmatist, but the label can be misleading. Holmes was too democratic for Peirce, too aristocratic for Dewey, and too agnostic for James. Peirce, for example, had objected to the idea of truth as whatever is capable of surviving the competition of the market. "Some people fancy that bias and counter-bias are favorable to the extraction of truth—that hot and partisan debate is the way to investigate," wrote Peirce. "This is the theory of our atrocious legal procedure. But logic puts its heel upon this suggestion."[38] For Peirce the pursuit of truth arose out of a genuine desire for knowledge, and thus its claims were not to be left to the vulgarities of competitive hustling and bargaining. Peirce also, it will be recalled, wanted his "community of inquirers" to remain apart from society and its pressures in order to monitor its own procedings and arrive at its own judgments. Dewey, in contrast, believed that philosophers should directly involve themselves in public affairs in order to address social problems. Holmes would have to choose between detachment and involvement when sitting on the Supreme Court. He would not have to choose a different definition of truth than that offered by Peirce. Holmes might change the venue and have disputes settled not in closed committees but in the open public. But it is worth recalling that Peirce rejected the traditional approaches to truth involving correspondence or coherence. On the contrary, given the epistemological problematics of truth, Peirce regarded it as a conditional prospect rather than as an incorrigible proposition, whatever idea was "fated" to win ultimate acceptance. Whether consciously or otherwise, Holmes simply carried Peirce's dictim to its logical conclusion and endowed truth with the "power" of gaining an audience and commanding recognition as a "fighting faith."

Curiously, Holmes was not saying anything that modern literary critics could deny, especially those who reject the idea of truth and the presence of an author as an intending agent. Holmes, too, insisted that the Constitution cannot embody any particular theory passed on by its authors. He also saw constitutional interpretations not as objective judgments but as in all likelihood the projection of the judge's own values, and law was not so much an agency of justice as an instrument of force. By warning judges not to confuse morality with law and logic with experience, Holmes was

37. Dewey, "Oliver Wendell Holmes," in *Character and Events*, vol. 1, 100–106.
38. Peirce, *Collected Papers*, vol. 2, 635.

also, like our contemporary theorists, directing attention to the brute world of power that cannot be overcome by love or reason. If law is to be interpreted as much by its impact as by its intent, the meaning of law can only be indeterminate. Thus in legal philosophy as well as in pragmatic philosophy the search for truth becomes the struggle for acceptance, whether in the marketplace, the committee, the courts, the schools, or the broader popular culture. If Holmes were living today he would perhaps have the last laugh watching contemporary radicals seeing themselves as Gramscian deconstructionists vying to wrest "hegemony" away from the ruling classes. Would he not see them as scrambling Social Darwinites competing with capitalists to win over the hearts and minds of the American masses? How can the contemporary radical critic subvert America's political culture when Holmes and the early Lippmann have already exposed the mechanistic and materialist basis of the Constitution and Adams had concluded that it had "expired" as the source of political authority?

To draw parallels between Holmes and contemporary cultural critics is merely a way of suggesting that he was one of the most modernist of modern thinkers. In some respects Holmes is almost postmodern in that the doubts and tensions that troubled other thinkers like Adams—the tension between knowledge and experience, events and meaning, truth and change—scarcely concerned Holmes. How did he manage to overcome such tensions? The modernist confronts problems for which he has no solutions and wonders whether life can be enjoyed if it cannot be edified. Holmes savored life. A natural skeptic, he felt no need to flee the "irritation of doubt" to arrive at settled beliefs. Holmes's proto-postmodernist response to the challenge of modernity departs from two traditions: the tense intellectual legacy of New England Calvinism and the high moral aspiration of New England Transcendentalism. Holmes's serene stance is all the more peculiar considering that he drew on no existing school of philosophy. Was he a pragmatist?

In an important article, "Justice Holmes, the Prediction Theory of Truth, and Pragmatism" (1942), the philosopher M. H. Fisch was one of the first to suggest the relationship of Peirce's and Dewey's philosophy to the new school of jurisprudence. Fisch cited Holmes's well-known statement that "the object of our study . . . is prediction, the prediction of the incidence of public force through the instrumentality of the courts," to support his argument that Holmes had been influenced by pragmatism. Holmes's membership in Cambridge's "Metaphysical Club," where, according to Peirce, the term *pragmatism* first began to be discussed, seemed more than coincidental to Fisch. Holmes's belief that law should be approached as a science also reinforced the impression that he was a pragmatist, as did his agreement with Dewey that Austin's treatment of law as simply command and compliance must be rejected. It could also be added that Holmes agreed with the pragmatists that history and historical knowledge had no decisive bearing on the present problems the courts must face. Yet despite these similarities it is theoretically difficult and factually awkward to classify Holmes as a pragmatist.[39]

If Peirce, James, and Dewey were not quite prepared to declare that pragmatism is, or can become, a science of prediction, neither was Holmes prepared to embrace the three philosophers as intellectual comrades in the struggle to overcome modernity. For one thing, he would not envision the Supreme Court as Peirce's "community of inquiry" that can claim to offer reliable judgments by virtue of standing above the community. Nor could he agree with James that human behavior defies patterns of rationally predictable conduct. He also interpreted Darwinism in a way that would have been upsetting to Dewey. Holmes saw the initial impact of evolution as reinforcing the conservative conviction that liberty meant opposition to government, that competition was the rule of life, and that the true test of ideas was not only their success but their survival in the marketplace. Although Dewey praised Holmes's presumed pragmatic mode of thinking, he seemed not to recognize that the legal philosopher arrived at opposite conclusions and regarded individualism as the strength of the Republic. Aside from these ideological and theoretical differences, Holmes's personal reservations about Peirce, James, and Dewey are even more telling.

"I feel Peirce's originality and depth," Holmes wrote to the philosopher Morris Cohen in 1927, "but he does not move me greatly—I do not sympathize with his pontifical self-satisfaction." Holmes ridiculed Peirce's alleged claim that he could, given time, "explain the universe." Holmes suggested that Peirce was reading his "cosmic principles" into the world so that his thinking would reflect what he wanted to believe.[40] He had a similar response to James. "As to pragmatism, I now see that the aim and end of the whole business is religion," he wrote to the British scholar Sir Frederick Pollack. Holmes admired James as "in large part an Irishman" possessed of an "aperçu of human nature" rarely found in strict logic; and he praised James for "pointing out that ideas were not necessarily faint pictures of original experience." Despite his awareness that James had put to rest the promise of truth as representation, he regarded the philosopher's book *Pragmatism* as "amusing humbug." James was "eternally try-

39. M. H. Fisch, "Justice Holmes, the Prediction Theory of Truth, and Pragmatism," *Journal of Philosophy* 39 (1942): 85–97.

40. Oliver Wendell Holmes to Morris Cohen, in "Holmes-Cohen Correspondence," ed. Felix S. Cohen, *Journal of the History of Ideas* 9 (1948): 34–35.

ing to get devout conclusions from skeptical premises, which I think very
possible; but I think he takes the wrong road. He believes in miracles if
you will turn down the lights."[41] Holmes wanted Peirce and James to
face the stark implications of modernity and to give up all wishful thinking
about God as a satisfying object of emotion whose existence will one day
find philosophical demonstration. When Holmes read Melville's *Moby
Dick* he thought of Pearson's *A Grammar of Science* and the inscrutable
mystery of reality.[42]

Holmes's opinion of Dewey indicates it was not only pragmatism's
softness on religion that bothered him but also its sentimentality toward
politics. For the most part Holmes found Dewey "unreadable," an ambitious, "cosmic" prose that suggests how "God would have spoken had He
been inarticulate but keenly desirous to tell you how it was." Nevertheless, Holmes praised parts of Dewey's *Human Nature and Conduct* as "like
shiverings of jade—subtle, sometimes epigrammatic," and *Experience and
Nature* he judged "profound and illuminating." While he confessed that
he would be hard pressed to sum up the latter text, he sensed that Dewey
held "more existence in his hand" and probed questions "more honestly"
than all living philosophers. But Holmes saw Dewey as the American
counterpart to Beatrice and Sidney Webb, Fabian Socialists who believed
that a gentle Marx was the answer to a harsh Malthus. Dewey "indicates
emotional attitudes that do not quite stir my sceptical mind," Holmes
wrote to Harold J. Laski. "He talks of the exploitation of man by man—
which always rather gets my hair up."[43] In Holmes's estimate, pragmatism lacked tough-mindedness and allowed sentiment to do the work of
thought. The challenge of modernity was not to find a philosophical or
political solution to it but to live with it in all its intellectual darkness and
fatality. Holmes had no objection to law being used to mitigate capitalist
oppression, but the human temptation to exploit could only be controlled
and not eliminated by judicial fiat. Dewey espoused the endless promises
of intelligence, Holmes the limited possibilities of law.

Holmes's stoical temperament made him equally impatient with Henry
Adams. Of Adams and his two brothers Holmes observed that they had
an "inward delicacy" of mind befitting their aristocratic background.

41. Oliver Wendell Holmes to Frederick Pollack, April 26, 1912, in *Holmes-Pollack Letters:
The Correspondence of Mr. Justice Holmes and Sir Frederick Pollack, 1874–1932*, ed. Mark De-
Wolfe Howe (Cambridge, 1961), vol. 1, 140, 191–92; Holmes to Lewis Einstein, June 18,
1908, in *The Holmes-Einstein Letters: Correspondence of Mr. Justice Holmes and Lewis Einstein,
1903–1905*, ed. James Bishop Peabody (New York: St. Martin's Press, 1964), 34–36.

42. Oliver Wendell Holmes to Harold J. Laski, April 14, 1921, in *Holmes-Laski Letters*,
ed. Mark DeWolfe Howe (New York: Atheneum, 1963), vol. 1, 256–57.

43. Holmes to Laski, June 14, 1922, ibid., 330.

Holmes felt that Adams had a right to pronounce himself a "failure," though he questioned the self-description as misleading. Adams's pronouncements on science and other matters Holmes found unconvincing. Although impressed by Adams's "noble" gestures as a close friend, Holmes grew weary listening to the historian describe how futile it was looking for a rational purpose in history. He explained why in a letter to Lewis Einstein:

> He was very keen and a thinker, but seems to me to have allowed himself to be satisfied too easily that there was no instruction for him in the branches in which he dabbled. When I would step in at his house on the way back from Court and found him playing the old Cardinal, he would spend his energy in pointing out that everything was dust and ashes. Of course one did not yield to the disenchantment, but it required so much counter energy in a man tired from his day's work that I didn't call often. And yet I met him casually on the street and often he was a delightful creation. He was kind, sad, and defeated, although another man would have thought the same life a success.[44]

Holmes would never be able to sympathize with this "delightful creation," an intellectual who drained the energies of those around him by refusing to stop asking unanswerable questions. The event that first defeated Adams intellectually lingered with Holmes emotionally. Adams was in his early twenties when the Civil War erupted, and for years afterward he would wonder whether the war could have been prevented and whether its outbreak signified the failure of the Constitution to mediate conflict as the framers had promised. A world of chance and contingency had no need of historians, Adams later concluded as he took refuge in irony and paradox. Holmes, in contrast, accepted the war as being as inevitable as it was normal. The modern anguish over the meaninglessness of events hardly touched Holmes, who regarded combat and struggle as part of the definition of life. Holmes would come to regard the law itself as the continuation of class warfare by more civilized means.

To use James's categories, Holmes's tough-mindedness contrasted with Lippmann's tender-mindedness as well as Adams's; the latter were rationalists who failed to make sense of a world that consisted in nothing more than the endless rush of experience. Holmes believed that writers like Adams and Lippmann found themselves disappointed only because they started out assuming that the world should be in consonance with their sense of reason. Yet Holmes marveled at Lippmann's prose and likened

44. Holmes to Einstein, May 26, 1926, *Holmes-Einstein Letters*, 253–54.

it to flypaper. "If I touch it, I am stuck till I finish it."[45] Stuck, but not seduced.

Legal Realism and Poststructuralism

The legal scholar who would transform American jurisprudence and remain an important influence from the Progressive era to the New Deal was born in Boston in 1841, three years after Adams's birth and four years after Emerson's famous Phi Beta Kappa address, "The American Scholar." In his later life Holmes would recall Emerson as the "early firebrand that burns to me as brightly as ever."[46] Holmes learned from Emerson that life is action and passion at the pitch of perception, and that in the experiment of living, risk and danger cannot be avoided. Such convictions Holmes carried with him into the Civil War as a twenty-year-old Harvard graduate. He served with gallantry as an officer and was severely wounded in three battles. During the war Holmes shocked Boston society by describing the affair as a regimented bore. But afterward he would look back on the Civil War as the high point of his life, a kind of epiphany that demonstrated how man, a weak, finite creature, was capable under stress of rising to miraculous feats of bravery. The war burned itself into Holmes's memory, and he would forever lecture on "the soldier's faith," emphasizing the importance of obstacles to the development of willpower, of valor as preferable to prudence, and of duty not to others but to oneself. It is misleading to see Holmes partaking of the New England Calvinist tradition. The "peaceable kingdom" of community and brotherly love had no place in Holmes's thoughts, nor did sin and the problem of evil. Social obligation and the classical principle of civic responsibility also cannot be clearly found in Holmes's priority of values. Instead he offers the solitary individual thriving in a world of force and energy as though the most important thing in life is not a cause but a challenge. A tall, handsome legal scholar, Holmes had an almost Weberian understanding that life embodied struggle and law legitimated it. Offering a public tribute to a fellow judge, Holmes advised Americans:

> But I know of no true measure of men except the total of human energy which they embody—counting everything, with due allowance for quality, from Nansen's power to digest blubber or to resist cold, up to his courage, or to Wordsworth's power to express the unutterable, or to Kant's speculative reach. The final test of this energy is battle in some form— actual war—the crush of Arctic ice—the fight for mastery in

45. Quoted in Steel, *Lippman and the American Century*, 175.
46. Holmes to Pollack, May 20, 1930, in *Holmes-Pollack Letters*, vol. 2, 264.

> the market or the court. . . . It is one thing to utter a happy
> phrase from a protected cloister; another to think under fire—
> to think for action upon which great interests depend.[47]

The Civil War experience turned Holmes into a fatalist who accepted
the truth and finality of the inevitable. The war itself may have brought
forth shining deeds of valor, but its meaning surpassed human comprehension. Not only history but even human beliefs are fated rather than
willed. Holmes's determinism departed from James's volunteerism. "All
I mean by truth is the road I can't help travelling. What the worth of
that *can't help* may be I have no means of knowing. Perhaps the universe,
if there is one, has no truth outside of the finiteness of man."[48] To James
he suggested that his definition of truth as that which he "can't help"
believe could only mean that there are as many beliefs as there are believers and as many truths as there are people. Something of a mystic as well
as a skeptic, Holmes remained intrigued with the unknowable, and he
felt in his bones, if not in his mind, that human beliefs had some vague
"transcendental basis in the sense their foundations are arbitrary."[49]
Holmes refused Pollack's suggestion that he give his concept of belief a
better philosophical explanation:

> I can't help is the ultimate. If we are sensible men and not
> crazy on-ists of any sort, we recognize that if we are in a
> minority of one we are likely to get locked up and then find a
> test or qualification by reference to some kind of majority vote
> actual or imagined. Of course the fact that mankind or that
> part of it that we take into account are subject to most of the
> same can't helps as ourselves makes society possible, but what
> interests me is that we start with an arbitrary limit which I
> know reason for believing is a limit to the cosmos of which I
> am only a small part.[50]

Holmes's outlook led him to assume that he could see the inner connection of all events and to accept whatever happens as fated to happen—a
vision of historical totality that Adams had searched in vain to find. The
philosopher Morris Cohen questioned Holmes's claim that some principle
of unity binds all things together and that the modern intellect must
"bow" before the cosmos. Cohen cited the example of Prometheus defying
the gods as more inspiring. "I do in a sense worship the inevitable,"

47. Holmes, "The Test Is Battle," in *The Mind and Faith of Justice Holmes*, ed. Max Lerner
(1943; New Brunswick: Transaction, 1989), 39.
48. Holmes to Pollack, Oct. 27, 1901, *Holmes-Pollack Letters*, vol. 1, 99–100.
49. Holmes, *Collected Legal Papers*, ed. Harold J. Laski (New York, 1920), 312.
50. Holmes to Pollack, Oct. 26, 1929, *Holmes-Pollack Letters*, vol. 2, 255–56.

Holmes admitted to Cohen. He also conceded that his hypothesis is not proved but more like a wager that helps his "emotional attitude toward the mystery of the world."[51]

Modernism and mysticism offer a curious combination. But in many respects Holmes was a precursor of postmodernism in sensing the dead end of all theoretical speculation. Somehow he could doubt the foundation of any objective reality and still value common sense as an act of intellectual modesty. To Lady Pollack he confessed the futility of pursuing further the riddles of philosophy:

> The fact that each has his more or less differing system; whether there is an objective reality in which is to be found the unity of our several compulsions or whether our taste in truth is as arbitrary as our taste in coffee and there is no objective truth at all, I leave to philosophers by profession. I think the law is a better calling—though I used not to.[52]

How did Holmes's antiphilosophical stance bear upon the development of American law? Adams, it will be recalled, feared that in the modern age law would simply be "police" after the Constitution had "expired" as an anachronism in an age of corporate power. To make and interpret law is the highest expression of authority, and the corrosions of modernity threatened law by leaving it without intellectual foundations. To the modernist mind law without morality is like philosophy without epistemology—a depressing subject:

> Law is born of the despair of human nature.
>
> —Ortega y Gasset[53]

Yet neither Holmes nor Dewey despaired.

The relationship of Dewey to Oliver Wendell Holmes, Jr., indeed the relationship of pragmatism to the study of law itself, deserves attention. In the area of law both Dewey and Holmes had to establish the relationship of government to the principle of sovereignty. As liberals both had to confront one of the questions of modernism: Can law be conceived as something "higher" than the ability to induce compliance? Does modern man respect the power of authority or the authority of power?

Holmes's response to the crisis of modernity was profoundly simple and simply profound. His genius was to shift legal thought from theory to practice. The student and scholar should study not what the judges

<hr>

51. Morris Cohen, "Justice Holmes," in *Mr. Justice Holmes*, ed. Felix Frankfurter (New York, 1931), 30–31; Holmes to Morris Cohen, Jan. 30, 1921, "Holmes-Cohen Correspondence," 27.

52. Holmes to Lady Pollack, Sept. 6, 1902, *Holmes-Pollack Letters*, vol. 1, 105.

53. José Ortega y Gasset, *Concord and Liberty* (New York: Norton, 1946), 29.

know but what they do, and regard law as a function of need rather than an embodiment of truth. The Constitution has less to do with the static textual phrases and clauses within it than with the changing context of the present environment in which it must function. Holmes was accused of undermining the place of morality in law. Whose morality? That of the interpreters of the Constitution or that of its authors? Holmes tried to show that there inhered in law no clearly objective moral content but rather the subjective biases of specific judges. In the notorious *Lochner* decision, in which the Supreme Court declared unconstitutional New York State's legislation protecting workers' health and welfare by limiting bakery workers' hours, Holmes, in a celebrated dissent, argued that his fellow justices were reading into the Fourteenth Amendment their own prejudice for laissez-faire economics. The decision as to the character of the country's economic system should be left up to the American people themselves, whose will is best expressed through the legislative branch of government.

Excluding ethical considerations from the purview of the Court, Holmes wanted to see law become more scientific and empirical. Specifically, he wanted to see judges consider law in light of its effects rather than its origins, and lawyers to inform their clients how they can expect judges to rule in particular cases. In its most practical sense law is what is possible, not what is ethical, and the client wants to know what he can get away with and how. Holmes knew that his theory of law was "cynical," but such a sardonic sensibility was necessary to anticipate what the courts would in fact rule. The idea of law as aspiring to be a predictive science was consistent with the Constitution. The framers, after all, wrote the document in expectation of what people *will* do, not what they *should* do. Holmes applied the same "science of politics" to the study of judges and their habits and propensities. "The prophecies of what the courts will do in fact, and nothing more pretentious, are what I mean by law."[54]

In divorcing law from morality and treating it as prospective advice and judgment, Holmes was not advocating relativism. Critics of pragmatic "legal realism" insisted that a lawyer informing clients what an actual court will decide is merely providing legal counsel that has nothing to do with the nature of law itself. "I don't care a damn if twenty professors tell me that a decision is not law if I know the courts will enforce it," Holmes exploded to Laski.[55] The critics argued that law remained inconceivable without values like innocence or fault, breach, responsibility, and culpability. Here Holmes was close to James and Dewey in

54. Holmes, "The Path of the Law," in *The Mind and Faith of Justice Holmes*, 75.
55. Holmes to Laski, Dec. 3, 1917, *Holmes-Laski Letters*, vol. 1, 115.

believing that the philosopher is not to evaluate the good and the bad in the older religious categories of crime, sin, and punishment. Holmes asked of the judge what James and Dewey asked of the philosopher: to probe not the endless question of intent but the more answerable question of effects, not the thought but the act and its repercussions. In *The Common Law* Holmes wanted criminal law to show not that the deed was "wicked" but that it was likely to be followed by "hurtful consequences." Actual intent was not a practical test, Holmes reasoned, for a man may innocently burn his backyard weeds with no thought of burning down his neighbor's house; but he is guilty of doing so because a "reasonable" person would have envisioned such consequences on a windy day. Holmes's doctrine of external reliability, far from relativizing morals, made subjects responsible for their actions regardless of their intentions.[56]

Yet as a modernist Holmes had no doubt that law itself was relative and temporal rather than absolute and timeless. Like all institutions, it evolved upward from the needs and pressures of a changing environment and not downward from divine, transcendental sources. Although possessed of mystical tendencies himself, Holmes saw nothing mysterious in the nature of law once its worldly operations could be observed. Like Veblen, Holmes believed that many modern rules and customs derived from archaic traits that the anthropologist uncovers. Holmes wondered why Charles Beard seemed so shocked to discover, in his *An Economic Interpretation of the Constitution*, that the framers thought realistically about reality. Only schoolchildren are taught to believe that their country's "founding fathers" were demigods devoted to the good of the nation. Did not Hamilton and Madison agree that power was the basis of politics and property the foundation of government? The Constitution was not born of moral principles, Platonic essences, absolute values, or any formal system of thought based on the rational coherence of logical deductions and inferences. In his most famous utterance, Holmes declared that the meaning of law cannot be found in the formal texts that inscribe it:

> The object of this book is to present a general view of the Common Law. To accomplish the task, other tools are needed besides logic. It is something to show that the consistency of a system requires a particular result, but it is not all. The life of law has not been logic: it has been experience. The felt necessities of the time, the prevalent moral and political theories, institutions of public policy, avowed or unconscious, even the prejudices which judges share with their fellow-men, have had a good deal more to do than the syllogism in de-

56. Oliver Wendell Holmes, Jr., *The Common Law*, ed. Mark DeWolfe Howe (1881; Boston: Little, Brown, 1963), 34–129.

termining the rules by which men should be governed. The law embodies the story of a nation's development through many centuries, and it cannot be dealt with as if it contained only the axioms and corollaries of a book of mathematics.[57]

How then does one tell the story of a nation's development? Holmes remembered Adams's nine-volume *History* as a "brilliant" account of America's past.[58] But Adams, curiously, saw no evidence of linear progress in America's development. Instead he depicted America's loss of ideological coherence once change and development took place and all "principles" surrendered to "circumstance" when each party vied for office in a political culture that had more to do with winning than with thinking and rewarded opportunity more than duty. Whether or not Holmes actually read Adams's *History*, he remained unmoved by the author's anguish. With the Social Darwinists Holmes believed instead that the study of history can demonstrate "a lively example of the struggle for life among competing ideas, and of the ultimate victory and survival of the strongest."[59] It was not only the survival of the powerful rather than the thoughtful that worried Adams. The historian knew that eighteenth-century truisms could not survive twentieth-century modernisms. The social contract theory of government was one such casualty. "Natural rights and natural liberties," wrote Dewey, "exist only in the kingdom of mythological social zoology."[60] Holmes agreed. "Nothing but confusion of thought can result from assuming that the rights of man in a moral sense are equally rights in the sense of the Constitution and the law."[61] If law was not an abstract problem of logic, neither were rights an inalienable principle endowed by nature. Adams had seen developing in the early nineteenth century what Holmes had discovered at the fin de siècle: the life of law would be not logic and ethics but interests and power. Adams saw the triumph of the real over the ideal as a historian's defeat, Holmes as a soldier's delight. Adams had started his career with the optimistic assumption that it was possible to follow the classical tradition and write history in such a manner that the American people would be inspired to engage in periodical recurrences to the principles of the original founding. He ended his nine-volume work, one recalls, convinced that a classical *ricorso* was impossible in a liberal America that would never be bound by the past. Ironically, Holmes reached the same conclusion for entirely different reasons.

57. Ibid., 5.
58. Holmes to Einstein, Feb. 1, 1927, *Holmes-Einstein Letters*, 263.
59. Holmes, *Collected Legal Papers*, 220.
60. John Dewey, *Liberalism and Social Action* (1935; New York: Capricorn, 1963), 17.
61. Holmes, "Path of the Law," 71–76.

The pragmatists James, Peirce, and Dewey saw little value in studying history because it was the future and not the past that held out the possibility of control by human intelligence. Holmes acknowledged that law embodied the history of a nation, but this only meant that law involved genetic growth rather than logical sequence. "The law, so far as it depends on learning, is indeed, as it has been called, the government of the living by the dead," Holmes wrote. "But the present," he continued, "has a right to govern itself so far as it can." Legal precedent and historical perspective were important but not essential. "Historic continuity with the past is not a duty, it is only a necessity." Holmes's desire to turn his profession into a science of law made him all the more impatient with history. "I look forward to a time when the part played by history in the explanation of dogma shall be very small, and instead of ingenious research we shall spend our energy on a study of the ends sought to be attained and the reasons for desiring them."[62]

Initially Adams felt that Americans should know history for the sake of memory, identity, and a sense of movement and direction. Holmes believed that one returns to the past in order to be more fully liberated from it. Of the survival of rules and conventions, Holmes stated: "Many might as well be different, and history is the means by which we measure the power which the past has had to govern the present in spite of ourselves, so to speak, by imposing traditions which no longer meet their original end. History sets us free and enables us to make up our minds dispassionately whether the survival which we are enforcing answers any new purpose when it has ceased to answer the old."[63] Much like the jurist Blackstone, Holmes would use history to uncover the original purpose of a rule, only to subvert it by showing that the conditions that gave rise to the rule no longer obtain. A historical accounting of law would therefore do as much to undermine it as to sustain it. In "Law as Civilization" Holmes explained why history is the least reverential of all subjects:

> A very common phenomenon and one very familiar to the student of history, is this. The customs, beliefs, or needs of primitive time establish a rule or a formula. In the course of centuries the custom, belief, or necessity disappears, but the rule remains. The reason which gave rise to the rule has been forgotten, and ingenious minds set themselves to inquire how it is to be accounted for. Some ground or policy is thought of, which seems to explain it and to reconcile it with the pres-

62. Holmes, "Learning and Science," in *Mind and Faith*, 34–35; *Collected Legal Papers*, 195.

63. Holmes, *Collected Legal Papers*, 225.

ent state of things; and then the rule adapts itself to the new reasons which have been found for it, and enters on a new career. The old form receives a new content, and in time even the form modifies itself to fit the meaning which it has received.[64]

As a skeptical modernist Holmes would use history to demystify existing rules by exposing their obsolete historical origins. This radically subversive stance contrasts strikingly with Burkean conservatism, which held that the origins of political institutions must be veiled in secrecy; and with ancient classical thought, which held that rules and institutions must never be regarded as deriving from human artifice. Holmes strips away God and nature and leaves political authority naked, devoid of any metaphysical status. The problem here is not simply Holmes's "antifoundationalism," which upholds the instrumental role of law at the expense of its inherent value. The dilemma is that he is left without any objective criterion for deciding which rules should be exposed as irrelevant and which should be supported as necessary. More specifically, Holmes's penchant for demystification was at odds with his fetish with survival as the test of strength and fitness. How could Holmes be so sure that the "rights of man in a moral sense" is a confusing and misleading concept when it survived two centuries of scrutiny and even outlived him to be incorporated into the charter of the United Nations? A Holmesian might reply that the concept is still useful because it continues to meet present needs. But the need from which it arose was the need to control despotic monarchy, the tyranny of the past, not the totalitarianism of the future. Given the survival theory of truth, would a Holmesian have to choose Stalin over Bukharin? Is the inevitable always the desirable? With Holmes we are still left with one of the dilemmas of modernism: power without authority, the efficacy of force to emerge triumphant, whether in the battlefield or in the courts.

Holmes's approach to truth also compounds the problem of modernism by relegating it to the competitive marketplace of ideas. In his Darwinian delight with struggle and his soldierly fascination with victory, Holmes came close to endorsing a theory of truth that Peirce scrutinized and rejected: truth as tenacity.

It is this preoccupation with what survives and perpetuates itself that warrants considering Holmes a precursor of postmodernism. Holmes saw power as some vague force determined to move toward its own ends regardless of the intention of human agents. (Adams sensed the same phenonenon, but he continued to quarrel with history rather than resign

64. Holmes, "Law as Civilization," in *Mind and Faith*, 53.

himself to it.) Humanism, the concern for values and moral considerations, was also rejected by Holmes as illusionary. So too objectivity.
In his criticism of utilitarianism, Holmes insisted that there can be no
impartially reliable concepts such as aggregate happiness. The judges will
invariably read into cases their own values without any awareness that law
offers no privileged perspective on truth and that all beliefs presuppose
prejudices. Holmes was honest enough to understand that he could only
describe the operation of law and not prescribe its spirit and substance;
unlike Dewey, he did not believe the scientific method could resolve
conflicting value preferences. His doctrine of judicial restraint, the doctrine that the legislative branch must decide matters of a quasi-
constitutional nature, aimed to make law more responsible to the needs
and desires of the community. Holmes's deference to the legislature was
his way of asking the court to be intellectually humble and admit that its
judgments may be no more than the will to impose its own values.

On that Nietzschean note it might seem that Holmes stands closer to
Adams than to the pragmatists. Peirce remained unaware that his "community of inquirers" might harbor prejudices despite the commitment to
science. And Dewey assumed that more education and more intelligence
could only mean more knowledge and a greater possibility for objectivity
and social responsibility. But in Holmes's vast writings one senses the
same perplexity Adams felt in trying to assert a generalization without
following it up with a battery of reservations. "The chief end of man is
to frame general ideas," Holmes wrote to Cohen, only to add, "and no
general ideas are worth a straw."[65] Despite their many differences, both
Holmes and Adams knew the meaning of knowledge without truth and
existence without foundations. Yet while Holmes could live with the
void, Adams could only shudder at the thought of it. Max Lerner explains
why:

> Like Henry Adams, Holmes was the flowering of an aristoc-
> racy that felt itself bewildered under the impact of the new
> industrialism. But while Adams analyzed with poignant
> awareness the sources of his defeat, Holmes gallantly and ro-
> bustly proclaimed that one could still live in a world like this.
> Even aristocrats could. The function of the aristocrat was to
> maintain the great tradition while the forces loose in an indus-
> trial world battled it out to a conclusion.[66]

The relationship of pragmatism to American law has been the topic of
many recent articles and symposia. Judge Richard A. Posner has written

65. Holmes to Morris Cohen, Apr. 12, 1915, "Holmes-Cohen Correspondence," 8.
66. Max Lerner, "Mr. Justice Holmes," in *Ideas Are Weapons* (New York: Viking, 1943),
57–58.

learnedly on the subject and shown how the pragmatic tradition of legal realism influenced Benjamin Cardozo, the scholar who announced that law was being "made" in the guise of being interpreted. Posner has no quarrel with modernist jurisprudence that submits legal doctrine to the pragmatic criteria of meaning, but he insists that there is no distinction between the "old" pragmatism and the "new." Yet the neopragmatism of Richard Rorty and others is so language-saturated that one might raise the question whether Holmes would applaud "the linguistic turn" in modern thought. No doubt he would agree with the "old" Nietzscheans who, like the Progressive historians, saw the rhetoric of objective reason as masking power and prejudice. But would he agree with the "new" Nietzscheans who are fixated on language as though it creates its own reality? Holmes once admonished the philosopher Max Otto: "Think things instead of words." Distrustful of the conventional language of law, Holmes could hardly reduce experience to language and declare that there is nothing beyond the Constitution as a "text."[67]

Recently it has been argued, most thoughtfully by law professor Thomas C. Grey, that Holmes's thinking was advanced to the point of anticipating ideas that later emerged in neopragmatism. Instead of conceiving law as founded in science and its factual claims, Holmes saw it as contextualist in that it embodied particular social practices and habits rather than reason, and thus it signified not objective truth and morality but the adaptive processes of evolutionary growth.[68] It might be suggested also that Holmes's sense of knowledge as power parallels the contemporary poststructuralist position, which depicts law as an interpretive act that, in effect, amounts to self-legitimation and the will to domination. Holmes, in fact, offered the same criticism of Rudolph Stammler as did the Nietzschean-influenced Weber. Both sought to appreciate law not as a logical relationship among concepts but rather as the data of empirically observable behavior, particularly observations of people and judges living by norms and habits that have little to do with categorical imperatives and much to do with power relations. Neither believed the meaning of law could be deduced from the precepts of justice.[69]

67. Richard Posner, "What Has Pragmatism to Offer Law?"; this article appeared in the "Symposium on the Renaissance of Pragmatism in American Legal Thought," *Southern California Law Review* 63 (Sept. 1990): 1653–70; see also Posner's introduction to *The Essential Holmes*, ed. Richard A. Posner (Chicago: University of Chicago Press, 1992), ix–xxxi; Holmes's letter to Max Otto was reprinted along with others in the *Journal of Philosophy* 38 (July 3, 1941): 391.

68. Thomas C. Grey, "Holmes and Legal Realism," *Stanford Law Review* 41 (Apr. 1989): 787–870.

69. On Stammler, see Laski to Holmes, May 30, 1926; Holmes to Laski, June 17, 1926, *Holmes-Laski Letters*, vol. 2, 90–91; Max Weber, *Critique of Stammler*, trans. Guy Oakes (New York: Free Press, 1977).

The crisis of modernity challenged the whole New England tradition of Brahmin aristocracy. Even though Holmes rose to the challenge, he, like Adams, has been the subject of considerable criticism, particularly by contemporary conservatives who claimed he shirked his responsibility of assuming political leadership in democratic America. Holmes's deference to the legislature amounted to "judicial abdication," declared Walter Berns. "He was not judging; he was refusing to judge." Relegating important matters of law to the representatives of the people could only mean that the Constitution must be, in Holmes's words, in "conformity to the wishes of the dominant power"—a thought too starkly crude for the conservative who wants power legitimated and rendered respectable. Thus Holmes's great teaching was also his great failing. "He taught judicial restraint, and he did so in a manner that exalted the legislative authority by depreciating constitutional authority."[70]

Holmes, Adams, Dewey, and other thinkers struggling with modernity knew that political authority had been eclipsed along with any notion of absolute value and truth. This recognition might be called the Hobbesian moment in American intellectual history. For American thinkers, especially those who recalled the scenes and still heard the cannons of the Civil War, could agree with Hobbes that government can exert authority only if it has the sanction of force. The inevitability of conflict and the finality of force Holmes never doubted. "I believe that force, mitigated so far as may be by good manners, is the *ultima ratio*," he wrote, "and between two groups that want to make inconsistent kinds of world I see no remedy except force." During the World War I period, when Dewey was advocating intervention, he fully agreed that law was synonymous with force as an instrument of social organization. "And what we call law may always, I suggest, be looked at as describing a method for employing force economically, efficiently, so as to get results with the least waste." Adams could also see no moral content in law and no higher authority in the Constitution other than the ability of the government to exercise its powers. All three thinkers concluded that there exist no general abstract principles in which concrete cases of the Constitution might be decided, and therefore law is a matter of irresistible force. With Peirce they would concur that when the Supreme Court is rendering a judgment it is not so much establishing a truth as "settling an opinion." But Adams and Holmes recognized that when opinions are resolved they still remain mere opinions, with no philosophical or scientific status. "The first requirement of a sound body of law is," Holmes announced, "that it should correspond

70. Walter Berns, "Oliver Wendell Holmes, Jr.," in *American Political Thought*, ed. Morton J. Frisch (New York: Scribner's, 1971), 167–90.

with the actual feelings and demands of the community, whether right or wrong."[71]

Adams could agree with Holmes that there is no guarantee that either a small community of scientific inquirers or the larger democratic community of citizens might hold the right feelings and ideas. And unlike their conservative critics, Adams and Holmes doubted that the Supreme Court could be entrusted with authority because its own judgments were merely forms of opinion. Skeptical of the truth-claims of the few as well as those of the many, the modernist seeks to limit the power of the courts so that law can neither condemn deviance nor coerce dogma. But Adams, in contrast to Holmes, was not content to identify law with force and authority with power. He realized, after all, that America had its birth in opposition to constituted authority, and the "conservative Christian anarchist" was always reminding readers that "resistance" was the very spirit of New England republicanism. Adams's many heroines defy Hobbes's dictum that obedience is founded upon fear, as does Dewey's wonderful remark that if power is all there is, humanity can "always kick back." If Holmes sided with the soldier under fire, Adams's heart went out to the rebel who made authority tremble, while Dewey looked to the schoolhouse to prevent problems ending up in the courthouse.

Adams and Holmes accepted the inevitability of democracy, perhaps even its desirability. Both also recognized that there was no way to stop people from heading for hell as a matter of right. Two of America's greatest thinkers were willing to live with democratic society and unwilling to lead it. Shouldering the burdens of modernism, they knew too much to do otherwise. The question that remains is whether society could lead itself.

71. Holmes is quoted in Lloyd Morris, *Postscript to Yesterday* (New York: Random House, 1947), 341; John Dewey, "Force, Violence, and Law," in *Character and Events*, vol. 2, 637; Holmes, *The Common Law*, 36.

9

Self and Society

The Socialization of Authority and the Fate of the Individual

The rise of American pragmatism has been generally interpreted as a response to the loss of certainty, especially the possibility of knowledge having access to the real, objective world or to the "higher" realm of metaphysical truth. Its genesis took place in a post-Darwinian culture where nature replaced scripture and philosophy left behind religion and turned toward scientific naturalism as a new outlook toward the universe. Yet pragmatism set out to overcome more than the familiar war between science and religion. In addition to secularizing the methods of knowledge, pragmatism also sought to question the authority of institutions whose legitimacy lay in historical origins, and it did so not only by invoking the new authority of science but also by turning to society as the cohesive basis of identity, meaning, and value. This substitution of society for history and even older philosophical stances raises several awkward issues.

For one thing, it marks a departure from Peirce's original formulation of pragmatism as resting on something more solid than the whims of society. The "fixation" of our beliefs, Peirce had warned, cannot be mere social convention, for anything contingent has no bearing on its truth and is more arbitrary than reasonable. Moreover, if society is the context of philosophy and language its medium, is not the ordinary and mundane its message? In the 1920s, the period in which American philosophy took the sociological turn, American literary intellectuals were writing of society as either dreary, petty, or oppressive. Pragmatism, however, embraced society as almost redemptive. One encounters here, it seems, another example of "American exceptionalism." For no other modern philosophy has so dignified the social.

Today many historians and literary scholars see pragmatism as entirely continuous with American ideals and institutions. This notion of consensus and continuity deserves scrutiny. A closer look at America's intellectual traditions may suggest that pragmatism represents a decisive break with the past in its adopting of society and its norms. Three generations of intellectuals, after all, insisted that the American character could best flourish to the extent it protected itself from the threat of natural society: the New England Calvinists, the framers of the Constitution, and the Concord Transcendentalists.

In John Winthrop's two sermons, "A Modell of Christian Charity" (1630) and his "Speech to the General Court" (1645), America's earliest settlers were presented with the commanding idea of spiritual authority as a warning against the encroachments of society and its temptations. The state of "natural liberty" inhabited by humanity unguided by grace can descend to a condition "worse than brute beasts" in which men and women are free to sin but incapable of obedience. Winthrop was trying to curb the need for the advent of temporal or social authority, which enters consciousness as an external compulsion when the individual senses the discrepancy between what he desires and what society permits. But Winthrop's message that true "civil liberty" elevates the human condition to a moral capacity to do that which is "good, just, and honest" proved too demanding to survive an emergent liberal culture, one in which Americans would look to the conventions of society, and not the voice of the soul, to know right from wrong.[1]

If the Puritans feared society unassisted by divine grace, the *Federalist* authors feared society uncontrolled by checks and balances. Looking to the "machinery of government," the framers sought to impose the political upon the social because society seemed so class-ridden that oppression and exploitation would break out if the few or the many, property or democracy, reigned unchecked by the Constitution's "auxiliary precautions." Left to its own devices, society must be regarded as suspect, since its members, acting not as responsible individuals but as "overbearing factions," lacked all means of regeneration and self-control.[2]

1. John Winthrop, "A Modell of Christian Charity" and "Speech to the General Court," in *The Puritans*, ed. Thomas Johnson and Perry Miller (New York: Harper, 1963), 194–203.
2. Those who did not see the necessity of the Constitution, those who, like Tom Paine, believed that society is founded on our wants and government on our wickedness, would be closer to the pragmatic effort to see society as the source of value. What complicates such a parallel is that Paine was also the spokesman for an emergent economic liberalism, the legacy of "individualism" that Dewey felt America must overcome. For the framers'

Emerson's essay "Self-Reliance" may indicate how far removed the Transcendentalists were from the pragmatists. True, both generations of intellectuals rejected the idea of a government of political controls and turned to nature and experience as the fount of value, and both sensed the absence of philosophical foundations and the construction of knowledge as a matter of either poetic imagination or willpower. Yet Emerson and Thoreau not only repudiated what Dewey would later regard as society's regeneration by means of participatory democracy in the public realm, they also saw themselves as romantic individualists resisting the strangulation of the self by society. In an age of an emergent mass democracy, Emerson and Thoreau advocated a solitary stance against the tyranny of the social. "In all of my lectures," wrote Emerson, "I have taught one doctrine, namely, the infinitude of the private man." Moreover, as Santayana observed, there are philosophical reasons why pragmatism may be seen as departing from its "ancestral transcendentalism," not the least of which is that Emerson and Thoreau would never have instrumentalized consciousness nor reduced truth to its practical meaning or mind to its biological operations. In denying consciousness a transcendental status, a pure diaphanous moment such as Emerson invoked in his description of the "transparent eyeball" and the "Oversoul," pragmatists were also viewing the self as socially constituted, the very thing Thoreau went into the woods to escape from when he told his fellow Americans that society "paws at me."[3]

The pragmatists did, however, carry on the Transcendentalist legacy of rejecting the weight of the past as a brooding memory, scorning political institutions as mechanisms of control and surveillance, and plunging forward into the stream of experience where everything is in a state of transition. What the Transcendentalists and pragmatists shared with the progressives was a critique of existing political institutions that claimed to have foundations capable of withstanding the challenge of change. All three generations of thinkers showed little respect for the Constitution that they were taught to venerate as schoolchildren.[4] Toward the end of

distrust of society unregulated by government, see the *Federalist*, nos. 1, 6, 10, 43, 51, and 63.

3. R. W. Emerson, "Journals," Apr. 7, 1940, in *Ralph Waldo Emerson: Selected Prose and Poetry*, ed. Reginald Cook (New York: Holt, Rhinehart, 1950), 475. For a view emphasizing the continuity between the Transcendentalists and the pragmatists, which focuses on James to the neglect of Dewey and Mead, see Richard Poirer, *The Renewal of Literature: Emersonian Reflections* (New York: Random House, 1987); for the opposite view, see George Santayana, *Winds of Doctrine and Platonism and the Spiritual Life* (New York: Harper, 1957), 124–38.

4. See John Patrick Diggins, *The Lost Soul of American Politics: Virtue, Self-Interest, and the Foundations of Liberalism* (New York: Basic, 1985).

the nineteenth century, when the Supreme Court began to issue constitutional judgments on matters of morals and social policy, the presumption of judicial review became more controversial than ever, and for progressive historians the problem now became not the maintenance of political authority but an inquiry into its legitimacy. This goal was achieved in Charles Beard's great classic, *An Economic Interpretation of the Constitution* (1913), which succeeded in delegitimating America's most sacred political institution by supposedly disclosing the squalid motives behind it. Yet perhaps Beard succeeded too well, for he had revealed not only what Arthur Bentley and Oliver Wendell Holmes would also acknowledge but what many of the Founding Fathers had realized all along: power is the basis of politics, property the foundation of government, conflict and struggle the essence of life, and law not the expression of justice but the despair of morality. Moreover Beard, Holmes, Bentley, Dewey, and a whole generation of social philosophers influenced by the methodology of pragmatism succeeded in convincing themselves that history could not be a source of authority. Thus Beard and the Progressive thinkers left America in the grip of a disturbing question: if the Constitution does not possess or transmit true authority, why are we obliged to return to it?

The answer given by most social theorists of the era is that we are not obligated to do so. The idea of America's "coming-of-age" implied not only that American culture must catch up with American energy but that America must liberate itself from a Puritanism that had sanctified the acquisitive way of life and from a Madisonian pluralism that had, through its mechanisms of countervailing checks and balances, institutionalized the values of competitive capitalism.[5] With the decline of religion as a viable intellectual proposition, and with the discrediting of the Constitution as a trustworthy arbiter of justice, American scholars felt they had to look elsewhere to find the source of moral and political judgment and to establish the basis for a unified system of authority that could ethically govern and discipline what Beard, Bentley, and Holmes saw as the relentless pressure of interest politics. What was needed was a new social theory that could provide an answer to the self-reliant individualism and the self-regulating political economy of the nineteenth century. The sociologist Charles Cooley explained why one could not look to the past for the answer:

> So strong is the individualist tradition in America and England that we hardly permit ourselves to aspire toward an ideal society directly, but think that we must approach it by some dis-

5. Van Wyck Brooks, *America's Coming-of-Age* (New York: B. W. Huebsch, 1915).

tributive formula, like "the greatest good of the greatest number." Such formulas are unsatisfying to human nature,
however justly they may give one aspect of the truth. . . . No
aggregation of merely individual good can satisfy the need of
the imagination for a unitary conception. . . .

It would be fatuous to assume that the market process expresses the *good* of society. The demand on which it is based
is a turbid current coming down from the past. . . . To accept
this stream as pure and to reform only the mechanism of distribution would be as if a city drawing its drinking-water from
a polluted river should expect to escape typhoid by using clean
pipes.[6]

All the Progressive sociologists—Albion Small, Edward Ross, Lester
Ward, James Mark Baldwin, and others—shared Cooley's indictment of
the older individualism that stalked the nation like a specter. The discipline of sociology was born and took its shape as an opposition to the
conservative doctrines of political economy. Yet unlike political scientists,
sociologists did not feel the overriding necessity to reform the machinery
of politics on the assumption that a good government would produce a
good society. On the contrary, they believed that a good society would
produce a good government if society and the larger collectivity could be
looked upon as constituting the true source of authority. To make their
case, American sociologists had to write upstream, so to speak, struggling
every foot of the way against the main currents of American intellectual
history, specifically the economic doctrines of nineteenth-century liberalism and the political doctrines of the eighteenth-century Enlightenment.
In their attempt to reorient the American value system sociologists had
to do nothing less than deny the empirical existence of the self and declare
that society constituted the representation of the self. To break down the
false dualism between society and the self they had to extirpate what
Small called the "preposterous initial fact of the individual" and affirm
the two major tenets of Progressivism: that man is social in nature and
society cooperative in spirit. The new sociological manifesto could be
summed up in five simple words: "One man is no man."[7]

The manifesto would have troubled the puritans, who feared allowing
society to come between man and God; the framers, who could trust the
one man but not the many; and the Transcendentalists, who believed
that collective man is no man. With the socialization of authority, with
the locus of inquiry now confined to social relations, the pragmatists told
Emerson, in effect, that there exists no sacred self to rely upon, and told

6. Charles H. Cooley, *Social Process* (New York, 1918), 417–18.
7. *American Masters of Social Science*, ed. Howard Odum (New York, 1927), 152.

Thoreau to come back from Walden Pond and enjoy the presence of others.

Charles H. Cooley and George H. Mead

One of the first American scholars to challenge older ideas of moral and political authority and develop a new theory of social authority was Charles Horton Cooley (1864–1929). A professor of sociology at the University of Michigan, Cooley had grown up in the late nineteenth century a shy, sensitive youth overawed by his hard-driving and success-oriented father and troubled by his own efforts to define himself as an individual. The problem that confronted Cooley was how to assert his independence from the conventional moral principles represented by the seemingly "inner-directed" universe of his father while at the same time salvaging the notion of moral authority. Cooley did so—to make a long and complex story short and simple—by conceiving society itself as the spiritual source of authority. In developing this bold vision he drew upon many mentors: Emerson, Goethe, Darwin, James Mark Baldwin, and above all William James. From James, Cooley derived the idea that the self was an object as well as a subject, that which is known as well as that which knows. Out of this dialectical interplay between the "I" and the "me," between what I think and that about which I think, arises the sociality of selfhood, the fascinating reflexive phenomenon Cooley termed "the looking-glass self." "Society," wrote Cooley, "is an interweaving and interworking of mental selves. I imagine your mind, and especially what your mind thinks about my mind, and what your mind thinks about what my mind thinks about your mind."[8]

Cooley aimed to demonstrate not only the two tenets of the new sociology: that the individual stood in a reciprocal relation to society and that the impressions people have of one another produce the "solid facts" of society. He also desired to find a basis for the regeneration of modern society by directing our attention to what he called the "primary groups," those "face to face" associations that develop in the family, among children's playmates, and in the neighborhood, and that nurture such sentiments as love, loyalty, and community spirit. Convinced that social science offered evidence for the existence of such behavior, he announced that one could find in William Graham Sumner's *Folkways* three universal ideals that seemed obligatory in all tribal communities: group loyalty, kindness to group members, and adherence to the customs of the tribe.[9]

8. Charles H. Cooley, *Life and the Student* (New York, 1927), 200–201.
9. Charles H. Cooley, *Human Nature and the Social Order* (New York: Schocken, 1964), 401.

How could Cooley translate such admirable archaic traits into workable modern principles? How could he make the descriptive speak for the normative? Certain that such ideals were authoritative by virtue of their hold over our allegiance, Cooley took up the question of authority in the most illuminating chapter of *Human Nature and the Social Order* (1902). Here he defined authority as the "sense of oughtness" that obligates us to do "right"; and authority is bound up with "conscience" as the rational comprehension of duty. But Cooley took pains to distinguish his discourse and analysis from the two traditional ideas of authority: the old Federalist notion of political or institutional authority, which seemed to Cooley (as it did to Lippmann and several others) to resemble nothing so much as a "machine controlled by the power of darkness"; and the old spiritual idea of authority, which "works through conscience and not outside it." The former idea Cooley would not deign to dignify with the status of authority; the latter he found misleading because conscience cannot be understood apart from the external social forces that impinge upon it.[10]

Cooley's attempt to liberate the concept of authority by socializing the concept of conscience proved fraught with theoretical difficulties. For one thing, his treatment of moral authority as a sociological phenomenon implied that religious commandments based on a sense of the supernatural could be explained on the basis of natural needs and conditions. Thus he believed that he could cite the discoveries of William Graham Sumner to affirm the dictates of John Winthrop. Historians of the Progressive era appear to have missed the quiet intellectual desperation of this heroic if futile effort. Cooley, to be sure, was attempting to use the knowledge of modern social science to revitalize the truths of classical religion; and he chose sociology as the best discipline for the reformation of society.[11] Yet each book Cooley wrote took him farther away from the redeeming heritage of spiritual authority he was trying to recapture. Let us consider the troika of conflicting aspirations that beset Cooley's mind and forced him, however inadvertently, to reduce the spiritual concept of authority from the sacred to the profane.

As a Christian, Cooley invoked the Winthropian ideals of love and affection as imperative norms that bind community and command and deserve our obedience. As a democrat, he looked to the people to judge right from wrong and thus collectively determine their duties and obligations. And—and this is the crux—as a sociologist he acknowledged that there was no "higher criterion of right than conscience" and that "social or moral science can never be a final source or test of morality," since we

10. Ibid., 358–401.
11. David Noble, *The Paradoxes of Progressive Thought* (Minneapolis, 1958), 103–24.

investigate only "the conditions and relations of the concrete right—the when, where, and why of what people *do* think is right." Insofar as there may be a test, it is "what *we* think," not what I or you know or claim to know, that must guide our judgments. Ultimately knowledge is phenomenological, a description of what we emotionally experience rather than an evaluation of what we intellectually comprehend: "What is felt to be right *is* right."[12] Authority rests on what we feel, and our feelings are determined by our imagining the feelings of others toward our own thoughts and feelings. Authority, then, involves not truth but opinion, not the rational recognition of obligations but the felt response to impressions. To wax Tocquevillian, one might say that Cooley first delivered the self to society, next located mind in the mirrored reflections of itself, then identified authority as residing in a conscience that has no consciousness of itself as itself, and concluded by turning the whole messy problem of what is "right" and what one "ought" to do over to the constraining opinions of others.

George Herbert Mead (1863–1931) also left the problem of authority where Tocqueville had found it. A professor of philosophy at the University of Chicago and a colleague of Dewey, Mead experienced in his early years, as did Dewey and Cooley, a crisis of religious belief, and he too, like William James, suffered intellectual and emotional traumas that came close to ending in anxiety attacks and nervous breakdowns.[13] In his moods of deepest depression he revealed, as he expressed in private letters written in the 1890s, an inability to function in a world without meaning and purpose. Clearly Mead's early alienation from the older orthodoxies reflected a craving for authority, a need to go beyond the skeptical negations of a youthful agnostic and affirm some positive system of ideas that would enable him to know the world and be at home in it. When he discovered Dewey's philosophy he could now see mind and society not as alienated but as organically related by the very nature of human activity. Soon Mead began to search for a moral equivalent of religion in the discipline of sociology, and eventually he developed a theory in which the genesis of the self emerges in the processes of the communicative interchange of language, gesture, and other forms of symbolic behavior.[14] Although he criticized Cooley's conviction that society inhered in the dialogic activities of mind and not in the "real" social world of human interaction, he fully endorsed the entire corpus of Cooley's scholarship. Mead no less than Cooley was attempting to use sociology to resolve the

12. Cooley, *Human Nature and the Social Order*, 359–73.

13. See the chapter on Mead in Neil Coughlan, *Young John Dewey: An Essay in American Intellectual History* (Chicago, 1975), 113–33.

14. George Herbert Mead, *Mind, Self, and Society* (Chicago, 1961).

crisis of authority in the modern age; and in his unfortunately neglected book, *Movements of Thought in the Nineteenth Century*—actually not a "book" but a collection of undergraduate course lecture notes published posthumously in 1936—Mead described how the great thinkers of the past century like Kant, Hegel, and Marx were attempting to resolve the problem left in the wake of the French Revolution: to replace the arbitrary authority of the older institutions of church and state and with a new rational authority, theories and intellectual systems that could explain how the order of society and direction of history flowed from the rational nature of man and from the rational character of society itself. An heir to this great tradition, Mead became convinced that the proper study of man is society and that the search for authority must begin and end within the dimensions of the social world.[15]

"Mead grows on me every day," Dewey wrote to James in 1892.[16] At the University of Chicago Dewey introduced Mead to resolutions of philosophical problems he was working on, particularly his revision of the reflex-arc concept, the notion of thinking as a stimulus-response affair. Dewey came to see that the mind is not only reactive but active and that it is wrong to believe that only the mind thinks and the body acts. Dewey's discovery that the mind is an integrated organism that behaves, at once hit Mead as a religious deliverance. "I have seen . . . that all matter, especially the human organism, becomes spiritual when one sees in it the processes of life and thought," he wrote his parents, "that the body and soul are but two sides of the same thing, and that the gulf between them is only the expression of the fact that our life does not yet realize the ideal of what our social life will be when our functions and acts shall be not simply ours but the processes of the great body politic which is God as revealed in the universe."[17]

Peirce also had some influence on Mead, though it remained less direct. Both agreed that philosophy entailed semiology, the theory of knowledge as a system of signs; both subscribed to a triadic scheme in which the subject responds to objects mediated by an interpretant that transmits the meaning of experience. The dictum that there could be no thought without signs would become fundamental to linguistic philosophy, and in our era French deconstructionists insist there is no reality but language and the interaction of the signifier and the signified. Although Mead agreed with Peirce about the importance of philosophy as a communicative process, he was less convinced that truth could be arrived at as long as inquiry

15. *Movements of Thought in the Nineteenth Century*, ed. Merrit H. Moore (Chicago, 1936).
16. John Dewey to William James, Feb. 8, 1892, James mss.
17. Mead, quoted in Coughlin, 148.

continued indefinitely. Mead's world was more spatial than temporal; he regarded thought less as a continuing process than as an immediate activity situated in a specific context in which metaphysical truth remained beyond the reach of pure philosophical reflection. If Peirce loved philosophy because it held out the possibility of discovering God, Mead loved society as the place where the self could be found. Ultimately Mead was a romantic as well as a pragmatist; like the poets of the nineteenth century, he wanted to regard the self as reflexive in order to overcome the dualism of subject and object. To the extent that the self-reflexive subject thinks about itself as something other than itself, it becomes its own object. The literary critic Kenneth Burke caught well what Mead was up to.

> The strategy of romantic philosophy (which Mead likens to the beginnings of self-consciousness at adolescence) was to identify the individual Self metaphysically with an Absolute Self, thereby making the reflexive act the very essence of the universe, a state of affairs that is open to lewd caricature. But Mead, turning from a metaphysical emphasis to a sociological one, substitutes for the notion of an Absolute self the notion of mind as a social product, stressing the sociality of action and reflection, and viewing thought as the internalization of objective relationships.[18]

While there are some differences between Peirce and Mead regarding theoretical matters, they shared a peculiar distinction in academic circles: neither published a book on philosophy during his long life, yet each would have a tremendous influence as his manuscripts were later discovered and made available to students and scholars. Mead has been regarded as a progenitor of "symbolic interactionism," a school of thought that sees the individual not as an object buffeted about by external or internal forces but as a dynamic agent engaged in ongoing activities involving thought, gestures, and conversation as well as action. Mead's influence has also been attributed to phenomenology, the study of the mind's reflexive examination of itself as the basis of getting at the bottom of experience— something Adams did all the time, only to discover that there was no bottom. And Mead has been regarded as a forerunner of some aspects of contemporary "critical theory" because he also regarded language and conversation as a means of approaching objective cognitive truth and responsible behavior. Out of conversation arises a "universe of discourse" in which the individual strives to understand and agree with the "generalized

18. Kenneth Burke, "George Herbert Mead," in *Philosophy of Literary Form*, 379–80; see also Charles W. Morris, "Peirce, Mead, and Pragmatism," *Philosophical Review* 47 (1938): 109–27.

other" that constitutes the whole community. If character and personality are a product of social formation, language and communication are the means through which human beings attain both identity and responsibility.[19]

"Mead's outlook is Aristotelian," observed the philosopher H. S. Thayer. Aristotle insisted that man achieves his genuine social existence participating in the polis, and Peirce, Thayer rightly notes, showed Mead that man is a sign-using creature and that all thought partakes of language and symbolization. But Thayer wonders how Mead can demonstrate that the self comes into being as it arises out of a social process. In a way, the problem of the self is similar to the problem of truth as defined by the pragmatists. If truth is not what exists but what comes into being in action and verification, is the self an identity or a social formation, a being or a becoming? "There is something unsettling about the phrasing when we speak of a human being 'becoming himself,'" Thayer wryly comments. "For surely by any ordinary criterion of identity, objects are identical with themselves and with nothing else. To say that a human being becomes himself is to say, then, that he becomes what he is and nothing else; true, but not impressive." Mead's courageous attempt to overcome the dualism of self and society is not only unimpressive in its circular tautologies but unconvincing when philosophy looks to sociology for functional answers to essential questions. "That one becomes what one is presupposes that one does not have the remotest idea *what* one is," wrote Nietzsche. Pragmatism changes the question from *what* to *how* and is content to describe how the self becomes itself as a process of growth without defining exactly what it is that undergoes the process. The self is not discovered but made, a descriptive process in which knowing can be nothing more than becoming, adapting, and fashioning. "Insist on yourself; never imitate." So advised Emerson. Pragmatism gives us sociology when we ask for poetry.[20]

To the extent that Mead has been described as partaking of an Aristotelian outlook, two matters deserve comment. For one thing, the idea that social order derives from the interaction of its members is a modern notion alien to Aristotle, who believed ties are forged on the basis of justice and friendship, sentiments that have less to do with civic virtue or democratic participation than with goods and skills that citizens produce and with

19. Hans Jonas, *G. H. Mead: A Contemporary Reexamination of His Thought*, trans. Raymond Meyer (Cambridge: Polity Press, 1985).

20. Thayer, *Meaning and Action*, 240; Friedrich Nietzsche, *Ecce Homo*, trans. R. J. Hollingdale (New York: Penguin, 1979), 64; Ralph Waldo Emerson, "Self-Reliance," in *Ralph Waldo Emerson: Selected Prose and Poetry* (New York: Rinehart, 1966), 187; on Dewey's difficulties dealing with the self, see Quentin Anderson, *Making Americans: An Essay on Money and Individualism* (New York: Harcourt, 1992).

mutual standards of obligation. Moreover, when Peirce, Mead, and the pragmatists broke with the Cartesian tradition, they denied that the mind was a presupposition of consciousness. Seeing mind as a linguistic phenomenon or a social product, they gave up any privileged status on the part of the conscious individual. Mead in particular would, like Dewey and Marx if not altogether like Peirce, explain consciousness by social life and not life by consciousness. But Mead's denial that the philosopher could have any idea of individual consciousness, of the self and its personal identity, denies private inwardness any cognitive status. One wonders, then, if Mead can be described as having an Aristotelian perspective when it comes to the problem of truth and the modern insistence on the generic social formation of knowledge. The philosophers of classical antiquity may have regarded politics as social in nature. But they also believed that to think socially and to thereby live according to the opinions of others was to remain in Plato's cave of impressions and shadows. "Know thyself!" How can the pragmatist fulfill the Delphic imperative if the self and society are one and the same?

Classical and Christian Morality and the Disappearance of the Self

The socialization of the self had important implications for the fate of ethical theory in America. Like Dewey, Mead refused to make a distinction between interests and ideals in order to separate egoistic behavior from conduct governed by higher principles. His conviction that the mind has the ability to take the role of others in regard to its own evolving conduct might possibly be compared to Kant's definition of judgment: "the elevation to a general standpoint which a person can determine only by putting himself in the place of others."[21] But Kant presupposed the individual self as free to choose to aspire to moral conduct out of a sense of duty and obligation. Mead wanted to see a wholly integrated society "in which everyone is going to recognize the interests of everybody else—for example, in which the golden rule is to be the rule of conduct, that is, a society in which everyone is to make the interests of others his own interests, while actually each person seems to be pursuing his own interest."[22] As a socially conditioned creature pursuing his own ends, man accepts the interests of others as legitimate and even identical to his own. Ironically, such a description could readily be accepted by the framers of the Constitution as grounds for establishing "checks and balances" to control power-seeking drives as a threat to liberty and property. It was precisely because human nature could not rise to reason and virtue to

21. Immanuel Kant, *The Critique of Judgment* (New York: MacMillan, 1892), 172.
22. Mead, quoted in Paul E. Pfuetze, *Self, Society, Existence: Human Nature and Dialogue in the Thought of George Herbert Mead and Martin Buber* (New York, 1961), 99.

become an ethical self that the framers described man as "irrational." And it was man acting in groups ("factions") who would be indifferent to all ethical appeals to citizenship and duty as he relentlessly pursued interests and power. Mead simply saw rationality and morality in all forms of pursuit defined as social action. Thus not only was conversation a healthy social interaction, so too was economic exchange. "One cannot complete the process of bringing goods into a market except by developing means of communication. The language in which that is expressed is the language of money." Marx denounced money as the "alienating medium" of mankind. Mead may never have been able to demonstrate how ethics could derive from economies; but perhaps he could show Marxists why "money talks."[23]

Mead's theory of the nature of the self and of society raises two serious and perhaps unresolvable questions, one involving identity, the other authority. Mead believed that consciousness and self-awareness would emerge from the ongoing social transactions in which the individual takes on a series of different roles, a process that would somehow enable the individual to come more and more to know his own self as he distinguished it from the roles he played in relation to others. Yet Mead never demonstrated how identity, in the form of a healthy, unified self that actually knows itself, can emerge from the conflicting demands of different social roles and the endless patterns of social interaction characteristic of modern industrial life. Nor did he explain how authority is possible—how, that is, it can be anything more than Tocqueville's nightmare: the arbitrary despotism of popular opinion.

It should be noted that Mead followed Dewey and Beard in rejecting the conviction that authority lies either in an idea that could compel the mind or in a past that could endow the present with knowledge. With Dewey he believed that the very term *authority* was synonymous with the Greek and Christian notion of universal and antecedent truth, and thus the search for authority in immutable ideas must be rejected as a false and almost childish quest for certainty and security. With Beard he argued, in *The Philosophy of the Present*, that history cannot be studied for what it reveals, since the past is always subjected to the continual appearances of "emergents," new problems and perspectives that reshape the past in the image of and according to the needs of the present and thereby render history as an objective reality beyond the grasp of contemporary man. Since knowledge could not be disclosed to consciousness through the study of ideas, and since it could not be apprehended in the study of

23. Mead on "bringing goods to the market" is quoted in Burke, who also made the quip about "money talks"; "George Herbert Mead," 381.

the past, Mead was forced to reject traditional philosophy and history as possible intellectual sources of authority and embrace the new discipline of sociology. Yet one wonders whether the problem of authority can be resolved merely by socializing the concept. What becomes of authority when its seat is no longer in imperative ideals that compel individual consciousness or in political institutions that govern conduct by force of law? The answer appears to be that society itself has assumed the role that was once played by church and state as the arbiters of conduct.

Mead and Dewey would perhaps be uneasy with that conclusion. Both saw the self as socially constituted and not necessarily socially determined, and on occasion they could be as angry with the suffocations of society as were Emerson and Thoreau. "It is naturally true," Mead wrote, "the the self exists over against other selves," a point he made in opposition to the Hegelian idea of a totalizing process that identifies external social reality with social experience. While unwilling to identify the whole of reality with the development of each and every social process, Mead did share Hegel's idea of the inner self striving dialectically for social recognition. The history of struggle and class conflict, Mead emphasized, indicates that individuals and groups realize themselves in opposition to others. Yet in the end what is to be realized is not Emerson's "aboriginal self" or any indwelling essence but the full flower of the "social self," which fosters "the capacity of the human individual to assume the organized attitude of the community toward himself as well as toward others."[24] In such a naturalistic scenario, the imperative of duty and obligation cannot emanate from any source that transcends the person or in any principle that can be distinguished from the undifferentiated whole. Authority, in short, has no content and meaning superior to or anterior to society, and it cannot command because the self belongs to "others."

Although contemporary scholars tend to see pragmatism as not only sustaining American ideas and ideals but perhaps even fulfilling them, when it comes to the socialization of the self, pragmatism departs emphatically from early American traditions. This intellectual break is not only true in respect to the Transcendentalists and the sense of the self as inviolate; it is also true in respect to the Puritans and the Founders and the self as the bedrock of personal responsibility. Although the Puritans regarded humankind as stained with sin and the framers saw political man as a creature of interest, both assumed that the individual could rise to saintly grace or virtuous citizenship providing human action was sufficiently autonomous so that the self could be both the judge of its

24. George Herbert Mead, *The Philosophy of the Act*, ed. Charles W. Morriss (1938; Chicago: University of Chicago Press, 1972), 625, 654–55.

own conduct and the agent of self-control. Dewey and Mead may have sublimated their religious heritage into society and thus continued the Christian duty of justifying society's ways to man; they could even show why adaptation is rewarded and deviance punished. But their sense of the self has no clear basis in Christian and classical traditions. Despite their differences, Christian and classical ethics depend upon the assumption that an internal self exists as the source of conscience, guilt, and responsibility. In denying the existence of truth as well as that of the self, pragmatists can hardly ask us to be true to ourselves. In pragmatism the self is a product created in social interaction, a "process" that becomes an object of its own awareness. With such awareness, we can know how our selves have come to be formed. The rest is history, the story of the self's development by forces beyond itself, by situations, systems, and structures within which the self resides, thinks, and acts. Ethics is no longer a matter of adhering to rules, obeying conscience, or aspiring to higher ideals. Morality is now a matter of engaging in practices in accordance with a community's conventions. To do the right thing is to do what comes socially.

One recalls Lippmann's definition of liberalism as the overthrow of authority and the search for its substitute. In America the search ended with pragmatism, which promised to take the place of traditional authority that had once rested on obsolete philosophical foundations. It might be said that in modern pragmatic sociology, authority is functional rather than foundational, what works, or, as Dewey put it, whatever "will do" in satisfying human need.[25] The ramifications of this modern surrogate for authority deserve examination.

Traditionally authority signified origins, not consequences, and thus inquiry into its nature involved a search for beginnings, foundings, roots. In pragmatism and sociology, however, the chronologically prior enjoys no superior status. In much of modern sociology the mode of investigation is not diachronic but synchronic, stressing spatial relations where things function instead of happen and where everything that stabilizes the system is legitimate and rational and nothing, theoretically, can be conceived to precede anything. Since rationality lies in its structure and function, there is no need to search for the origins of its authority. As the logic of relations replaces the logic of development, society no longer belongs to an order of events subject to causal explanation; hence one need not obey society, one merely goes along with it.

25. "Not stern moralists alone but everyday experience informs us that finding satisfaction in a thing may be a warning, a summons to be on the lookout for consequences. To declare something is *satisfactory* is to assert that it meets specifiable conditions. It is, in effect, a judgment that the thing 'will do.' It involves a prediction; it contemplates a future in which it will continue to serve; it will do." John Dewey, *Quest for Certainty*, 260.

Is political philosophy now obsolete? In his important book *Social Organization* (1909), Cooley rejected the eighteenth-century notion of free individuals banding together to create civil society and government by contract. "This doctrine," he rejoined, "is wholly at variation with evolutionary thought. To the latter, society is an organic growth; there is no individual apart from society, no freedom apart from organization, no social contract of the sort taught by these philosophers."[26] Cooley was certain that such doctrines were based on false conceptions of both nature and human nature.

The eighteenth-century framers could scarcely locate the source of freedom in society and social organization, those "artificial" creations inhabited by irrational factions. Although the political and the social never remained completely distinct in Enlightenment thought, and although Madison and others conceded that "all governments rest on opinion," the case for freedom rested on a specific understanding of the workings of nature and human nature. Jefferson, who was more concerned about upholding rights than about controlling power, believed natural rights "inalienable" because they are part of man's essential nature. In contrast to the framers, Jefferson had more trust in human nature and its rational capacity to submit to objective knowledge. His distrust of metaphysics made him trust material fact all the more. As Jefferson put it, "the opinions and beliefs of men depend not on their own will, but follow involuntarily the evidence proposed to the mind."[27] That the will be determined by evidence independent of mind and will may have compromised the Enlightenment idea of human freedom. But this ambiguity only indicates that for some Enlightenment thinkers reality had a status to which all subjective perceptions must defer. And nowhere but in the solid, indubitable ground of reality could authority be anchored. That society is created by man is precisely why society can at best be the sphere of convention that may sustain the social order but not the source of authority that legitimates it.

Dewey and the pragmatists, of course, questioned Jefferson's political vocabulary as well as his philosophy. But so did eighteenth-century exponents of the American "counter-Enlightenment." Yet as we shall see in the last chapter, even thinkers like John Adams, who was almost postmodern in sensing the limits of knowledge and the ambiguity of power, seem closer to contemporary Protestant neoorthodoxy than to pragmatism or neopragmatism. Adam's Humean skepticism was reinforced by Calvinism, a theology that distrusted society as the place where humankind

26. Charles H. Cooley, *Social Organization* (New York: Schocken, 1962), 47.
27. Jefferson, quoted in Morton White, *The Philosophy of the American Revolution* (New York, 1978), 198.

experiences alienation to the world of things and external objects. Earlier
Protestant notions of authority and morality rested on the spiritual foundations of individualism and acknowledged no mediating norms between
God and man. No external social norm could guarantee the quality of
motives necessary for salvation amid the infinite possibilities of good and
evil in the secular world. Reinhold Niebuhr, reflecting on the curious
antinomian and authoritarian countercurrents in Protestantism, explained
why classical religious authority transcends circumstances and norms and
cannot be readily translated into society's sanctions: "The will of God is
the norm, the life of Christ is the revelation of that will, and the individual
faces the awful responsibility of seeking to do God's will amidst all the
complexities of human existence with no other authoritative norm but the
ultimate one."[28]

In modern sociology, trying to find the source of ultimate authority is
no longer an "awful responsibility." Knowledge, duty, and authority are
not to be sought in God's inscrutable will but in society's observable
ways.

The Opposing Self: Lionel Trilling

The ways of society, however, hardly provide the rhythms of life for the
American intellectual. Society never made much sense to Henry Adams,
who often depicted it in zoological terms: "Society in America was always
trying almost blindly as an earthworm, to understand itself; to catch up
with its own head, and to twist about in search of its tail."[29] It was not
only the "conservative Christian anarchist" who felt ill at ease with society
and its irrational ways. Dewey, Cooley, and Mead were all figures in
America's liberal culture. Yet many aspects of that culture not only resisted the socialization of authority but rejected the argument that the self
has no independent existence and that truth and reality are experienced
in and through the opinions of society. When Emerson called upon each
American to "trust thyself" he was affirming in prose and verse what
Jefferson had affirmed in the Bill of Rights: the sovereignty of the individual mind against the molestations of society or the state. In American
literature one finds writers affirming the integrity of the self against the
pressures of society as the very definition of moral character. It would be
a false nostalgia to look to literature to find the old moral absolutes that
can solidify the quicksand of modern relativism. But it is in literature,
and not necessarily in modern sociology, that values become real because
they invariably involve the conscious act of choice. And it is perhaps

28. Reinhold Niebuhr, *The Nature and Destiny of Man* (New York, 1941–43), vol. 1, 60.
29. Adams, *Education*, 237.

relevant that one has to turn to literature to discover the many real meanings of authority, whether it be to Melville's *Billy Budd* or Twain's *Huckleberry Finn*. Here we may learn that liberty is bound up with the fate of
authority and that both can survive only on the basis of definite laws
superior to human sentiment and will; or we may discover that the authority of social convention, the respectability of polished shoes and starched
collars, must be resisted so that the spirit can escape the suffocation of
the self by society.

The problematic relationship between self and society may not be a
problem to modern sociology, but it emerges as the agony and the genius
of modern literature. To writers, the socialization of authority and its
accompanying loss of authentic selfhood is not so much liberating as
alienating. Hermann Hesse wondered why it was almost impossible to
live in obedience to the promptings of one's true self. F. Scott Fitzgerald
had an answer. Fitzgerald concluded his first novel with the utterance,
"I know myself, but that is all," only later to come to the realization that
he did not know himself, that indeed he had no self, and that he had
lost his identity without knowing it—a discovery that led to his nervous
breakdown.[30] Fitzgerald's Gatsby paid the price for allowing himself to
be taken in, "integrated" by those very American values that seem so
nourishing to sociologists, and the lesson was not lost upon the writers
of the twenties. One can read almost the whole corpus of the literature
of the "lost generation" as a countercurrent to modern sociology. "Primary
group" associations hardly seemed nurturing to Sinclair Lewis, Sherwood
Anderson, and other novelists in flight from small-town life; technology
and organization, the inventions of the modern industrial age that Cooley
looked to to revitalize "face to face" relationships, led John Dos Passos to
depict in the very structure of his narration the facelessness and home-
lessness of the modern condition; and as for the family, the presumed
source of warm, healthy emotional growth, one merely has to survey the
drama of the twenties, from Eugene O'Neill to Sidney Howard, to discover what that sticky primary unit does to children, women, and man-
hood. To read O'Neill against Meadian sociology is to know what it
means when characters cannot distinguish reality from illusion, wear actual masks to change roles in desperate attempts to find their identities in
personae, struggle to comprehend the tension between impulse and
thought that divides the self from itself, and finally confront the terrifying
proposition that only "pipe dreams" make possible an existence without
God. Cooley and Mead might cheerfully deny the ontological status of

30. F. Scott Fitzgerald, *This Side of Paradise* (New York: Scribner's, 1970), 282; *The
Crack-Up*, ed. Edmund Wilson (New York: J. Laughlin, 1956), 78–79.

the self, but it took novelists and playwrights to actually experience the metaphysical dread of that proposition.

O'Neill's quarrel was with God. Some nineteenth-century romantic thinkers read God into nature when they tried to reconcile the objectivity of the world with the subjectivity of experience, of fact with value, to ward off the specter of alienation. Reviewing Mead's *Currents of Thought in the Nineteenth Century*, Dewey wrote that his late colleague "shows clearly the connection of the scientific postulate as to the intelligibility of nature with earlier theological notions, and brings out the otherwise surprising fact that the emphasis of the Romantic philosophers upon individual consciousness makes explicit the earlier religious idea that nature is but a theatre in which is enacted the drama of the human soul."[31]

Dewey's assimilation of self and society, and Mead's likening nature to a theater and society to a stage on which one plays out roles, served to overcome the dualism of subject and object. Yet when one realizes that actors are not the identities they play, one is reminded by Diderot's *Rameau's Nephew*, wherein the protagonist goes through life manipulating his roles in accordance with society's demands. Hegel took Diderot's character to be the supreme example of self-estrangement, a creature so alienated he could hardly experience his own alienation. This notion of role playing and what sociologists later would call the "looking-glass self" can be found in the writings of eighteenth-century writers Adam Smith, Adam Ferguson, and John Adams, and other thinkers influenced by the Scottish Enlightenment, where the theoretical foundations of modern capitalism were first developed. And here one encounters a revealing irony.

In *Individualism Old and New* (1930), Dewey put forth a familiar argument that has remained an unquestioned truism in modern political thought:

> It is not too much to say that the whole significance of the older individualism has now shrunk to a pecuniary scale and measure. The virtues that are supposed to attend rugged individualism may be vocally proclaimed, but it takes no great insight to see that what is cherished is measured by its connection with those activities that make for success in business conducted for personal gain. Hence, the irony of the gospel of "individualism" in business conjoined with suppression of individuality in thought and speech. One cannot imagine a bitterer comment on any professed individualism than that it subordinates the only creative individuality—that of the

31. John Dewey, "The Work of George Mead," *New Republic* 137 (July 22, 1936): 329.

mind—to the maintenance of a regime which gives the few an opportunity for being shrewd in the management of monetary business.[32]

One can sympathize with Dewey's position at the outset of the depression. Yet there is no irony or inconsistency in the situation he describes. The real irony is that while Dewey and Mead saw social interaction as an answer to private individualism, Scottish philosophers saw the social self as the basis for the rise of modern capitalism. The idea that society is the theater in which people act as individuals in the scramble for wealth symbolized in consumption, and at the same time act as conformists in seeking social recognition, is an idea as American as Tocqueville and had its first formulations in the writings of Smith and Adams. If man truly knew his identity, if he were self-reliant and uninterested in fame and fortune, he would not be motivated to "emulate" and compete to prove himself in the eyes of others. Dewey assumed that he had to demonstrate why the distinction between public and private and society and self is false. Yet the original theory of laissez-faire, as opposed to Weber's interpretation of Calvinism as the stimulus of capitalism, assumed that the self is a social formation and that economics is a social phenomenon requiring no commanding authority. Dewey believed that pragmatism had extirpated dualism for good, dissolved into social relations every absolute, and demonstrated how truth can be made and values created when desire experiences satisfaction. So did capitalism.[33]

It is no wonder that America's pragmatic liberalism, sharing the same antimetaphysical premises of capitalism, proved inadequate in challenging the old order by presenting a genuine alternative. The pragmatic socialization of the self becomes even more troublesome when one considers Dewey's political prescriptions for America. Dewey assumed that once economic individualism is overcome the truer individuality of the creative mind will be free to think for itself. Dewey had no use for Tocqueville and hence could not bring himself to see the mind as more the creature than the creator of social forces. His hope rested on the assumption that economics and politics are different activities, one signifying material profit, the other virtuous participation; and the assumption that whatever ails American democracy has little to do with the realities inherent in democracy itself. "We have every reason to think that whatever changes

32. Dewey, *Individualism Old and New* (1930; New York: G. P. Putnam's, 1962).
33. Unlike Adam Smith and the Scottish philosophers, later writers saw capitalism's overcoming of dualism, of the tension between subjective spirit and objective formation, as not liberating but distorting and even tragic. See Georg Simmel, *The Philosophy of Money* (London: Routledge, 1978).

may take place in the existing democratic machinery," advised Dewey in 1927, "they will be of a sort to make the interest of the public a more supreme guide and criterion of governmental activity, and to enable the public to form and manifest its purposes still more authoritatively. In this sense the cure for the ailments of democracy is more democracy."[34]

The problem with Dewey's formulation is that the more democracy the more politics, and the more politics the less the public can become the "supreme guide and criterion" of government. Unless the public, which Lippmann once described as a "phantom," can be identified as a single voice articulating similar values and interests, can democracy become anything more than a spray of disparate desires? Does it follow that when politics is seen as social interdependence the public good manifests itself?

One can share Dewey's hopes in the face of the social injustices of his era; it is more difficult to accept his assumption that political democracy is the answer to economic liberalism. Given the social nature of existence, democracy and capitalism operate from the same premise in reaching a mass audience with programs to be packaged for voters and buyers. The more democracy, the more political leaders must sell themselves, and to do so they must appeal to the electorate on its terms while at the same time trying to convey their own individuality. But in Dewey's conflicting preferences for individuality as freedom of mind, and society as the seed of the great community, lies a paradox that can be posed as a question: Can one be both social and individual?

Democratic politics depends upon candidates persuading voters that one is sincere and has individual convictions, an act that requires consistency in a democratic environment of diversity. The candidate strives to project strength and sincerity and at the same time reach differing interest groups, with the result that he or she evades or takes conflicting positions. The sight of a politician hedging or trimming, and enduring all sorts of indignities, suggests not so much sincerity as weakness and desperation. Asking to be trusted, the candidate is then seen to be surrendering personal conviction to pragmatic compromise and hence proving himself unreliable and unworthy. The paradox is that the more he tries to persuade, the more unpersuasive he becomes. Voters are eager to know what earlier sociologists claimed has no existence—the individual's authentic self. In this behavior the American is simply continuing to ask what has been demanded since the age of Jackson: that our representative play no feigning role for political purposes, that he or she be a "natural" leader

34. Dewey, *Public and Its Problems*, 146.

rather than a social creature so that politics can, as Emerson put it, rise to "culture" rather than sink to "cunning."[35]

Not until the 1960s did American sociology begin to question the premises of social interaction as the only take on reality. George Homans and Dennis Wrong criticized their profession for perpetuating an "oversocialized conception of man" that failed to penetrate the whole domain of human sensibility and awareness.[36] Yet the most telling critique of modern sociology had actually been implied a decade earlier in David Riesman's *The Lonely Crowd* (1950). Here Riesman argued that the old American character governed by the "inner-direction" of an intact, firm moral self had succumbed to the "other-directed" man, a "personality" so perfectly integrated that he represented a threat to the liberal tradition of individualism. A few years after the appearance of Riesman's dissenting classic another statement in defense of the liberal tradition against modern sociology appeared in two books written by Lionel Trilling, first *The Opposing Self* (1957) and then *Sincerity and Authenticity* (1972). It is no coincidence that Trilling wrote two reviews praising the work of Riesman, for both authors recognized that meaning and value derived as much from individual consciousness as from collective interaction, and both affirmed the self that can resist and oppose. Ironically, a contemporary sociologist and an urbane literary critic were willing to return to the old-fashioned liberal idea that the individual must be the judge of authority even though he is not the absolute source of it. But this idea, Trilling noted, requires almost an act of faith, so difficult is it to maintain a conception of the individual in the modern age. Reisman wrote his book inspired by the "poetry of individualism," and Trilling tells us why the simple equation of authority and society can only result in a conformity that is death to human consciousness:

> And it is this faith that makes it possible for him to assert what in our day will seem a difficult idea even to people of great moral sensitivity—that one may live a real life apart from the group, that one may exist as an actual person not only at the center of society but on its margins, that one's values may be none the less real and valuable because they do not prevail and are even rejected and submerged, that as a person one has not ceased to exist because one has "failed."[37]

35. Ralph Waldo Emerson, "Politics," *Selected Prose and Poetry*, 193–207.

36. George C. Homans, "Bringing Men Back In," *American Sociological Review* 24 (1964): 809–18; Dennis Wrong, "The Oversocialized Conception of Man in Modern Sociology," *American Sociological Review* 26 (1966): 183–93.

37. Lionel Trilling, *A Gathering of Fugitives* (Boston, 1956), 107.

Trilling's concern about the moral fate of the individual came after he had taken some interest in Dewey's pragmatism in the thirties. No thinker since Emerson has reflected so astutely on the condition of selfhood and society as an unresolved dilemma.

Lionel Trilling was an intellectual's intellectual, a mind devoted to minds who lived for ideas as analytical tools that would save us from the "weightlessness" of being.[38] Born in New York to a Jewish immigrant tailor and an English-reared mother, Trilling attended Columbia University and embraced cosmopolitanism as an escape from the ethnic constraints of his youth. He studied literature, particularly the British Romantics, and in graduate school wrote his dissertation on Matthew Arnold. The first Jew promoted to the rank of full professor at Columbia, Trilling became a highly respected teacher sometimes referred to as "the lion" because of his imposing presence. So supple, probing, and aspiring was Trilling's mind that in the fifties he appealed to students who would move in opposing directions—to New Left radicalism, neoconservatism, and countercultural bohemianism. If Dewey helped save America's schoolchildren from boredom, Trilling saved graduate students from cynicism.

As a New York intellectual, Trilling became one of those in the wonderful "herd of independent minds," Jewish writers who defined themselves by arguing ideas instead of accepting them. Most of these writers aspired to urbanity and cosmopolitanism and rarely pined for community and the primary face-to-face relations so dear to sociologists. As Thorstein Veblen noted, the "intellectual preeminence" of Jews derives from their marginal status as a rootless people with a wandering curiosity, uninhibited by existing conventions, and thus always in "the vanguard of inquiry."[39] Dewey, one recalls, believed Lippman's concealed Jewish background rendered him insecure and explained his recourse to the absolutes of classical philosophy. Trilling and other New York intellectuals, however, embraced modernity, relished complexity and ambiguity, and at the same time esteemed conservative writers like T. S. Eliot.

Was Trilling a pragmatist? The philosopher Cornel West has put Trilling in an interesting category: "The Pragmatist as Arnoldian Literary Critic."[40] Both Trilling and Dewey, West rightly points out, saw knowledge as basically a criticism of life, believed that neither philosophy nor

---

38. Lionel Trilling, *Sincerity and Authenticity* (Cambridge: Harvard University Press, 1972), 156.

39. Thorstein Veblen, "The Intellectual Preeminence of Jews in Modern Europe," in *Essays in Our Changing Order* (1934; New York: Augustus Kelley, 1964), 219–34.

40. Cornel West, *The American Evasion of Philosophy: A Genealogy of Pragmatism* (Madison: University of Wisconsin Press, 1989), 164–81.

poetry could avoid politics and social issues, and emphasized humanistic values grounded in experience. We have seen how Trilling admired one of Dewey's early essays for trying to bridge the gap between poetry and science; and, as the historian Thomas Bender has reminded us, Trilling used Dewey's *Ethics* when appraising the novelist Dos Passos—another writer troubled by the individual's relation to society.[41] Trilling did wrestle with the issues of choice, agency, and responsibility, and he did desire to see literature as an instrument of practical value as well as aesthetic pleasure. Yet a pragmatist of the Dewey-Mead school could hardly have written *Sincerity and Authenticity*. How can one be true to one's self if the self has no ontological status apart from society and its discontents?

It is a measure of Trilling's rich mind that critics saw his description of the "conditioned self" as politically conservative, when the idea of the self's social formation had actually been a liberal proposition. But his analysis of the socially constructed self reflected a reaction to his earlier exploration of the Jamesian self as freely willed. Later, as he studied Nietzsche and Freud, he saw the self as inherently at conflict with itself, a view closer to Adams than to Dewey. Trilling did not deny the social determinants of literature, but the idea of a social self seemed as stultifying to him as the idea of uninhibited will seemed dangerous. Society may be the focus of literature, but does all meaning and value pertain only to the sphere of social implications? Dewey and Mead assumed that morality derives from social interaction; Trilling observed that in *Huckleberry Finn*, supposed social values like freedom and moral responsibility take place outside of society, where the drives of status and success give way to the bonds of human affection.[42]

Dewey valued democracy and equality; Trilling hierarchy and order. Dewey embraced the instrumental, Trilling the contemplative. Dewey sought to confront discordance and contingency to control power; Trilling invoked Keats's "negative capability" to be able to live with doubt, uncertainty, tension, and unresolved paradox. Dewey insisted that the object is mediated in the act of knowing it; Trilling continued to value Arnold's dictum on the function of criticism: "to see the object as in itself it really is."[43]

With Dewey and Trilling we are in a world of mutual sympathies but entirely different perspectives. Seeing change as one of the main problems

41. Thomas Bender, "Lionel Trilling and American Culture," *American Quarterly* 43 (June 1990): 324–47.

42. Lionel Trilling, *The Liberal Imagination: Essays on Literature and Society* (1950; Garden City, N.Y.: Anchor, 1957), 100–113.

43. Lionel Trilling, *Beyond Culture: Essays on Literature and Learning* (New York: Viking, 1968), 160.

of the modern predicament, Dewey and the pragmatists saw intelligence functioning as an organism of adjustment, adaptation, and control. Trilling saw the main problem of modernity as the tension between freedom and convention and the perplexities of imagination and reality. In *The Liberal Imagination* (1950), Trilling criticized intellectuals for validating only those ideas that can be rationally organized so as to explain reality, whereas true literature should provide an account of "variousness, possibility, complexity, and difficulty." The naturalistic novelist Theodore Dreiser sought to sink mind into the common details of social life, just as Beard sought to interpret the Constitution by focusing the reader's mind on its economic details. Both the novelist and the historian assumed that reality can be known if social and economic facts are allowed to speak for themselves in all their grim and sordid implications. Trilling protests such writing, but not because it fails to depict society as the healthy arena of social interaction. Instead he quotes the more sympathetic F. O. Matthiessen: "The liability in what Santayana called the genteel tradition was due to its being the product of mind apart from experience. Dreiser gave us the stuff of our common experience, not as it was hoped to be by any idealizing theorist, but as it actually was in its crudity."[44]

Should mind be reduced to "common experience" and life be left submerged in its social existence? For Trilling there would remain a dialectical tension between the self and the culture that conditioned it, which made the autonomy of the authentic individual an impossibility. At the same time, Trilling saw the self expressing its being not necessarily in adjustment but often in defiance. Only a philosophy determined to destroy all dualisms would allow society to take on values that once belonged to the sacred. Trilling agreed with Freud that the self must maintain a standing quarrel with culture precisely because there is no going beyond it. Dewey regarded philosophy and society as inseparable aspects of the same experience. Trilling withheld assent to any idea that left no possibility of resisting its conclusions. Starting out with Arnold, Trilling ended his career in praise of Freud and Nietzsche, who sought to sustain the meaning of human existence by interrogating it.

It would be fitting to conclude this book with Trilling, who once wrote with esteem on John Dewey and Henry Adams, as though America needed both its optimistic thesis and its negative antithesis, which indeed it does. But American pragmatism has enjoyed a revival in recent years. The revival, coming after two decades of decline following the Second World War, is so richly provocative that the liberalism Trilling found deficient because of its claim to know reality has undergone a transforma-

---

44. Trilling, *Liberal Imagination*, xiii, 1–19.

tion, especially in the writings of Richard Rorty. Nietzsche once warned that if we gaze into the abyss, the abyss will gaze back into our own thoughts. Rorty suggests that if we gaze into the abyss in search of the foundations of knowledge, Dewey will smile back in the company of Nietzsche. In the abyss of nothingness one will also find none other than Adams, grinning back wickedly.

10

The Decline and Revival of American Pragmatism

"The Corruption of Liberalism"

One reason for pragmatism's decline in the years following World War II involves controversies bitterly debated in America upon the outbreak of the war in 1939. Later the subsequent cold war raised another argument producing a strangely different line of reasoning. In the first episode, pragmatism was alleged to have rendered America vulnerable against fascism; in the second, impregnable against communism. The image of pragmatism moves from weakness and vacillation to strength and flexibility, only to take on another image with the Vietnam War—arrogance and pride.[1] Seldom did these images illuminate the real issues of the historical moment, but they suggest the extent to which the career of pragmatism cannot be separated from the politics of liberalism.

In 1940, shortly after the fall of France, Lewis Mumford resigned from the *New Republic*'s editorial board after publishing "The Corruption of Liberalism." Mumford had been a great admirer of Henry Adams, and in a symposium in the *New Republic*, "Books That Changed Our Minds," he hinted that Adams, together with Nietzsche and Oswald Spengler, had despairingly sensed the advent of something resembling fascism as the last gasp of civilization.[2] Whatever caused fascism, Mumford believed

---

1. See, for example, Ralph Booth Fowler, *Believing Skeptics: American Political Intellectuals, 1945–1964* (Westport, Conn.: Greenwood Press, 1978); and, with more shrill than substance, Marian J. Morton, *The Terrors of Ideological Politics: Liberal Historians in a Conservative Mood* (Cleveland: Case Western Reserve Press, 1972).

2. Lewis Mumford, "Spengler's 'The Decline of the West,'" in *Books That Changed Our Minds*, ed. Malcolm Cowley and Bernard Smith (New York, 1939), 215–25.

he could explain the shortsighted failure of American intellectuals to answer fascism with a call to arms.[3] America's foremost architectural critic distinguished two traditions: first, "ideal liberalism," which drew its strength from classical humanism, respected historic continuity and universal moral values, and practiced personal responsibility; second, "pragmatic liberalism," which derived from eighteenth-century rationalism, rested on utilitarian, quantitative standards assuming the relativity of all values, and optimistically looked to science to solve problems. Mumford was certain that pragmatic liberalism paved the way for fascism by refusing to recognize evil and the necessity of coercion in human affairs. With eyes fixed on the environment and on the "muddled nonsense" of economic determinism, pragmatic liberals would never know that "it is not in Ricardo or Marx or Lenin, but in Dante and Shakespeare and Dostoevski, that an understanding of the true sources of fascism is to be found."[4]

The impression that an "arid pragmatism" left America unprepared for Hitler also spirited the critiques of other writers after the outbreak of World War II. In "Our Guilt in Fascism," Waldo Frank indicated the "empirical rationalism" of the eighteenth century for denigrating such concepts as tragedy, sin, and God, accepting instead a "modernist solipsist religion of things and words," and dismissing the "pre-rational" world where "primordial intuitions" make possible the apprehension of reality as an "organic" wholeness. To empirical rationalism Frank opposed "The Great Tradition," the medieval legacy of faith and reason that had reached its "Gothic height" in Aquinas's philosophy. In "The Irresponsibles," Archibald MacLeish, the distinguished poet and Librarian of Congress, agreed with the humanist argument that modernisms like Freudianism, Marxism, and pragmatic naturalism undermined the will to fight fascism. MacLeish attributed the reluctance to become involved to the notion of objective science and impartial art that rendered the intellectual a detached spectator. He traced the American writers' irresponsible behavior to the "lost generation" of the twenties, when philosophers and poets turned to culture as a refuge from politics.[5]

The Mumford-Frank-MacLeish thesis on pragmatism seemed to confirm what Niebuhr had worried about earlier in the thirties. Striving to be a moral person in an immoral world, the pragmatist seeks to avoid power and conflict and continues to trust reason and goodness. But Nie-

3. This subject is more fully explored in the author's *Mussolini and Fascism: The View from America* (Princeton, 1972).

4. Lewis Mumford, "The Corruption of Liberalism," *New Republic* 102 (Apr. 29, 1940): 568–73.

5. Waldo Frank, "Our Guilt in Fascism," *New Republic* 102 (May 6, 1940): 603–8; Archibald MacLeish, "The Irresponsibles," *Nation* 150 (May 18, 1940): 618–23.

buhr believed that if pragmatism suffered from illusions it was close to the Christian sin of pride in trying to maintain a posture of innocence in a guilt-ridden universe. The secular, humanist critique of pragmatism derives from different convictions and seemingly leads to hopeless confusions.

The secular critique of Mumford, Frank, and MacLeish extended an assault on pragmatism that had its origins in an earlier context of society and culture. But the critique involved descriptions and categorizations that made pragmatism almost unrecognizable. MacLeish, for example, insisted that the intellectual's reluctance to fight fascism reflected his alienation from American society and political life. Yet in an earlier analysis Frank claimed that pragmatic intellectuals were too integrated with native values. In *Our America* (1919), Frank depicted pragmatism as embodying the prioneer mentality of pushing ahead, "getting on," and of success and utility at the cost of desire and its fulfillment. "The legs of the pioneer had simply become the brains of the philosopher."[6]

Mumford's wartime critique similarly elaborated an earlier attack, in this instance leveled at Dewey in *The Golden Day* (1926). Here Mumford claimed that the pragmatist's rush to organize intelligence resulted in a routine procedure that stifled imagination and impulse. Mumford acknowledged that much of his critique derived from Randolph Bourne's World War I writings. But in the twenties the issue was no longer war and peace. Instead Mumford condemned pragmatism for exacerbating the alienation it had once set out to overcome. Pragmatism lacked a "tragic sense of life," devalued the past as a hindrance to progress, demanded that thinkers adjust to circumstances rather than make circumstances conform to human needs and desires, and, by advising intellectuals to learn the secrets of nature, made power the sole object of knowledge. Mumford wanted America to drop pragmatism and reconsider its own intellectual heritage. He identified with the metaphysical angst of Melville, the pastoral idyll of Thoreau and Emerson, and the high cultural traditions of Matthew Arnold. After World War II he would write "An Apology to Henry Adams," praising the historian against his critics, who claimed he had misunderstood science, for presaging the terrifying implications of atomic energy once radium had been discovered.[7]

The Mumford-MacLeish-Frank argument would have Americans believe that there existed, on the one hand, an "ideal liberalism" devoted to universal values and an organic relation to life, and, on the other, a "prag-

6. Lewis Mumford, *Our America* (New York, 1919), 26–29.

7. Lewis Mumford, *The Golden Day* (New York, 1926): "An Apology to Henry Adams," *Virginia Quarterly Review* 38 (1962): 196–217.

matic liberalism" committed to the abstractions of the eighteenth-century Enlightenment and indifferent to values deriving from "pre-rational" sources. A curious distinction. Did not Dewey insist that human nature must be conceived organically, that intellect cannot be severed from its natural connection with human activity, and that pragmatism aims to bring philosophy into a vital relation with life? Moreover, when Mumford cited Adams and Emerson as some of the heroes in his critique of pragmatism, he ignored Dewey's own admiration of Emerson and Adams's belief in the scientific ideals of the Enlightenment, however eroded they may be by the acids of modernity. Consider also Bourne's critique, which Mumford employed. When Bourne attacked Dewey for exalting technique at the expense of value, he meant to demonstrate that such a rationale could justify America's entry into the First World War as a consequence of equating involvement with responsibility and thought with action. If the same mentality could lead Dewey to advocate noninvolvement in the Second World War, surely the connection between a philosopher's mode of thinking and his specific political position must be ambiguous.

Even more questionable was the accusation that pragmatic liberalism was inadequate to the challenge of totalitarianism because it had its roots in eighteenth-century rationalism. One need only read the doctrinal writings of Mussolini and Hitler to realize that fascism itself set out to repudiate the eighteenth-century Enlightenment. Against the scientific ideals of reason and objectivity, fascism offered the mystical idea of transcendence, the purity of soil and its elemental union with nature, biological vitalism and the power of the irrational, and the "organic" bonds of community. Considering that fascism was at war with liberalism, rationality, and modernity, it almost seems as though America's critics of pragmatism wanted to fight fascism with fascism.[8]

"The New Failure of Nerve": Sidney Hook's Response to Mortimer J. Adler and Allan Bloom

One of the assumptions of the critics was that a culture dies from the top down, not because the economy or the environment are determining forces, as the Marxist and pragmatist insisted, but because the ideas and values are false and corrupting or perhaps even nonexistent. A culture commits suicide when it loses the capacity to instill values and sustain

8. On the antimodernity motif see Wolfgang Sauer, "National Socialism: Totalitarianism or Fascism?" *American Historical Review* 73 (1967): 404–24; see also Diggins, *Mussolini and Fascism*, 444–48.

convictions. A philosophy committed to procedure and method as opposed to content and substance, a philosophy that would instruct people how to examine thoughts but not necessarily what thoughts to believe, pragmatism may have been vulnerable to the accusation that it lacked the intellectual foundations to oppose fascism. But the religious case against pragmatism went further than the humanist critique by specifying what American philosophy needed in order to take a militant stand against totalitarianism—nothing less than knowledge of God.

In fall 1940, when western Europe had been falling to Hitler's *Wehrmacht*, a national conference took place at New York's Jewish Theological Seminary on the subject of "Science, Philosophy, and Religion in Their Relation to the Democratic Way of Life." Mortimer J. Adler, the University of Chicago Thomist philosopher, delivered a stinging address, "God and the Professors," claiming that fascism exposed the spinelessness of the modern mind in all its uncertainty and hesitating cowardice. American professors had succumbed to "positivism," a more serious threat to democracy than even Hitler, whose "nihilism" was at least "more honest and consistent, less blurred by subtleties and queasy qualifications." Positivism and the naturalism that pragmatism had built upon denied everything Adler wanted to affirm: that philosophy is superior to science because it can address ends and values; that philosophy and science are logically independent of one another, and hence the truths of one cannot be discredited by the discoveries of the other; that the highest form of knowledge is metaphysics, for it alone can demonstrate the existence of God "by appealing to the evidence of the senses and the principles of reason, and without any reliance upon articles of religious faith."[9]

Curiously, some of what Adler had to say in defense of philosophy anticipated the recent poststructuralist critique that philosophy is not so much the pursuit of truth as an exercise in "discourses," "language games," or interpretive "construals" in which nothing can be confirmed as corresponding to reality as it really is. "Those who say that philosophy is just another kind of knowledge but not superior to science," declared Adler, "might just as well call philosophy opinion and deny its existence."[10] But Adler was a scholastic who conceived of philosophy as a supernatural vocation, believed democracy must be established on metaphysical principles, and assumed the mind can apprehend reality and the truth of propositions beyond the words that represent them. In Adler's

9. Mortimer J. Adler, "God and the Professors," in *Science, Philosophy and Religion: A Symposium* (New York, 1941), 37–38, 121; Adler's controversial address is conveniently reprinted in *Pragmatism and American Culture*, ed. Gail Kennedy (Boston, 1950), 67–76.

10. Adler, ibid., 73.

indictment, pragmatism's effort to incorporate modernity signified the end of philosophy, since modern thought no longer had a theoretical foundation, an absolute beginning, a base or starting point that guaranteed certainty. Only a return to the premodern world of St. Thomas Aquinas and Aristotle could guarantee the existence of God as the ultimate reality and the "Unmoved Mover." By implication, Adler's quarrel was not only with the pragmatists but with Henry Adams, who doubted what Adler thought possible: to bring the Thomistic synthesis of faith and reason into the twentieth century. Did America need a method or a miracle?

"Tout commence en mystère et finit en politique," wrote the French Catholic Charles Peguy. Substitute *philosophy* for *mystery* and we have an exact description of how Adler's quarrel with pragmatism evolved. "We do not have to wait until this Conference is over to discover its futility and the reasons therefor," Adler stated in reference to preparing America for a showdown with the Third Reich. "The glorious, Quixotic failure of President Hutchins to accomplish any of the essential reforms which American education so badly needs, demonstrates the point for us. In fact, if he *could* have succeeded, this Conference would not be necessary now." [11]

In 1936, Robert Hutchins, the young, dynamic president of the University of Chicago, published *The Higher Learning in America*, a manifesto calling for a comprehensive revision of the undergraduate curriculum. Sharing many of Adler's convictions, Hutchins proposed that instruction be organized around "the Great Books of the Western World" and taught in the spirit of the Socratic dialogue. He also insisted that metaphysical philosophy be at the summit of the curriculum instead of science, which confines itself to the domain of natural knowledge. Unlike Adler, Hutchins doubted that God's existence could be proven, but he did believe reason sufficient to track down the truths of "natural law." He also saw no conflict between metaphysics and modernity. An exploration into the nature of final causality and an inquiry into the nature of being remained the only way to explain the things of life that come into existence and pass away. Metaphysics promised what Adams, Dewey, and most modernist thinkers thought beyond the realm of knowledge: mind's ability to attain truth and certainty. Thus philosophy cannot culminate in science and the method of verification, which makes truth a matter of experimental prediction rather than rational demonstration. Convinced that logic transcends experience, Hutchins reasoned syllogistically from premise to conclusion with supreme confidence. "The aim of higher education is wis-

11. Ibid., 69.

dom. Wisdom is knowledge of principles and causes. Metaphysics deals with the highest principles and causes. Therefore metaphysics is the highest wisdom."[12]

As a philosopher who thought he had once demonstrated the futility of the "quest for certainty," John Dewey could hardly allow Hutchins to take the lead in reforming American education. When Hutchins's book received favorable reviews in the popular press, Dewey felt the need to reply in the more obscure left-wing journal, *Social Frontier*. Dewey reiterated his conviction that older metaphysics rested on the false Thomist premise that man is everywhere and always the same, and therefore the aim of philosophy is to discover universal truths and first principles. Dewey feared that Hutchins's proposals would take America down the road of absolutism and authoritarianism and that the University of Chicago would become a bastion of Catholic dogma with Adler explicating Aquinas's *Summa Theologica*. And, inevitably, what began as a philosophical dispute ended in political accusation:

> I would not intimate that the author has any sympathy for fascism. But basically his idea as to the proper course to be taken is akin to the distrust of freedom and the consequent appeal to some fixed authority that is now overruling the world. . . . Doubtless much may be said for selecting Aristotle and Saint Thomas as competent promulgators of first truths. But it took the authority of a powerful ecclesiastical organization to secure their wide recognition. Others may prefer Hegel, or Karl Marx, or even Mussolini as the seers of first truths; and there are those who prefer Nazism. As far as I can see President Hutchins has completely evaded the problem of who is to determine the definite truths that constitute the hierarchy.[13]

With Dewey first "intimating" that Hutchins harbored fascist sentiments, Adler could not resist the temptation, several years later, to describe America's positivist professors as posing a threat more dangerous than Hitler. But the political polemics only clouded the philosophical issues and precluded any grounds for reconciliation. Actually, Hutchins's proposals, rather than imposing authority and hierarchy, aimed to democratize the university by eliminating the faculty rank system and by making the classics accessible to all students. In his reply to Dewey in the *Social Frontier*, Hutchins denied that science would have no central place in his

---

12. Harry S. Ashmore, *Unseasonable Truths: The Life of Robert Maynard Hutchins* (Boston, 1989), 154.
13. Dewey's review in the *Social Frontier* is quoted in Ashmore, 156.

curriculum and that the campus must remain aloof from society. He also agreed with Dewey that first principles must be put to the test of research and contemporary experience. Yet the two educators could hardly reconcile one philosophical issue that goes to the heart of modernism. Did the rise of science make possible genuine progress and thereby render irrelevant the wisdom of ancient thinkers? If science shows man how to control nature, how can he learn to conform to it? Ultimately Hutchins was a dualist who could not accept the ethical naturalist's fusion of fact and value. Thus what angered Dewey was the subordination of science to philosophy. "Are we compelled to hold that one method obtains in the natural sciences, and another, radically different, in moral questions?" demanded Dewey. "We are compelled to hold just that," Hutchins replied, "because moral questions are not susceptible to scientific treatment."[14]

When Adler delivered his "God and the Professors" address in 1940, Sidney Hook replied in the New Republic with a forceful rebuke, "The New Medievalism." Hook saw Adler's call for return to a theologically grounded philosophy as the beginning of a modern "Inquisition" since there was no way to define true religion. Only science, Hook noted, had succeeded in reaching universal agreement, mainly because its methodology refused to accept self-evident truths and instead submitted all truth-claims to empirical inquiry and the test of verifiable consequences. To Hook and Dewey science was sufficient to meet the challenge of modernism.[15]

The unswerving commitment to science created some unacknowledged difficulties for American pragmatism. Since science could offer only a prediction theory of truth, the nation could hope to reach agreement only in the future, when whatever problem was at hand had been settled. Such a theory could hardly help the American public decide whether to enter the war. Nor would it be of much use in defining America's political culture. The foreground orientation of thought made an idea potential rather than actual, not what is or what was but what is to be. Can America develop its political values from the future instead of the past? As a political philosopher Dewey fervently believed in community, and at times he thought he saw it flowering in Jefferson's eighteenth-century America, the land of self-evident truths and individual natural rights. Yet while Dewey's political philosophy aspired to community, he did not believe America needed a common philosophical foundation. At the same

14. Quoted in Ashmore, 159.
15. Sidney Hook, "The New Medievalism," New Republic 103 (Oct. 28, 1940): 602–6; reprinted in Kennedy, ed., 76–80.

time, Adler and Hutchins, who also believed American individualism needed to be curbed by moral community, sought such an ideal not in America's past but in medieval history, religion, and philosophy, the hierarchical stage of order that had broken down more than three centuries before the Republic had been founded. If medieval philosophy could barely survive European feudalism, how could it take root in American liberalism?

The relationship of philosophy to politics turned out to be more ambiguous than either Dewey or Adler was aware. Dewey's assumption that only a scientific outlook was progressive could hardly account for many episodes in American history, abolitionism and the Social Gospel, for example, that were influenced by religion. Similarly, Adler assumed that the conference he was addressing would not have been necessary, and America would have been fully prepared to enter the war, as he himself advocated, had Hutchins's educational proposals been carried out. Presumably acquaintance with the "Great Books" and knowledge of natural law would have educated Americans in moral and political responsibility, making them aware of evil and the necessity of combatting it. The only problem with Adler's argument is that Hutchins himself opposed America's entry into the war! So much for the "highest wisdom" of metaphysics.

Even more than Dewey, Hook spent his entire intellectual life waging war against metaphysics. Dewey sublimated metaphysics into his philosophy of experience and, as with religion, he assumed that education is preparation for the future and that American redemption lay in "a common faith," not in the supernatural as such but in the "*active* relation between ideal and actual."[16] Although Hook would make no concessions to religion and disagreed with Dewey about even mentioning the word *God* in philosophical discourse, Hook paid the Supreme Being the supreme compliment: from his first writings as a youth to his last written from a hospital deathbed, Hook quarreled with Him with the passion of Job and the wit of Groucho Marx.

Born in 1903, Sidney Hook grew up in a slum neighborhood in Brooklyn, raised by a mother busy earning the household income to compensate for a husband confined to a home for the incurably ill. Hook's atheism and defense of euthanasia derived from witnessing such suffering in his younger years. He would go on to demand that the world be analyzed rationally, and anything beyond a naturalistic account he would dismiss as metaphysical moonshine or theological superstition. "What is Heidegger trying to say?" he exploded after reading *Sein und Zeit*. He wrote his

16. John Dewey, *A Common Faith* (New York, 1934), 34–35.

dissertation under Dewey at Columbia University, and in that work and in subsequent others he challenged the cognitive legitimacy of metaphysics and ontology. The problem with metaphysics, Hook insisted, is that it shuns the practical for the ineffable and misleads philosophers into assuming that they can say something profound about the obscure and opaque.[17]

In the thirties Hook spent much of his time writing about Marxism in an attempt to reconcile it with native American pragmatism. Before long Hook had to concede, in a wonderfully witty series of debates with Max Eastman, that Marxism itself, especially the concept of the dialectic and all the Hegelian smoke and mirrors, may indulge in the scandal of metaphysics. Nevertheless, Hook was the first philosopher in the Western world to locate freedom in Marx's notion of "praxis" in order to salvage democratic socialism from Leninism and the theory of party dictatorship.

Although Hook could never get Dewey interested in Marxism, it was Hook who carried on the torch of pragmatism when his mentor withdrew from the battle in the post–World War II years. In several books and numerous articles Hook answered the criticisms that had been leveled at pragmatism by humanists, organicists, theists, existentialists, and Freudians. Does pragmatism lack a sense of tragedy? Pragmatism's noble sense of tragedy, Hook replied, lies in its recognition that human action is fraught with moral ambiguity regardless of intentions. "Many have been the attempts to escape the antinomies between the right and the good by defining the good as the object of right or the right merely as the means to the good. All have failed." It was Hook who took on Allan Bloom's thesis, spelled out in the best-selling *The Closing of the American Mind*, that America suffers from too much relativism and settles for pragmatic expediency instead of aspiring to the timeless truths of classical antiquity. "The difficulty with Bloom's position is that, like Leo Strauss, he had not emancipated himself from the Greek notion that the cosmos is also an ethos, and that what is good and bad, right and wrong for man is essentially related to the cosmic order rather than to the reflective choices of men and women confronted by problems of what to do." Dewey could not have said it better—particularly Dewey![18]

Hook carried on Dewey's thought and spirit but not exactly his character and temperament. To compare the two is to compare a saint to a

17. Sidney Hook, *Out of Step: An Unquiet Life in the Twentieth Century* (New York, 1987); *The Quest for Being* (New York, 1950); John Patrick Diggins, "The Man Who Knew Too Much: Sidney Hook," *New Republic* 203 (Dec. 3, 1990): 27–34.

18. Hook, *Pragmatism and the Tragic Sense of Life* (New York, 1974), 3–25; Sidney Hook, "The Closing of the American Mind: An Intellectual Best Seller Revisited," *American Scholar* 58 (1989): 123–35.

street fighter. Where Dewey would gently correct an opponent, Hook would announce he was going to prove his foe "not only wrong but demonstrably wrong." Hook seemed to be born for argument and disputation, and he could seldom resist the polemicist's instinct for annihilation. Always loving a good fight, a raging rationalist at once scrappy, aggressive, and witty, Hook was the Jake LaMotta of American philosophy.

In the war years the religious assault on pragmatism and science continued in the *Catholic World* and in Protestant publications as well. In response, Hook organized a symposium in the *Partisan Review* that he aptly titled "The New Failure of Nerve." Hook borrowed the phrase from the classicist Gilbert Murray, who had used it to describe the ancient Greeks' loss of confidence in reason and in themselves as they desperately turned toward spiritual shelter in mysticism and pessimism. Hook argued that in times of crisis the cool prudence of empirical knowledge remained the surest guide, and that modern democracy need not rest on antiquated philosophical presuppositions. In his contribution, Dewey demonstrated that naturalism had many of its roots in Aristotle's teachings—until the Catholic Church overlaid them with supernatural beliefs. The question whether standards and rules had to be regarded as absolute was one Dewey had addressed since the turn of the century. But during the war pragmatism became identified with relativism and various other isms that supposedly had spawned European totalitarianism. Hook and Dewey could rightly point out that fascism and communism had little to do with intelligence and the methods of science and everything to do with emotion and the madness of dogma. The spectacle of the fanatical ideologue claiming to possess ultimate truth made it all the more clear why American philosophy must shun absolute foundations. To be able to live without truth and certainty, to have the courage to face life as Melville faced the void, is the challenge of modernism. For once Adams, who rejected Pascal's wager because religion meant submission to authority and the end of curiosity, would be on the side of the pragmatists.[19]

Communism and the Vietnam War

The attack on pragmatism on the part of Catholics and "organic" liberals after the outbreak of World War II did not let up with the Allied victory—and, it should be noted, the heroic performance of American soldiers, many of whom had been brought up on "progressive education." One Jesuit professor even blamed the death camps on the modernist and

19. Sidney Hook, "The New Failure of Nerve," *Partisan Review* 10 (Jan.–Feb. 1943): 2–23; John Dewey, "Anti-Naturalism in Extremis," ibid., 24–39.

pragmatist denial of natural law.[20] This intellectual warfare involved more than rival philosophical camps struggling to claim America's political soul. Occasionally some pragmatic liberals themselves had second thoughts about the adequacy of pragmatism when confronting the ideologies of totalitarianism. The UCLA philosophy professor Donald A. Piatt advised Dewey that the best way to "save your pragmatism from the relativists and fascists" is to "somehow . . . reinforce absolutes." Pragmatic philosophy may conclude that values grow out of changing conditions, but people will be moved only by being shown why "moral standards" are separate from values and are "authoritative."[21]

"Authority," "authoritative," "absolute"—such terms were so alien to Dewey that he must have grimaced as he read the above letter. In 1918, in the midst of the First World War, Dewey delivered an address titled "Philosophy and Democracy." Here he argued that the quest for absolute ideas, the aspiration to grasp some supreme and total reality, would lead not to authoritative knowledge but to authoritarian politics. All claims into the ultimate nature of things cannot avoid the conclusion that "some realities are superior to others," and such claims will work on behalf of a "regime of authority" that identifies with what is accepted as the higher and truer. Conversely, Dewey believed that philosophical humility, the recognition that the world is contingent and knowledge finite, is more conducive to democracy and human freedom, since no regime can claim to have its legitimacy based upon privileged knowledge.[22] While many critics of pragmatism and even a few liberal pragmatists themselves worried that relativism led to fascism, Dewey was convinced that fascism sprang from "foundationalism," to use the contemporary expression of neopragmatists who insist that philosophy can get along without Cartesian certainty. Yet Dewey's predicament anticipates the dilemma of post-structuralism as seen by its critics in our day. While the recognition that philosophy cannot provide knowledge that transcends the contingencies of history leads to a healthy skepticism, it may also leave history vulnera-

20. "The fire of human liberty is extinguished, because there are no inalienable natural rights; there are no inalienable rights, because there is no natural law; there is no natural law, because there is no eternal law; there is no eternal law, because there is no God—no God, that is, but Caesar. Would you judge this philosophy by its fruits? Then behold the rotting corpses, the mangled bodies, the crippled minds, the broken hearts, the crushed liberties—the stench of physical and spiritual death—in the lands across the seas." William J. Kenealy, "The Majesty of the Law," *Loyola Law Review* (1950), reprinted in *American Ideas: Source Readings in the Intellectual History of the United States*, ed. Gerald Grob and Robert Beck (New York, 1963), 333–47.

21. David A. Piatt to John Dewey, August 2, 1939, Dewey mss.

22. John Dewey, "Philosophy and Democracy" (1718), in *Middle Works, 1899–1924*, vol. 2, 43–53.

ble to politics and its corruptions. If there is no way of attaining truth in respect to beliefs about the world, and if pragmatism confines itself to formal method alone, how can it answer to power? Can one know what is morally wrong without knowing what is objectively right?

Modernism is the predicament of life without any truth rooted in fixed principles, and pragmatism arose in an attempt to cope with the modern condition. How well did it cope in respect to political freedom and totalitarianism? A brief discussion of Dewey's relation to Soviet communism may suggest that philosophy need not possess absolute truth in order to combat particular falsehoods. A discussion of pragmatism and the cold war may also help explain why the philosophy that had dominated American culture for a half-century suffered an eclipse after the McCarthy era of the fifties.

Dewey visited the USSR in 1928 and returned to inform Americans about the "Great Experiment." He found Russia a society in "transition" and in "a state of flux," a country still struggling to overcome the legacy of civil and foreign war, famine and blockade. Whether Bolshevism would "annul itself" as a result of history's dialectic, and whether the dictatorship of the proletariat would negate itself as a historical stage that is "destined to disappear in a new synthesis," only time would tell, observed Dewey as he expressed little interest in theoretical matters. He was impressed in particular by the great strides in the school system, whose curriculum was facilitating the transformation from a peasant-bred individualist psychology to a modern collectivist economy. Dewey sensed the presence of repressive measures, and he was completely aware that education was as much a matter of propaganda as of pedagogy. But he believed that the creative energies unleashed by the five-year plans would continue and that the repressions would relax as Russia felt more secure. With his great faith in scientific methodology, Dewey could criticize the Right and the Left: the capitalist who predicts that the Soviet Union cannot work because it is building on the illusions of socialism, and the Marxist who claims it will work because it has repudiated the institutions of capitalism. "Not being an absolutist of either type, I find it more instructive to regard it as an experiment whose outcome is quite undetermined, but that is, just as an experiment, by all means the most important one going on upon our globe—though I am quite frank to say that for selfish reasons I prefer it tried in Russia than in my own country."[23]

Dewey's *Impressions of the Soviet Union* (1929) is an understandable docu-

23. John Dewey, *Character and Events* (New York, 1929), vol. 1, 378–431; this anthology contains Dewey's writings on Russia, which first appeared in the *New Republic* and were also published as *Impressions of the Soviet Union* (New York, 1929).

ment, and in some respects no different from what other American writers and even industrialists and financiers would say in praise of Russia's economic programs during the Great Depression—in contrast to a Weberian perspective, which would have perceived the persistence of power and domination. But with the coming of the cold war the book would be held up as evidence that America's leading philosopher was a communist propagandist.[24] The charge mistook a travelogue for a treatise.

In his reflections on the Soviet Union Dewey paid little attention to Marxism. He assumed instead that ideological doctrine would wither away as Russia faced the practical tasks of overcoming backwardness. The reluctance to take seriously communist doctrine disappointed Hook, who in 1933 had used theory to justify party dictatorship and the crushing of all opposition tendencies.[25] Yet Hook remained skeptical of the communist dogma of inevitability and denial of human agency and, like Dewey, he viewed the Soviet Union as an exciting test-case of economic modernization by political means. By viewing communism as an "experiment," Dewey and Hook could judge the Soviet Union according to pragmatic criteria and look to the practical consequences of Stalinism regardless of the theoretical validity of Marxism. Both American philosophers changed their minds about the Soviet Union within two years. The use of force and violence, the conflict between means and ends, the "excess of dogma and indoctrination," and the mystique of historical inevitability and party infallibility were all grist for Dewey's critique in "Why I Am Not a Communist," a testament written in 1933 that summed up reservations that began in 1931.[26] Dewey raised the same points in his debates with Trotsky, as we have seen. During World War II, when critics were equating pragmatism with fascism, Dewey was protesting the pro-Stalinist propaganda film *Mission to Moscow*.[27] In March 1944, at the height of Soviet popularity in America, Dewey expressed his frustration to Hook about the pro-Soviet writing in the *Nation* and the *New Republic*. "The failure of nerve persists and intensifies—temporarily at least there is no let up in appeasement of Russia. It's wonderful how those persons who were very critical of British appeasement of Hitler, pointing out it is more likely to produce war than the other course, now urge the same course with Stalin."[28]

24. John Dewey to W. R. Houston, Apr. 22, 1946, Dewey mss.
25. Sidney Hook, *Toward an Understanding of Karl Marx* (New York, 1933).
26. John Dewey, "Why I Am Not a Communist," *Modern Monthly* 8 (April 1934): 135–37; see also the important study by Frank A. Warren, *Liberals and Communism: The "Red Decade" Revisited* (Bloomington, 1966).
27. John Dewey to "Robby Dear" (Tuesday, 11th, no month, 1943), Dewey mss.
28. John Dewey to Sidney Hook, Mar. 8, 1944, Hook mss.

These courageous stances in the latter part of Dewey's career give the lie to three impressions about the anti-Stalinist Left in America: that liberalism capitulated to communism in the thirties, that pragmatism ill-prepared America to deal with totalitarianism, and that former communist sympathizers who turned anticommunist became hardened cold warriors who must bear responsibility for McCarthyism and subsequent tragedies like the Vietnam War. None of these descriptions applies to Dewey, who hardly had to read St. Thomas to understand the menace of Stalinism as well as fascism.

Nor did Dewey become, as did Hook, an embittered anticommunist cold warrior. Although he could never forget how American communists tried to "wreck" the New York teachers' union, he drew back from joining the ranks of ex-Trotskyists, socialists, and liberals in their almost apocalyptic fears of Soviet expansionism. Earlier, after the Nazi-Soviet nonaggression pact, he resigned as honorary chairman of the Committee for Cultural Freedom; and, in 1944, he refused Reinhold Niebuhr's plea that he reconsider his reservations about rejoining on the grounds that too much attention was being focused on the communist issue. In 1949, he publicly criticized Hook's efforts to have active communists disqualified as teachers for violating "professional ethics." All along Dewey remained critical of the Soviet Union but optimistic about the future. Dewey died in 1952, a year before Stalin's death. Always a man of good hope, he would not have been surprised by *glasnost*. "The Russians," he wrote to a friend in 1946, "are and will be a great people—when they get the chance."[29]

In liberal circles the philosophy of pragmatism remained influential even after Dewey's death at the remarkable age of ninety-two. In 1950, the historian Henry Steele Commager praised pragmatism in *The American Mind*, describing it as deriving directly from the country's historical experience and becoming, in the twentieth century, "almost the official philosophy of America." A few years earlier Lloyd Morris, in the popular *Postscript to Yesterday*, observed that "by the mid-nineteen forties, pragmatism had touched the lives of two generations of Americans. Perhaps never before had a philosophy been applied so hopefully, over so wide an area, to shape the minds of youth to the uses of a greater freedom." In the anthology *Pragmatism and American Culture*, editor Gail Kennedy suggested that the debates about pragmatism came close to putting "American civilization itself . . . on trial." In 1957, the philosopher Morton White added an epilogue to his 1949 book, *Social Thought in America*:

29. Dewey to Hook, Nov. 16, 1939; June 27, 1949; July 2, 1949; Hook to Dewey, July 18, 1949; Reinhold Niebuhr to Dewey, May 22, 1944, Hook mss. Dewey to Houston, Apr. 22, 1946, Dewey mss.

The Revolt against Formalism. Here he took on two critics of pragmatism, Walter Lippmann and Reinhold Niebuhr, by questioning the philosophical validity of natural law and the unscientific status of original sin. During the fifties the Columbia University philosopher Charles Frankel also defended—against, curiously, the assault of both religious and relativist thinkers—pragmatism and the adequacy of old-fashioned rational intelligence in a book with the revealing title, *The Case for Modern Man.* In view of the prestige that pragmatism enjoyed in the fifties, what accounted for its eclipse the following decade?[30]

A partial answer requires considering what came to be regarded as the antithesis of pragmatism—the bugaboo of "ideology." The sixties opened with Daniel Bell's much discussed (and seldom read) *The End of Ideology.* Bell had in mind the "exhaustion" of utopian and cataclysmic ideas once associated with radicalism in general and Marxism in particular. In the long view Bell's forecast proved correct as Marxism eroded not only in the West but even in the third world during the late seventies and eighties. But in the sixties Bell's book helped create the impression that America must continue to remain free of ideology and adhere to its tradition of sober, prudent practicality. Earlier, a year after Dewey's death, Daniel J. Boorstin wrote *The Genius of American Politics* in an effort to warn Americans that fascism and communism were "garret-spawned" ideologies on the part of theory-struck intellectuals, whereas the virtue of America was to accept the "givenness" of experience and be "doctrinally naked." With the cold war seeming to determine intellectual categories, the impression grew that ideology meant a dogmatic and even fanatical refusal to come to terms with reality. After witnessing the horrors of totalitarianism, American writers viewed the communist mentality as "a mania of absolutism" (Reinhold Niebuhr), the curse of the "monist and dogmatist" (Arthur Schlesinger, Jr.), the "tyranny of logicality" (Hannah Arendt), the substitution of mystical "faith" for "critical intelligence" (Hook), and the translation of "universal principles" into their "utter depravity in action" (Hans Morgenthau).[31] In America's political culture ideology came to mean everything alien and dogmatic, whereas pragmatism stood for flexibility,

30. Henry Steele Commager, *The American Mind: An Interpretation of American Thought and Character since the 1880s* (New Haven, 1950), 95–98; Lloyd Morris, *Postscript to Yesterday* (New York, 1947), 368–69; *Pragmatism and American Culture,* ed. Gail Kennedy (Boston, 1950), viii; Morton White, *Social Thought in America: The Revolt against Formalism* (Boston, 1957), 247–80; Charles Frankel, *The Case for Modern Man* (New York, 1956); see also David A. Hollinger, "The Problem of Pragmatism in American History," *Journal of American History* 67 (June 1980): 88–106.

31. Daniel Bell, *The End of Ideology: On the Exhaustion of Political Ideas in the Fifties* (New York, 1960); Daniel J. Boorstin, *The Genius of American Politics* (Chicago, 1953); Reinhold Niebuhr, *The Irony of American History* (New York, 1952), 85; Arthur Schlesinger, Jr., "Varieties of Communist Experience," in *The Politics of Hope* (Boston, 1962), 292; Hannah

adaptability, and the capacity to confront the world without illusions. On the one side absolutism and the mythologies of history, on the other experimentalism and the methodologies of science. In the polarization of images "pragmatic realism" seemed virtually to define America's political character, and since pragmatism had all along prided itself on being able to cope with a world of change, it seemed that modernism had won the war with Marxism.

That impression collapsed in the mid-sixties when young Americans were asked to fight in Vietnam. If the Soviet Union's effort to expand communism appeared doctrinaire, utopian, and brutal at the same time, how could a student view America's effort to expand democracy to a part of the world where the bright sun of liberalism had never shone? Even if the Vietnam War could be regarded as an exercise in power diplomacy rather than democratic idealism, how long must an "experiment" be tried before a people and their leaders admit its failure? Understandably, the New Left of the sixties reversed the ideology-pragmatism distinction and judged America to be utopian and resistant to reason. To bring democracy to the Mekong Delta was another example of "crackpot realism" (C. Wright Mills). American foreign policy seemed less devoted to "pragmatic realism" than to the impossible extremism of the fanatic, whom Santayana once defined as a person who redoubles his effort when he has forgotten his aim. Almost everything that pragmatism stood for—the reliability of experimental method, the objectivity of scientific knowledge, and the superior efficacy of technology—appeared to be the bright illusions of ideology in the dark jungles of Vietnam.[32]

The Vietnam War only magnified a problem that had been potential in pragmatism all along. When pragmatism, or any philosophy, allows itself to enter the arena of politics and becomes identified with a policy decision, whether it be a foreign war or a domestic social program, it risks losing its status as a science concerned only to judge the consequences of an idea after it has been put into practice. For once a decision is made to pursue a policy, those supporting the decision are so identified with it they can hardly judge its outcome objectively. Instead the temptation is to stay the course because pride will not admit human fallibility and politics will not allow public honesty. To be sure, the Vietnam War had been supported by all kinds of political thinkers, even critics of pragmatism. But no other philosophy holds that man knows best what he does

Arendt, *The Origins of Totalitarianism* (New York, 1958), 472–73; Sidney Hook, "Communism and the Intellectual," in *The Intellectuals*, ed. George B. de Husar (New York, 1960), 354–64; Hans Morgenthau, *Politics among Nations* (New York, 1960), 259; see also Fowler, *Believing Skeptics*.

32. C. Wright Mills, "Letter to the New Left," in *The New Left: A Collection of Essays*, ed. Priscilla Long (Boston, 1969), 14–25.

and that the ideas he acts upon are tested in encounters with experience. Yet the premise that experimental knowledge is self-correcting offers no clear guidance as to how to proceed when error has been committed. Of the Vietnam War Sidney Hook recalls in his autobiography: "I agreed that it was a mistake for the United States to get in, but that it would be an even greater mistake to get out before the independence of South Vietnam was recognized." Since North Vietnam had no intention of granting such recognition, the only alternative was to get further in. Thus the war escalated, and the pragmatist's inseparable unity of means and ends—argued so elegantly by Dewey in his debates with Trotsky—broke apart in a political culture that continued the unworkable to reach the unreachable.

History has seldom been kind to the pragmatist, who refuses to show how knowledge becomes possible, actual, and reliable rather than simply virtual and potential. One Vietnam veteran, now a professor, convinced that tragic episodes like that war are possibly beyond understanding, quotes T. S. Eliot: "We had the experience, but missed the meaning." Dewey's idea that experience is something that is "had" rather than "known," and his insistence that ideas must be congruent with experience without specifying what they take away from it, reinforces Lovejoy's thesis that pragmatism deprives knowing of any status other than a wishful projection into the future. "I am about to have known," is Lovejoy's apt formulation of a philosophy that is supposed to be practical, but when applied to politics turns out to be almost futile. Santayana, who had his own political mistakes to account for, at least saw that history, and the events and occurrences that pragmatism promises to comprehend in order to control, cannot be both the basis of knowledge and the criterion to which it appeals. "Experience abounds, and teaches nothing."[33]

As the campus confrontations of the sixties spread across the country, New Left journals denounced the "bankruptcy" of American liberalism and along with it pragmatism. Both were blamed for racism, imperialism, and oppression—the usual round-up of charges. Nothing new could be seen in this stale indictment, which echoed much that Old Left communists said of the "reactionaries" Hook and Dewey.[34] But barely noticed was something startlingly new in the annals of Marxist radicalism. "Rea-

---

33. Sidney Hook, *Out of Step*, 583; the professor quoting Eliot is Michael Norman, "About Face," *New York Times Magazine*, Oct. 11, 1992, p. 14; Lovejoy is quoted in George S. Dicker, "Knowing and Getting to Know in John Dewey's Theory of Knowledge," *Monist* 57 (April 1973): 191–219; George Santayana, "Apologia Pro Mente Sua," in *The Philosophy of George Santayana*, ed. Paul Arthur Schilpp (LaSalle, Ill.: Open Court Press, 1940), 540.

34. John Patrick Diggins, *The Rise and Fall of the American Left* (New York, 1992), 231–38; V. J. McGill, "Pragmatism Reconsidered: An Aspect of John Dewey's Philosophy," *Science and Society* 3 (Summer 1939): 299–322.

son," the great promise of the Enlightenment, was now seen as a form of domination rather than liberation. New Left theorists learned this critique from Herbert Marcuse, Max Horkheimer, and other members of the "Frankfurt School" who arrived in America as refugees from Hitler's Germany and taught the sixties generation the principles of "critical theory." Romantic pessimists, the Frankfurt scholars saw pragmatism as another form of positivism and scientific control, progress as the illusion of change in a world of repetition and regression, and technology, consumption, and popular culture as the pacifying apparati of mass society. The more philosophical of the New Left journals became thick with the language of "alienation," "reification," and "negation." So pervasive was the influence of the Frankfurt School that many New Left activists seemed unaware of their own ideological origins. When Tom Hayden wrote the "Port Huron Statement" in 1962, he followed the advice of Arnold Kaufmann, his University of Michigan philosophy teacher, and drew upon Dewey's political writings to develop the idea of "participatory democracy." But the New Left students who retained an interest in philosophy turned to the Frankfurt scholars and looked to Hegel's dialectical mode of thinking as a deliverance from the blind alley of history.[35]

To suggest that liberal pragmatism became a casualty of the cold war is far from the whole story of the philosophy's decline in the post–World War II era. Since the twenties and thirties disillusioned writers of the "lost generation" and militant Marxists had attacked pragmatism for its unflinching optimism, its superficial faith in science and technology, its innocence of corporate power, and its alleged unconcern about the cultural deprivations of the American environment. In the fifties some elements of this older critique appeared in Trilling's *The Liberal Imagination* (1950) and in Louis Hartz's *The Liberal Tradition in America* (1955). A political liberalism resting on the philosophy of pragmatism placed too much emphasis on action and organization and not enough on reflective ideas that crackled with irony and complexity. As part of the liberal consensus, pragmatism had prevailed only in an American political culture that took its ends for granted as it focused on means. Pragmatism rendered American life prudent, flat, and linear when it should be bold, tense, and paradoxical.[36]

Since the twenties many followers of Freud had doubted that Dewey's vision of man as a biological organism could be reconciled with the psychoanalytical vision of the human psyche as tragically divided. In the

35. The full text of Hayden's "Port Huron Statement" is reprinted in James Miller's excellent book, *Democracy Is in the Streets* (New York, 1987).

36. Lionel Trilling, *The Liberal Imagination: Essays in Literature and Society* (New York, 1950): Louis Hartz, *The Liberal Tradition in America* (New York, 1955).

post–World War II years, pragmatism was further challenged by existentialism, a philosophy more responsive to crisis situations in which man must face the immediate agony of choice instead of deferring to science and its slow accumulation of data. Existentialism opened up a vision of the world that would have been familiar to Adams, James, and Niebuhr, but not necessarily to Dewey, Peirce, and Mead: Beyond everything finite there is nothing ultimate, neither God, nor nature, nor society; only existential reality experienced not as a problematic situation but as a dreadful encounter with the meaninglessness of life as man becomes aware of his finitude, frailty, and fear of approaching death. To the extent that Deweyan pragmatism had been reluctant to address such subjective issues as love, death, and the meaning of existence beyond the biological context, existentialist and Freudian thinkers could rightly wonder whether it had fully addressed the problems of modernism that elude objectivity and reason. Some existentialist theologians even suggested that pragmatic naturalism, rather than relating man to the ongoing processes of nature, left him "a stranger in the universe," a wanderer in the factual world of science in search of the human world of value.[37]

Meanwhile the world of science seemed to be shrinking in its claims to comprehension. The promises of scientific pragmatism proved to be disappointing in the academic disciplines. Ernest Nagel was one of the last of the Columbia University naturalists to defend social inquiry on an empirical basis in his seminal *The Structure of Science* (1961). Nagel held that social and historical events could be explained only if they could be subsumed under some natural law or what philosophers call "nomological statements" pertaining to rules of regularities and of reasoning itself. This "covering-law" theory (William Dray's term) most likely would have pleased Adams and Peirce, who also desired to find a scientific explanation that would connect particular events to general laws as the sufficient condition for their occurrence. But not much came of this empirical theory when applied to research, and before long historians joined nonpragmatic philosophers in insisting that explanations may have more to do with unpredictable and arbitrary decisions and reasons on the part of the individual than with laws supposedly governing or "covering" general causes.

The limitations of pragmatism when applied to the social sciences were nothing compared to the inhibitions of pragmatism when confronting the advent of analytical philosophy. This transatlantic sea change is well known to philosophers. It could be termed the Anglo-Austrian invasion, since it derived from the British philosophers Bertrand Russell and G. E.

---

37. Will Herberg, *Judaism and Modern Man* (New York, 1951), 16–23.

Moore and the brooding Viennese genius Ludwig Wittgenstein. Sensing the long impasse of metaphysical philosophy, such thinkers called for an investigation not of ideas in the mind but of the language through which the mind expresses its thoughts. Russell and Wittgenstein had been impressed with the purity of mathematical knowledge, and they believed that a similar precision of logical technique could be applied to an analysis of language, statements, and propositions. The analysis would confine itself strictly to the clarification and definition of terms and concepts. This devotion to the linguistic scrutiny and taxonomic discrimination of the meaning of words began to dominate American philosophy in the postwar years. According to some critics, analytical philosophy turned the discipline into a boring, bloodless affair of academic disputations that inhibited fresh philosophical thought. "American philosophy is dead," Lewis S. Feuer informed readers of the *New York Times* in 1966. Feuer doubted, perhaps half in jest, that James, Dewey, Freud, or Einstein would be able to obtain a Ph.D. in any of the country's philosophy departments because their ideas would not pass the language test of formal logic.[38] But later in his life Wittgenstein rejected his own philosophy for being content with a passive study of propositions. Language, Wittgenstein now pointed out, neither functions as a picture or mirror of reality nor possesses a logical structure. Rather than correspond to anything, language is itself an activity, and it can only be understood in view of its particular usages in specific situations. With this new appreciation of language as an instrument, as a resourceful tool that makes thought possible, the stage was set for the revival of American pragmatism.

Epistemology Is Dead, Long Live Pragmatism: Richard Rorty's Quarrel with Philosophy as Theory

It is about time to get rid of the habit of overestimating philosophy and thereby asking too much of it. It is necessary in the present plight of the world that there be less philosophy, but more attention to thought, less literature, but more cultivation of the letter.

Future thought is no longer philosophy, because it thinks more originally than metaphysics. But neither can future thought, as Hegel demanded, lay aside the name "love of wisdom" and become wisdom itself in the form of absolute knowledge. Thought is on its descent to the poverty of its provisional essence. Thought gathers language in simple speech. Language is thus the language of Being, as the clouds are the clouds of the sky. Thought by its speaking traces insignificant

38. Lewis S. Feuer, "Death of American Philosophy," *New York Times Magazine* (Apr. 29, 1966), 30.

furrows in language. They seem even more insignificant than
the furrows the peasant with deliberate steps traces in the
field.

                    –Martin Heidegger, "Letter on Humanism" (1947)

In the 1960s, when pragmatism had fallen on hard times, Princeton
University professor Richard Rorty was beginning to work quietly on
ways in which philosophy might overcome its analytic impasse. Few
scholars anticipated that Rorty's work would lead to a reconsideration of
pragmatism as a profound contribution to modern philosophy and as the
answer to the problem of modernism itself. But in the late seventies his
writings were widely discussed, and by the mid-eighties he became the
subject of conference symposia and international philosophy journals as
the term *Rortyan* signified an exciting new development in American philosophy.

Rorty's emergence as the most provocative and controversial modern
American philosopher is remarkable in several ways. Where most philosophers believed it necessary to move beyond pragmatism, Rorty argued
that it was necessary to return to it. Many academic intellectuals felt that
America should learn from European thinkers; Rorty became convinced
that Europe could learn from America as well. And while philosophers
and intellectual historians continued to look for the basis of action in ideas
and theories that might account for human conduct, Rorty claimed there
are no criteria, beyond a person's own beliefs and practices, for judging
conduct or theorizing about events, since knowledge lacks the external
foundations to do so. What Rorty wants to tell modern man could have
been the message that Dewey might have told the young Henry Adams
in the nineteenth century and that John Locke told Englishmen in the
seventeenth century: What we cannot know we need not worry about.
No truth, no sweat.

Rorty's conclusion that philosophical theorizing about truth is a waste
of time took considerable time to reach. It stemmed from his reconsidera-
tions of the whole possibility of knowledge and his assumption that epistemology was dead. No basis of objective knowledge can constrain our
thoughts and guide our actions, for nothing exists inside thought that is
capable of being introspectively discoverable and nothing outside action
capable of being cognitively knowable. We are what we do.

Rorty and many of his readers assumed that this rejection of the theoretical foundations of knowledge derived from twentieth-century European philosophy until it occurred to Rorty himself to demonstrate its
parallels with pragmatism and the rejection of epistemology for experimentation. Many of Rorty's growing number of critics also see as threatening his redefinition of philosophy as an enterprise without a theoretical
base on which knowledge rests. Yet to the student of American intellec-

tual history Rorty's reorientation of philosophy seems less threatening than familiar, as though it sprouted on native ground.

In America the revolt against theory long antedated the arrival of European existential philosophy by way of the neopragmatists of our time. The revolt began after the decline of Puritanism and manifested itself in the founding of the Republic in 1787. At the Philadelphia Convention no one spoke of "clear and distinct" ideas arrived at through Cartesian reasoning. Drawing upon David Hume, the Constitution's framers insisted that all governments rest on "opinion" and not a true knowledge. The *Federalist* authors distrusted the "theoretic politician" who refused to heed the lessons of experience and remained hooked on abstractions. The higher wisdom of classical philosophy proved useless to the framers, who sought not to inform Americans what they "ought" to do but instead to predict what they would do. As will be noted in the next chapter, the framers structured the Constitution without resorting to foundational ideas. Even Jefferson, who had no hand in the Constitution, looked to the life of action to save America from the perils of metaphysics; and, as Adams pointed out, once in office Jefferson abandoned the theory of republicanism as a hindrance to growth and success. Later in the nineteenth century the Transcendentalists also felt, for entirely different reasons, that Americans would do well to leave the authority of theory to the musty doctrines and libraries of the Old World. Emerson wanted Americans to trust themselves and think from within, and Thoreau asked the intellectual why he thought he could sit down to write before he had stood up to live. Their French contemporary Tocqueville observed that "less attention . . . is paid to philosophy in the United States than in any other country in the civilized world." The revolt against philosophical theory culminated in pragmatism, and Giovanni Papini's remark that pragmatism was a philosophy for getting along without philosophy only reinforced Tocqueville's observation that Americans were too result-oriented to be bothered with speculative inquiry. But even with pragmatism's demise in the mid-twentieth century the antitheory animus continued as strong as every.[39]

39. John Patrick Diggins, "Theory and the American Founding," in *Theory in America*, ed. Leslie Berlowitz, Denis Donoghue, and Louis Menand (New York, 1988), 3–25; Alexis de Tocqueville, *Democracy in America*, ed. J. P. Mayer (New York: Anchor, 1969), 429. In his chapter "Concerning the Philosophical Approach of the Americans," Tocqueville observed that people in the new republic never read Descartes because they already had a "philosophical method" influenced by Protestant Christianity and energized by a society pregnant with the promise of prosperity. "Consequently each man undertakes to be sufficient unto himself and glories in the fact that his beliefs about everything are peculiar to himself. No longer do ideas, but interests only, form the links between men, and it would seem that human opinions are no more than a sort of mental dust open to the wind on every side and unable to come together and take shape" (*Democracy in America*, 432–33).

Daniel J. Boorstin's *The Genius of American Politics* sought to explain Americans to themselves. Much like Rorty, Boorstin told the people that they did not need theory because the country had always been more concerned with processes than with purpose. Doctrines, treatises, and systems were alien to a national character more interested in improving life than in perfecting thought. After the decline of Calvinism, the "genius" of Americans was that they came to accept the "growing sense of 'givenness,' the growing tendency to make the 'is' the guide to the 'ought,' to make America as it was (or as they now made it) a criterion of what America might be." Boorstin even used, whether consciously or inadvertently, Hegel's concept of the "Preformation Hypothesis." Boorstin referred to the "preformation ideal" to suggest that values exist in a "perfectly preformed theory" that renders unnecessary the mind's reflective activity. It is "the idea that all parts of an organism pre-exist in perfect miniature in the seed. . . . It assumes that the values and the theory of the nation were given once and for all at the very beginning." Together with the "preformational" concept Boorstin offered a kind of Whitmanesque metaphor that could lead Americans into believing that they were growing not out of but into a theory: "Our theory of society is thus conceived as a kind of exoskeleton, like the shell of a lobster. We think of ourselves as growing *into* our skeleton. But we always supposed that the outlines were rigidly drawn into the beginning."[40]

The suspicion of theory and of the abstractions of philosophy goes deep into American history. Rorty's message about the limitations of philosophy derives in large part from Martin Heidegger, the existentialist who taught that philosophy must be rethought and discourse reexamined to see if words might possibly be immediate to their objects. But Heidegger's suggestion, quoted above, that the furrow dug by the peasant may be more significant than the imprint thought leaves on language is as American as peanut butter. Did not Jefferson advise that on many important questions the plowman is wiser than the professor?

Richard Rorty was born in New York City in 1931. His father, James Rorty, was an ex-Trotskyist and close friend of Hook, "a man upon whose knees," Richard Rorty later recalled, "I was bounced as a baby." In the late eighties Hook and Rorty had friendly debates on interpreting Dewey's legacy. To Hook pragmatism always meant empirical science and the scientific method; Rorty sought to make pragmatism more poststructuralist and language-sensitive. In the fifties Rorty started his graduate work at the University of Chicago and finished at Yale. Studying the history of philosophy reinforced his conviction that the analytic critics

40. Boorstin, *Genius of American Politics*, 1–34.

were correct to see the problems of philosophy deriving from unconscious use of language conventions. But he later became convinced by Wittgenstein that logical empiricism could not fulfill its promise to use language to clarify meaning, since language itself constitutes rather than reflects reality, and its meaning lies not in its logical function but in its practical use. But after this "linguistic turn," what then? Is there any escape from the world of words?[41]

The thought that there was nothing beyond language except death filled Heidegger with dread. In the twenties, at a time when empiricists and pragmatists relegated metaphysical questions to the Middle Ages, Heidegger looked to metaphysics as an inquiry into the void to wonder why "something" should be preferred to "nothing" and what it means not to know but to be. With Heidegger's writings existentialist philosophers pondered the implications of *Dasein*—"being there"—in a time-saturated world with an unchangeable past and an unforeseeable future. In the thirties Heidegger would support the Third Reich, an affiliation that should give Catholic critics of pragmatism some doubts about metaphysics providing immunity to the totalitarian temptation. But Heidegger's metaphysical as well as political desperation suggests that modernism as the problem of philosophical unbelief reflects an earlier loss of religious conviction.

Raised a Catholic and educated in a Jesuit seminary, Heidegger felt the loss of faith almost as deeply as Dewey felt his "inward laceration" and "unnatural wound" when he first thought that nature would have no place for spirit. Heidegger soon discovered that the church had no answers other than dogmatic incantations and that even Kant's arguments for God's existence had no proof other than desperate intuitions. Heidegger's own explorations into the nature of "Being" led him to formulate the notion of *Dasein* to suggest the mundaneness of everyday existence and of humankind's involvements, which conceal from consciousness the deeper awareness of alienation, an awareness brought on by anxiety, particularly about the finality of death. Shakespeare's observation that all life is a preparation for death had its modern expression in Heidegger's sense of philosophy as a meditation on mortality. The inevitable approach of death forces the mind to ask what it wants to choose from life so existence might be "authentic" rather than automatic. But in Heidegger's greatest work, *Being and Time* (1927), the philosopher decides that human existence has no metaphysical grounds; it originates in the abyss of emptiness and

41. Marina Martin, "Intrevista: Richard Rorty el 'liberal trágico,'" *Revista de Occidente* 90 (Nov. 1988): 103–12; Richard Rorty, *Objectivity, Relativism, and Truth* (New York, 1991), 15–17.

culminates in the annihilation of death, a nothingness that man cannot know as fact or experience as emotion.[42]

Heidegger's philosophy seems so morbidly existential as to be closer to Melville's metaphysical angst than to Dewey's methodological wholesomeness. But what Rorty appreciated was Heidegger's sense that philosophy has no way of knowing truth and reality as traditionally conceived to be standing apart from the thinker. It was not, Rorty insists, that Heidegger saw philosophy as having been following a futile course of inquiry and thus in need of being brought back to its proper task. Much like Wittgenstein and Dewey, Heidegger saw philosophy as an illusionary quest in search for something above, beyond, or below, an origin, groundspring, or foundation. Recognizing that both the idealist and the realist offer only a representation of thought and not the thing represented, Heidegger turned to phenomenology to explore the themes of ontology in order to investigate not how truth is found but how "Being" might reveal itself. But he realized that man himself is Being and there is no way to step outside of it to study it.[43]

Although Hook dismissed Heidegger's *Being and Time* as metaphysical rubbish, the text contains some parallels with pragmatism, particularly the rejection of theory and abstract understanding in favor of the ordinary world of experience. Heidegger felt surest about knowledge related to practical activities. "I experience an object most primordially when I am using it," he wrote, with the primordial implying what is closest to the concerns of everyday living. We can know the world only to the extent that we become involved in it by way of the tools and techniques we employ. Thus the primordial is the practical, and for Heidegger human existence is basically worldly, the banal tasks to be performed by man as *homo faber* who encounters life in work and makes and builds so that he may "think for the sake of dwelling."[44]

Wittgenstein's conviction that to know could at most be knowing how to function and carry on, and Heidegger's conviction that awareness of the existential void is necessary to learning endurance and resoluteness, could be assimilated with Dewey's teaching that philosophy is about

42. Martin Heidegger, *Being and Time*, trans. J. Macquarrie and E. S. Robinson (New York, 1962). Before Rorty's impact Heidegger's philosophy was first introduced to Americans by Hannah Arendt, William Barrett, and Marjorie Greene. See the illuminating interview in "Heidegger and Modern Existentialism; A Dialogue with William Barrett," in Bryan Magee, *Men of Ideas: Some Creators of Contemporary Philosophy* (New York, 1982), 57–75.

43. Richard Rorty, *Philosophy and the Mirror of Nature* (Princeton, 1979), 357–94; *The Consequences of Pragmatism: Essays 1972–1980* (Minneapolis, 1982), xxi–xxii, esp. chap. 3 on the comparison of Heidegger and Dewey, 37–54.

44. Martin Heidegger, *Poetry, Language, Thought*, trans. Albert Hofstadter (New York, 1971), 145–86; *An Introduction to Metaphysics*, trans. R. Mannheim (New York, 1961).

adapting and coping. Dewey, Heidegger, and Wittgenstein also insisted, as Rorty notes, that philosophy is similar to human existence in that it can be understood only historically, that is, in the context of changing situations as the mind responds to problems and expresses needs and desires. Philosophy requires no theoretical foundations if it attends to practice and studies how knowledge is used.[45]

Rorty could well have made a case for reviving pragmatism by drawing upon American intellectual history. Ben Franklin, after all, advised Americans that the test of an idea is not its truth but its usefulness. But Rorty had his own reasons for turning to French poststructuralists like Jacques Derrida, whose philosophical mission was to demonstrate not the utility of knowledge but its duplicity. With Derrida the postmodernist mind reaches the Hegelian heights of self-awareness, and once the mind attains knowledge of itself and its operations, it experiences the exhilaration of "the self-destruction of reflection" (Rodolphe Gasché).[46] Once it is recognized that knowledge is made rather than found, that thinking can express no truth apart from the conditions of its production, and that language makes and unmakes the world according to human needs, we can see why postmodern philosophy commits suicide as the only way to extirpate the false dualisms that trouble the mind. And this war against dualism is as much religious as philosophical.

Curiously, Dewey came from a devout Protestant background and Derrida from an orthodox Jewish heritage.[47] Both looked to philosophy to overcome the supposedly false oppositions imposed by religion (good and evil, spirit and flesh, etc.), what some poststructuralists call "binary oppositions." And both would abolish the various conceptions of certitude, even that of presence itself. Everything is "always already," Derrida insists, since what exists or happens can only come before our thoughts as represented. Derrida claimed that "Being" itself is an illusion of Western metaphysics, for there exists only writing, linguistic traces of a subject long gone as the author disappears into a text open to multiple interpretations. Almost a century earlier James wrote of the "specious present" and Dewey of the "present-as-absent" to suggest, among other things, that consciousness of temporal experience can never be "now" since awareness is retrospective, a mode of memory rather than a moment of perception. But initially poststructuralism arrived in America not by way of Chicago pragmatism or even New England transcendentalism—Emerson's "oversoul" had also abolished time and tried to inform Americans that presence,

45. Rorty, Consequences of Pragmatism, 37–54.
46. Rodolphe Gasché, The Tain of the Mirror: Derrida and the Philosophy of Reflection (Cambridge, 1986), 35–54.
47. On Dewey's religious background, see Kuklick, From Churchmen to Philosophers.

like common life itself, is an "endless succession of phantasms." Instead poststructuralism arrived in large part from France and the new school of thought known as "deconstruction."[48]

If Nietzsche's problem was that God is dead, Derrida's pleasure is that language is alive, so alive, boundless, indeterminate, and opaque that any attempt to interpret its message is an attempt to impose one's own interpretation and treat it as a discovery. The will to believe in God and the will to interpret a text turns out to be merely the will to power disguised as prayer or profundity. Starting with Ferdinand Saussure's thesis that language is a system of self-constituting signs, Derrida demonstrated that the signifiers—statements, words, gestures, or whatever—bounce off one another rather than refer to the object signified. Derrida claimed that once the unintended movements of signifiers, the associations, affiliations, images, and puns in a written text, are revealed, the author's own purpose and presence has disappeared from the text. Thus the reader is left staring at words without objective references, and as the eyes blink there is only rhetoric without reality, names without things, metaphors that arise out of metaphorization, an endless chain of signs and signifiers in which meaning is hopefully deferred until it is discovered to be hopelessly absent.

Although Derrida's teachings caught on primarily among American literary critics, he actually set out to undermine philosophy, both ancient and modern. Classical philosophers believed truth accessible to reason once the "idols" of opinion were toppled; modern, analytical philosophers believed meaning could be established by removing metaphysics and purifying language by discovering the rules by which pure speech may be established. Derrida insisted that speech is itself an ungovernable script, that there is no such thing as unmediated expression and transparent language, and that truth cannot be grounded in reality whose representation consists in a web of signifiers that refer to each other and not to something beyond appearances and opinion. With the real not so much represented as dissolving before our eyes, meaning disappears from writing and a text can be shown to be saying nothing. Derrida's method was to uncover systematic incoherences within a text, rhetorical devices, "metaphorical redoubling," and other sudden twists, reversals, and betrayals that bring out the tensions in Western metaphysical thought. He sought to "deconstruct" the philosophical presuppositions that inhere in a text to show that there is nothing outside the text that justifies its

48. Jacques Derrida, *Of Grammatology*, trans. G. C. Spivak (Baltimore, 1982); on James and Dewey and the absence of presence, see Arthur O. Lovejoy, *The Reason, the Understanding, and Time* (Baltimore, 1961), 194–95; Ralph Waldo Emerson, "The Over-Soul," in *Ralph Waldo Emerson: Selected Prose and Poetry*, ed. Reginald L. Cook (New York, 1966), 125–43.

linguistic constructions. When words become unpersuasive, the philosopher, Derrida observed of Aristotle, searches for other words, expressions, and metaphors in a ceaseless "play of substitutions."[49] Convinced that reality itself is a textual construction, Derrida set out to deconstruct metaphysics by demonstrating that traditional binary oppositions— mind/body, presence/absence, existence/essence, male/female, good/evil, knowledge/power—were false dualisms sanctioned by social practice.

Rorty titled his essay on Derrida "Philosophy as a Kind of Writing." Influenced by Thomas Kuhn's *The Structure of Scientific Revolutions*, Rorty claimed that philosophy has been governed by paradigmatic linguistic conventions just as physics tries to find the significance of invisible things by developing new models to read "the Book of Nature." Rorty wanted philosophers to recognize that after Wittgenstein, Heidegger, and Derrida, philosophy had lost its innocent assumption that it can tell the truth. For telling and proving by words is simply a narration that cannot be tested for representing accurately what exists beyond the text. Thus philosophy should become the self-conscious activity of language, a way of writing and not necessarily a way of knowing. The deepest matters of metaphysics and ontology, God's existence and man's ultimate significance, are unknowable because inexpressible. Language conventions are so conditioned that the philosopher as writer can only name and rename God and man rather than show or prove them to be immediate to expression and thus cognitively possible objects. "Derrida is in the same situation in regards to language that many of us secularists are in in regards to God," observed Rorty.

> It isn't that we believe in God, or don't believe in God, or have suspended judgment about God, or consider that the God of theism is an inadequate symbol of our ultimate concern; it is just that we wish we didn't have to have a view about God. It isn't that we know that "God" is a cognitively meaningless expression, or that it has its role in a language-game other than fact-stating, or whatever. We just regret the fact that the word is used so much. So it is for Derrida with the vocabulary of Kantian philosophy. His attitude toward centuries of worry about the relation of subject and object, representations and the real, is like the Enlightenment attitude toward centuries of worry about the relation between God and man, faith and reason.[50]

49. Jacques Derrida, *Margins of Philosophy*, trans. Alan Bass (Chicago, 1982), 242–43, 249.

50. Rorty, *Consequences*, 97–98.

Henry Adams, one remembers, wondered whether God could be a person or a thing and knew that modern philosophy could demonstrate nothing on the subject. The situation in the Middle Ages was different. To the medieval philosopher, Adams wrote, "words had fixed values, like numbers, and syllogisms were hewn stones that needed only to be set in place, in order to reach any height or support any weight."[51] But in modern thought words cannot reach any truth or support any proposition.

How, then, can postmodern philosophy deal with power? That question makes Rorty's comparison of Dewey to Michel Foucault all the more perplexing. Somewhat like Adams and Niebuhr, and completely unlike Dewey, Foucault saw the hidden movement of power as the historian's challenge to disclose, and power had less to do with class conflict than with common attitudes, sentiments, and visions toward authoritative symbols that had the capacity to elicit compliance and obedience. Foucault also saw reason culminating in science and technology to the exclusion of all that was irrational and eccentric. But Foucault's focus was primarily language, particularly the episteme and discursive formations that shape rules and classifications, which in turn permit some phenomena to be seen as true, rational, and moral and others as false, deviant, and immoral. Foucault was indifferent to the whole issue of causation, and thus he treated language as an activity without an agency, an effect-producing process with no apparent human purpose. Foucault depicted the human subject disappearing from history altogether. All that will remain is power, not so much in the vulgar sense of an omnipresent system of coercion but as an unseen force that follows the logic of organization and silently imposes itself on social relations, not domination but a "capillary" insinuation from the center outward. The ascendancy of power and the eclipse of man as subject meant the death of humanism, which traditionally implied some external standard of reason from which the meaning and direction of history could be explained. For Foucault knowledge cannot penetrate power because what comes to be accepted as truth is itself a product of the relentless activity of power as the capacity to win and command such acceptance. The idea of a rational man in control of his destiny will soon fade away, Foucault chillingly observed, like a human image on the sand erased by the incoming tide.[52]

What Rorty found attractive in Foucault was their common conviction that knowledge derives from language and discourse and that traditional

51. Adams, *Mont-Saint-Michel and Chartres*, 325.
52. Michel Foucault, *The Order of Things: An Archaeology of the Human Sciences* (New York: Vintage, 1973), 387; Foucault's description of power as "capillary" is in *Power/Knowledge: Selected Interviews and Other Writings, 1972–1977: Michel Foucault*, ed. Colin Gordon (New York, 1980), 39.

notions of rationality, objectivity, and representation must be rejected.
Rorty quoted Foucault as saying that "we should not imagine that the
world presents us with a legible face . . . [we] must conceive discourse
as a violence we do to things." Rorty completely agreed with Foucault
that the world is not discovered in thought but instead emerges in discourse, and he proceeded to explain why "we should see Dewey as having
already gone the route Foucault is traveling," that is, "against the notion
of knowledge as correspondence to nonrepresentations," a route in which
there is no transcendental subject but simply a traveler negotiating a
text.[53]

Rorty's *Philosophy and the Mirror of Nature* (1979) first put forth the case
for seeing Dewey as a precursor of poststructuralism. The thesis would
be elaborated in subsequent books and articles, but that book, as well as
Rorty's address to the American Philosophical Association in the same
year, jarred his colleagues with the call for the "end of philosophy." Rorty
used the writings of European poststructuralists and those of Dewey to
argue that the whole tradition of Western philosophy, which began with
Descartes and reached its complete expression in Kant, could now be
dismissed since it was clear that all representational theories of knowledge
had collapsed. Truth as a matter of correspondence to reality proved to
be a metaphysical illusion, with mind pictured as a "glassy essence" that
could mirror the objects it sought to know. In place of traditional philosophy, Rorty called for a hermeneutical approach to knowledge that acknowledged the impossibility of discovering absolutely indubitable, universally valid, objective truths and instead confined itself to refining
discussion and interpretation. The Rortyan turn was offered as "an expression of hope that the cultural space left by the demise of epistemology
will not be filled—that our culture should become one in which the demand for constraint and confrontation is no longer felt." Philosophy could
continue not as knowledge and vision but as voice and conversation, especially "the conversation of mankind." The aim is not to prove what one
knows but to justify what one says. "If we see knowing not as having an
essence, to be described by scientists or philosophers, but rather as a
right, by current standards, to believe, then we are well on the way to
seeing *conversation* as the ultimate context in which knowledge is to be
understood."[54]

Rorty would have nothing to do with Peirce's version of pragmatism.[55]

53. Rorty, *Consequences of Pragmatism*, 205.
54. Rorty, *Philosophy and the Mirror of Nature*, 315, 389.
55. On Peirce, Rorty takes a different position than other neopragmatists like the American Richard Bernstein and Europeans such as Karl-Otto Apel and Jürgen Habermas. See
Habermas and Modernity, ed. Richard Bernstein (Cambridge, 1985).

Peirce had once held out the possibility that knowledge could converge upon the real, providing inquiry continued unobstructed and indefinitely. Dewey, too, believed in the efficacy of scientific investigation and not necessarily in the possibility of rhetorical persuasion alone. Another philosopher who has done much to revive pragmatism, the Frankfurt School disciple Jürgen Habermas, sought to carry on the Peircean method of philosophy and extend it beyond science to the sphere of social problems. If Rorty desired to bring poststructuralism to America to reaffirm pragmatism, Habermas sought to bring pragmatism to Europe to get rid of poststructuralism.

In Defense of the Enlightenment: Jürgen Habermas and the Promise of Communicative Action

American academic poststructuralists might have agreed that classical philosophy had come to an end, but they disagreed about where to turn for a solution. While several literary scholars tended to embrace Derrida, Foucault, and the omnipresence of language as either the illusion of authorial presence or a subtle domination by representation, some scholars in history and the social sciences found Habermas's writings more congenial to their political hopes for overcoming modernity.[56] Habermas had been associated with the Frankfurt School of "critical theory," whose members, German refugee intellectuals in America, had enormous influence on the sixties generation—a further reason why pragmatism suffered an eclipse until the eighties, when Rorty made it clear that pragmatism cannot be equated with positivism.

The Frankfurt thinkers opposed a scientific, positivistic reading of Marxism that substituted dogmatic certainty for dialectical irony, Stalin for Hegel. Their idea of "critical theory" aimed to liberate consciousness from economic and historical materialism. In addition to revising Marxist orthodoxy, critical theorists like Adorno and Horkheimer indicted the eighteenth-century Enlightenment as an intellectual scandal for treating nature as "mere objectivity" and thereby turning knowledge into power, allegedly the first step in the domination of man by man. Although the leading heir of the Frankfurt school, Habermas became critical of his mentors' scorn for the Enlightenment, and indeed set out to show how reason and the values of systematic philosophy might be restored.[57]

56. See the special issue "On Habermas," *Telos*, no. 49 (1981), 3–60.
57. The literature on the Frankfurt School is vast; the best place to begin is Martin Jay, *The Dialectical Imagination: A History of the Frankfurt School and the Institute of Social Research, 1923–1950* (Boston, 1973); and David Held, *Introduction to Critical Theory: Horkheimer to Habermas* (Berkeley, 1980).

"Marxism exists in nineteenth-century thought like a fish in water: that is, it is unable to breathe anywhere else."[58] So proclaimed Foucault. Habermas wanted to prove that the fish could breathe healthily in the mid-twentieth century providing that Marx's theory be reconstructed. Habermas's *Knowledge and Human Interests* (1968) aimed to reorient Marxist thought from labor and the forces of production to action and the possibilities of reflection. The Marxist tradition, concentrating on historical development and the "iron laws" of nature, ignored human agents as capable of reflecting upon their historical situation and, by acting upon it, playing a causal role in the transformation of society. Habermas also wanted to dispel the fear of instrumental rationality, the Weberian notion that scientific knowledge could offer nothing more than the manipulation of technical control, a tendency that could turn every modern society into the "iron cage" of soulless bureaucracy. In addition, he addressed the problem that plagued Adams: the specter of interests and power determining historical events while the masses of people remain unaware of the meaning of their situation and even of their actions. The victory of material interests in America's political culture troubled Adams as a violation of both the classical principle of virtue and duty and the Christian principle of love and sacrifice. In Habermas there is no hint that interests are degrading or even distorting.

Habermas set out to resolve the issue much as Dewey had done in his early college lectures on the eighteenth-century problem of altruism versus egoism. For Habermas, too, interests coincide with cognition, since all knowledge arises out of problems that humans encounter in a changing environment. Knowledge can be neither purely objective nor disinterested but instead is historically situated and interest-grounded. Human needs and purposes constitute knowledge through which reality is interpreted and acted upon, and it is through work and interaction that the human species reproduces itself. Although Habermas was addressing both Kant and Marx (the former because of his ahistorical conception of how knowledge is obtained, the latter because he analyzed action only in relation to labor and necessity), his new social theory had relevance for American political thought as well. The framers of the Constitution believed that because human nature is governed by "passions and interests" political behavior would be irrational, that is, incapable of devoting itself to the public good; hence all collective activity ("factions") must be controlled by the "new science of politics." The science of control Habermas dismissed as the fixation of positivism that ignored the possibility of human reflection and understanding as men interact as social beings. Out of

58. Foucault, *The Order of Things*, 262.

necessity men may act from interests, but somehow rational self-reflection elevates action to higher comprehension of human possibility that promises liberation from domination. Interest-bound knowledge moves from labor and practical technique to communication and mutual self-reflection, processes that enable men and women to come to an awareness of their situation and to create knowledge that furthers their capacity for rational and responsible action.[59]

Habermas's analysis in *Knowledge and Human Interests* is partly and inadvertently Deweyan and fully and consciously Meadean in its emphasis on social interaction as dialogical and communicative. But the American philosopher he first drew upon was Peirce, the founder of pragmatism, who perhaps did more than any other thinker to address the problem of reality and its uncertain representations, the whole modernist dilemma of the world-word relationship, of truth as correspondence to something external to language.

Habermas praised Peirce as the "first to treat the dimensions of a self-reflecting philosophy of science." In contrast to the positivist Ernst Mach, who gave little thought to the role that the knowing investigator plays in constituting the world, Peirce showed how it was possible in science to allow for such a subjective role and still come to objective conclusions. As indicated in chapter 4, Peirce sought not so much to plumb the metaphysical depths of philosophy as to refine and render systematic the methodology of scientific inquiry. Habermas welcomed Peirce's efforts to clarify the "logic of procedure with whose aid we obtain scientific theories." All human thought, Peirce and Habermas agree, contains arbitrary and accidental elements, but with enough information and sustained, systematic inquiry, opinions will gravitate toward truth defined as "final agreement"—until further evidence and argument calls for reconsideration and revision. Science need not require a transcendental consciousness since reality discloses itself in the process of inquiry. And since there are no uninterpreted facts, even scientific knowledge has a semiotic component. While Habermas agrees with Peirce that all knowledge is discursive, it does not follow that all knowledge is mind-dependent. For Habermas also agrees with Peirce that often the stimulus to thought originates beyond the "compass of interpretations," which attests to reality independent of mind. Reality's capacity to resist false interpretation, what Peirce described as truth's struggle for recognition, awakens doubt about habitual thought and hence prompts inquiry. What makes scientific progress possible is not the production of true statements about reality but the willing-

---

59. Jürgen Habermas, *Knowledge and Human Interests*, trans. Jeremy Shapiro (Boston, 1971), 3–90.

ness of investigators to arrive at an uncompelled consensus that satisfies doubt and settles opinion. Thus Peirce helped modern thought overcome the Cartesian obsession with foundationalism and indubitability. True scientific inquiry approaches reality not as foundational but as hypothetical, not what *is* in and of itself but what becomes represented in propositions that are always testable and falsifiable.[60]

While Habermas appreciated Peirce's basing scientific inquiry in the context of a practical, problem-solving activity, he sought to move beyond Peirce and to show why inquiry need not culminate in "success" and technical control and why the operations of mind need not be regarded as similar to the properties of matter. To Habermas matter may be known through inductive, deductive, and abductive statements as well as syllogistic reasoning; but mental activity is essentially dialogic and is distinguished from the objectified processes of nature. The community of investigators must therefore use language that avoids replicating the material universe so that scientific inquiry may recognize its "transcendental functions." Rather than imitate the mechanisms of nature, scientific language "arises from symbolic interaction between societal subjects who reciprocally know and recognize each other as unmistakable individuals. This *communicative action* is a system of reference that cannot be reduced to the framework of *instrumental action*." Science cannot be reduced to mere prediction and control as long as investigators recognize that human life, unlike the events of nature, requires interpretation, meaning, and understanding, which in turn must involve the communication of individuals with one another.[61]

Habermas's reorientation of Marxism from labor and production to language and communication had been facilitated by another American pragmatist, George Herbert Mead. In addition to drawing upon the European hermeneutical tradition, where understanding involves the interpretation of meaning and no truth-claim can be immune to criticism, Habermas found in Mead's *Mind, Self, Society* the basis for his argument that understanding of meaning can only come from conscious verbal interaction.[62] Desiring to free the concept of rationality from its instrumental connotation of integration and technical control, Habermas was forced, he told an interviewer, "to stick more closely to the history of theory, for example to George Herbert Mead's theory of symbolically mediated interaction, in order to show that the pragmatic tradition already contained this concept of rationality."[63] Mead's notion of symbolic interaction

60. Ibid., 90–139.
61. Ibid., 137.
62. Jürgen Habermas, "Summation and Response," *Continuum* 8 (1980): 126.
63. *Habermas: Autonomy and Solidarity: Interviews with Jürgen Habermas*, ed. Peter Dews (London, 1986), 104.

opened up the possibility of seeing communication as mediated by linguistic symbols and gestures that make the content of verbal exchange have the same meaning to different individuals engaged in discourse. Thus from the materials of American philosophy and sociology Habermas was able to develop his concept of communicative rationality that would be bound to "an ideal speaking-situations, and that means a way of life in which unforced universal agreement is possible."[64]

Why should speech be capable of redeeming alienated humankind from its frailties and fantasies? Habermas elaborated his argument in *The Theory of Communicative Action* (1981). Here he no longer emphasizes the self-reflection that occupied *Knowledge and Human Interests* and instead concentrated on the intersubjective nature of communication as a dialogic process. The later book was also more concerned with conditions and competencies than with consciousness, that is, with the rules and setting that minimize distorted communication and make possible an optimum speech environment. Habermas termed his project "universal pragmatics," a phrase that presumes the existence of universal conditions of meaning and understanding and the possibility that speech can do the work of philosophy and free man from the bondage of false opinion. At the risk of oversimplification, one might say that communication is to Habermas what education was to Dewey: progressive stages of moral growth.

Habermas sought to reconstruct language, not deconstruct it. Communication presupposes that speakers justify their positions and truth-claims, that they be accountable for what they say. Habermas is, of course, treating communication as speech and not writing, and thus the speaker, unlike the author, remains a witness to his own statements and can be interrogated instead of disappearing from the text under the suspicious gaze of the deconstructionist. But "interrogation" is too strong a word to capture Habermas's sense of a communicative community as a gentle endeavor to reach mutual understanding through the acceptance of rules of speech, argument, validity claims, and models of linguistic interaction involving comprehensibility, appropriateness, and sincerity. "The goal of coming to an understanding is to bring about agreement that terminates in the intersubjective mutuality of reciprocal understanding, shared knowledge, mutual trust, and accord with one another." If truth cannot be found in philosophy it can be talked into existence in sociology. To agree is to accept.[65]

Habermas may have succeeded in assimilating his version of pragma-

64. Habermas, "Summation and Response," 126.

65. Jürgen Habermas, *The Theory of Communicative Action*, vol. 1: *Reason and the Rationalisation of Society* (Cambridge, 1984); Habermas's description of the goal of communication is in his "What Is Universal Pragmatics?" in *Communication and the Evolution of Society* (Boston, 1979), 3.

tism with that of Mead in order to reaffirm the possibility of democracy and philosophy. But unless one assumes that all of American history exudes a pragmatic ethos, one can ask what Emerson and Tocqueville would say to the idea that conscience must yield to conversaton and that public opinion is rational and tolerant rather than arbitrary and tyrannical. The philosopher that Habermas set out to refute was actually the German philosopher who admired Emerson for worshiping the "Oversoul" because he agreed with Tocqueville that democracy is a threat to the solitary self—Friedrich Nietzsche.[66]

In *The Philosophical Discourse of Modernity* (1987), Habermas went after the "French Nietzscheans" Derrida and Foucault. Their intellectual crime? Obliterating the categories of knowledge and treating morality and the life of reason as the will to power, which the will itself "so radiantly conceals." Nietzsche himself betrayed all allegiance to the Enlightenment. His "drive to metaphorize" deconstructed the claims of language and communication, reducing statements to the fictions of figural representations. The French Neitzscheans carry on this wreckage of wisdom. Foucault with his obsession with power, and Derrida with his playful annihilation of meaning, surrender reason to language, logic to rhetoric, and thought to text. This Nietzschean engagement in a sustained act of intelligence in order to deny the value of intelligence is, according to Habermas, "a performative contradiction."[67]

Following the debates over poststructuralism, a student of American history cannot help but wonder what all the fuss is about. Centuries before Nietzsche, New England Calvinists used the faculty of reason to criticize reason, as did the framers of the Constitution. The poststructuralist assault on Descartes would surprise neither Adams nor Dewey, who were amused to read the philosopher trying to prove through reason the validity of a religious faith that denied the authority of reason. Habermas fears that the French Nietzscheans, in subverting the principle of the Enlightenment, leave the moden condition in a universe of power and domination with knowledge reduced to an illusion. But in American history this situation had been faced and surmounted. Among the first doubters of the efficacy of reason and the adequacy of language were American historians concerned about the foundations of American history. More than a half-century before Derrida and Foucault, these historians found themselves stumbling into the void of nothingness, feeling the omnipresence of power, traversing the quicksands of relativism, and yet still believing in progress!

66. Nietzsche on Emerson is in *The Portable Nietzsche*, ed. Walter Kauffmann (New York, 1954), 522.

67. Jürgen Habermas, *The Philosophical Discourse of Modernity: Twelve Lectures* (Cambridge, 1987), 51–74, 83–105, 122, 185.

The Case of the
Progressive Historians

It may seem strange to bring into a discussion of European poststructuralism the American progressive historians Charles Beard and Carl Becker. Does not such a treatment yank them out of their context in American history in the early part of the twentieth century? Not necessarily. The American historians were familier with Nietzsche and various currents of European relativist thought, and as with the poststructuralists, for the progressives the problem of history also begins with the problem of the Enlightenment.

The progressive historians Beard and Becker did as much to challenge the Enlightenment as any European poststructuralist. Both had great admiration for Henry Adams, possibly because all three historians wanted to believe in the values of the Enlightenment, only to discover that their investigations showed ideas being betrayed by action. Language, particularly the language of politics, seldom corresponded to behavior. Thus Adams compared Jefferson's theoretical writings against his political conduct to suggest that doctrine had little bearing upon deed. Beard claimed it a "myth" to think that one could establish the original intentions of the framers of the Constitution, and "the idea that it could be understood by a study of its language . . . is equally mythical." Becker critically examined the truths of the Declaration of Independence against its cognitive claims and left the document in doubt about its self-evident truths. The Declaration, like the Constitution, had more to do with rationalization in the service of interest and power than with reason and truth. The Declaration is so rhetorically plotted, Becker argued, that the reader is not to know and perhaps the author not to acknowledge the actual motives for rebellion: the denial of legitimate authority in England in the vocabulary of tyranny and the transfer of power to America in the name of liberty. Reading the text against itself, Becker brought out what went unsaid so as to show that the language, despite its felicity of expression, may have borne no testimony to what was going on.[68]

Consider as well Becker's devastating critique of the Enlightenment in *The Heavenly City of the Eighteenth-Century Philosophers.* Becker depicts French thinkers using secular language to worship new ideas in order to satisfy the same older religious hunger for meaning and purpose that characterized the Middle Ages. Thus virtue replaces grace, perfection substitutes for salvation, and "Nature" and "Reason" take the place of God and religion as the ultimate authority. Were the *philosophes* schizoid? Their epistemology taught them that man and nature were one; their

68. Charles A. Beard, *An Economic Interpretation of the Constitution* (New York, 1913), 1–18; Carl L. Becker, *The Declaration of Independence* (New York, 1922).

politics forced them to consider existing society as unnatural. Driven by "the will to know," were the *philosophes* obeying knowledge or using it? In "The Dilemma of Diderot," Becker describes *Rameau's Nephew* as a study in beyond good and evil, a protagonist who turns the categories of the Enlightenment back upon itself. If truth is what is useful and happiness is virtue, everything is permissible. The Enlightenment's premises contradicted its promises. The *philosophe's* illusion of disinterestedness and objectivity continued in Western historiography. Becker quoted Nietzsche's description of the scientific historian: "a mirror: accustomed to prostration before something that wants to be known, . . . he waits until something comes, and then expands himself sensitively, so that even the light footsteps and gliding past of spiritual things may not be lost in his surface and film." The notion that the object of knowledge could be obtained without being interpreted, that truth was there to be found, was to Becker an illusion at once amusing and appalling:

> Thus the scientific historian deliberately renounced philosophy only to submit to it without being aware. . . . With no other preconception than the will to know, the historian would reflect in his surface and film that "order of events throughout past times in all places"; so that, in the fulness of time, when innumerable patient expert scholars by "exhausting the sources," should have reflected without refracting the truth of all the facts, the definitive and impregnable meaning of human experience would emerge of its own accord to enlighten and emancipate mankind. Hoping to find something without looking for it, expecting to obtain final answers to life's riddle by resolutely refusing to ask questions—it was surely the most romantic species of realism yet invented, the oddest attempt ever made to get something for nothing![69]

In exposing the hopeful certitudes of the Enlightenment, in showing the Revolution as a declaration of knowledge in the service of power and the Constitution as a discourse on liberty at the service of property, Becker and Beard desanctified and demystified the American past with all the debunking delight of a contemporary deconstructionist. Like the poststructuralist, Becker and Beard doubted that the role of reason explained the past, that language mirrored reality, and that truth could be discovered as an act of research rather than produced as an act of rhetoric. But there remains a telling twist.

69. Carl L. Becker, *The Heavenly City of the Eighteenth Century Philosophers* (New Haven, 1932); Becker's "The Dilemma of Diderot" is in *Everyman His Own Historian: Essays on History and Politics* (Chicago, 1966), 262–83; his discussion of Nietzsche and his own statement is in the title essay, "Everyman His Own Historian," 249–50.

Where French deconstructionists complain that they cannot find truth but only power, Becker and Beard later recognized that they were naive to think that reason would fulfill the Enlightenment's promise to provide an answer to power. That knowledge would be incapable of generating its own opposition to power because knowledge itself is a form of power came to seem to them as inescapable as the relationship of liberty to property. In *Progress and Power* (1936), Becker explained how humankind from the beginning of known history had implemented itself with power and, as Francis Bacon long ago pointed out, how human knowledge and human power come together as an instrument of inquiry and change. The deconstructionist notion that Enlightenment knowledge was logically distinct from power rested on the assumption that whatever came to be known must be accepted under conditions free of distortion and coercion. But that assumption, having never taken root in the American Enlightenment, which had been infused with strong doses of Scottish and Calvinist skepticism, scarcely stymied Becker and Beard. Power was not only essential to progress but it did not require knowledge, or at least, as will be discussed in the next chapter, foundational knowledge, for its control.

Could America dispense with the Enlightenment? It should be remembered that when Becker advised Americans to continue to believe in the ideals of the Enlightenment, after the outbreak of World War II and the threat of totalitarianism, it was not because he himself now believed that the Declaration had philosophical foundations but simply that its pronouncements "still glitter." Similarly, Beard advised that the Constitution can be defended as a "useful fiction" requiring no metaphysical grounding. "All our comprehensive ideas or theories that purport to universal history, including . . . American history specifically, are in the nature of fictions, that is, interpretations into which enter either elements of knowledge, imagination, conviction or belief." Becker's "Everyman His Own Historian" asked professional historians to join the average citizen and serve as "bards and story tellers of an earlier age" in narrating a useful past for present purposes. Like Rorty and today's liberal poststructuralists, Becker and Beard ended their careers believing that scientific method is enhanced by prescriptive rhetoric as facts and fictions blur, and empirical verification competes with the literary imagination.[70]

Thus in certain respects Becker and Beard made "the linguistic turn" in contemporary thought almost a half-century before the modernist philosopher advocated it. It seems ironic that pragmatism, which at one time had promised to translate all problems of knowledge into problems of

70. Charles A. Beard, *The Republic* (New York, 1943), 339; Carl L. Becker, "What Is Still Living in the Political Philosophy of Thomas Jefferson?" American Philosophical Society, *Proceedings* 84 (1943): 201–10; Becker, *Everyman His Own Historian*, 251.

scientific investigation, ended up having literature replace science. But where else could the historian go if the past remained inaccessible to scientific observation and experimentation? Whether or not Becker and Beard saw how pragmatism had paved the way for the skeptical assault on the philosophical status of ideas, they themselves carried out its logic. Once one looks for the meaning of language in its usage, and once one sees the inseparability of knowledge and interests, there is no difficulty in seeing the Declaration and the Constitution as justifications and rationalizations. Dewey himself dismissed as unknowable nonsense many of the Enlightenment's major assumptions, particularly the social contract theory of the origins of government, the doctrine of natural rights, and the Newtonian worldview of the unified, coherent universe. His collaborator Arthur Bentley dismissed such notions as the "spooks" of metaphysics.[71]

Jürgen Habermas, of course, is well aware that all forms of modern thought have turned the eighteenth century into a lost intellectual world; but he believes the philosophies of Peirce and Mead can help in the restructuring of modern social theory. Richard Rorty similarly is aware that the ideas of the past are lost once a deconstructionist shows a thinker to be assuming he is proving truths when he is actually producing words; but he too believes that pragmatism has not exhausted its promise of bringing knowledge to bear upon modernity. One philosopher places his hopes in communication, the other in conversation. Confronting the dilemma of modernity, both believe philosophy can talk its way out of the problems it has thought itself into. Can it?

71. John Dewey and Arthur F. Bentley, *A Philosophical Correspondence*, ed. Sidney Ratner and Jules Altman (New Brunswick, N.J., 1964).

11

Conclusion: Poststructuralism and America's Intellectual Traditions

Philosophy as "Prophylactic": The Lost Legacy
of the American Founders

When did philosophy allegedly come to an "end"? Did it do so in 1979, when Richard Rorty, drawing on Heidegger and Wittgenstein as well as Dewey, announced its terminal illness? Or did it do so in 1788, two centuries earlier, when the American founders announced its finite limitations in the creation of a government? Although a concluding chapter usually brings things forward to the present, in the instance of this study the present can best be clarified, and perhaps made more at ease with itself, by returning to the past.

The recent effort to assimilate American pragmatism with European poststructuralism aimed to demonstrate how conventional philosophical investigation had reached an impasse with Dewey and James on this side of the Atlantic, and with Nietzsche and Heidegger on the other. The "French Nietzscheans" Foucault and Derrida can be seen to be dealing with the world linguistically just as the earlier pragmatists dealt with it instrumentally because both had to confront a world that could only be described and acted upon. For both schools of thought history is there to be overcome, since the ideas held by past thinkers (with some exceptions) rested on the false consciousness of foundationalism.

Is it really the case that the past has little to teach the present? When one studies the problems of postmodernism from the perspective of American intellectual history, the theoretical crises of our times seem less urgent. Could it possibly be that some American thinkers lived with the

427

postmodern condition in premodern times? Consider the prevalent themes in European thought for the past two decades:

(1) The rejection of philosophy as the search for foundations, whether they be origins or ends, or absolute, indubitable, necessary truths.

(2) The deconstruction of language in order to expose the absence of intention, the indeterminacy of meaning, and the unreliability of words without reference to objects beyond the text.

(3) The reality and ubiquity of power, whether submission of the subject or the autonomy of the system, whether coercive or consensual, whether inherited from traditional mechanisms of domination or emerging from new knowledge productions.

These three problematics, especially numbers 3 and 1, the convictions that power cannot be eradicated by the rational promises of philosophy and that philosophy itself must limit its knowledge-claims, have characterized much of American thought since the beginning of the Republic.

Poststructuralists claim that the Enlightenment went wrong because it carried on Descartes's "logocentrism" and assumed that reason logically preceded language and that objects cognitively presided in the mind, a rationalism that Kant continued by making consciousness and intentionality the focus of knowledge. The American founders, however, took their guidance from Locke and Hume rather than Descartes and Kant, and as a result the framers of the Constitution had little faith in the notion that a self-conscious citizenry would be rational and capable of respecting reason and the rule of law. Man's reason, when acting alone, may be "timid and cautious," Madison observed, but when acting collectively "factions" become assertive and indifferent to legality. "In a nation of philosophers, this consideration ought to be disregarded. A reverence for the laws would be sufficiently inculcated by the voice of an enlightened reason. But a nation of philosophers is as little to be expected as the philosophical race of Kings wished for by Plato."[1]

Although the framers were steeped in political philosophy, the American founding itself had no foundations in "enlightened reason" enabling citizens to live in and for truth, not even the "self-evident" truths of Jefferson's Declaration, which are nowhere to be found in the Constitution. To the framers the task of reason was to tell the people how unreasonable they are.

The *Federalist* authors used reason and rational persuasion to convince readers that the "passions and interests" are so irrepressible that America cannot expect reason or virtue of either its leaders or its followers. The framers reminded Americans that there may be no human subject, no rational agent capable of standing outside the arena of conflict and struggle

1. *Federalist*, no. 49.

and enjoying a privileged grasp of the truth of things by virtue of possessing Descartes's "clear and distinct" ideas. Hamilton and Madison took
pains to point out that readers as well as authors of the *Federalist* must
not "assume an infallibility in rejudging the fallible opinions of others."
They also saw that knowledge and judgment cannot restrain power, since
all truth-claims are inextricably bound up with interests, power, and
desire. "No one is allowed to be a judge in his own cause; because his
interest would certainly bias his judgment, and, not improbably, corrupt
his integrity." Regarding interests and "self-love" as the basis of action,
the framers felt that they must work with "the defect of better motives,"
with defective and distorting human sentiments and beliefs, which render
all political discourse obscure and problematic.[2]

The American framers no less than the later French deconstructionists
had a keen sensibility toward the equivocating and obfuscatory moves of
language.[3] Habermas's worry that poststructuralism threatens the values

2. In one rare instance Hamilton cites certain "axioms" as "primary truths or first principles," such as the whole is greater than its parts. These principles "contain an internal
evidence which, antecedent to all reflection or combination, commands the asset of the
mind." But Hamilton then proceeds to explain why the "objects of geometrical inquiry"
have little chance of influencing morals and politics. These topics arouse so much emotion
that thought becomes obstinate and obscure. "The obscurity is much oftener in the passions
and prejudices of the reasoner than in the subject. Men, upon too many occasions, do not
give their own understandings fair play; but, yielding to some untoward bias, they entangle
themselves in words and confound themselves in subtleties."
That "words," the very invention of human thought, come between knowledge and its
object indicates that the framers scarcely regarded language as transparent. When Madison
wants to explain the division of power he is aware of the difficulty of using classification
and definition. "The faculties of mind itself have never yet been distinguished and defined
with satisfactory precision by all the efforts of the most acute and metaphysical philosophers.
Sense, perception, judgment, desire, volition, memory, imagination are found to be separated by such delicate shades and minute gradations that their boundaries have eluded the
most subtle investigations, and remain a pregnant source of ingenious disquisition and
controversy." The subtle gradations are even more pronounced in social phenomena. "When
we pass from the works of nature, in which all delineations are perfectly accurate and
appear to be otherwise only from the imperfections of the eye, which surveys them, to the
institutions of man, in which the obscurity arises as well from the object itself as from the
organ by which it is contemplated, we must perceive the necessity of moderating still further
our expectations and hopes from the efforts of human sagacity." Three sources of obfuscation
impede a clear definition of the branches of government: "indistinctness of the object,
imperfection of the organ of conception, inadequateness of the vehicle of ideas." The last
impediment poses a "fresh embarrassment" in political discourse, for language as the vehicle
of ideas may distort reality rather than reflect it. *Federalist*, nos. 31, 37.

3. The use of words is to express ideas. Perspicuity, therefore, requires not only
that the ideas should be distinctly formed, but that they should be expressed
by words distinctly and exclusively appropriate to them. But no language is
so copious as to supply words and phrases for every complex idea, or so
correct as not to include many equivocally denoting different ideas. Hence it
must happen that however accurately objects may be discriminate in them-

of the Enlightenment may be more appropriate to Europe than to America. The thinking of Hamilton and Madison represented a curious blend of Humean skepticism about knowledge and Calvinist pessimism about human nature. Significantly, eighteenth-century French writers did criticize the U.S. Constitution for abandoning the promises of classical political philosophy and the prospect of human progress if not perfectibility. Specifically, they scolded the framers for burdening the young Republic with excessive reliance on controlling mechanisms, such as the separation of power, instead of centralizing all authority in a single national assembly that would represent a virtuous citizenry. John Adams answered the French critics in his three-volume *Defense of the Constitutions of the Government of the United States of America* (1787–88). Adams responded to critics like Baron Turgot by arguing that "the people" cannot be represented as a coherent entity because in daily life people do not all gather together at the same time and place, reason alike and deny their differences, and thereby arrive at common conclusions that would constitute a sovereign general will. By demonstrating that a phrase like "the people" may exist linguistically while having no basis in the real world, Adams was trying to disassociate representation from its purported reference. As though presaging twentieth-century poststructuralists, Adams examines the rhetorical complacencies of political thought and leaves classical political philosophy in shambles.

Adams's three-volume treatise, a rambling work rarely read by recent scholars, who assume its author was upholding classical republicanism, deserves our attention not only because of his refutation of that tradition but even more because of the way he shows past thinkers to be using language to repress truth instead of reveal it. In the case of Machiavelli, for example, Adams showed how rhetoric is the manipulation of effect upon readers in the guise of offering a discourse on reality. Adams, in short, undermined Machiavelli by demonstrating that what he says is not necessarily what he means and thus there may be no reliable presence of clear meaning in his writings. While writing about virtue and duty, Machiavelli himself is thinking about power and opportunity.

Adams scrutinized, among other works, Machiavelli's *History of Florence* to demonstrate that the text contradicts itself despite the author's inten-

---

selves, and however accurately the discrimination may be considered, the definition of them may be rendered inaccurate by the inaccuracy of the terms in which it is delivered. And this unavoidable inaccuracy must be greater or less, according to the complexity and novelty of the objects defined. When the Almighty himself condescends to address mankind in their own language, his meaning, luminous as it must be, is rendered dim and doubtful by the cloudy medium through which it is communicated.

Federalist, no. 37.

tions. "One is astonished at the reflection of Machiavel, 'such was the spirit of patriotism amongst them on those days, that they cheerfully gave up their private interest for the public good,' when every page of his history shows, that the public good was sacrificed every day, by all parties, to private interests, friendships, and enmities." In another instance Adams, citing Thucydides, observed that "words lost their signification: brutish rashness was fortitude; prudence, cowardice; modesty, effeminacy." With language and meaning so indeterminate, Adams had no difficulty showing how Machiavelli manipulated rhetoric to flatter the citizens of Rome. "It was very provoking to read these continual imputations to fortune, made by Machiavel, of events which he knew very well were the effects of secret intrigue." Adams felt the need to decode *History of Florence* to expose its rhetorical devices and linguistic maneuvers that concealed what its author refused to admit: that power eluded his grasp because his "pious exhortations" about civic virtue deliberately excluded the darker truths of Christianity. Adams, in short, "deconstructs" Machiavelli by showing him to be repressing "what he knew very well were the effects" of a human nature stained permanently by original sin.[4]

Adams's exposing Machiavelli's attempt to conceal religious thoughts from political theory is curiously ironic. Ever since Nietzsche, modern thinkers have regarded Christianity as an internalized psychic wound of repression that leads to guilt and meek submission. Instead of confronting and refuting the teachings of Christianity, Machiavelli, in Adams's account, is vainly trying to repress a repressive theology for the sake of republican liberty. But Adams questions not only the validity of Machiavelli's arguments but the sincerity of his expressions. *History of Florence* is interrogated and read against itself to disclose the text's implicit subversion of its explicit pronouncements. Adams's *Defense* suggests that even in the eighteenth century no political treatise could resist textual scrutiny when studied by a Calvinist who holds gnawing suspicion to be the critic's highest obligation.

Contemporary poststructuralist thought need not trouble the student of American intellectual history. While Adams showed how political thought constructs its arguments by excluding contrary thoughts, Jefferson insisted that political philosophy requires no grounding in philosophical absolutes. Although a curious and speculative thinker himself, Jefferson regarded the function of philosophy as "prophylactic" (Boorstin's apt term), a discipline that should be steering the thinker away from error rather than falsely leading him to truth. Jefferson viewed metaphysics as

4. John Adams, *Defense of the Constitutions of the Government of the United States of America* (1787–88; New York: DeCapo Press, 1971), vol. 2, 30, 52–58, 103, 109.

the disease of philosophy, which, instead of chasing "abstractions," should be "clearing the mind of Platonic mysticism and unintelligible jargon."[5] Thus early American thinkers presaged the contemporary distrust of philosophy and language. What of power?

The poststructuralists have been praised as the "masters of suspicion" because of their Nietzschean penchant for seeing power everywhere where language tries to conceal its presence. So did the American rebels of '76. In Bernard Bailyn's account of the ideological origins of the American Revolution, suspicion of power became almost paranoiac, as though the colonists were recoiling from an omnipresent malignancy possessed of "an encroaching nature," which, if unarrested, "creeps by degrees and swallows the whole." Whether concealed or conspiratorial, power had been successfully opposed when the colonists took up arms against it. But if power could only be dealt with by military force in the Revolution, how was its menacing nature to be subdued in the Constitution?[6]

Currently an impression has been circulating that the eighteenth-century Enlightenment regarded power and knowledge as logically distinct. In Europe in particular, political power was seen as arbitrary and threatening, and thus the Age of Reason would bring forth knowledge that would be systematic and liberating. Presumably knowledge could have nothing to do with power because whatever comes to be validly known must be accepted under conditions free of coercion and distortion. Thus today's poststructuralists delight in ridiculing French *philosophes* for allegedly distinguishing knowledge from power and failing to see that knowledge would come to be a form of power itself. Yet the American framers never made the assumption—as did Dewey a century later with his faith in the emancipatory role of "intelligence"—that knowledge would emerge as a rational answer to the irrationalities of power.

At the time of the Constitutional Convention the framers saw power as springing from the alienated (i.e., "fallen") human condition, and thus, like "passion," it was impossible to restrain by appeals to moral and political authority. Instead its expansionist tendencies had to be checked by its balanced dispersion so power is "counterpoised" (Arthur O. Lovejoy's expression) to control its effects. Like the poststructuralists, the *Federalist* authors saw all action as power-driven. John Adams had a pre-Nietzschean insight that people of superior knowledge and education would become a new aristocracy and, in the name of virtue, mask its

5. Daniel J. Boorstin, *The Lost World of Thomas Jefferson* (New York, 1948); Jefferson on philosophy "clearing the air" is in his letter to Dr. Benjamin Waterhouse, Mar. 3, 1818, in *Thomas Jefferson: The Life and Selected Writings*, ed. Adrienne Koch and William Peden (New York, 1944), 685–87.

6. Bernard Bailyn, *The Ideological Origins of the American Revolution* (Cambridge, 1968), 55–93.

drive to domination. Precisely because Adams and the framers claimed no privileged access to metaphysical certitude they felt that "power must be opposed to power, force to force, strength to strength, interest to interest, as well as reason to reason, eloquence to eloquence, and passion to passion." Clearly the framers did not commit the Enlightenment fallacy and count upon reason to generate its own challenge to power. Nor did they claim access to truths the authority of which could compel man's political obedience and eliminate conflict and diversity so that society would be more in harmony with nature. Neither did they claim, in a tradition that the poststructuralists see as running from Plato to Kant to Rousseau, that political unity must be sustained because diversity and plurality meant the loss of rationality and authority. Their idea of a "mixed government" implied that if the new republic was to be founded upon a consensus, it was an understanding that conflict, even a class conflict that envisioned the few oppressing the many and the many the few if both elites and popular factions were not controlled, was an inevitable aspect of the human condition, "sown" into the nature of man, as Madison put it.[7]

The curious synthesis of Calvinist pessimism and Scottish skepticism that influenced the framers distinguishes the American Enlightenment from the French. Adams, Hamilton, and Madison had been influenced by the Scots Adam Smith, David Hume, and Adam Ferguson. Thus the later poststructuralist thesis that history lacks a rational subject, a conscious, intending agent whose actions shape events and produce desired outcomes, would not be so strange a thought to eighteenth-century thinkers, who viewed history and society as the result of human action but not necessarily of human design, purpose, and intention. The Constitution itself was deliberately designed in mechanistic rather than in moral terms so that after its enactment it would as a system function apart from human agency. The Federalist authors insisted that they could not deal with the irrational causes of factions but must instead restrain their effects, and they could not count upon the future appearance of "enlightened" leaders and thus must rely upon structural organization. The only invention that could handle the tumultuous human behavior expected, the "passions and interests" that are incapable of self-government, would be what James Russell Lowell later called the Constitution—"a machine that would go by itself."[8]

What explains the framers' ability to grapple with the ferocity of power

---

7. Arthur O. Lovejoy, *Reflections on Human Nature* (Baltimore, 1969), 37–66; Adams is quoted in Adrienne Koch, *Power, Morals, and the Founding Fathers* (Ithaca, 1961), 82; *Federalist*, no. 10.

8. Michael G. Kammen, *A Machine That Would Go of Itself: The Constitution in American Culture* (New York: Knopf, 1986).

without access to foundational knowledge? Could it be that they were beneficiaries of the Christian heritage that Machiavelli sought to exclude from political thought, the same heritage that contemporary Nietzscheans see as the theological temptation of the weak while Marxists dismiss it as the controlling ideology of the ruling classes? The pragmatist, Marxist, and poststructuralist all espouse turning to either science or language to move beyond the inadequacies of traditional philosophy. None considers the older insights once valued in religion.

Niebuhr and the Illusions of Poststructuralism

Neopragmatism and poststructuralism have led to a growing impression, not among the public but in the academic world of heady "theory," that the search for truth must be forsaken as a quaint illusion from a previous age of innocence. In the absence of knowledge the world consists in structures of domination that move almost invisibly without any apparent human agent. With the "end" of philosophy there remains, in short, only power and its scarcely felt molestations.

In recent years many students and scholars who have fallen under the spell of this style of thinking have convinced themselves that knowledge has lost its capacity to deal with the world of power. Why? Because all knowledge-claims can no longer be regarded as grounded in the objectively true and real. The two authorities often cited to reinforce the death of knowledge, whether the postmortem is delivered by poststructuralists, critical theorists, or deconstructionists, are Nietzsche and Heidegger.

Introducing Reinhold Niebuhr into the poststructuralist dialogue offers the possibility that his writings, also steeped in Nietzsche and Heidegger, are far more constructive about the human predicament. Niebuhr can accept the limitations of knowledge and still teach us how to think about power. We may not be able to speak truth to power, since truth can no longer be entertained after the erosions of modernity. But Niebuhr enables us to see the truths that reside in power itself and to face the world of power politics as an inescapable confrontation with our own human nature. As a Christian existentialist, Niebuhr shows us how to put the pessimistic wisdom of tragedy and irony to positive use.

The argument put forth here suggests that the pragmatists and poststructuralists, or at least those thinkers who believe they have overcome the cognitive illusions of the past by "problematizing" knowledge, are themselves under the illusion of their own originality, not to say profundity. As a pragmatist Dewey dispensed with traditional notions of truth and turned to science; as a neopragmatist Rorty replaces the methodology of science with the contingencies of language and convention. This American move toward European poststructuralism challenges the traditional promises of human reason, and it does so by taking the following positions, which may be regarded as the author's eleven theses on what we in American history always wanted to know until we came to realize that we already know it—thanks to Niebuhr and the Calvinists.

(1) A critique of the eighteenth-century "logocentric" Enlightenment for assuming that pure, transparent reason operates in human faculties and in the processes of nature and that the self is the reference point of reason. Instead the poststructuralists, especially the critical theorists of the old Frankfurt School, depict the Enlightenment *philosophes* as subduing nature by trying to master the environment by manipulating it.

(2) The illusion of truth and the impossibility of access to any absolute or any form of unmediated knowledge.

(3) Yet a modern predicament which sees humankind desperately in need of what it cannot attain.

(4) Thus the human subject is driven to assume that truth can be found as an act of uncovering or recovering because the rationalist mind presupposes the presence of what it is looking for (Heidegger) and treats as objective discovery what is actually imposed interpretation (Nietzsche).

(5) As a result thinkers are tempted by the will to believe and regard their beliefs as found rather than made, uncovered rather than invented, a matter of proof instead of persuasion.

(6) The beliefs held and imposed are essentially expressions of the will to power, and words like *freedom* and *virtue* conceal the domineering motives behind them.

(7) An ironic perspective that sees meanings reversing themselves and consequences defying the best of intentions.

(8) The "linguistic turn": the conviction that all human cognition is inescapably verbal or textual and consists of a web of unstable, dancing signifiers having no reference to a reality beyond the text; words full of sound and fury signifying not nothing but almost everything, as though the script were out of control; philosophers assuming they are looking for truth and waking up to realize they are only writing words about words, manipulating metaphors, alternating verbal images—just what I'm doing now!

(9) Antiessentialism. Since our mental and physical activities are productions that bring thoughts and things into existence, there is no essence beyond or behind them, nothing that can be traced back to nature, first principles, self-evident truths, and the like.

(10) Antifoundationalism. Once upon a time when beliefs were justified they were founded upon something bedrock, immediately given, self-evident, unconditional, indubitable, something that is self-explanatory

and self-justifying, some antecedent reality, some presence that exists prior to its being known, something, anything, upon which thought can be said to rest. No more. The poststructuralists say of foundational knowledge what Gertrude Stein was reported to have said about Oakland, California: "There's no there there."

(11) Knowledge is power and power is knowledge. Supposedly, knowledge was once seen as logically separate from power because it presumably derived from uninhibited free inquiry. But for the poststructuralist knowledge is a form of communication and persuasion, and to the extent it commands attention and wins acceptance, knowledge embodies power, even the power it was supposed to resist. For Foucault in particular, knowledge as an act of writing is an effort at self-determination in full awareness that the whole process of knowing is contingent, and thus the conscious thinker must reflect back on how the self constitutes itself. One searches for knowledge and produces power as discourse. What can be known is only what can be said, and what is said, uttered, or proclaimed should be seen as strategies of power and domination, intended or otherwise.

Since our linguistic assertions can only be interpretations, and since interpretations are little more than efforts at self-legitimation, can knowledge be free of interest and power? Can reason be rational?

Once such questions are raised we can begin to see that Niebuhr was something of a poststructuralist before the term came into being. But whereas the neopragmatist prides himself on being "postmodern," Niebuhr could draw upon premodern thinkers and demonstrate their relevance to the modern human condition. Earlier in history religious thinkers who never presumed to know truth and reality were more troubled by their inability to know God. They too believed that what little knowledge could be obtained would come from reading a text, and the Bible informed them that after the Fall humankind was left alienated not only from knowledge of God but from knowledge of self. Henceforth the mysteries of the human heart made it almost impossible to be sure whether one's actions benefit or harm others. Long before Nietzsche, St. Augustine showed that even the best intentional exercise of power may be an act of domination, whether in the name of solidarity or salvation. The historian Perry Miller demonstrates how this "Augustinian strain of piety" influenced the New England Puritans, sensitizing them to "interrogations externally posed by human existence" and to what our contemporary deconstructionists would call "the hermeneutics of suspicion," the mind's anguish at never knowing directly the object it interprets.[9] The Pascalian-

9. Perry Miller, *The New England Mind: The Seventeenth Century* (1939; Boston: Beacon, 1964), 3–34.

Augustinian strain of thought can be traced to Hawthorne and the obscurity of motivation and to Melville and his sense of nothingness behind the whiteness of the white whale, "the inscrutable thing" that turns the search for the absolute into a journey of self-annihilation. Knowledge comes at the price of sorrow and gloom, illuminating darkness rather than truth. Epistemological pessimism runs as a continuous current in American intellectual history, and in the twentieth century it reaches its profoundest depths in the theology of Reinhold Niebuhr.

The criticism of the Enlightenment leveled by contemporary poststructuralists had its predecessor in Niebuhr's writings a half-century earlier as well as in the religious writers who voiced their doubts at the dawn of the "Age of Reason." Niebuhr's indictment of the "children of light" contains the following ingredients: the exposure of reason as hubris and the refusal to see reason and justification as tainted with rationalization; the futility of all explanatory ideas in understanding meaning and representing reality; the darkness of finitude felt as primordial mystery; the inner discordance within the human spirit reflecting the disharmony in man's relation to the universe; the acceptance of inevitable defeat and the imperative to continue the struggle with no victory in sight; the irony of intentions and consequences and the tragedy inherent in all situations when decisions must be made with no assurance of the right, good, and just; the indeterminacy of language and the opaqueness of symbols and images; the "aporia," or impasse, that arises when words, even scriptural passages, are used to grasp the fragmentary character of all historical apprehensions of the truth; the importance of anxiety as the precondition of both sin and freedom, guilt and human creativity; and the self-deceptions of philosophy, science, and religion in pretending to resolve the problems of modernity. In *Beyond Tragedy*, Niebuhr admired Nietzsche for exposing philosophy's claims to knowledge and for having recognized the sense of tragedy in a superrational quest for meaning and morality.[10] In his magisterial treatise, *The Nature and Destiny of Man*, Niebuhr described Kierkegaard's analysis of the connection of anxiety to sin as "the profoundest in Christian thought." In the same work he quoted from *Sein und Zeit* to show Heidegger explaining how existence itself creates anxiety as human beings become aware that life is both potentiality and contingency. In Heidegger as in Niebuhr one discerns the idea of the "fall" as an alienation from God that hurls humankind into the world, "thrown" there, like the roll of the dice, so that there is no point in reasoning "Why?"[11]

10. Reinhold Niebuhr, *Beyond Tragedy: Essays on the Christian Interpretation of History* (1937; New York: Scribner's, 1965).

11. Niebuhr, *The Nature and Destiny of Man: Human Nature* (1941; New York: Scribner's, 1964), vol. 2, 183–84.

The parallels between Niebuhr and the contemporary sages Foucault and Derrida, as well as the older Frankfurt scholars Theodor Adorno and Max Horkheimer, are striking. Not only do all such thinkers interrogate the Enlightenment to expose the illusions of reason and progress, but Niebuhr even sees the same alienation from nature as humankind assaults the environment in an effort to wrest value from it. "The conquest of nature, in which the bourgeois mind trusted so much, enriches life but also imperils it," wrote Niebuhr in *The Children of Light and the Children of Darkness*.[12]

Long before the poststructuralists Niebuhr also approached knowledge and history as ironic in that ideas could carry ambiguous and contradictory meanings and events could have unintended consequences. Niebuhr's *The Irony of American History* reads like a poststructuralist critique of our country's rhetorical pretensions. As a people Americans have always assumed their innocence and virtue because the country was founded in an act of repudiating the corruptions of the Old World. Yet the colonists proceeded to work the materials of the environment, and their heirs transformed the continent through industry and technology to produce, in mid-twentieth century, the greatest power-machine in the world. Like Foucault and Derrida, Niebuhr shows political leaders to be uttering soothing words to avoid facing the harsher reality of power and guilt. Thus in the name of the "dignity of the individual" America found itself fighting a cold war that required the massive concentration of nuclear weapons whose presence, though perhaps necessary, violated the individual's essential freedom of decision-making and capacity for self-determination. Niebuhr never went so far as to suggest that Americans live under the tyranny of language, as though the republic were a rhetorical dictatorship. But he did show why political language that speaks of virtue and innocence can only be distrusted as a sinful misuse of words, usually by members of the privileged classes who mistake their power and wealth for "moral excellence."[13]

The critiques of Marxism by Niebuhr and the poststructuralists are not only similar but virtually identical. Both expose the Marxist philosophy of history as a false teleology that dramatizes truth and freedom emerging triumphant from conflict and struggle. What Niebuhr calls redemptive history the poststructuralists call "metanarrative." Even more amazing, both Niebuhr and the poststructuralists praise Marxism for revealing the false moral claims of the bourgeoisie and unmasking the ways the domi-

---

12. Niebuhr, *The Children of Light and the Children of Darkness* (1943; New York: Scribner's, 1960), 1–41.

13. Niebuhr, *Moral Man in Immoral Society* (1932; New York: Scribner's, 1960), 113–41.

nant classes rationalize their interests by invoking "natural law" or the "free market"; they then turn the critique around and show that Marxism has its own ideological taint in promising a future of social harmony free of power and coercion. The communist as well as the capitalist presumes to know how to make power disappear, in one case by eliminating property and in the other by reducing government to a night watchman. Niebuhr's own critique of liberal capitalism combines Marxism and poststructuralism to demonstrate the absence of what the profit-seeking capitalist assumes to be present: a rational, autonomous, prudent, responsible self. Where Niebuhr departs from Marxism and partakes of poststructuralism is in the common conviction that social conflict is inevitable and power relations inescapable.

Perhaps one reason Niebuhr and the poststructuralists see things so similarly is that both are historicists who recognize the hermeneutical predicament. Humankind can be understood only historically, and knowledge itself is conditioned and mediated by its historical context. Language, one of humankind's proudest creations, defeats the effort of human reason to get beyond the limits of the text. The literary critic can no more establish an author's intent by reading his or her book than can a theologian divine God's purpose by reading the Bible. Thus when we read contemporary poststructuralists we find what we earlier had found in reading Niebuhr: finitude, contingency, opacity, and irony.

Yet what we fail to find in the poststructuralists, hope and possibility, we are encouraged when we find these qualities in Niebuhr. His theology and philosophy of history offers not poststructuralist constraints and incarcerations but indeterminate potentialities for freedom. Where the poststructuralists emphasize systems and structures, Niebuhr believed in the possibilities of human agency.

One possibility is the human capacity for transcendence. Human beings are creatures of history, yet desire to be more than products of time and place. The paradox is that human beings are mortal and finite yet capable of looking beyond their natural condition to seek self-transcendence. This alienated striving for moral wholeness is driven by angst and guilt, which in turn give civilization an "uneasy conscience" that makes possible social justice and the Christian concept of love. Our finitude is our fate, but out of contingency can arise a noble dignity. Moral truth need not have access to metaphysical truth. A morality that arises out of guilt to reach the state of grace can take place within the fragmentary nature of human existence:

> Nothing that is worth doing can be achieved in our lifetime; therefore we must be saved by hope. Nothing which is true

or beautiful or good makes complete sense in any immediate context of history; therefore we must be saved by faith. Nothing we do, however virtuous, can be accomplished alone; therefore we are saved by love. No virtuous act is quite as virtuous from the standpoint of our friend or foe as it is from our standpoint. Therefore we must be saved by the final form of love which is forgiveness.[14]

Another essential quality of thought is present in Niebuhr and absent in the poststructuralists. Foucault claims that we produce power in the guise of knowledge and, hence, we create or reproduce structures of domination. Even something so innocent as the act of writing is a "discursive practice" to persuade others to accept, and thereby to submit to, our interpretations as legitimate. But since Foucault describes history as a series of seemingly causeless events, a strange, surrealistic scenario in which power is exercised in general while being possessed by no one in particular, he presents us with a theory of oppression without an oppressor. Where the "decentering" strategy of the poststructuralist leaves the impression that there is no core but only surfaces and margins and manifestations without meanings, Niebuhr's anthropological premise puts the sin-prone ego at the center of things. The poststructuralist has no place for either sin or transcendence. Without a human subject, how can there be either guilt or grace? Yet, curiously, Foucault comes close to Niebuhr's idea of sin in his conviction that discursive practices reflect self-aggrandizement in the service of interest and power. To Niebuhr the basis of sin is the dread of emptiness, the urge to complete the incomplete by asserting the self. A Niebuhrian could readily "deconstruct" the poststructuralist by demonstrating how the language of systems and structures, of arrangements and rules, and of other images of confinement and metaphors of power, precludes an author from allowing the prospect of human evil to emerge in the text. If it is already presupposed that actions have no explanation and events no origins, how could there be original sin?

In the chapter titled "The Tower of Babel" in *Beyond Tragedy*, Niebuhr suggests that only an intellectual suffering from the Christian sin of pride would presume that language should be so transparent as to represent accurately the real. On the question of language one may also discern differences between Niebuhr and the poststructuralists. When it is asserted that power resides in language as persuasion and distortion, the implication seems to be that language can only do wrong and is helpless to do the right thing. Niebuhr might agree about the duplicities of lan-

---

14. Niebuhr, *The Irony of American History* (New York: Scribner's, 1952), 63.

guage but not, ironically, because language is power. On the contrary, language is impotent in the face of fallen human nature. Words are not power. If they were, if they could effectively persuade the collective mind of nation-states, if language could actually produce effects and influence events, then aggression and war could be prevented by force of proclamation alone. The Kellogg-Briand Peace Pact of 1928 amounted to such a rhetorical renunciation of war. Nations rushed to sign it. But it was a treaty, indeed a verbose "text," that had almost no influence on world affairs.

Thus one can only speculate as to how Niebuhr might have responded to Rorty's neopragmatist turn toward language as redemptive. Dewey, as mentioned above, believed that scientific intelligence and the "method of discussion" remained viable resources in facing a world of conflict and aggression. One may also wonder who is further removed from the illusions of the Enlightenment and closer to the modern sensibility of finite humanism: the philosopher who may overestimate the possibilities of language or the theologian who sought to return the riddles of human nature to political discourse.

Rorty has suggested that the modern-ironist-language-oriented philosophers, whose exemplars are Heidegger, Nietzsche, and Derrida, "define their achievement by their relation to their predecessors rather than by their relation to the truth."[15] Niebuhr would agree, only now we would have the theologian seeing an affinity with Heidegger's Christian skepticism and the philosopher claiming Heidegger belongs to Dewey and American pragmatism. Recently it has been pointed out that Heidegger's pragmatism involves the primacy of practical understanding and purposeful action, elements close to Dewey's idea of knowledge as instrumental.[16] Niebuhr appreciated in Kierkegaard and Heidegger the existentialist themes of irony, paradox, ambiguity, uncertainty, and dissonance. And he admired such tensions in James's philosophy, where the sense of reality remained open, unfinished, contingent, and pregnant with novelty. But Niebuhr, one recalls, regarded Dewey as an example of moralist man in a Machiavellian world, an American innocent who believed that all that stood in the way of progress was ignorance and bias, the failure to develop intelligence through education and the failure to turn to science to resolve problems. Would not a Foucauldian poststructuralist be amused by Dewey's convictions that intelligence could generate its own rational solution to power and that injustice and conflict will yield to education and

15. Richard Rorty, *Contingency, Irony, and Solidarity* (New York: Cambridge, 1989), 79.
16. Mark Okrent, *Heidegger's Pragmatism: Understanding, Being, and the Critique of Metaphysics* (Ithaca, New York, 1988).

science? A Niebuhrian would also be unconvinced by Rorty's hope that
the problems of modernity will yield to conversation and solidarity. Does
power disappear once life is reconceived as dialogue and the self relocated
within the group? For Rorty everything depends not upon what can be
known but upon how things are talked about and described in a vocabulary that purports to elevate knowledge by edifying it. How can a description of the corruption of self-interests, however fresh and vivid, also constitute its correction?

To bring Niebuhr into the poststructuralist discourse means going
backward in time to early religious thinkers. The postmodern philosopher
would perhaps dismiss the notion of original sin as an example of essentialism, and the social scientist would remind us that the natives of Samoa
were innocent of sin and guilt. But long before Margaret Mead made that
point Henry Adams discovered it in his travels. Yet Adams would have
been able to appreciate both Niebuhr's Christian existentialism and the
brooding, and at times somewhat playful, nihilism of the poststructuralists. For New England Calvinism also depicted man as an absence, a
mind that had no free will and no sufficient faculty of reason. Man was
made to feel that he was nothing because God was everything. Told in
sermons that the will cannot be its own cause, the early Christian felt the
abyss of helplessness. "In God's providence," observed Adams of the
Middle Ages, "man was nothing." Jonathan Edwards, the great eighteenth-century theologian, told Americans that they must stare into the
bottomless metaphysical pit to appreciate why virtue is beyond rational
comprehension and why motives for doing good cannot have a point of
origin or a pragmatic meaning. "And if it be inquired, what that virtue
is, which virtue consists in the love of the love of, it must be answered,
it is the love of virtue. So that there must be the love of the love of the
love of virtue, and so on *ad infinitum*. For there is no end of going back
in a circle. We never come to any beginning, or foundation. For it is
without beginning and hangs on nothing."[17]

It would seem that Adams and Niebuhr, who retained some of the
riddles of Calvinism in their philosophical outlook, were closer to the
European poststructuralists than the first generation of American pragmatists, who subordinated religion to science. Yet Habermas and Rorty
believe that the reconstruction of modern thought can best begin with
the more optimistic legacy of pragmatism. Taking up where conventional
philosophy supposedly ended, neopragmatism promises to restart the con-

17. Henry Adams, *Mont-Saint-Michel and Chartres* (1904; Garden City, N.Y.: Anchor,
1959), 409; Jonathan Edwards, "The Nature of True Virtue," in *Jonathan Edwards: Representative Selections*, ed. Clarance H. Faust and Thomas H. Johnson (New York: Hill and Wang,
1962), 353.

versation and continue the edifying processes of communication. It seems that we are to communicate amid our uncertainties, motivated by nothing more than the will to continue, and wondering whether we are to be moved by beautiful words or by powerful thoughts. The language of religion once aspired to penetrate the soul and open the heart. To what does the language of social science aspire?

The Limits of Communication: Habermas

Habermas's valiant defense of the Enlightenment, articulated in the eighties, proceeded seemingly unaware that the American Enlightenment had a different message about power and knowledge than the French and German counterparts. Nor, of course, was Habermas aware of Niebuhr and the Calvinist tradition. The indifference to religion in poststructuralist thought may be due to the fact that many of its post–World War II thinkers were attempting to move beyond Marxism without abandoning a secular analysis of history. The proper study of mankind is not man and his spiritual anxieties but language and its social activities. All that needs to be known is produced by the processes of communication. Even the scientific universe, no less than the older metaphysical cosmos, is a product of human faculties. Because Habermas regards language as the ultimate philosophy, he disagreed strongly with the view of the French Nietzscheans that language is the duplicitous deferral of meaning or the verbal chains of epistemic confinement. Rather than language being mischievous or oppressive it is reliable and progressive. The social function of language shows how man can be freed from his subjectivity, from, that is, the Hegelian notion that reason and rationality reside within the individual behind whose back "history" moves to unfold human destiny. The "universal pragmatics" of language also shows how communication can liberate thought from relativism and establish normative standards in a world without philosophical foundations.

Modernist writers like Adams, Niebuhr, and Nietzsche assume that man is free to believe and condemned to doubt—unless, out of weakness and timidity, he finds in objects only what he has imported into them. Habermas starts from the opposite assumption: man finds in objects his own desperately distorted meanings because he is not free to think rationally in full awareness of the conditions that hinder freedom. Habermas's sensibility to "domination" is similar to Marx's sensibility to "alienation" in that both conditions stunt human consciousness. But Habermas shifts orientation from labor acting upon nature within the forces of production to language interacting in communicative situations to reach a normative consensus. His aim is to overcome domination by establishing the "ideal

speech situation" in which all propositional statements and practical questions are freely resolved without intimidation, manipulation, or coercion.
Whether it be through the method of "discursive justification" or the
"force of the better argument," members of the communicative community decide without recourse to any criterion of truth other than that
arrived at through the "finely woven net of linguistically generated inter-
subjectivity."[18]

Habermas drew much of his analysis from European thinkers, especially the speech-act theory of John Austin, the linguistic philosophy
of Wittgenstein, and the philosophical hermeneutics of Hans-Georg
Gadamer. Language as speech has a binding quality in that utterances
occur in concrete social situations and speakers communicate statements
that are cognitively testable and for which they remain personally responsible. But Habermas's notion of "universal pragmatics" also derived from
American sources, especially Peirce and the scientific method of organizing the procedures of knowledge communally, and Mead and the fundamental social basis of human nature expressed in symbolic interaction.
Significantly, when Habermas's critics claim that his communicative theory is so all-absorbing as to submerge the individual into the social and
to rid all dissent and deviancy in the name of consensual harmony, he
cites Mead's point that individuation and socialization are two aspects of
the same linguistic process that turns private persons into public actors.
And when critics insist that "universal pragmatics" is a "totalizing" obsession that aims to impose moral order, Habermas can cite Peirce's thesis
that establishing the necessary conditions for comprehension and agreement is an ethical imperative that must transcend differences. "There is
never too much universalism but not enough," Habermas recently told
an interviewer.[19]

Habermas's drawing upon pragmatism to defend the Enlightenment,
itself a universal aspiration, makes sense in the context of American progressive thought. The hope for an ideal communicative environment follows from the same pragmatic assumption that modern society suffers
from cultural lag as the forces of change render obsolete older thoughts
and values. Both Habermas and the pragmatists believe that there can be
no return to historically surpassed forms of life; hence the need for new
habits of thought to catch up with and adapt to new conditions. To
the pragmatists' expectations for science and education, Habermas adds
discourse and communication. But Habermas is closer to Dewey than to
Peirce, who never extended his ideas of community inquiry and consen-

18. Habermas, *Philosophical Discourse of Modernity*, 346.
19. Habermas, "Être Résolument Moderne," *Autrement Revue* 102 (Nov. 1988): 23–29.

sual agreement beyond the field of science. Moreover, as Karl-Otto Apel has noted, Peirce's notion of consensual truth involved the "self-surrender" of the individual investigator, whereas Habermas wants to reconcile individual submission and individual self-expression by allowing the thoughts of all participants to be heard.[20]

And once heard, what then?

In American society the expression "I hear you" is meant to convey that the listener understands perfectly what the speaker is saying. It also implies that the listener does not necessarily accept what the speaker is saying and that therefore agreement does not logically follow from understanding. Even in an "ideal speech situation," perhaps an academic or scientific committee where argumentative discourse proceeds with complete commitment to truth, sincerity, and rational justification, a conclusion might be reached that simply allows each member to choose freedom rather than truth, private conviction rather than public consensus, the reasonableness of differing rather than the necessity of deferring and conforming. Committee members understand one another and conclude the meeting by agreeing to disagree.

Peirce believed members of a scientific inquiry would desire to reach agreement because he himself psychologically and morally identified his entire being with a larger whole and ongoing process. But Habermas's theory of communicative action presupposes an ethical imperative without explicitly articulating it. Thus Richard Bernstein has rightly criticized Habermas's failure to specify what it is that will motivate agents to want to overcome the distortions and dominations that inhibit agreement arrived at through communicative competence.[21] From a different angle, Richard Rorty questions whether Habermas can develop a "universal pragmatics" and a "transcendental hermeneutics" on the basis of linguistic processes. Rorty judges Habermas's efforts to be a futile search for an Archimedean or Kantian standpoint to provide universalistic criteria for justifying truth-claims. A pragmatism truly carrying on the spirit of Dewey would stick to the concrete and experimental rather than the abstract and theoretical and take its shape from "the meaning of the daily detail" (Dewey's expression). Sufficient consensus can be reached, Rorty suggests, not by philosophy grounding itself in epistemological foundations but by society asserting itself in harmonic resolutions. Whereas Habermas places all his hope in a systematic methodology of discourse

20. Karl-Otto Apel, "C. S. Peirce and the Post-Tarskian Problem of an Adequate Explication of the Meaning of the Truth: Toward a Transcendental-Pragmatic Theory of Truth, Part II," *Transactions of the Charles S. Peirce Society* 18 (Winter 1982): 3–17.

21. Richard J. Bernstein, *The Restructuring of Social and Political Theory* (New York, 1976), 219–25.

practice based on an implicit Peircean belief that man identifies with consistency and community, Rorty simply looks to "solidarity" to give philosophy its afterlife less in knowledge than in sentiment.[22]

Yet in American history solidarity eluded not only the socialists but even the sociologists. While Habermas feels it urgent to clarify the formal characteristics of speech-acts, long ago sociologists at the University of Chicago felt the need to admit that speech can be divisive as well as cohesive. Robert Park, Mead's close associate, explained how he and members of the sociology department set out to prove that communication could be the basis of moral order in a new urban age. As they discovered that communication increased individual self-consciousness and even feelings of isolation, Park reread James's "A Certain Blindness in Human Beings" to appreciate the paradoxical dimensions in the phenomenon. The Chicago sociologists had assumed, with Dewey, that discussion would be integrative and enhance the "I-Thou" relationship and thereby overcome divisiveness and conflict. Instead the opposite took place: "The outcome of discussion is usually to lay bare the submerged hypotheses, not to say submerged complexes, on which divergent opinions are based. This sometimes leads to agreement, but it sometimes reveals differences so profound and so charged with emotion and sentiment that further discussion appears unprofitable, if not impossible. When that happens to individuals there seems to be no way of carrying on the controversy except by fighting." In his final estimate in "Communication and Culture" (1938), Park became convinced that the activity of speech is pregnant with irony and duality; it could enhance communication and also intensify competition.[23]

Whether communication results in conflict or agreement, Habermas's theory advances by retreating. After reorienting social theory from production to reflection, his own reflections take us back to the Marxist fetish of production. The philosopher cannot know truth as correspondence or coherence, Habermas concedes as a postmodernist. But the philosopher can do something about it by arranging for the possibilities of its occurrence in an ideal speech setting. What cannot be known epistemologically can be produced organizationally in a proper environment that nurtures its discursive habits.

Habermas's communication theory may help salvage Marxism from the suspicious gaze of the deconstructionists, who see the theory as trying to regularize the rules of language to compensate for the disorders of modern

22. Rorty, *Mirror of Nature*, 379–82; see also Rorty's "Habermas and Lyotard on Postmodernity," in *Habermas and Modernity*, ed. Richard J. Bernstein (Cambridge, 1985), 161–76.

23. Park is quoted in Fred Matthews, *Quest for An American Sociology: Robert E. Park and the Chicago School* (Montreal: McGill-Queens University Press, 1977), 146–53.

life; but it also does much to aid and comfort the capitalist. Often Habermas's proposals remind the student of American history of the developments in the fifties that led to such critical books as David Riesman's *The Lonely Crowd* and William Whyte's *The Organization Man*. As suggested in the chapter on Peirce, America's business managerialists also advocated a more rational society based upon cooperation, seminar discussion sessions, teamwork, and "togetherness." The assumption held that entrepreneurs could arrive at decisions collectively that they would carry out individually. A further assumption held that "group think" would reduce conflict and offer intimate identity in a heartless, competitive world. Capitalists could not agree more that truth, like profits, is not discovered but produced to overcome problems and satisfy needs. The capitalist not only produces but delivers whatever consumers demand. The capitalist gives us the "free market" and consumer sovereignty and the Marxist gives us the "ideal speech situation" and discursive rationality. An unfair comparison, to be sure; but no system of organization better recognizes social relations as an affair of signs, symbols, and associations than does capitalism. The literary critic Kenneth Burke even explained why modern capitalism functions symbolically as a surrogate for older religions. "And as the communion service, wherein men make themselves one by partaking of a substance in common, contains a dialectic of the one and the many, since the rite is social in its emphasis but permits individual appropriation of the sacramental substance, so the philosophy of the market points to the public benefits that follow from individual acquisition."[24] Habermas's shift from what might be termed a labor to a linguistic theory of value is perhaps necessary but not without an embarrassing irony. For capitalism, too, is a speech act with all the "illocutionary force" of a promissory note, a means of communication in which "money talks"![25]

Habermas's hope that consensus can take the place of the older categories of correspondence and coherence as a means of getting around the problem of truth raises the problem of error. His procedure is basically Peircean: a consensus arrived at by investigators whose views have no object of knowing but only ways of discussing and communicating. Can a consensus be freely and constructively arrived at and still be wrong? If

24. Kenneth Burke, *A Grammar of Motives* (Berkeley: University of California Press, 1969), 94.
25. Habermas does discuss money as a medium for coordinating action in Sociological analysis (*Discourse of Modernity*, 350–51); Burke noted the way Mead referred to money as a form of language in his review of the posthumously published *The Philosophy of the Act*, in Burke's *The Philosophy of Literary Form* (Berkeley: University of California Press, 1973), 379–82.

the consensus is merely the agreed interpretation, and the interpretation commands assent not because it is closer to the truth of things but rather because it better carries the force of the prevailing argument, how can community participants know that the consensus is not merely another contrived point of view that reconstructs reality rather than represents it? Without the possibility of error disturbing the community of communicators, where arise the grounds for doubt whose irritating nature compels the thinker to move beyond settled agreement and initiate new inquiry? And if the purpose of communication is to reach understanding and agreement, what becomes of curiosity, which often arises when things are not understood?

"Truth is public," declared Habermas in explicating Peirce's logic of inquiry.[26] The private views of individuals can never refer to what is real, Habermas insisted; nor can individual subjectivity provide usable knowledge, since it merely expresses the existing value system and therefore cannot offer an independent means of critically evaluating society. Thus the communicative community is to overcome subjectivity by allowing each individual to participate openly and freely without fear of ridicule or repression. But the public arena, as Tocqueville observed, may be just as despotic even in a democracy, a "tyranny of the majority" that silences dissent and jeopardizes liberty. Habermas wants his ideal speech situation to be completely free and unrestrained; yet considering the abundance of rules governing the use of language, it almost seems that the Marxist is trying to get from communication what the Catholic wants to get from confession. The philosopher and the priest want to break down the sin of privacy.

One needs to turn to literary sensibility to appreciate the possibility that truth may better reside in private thoughts than in public acts. The novelist makes it clear why it is necessary to play off dialogue against monologue: the former conveys what is said, the latter reveals what is meant. Words make conversation possible; but thoughts make some truths knowable. And in some settings thoughts cannot be uttered publicly because what seems "true" to the mind is too real to be surrendered to the world of discourse. The creative writer may feel that the realities of inner experience can have no accurate expression in the more objective world of language and social relations. Habermas wants to collectivize the definition of truth just as Dewey wanted to democratize the discourse of knowledge. But if truth is public, if it comes into existence only in communication, would not speech have to become so perfected as to be transparent? The philosopher has lost hope that truth can be found in thought,

---

26. Habermas, *Knowledge and Human Interests*, 100.

yet society can expect it to be established in speech. If philosophy becomes so content as to allow communication to assume its new role in intellectual life, one might consider Stendhal's observation: "Speech has been given man to hide his thoughts." And Nietzsche's: "Every deep thinker needs a mask."[27]

Closer to home, one could cite a number of writers to suggest that the American mind resists the appeal of communicative consensus. Thoreau wanted Americans to speak to nature; Melville's Bartleby "preferred not to" reply to others; Whitman chose poetry to sing of himself, and T. S. Eliot did the same to argue with himself. Lippmann believed that language, "a dictionary of faded metaphors," could not be trusted to form public opinion; and Santayana warned that to leave truth to the unfolding of a democratic consensus was to leave it to chance. Given these capricious ironies of democratic society, perhaps F. Scott Fitzgerald offered the best definition of freedom: "Remember this—if you shut your mouth, you have your choice."[28]

Habermas's proposal is alien to the rebellious spirit of American culture. It is also alien to the conservative prudence of the framers of the Constitution, perhaps the first political philosophers to realize that liberty depends upon diversity rather than unanimity, conflict rather than consensus. Jefferson thought uniformity would threaten politics with dullness as it had threatened art with death. But the Founders' expectations of diversity and conflict proved erroneous, and by the time of the Jacksonian era it took Tocqueville to observe uniformity everywhere in America. The new democratic society, Tocqueville explained, would perish were it not for the common values and mores that Americans shared, the "habits of the heart" that evolve in an open, fluid society without fixed class structures. Henceforth the best of American minds would sense the dual nature of American freedom, which could both liberate and oppress at the same time, as though the individual psyche, fleeing the state and succumbing to society, remained frozen in an unresolved contradiction. Observing that "the New England conscience is responsible for much that seems alien to the New England nature," Henry Adams also believed, as did Lippmann, Santayana, and others, that discourse and communication had little bearing on conduct. "The New England temper distrusts itself as well as the world it lives in, and rarely yields to eccentricities of conduct. Emerson himself, protesting against every usual tendency of soci-

27. Stendhal's observation is actually a quote from a certain R. P. Malagrida in *Scarlet and Black* (London: Penguin, 1953), 152; Friedrich Nietzsche, *Beyond Good and Evil*, trans. Marianne Cowan (Chicago: Gateway, 1955), 48.

28. Lippmann, *Public Opinion*, 66; George Santayana, *Dialogues in Limbo* (Ann Arbor: University of Michigan Press, 1957), 89–123; F. Scott Fitzgerald, *The Crack-Up*, 210.

ety, respected in practice all its standards." Society's standards intimidate the best of writers, and even religion, a progressive force that once stood for liberty against tyranny and slavery, can be oppressive and distrustful of progressive ideas. Dreading public disapproval, Mark Twain admitted to having "suppressed a book which my conscience tells me I ought to publish," a book on atheism, a subject more feared in America than fear itself. In America conscience and consensus were at war. Twain could remind the postmodernist thinker why an ideal speech situation is improbable and why democracy and the pressures of society combine to make cowards of us all.[29]

When one takes Habermas's "Truth is public" beyond the range of science, where Peirce had left it, the declaration seems too sweeping. Surely it is not always the case that truth emerges in society rather than in soliloquy. If it were the case, playwrights would not have to resort to interior asides to convey the truths that have no name. The truths that must meet the inevitable requirements of an ideal speech situation may be bearable because bland, agreeable because sayable.

Turning from Habermas to Rorty, there is no burden of truth to bear, no distinction between what is said and what is known, no transcendental basis of cognition, no nonhuman reality to constrain thought but plenty of historical contingencies to provoke it, no moral order to discover but a challenging idea of solidarity to develop, no knowledge to be found but instead a discourse to be narrated, no loneliness of thought but a liveliness of conversation as its own excuse for being. Rorty wants philosophers to turn toward literature for guidance. "Mr. Mark Twain," Huck Finn surmised, "he told the truth, mainly."[30] For Rorty the tale is more important than the truth, the whole tale and nothing but the tale, mainly.

Rorty's Political Thought and the Deweyan Legacy

At once influential and controversial, Richard Rorty is a unique figure in American intellectual life, a searching, profound scholar who has ceased believing in the promises of philosophy without ceasing to be credulous about the possibility of knowledge by other means. Not surprisingly, he has had a greater impact on literary theorists and intellectual historians than upon American philosophers themselves. In light of the scholarly growth-industry on Rorty's thoughts, one is reminded of W. H. Auden's

29. Henry Adams, *The Life of George Cabot Lodge* (Boston: Houghton Mifflin, 1911), 50, 146; the Twain quotes are in Van Wyck Brooks, *The Times of Melville and Whitman* (London, 1949), 354–55.

30. Twain is quoted in Lewis Leavy, "Mark Twain," in *American Writers*, ed. Leonard Ungar (New York: Scribner's, 1974), vol. 4, 190–213.

lines, composed after World War II, on the English professor who continues to write even though the existentialist philosopher claims that mind has nothing to say:

> The sons of Hermes love to play,
> And only do their best when they
>   Are told they oughtn't;
> Apollo's children never shrink
> From boring jobs but have to think
>   Their work important.

> In fake Hermetic uniforms
> Behind our battle-line, in swarms
>   That keep alighting,
> His existentialists declare
> That they are in complete despair,
>   Yet go on writing.[31]

An awareness that language threatens the presence of mind can only provoke philosophers to go on philosophizing and do what "they oughtn't." Plato attributed to the body and its animal needs the same impediments to reason that Derrida attributes to language and its equivocations. From such an argument "Plato concludes," wrote Lippmann, "that the only pure philosopher is a dead one."[32] Does it follow that the only pure deconstructionist is a silent one? Yet Plato wanted to conceive philosophy as dialogue just as Rorty wants to continue it as conversation.

Rorty's postmortem treatment of traditional philosophy is not without political implications. Both the Left and the Right have been hostile to his neopragmatist alliance with poststructuralism. The radical claims that Rorty's idea of "conversation" is a dangerous delusion, since it can seldom be free of inhibition, in the same way that all "ungrounded discourses" have been "decisively coopted by late capitalist culture."[33] Neoconservatives regard pragmatism's embrace of deconstruction and its determination to render all meaning and value indeterminate as further evidence that American liberalism contains a suicidal death wish.[34] Such criticisms would have been familiar to Dewey, who was accused by the Left of avoiding the question of power and by the Right of undermining the idea of truth. At the same time today's liberal pragmatist reminds Rorty that

---

31. W. H. Auden, "Under Which Lyre," in W. H. Auden, *Selected Poems*, ed. Edward Mendelson (New York: Vintage, 1979), 178–83.

32. Lippmann, *Preface to Morals*, 159.

33. Frank Lentricchia, "Rorty's Cultural Conversation," *Raritan* 3:1 (1983): 136–41.

34. Gertrude Himmelfarb, "The Abyss Revisited," *American Scholar* 16 (1992): 337–48.

Dewey's daily passion was not conversation but participation, civic activity rather than verbal loquacity.[35]

Since Dewey had been the guiding light of American liberalism, it is understandable that philosophers and political theorists would be deeply concerned about where Rorty seems to be taking modern thought.[36] In the eighties, a decade dominated by the presidency of Ronald Reagan and the ascendancy of neoconservative think tanks proffering advice on every subject under the sun, Rorty wrote two essays, "Postmodernist Bourgeois Liberalism" (1983) and "The Priority of Democracy to Philosophy" (1987), to chart the future of liberal pragmatism.

Seeking to dephilosophize politics, Rorty wanted to see America choose tradition rather than moral law, the conventions of an ongoing community rather than the general principles of a static theory. With Jefferson America got off to a good start in substituting experience for doctrine. "It does me no injury for my neighbor to say that there are twenty Gods or no God," declared Jefferson. Rorty took Jefferson to mean that politics could be "separated from beliefs about matters of ultimate importance." Just as Jefferson found the vocabulary of theology "useless" for the needs of society, Rorty judged the vocabulary of philosophy of little value in the reconstruction of social theory. Rorty preferred John Rawls's *A Theory of Social Justice* for developing a political philosophy with a mode of reasoning requiring neither a reductive logical analysis that would discover moral rules nor a neo-Kantian, ahistorical essence that would ground

---

35. Robert Damico, "Impractical America," *Political Theory* 14 (1986): 83–104.

36. Rorty's "end of philosophy" declaration has had the effect of revitalizing philosophical debate. The literature is vast; I have benefited from the following: *Reading Rorty*, ed. Alan Malachowski (Cambridge Mass.: Blackwell, 1990); Joseph Margolies, *Pragmatism without Foundations: Reconciling Realism and Relativism* (Oxford: Blackwell, 1986); R. W. Sleeper, *The Necessity of Pragmatism: John Dewey's Conception of Philosophy* (New Haven: Yale University Press, 1986); Sandra B. Rosenthal, *Speculative Pragmatism* (Amherst: University of Massachusetts Press, 1986); C. G. Prado, *The Limits of Pragmatism* (Atlantic Highlands, N.J.: Humanities Press International, 1989); Edward Pols, *Radical Realism: Direct Knowing in Science and Philosophy* (Ithaca: Cornell University Press, 1992); Stanley Rosen, *Hermeneutics as Politics* (Oxford: Odeon, 1987); *Redrawing the Lines: Analytic Philosophy, Deconstruction, and Literary Theory*, ed. Reed Way Dasenbrock (Minneapolis: University of Minnesota Press, 1989); Richard J. Bernstein, *The New Constellation: The Ethical-Political Horizons of Modernity-Postmodernity* (Cambridge: Polity, 1991); Gary Brodsky, "Rorty's Interpretation of Pragmatism," *Transactions* 17 (1982): 311–38; James Gouinlock, "What Is the Legacy of Instrumentalism? Rorty's Interpretation of Dewey," *Journal of the History of Philosophy* 28 (1990): 251–69; Anthony J. Cascardi, "The Genealogy of Pragmatism," *Philosophy and Literature* 14:2 (1990): 295–303; Daniel W. Conway, "Taking Irony Seriously: Rorty's Metaphysical Liberalism," *American Literary History* 3 (1991): 198–208; Abraham Edel, "A Missing Dimension in Rorty's Use of Pragmatism," *Transactions* 21 (1985): 21–37; Walter Watson, "Systematic Pluralism and the Foundationalist Controversy," *Reason Papers* 16 (1991): 181–203.

morality in rationality and duty. Justice need not be justified by reference to an antecedent principle but instead by a "deeper understanding of ourselves and our aspirations" based upon the experience of history and the "traditions embedded in our public life." What was true of law and justice was also true of the disciplines of philosophy and even history. By turning to Dewey and the deconstructionists and avoiding the philosophical vocabulary of Descartes, Hume, and Kant, "we shall be able to see moral progress as a history of making rather than finding, of poetic achievement by 'radically situated' individuals and communities, rather than as the gradual unveiling, through the use of 'reason,' of 'principles' or 'rights' or 'values.'"[37]

Why do American intellectuals refuse to heed Rorty's advice to shun the search for foundations and work on the surface of common life? Rorty believed that intellectuals reach for "higher principles" than American conventions because their native country morally discredited itself in the Vietnam War. But Dewey, Rorty insisted, would want American scholars to converse with their fellow citizens instead of taking the high philosophical ground:

> The political discourse of the democracies, at its best, is the exchange of what Wittgenstein called "reminders for a particular purpose"—anecdotes about the past effects of various practices and predictions of what will happen if, or unless, some of these are altered. The moral deliberations of the postmodernist bourgeois liberal consist largely in this same sort of discourse, avoiding the formulation of general principles except where the situations may require this particular tactic—as when one writes a constitution, or rules for young children to memorize. It is useful to remember that this view of moral and political deliberation was a commonplace among American intellectuals in the days when Dewey—a postmodernist before his time—was the reigning American philosopher, days when "legal realism" was thought of as desirable pragmatism rather than unprincipled subjectivism.[38]

Rorty's claim that Dewey shared his assumption about the primacy of democracy to philosophy generated considerable controversy. The most spirited response came from Richard Bernstein, a fellow philosopher who had been a student with Rorty at the University of Chicago. Bernstein criticized Rorty's deconstruction-drenched, "aestheticized pragmatism"

---

37. Richard Rorty, "Postmodernist Bourgeois Liberalism," *Journal of Philosophy* 80 (Oct. 1983): 583–89; "The Priority of Democracy to Philosophy," in *The Virginia Statute of Religious Freedom*, ed. Merrill Peterson and Robert Vaughan (Cambridge, 1988), 257–82.

38. Rorty, "Postmodernist Bourgeois Liberalism," 590–91.

for insisting that liberal democracy needs no philosophical justification. Bernstein also held that democracy need not be deduced from premises about human nature or the self. But Rorty's call for turning to conventions and traditions offered no criterion for clarifying which are to be chosen. Paradoxically, while Rorty claimed there could be no philosophical resolution to the competing conceptions of the good life, he advocated adhering to conventions that presuppose such a consensus. Moreover, although he subscribed to Nietzsche's thesis that there are no facts but simply interpretations, Rorty appealed to a collective "we" as though he had discovered what he had actually constructed. Bernstein charged Rorty with substituting one myth for another, the "historical myth of the given" for the "epistemological myth of the given," as though history could have foundations while philosophy is denied them. Thus Rorty can criticize "realism" on the grounds that there is no "fact of the matter" independent of interpretation and at the same time invoke a common historical heritage as though there were and it only remained to be found. Bernstein asked readers to consider Peirce, Gadamer, and Dewey. In their vision of philosophy as a dialogue there exists something "other" to which we must be responsive, whether it be a partner, a text, or a tradition. Rorty's view of liberal democracy had no deteminate content save what his own "idiosyncratic desires" read into it, which amounted to a "will to power, our will to self-assertion." Conversation is not a dialogue for Rorty but a creation that allows the ego free rein uninhibited by epistemic conditions. Thus "for Rorty there never seem to be any effective constraints on *me* and *my* interpretations. This is why Rorty's constant references to 'we,' a common tradition, a shared consensus appear to be hollow—little more than a label for a projected 'me.'"[39]

Curiously, Rorty's reply to Bernstein turned out to be more political than philosophical. Both the critique ("One Step Forward, Two Steps Backward") and the response ("Thugs and Theorists") were first delivered to the Yale Law School's Legal Theory Workshop and then published in *Political Theory*, a journal that emerged from the activist sixties generation of graduate students committed to democracy but dissatisfied with liberalism. In elaborating his "political credo," Rorty meant by "thugs" the ruling elites who use whatever means necessary to hold onto power and wealth, whether they be the plutocratic advisers to the Reagan administration, the *nomenklatura* in Moscow, or the Ayatollah sycophants in Iran. Such a lineup of suspects meant that older ideological categories no longer pertained. In the spirit of Dewey, Rorty asked liberals to stay clear of

39. Richard J. Bernstein, "One Step Forward, Two Steps Backward: Richard Rorty on Liberal Democracy and Philosophy," *Political Theory* 15 (Nov 1987): 538–63.

Marxists who continued to regard theory as a mystique rather than a method, ignored the "red menace," and believed existing evils "integral" to liberalism and hence beyond democratic reform. Although Rorty well recognized that Habermas is a social democrat with a passionate commitment to reform, he saw the German philosopher nostalgically trying to salvage a nineteenth-century doctrine and vocabulary. Bernstein, who first introduced Habermas to American social theorists, suffered the same illusion. "Bernstein resembles Habermas in thinking that there is still something to be milked out of Marxism." One recalls that decades earlier Hook could never convince Dewey to allow himself to be weaned on the wisdom of dialectical materialism. Thus in this instance Rorty could rightly claim that Dewey "thought of himself as freeing us up for practice, not as providing theoretical foundations for practice."[40]

American pragmatism seems to have a split personality. If Rorty endeavored to relate Dewey to poststructuralism to demonstrate why philosophy cannot tell us much about knowledge and truth, Bernstein endeavored to relate Peirce to Habermas to demonstrate why philosophy can have foundations in a systematic mode of inquiry that constrains thought and yields some measure of objective knowledge. One philosopher believes consensus will emerge from the language of solidarity by means of narration, the other from the logic of inquiry by means of linguistic signs.

Although Rorty agreed politically with Habermas in seeing capitalism and liberal democracy as the inevitable features of modernity, he disagreed philosophically that the directions of modernity have a theoretical solution—especially in what the German Peirceans called "logical socialism," a phrase that Peirce briefly toyed with to imply that the debilities of individualism might possibly be transcended through the long, undisturbed processes of inquiry.[41] Rorty came to doubt Peirce's dictum that "what would be believed at the end of inquiry" could provide a convincing definition of truth. Habermas built much of his theory of knowledge acquisition on Peirce's theory of inquiry, but Rorty saw no foundations there as well. Habermas's notion of rational consensus seemed to Rorty too schematic and prone to compress all viewpoints into a "commensurable" mold. Habermas's project for an ideal speech situation echoed Kant's conditions of possibility for approaching "pure understanding," an illusionary quest for purity and innocence. No transcendental possibility of cognition enables us to stand outside our views of the world and evaluate them from some universal standpoint. What we view, we view, and no

---

40. Rorty, "Thugs and Theorists," ibid., 564–80.

41. Karl-Otto Apel, *Charles S. Peirce: From Pragmatism to Pragmaticism* (Amherst: University of Massachusetts Press, 1981), 53.

amount of inquiry will restore older notions of reason and truth. Foucault made Rorty aware that the results of inquiry may be merely another practice of justifying this or that. The whole question of truth, Rorty concluded, should be dropped from philosophy as "misguided."[42]

Although American scholars have welcomed Rorty's revival of pragmatism, they are less enthused about his relating America's one original contribution to philosophy to European poststructuralism and especially French deconstruction.[43] Yet Rorty has some grounds for developing the relationship. For James and Dewey—though not necessarily Peirce—also rejected the conventional conceptions of knowledge in which truth corresponds to reality or coheres with a larger system where its presence entails every other truth. In addition, the antidualist stance might have prepared James and Dewey to endorse the "philosophy of difference," the Heidegger-inspired conviction that distinctions between essence and appearance, subject and object, and the rational and emotional are only linguistic conventions. Derrida's analysis not of the author's intent but of the unintended, ironic effects of his language displaces the conceptual order of thinking as well as the classical dualisms that the pragmatists also wanted to see extirpated. What Rorty has called "antifoundationalism" might also be taken as another way of saying that pragmatism and poststructuralism remain skeptical of authority as a commitment to something external, whether it be reality, objectivity, or causality. Seeing no distinction between discourse and doctrine, Rorty substituted edification for instruction to suggest that we need to find better ways of speaking so that the search for knowledge yields to education as self-formation, learning not what is "out there" in the world but how to cope with it. What came to be discredited in pragmatism as well as deconstruction was logocentrism—the claim of thought to have grasped reality and reason to have represented it. Since reality cannot be known, Rorty urged Americans to follow James and Dewey and ask what it would be like to believe in one or another of our versions of it and to look to the consequences of ideas rather than their supposed truth-properties.

In relating pragmatism to the writings of Derrida and Foucault Rorty may have pushed the French connection a little too far. Rorty and some poststructuralists see the scientific method as limited, an interpretive construction of data even if it emerges from the laboratory as pure factual discovery. Yet to Dewey science was cherished not because it could accurately represent reality or reveal the structure of things known. On the

42. Rorty, "Habermas and Lyotard on Modernity," in *Habermas and Modernity*, 161–75; "Life at the End of Inquiry," *London Review of Books* (Aug. 2–Sept. 6, 1984), 6–7.

43. See, for example, James T. Kloppenberg, "Objectivity and Historicism: A Century of American Historical Writing," *American Historical Review* 94 (Oct. 1987): 1011–30.

contrary, science offered the only discipline that could move thought from interpretation to action to judge what a thing will do when experimented upon. "*The* method of physical inquiry is to introduce some change in order to see what other change ensues," observed Dewey.[44] Where some poststructuralists seem content to deconstruct the world by exposing the vulnerability of its interpretive representations, the pragmatist insists, with Marx, that the challenge of philosophy is not to interpret the world but to change it. Introducing change brings about variation in the things studied in order to "elicit some previous unperceived qualities" that are the consequence of altering the conditions of perception. To experiment holds out the possibility that the investigator can look for "a new truth" emerging from the changed conditions resulting from inquiry.[45] With poststructuralism, however, the reduction of truth to the contingencies of interpretation precludes the possibility that reason can provide a new truth for what had been deconstructed. Poststructuralism denies the newness of the future just as pragmatism denies the presence of the past.

Obviously, then, poststructuralism rejects two articles of faith that Dewey upheld throughout his life: the idea of progress as experiments directed toward human "ends-in-view," and the institution of education as the agency of change challenged by society's "problematic situations." The poststructuralist regards progress as the illusion of change masking the reality of repetition, and what he or she thinks of education should perhaps never be told to schoolchildren. What would Dewey have made of the poststructuralist premise that knowledge cannot escape its complicity with power, so that in the classroom, instruction amounts to domination? To Foucault the school is little more than a prison, and the relationship of teacher to students is further evidence that power is constitutive of all social relations. Foucault's conviction that progress augments rather than limits the scope and substance of power and that power organizes itself as knowledge imposing its claims on society is a Weberian thought that resonated in Adams and Niebuhr, and particularly in Carl Becker's *Power and Progress* (1936).

In following the pragmatic tradition and treating knowledge as what comes to be validated by conventional methods of validation (and interpretation), Rorty overlooks the poststructuralist point that what comes to be accepted is at the expense of what has been excluded. Consensus by its nature drives out conflict, and normal paradigms of thought scarcely

---

44. Dewey, *Quest for Certainty*, 84.

45. Ibid., 87; "William James," in *John Dewey: Middle Works, 1899–1924*, ed. Jo Ann Boydston (Carbondale, Ill., 1982), vol. 12, 220.

acknowledge the abnormal, deviant, and unreliable, which Jonathan
Culler quaintly specifies as "women, children, poets, prophets, mad-
men."[46] Distinctions between poststructuralism and pragmatism extend
beyond the uses of language. Foucault and Dewey, whatever their agreement about the end of epistemology, are at cross-purposes and trying to
prove the opposite "truths" about the human condition.

Foucault enjoyed considerable influence with the sixties generation, or
at least those former New Left activists who became disenchanted with
Marxism and found themselves looking for an alternative explanation of
domination and oppression that offered something other than the stale
categories of class, labor and capital, and the mode of production. Foucault concentrated on language and discourse to demonstrate that all that
is strange and discordant has been suppressed, pushed out of sight, mar-
ginalized not by the creatures of capitalism but by society's quiet processes of cognition and recognition. Such an argument is alien to Dewey's
evolutionary theory of the mind, which sees intelligence itself springing
to life as it responds to "discordance" and the disruptions and discontinuities that are part of the "precarious nature of existence."[47] Foucault,
in contrast, sees humankind as historically constructed by subjugating
language conventions whose normalizing pressures inhibit freedom by
channeling activity toward socially accepted ends. Dewey believed that
when man's activities experience constraint he learns to adapt to changing
conditions or to address the new problematic situation by the intelligent
transforming of the inhibiting environment. Foucault's theory of the mar-
ginalization of mind is incompatible with Dewey's theory of the origina-
tion of mind, in which encounters with the alien and discordant produce
the discomfort of doubt that prompts inquiry. In Dewey's Darwinian
"emergent" theory, the mind is an organism of adaptation and control in
which the self struggles for self-realization. In Foucault's poststructuralist
"dissolving" theory, the mind is a social construction in which the self is
appropriated by discursive practices and disappears from itself, a loss so
unaware of its own absence that the self is too alienated to experience its
own alienation. To Dewey adaptation and self-realization progress together; to Foucault the only hope is maladaptation and resistance—all
power to the marginals and misfits. In American intellectual history Foucault's anarchist message might have found a warm response in Thoreau,
Veblen, or the young John Dos Passos. But it is difficult to imagine
Dewey feeling comfortable with a philosopher who denies progress, sees

46. Jonathan Culler, *On Deconstruction: Theory and Criticism after Structuralism* (Ithaca,
1982), 152–55.
47. Dewey, *Experience and Nature*, 40–77.

power as a production of knowledge, and values madness as healthier than reason.

If Foucault's obsession with power might cause Dewey to wince, one can well imagine his response to Derrida's obsession with language. In poststructuralism the great promise of the Enlightenment, communication and the dissemination of ideas, liberates humankind from ignorance only to imprison the modern mind in discourse in which nothing is present except scriptural signs with no objects beyond the text. With the sovereignty of language replacing the rationality of the self-conscious subject, words refer only to other words and no meaning exists outside a linguistic system. One disturbing implication of the "linguistic turn" in postmodern thought is that the eighteenth-century principles of liberty and natural rights can no longer be asserted by reference to Jefferson's "Nature and Nature's God." The *Federalist* authors held that liberty could be preserved by balancing power, not by articulating truths about nature and God. What, then, of Jefferson's sacred Declaration?

Most likely the deconstructionist would declare that "we hold these truths not to be self-evident but to be linguistically created and interest-mediated," and proceed to defend rebellion against tyranny as one power system replacing another, with no appeal to a "higher" authority.

Curiously, Dewey himself remained skeptical of the language of natural rights. "These words are to be taken literally, not rhetorically, if one wishes to understand Jefferson's democratic faith." But Dewey cannot take the author of the Declaration literally. "The terms in which Jefferson expressed his belief in the moral criterion for judging political arrangements and his belief that republican institutions are the only ones that are morally legitimate are not now current," he wrote after the outbreak of World War II. "It is doubtful, however, whether the defense of democracy against the attacks to which it is subjected does not depend upon taking once more the position Jefferson took about its moral basis and purpose, even though we have to find another set of words in which to formulate the moral ideal served by democracy."[48]

Dewey's advice is perfectly Rortyan: what we cannot prove philosophically we redescribe rhetorically. The debate that has been raging the past decade over Rorty's use, or abuse, of Dewey deserves discussion. The historian Robert Westbrook made the point that Rorty was seeking to "deconstruct" philosophy while Dewey all along sought to "reconstruct" it.[49] True, Dewey continued throughout his intellectual life to develop

48. John Dewey, *The Living Thoughts of Thomas Jefferson* (New York: Fawcett, 1963), 34–35.

49. Robert Westbrook, *John Dewey and American Democracy* (Ithaca, 1991), 540.

systematic methods of knowing and to call for a public philosophy to overcome the debilities of liberal individualism. No doubt Dewey would be aghast to see the poststructuralist's critique of science, language, education, social intelligence, and the promises of inquiry. But in a theoretical sense all this is beside the point.

As an antifoundationalist, Rorty need hardly feel obligated to render neopragmatism consistent with every aspect of classical pragmatism. There can be no "essential Dewey" if one chooses to read him as he advised us to read reality—as a phenomenon always in transition, the potential nature of which can be known only by changing it. Rorty is perfectly frank in telling us that he picks and chooses what he wants from past thinkers in order to reinterpret texts in light of what he regards as important for our purposes. Hence he distinguishes "historical reconstruction," which is strictly contextualist and aspires to establish an author's intent, from "rational reconstruction," which seeks to make the dead our "conversational partners" even if we might anachronistically impose our problems upon them.[50] Thus Rorty reconstructs a "hypothetical Dewey" to explore what is still living in the philosopher's thought and to simply ignore what is unconvincing and outdated.[51] In a way Dewey himself advised the same procedure when he suggested that we should retain Thomas Jefferson's values while rejecting his outmoded eighteenth-century language and concepts. Whether one is justified in claiming that we can retain and even expand Dewey's values while rejecting his cherished scientific method is the crux of the controversy between Rorty and his many critics. But as far as intellectual history is concerned, Rorty's antifoundationalism and antiessentialism render him free to do what he wants with Dewey, just as Dewey believed himself free to do what he wanted with Jefferson, and Jefferson felt free to do what he wanted with Jesus.

Yet Dewey doubted the adequacy of Jefferson's terminology only because he doubted the philosophical grounds of the political ideas the "words" purported to represent. Did he question the reliability of language itself and privilege it over action and experimentation?

Dewey seemed unaware that philosophy is a species of writing and subjected to all the figurative problems of textual discourse. Dewey and his collaborator Arthur Bentley saw language as equivalent to thinking

50. Richard Rorty, "The History of Philosophy: Four Genres," in *Philosophy in History*, ed. Richard Rorty, J. B. Schneewind, and Quentin Skinner (Cambridge: Cambridge University Press, 1984), 67–74.

51. Rorty, "Between Hegel and Darwin," paper delivered at the conference on the Life Sciences, Social Sciences, and Modernity in the Western World, Bellagio, Italy, May 22, 1990.

and both as forms of action in which there is no dualism between words and thought and knowing and the known. According to Sidney Ratner, Dewey agreed with Wittgenstein and other "ordinary language" theorists who saw thought as bound up with its linguistic formulations and language as an instrument whose usage determined the meaning of words.[52] Hence Dewey was closer to speech-act theory than to later Derridean deconstruction. The latter focuses on the delusions of intertextual discourse wherein the author is absent to make clear his intentions; the former looks to intersubjective agreement made possible by the presence of speakers and listeners who share a common understanding of objects that words signify. In this respect Dewey anticipated Habermas's view of language as purposive action expressed in communication. But Dewey was innocent, as was much of modern philosophy until Nietzsche, of the abyss lurking behind textual communication. Reading Jefferson, Dewey doubted his utterance, not his presence.

When Dewey remarked, on his ninetieth birthday, that "democracy begins in conversation,"[53] he most likely regarded language as speech rather than script. "Language is the cherishing mother of all significance," he wrote in *Experience and Nature*. Earlier in his career he informed students in his lectures that language was as natural to social behavior as a bodily function. "Language performs the same function in society that nerve fibres do in the body. It is through the institutional organization of language that we have defined our social sensorium."[54] Where Dewey saw in language the power of social cohesion, the poststructuralist sees in it the pleasures of linguistic disruption. To Foucault, language confines, restricts, excludes, incarcerates; to Derrida, it reverses meanings, contradicts syntax, betrays purposes; to Dewey, it stabilizes meanings and synthesizes ends and methods. "Continuity of meaning and value is the essence of language," he wrote in *Art as Experience*.[55] A philosopher who believed that "society exists in and through communication" could hardly proclaim that language destabilizes meaning by exposing truths as fictions hidden in rhetoric. In his essay "Events and Meanings," Dewey advocated conversation and storytelling to overcome the growing sense of the meaninglessness of history, an attitude best expressed by those "extreme modernists" who, like James Joyce, "string words together in a jumble."

52. Sidney Ratner's comments on Dewey and language are in his introduction to *John Dewey and Arthur Bentley: A Philosophical Correspondence, 1932–1950*, ed. Sidney Ratner (New Brunswick, N.J., 1964), 46.

53. *Dialogue on Dewey*, ed. Corliss Lamont (New York, 1959), 88.

54. Dewey, *Experience and Nature*, 186; "Political Philosophy" (1892), Dewey mss., 102 62/x, p. 52.

55. Dewey, *Art as Experience*, 240.

Dewey assumed that narration could be sufficient to overcome what the modernist mind regarded as chaos and entropy, the "nightmare" of causeless happenings and convulsions. "Events that have no attributed meanings are accidents and if they are big enough are catastrophes. By sufficient preliminary conversation you can avert a catastrophe. For nothing is a catastrophe which belongs in a composed tale of meanings."[56]

Compared to Dewey, Rorty is much more aware of the equivocal, subversive, decentering, and obliterating nature of language that defies and deconstructs its author's own purposes. Yet he also believes that the philosopher can turn to writing and narration to render meaningful and hopeful the quixotic and capricious spectacle of existence in the modern world. It should be recalled that the shocks of the two world wars and the tragic catastrophes of Hiroshima and the Holocaust scarely compelled Dewey to follow his own advice and compose a new tale of meaning for our times. In this respect Rorty can only follow what Dewey offered as a theoretical possibility and not an actual achievement. Yet if Rorty believes in anything it is the irrelevance of theory and the imperative of practice.

Against Theory and the Limits of Redescription: Thorstein Veblen

In a symposium later published as *Against Theory: Literary Studies and the New Pragmatism*, Rorty spelled out his credo first intimated in *Philosophy and the Mirror of Nature*. Since theory has no foundations in origins, causes, or antecedent ideas independent of the knowing subject, there can be no basis in theory to which practice must conform. The pragmatist denies there can be any direct encounter with reality and that knowledge can be identical with its object. Insisting that pragmatists "are supposed to treat everything as a matter of choice and context and nothing as a matter of inherited properties," Rorty advised literary critics to forget trying to establish an author's meaning and intent and choose a context for a text and openly acknowledge "the advantages of doing so." Literary interpretations, like beliefs, cannot be grounded in anything whose source is not also another interpretation and belief. Rorty agreed with the literary critic Stanley Fish that practice cannot be derived from theory, since no account of theory can be anything other than another interpretation of theory. "Pragmatists and Derrideans are, indeed, natural allies," declared Rorty. When philosophical argument fails, pragmatists follow Heidegger and Derrida and resort to narrative to explain how we "got into our present

56. Dewey on society existing through communication is quoted in Frederick Matthews, *Quest for American Sociology*, 146; Dewey, "Events and Meanings," in *Character and Events*, vol. 1, 129.

dead end." Rorty urged that we give up speculative theory and observe what happens in language practices as one way to continue the conversation of mankind.[57] Although he has recently reconsidered the fetish of interpretation, Rorty's original sense of practice tended to privilege language over action.[58] We employ narrative to find out how we have arrived at our present dilemmas, and we engage in redescription as a possible means of overcoming them.

But only if literature and conversation were perfectly synonymous with life could we write and talk our way out of such dilemmas. How long would William James listen to Richard Rorty?

> As long as one continues *talking*, intellectualism remains in undisturbed possession of the field. The return to life can't come about by talking. It is an *act*; to make your return to life, I must set an example for your imitation. I must deafen you to talk, or to the importance of talk, by showing you, as Bergson does, that the concepts we talk with are made for purposes of *practice* and are not for purposes of insight.[59]

Rorty's proposal to turn philosophy, and indeed many other disciplines, into a species of language hangs on the adequacy of conversation and narration. With Heidegger he reflects on the meaning of "our present dead end" as a language condition, whereas James and Dewey regarded problems as the precondition for action. Even if it could be shown that language as a practice without theoretical foundations still furnishes the description of where we are, neopragmatism offers as a solution what Adams described as the problem: Without theory Americans can make history but not know it.

It may be difficult to imagine Dewey going all the way with deconstruction and according priority to structure over subject, language over action, and power over authority. Pragmatism was supposed to resolve the crisis of modernism, not to "discourse" about it. Yet when it comes to the priority of practice over theory, Rorty stands on solid ground. Dewey himself regarded theory as superfluous and class-biased. Since Dewey's position has been almost universally endorsed by liberals and radicals, especially those impressed by Marx's similar notion of "praxis," the issue of theory and practice needs to be explored to consider its ironic political

57. Richard Rorty, "Philosophy without Principles," in *Against Theory: Literary Studies and the New Pragmatism* (Chicago, 1985), 132–38.

58. Richard Rorty, "Intellectuals in Politics," *Dissent* 38 (Fall 1991): 483–90.

59. William James, "The Continuity of Experience," in *Writings of William James*, 297; "Pragmatism's Conception of Truth," ibid., 435.

implications, which could possibly make practice conservative and theory subversive.

The point has been made earlier that Dewey perceived a social distinction between the dualisms of theory and practice and knowing and doing. In classical antiquity knowing represented the authority belonging to the leisure class, and doing represented the obedience of those who must labor. Dewey's quarrel with classical philosophy involved, among other things, the hierarchical scheme that had rational thought aspiring to the necessary and immutable at the apex of the social order untouched by any suggestion of "practical activity—in short, a matter of strictly *contemplative* beholding." Dewey noted that Aristotle associated theory with "*Theos*, God," and the etymological root of the term could also be found in "*theater* as a place for *looking* at a spectacle which is *there* to be seen."[60] To know is not to produce knowledge but to behold timeless truths that disclose themselves in contemplation. Such assumptions, Dewey insisted, could not survive the rise of modern science, wherein truth is not revealed but made by *homo faber* acting upon the materials of existence. Henceforth, modernity meant practice and the making of things as opposed to theory and the discovery of causes.

Rorty, Fish, and other neopragmatists also argue that practice is to replace theory because the latter has no foundations in thought or in any idea that can stand apart from action and constitute a judgment upon it. But without some transcending theoretical perspective, will not all thinking succumb to subjectivity? On the contrary, the neopragmatists believe that the constraints of collective intellectual practices will prevent individual thinkers from pursuing their preferences. Antifoundationalism, Fish assured literary critics, is not out to undermine shared standards and public conventions. Such anarchy would follow "only if antifoundationalism is an argument for unbridled subjectivity, for the absence of constraints on the individual; whereas, in fact, it is an argument for the situated subject, for the individual who is always constrained by the local or community standards and criteria of which his judgment is an extension." Antifoundationalism may be against philosophical truth but not against social authority. As scholars "you will always be guided by the rules or rules of thumb that are the content of any settled practice, by the assumed definitions, distinctions, criteria of evidence, measures of adequacy, and such, which not only define the practice but structure the understanding of the agent who thinks of himself as a 'competent member.' That agent cannot distance himself from these rules, because it is

60. Dewey, "Reflections," 102 59/9, pp. 12–13; Dewey mss.

only within them that he can think about alternative courses of action, or, indeed, think at all."[61]

Does Fish's argument for rule-bound interpretive communities advance knowledge or simply redefine it? The same dilemma of establishing objectively determined meaning applies to history as it does to the texts, whether literary or legal, that Fish has in mind. Adams, it will be recalled, concluded that American history had no rational meaning since its people and leaders were rarely fully conscious of their actions, many of which resulted in ironic consequences. Adams left the formal subject of history with the suspicion that the world was racing ahead of mind, taking "leaps" that put the production of energy ahead of intellect to the point that the future could be out of control.

Observe how the neopragmatist promises to regain control, if not of the world then at least of the text, which for many literary critics is the world. In theory a text without a consciously intending author in control of the play of words leaves the critic without an authoritative interpretation of meaning. But the neopragmatist shifts the problem of meaning from the text to the reader, not as an individual but as a collective entity. It is how the community of interpreters experiences the text that establishes its meaning. Translated into history, one would say that the meaning of history is the experience Adams had in studying it. And if he experienced meaninglessness, the neopragmatist would invite him to join a community of scholars where different interpretations would be thrashed out and revised, and thus meaning and understanding could be stabilized without resorting to an illusionary theoretical foundation of knowledge. The point seems to be not so much to know history as to react to a historical text in order better to share the experience. Unwilling to reduce knowledge to experience, and knowing full well that any inquiry without access to its object risks arriving at false conclusions, Adams concluded, "Silence is best."

The Fish-Rorty case against theory derived from the antifoundationalist conviction that theory cannot transcend its own contextual conditions to guide practice. Historicism had made the modern mind aware that theory has no atemporal character of rational judgment. Rather it expresses the conventions, interests, and practices of a given situation and thus cannot attain the disinterested objectivity that would make it truthful instead of conditional. Such reasoning, while perhaps epistemologically persuasive, fails to consider nonphilosophical grounds for continuing the distinction between theory and practice. Theory may be regarded as a mode of

61. Stanley Fish, "Consequences," in *Against Theory*, 107–31, quote on 113.

thinking that resists translation into practice because the thinker refuses to identify with society's "settled" conventions. In this sense theory claims not to represent truth but to question it. Fish and Rorty may be right to insist that antifoundationalism does not lead to anarchy; the real question is whether it leads to conformity.

Thorstein Veblen's critique of pragmatism as well as of American society in general suggests that a writer can distance himself from existing rules and practices and devise new rules, of evidence as well as of expression, to bring to light the unsettling truths about the modern world. Veblen coined the phrase "idle curiosity" to hint that pragmatism embraced practical action out of fear that theoretical speculation wasted itself in pursuit of the otiose and useless. In contrast to idle curiosity, which is "unintended and irrelevant" to practical concerns but strives "toward a more and more comprehensive system of knowledge," pragmatism offers "didactic exhortations to thrift, prudence, equanimity, and shrewd management." Fish and Rorty sought to anchor knowledge in the sense of "competency" that inquirers feel by following accepted practices. Yet if practice itself is to guide thought and thought is constrained by the established conventions of a community, who would challenge existing conventions, and whence would come the "irritation of doubt" that prompts fresh inquiry? In his essay "Kant's Critique of Judgment," Veblen indicates why theoretical wonder is the driving force behind the mind's desire to think about what it cannot know:

> The unrest felt on account of the inharmonious and forced activities of the faculties, when engaged about a mere manifold or a discordant miscellany, drives the mind to seek a concord for its own activities, and, consequently, a reconciliation of the conflicting elements of its knowledge. The reason for the unrest felt in contemplating external things simply as individual and unconnected things lies in the fact that the mind is adapted to conceive the subject-matter of its knowledge in the form of a connected whole. If the mind had not an inherent capacity for thinking things as connected into a totality, or at least as being connected in a systematic way and under definite laws, it could not feel the lack of totality in contemplating things under the mere form of juxtaposition in time and space. It would not be dissatisfied with things as mere data if it knew of nothing better; and it would not seek for anything different if the conception of things, as a mere congeries, satisfied the requirements of its normal activity.[62]

62. Thorstein Veblen, *The Place of Science in Modern Civilization and Other Essays* (1919; New York: Capricorn, 1969), 1–31; "Kant's Critique of Judgment," in *Essays in Our Changing Order*, ed. Leon Ardzroni (1934; New York: Augustus Kelley, 1964), 175–93, quote on 191.

Fish insisted that practice requires no theoretical guidance because thought and action will be restrained by "the content of any settled practice," and Rorty insisted that "nothing counts for justification unless by reference to what we already accept."[63] Veblen believed the genuine seeker of knowledge must be dissatisfied with all that settles into our conceptions of "normal activity." Veblen hailed the Jewish intellectual whose lack of allegiance placed him in "the vanguard of inquiry" because of his restless, nomadic "immunity from the inhibitions of intellectual quietism."[64] Fish and Rorty liberated the intellectual from theory only to inhibit him in practice as conforming to the accepted and settled. Since theory, like "idle curiosity," cannot give us anything knowable, the point of pragmatism was to make life bearable. The rejection of theory actually antedates pragmatism. At the time of the Enlightenment, with the rise of modern experimental science, theoretical curiosity came to be regarded as, in Hans Blumenberg's words, "an attitude of inescapable resignation because it has no motive for its progress but rather dwells persistently on each of its phenomena and loses itself in admiration of it."[65] It seems today that the same could be said of practice as an inescapable resignation to a community's existing conventions and the practitioner's own admiration of himself as a "competent member."

"Cultural anthropology (in a large sense which includes intellectual history) is all we need."[66] So advised Rorty with supreme confidence. Theory and systematic philosophy based upon epistemological foundations must give way to a study of how cultures view themselves and justify their practices in common discourse. Scholars can engage in a study of beliefs and values not to judge their truthfulness but to describe their function, in order, presumably, to better redescribe new possibilities as a creative effort. Whether Rorty was suggesting that authors can write about what "is" in order to develop redescriptions of what "ought" to be may not be the issue in philosophy but it is all too familiar in intellectual history. Consider the heroic efforts of Veblen to fulfill precisely this role of the social critic as both descriptionist and moralist.

Veblen set out to free economics from all metaphysical foundations in natural law and classical market axioms, and, as well, all postulates and theories that imputed to objects human significance, propensities, causes, purposes, and other tropismatic habits of mind that give meaning to what

63. Fish, "Consequences," 113; Rorty, *Philosophy and the Mirror of Nature*, 357–394.
64. Veblen, "The Intellectual Pre-eminence of Jews in Modern Europe," in *Essays*, 219–31.
65. Hans Blumenberg, *Legitimacy of the Modern Age*, trans. Robert Wallace (Cambridge: MIT Press, 1983), 388.
66. Rorty, *Philosophy and the Mirror of Nature*, 381.

is essentially mechanical. Veblen also turned to the study of cultural anthropology to describe differing tribal customs and to make ironic comparisons between savagery and modernity. As if a proto-poststructuralist, he sought to deconstruct the conventional hierarchical oppositions that privilege the former term over the latter: male/female, civilization/barbarism, leisure/labor, reason/instinct, practicality/curiosity, normal/abnormal. Through such "perspective by incongruity," in Kenneth Burke's apt phrase, Veblen put America through a kind of transvaluation of its own values by showing that the Protestant ethic existed in belief but not in practice. As in primitive society, wealth and property represent not reward for labor and savings but predation and exploitation. Whatever the moral maxims in discourse, in the distribution of status the possession of money commands more esteem than the production of goods. In Veblen's America the masses of people saw themselves as dedicated workers and rational consumers practicing industry and frugality. Veblen drew on anthropology to challenge that self-image by redescribing modern society as carrying forward tribal and feudal customs that valued leisure over labor and wasteful consumption over useful production. It was, in short, precisely the opinions, beliefs, and practices of Americans that posed the problem of hegemony and false consciousness. Even workers accepted the cultural authority of the rich and the symbolic trappings and trophies of unearned wealth. The triumph of capitalist culture could be explained by semiotics as Veblen demonstrated consumer commodities radiating as "signs," nonhuman objects that nevertheless convey the human meaning of success. He went beyond Marx to demonstrate what French poststructuralists are only beginning to grasp in our times: that economics is as much a language as literature, and that reification manifests itself in consumption rather than in production.[67]

Thus Veblen narrated the evolution of modern economic society, provided an anthropological description of society's contemporary practices to unveil the persistence of archaic traits, even gave a vivid account of "the barbarian status of women," and tried to redescribe the whole depressing scenario by reversing hierarchical oppositions in order to show America betraying its ideals of honest workmanship to the pecuniary images of success and respectability. Veblen fulfilled almost all the requirements of Rorty's model of the poststructuralist thinker. He turned against economic theory, adopted anthropology as a means of redescribing what passed for social reality, and tried to break down disciplinary barriers by using social psychology to illustrate the irrationalities of consumption

67. I have developed these themes in *The Bard of Savagery: Thorstein Veblen and Modern Social Theory* (New York, 1978).

deriving from envy and emulation (Heidegger saw such irrationalities reflecting "the emptiness of Being").[68] He also wanted to mitigate human suffering and humiliation by showing the masses that there is nothing intrinsically shameful in work and by showing women how they have come to be relegated to the role of idle consumers no matter how much they want to be active producers. As much as Rorty, Veblen believed in solidarity as the continuous struggle for freedom that begins in the creative imagination; and as much as the modern deconstructionist, he sought to liberate language by destabilizing conventional meanings through the inventions of new, arresting phrases like "conspicuous consumption," "honorific waste," and "trained inability." With a new vocabulary Veblen could redescribe the American leisure class as though he were an ethnographer observing Polynesian rituals. He deconstructed economics so that modern society could see the symbolic meanings of wealth. Long before Pierre Bourdieu and other French postmodernists, he exposed higher education as a system of status rivalry and class pretension, "a study in total depravity."[69]

But in the end Veblen failed and judged himself a failure. The indulgent America he found developing in the 1890s continues its "invidious distinction" between wealth and work in the 1990s, and higher education has become a cushy residence of bureaucratic administrators and sinecured professors—the leisure of the theory class. Thus narrative redescription, like philosophy itself, according to Rorty, makes nothing happen. The turn toward anthropology was politically useless as contemporary American society went about its insensate ways. It should be noted that Veblen studied the practices of people and not necessarily their beliefs, what they did in their actions and not simply what they claimed as their intentions. Anticipating the advice of the neopragmatist, he did not feel practices must be theoretically grounded. But what the neopragmatists hail as liberating, society's stabilizing conventions, Veblen saw as suffocating.

In many respects Rorty's attempt to update American pragmatism by turning to European poststructuralism offers as a solution what in fact may be the heart of the problem: the proposal that America needs no theory to guide action but simply a better description of practice. It should be recalled that an alternative account of American history and society, as opposed to the image American people held of themselves, was precisely what earlier progressive scholars tried to present. In the late

68. Martin Heidegger, *The End of Philosophy*, trans. Joan Stambaugh (1954; New York: Harper and Row, 1973), 107.
69. Veblen, *The Higher Learning in America* (New York, 1914).

nineteenth century Americans had conceived themselves as self-sufficient individuals blessed with an impartial, just government founded upon a divinely inspired Constitution. Authors like Beard, Becker, and Bentley redescribed Americans as people of interest-group politics living under a constitutional government that protected property and perpetuated corporate power. This turning from ideals and theories to address the social facts of industrial society came to be known as "realism," uncovering not the smiling but the sordid aspects of American life. But the effort at redescription, in contrast to some of the sensationalist journalism of the "muckrakers," did little to arouse the people into protest and reform. A cool, scholarly debunking of national self-conceits proved insufficient; for whatever reason, the ruling classes won the battle for hegemony. One wonders, then, what Dewey would think of redescription that turns out to be a method that failed to introduce change and left things as they were.

Rorty called for redescribing our view of the world, the self, and the past on the assumption that we are what we think and say we are through words. Recognizing the ironic nature of vocabulary, that "anything can be made to look good or bad by being redescribed," Rorty wanted to make us aware that the human condition is a result of social and historical circumstances, a matter of contingency rather than the necessity of any essential human nature or national character. Rorty would agree with George Santayana's observation that "discourse is a language, not a mirror," and that the "truth which discourse can achieve is truth in its own terms, appropriate description."[70] Since descriptions can refer only to other descriptions, what is described is not as important as how it is conveyed. The edifying description that Rorty feels is not only appropriate but imperative is human "solidarity," a moral possibility that could be created by redescribing the world in ways that help us see the effects of our indifference to the cruel fate of others. Redescription would not be a matter of inquiry but one of imagination. "This process of coming to see other human beings as 'one of us' rather than as 'them' is a matter of detailed description of what unfamiliar people are like and of redescription of what we ourselves are like."[71]

Ironically, what Rorty has been advocating in his recent writings had already been carried out by American historians two decades earlier. In the field of social history especially, New Left labor historians redescribed the American past in ways that satisfied the ideological needs of the present in order to tell us "what we ourselves are like." Nineteenth-century

70. Santayana, *Animal Skepticism and Other Essays* (New York: Dover, 1955), 179.
71. Rorty, *Contingency, Irony, Solidarity* (New York: Cambridge University Press, 1989), xvi.

workers appeared in history texts as endowed with class consciousness, community spirit, and a commitment to the solidarity of "moral economy," and Marxist and feminist scholars could seldom agree whether we are to share the sufferings of the workers or sing of their triumphs in resisting capitalism and its lust after hegemonic domination.[72] But whether workers were heroes or victims, Marx must have been wrong when he wrote in the preface to *Das Kapital*: "We suffer not only from the living but from the dead. *Le mort saisit le vif!*"[73] The radical historian reverses the dictum: the living can make the dead say what needs to be heard. Both Marx and Dewey believed that the past is beyond redemption and thus the meaning of history lies in the future. But the radical historian and the neopragmatist can refashion the past to the requirements of the contemporary imagination. If textual reality is the only reality, redescription is the will to believe that the world can be changed by writing about it.

Rorty's advocating the strategy of redescription contains an embarrassment if considered as part of the pragmatic theory of knowledge. For the pragmatist recognizes that the truth of any proposition pertaining to things not observable in the present or testable in the future has no means of verification and therefore no meaning itself. But even when statements refer to events or ideas not now present, they can have some validity if a sense of continuity can be established by showing how present realities are the effects of past tendencies. Dewey emphasized that the pragmatist can confirm statements about the past only by showing how subsequent consequences developed from events contained in those statements and how the consequences continue up to the present. Yet this feat of demonstration by tracing is precisely what a radical redescription of American history falls short of accomplishing. Whether studying nineteenth-century workers, the black family after emancipation, or the American Revolution as respective expressions of class, filial authority, and political ideology, the historian cannot demonstrate in what ways "class solidarity," "household stability," and "civic virtue" are historically real and true because we can today see and appreciate their observable effects. Historians can "discourse" forever about the Machiavellian or Marxist "moment" in American history. But how does the earnest labor historian get from Jacksonian artisans and their soft patriotic hearts to New York construction workers and their hard patriotic hats? "Appropriate description" indeed!

Rorty's advocacy of redescription as a means of improving the way we

72. John Patrick Diggins, "Comrades and Citizens: New Mythologies in American History," *American Historical Review* 90 (June 1985): 614–38.

73. Karl Marx, *Capital: A Critical Analysis of Production* (Moscow: Progressive Publishers, n.d.), vol. 1, 20.

see the world has its predecessors, not only the rhetorical theories of Kenneth Burke but perhaps even those of the seventeenth-century New England Puritans, who, finding reason corrupt and the will decayed, often put their trust in words. Even the Enlightenment turned to literature as much as to philosophy. What, after all, was the Declaration of Independence if not a new way of looking at things composed by an author whose immediate liberal politics compelled the announcement of self-evident truths and whose earlier Lockean philosophy denied their existence? Rorty's strategy is also perfectly consistent with pragmatism's ambition to use knowledge to enable humankind to achieve more satisfying relations with the environment and to cope better with the instabilities of experience. Yet one wonders about the fate of historical study if a pragmatic criterion of present usefulness should determine how the past is viewed. Would Rorty accept Parson Weems as a proto-poststructuralist who once gave young Americans the appropriate myths about George Washington? Our first film star president also approached American history as the work of text and speech rather than fact and research. In his first inaugural address Ronald Reagan invoked both John Winthrop and Thomas Paine, seemingly unaware that what the former wanted to uphold the latter wanted to destroy. The address was also edifying in that it relieved Americans from any sense of guilt and responsibility and had them believing that the "city upon a hill" was Beverly Hills. Who will save American history from its redescribers?

Emerson, Silence, and the Limits of Persuasion

"He was born a philosopher, and a man of few words." Benedetto Croce quoted the statement of a fellow Italian to suggest that a person could be a philosopher without writing philosophy or talking much about it. The description may be true of "working men and peasants" because they "think and speak wisely and are secure in the possession of the substantial truths."[74] Uncertain about any truth, Rorty wants the postmodernist writer to be of many words, as though he thinks with his tongue in the "conversation of mankind."

Emerson offered America a different perspective on philosophy. We can avoid talking about what we do know because perception requires neither representation nor explanation. "Good as discourse is, silence is better, and shames it," wrote Emerson. "The length of discourse indicates the distance of thought betwixt the speaker and the hearer." Emerson defined philosophy as the "account the human mind gives to itself of the

---

74. Benedetto Croce, *My Philosophy: Essays on the Moral and Political Problems of Our Time,* trans. E. F. Carritt (1949; New York: Collier, 1962), 241.

constitution of the world," and it was more important to receive the account than to convey it. "If I speak, I define and confine, and am less." Speech requires the presence of others and demands their attention, whereas "silence is a solvent that destroys personality and gives us leave to be great and universal."[75]

In his essay on Emerson, Dewey demurs from the notion that poetry could replace philosophy as a kind of private recollection of the rationality of all things in the beauty of nature. Although an admirer of Emerson, Dewey could hardly endorse the suggestion that character and disposition can replace discourse and conversation and that silent apprehension affirms what reason and argument destroy. "The desire for an articulate, not for silent, logic is intrinsic with philosophy," wrote Dewey. "The unfolding of the perception must be stated, not merely followed and understood. Such conscious method is, one might say, the only thing of ultimate concern to the abstract thinker. Not thought, but reasoned thought, not things, but the ways of things, interest him."[76]

Rorty seems to stand somewhere between Dewey and Emerson. While he wants philosophy to be articulate and is less interested in thought than in discourse, he also assumes that imagination may proceed where understanding falters. Since the philosopher *qua* philosopher cannot possess well-grounded beliefs, there is no use elaborating reasons for holding them. Like Emerson, Rorty favors anecdote, epigram, and aphorism. If Emerson was, as Santayana put it, "a Puritan whose religion was all poetry," Rorty is a pragmatist whose philosophy is all colloquy.[77] Yet while Emerson believed truth is to be discovered by the self-reflecting self and that talk alienates speaker and hearer, Rorty insists there is neither truth nor self, and thus the life of the mind must continue as discourse rather than disclosure, action and conversation instead of the silent moments of solitude and stillness. Postmodernist thought will go forward as a linguistic enterprise, and if philosophy cannot let go of its conventional categories of analysis, "postphilosophy" can turn to other disciplines and offer a narrative account of their respective subjects, whether history, poetry, or anthropology.

In his most recent writings Rorty replaces "the end of philosophy" with a kind of Emersonian self-creation, an urge to absorb and assimilate all ideas fit for language, yet without Emerson's confidence in self-

75. Ralph Waldo Emerson, "The Poet," in *Selected Prose and Poetry*, ed. Reginald L. Cook (New York, 1966), 316–40; "Plato, or the Philosopher," in *Representative Men: Seven Lectures* (New York: Hurst, n.d.), 28–58; some quotes are also from John Dewey, "Ralph Waldo Emerson," in *Characters and Events*, vol. 2, 69–77.

76. Dewey, "Ralph Waldo Emerson," 70–71.

77. Santayana, "Emerson," in *Santayana on America*, 266.

reliance, God, Nature, and the "transparent eyeball" that perceives beyond the real and accepts words as coexistent with reality. With the
poststructuralist attack on humanism, there can be no talk of self, mind,
soul, and other intuitions precious to Emerson. Instead the world is the
"prison-house of language" rather than the externalization of the soul, and
philosophy becomes what can be thought in conversation rather than
what can be known and believed in contemplation. In Emerson "man-
thinking" is presented not only as a linguistic formulation but more emphatically as a deliberate self-creation in which "in the order of genius
the thought is prior to the form."[78] Assuming the opposite and holding
that the word precedes all else, Rorty limits what philosophy can prove
to demonstrate what language can produce, and what he wants to see
produced in contemporary America is an idea that could never get itself
established in historical America—the idea of solidarity.

A certain spiritual solidarity characterized the moral community of
seventeenth-century New England Puritans. But their theology had, or
was seen to have, firm philosophical foundations. Rorty rejects all previous thinkers who assumed that philosophy had foundations external to
itself on which its knowledge could rest, and he believes that he can
successfully combine antifoundationalism with social criticism. The
Transcendentalists had recourse to nature when criticizing society. But
with Rorty nature cannot be a norm if it exists not immediate to the
"transparent eyeball" but in the flickering, contingent perceptions that
stem from social conventions. Thoreau flees to the woods to escape society's conventions, which "paw" at him, and Twain identifies freedom
with the Mississippi River. To Rorty the core of American identity lies
not in flight but in talk. This turn toward conversation and narration
requires a willing suspension of disbelief in our own desire to get to the
bottom of things, to "dive deep," as Melville put it, to penetrate beyond
conventions and even the reach of words themselves. But perhaps Rorty
would remind us that Billy Budd had to hang from the gallows because
he could not speak. We ignore "the linguistic turn" at our peril.

Rorty's neopragmatism offers neither an epistemology with which
thought might be made to correspond to reality nor a metaphysics with
which we can search for the meaning of something beyond the babble of
conversation. Instead this new antidualistic philosophy becomes a language activity provoked by the way things are said rather than known,
presented rather than proven. And history becomes the study of "genealogy," the study of the conditions that allow specific knowledge assertions
to win acceptance, to become justified and legitimated. Both philosophy

78. Emerson, "The Poet," 320.

and history thus become forms of narration, not inquiries into the nature or causes of things, but descriptions of how things developed and how we came to be who we are. As to morality, Rorty advocates turning to literature to find a vocabulary of ethical vision and reflection. Authors such as Marcel Proust, Vladimir Nabokov, and George Orwell illuminate how to master contingencies and how to reveal the suffering brought by power, deception, and cruelty. The ultimate ideal for Rorty is solidarity, a sentiment that enables humankind to sympathize with the suffering of others. Solidarity has nothing to do with the search for truth and objectivity; it is an invention, not a discovery, a statement rather than a substance. Its domain is language, and presumably its values can be made to move from literature to life.

To Rorty and the French poststructuralists the turn from philosophy to literature seemed the only alternative once philosophy lost its innocent assumption that it could find indubitable foundations on which to develop demonstrable propositions. Pragmatists and poststructuralists share a common revolt against Cartesian rationalism. Descartes's confidence that knowledge could be deduced from immediate awareness seemed naive to modernist thinkers too aware that the immediacy of subjective awareness may be only a linguistic construction to conceal the fear of nothingness, the anxiety of the "I" in knowing that the self is simply a word. As one critic said of Descartes, although his method proclaimed the sufficiency of reason, it amounted to "believe in believing."[79] Henry Adams, one recalls, loved to quote Pascal's point against Descartes that he doubted not God but reason. It should be remembered that religious thinkers like Pascal pronounced modern philosophy dead before it came to life. Accepting humility in the face of mystery, premodern philosophers sensed the impossibility of mind knowing its object, whether the object be factual truth or moral principle. Poststructuralism emerged as original in the post–World War II period to the extent that many of its proponents came from a Marxist background (Derrida is an exception), and their disillusionment with Marxism as a "science" led to a critique of the Enlightenment and the promise of truth and objectivity. Yet earlier critics of the emerging Enlightenment, the Calvinists in America and the Catholics and Jansenists in Europe, also tried to warn the coming modern world about the limits of reason.

Centuries ago, before the rise of modern science and the discovery of the new world, it was assumed that knowledge resided between the covers of books and that writing and communication, rather than the study of ·

---

79. The phrase is quoted in Lucien Goldman, "Pascal and Dialectical Thought," from Goldman's *Le Dieu Cache*, reprinted in *Philosophical Forum* 23 (1991–92): 9–19.

nature and human behavior, provided the linguistic tools to get at the truth of things. To believe in the words of the Gospel was to believe in textual truth independently of the context that explains it. Neopragmatists like Rorty and Habermas, while fully aware that knowledge is contingent upon the conditions of its production, regard philosophy as a matter more of justification than of explanation, and hence they call for a return to writing and conversation—precisely where Pascal wrestled with the limits of knowledge in investigating truth and rhetoric. Most people, Pascal observed, "are brought to believe, not because the thing is proved, but because it pleases." To attempt to persuade others when there can be no way of demonstrating the truthfulness of a proposal means that we can only appeal to what others want to hear and indulge their desires. "Thus the art of persuasion consists as much in pleasing as in carrying conviction, so much are men inclined to be governed by caprice rather than by reason." Rorty claims there need be no objectivity to persuade people of the virtues of solidarity, and he assumes that people practicing solidarity with fellow human beings will somehow be moved to diminish the extent of suffering and humiliation in the world. It seems solidarity is to perform the old function of religious conscience without invoking guilt and responsibility. Yet without the appeal to God and "bad faith," without the existence of objective standards of justice, there remains only the appeal to pleasure, emotional preference, or what the early pragmatists called "satisfaction." Such appeals to emotions without reasons are appeals that can only arouse notions that "change from one hour to the next," observed Pascal. A speaker who has no foundations and listeners who have only their emotions would leave Rorty's beloved idea of solidarity to whim. "I cannot say whether there are any strict rules for adapting discussion to the inconstancy of human caprice," Pascal concluded.[80]

Rorty insists that the truth-value of solidarity depends upon not its source but its production, and thus, as with Habermas's theory of communication, Rorty wants to see solidarity come into existence as a literary act. But why language that is not stable enough to support truth can be clear enough to forge solidarity as a unifying principle held by different people remains unexplained. If language as a means of expression can be shown to subvert its author's own intentions, one can only wonder about the status of language as a means of realization.

Rorty's quest for solidarity compounds the problems in Dewey's older quest for community. If solidarity is essential to reducing human misery, what qualities and values reside in collective thought that can move people

80. Blaise Pascal, "The Art of Persuading," in *The Essential Pascal*, ed. Robert W. Gleason, S. J., trans. G. F. Pullen (New York, 1966), 314–27.

to do as a group what they are apparently unwilling to do as individuals? Rorty claims that we are motivated to moral obligation simply by identifying with the solidarity of a group in which the possessive "I want" is transformed into the collective "we want."[81] Somehow in solidarity there is an invisible hand that works like alchemy, converting the private vices of individual pursuits into the collective virtues of benevolent purposes. What's good for "us" is good for all! It should be noted that in certain schools of thought, the moral philosophers of the Scottish Enlightenment, for example, it was assumed that humankind has the capacity for responding to the misfortunes of others because of the innate sentiments of "sympathy," "pity," and "conscience." But poststructuralism refuses to conceive of human nature as having foundations in inborn propensities. Thus literature is to do the work of morality; the appeal is to our imagination rather than to our instincts. In a world of words we are little more than our vocabularies, and solidarity is born of persuasion, the will to believe in the potency of metaphor.

Yet the poststructuralist still must wrestle with the issues of the pragmatist. Dewey once tried to convince Americans that they could move from "scientific method" to a sense of solidarity and social responsibility based on his organic metaphors. The literary critic Kenneth Burke observed that Dewey's proposal "serves primarily as a lawyer's brief, in that it persuades without exposing the crucial steps in its persuasion. Philosophical tracts, if they are of worth, seek to persuade; but the difference between them and Ciceronian exhortation, . . . is that they try at the same time to expose their methods of persuasion." Without such methods we have only what Pascal called the language of pleasure (*langage de volupté*) and persuasion by seduction (*convaincre d'agrément*).[82]

Before we allow ourselves to be seduced, it should be noted that solidarity, instead of being morally edifying, can be brutally discriminating, as in ethnic, religious, or racial solidarity and their "cleansing" bloodbaths. But curiously, Rorty seeks to see solidarity exist as a political reality for much the same reason Adams reconstructed the Virgin as a literary possibility—to appreciate the exercise of mercy and compassion. Both the philosopher and the historian want to persuade us not what is but what might be as a product of the literary imagination. "Do we attain reality by making a silhouette of our dreams?" asks Santayana.[83]

Apparently Rorty, who endorses Freud's view that wish is father to

81. Rorty, *Contingency, Irony, Solidarity*, 195.
82. Kenneth Burke, *The Philosophy of Literary Form* (1941; Berkeley: University of California Press, 1973), 391; Paul de Man, "Pascal's Allegory of Persuasion," in *Blaise Pascal*, ed. Harold Bloom (New York: Chelsea House, 1989), 135–54.
83. Santayana, *Reason and Common Sense* (1922; New York: Collier, 1962), 178.

thought and that people are their beliefs and desires, would reply yes to Santayana's question. For our dreams are part of our identities and silently bespeak our self-descriptions.[84] The problem still remains how to make solidarity a dream that will survive the morning's cold analysis. To Rorty the term signifies a compassionate principle of reaching out to the misfortunate, a curious, if noble, sentiment coming from Nietzschean-influenced poststructuralism. But a deconstructionist would have no trouble seizing on the prefix *solid* to suggest a masculine resistance to sentiment on the part of a group seeking to promote its own interests. Simply because in theory the epistemologist can prove that there is no self, and the poststructuralist that there is no center, does nothing to eliminate the reality of self-centeredness that sees itself as solidarity. With no theory to govern practice, with no judgments referring to what is right and no action performed for duty's sake, with nothing existing outside our own thoughts and conversation, Rorty's faith in self-description can easily slip into the sin of self-deception.

The Return to History and the
Temptation of "Agreeable Tales"

Rorty's calling upon the poststructuralist to turn to history as an edifying discipline, especially intellectual history and historical narrative, contains several curious ironies. For one thing, no previous American pragmatist had assumed such a positive attitude toward the study of the past. Peirce, James, Dewey, and Mead, while conceding that history might illuminate how problems evolved, looked to the future confirmation of experimental procedures to formulate hypotheses and await results. In Dewey's hand, as we have seen, pragmatism also promised to prepare us to meet events, not necessarily by understanding history so much as by acting upon it. The past served as a condition of praxis rather than a source of knowledge and direction. It was there to be used instead of preserved and obeyed. History had no authority.

In bringing history back into the study of philosophy Rorty broke with the analytical tradition, which had emphasized the physical sciences and mathematics, the realm of indubitable facts and objective laws. But Rorty has also reappropriated the past as a contemporary poststructuralist, and the union of history and philosophy suggests another curious irony in the revival of pragmatism.

The poststructuralist seems to be of two minds about history. On the one hand, the traditional concept of history, with its epistemological implications of factual foundations and causal understanding, is suspect to

---

84. Rorty, "Freud and Moral Reflection," in *Pragmatism's Freud: The Moral Disposition of Psychoanalysis*, ed. Joseph H. Smith and William Kerrigan (Baltimore, 1986), 1–27.

the poststructuralist, whose reading of texts leaves no room for a centered subject capable of historical consciousness but only written traces on the page, words that refer not to past realities but to rhetorical strategies. On the other hand, the poststructuralist likes to use history against philosophy to undermine its claim to all trans-historical understanding. The poststructuralist allies with "postphilosophy" to expose historical narration not as a presentation of the past but as an inscription of it in the form of a text that produces its own constructions; and, conversely, he or she uses history to demonstrate that all philosophical knowledge is contextual and, hence, impeachable. Thus the philosopher subverts history by showing how it is imprisoned in textuality while at the same time subverting philosophy by showing how it is imprisoned in historicity.

Although Rorty is willing, indeed almost eager, to give up on conventional philosophy, he is reluctant to call for the end of history as well. Instead he wants to use history in at least four discrete ways.

First, he seeks to give philosophical inquiry an edifying historical dimension by having the history of philosophy supplant analytic and systematic philosophy. Alfred North Whitehead is one of his examples of a philosopher who helps makes sense of modern culture by telling the story of philosophy, a "sage" who "tries to pull together Wordsworth and Einstein and Darwin and the Gospels."[85] Rorty is careful to make clear that there are no "enduring problems of philosophy" like free will that philosophers of all times have worked on in similar ways. Rather a historical account of philosophy simply enables us to see how we have gotten from there to here, how things have changed, and how philosophical ideas came to be legitimated through extraphilosophical discursive practices.

Rorty also wants philosophy to be done historically in order to appreciate it as reactive and dialogic and thereby to see the history of ideas as a series of points of view that arise from the conditions of argument and discourse. Such finite viewpoints suggest that history contains no telos, no objective verities unfolding with the passing of events. Since each philosophy belongs to its own time, the poststructuralist recognizes that all thinking must face a rendezvous with historicism.

So far Rorty's prescriptions should create no difficulty for the intellectual historian. But the third way in which he wants to use history does cause one to wonder how useful history can be to the historian confronted with modernity. "The history of inquiry," Rorty argues, "is a matter of understanding the justifications which people had for saying what they did."[86] Rorty favors such an approach because truth becomes less "mind-dependent" and epistemological and more a matter of finding out what

---

85. Rorty, "What Are Philosophers For?" *Center Magazine* 16 (Sept.–Oct. 1983): 40–51.
86. Rorty, "Realism and Reference," *Monist* 59 (July 1976): 321–40.

thinkers in the past were talking about and how they defended their thoughts. Ultimately Rorty is offering something like a sociology of knowledge approach by treating the act of justification as a social phenomenon. In this case the historian defines knowledge as understanding the social practices in which beliefs come to be justified. Leaving aside the question whether a justification explains what is being said or whether professed beliefs are actual causes of ideas, one wonders in what way Rorty's methodological advice really advances historical understanding. The American colonists, for example, justified their denial of British sovereignty on the grounds of natural liberties and rights deriving from "Nature," itself a philosophical foundation the neopragmatist rejects. Should, then, the American Revolution be judged illegitimate?

Consider how Niebuhr approached the problem of human reasoning as justification. Like Rorty, Niebuhr sought to give historical depth to philosophical inquiry, and he too believed it more important to discover how ideas were used than to try to establish how they represent the nature of knowledge. In a chapter aptly titled "The Tower of Babel" in *Beyond Tragedy*, Niebuhr traces how in various epochs writers claimed universal values while remaining blind to particular interests inherent in prevailing social structures.[87] The Middle Ages saw itself as a Christian culture enforcing the theory of a just price, seldom acknowledging that it benefited primarily the feudal landlords who were the borrowers at the expense of the city artisan producers. Bourgeois society then emerged along with the universal aspirations of modern science and the principle of timeless natural laws, and merchants refused to see their private interests insinuating themselves into such objective conceptual claims. In the twentieth century, Marxism, the one modern philosophy that supposedly recognized the finite perspective of all cultures and the false claims of impartiality, proceeded to erect a concept of a future classless society that would render identical all interests and thereby achieve universal truth. Thus, in regard to Rorty's advice to concentrate on the "justifications people had for saying what they did," a Niebuhrian would regard intellectual history as the systematic study of illusion and self-deception. A neopragmatist who shares Rorty's appreciation for irony might value Niebuhr's parables of Christian pride. But what becomes of Dewey's faith in science and progress?[88]

Whatever the position of the pragmatist, a Niebuhrian and a Nietzschean can agree that the human condition is a mystery of the spirit and not of nature, of life without God and not life without science, of language

87. Niebuhr, *Beyond Tragedy*, 27–46.
88. Dewey, "Has Philosophy a Future?" (1949), *Later Works*, vol. 16, 359–67.

without faith and not only philosophy without foundations. It is telling that Niebuhr praised the postmodernist Nietzsche, and not the progressive Dewey, for seeing that the justifications people have for their utterances probably reflect their corruptions more than their convictions. "It is this penetration into the dishonesty of rational idealism which establishes affinities between Nietzsche and classical Christianity."[89]

In addition to turning to history for a sense of continuity and change, an appreciation of the historical conditions of all knowledge, and an understanding of how beliefs are justified, Rorty offers still another reason for using the past. Rorty proposes that history is a matter of telling rather than knowing, a story that narrates rather than an analysis that explains. "The creation of imaginary significations which enable us to tell each other new stories about who we are, why we are good, and how we can become better, has gradually become, between Kant's time and ours, the province of *narrative* rather than *theory*," he wrote in response to Cornelius Castoriadis's criticisms of "the end of philosophy." "*Theories* about the nature of Humanity have been gradually displaced by *narratives* about how we, we Europeans, came to be what we are, of how we live now, and how we might someday live. Already in Hegel's partial historicization of philosophy we see the beginnings of a turn from theorizing to storytelling." The turn to narrativity means the end of philosophy if we drop all reference to a "True Self, a Real Human Nature" at the basis of human existence. Philosophy would then end when people "ceased to think of themselves as 'born free' and instead saw freedom as simply a relatively recent, glorious, European invention—and none the worse for having been invented rather than discovered."[90]

Why does it follow that theories about human nature are to be replaced by narratives about human life? Cannot the turn toward narration be regarded as another temporary product of history rather than a final description of the modern condition? The poststructuralist prides himself on seeing history and contingency where others supposedly see theory and necessity. And seeing all language constructions as indeterminate productions, the neopragmatist wants us to appreciate how things can be changed by being redescribed. But the spectacle of power and evil may not be contingent and instead defy the philosopher who assumes that reality, known only as interpreted, can be reinterpreted to suit political purposes. Experimenting with vocabularies can do little to change determinate phenomena that exist independently of language. In concentrating

89. Niebuhr, *Nature and Destiny of Man*, vol. 1, 91.
90. Rorty, "Comments on Castoriadis's 'The End of Philosophy?'" *Salmagundi* 82–83 (Spring–Summer 1989): 24–30.

on language, the neopragmatists look "only to the shell and husk of history," as Edmund Burke put it two centuries ago, sensing that language fixation is the focus of the thinker who refused to acknowledge that the wicked inventiveness of power eludes its passing representations:

> You might change the names. The things in some shape remain the same. A certain *quantum* of power must always exist in the community, in some hands, and under some appellation. Wise men will apply their remedies to vices, not to names: to the causes of evil which are permanent, not to the occasional organs by which they act, and the transitory modes in which they appear. Otherwise you will be wise historically, a fool in practice. Seldom have two ages the same fashion in their pretexts and same modes of mischief. Wickedness is a little more inventive. Whilst you are discussing fashion, the fashion is gone by. The very same vice assumes a new body. The spirit transmigrates; and, far from losing its principle of life by the change of its appearance, it is renovated in its new organs with the fresh vigour of a juvenile activity. It walks abroad; it continues its ravages; whilst you are gibbeting the carcass, or demolishing the tomb. You are terrifying yourself with ghosts and apparitions, while your house is the haunt of robbers. It is thus with all those, who attending only to the shell and husk of history, think they are waging war with intolerance, pride, and cruelty, whilst, under the colour of abhorring the ill principles of antiquated parties, they are authorizing and feeding the same odious vice in different factions, and perhaps in worse.[91]

Rorty assumes that history can function the same way as a redescriptive narrative, a rhetorical means through which experience can be made to be edifying and communicated to others. The author can endow the past with meaning and wrest coherence by the employment of rhetorical forms because the past itself has no existence prior to its textualization. Such an approach to history cannot be said to distort the past if reality itself remains unknowable.

Curiously, Rorty comes close to the conclusion Henry Adams arrived at a century ago—only the latter saw it as the end of history while the former regards the conclusion as the point of departure for history's redefinition. Adams, too, began to sense that history could not be known but only told. But Adams doubted that he could even narrate a story or draw on the tales of Walter Scott and Alexandre Dumas. In his studies

---

91. Quoted in Conor Cruise O'Brien, *The Great Melody: A Thematic Biography of Edmund Burke* (Chicago: University of Chicago Press, 1992), 604.

on Tahiti and "The Primitive Rights of Women," Adams delved into anthropology and used Homer to speculate on the origins of patriarchal authority. But narrative alone could not satisfy Adams's hunger for truth that once was assumed to reside behind the flux of events. "He had no fancy for telling agreeable tales to arouse sluggish-minded boys, in order to publish them afterwards as lectures." To substitute form for content, to mold the past into a narrative because the past itself lacks coherence, seemed to Adams a desperate deception. The conclusion of his lament, quoted in full in an earlier chapter, bears restating here. "A teacher must either treat history as a catalogue, a record, a romance, or as an evolution; and whether he affirms or denies evolution, he falls into all the burning faggots of the pit. He makes of his scholars either priests or atheists, plutocrats or socialists, judges or anarchists, almost in spite of himself. In essence incoherent and immoral, history had either to be taught as such—or falsified."[92]

To write history without a means of representing it, to narrate a tale in an effort to account for an event, to assume one could explain something causally, to analyze why it happened by telling its story, seemed to Adams a falsification of history's resistance to human reason. History as an intellectual problem begins in the absence of immediate understanding, due not only to the linguistic mediation of texts but also to the inscrutabilities inherent in a reality that cannot be emplotted as chaos and contingency, or at least not in any edifying ways that would make people feel good about themselves. Understanding the past requires establishing invariant patterns, causal connections, and conscious intentions on the part of agents—all of which eluded Adams. He knew that the classical writing of history had come to an end, but he was not prepared to embrace the modernist version and make history pragmatically useful at the expense of its inherent tensions and uncertainties. To rephrase Karl Lowith's formulation: as a classical historian Adams asked why events happened; as a modernist the pragmatist asks how we shall push ahead. Unable to answer the first question, Adams could not move on to the second without self-deception. The pragmatist asks not "whence" but "whither," and off we go!

What makes Adams's mind so richly tense is not only his sensing the rift between classical and modern views of history but also his making the shift from what today would be called structuralism to poststructuralism. In a sense there are two Henry Adamses. When he set out to write his magnum opus on the history of the early American republic, he wrote the first six chapters on topography and national character, with little

92. Adams, *Education*, 300–301.

CHAPTER ELEVEN

mention of people or events. But as the story unfolded he believed he
could reconstruct the exact sequence of cause and effect to explain, among
other developments, the War of 1812. His search for what he later called
a "spool" on which to wind the thread of connections to obtain causal
understanding was similar to the structuralist's search for a "code" or
underlying pattern in history and society that would yield order and
stability. But Adams began to doubt that American leaders were conscious of their actions and the American people reflectively aware of what
was happening to them. Unable to find either human consciousness or
meaningful necessity in American history, Adams turned to speculating
on the future while doubting his ability to understand the past. The
pragmatist and the poststructuralist also question whether knowledge derives from a rational subject who sees the world purely through the faculties of knowing. The later, second Adams could share such a perspective
to the extent that he moved from structuralism to poststructuralism, from
a search for laws immanent in history to a recognition of his own incapacities of knowing. But Adams's skepticism was so total that he would not
readily be able to accept the pragmatist solution that all knowledge awaits
action and the poststructuralist solution that all knowledge asserts itself
as narration. Human deeds and language can tell us only what people did
and thought, not what they knew and understood, and Adams delighted
in showing that Jeffersonian America did not seem to know what it was
doing when the country deviated from its earlier conception of simple
republicanism.

Adams scarcely saw the human condition as one of linguistic entrap-
ment alone, as though all the world were not the playwright's stage but
the poststructuralist's text. In *Mont-Saint-Michel and Chartres* Adams does
examine how beliefs are justified, not only in language but in art, cathedrals, symbols, and images, and he emphasized that the great intellectual
debates of the Middle Ages involved rhetoric, analogies, metaphors, definitions, and dialectics. In the *Education* language itself often became the
source of symbols, with the setting of Quincy representing multiplicity
and Boston unity. But language is used to convey what thought cannot
express, and for Adams the human condition lay not in the efficacy of
rhetoric and discourse but in the inadequacy of reason and resolution.
Most likely he would have agreed with Lionel Trilling, who said of
Nietzsche: "It is not words that make our troubles, but our own wills.
Words cannot control us unless we desire to be controlled by them."[93]

Many poststructuralists insist that language does influence, if not completely control, our minds and thoughts. Yet they also insist that our

93. Lionel Trilling, *The Liberal Imagination*, 187.

beliefs and practices must not be controlled by theory on the grounds that there exist no deeper philosophical conditions for knowledge than our socially accepted conventions. Adams's reflections on this issue are worth pondering before we accept the "end of theory" along with the end of almost everything else that postmodernism pronounces dead on arrival.

Adams criticized Jefferson for misconceiving the nature and direction of America in his years as spokesman for the Virginia idyll of simple agrarian republicanism, which had envisioned minimal government and a world of peace and harmony. "He was a theorist, prepared to risk the fate of mankind on the chance of reasoning far from certain of its details," an aloof dogmatism that made him a proud "martyr to the disease of omniscience." But Adams was happy to report that "Jefferson wanted to put his theories into practice only at such time as he had not the power, and when he had the power he carefully abstained from theorizing."[94] Every president becomes a pragmatist at last! Adams had no quarrel with the Federalist conviction that politics must be governed by circumstances rather than principle. Indeed the life of John Randolph dramatized the plight of a stubborn theorist who saw every move and development as a betrayal of republicanism. Unable to adapt to changing conditions and unexpected events, even more unwilling to compromise principles, Randolph ended his career on the verge of madness. Aware that change is the rule of life, Adams nonetheless could not celebrate the erosion of theory and political philosophy as America developed in ways unanticipated by its founders. For without the authority of theory, practice became little more than the demand of interest politics. As noted earlier, Adams saw that politicians of both parties "cared nothing for fine-spun theories of what government might or might not do, providing government did what they wanted." Without theory to guide practice, practice becomes the will to power and politics the reign of arbitrary desire.

In Dewey's pragmatism the unity of theory and practice and ends and means offered the possibility of overcoming the dualisms of philosophy by viewing all thinking as a kind of deferred social interaction rather than immediate autonomous reflection. Dewey's notion of ideas as "plans of operation" is similar to Rorty's and Fish's position that all we need to know arises from the content of our practices in actual situations. Their denial that theory can be allowed to govern practice from a transcending standpoint reinforces Dewey's conviction that no judgment can be imposed on a situation with standards external to the situation being judged. As to truth, both the neopragmatist and the poststructuralist agree that

---

94. Henry Adams, "Von Holst's History of the United States," in *The Great Secession*, 277.

it is no longer a problem in life, since it can neither be found in thought nor be stabilized in language. Truth will take care of itself once thinkers cease theoretical speculation and get on with narrating stories rather than perfecting philosophy. The neopragmatist lives for discourse and action. To think about thinking in the hope of reaching the object of thought is as hopeless as swimming against a riptide.

In his worst moments Adams knew the meaning of hopelessness. But what the poststructuralist experiences as liberation he felt as frustration. Although Adams well knew the mind had its limits, he desired to push the limits of thought into the unknown.[95] Pragmatism promised to overcome almost any difficulty encountered in a "problematic situation"; Adams savored the situation itself as though the irritation of doubt and darkness were a natural habitat. Yet Adams anticipated the "end of philosophy" with such prescience that in many respects he, rather than Dewey, should be regarded as America's precursor of poststructuralism. Consider the criteria with which Rorty has defined the ideal poststructuralist thinker.

Rorty advises the "post-philosopher" to be reactive rather than systematic, more involved in dialogue than in thesis, and he instructs the thinker-as-writer to cut across disciplines and use whatever genre necessary in edifying the human situation. Adams described *Mont-Saint-Michel and Chartres* as a "talk" by an uncle to his nieces, a vehicle for storytelling, and here and in other works he resorted to art, anthropology, religion, philosophy, poetry, and the novel as modes of representing the past plight of men and women struggling with nature and convention. Rorty's conviction that reality is contingent, and that the liberal must be an ironist who espouses political values in full knowledge that such values have no philosophical foundation, could well be a portrait of Adams. The conservative Christian anarchist undertook the futile task of trying to preserve by remembrance what could not be demonstrated by science. The historian also saw events as unpredictable and incoherent; and, like Max Weber, he knew that the object of value could no longer have any basis in reason. Adams, too, believed there could be no explanation of things by reference to their essential nature, and he also felt disinherited from the eighteenth-century Enlightenment and his ancestors' faith in the capacity of rational intelligence to overcome the riddles of existence.

Rorty has noted how Foucault's "structures of power" can be linked to Derrida's "structures of culture" to appreciate better humankind as shaped and endlessly reshaped by the changing conditions of existence, from

95. The idea, implied by many poststructuralists, that because the mind has its limits we must face the "end of philosophy," is curious and not a little melodramatic. The point is often made by Heideggerians. But it may be worth noting that two outstanding students of Heidegger, Hannah Arendt and Leo Strauss, went on to write books on philosophy.

which there is no appeal to anything beyond existence. Adams similarly could offer humankind no redeeming philosophic vision. Adams's debates with James highlight the difference between the philosopher who saw indeterminism everywhere except in the exercise of free will and the historian who saw indeterminism everywhere except in the persistence of power. As a philosopher Foucault saw the ubiquity of power and the complicity of knowledge in its production; as a historian Adams saw the movement of power and the impotence of mind to oppose it and, as well, the complicity of science in the generation of energy that would lead to entropy.

Adams's reflections on power are in some respects more penetrating than those of the poststructuralists. Foucault likened power to a "capillary" phenomenon, not something that is suddenly imposed downward but something that slowly insinuates itself outward and adheres to whatever it touches.[96] With Adams power is also not simply coercion and domination. But where Foucault refused to identify the origins of power, and hence described a world weighted by invisible structures without an oppressor, a contingent world where power remained the only constant, Adams suggested that power is the ironic outcome of freedom itself. He too sought to make modern man conscious of the limitations of consciousness and of the tendency of knowledge-productions to bring forth new power systems. In Foucault's analysis, power is a product of knowledge as a form of discourse without an intending agent. In Adams's analysis, power derives from knowledge in the Baconian sense of the conscious domination of nature and the technological urge to improve material existence. Thus where the poststructuralists treat power as restriction imposed by linguistic epistemes, Adams treats it as acceleration liberated by humankind's own inventions. Like Niebuhr and Weber, Adams saw power as expressive of history as a spectacle without rational meaning. Knowing that philosophy had come to its end, Adams turned to physics, and he equates it with history to show that even human reason defeats itself by identifying with power. The literary critic R. P. Blackmur captures elegantly Adams's effort to make the modern mind aware of its own coming extinction:

> His dynamic theory of history begins by treating man as physics treated nature: as the development and economy of force. The sun, man, a mathematical point, were all forces, since all did the work; therefore, the same laws applied to each. Thus Adams reversed the common assumption that man

96. Foucault, *Power/Knowledge: Selected Interviews and Other Writing by Michel Foucault, 1972–1977*, ed. Colin Gordon (New York, 1980), 39.

captures forces, and made the dynamic assumption that forces capture man: man, he said, "is the sum of the forces that attract him." By such a theory man is reduced, like nature herself, to the movement of inertia: which may be deflected, intensified, accelerated, but must in the end be degraded, according to law, and to come to nothing; or at any rate must reach the extinction in man of everything hitherto held human, including the power to envisage and react to his fate.[97]

In poststructuralist thought power is generally depicted as outside the subject inhering in some unseen constraint against consciousness and freedom. To Adams the Virgin and the Dynamo exuded the imagery of power and energy and as symbols elicited excitement, hope, and awe. Power is the object's capacity to attract subjects into beliefs, however illusory, and "only the attraction will vary according to the value the mind assigns to the image of the thing that moves it." Like Nietzsche, Adams set out to articulate the conditions of truth only to conclude that all beliefs are pulled toward power as the unmentionable object. In his "Letter to American Teachers of History," Adams cites Schopenhauer's and Nietzsche's theory that energy is identical to will, and he noted as well that in modern physics the laws of energy have replaced older metaphysical philosophy and its timeless categories. But Adams questions the equation of will and energy, and perhaps that questioning reinforced James's objection to his friend's using, or abusing, the second law of thermodynamics. Adams saw little encouragement in will and vitalism, since modern science depicted life as becoming so developed and specialized that the instinct to variation is enfeebled. Adams's speculations on the exhaustion of energy may have been fanciful, but what better way to ask the modern mind to watch itself whoring after power only to be degraded and come to nothing.[98]

Although Adams did not necessarily attribute the human condition to language and its mediations, he was not innocent of the importance of writing and the contingency of all philosophical vocabularies, political ideas, and linguistic constructions. In trying to understand experience, Adams recognized, as Blackmur noted, that the literary means used to convey the sense of experience alters its object in the process of expressing it.[99] Adams delighted in the nominalist-realist controversies of the Middle Ages, and he saw that philosophy amounted to a conversation, or, more exactly, "the art of dispute—dialectics."[100] The purpose of scholastic disputation was edification and clarification, making things convincing and

97. R. P. Blackmur, *Henry Adams* (New York, 1980), 264.
98. Adams, *Degradation*, 289.
99. Blackmur, *Henry Adams*, xix.
100. Adams, *Mont-Saint-Michel and Chartres*, 323.

clear to others. No less than the poststructuralist did Adams become interested in exploring how humanity attempts to rationalize itself. But Adams remained ambivalent about examining the ways of legitimation, especially the justifications of religious beliefs. It will be recalled that Aquinas's attempt to synthesize faith and reason risked destroying both by refusing to leave Christianity in mystery and paradox. Moving from Adams's treatment of the Virgin to Aquinas's treatment of God, one moves from persuasion by enchantment to conviction by argument, a move that threatened the cathedral's foundations and philosophy's as well. Philosophy even as conversation can lead to doubt and dissolution instead of solidarity and organic unity.

Yet like the poststructuralists, Adams could hardly bring himself to call for a return to orthodox philosophy and its reassuring certitudes. While Adams may have reached different conclusions than our contemporary neopragmatists, he presaged the poststructuralist conviction that modern philosophy must reject the entire edifice of Catesianism. In *Esther*, as noted earlier, Descartes's ways of reasoning are ridiculed, and in *Mont-Saint-Michel and Chartres* Adams favors Pascal's skepticism over Descartes's assumption that all we need to know is "imprinted" in our mind. Adams would be right at home with the poststructuralist critique of Descartes's logocentrism and the metaphysics of presence that presumes a knower consciously present in the act of knowing and a mind directly apprehending reality. Adams also questioned the Cartesian assumptions that knowledge increases as one understands the mind's operations and that the believer can learn about the content of beliefs by understanding the processes of thought. "Of all studies," he wrote in the *Education*, "the one he would rather have avoided was that of his own mind." Only a mind convinced that it knows itself will believe in its own logically possible ideas. Adams's copy of *Oeuvres de Descartes* is full of marginalia making distinctions between consciousness and reason to suggest that the philosopher confuses the awareness of oneself thinking as proof of that which one thinks, as though the activity of thought guaranteed the object of thought. Just as the poststructuralist takes pleasure in demonstrating that the writer cannot prove anything conceptual beyond the text, Adams delighted in demonstrating that Descartes could not prove the existence of God "hors de sa pensée." Whether ideas are formed by the mind or found innately in it, the mind itself remained a mystery to Adams. "Nearly all the highest intelligence known to history had drowned itself in the reflection of its own thought."[101]

Moving in the opposite direction to Rorty, Adams resorted to philoso-

101. Adams, *Education*, 432; on Descartes, see Baym, *The French Education of Henry Adams*, 183–208.

phy for answers that could not be found in history. "He got out his Descartes again; dipped into his Hume and Berkeley; wrestled anew with his Kant; pondered solemnly over his Hegel and Schopenhauer and Hartman; strayed gaily away with his Greeks—all merely to ask what Unity meant, and what happened when one denies it." But philosophers seldom do so, Adams observes, for thinkers project their needs and desires onto the world. Some of the poststructuralists tell us we cannot have knowledge of external objects because the mind cannot transcend the medium of its own operations. Adams explained the same situation less prosaically and more playfully:

> As history unveiled itself in the new order, man's mind had behaved like a young pearl oyster, secreting its universe to suit its conditions until it had built up a shell of *nacre* that embodied all its notions of the perfect. Man knew it was true because he made it, and he loved it for the same reason. . . . The man's part in his Universe was secondary, but the woman was at home there. . . . She conceived herself and her family as the centre and flower of an ordered universe which she knew to be unity because she had made it after the image of her own fecundity; and this creation of hers was surrounded by beauties and perfections which she knew to be real because she herself had imagined them.[102]

But neither woman nor man can ignore the realities that science brings forth, visions of chaos and uncertainty alien to the mind. The plight of the modern mind resembles the parable of the "Fall," with Adam and Eve driven out of paradise by their own actions. "Neither man nor woman ever wanted to quit this Eden of their own invention, and could no more have done it of their own accord than the pearl oyster could quit its shell; but although the oyster might perhaps assimilate or embalm a grain of sand into its aperture, it could perish in face of the cyclonic hurricane or the volcanic upheaval of its bed. Her supersensual chaos killed her." Even if mind resides in its own creations, it could be subject to "a new avalanche of unknown forces that had fallen on it," forces that must either be controlled by the creation of a new philosophical universe or be submitted to as the mind is absorbed into the swirl of entropy and chaos.[103] With the possible disappearance of mind as self-conscious subject, we are in the world of poststructuralism. Reflecting on the forces that determine the mind, Adams depicts the mind as the creator of its own inventions and the victim of its own creations.

For Adams as well as Rorty the problem of philosophy is the problem

102. Adams, *Education*, 431–32, 458–59.
103. Ibid., 459–61.

of mind as eyeball. If the former chides the mind as too theoretically inquisitive for its own good, the latter criticizes it as too intellectually proud to settle down into the mundane world of practice. Instead the mind conceives itself as window, mirror, and "glassy essence," the conceit of omniscience by virtue of a transparence that presumes to represent nature without refraction or mediation. In words that presage Rorty's expressions, Adams describes "the trap of logic—the mirror of the mind," the assumption that knowledge knows itself in self-reflection. Entrapped by the promise of pure reflection, the philosopher's "search for a unit of force led into the catacombs of thought where hundreds of thousands of educations had found their end. Generation after generation of painful and honest-minded scholars had been content to stay in these labyrinths forever, pursuing ignorance in silence, in company with the most famous teachers of all time."[104]

Why did scholars choose to remain in the labyrinths and silently pursue the void instead of building a ladder of narration with which they could talk their way up and out of the catacombs? Perhaps for the same reason that Adams chose to remain prostrate before the abyss of his own ignorance. Almost a century before the neopragmatists, Adams knew that philosophers had all along assumed that truth could be found because they could no more live without foundations than historians without facts or theologians without God: "Nihilism had no bottom. For thousands of years every philosopher had stood on the shore of this sunless sea, diving for pearls and never finding them. All had seen that, since they could not find bottom, they must assume it."[105]

Richard Rorty's call for taking up history returns us to the beginning of our story, with Henry Adams undertaking a monumental narration of the early Republic in the hope of finding out how America came to be what it is. Rorty's return to pragmatism represents a return not to philosophy as such but to the history of philosophy and intellectual history, disciplines now defined as language activities that hold out the possibility of understanding how past beliefs came to be justified. And if the neopragmatist discovers that at every turn and development Americans were left with no system of legitimation other than power and interest?

Bolingbroke advised us that "history is philosophy teaching by example." Rorty also makes history a matter of edifying illustrations. But whereas Bolingbroke believed that the historian could look for "repeated exemplifications of fixed rules,"[106] Rorty insists that the philosopher-historian can look for no noncontingent principles and must be content

104. Ibid., 429–30.
105. Ibid., 430.
106. On Bolingbroke, see Arthur O. Lovejoy, *Essays in the History of Ideas* (1948; New York: Braziller, 1955), 176–80.

with the genealogy of ideas rather than their veracity, with the processes by which humans living in the past formed their opinions rather than understanding them as resting on foundations. "Every philosophy is under the illusion," wrote Niebuhr, "that it has no illusions because it has discovered the illusions of its predecessors."[107] In turning toward language, discourse, and conversation, is not neopragmatism under the illusion that philosophy can continue as a linguistic exercise and history can survive as a tale told by a narrator who admits to being unable to know the reality of past events? One can grant the neopragmatist thesis that past ages mistakenly assumed that thought had the capacity to discover something beyond time and chance. But, sinful creatures that we are, we can hardly escape our own illusion that words will suffice as persuasion serves as proof and conversation replaces conviction.

Rorty hopes to find solidarity as much as Adams once set out to find unity. But Adams saw through the projections of his mind, and he would be the first to admit that the Virgin amounted to an imaginative reconstruction that would deconstruct once the text collapsed from the weight of its own metaphorical strategies. Under Rorty the promise of pragmatism has moved from science and technology to script and vocabulary, from controlled experimentation to constructed narration. Solidarity can be talked into existence as a sentiment produced by the power of rhetorical persuasion. In some respects pragmatism still remains what it was for James, Peirce, Dewey, and Mead: not only a plan of action but a philosophy of hope. But with Rorty the future of pragmatism depends on the textuality in which it inheres, and history becomes a matter more of words than of events. One might say of Rorty's postmodern world, in a twist on what Adams said of Aquinas's medieval world, Never let us forget that language alone supports it; and if language fails to fulfill the promise of pragmatism, philosophy is lost, history turns itself over to literature, and theory succumbs to the temptation to tell agreeable tales.

The temptation could be debilitating instead of edifying. Such a scenario deprives intellectual history of its erotic attractions by giving us the climax of knowledge before we enjoy the pleasures of knowing. "Unphilosophical philosophy," wrote Oswald Spengler in 1918, the kind of inquiry that turns questions of what it is into what it has become, of metaphysics and causality into genealogy and morphology, will be "the last that West Europe will know."[108] What Spengler called "the autumn of our spiritual-

107. Niebuhr, *Beyond Tragedy*, 223.
108. Spengler's *The Decline of the West* came out in 1918, the year of Adams's death. Spengler praised Nietzsche in ways that Adams might be praised, as a seer who had "thoughts out of time," a prophet of the end of philosophy and history who, like Spengler

ity" could be, for the historian, the winter of our defeat. Without questions of causality and reality, without the "whence" of things, what becomes of Peirce's "irritation of doubt" and Weber's dictum that "fundamental doubt is the father of knowledge"? Without the possibility of discovery, how can the study of history sustain curiosity? Before accepting the "end" of philosophy, we should remember that it began in wonder.

---

himself, remained skeptical of the surrogates for classical knowledge seen in life as a living organism expressing itself symbolically:

> Systematic philosophy . . . lies immensely far behind us, and ethical [philosophy] has been wound up. *But a third possibility, corresponding to Classical Scepticism, still remains to the soul-world* of the present-day West, and it can be brought to light by the hitherto unknown methods of historical morphology. That which is a possibility is a necessity. The Classical scepticism is ahistoric, it doubts by denying outright. But that of the West, if it is an inward necessity, a symbol of the autumn of our spirituality, is obliged to be historical through and through. Its solutions are got by treating everything as relative, as a historical phenomenon, and its procedure is psychological. Whereas the Sceptic philosophy arose within Hellenism as the negation of philosophy— declaring philosophy to be purposeless—we, on the contrary, regard the *history of philosophy* as, in the last resort, philosophy's gravest theme. This *is* "skepsis," in the true sense, for whereas the Greek is led to renounce absolute standpoints by contempt for the intellectual past, we are led to do so by comprehension of that past as an organism.
>
> In this work it will be our task to sketch out this unphilosophical philosophy—the last that West Europe will know. Scepticism is the expression of a pure Civilization; and it dissipates the world-picture of the Culture that has gone before. For us, its success will lie in resolving all the older problems into one, the genetic. The conviction that what *is* is also *has become*, that the natural and cognizable is rooted in the historic . . . leads directly to the fact that everything, whatever else it may be, must at any rate be *the expression of something living*. Cognitions and judgments too are acts of living men. The thinkers of the past conceived external actuality as produced by cognitions and motivating ethical judgments, but to the thought of the future they are above all *expressions and symbols*. *The Morphology of world-history becomes inevitably a universal symbolism.*

Oswald Spengler, *The Decline of the West*, trans. Charles F. Atkinson (1918; New York: Knopf, 1926), 45–46; Weber on doubt is in *Methodology of Social Sciences*, 7; Weber also referred to pragmatism as an "anti-philosophical philosophy" that never claimed it can or should represent the being or essence ("*sein*") of events. See *Archiv für Sozialwissenschaft und Sozialpolitik* 29 (1909): 615–20.

Index

Abelard, 173

Abstract expressionism, 118

Action: communicative action, 420, 445; consciousness and free action, 80; *Federalist* authors on, 432; James on, 129–30; and language, 463; Peirce on, 166; philosophy and political action, 48; Rorty on, 407; as test of knowledge, 255; and values, 256; Weber on, 47–48; and will, 146

Adams, Brooks, 99

Adams, Charles Francis, 57, 58, 63

Adams, Charles Francis, Jr., 257

Adams, Henry, 55–107; Adler on, 391; on American history, 17–19, 22–23, 221, 465, 483–84; as antimodern modernist, 27; on Aquinas, 94, 152; and art, 96, 100, 128; and authority, 44, 55–58, 91, 93, 95–98, 106, 112, 170, 221; on belief, 15, 489; on Calvinism, 35, 89, 96; and Cameron, 101, 102, 105, 208; on chaos, 183, 490; on Chartres cathedral, 90–91; choice of a vocation by, 114; on Christianity, 32, 184; and the Civil War, 62–63, 278; on the classical ideals of politics, 60–67, 291–93; on communication and conduct, 449; on consciousness, 145; on conservatism and capitalism, 50; on the Constitution, 66, 225–26; on curriculum, 306; on Darwinism, 88, 179; *Democracy*, 65, 89, 103, 104, 148; on Descartes, 151–52, 174, 489; detachment of, 31; and Dewey, 2, 4, 7, 9–10, 16–17, 21, 206–7, 223, 226–27, 231–32, 250–51, 293; on doubt, 189, 190; dualism of, 40, 183–84; the Dynamo, 31, 98; on education, 68–69, 97, 101, 121, 207, 306–7, 316; Eliot on, 101; on the Enlightenment, 31; and entropy, 84, 87, 104, 181, 490; on eroticism, 102; *Esther*, 103, 104, 148–49, 151; and experience, 44, 175, 488; on faith, 149–50, 185, 187; on the family, 97–98; on force, 181; on God, 151–52, 184–85, 415; Harvard resignation, 67–68; on Hegel, 150; and history, 17, 20–21, 36–37, 44, 71, 78, 80–83, 97, 106, 108–11, 170–73, 195–96, 250, 258, 293, 465, 482–83; *History of the United States of America during the Administrations of Thomas Jefferson and James Madison*, 71–72, 75, 79, 171, 353; and Holmes, 346–47, 353, 354, 356, 358–59; on institutions, 123; on interest, 215, 418; Italian travels, 64–65; and James, 24, 30, 73, 89, 98, 100–101, 108–13, 116, 127, 131, 141–42, 144–51, 155; on Jefferson, 17, 37, 184, 408, 423, 485; on knowledge, 101, 179; on language, 484, 488; on the legitimation of belief, 15, 489; "Letter to American

495

512

Puritanism: Adams on, 35, 72–73, 89; in American political culture, 23; Augustinianism of, 436; and communal society, 301; and redescription, 472; on the self, 373; on society, 301, 361; spiritual solidarity of, 474

Quest for Certainty, The (Dewey), 217, 218, 244, 246, 334

Radical empiricism, 123, 125–26, 128, 165
Radium, 81, 82, 87, 176, 182
Randolph, John, 75, 485
Rationalism: Adams as rationalist, 125; Dewey on, 218, 224; empirical rationalism, 387; James transcending empiricism and rationalism, 124–25; and Kant, 428; poststructuralism and pragmatism on, 475; and religion, 150
Rationality, 420
Ratner, Sidney, 251
Rawls, John, 452
Reagan, Ronald, 452, 472
Realism: Adams on, 173–74; critical realism, 175; and idealism, 125; and James, 135, 136, 144; legal realism, 351, 357; and nominalism, 166, 173–74; and Peirce, 165, 175–76, 200; Rorty on, 454
Reason: Adams on, 51, 185; the American founders on, 428; and authority, 188; and democracy, 331; Dewey on, 227; and faith, 95, 185; *Federalist* authors on, 428; Hutchins on, 391; Madison on, 428; the New Left on, 403–4; Niebuhr on, 437; Peirce on, 175; poststructuralism on, 435; rationality, 420; relativism and historicism of, 188; using reason to criticize reason, 422; Weber on, 51. *See also* Rationalism
Redescription, 469–72, 481–82
Reed, John, 325
Relativism: and Adams, 170; and Beard, 170; Bloom on, 395; and Dewey, 308; and fascism, 397; and Holmes, 351; and modernism, 188; and Peirce, 176, 186, 188; and pragmatism, 396
Religion: Adams on, 36, 51, 72–73, 98, 150–51, 184–85; and authority, 90; and capitalism, 447; Dewey on, 34, 51, 212–17; and empiricism, 150; as experience not knowledge, 34; faith, 148, 149–150,

185, 187; Hook on, 394; James on, 30, 34, 121, 130–31, 150–51, 155–56; and knowledge, 34; Lippmann on, 329, 336; and modernism, 29, 410; Peirce on, 184–85, 187; and politics, 96; and poststructuralism, 443; pragmatism on, 34–35; and rationalism, 150; and science, 28, 51, 89, 154, 185, 212–17; and sex, 121; Weber on, 36, 51; and the will to believe, 149. *See also* Christianity; God
Representation, 16, 262, 416, 430
Riesman, David, 381, 447
Robinson, James Harvey, 261
Roosevelt, Eleanor, 22
Roosevelt, Theodore, 24, 106, 164
Rorty, Richard, 450–62; on action, 407; and Adams, 486, 489–91; on antifoundationalism, 456; and Bernstein, 453–55; on consensus, 445; on Derrida, 414, 441; and Dewey, 3, 51–52, 416, 451, 453, 459–62; on the end of history, 479; on the end of philosophy, 11, 416, 427; and Foucault, 415–16, 456; on foundationalism, 15; on Habermas, 445, 455; on Heidegger, 411, 441, 463; on history, 15, 478–482, 491–93; and Hook, 409; on inquiry, 455, 479; and James, 463; on knowledge, 407, 416, 476; on language and philosophy, 414, 463; on legitimation of belief, 15; and literature, 475; on Marxism, 455; on modernity, 11, 455; on morality, 475; on nature, 474; and neopragmatism, 11, 341, 357, 451, 474; and Niebuhr, 441, 442; on Nietzsche, 441; and Peirce, 11–12, 416–17, 455; and persuasion, 476; on philosophy, 11, 406–17, 416, 463, 473–74, 476, 479; on politics, 452; on postphilosophy, 486; on pragmatism, 49, 249, 407, 409, 416, 456; on pragmatism and poststructuralism, 49, 416; on realism, 454; redescription, 469–72; on science, 456; on solidarity, 470, 475, 476–78, 492; on theory and practice, 462–64, 467; on truth, 407, 456
Rousseau, Jean-Jacques, 121, 299, 300, 323
Royce, Josiah, 200
Rugg, Harold, 312
"Rule of Phase Applied to History, The" (Adams), 83
Russell, Bertrand, 134, 235, 236, 405, 406